W9-BOF-205

COGNITIVE DEVELOPMENT IN CHILDREN

Cognitive Development in Children

Five Monographs of the
Society for Research
in
Child Development

With an Introduction by Roger Brown

THE UNIVERSITY OF CHICAGO PRESS

CHICAGO AND LONDON

International Standard Book Number: 0-226-76755-8
Library of Congress Catalog Card Number: 78-103676

The University of Chicago Press, Chicago 60637
The University of Chicago Press, Ltd., London

CONTENTS

CONTENTS

CONTENTS

INTRODUCTION

The Social Science Research Council (SSRC) has a wonderful ability to detect intellectual developments in an early "critical period" when they can benefit maximally from a little enrichment. Ten years ago somebody or other in the SSRC detected the sap beginning to flow in the field of cognitive development and decided to bring together a few young researchers and see what would happen. The result was the creation in June 1959 of the Committee on Intellective Processes Research with, eventually, the following membership: Roger Brown, Jerome Kagan, William Kessen, Lloyd N. Morrisett, Paul H. Mussen, A. Kimball Romney, and Harold W. Stevenson; staff, Francis H. Palmer.

The committee promptly laid out a five-year program. There would be six research conferences and each conference would be reported as a monograph; and after all the conferences, there would be a summer institute offering courses in cognitive development for advanced graduate students. The Carnegie Corporation funded the venture, and surprisingly, five years later it had all been carried out exactly as planned. And there we were at the University of Minnesota, which had sponsored the institute, holding a last meeting with a representative of the SSRC. That last meeting, in 1964, had a remarkable quality which I am sure we all still remember. It was clear that the committee's business was done, and there was no reason not to dissolve, but we found it hard to face the death of the group. It had had so much vitality that we could not quite believe that the world in general and the SSRC in particular could face its end with equanimity.

What were the forces which had begun to revitalize the study of cognitive development in the late 1950s and which flowed through the conferences and monographs of our committee? Here are some that occur to me:

1. Computer simulation of cognitive processes. This was not a force in any very direct way. We had no conference directly on the subject and rather seldom talked about it. But computer simulation had liberated all of our imaginations. Since machines—hardware—could accomplish information processing of great complexity, it was obviously perfectly scientific and objective to attribute such processing to the human brain. Why limit the mind to association by contiguity and reinforcement when the computer,

admittedly a lesser mechanism, could do so much more? The computer freed psychologists to invent mental processes as complex as they liked.

2. Study of systems of intellectual content. In an earlier period, psychologists, when they wrote about speech or reading or mathematics or moral reasoning or logic, conceived of human knowledge in these various areas in lay terms or in terms congenial to some simplistic psychological theory. There was precious little study of the disciplines themselves. In the past decade a good many developmental psychologists have "minored," either as students or, later on, as professionals, in one of the intellectual-content fields. What brought about the change? A number of things, but of particular importance was the curriculum reform movement in the early 1960s. This brought mathematicians and physicists and linguists into contact with psychologists. It made them interested in psychological theory, and it helped to make us interested in the content of intellectual systems, with the result that our conceptions of *what* is learned when a language is learned, or when principles of moral reasoning or arithmetic are learned, have immeasurably deepened in recent years.

3. America's discovery of Jean Piaget. For something like twenty-five years most American psychologists had been unable to understand what Piaget was up to with his studies of the child's conception of number, physical causality, space, geometry, quantity, and so on. Whatever his program was, we were pretty sure that it was less scientific than discovering the universal laws of learning. Then computer simulation, psycholinguistics, curriculum reform, and mathematical models altered our notions of the scientific enterprise in such a way as to cause us to see Piaget as a very modern psychologist. To see that he was, in fact, the great psychologist of cognitive development.

4. The expanding domain of cognition. Personality theory and social anthropology have increased their concern with cognition in the past decade. Jerome Kagan, George Kelly, Riley Gardner, and others have shown that personalities may be characterized by cognitive styles, characteristic ways of processing information, as well as by need systems and favored defenses. The ethnoscience group within anthropology has shown that a culture is a system of perceptual and conceptual categories as well as a set of values and a bundle of customs. Using componential analysis and related techniques, the cognitive anthropologists launched the comparative study of such semantic domains as kinship, color, plants, and diseases.

These, then, were some of the new forces. What they caused the committee to produce were the following:

1. Conference on thought in the young child with focus on the work of Piaget, Inhelder, and their Genevan colleagues, held in Dedham, Massachusetts, in 1960. Reported in SRCD monograph, vol. 27, no. 2 (1962), edited by William Kessen and Clementina Kuhlmann.

2. Conference on basic cognitive processes in children, with an emphasis on concept formation and cognitive style, held in Minneapolis in 1961.

Reported in SRCD monograph, vol. 28, no. 2 (1963), edited by John C. Wright and Jerome Kagan.

3. Conference on first-language acquisition held in Dedham, Massachusetts, in 1961. Reported in SRCD monograph, vol. 29, no. 1 (1964), edited by Ursula Bellugi and Roger Brown.

4. Conference on mathematical learning held in Berkeley, California, in 1962. Reported in SRCD monograph, vol. 30, no. 1 (1965), edited by Lloyd N. Morrisett and John Vinsonhaler.

5. Conference on European research in cognition development held in Voksenäsen, Oslo, Norway, in 1962. Reported in SRCD monograph, vol. 30, no. 2 (1965), edited by Paul H. Mussen.

6. Conference on transcultural studies in cognition held in Mérida, Yucatan, in 1963. Reported as vol. 66, no. 3, part 2 (1964) of the *American Anthropologist,* edited by A. Kimball Romney and Roy Goodwin D'Andrade.

The Institute on Cognitive Development held at the University of Minnesota in 1964 offered the following courses:

1. The acquisition of a first language. (Roger Brown)
2. Personality and cultural influences on the development of intellectual processes. (Jerome Kagan)
3. The developmental theories of Jean Piaget. (William Kessen)
4. Learning and development. (Harold W. Stevenson)

The intellectual highlights of this long effort, beyond those for which members of the committee were responsible, are also numerous: Bärbel Inhelder's succinct and lucid exposition of Genevan psychology; the discussion of computer simulation of thought by Herbert Simon and Allen Newell; Eleanor Gibson's first efforts to analyze English graphemes into distinctive features; the report by Jerome Bruner and Rose Olver on equivalence transformations in children; Noam Chomsky's introduction of the distincton between "competence" and "performance"; Patrick Suppes' work on the behavioral foundations of mathematical concepts; A. V. Zaporozhets' review of Soviet research on the development of perception in the preschool child; and many more.

Of course not all the "souvenirs" of the conferences are intellectual. All of us remember the first meetings with Bärbel Inhelder, her great charm and intellectual vitality. She became our good friend and a kind of informal European auxiliary of the committee. All of us remember the striking contrast in atmosphere between the first and last evenings at Voksenäsen. Voksenäsen is a kind of inn high above Oslo, and the conferees, European and American, lived together there for nearly a week. On the first evening, before dinner, we wandered down to the drawing room and sat stiffly, listening to a very middle-European string ensemble play selections from *La Boheme,* all the while shooting suspicious looks back and forth across a nearly visible iron curtain. For at this conference the Americans met not only with British and Genevan psychologists but with A. V. Zaporozhets

(USSR), Hanuš Papoušek (Czechoslovakia), Zofia Babska (Poland), and Alina Szeminska (Poland). The dinner on the last evening was an un-curtained love-feast with warm toasts and expressions of affection and plans for reunion.

Then there was Yucatan. Probably my memory is idiosyncratic here, and it certainly is my own fault. The doctor of tropical medicine at the Harvard Health Services paled when I told her where I was going and made me vow that I would drink no unbottled liquids and would remember that ice is made of water which may or may not have been bottled and that no one when he brushes his teeth can avoid swallowing at least a little water. So I lived on cautious sips of warm orange soda and kept my lips tight in the shower and left as soon as the meetings were over. The doctor of tropical medicine was content, but I wish I had feasted on tortas and refried beans and gone to see the wonderful ruins at Chichén Itzá.

The decision now to publish as a single volume the five conference reports that originally appeared as SRCD monographs (minus only the discussion sections) is a happy one. We are grateful to the Society for Research in Child Development and to the University of Chicago Press for making it possible. The book is perhaps that symbolic continuation of the life of the committee that we hankered after at the last meeting in Minneapolis in 1964.

ROGER BROWN

I

THOUGHT
IN THE YOUNG CHILD

Report of a Conference on
Intellective Development
with Particular Attention to the Work
of Jean Piaget

EDITED BY
WILLIAM KESSEN
CLEMENTINA KUHLMAN

1

HISTORICAL AND BIBLIOGRAPHICAL NOTE

JOHN H. FLAVELL
University of Rochester

INTRODUCTION

Jean Piaget—developmental psychologist and philosopher, logician-mathematician and educator—is surely one of the remarkable and impressive scholars of contemporary social science. During the past 40 years he has put together a psychological corpus of considerable magnitude and scope:[1] a very detailed theory of intellectual and, to a lesser extent, perceptual development from birth to maturity; a theory of perceptual functioning *per se*, apart from his work on perceptual and intellectual development; miscellaneous theoretical sorties into logic, genetic epistemology, education, and neurophysiology; and finally, as buttress for the theoretical superstructure, a large and diverse body of ingenious experiments.

This paper is concerned with two facets of the man and the system. First, a brief chronology of his life and his work: what he has done, is doing, and will probably do in the future; and second, an account of the relation between his system and the psychological public-at-large.

THE MAN AND HIS WORK

Jean Piaget was born on August 9, 1896, in Neuchâtel, Switzerland.[2] He was a studious child and, as is clear from his childhood achievements, a decidedly precocious one. He was early addicted to scientific, especially biological, study and relates successive interests in mechanics, birds, fossils, and sea shells between the ages of 7 and 10. As a portent of scholarly productivity to come, he published his first scientific paper at the age of 10— a one page note on a partly albino sparrow he had observed in a public park. Shortly after, he contrived to serve after school hours as a volunteer laboratory assistant to the director of the local natural history museum, a mala-

---

[1] It should be understood that "he" and "Piaget" refer throughout these pages to Piaget *and* his many able assistants and collaborators over the years.

[2] Much of the following material on Piaget's life is drawn from his autobiography (1952a, pp. 237-256).

3

cologist or specialist in molluscs. During the four years he worked with the director, and in the ensuing years until 1930, he published about 25 papers on molluscs and related zoological matters, of which some 20 were in print before he reached the age of 21. His precocious productivity resulted in some humorous episodes; for example, he was offered (on the basis of his publications) the position of curator of the mollusc collection in the Geneva museum while still in secondary school! He pursued his formal higher education at the University of Neuchâtel, where he received his baccalaureate degree in 1915 and, following a dissertation on the molluscs of Valais, his doctorate in the natural sciences in 1918.

Throughout his adolescent and postadolescent years, Piaget read extensively in philosophy, religion, biology, sociology, and psychology—always taking copious notes on problems which occurred to him as he went along. One outcome of all this reading and rumination was a brief bout of ill health; the other was a philosophical novel (1918). Here and in his unpublished notes are ideas prophetic of theoretical concepts which were fully elaborated only much later. Three of these can be seen in some detail.

First, from reading Bergson and others he acquired the view that biology ought somehow to contribute to the solution of classical epistemological problems. At the same time, however, he sensed that some other, as yet unrealized, discipline was needed to mediate between the two. In subsequent years, developmental psychology came to serve as the mediator and a series of works on genetic epistemology was the final outcome (1950, 1957a). His early biological training and orientation are readily apparent in all his theorizing about mental development; as one symptom, he is fond of referring to the ontogenesis of thought as "mental embryology" (e.g., 1947).

Second, he came to believe that external actions as well as thought processes admit of logical organization and, indeed, that logic itself may stem from a sort of spontaneous organization of acts. In his later work, this notion seems to have been expressed in two related forms: first, that logical structures can be used to describe the organization of concrete, motor acts as well as that of symbolic, interiorized "thought" in the conventional sense (1937a); second, that all thought is essentially interiorized action from which it follows that the organization of overt action and of inner thinking can be characterized in the same general way, can be placed on the same continuum (1949a).

Finally, and perhaps most important, it was in this early, "prepsychology" period that he began formulating tentative views about totalities— Gestalt-like structures-of-the-whole—and about the possible kinds of equilibria which could characterize such structures. In any structure consisting of parts of a whole containing these parts, he believed there are only three possible forms of equilibrium: predominance of the parts with consequent deformations of the whole, predominance of the whole with consequent deformation of the parts, and reciprocal preservation of both whole and parts. Of these three, only the last is a "good" and "stable" equilibrium, the others deviating to a greater or lesser degree from this optimum. Piaget asserts that even at that time he believed that the third, stable form of equilibrium characterized the organization of intelligence at its higher levels, while the inferior forms would describe the structure of perception. It is interesting to note that, although almost all his writing from the early 1920's reflect—in greater or lesser degree—preoccupation with problems of equilibrium, the definitive statement on cognitive development as an equilibration process—a notion now at the heart of Piaget's thought—was published some 40 years after these adolescent musings (1957b).

After receiving his doctorate in 1918, Piaget left Neuchâtel in search of some training and experience in psychology. During the next year or two he wandered from place to place, not finding any problems in which he could really get involved. His activities included academic and practicum work at the laboratories of Wreschner and Lipps, at Bleuler's psychiatric clinic, and at the Sorbonne. While studying at the latter, he was offered the opportunity to work in Binet's laboratory at a Paris grade school. Simon, who was in charge of the laboratory, suggested that Piaget might undertake the project of standardizing Burt's reasoning tests on Parisian children. Although Piaget began his task without enthusiasm, his interest grew when he began the actual testing. He found himself becoming increasingly fascinated, not with the psychometric and normative aspects of the test data, but with the processes by which the child achieved his answers—especially his incorrect answers. By adapting psychiatric examining procedures he had acquired at Bleuler's clinic and in practicum courses at the Sorbonne, he was using the "clinical method" of searching questions, of following the child's thought wherever it leads, and so on, a method which was later to become a Piagetian trademark.

During the next two years he continued to do research on the child's responses to the Burt test questions and to other stimulus situations. He published the results of these first psychological experiments in a series of four articles (Piaget, 1921a, 1921b, 1922; Piaget and Rossello, 1921). One of the four (1921b) was accepted for publication by Claparède at Geneva, editor of the *Archives de Psychologie*. Claparède, evidently impressed by this one sample of Piaget's work, thereupon offered him the job of Director of Studies at the Institut J. J. Rousseau in Geneva. In this position he was to have ample research time and an almost completely free hand in developing his own program of child study. Piaget accepted the job on trial in 1921 and shortly after embarked on a series of studies which was to make him world famous before he was 30 years old.

Piaget's studies of the child's language, causal reasoning, "theories" about everyday phenomena, moral judgment, etc., conducted in the period from 1921 to 1925 are still by far his best known works. These experiments are described in his first five books (1924b, 1924c, 1926, 1927b, 1932) and in a lesser-known series of important articles (1923, 1924d, 1925, 1927a, 1929b, 1931; Krafft and Piaget, 1926; Margairaz and Piaget, 1925). In his autobiography (1952a), Piaget offers some interesting comments on this early, highly controversial work. First, it is clear that these studies were planned and conducted primarily to provide data for the systematic and comprehensive epistemology which, since his youth, had been one of Piaget's chief preoccupations. That is, only to the naive reader were the famous five books merely empirical studies of child thought. Second, it is also clear that he regarded them as tentative and sketchy first drafts to be followed by a later, more careful and comprehensive work. He was greatly surprised at the widespread attention they received and apparently a little dismayed that preliminary ideas should be treated by others as final statements of position. Finally, whatever shortcomings others have found in these studies, Piaget himself was in retrospect impressed by two essential ones. First of all, only an incomplete picture of cognitive structure and its development can be gained by the study of verbally-expressed thought alone, that is, by questions put to the child in the absence of concrete manipulanda towards which the child's responses can be directed. Yet the 1921 to 1925 work was almost wholly of this type. It was only later that Piaget became clearly aware, through the study of infants and the restudy of school-age children, of the necessity of distinguishing between logic-in-action, logic applied to concrete givens, and—the kind of behavior with which most of the early work dealt —logic applied to purely symbolic, verbal statements.[3] The second shortcoming, related to the first, was one of which Piaget was fully aware in the early 1920's but was unable to remedy until later. In accord with his concern about part-whole relations mentioned earlier, he strove in vain to find general constructs which would adequately describe logical operations. To be sure, the distinction between reversible and irreversible thought had already been made (e.g., 1924b, 1924d). However, the actual embedding of the reversibility concept into specific structures, such as the *groupings* of middle childhood and the *groups* and *lattices* of adolescence, was a much later development.

Two other developments of importance occurred during Piaget's early incumbency at Geneva. First, he read the work of the Gestalt psychologists with great interest but reacted to it with mixed feelings. He was gratified to learn that others had succeeded in formulating a coherent theory concerning part-whole relationships, a theory which could be experimentally fruitful. However, he early became convinced that the Gestalt doctrine of nonadditivity of parts within a whole (whole not equal to the sum of the parts), while correctly describing the structure of perception, did not apply

---

[3] Although Piaget does not mention this in his autobiography, early writings show that the distinction between concrete operations, bearing on sense data, and formal operations, or "operations to the second power," performed on the codified *results* of prior concrete operations, was already dimly sensed (1922, 1924d).

to the equilibrium states which logical operations tend to achieve. To be sure, as was mentioned above, the *specific* nature of such equilibrium states and of the algebraic structures describing operations-in-equilibrium was not yet elaborated. At this time Piaget maintained that the Gestalt structures were not descriptive of logical operations; in later publications, he was to treat the relation of Gestalt theory to his own system more fully (1936, 1937b, 1954, 1955b).

A second, and in a sense less important, trend during the early 1920's was what one writer has called Piaget's "flirtation" with psychoanalytic theory (Anthony, 1957). It is clear that Piaget read Freud and, in accord with his development-of-intelligence orientation, was particularly interested in the psychoanalytic conception of cognitive as opposed to affective functioning. Thus, there is an interesting early attempt to compare the structure of unconscious adult thought, conscious adult thought, and the conscious thought of the young child (1923). Similarly, in discussing the phenomenon of *artificialism* he draws upon Freudian theory to explain certain childhood myths (1926). However, it seems clear that the flirtation, if it can be called such at all, eventuated in no sustained affair or marriage; as his own studies proliferated and his own theoretical system assumed form and substance, references to psychoanalytic theory tend to drop out. Only once in later years, to this writer's knowledge, did he make any really detailed comparison between aspects of his theory and aspects of Freudian theory (1945), and here his treatment of the latter was more critical than sympathetic. This is of course not to say that the two systems cannot be and have not been interrelated with profit; there is Wolff's monograph (1960), and several other attempts at interrelation (Odier, 1956; Anthony, 1956a, 1956b, 1957). However, it is safe to say that Piaget *himself* has neither been profoundly influenced by Freud nor has he tried to wed the two systems.

In 1925 Piaget was given a part-time appointment at the University of Neuchâtel and until 1929 divided his activities between Neuchâtel and Geneva. This four-year period was a busy one for him, since his research activities had to compete with a heavy teaching load. These activities consisted principally of two distinct but related lines of investigation. First, he began preliminary work on the child's reaction to changes in the shape of plastic substances like clay, that is, transformations of shape which leave invariant or "conserved" the mass, weight, and volume. These early studies were important for two reasons. First, they comprised the first experiments in which the shift to less exclusively verbal tasks becomes apparent. Second, they were the germ of a whole rash of experiments of classification, number, quantity, time, space, measurement, velocity, and so on—many involving this matter of "conservation," or the finding of invariants amidst transformations—published in book after book from about 1940 on.

But the 1925 to 1929 era saw an even more significant development in Piaget's work, a series of investigations of cognitive evolution in infancy.

With his wife's assistance (Valentine Chatenay, a former student at the Institut J. J. Rousseau), he spent a great deal of time carefully observing both spontaneous and elicited behavior in his own three infants. This work was reported in most complete form in three books (1936, 1937a, 1945) and one article (1927c) but is also summarized in many other places (e.g., 1937b, 1946c, 1953). These investigations of infant behavior did more than simply provide Piaget with needed data on the early foundations of cognitive development. They also clarified his thinking on fundamental problems such as the specific nature of cognitive adaptation and the relation between cognitive organization in the initial presymbolic, sensory-motor period and in the subsequent periods of symbolic thought. It was also during the 1925 to 1929 period that Piaget finally concluded his work in the field of malacology. Although he never again did experimental studies in this area, a number of conceptions based on this work has survived as an integral part of his system, most notably in his views on organism-environment relationships, both biological and psychological (1936).

In 1929 Piaget returned to full-time status at the University of Geneva, becoming assistant director and later (in 1932) co-director of Institut J. J. Rousseau. During the 1929 to 1939 interval, Piaget became involved in two time-consuming administrative enterprises. First, the Institut, hitherto a private organization, became affiliated with the University of Geneva, and Piaget was the prime mover in the reorganization which followed. Second, he became director of Bureau International d'Education, a newly-formed intergovernmental organization which has since become jointly affiliated with and sponsored by the International Office of Education and Unesco. Although the job was a time-consuming one, it gave Piaget an opportunity to work towards a translation of developmental findings into educational practices. To this end Piaget and his co-workers have in the subsequent decades written extensively on the application of his theory to pedagogic methods (e.g., 1951, 1956a; Aebli, 1951). In the postwar years, Piaget has remained active in educational affairs, both with the Swiss government and with Unesco.

The period 1929 to 1939 saw a number of significant scientific activities. First, the teaching of a course on the history of scientific thought gave Piaget an excuse to pursue, more intensively than before, serious reading in the history of mathematics, physics, and biology. Although he had already expressed tentative concepts related to genetic epistemology (1924a, 1929a), the later, systematic opus on this subject (1950) seems largely to have been the fruit of his extensive reading and reflection during this 1929 to 1939 period.

The second major achievement was the resumption, on a larger scale and with the help of Szeminska, Inhelder, and others, of his earlier, preliminary studies of number and quantity concepts. Portions of this work were first described in several articles and monographs in the middle to late

1930's (1937d; Piaget and Szeminska, 1939; Inhelder, 1936; Szeminska, 1935). In 1941, a fuller account was presented in two books (Piaget and Szeminska, 1941; Piaget and Inhelder, 1941). This empirical work was significant on two counts. First, it constituted a systematic redirection of attention towards the intellectual constructions of early through middle childhood after an interlude of several years studying infant development. This renewed attack was to be more concerted and enduring than the famous work of the early 1920's directed towards the same subject population. A wide variety of what might be called the grand classes or modes of experience were eventually studied: first, number and quantity, and later, movement, velocity, time, space, measurement, probability, and classification. These experiments include some of the most original and ingenious ones Piaget has done.

Perhaps more important, the second series of studies of middle childhood, unlike the first, provided Piaget with long-awaited insight into the structural properties of thought. Beginning in 1937 (1937c, 1937d, 1937e) he introduced the concept of *grouping* (*groupement*). The notion that a group-like structure might serve as a theoretical model for cognition had, however, originated prior to this. Thus, Piaget had previously posited something called the *group of spatial displacements* as a model for the spatial behavior of the 18-month-old (1937a) and, as was mentioned above, had even earlier spoken of "reversibility" (a group property) in describing child thought in the middle years (1924b). However, the application of logico-algebraic concepts to intellectual structures was to be far more comprehensive and ambitious. In 1942 Piaget published a systematic and detailed description of the eight groupings which concrete operations form (1942). In 1949 there followed a more rigorous treatment of the same groupings plus a description of certain structures believed to apply to adolescent cognition (1949b). Finally, three years later, Piaget wrote a thin but forbidding book on the same general subject (1952b). It is difficult to overemphasize the importance of this shift towards logico-algebraic models for the form and content of Piaget's writings in the last 20 years. Unlike the earlier work, experimental data since 1940 or so are systematically interpreted in terms of these structural models, and they serve to unify and to permit comparisons among diverse findings in a way not possible in the earlier work. The Piaget of the 1920's and 1930's could in a sense be described as a theoretical pluralist: the parade of separate descriptive-explanatory concepts includes *egocentrism, syncretism, juxtaposition, realism, animism,* and others. Whatever their shortcomings may be, the development of a set of explicit logico-mathematical models for cognitive structure has lent a distinct conceptual unity and order to the Piaget of 1940 on. Knowing something about these models, one can predict with high probability how he will nowadays interpret any new set of behavioral data.

From 1940 until the present time Piaget has been engaged in a variety of activities. To begin with those of an administrative and academic nature, he assumed the directorship of the Psychology Laboratory at Geneva in 1940. He continued to edit the *Archives de Psychologie* with Rey and Lambercier and became first president of the newly-formed Swiss Society of Psychology, assuming joint editorship of its journal, the *Revue Suisse de Psychologie,* in 1942. He managed to give a lecture series in Paris in 1942 during the German occupation and delivered a briefer series after the war in Manchester, England; these lectures were subsequently translated and constitute the principal English summaries of Piaget's system (1946c, 1953). He received honorary degrees at various universities, including Brussels and the Sorbonne. Finally, as was mentioned, he remained active in the International Office of Education and, after it was organized, Unesco.

Research activities since 1940 divide into three major classes. First of all, there is the aforementioned series of studies on the cognition of number, quantity, space, and so forth (1946a, 1946b; Piaget and Inhelder, 1941, 1948, 1951; Piaget, Inhelder, and Szeminska, 1948; Piaget and Szeminska, 1941). The most recent work in this series is a volume on elementary classifying and serializing behavior (Inhelder and Piaget, 1959), and a book on imagery is in preparation (*ibid.,* p. 10, footnote). Two other volumes in the same vein are of particular interest. First, there is a book by Inhelder which describes the application of the quantity research to the diagnostic testing of mental defectives (Inhelder, 1943). Later, in collaboration with Piaget, she did a very interesting series of studies of scientific reasoning in adolescence (Inhelder and Piaget, 1955). This important work, besides constituting the only major study of adolescent thought by the Geneva group, also contains a thorough theoretical analysis of concrete operations, formal operations, and the relations between the two.

The second major project is a long series of perception experiments which have largely been published in the Swiss journal *Archives de Psychologie* since 1942. These perception studies, reported in some 40 articles at this writing, are more rigorous and quantitative than has typically been the case for the experiments on intellectual development.[4] To put it another way, these studies appear to the reader much more like conventional perception experiments—in methodological and expository form if not in content—than his intelligence experiments resemble conventional cognitive experiments. Again, quite unlike the case with his intelligence theories, the perceptual theory which has emerged from these investigations is intended to predict perceptual behavior quantitatively and in detail, given known parameters of the perceptual field (e.g., 1955a, 1960; Piaget, von Albertini, and Rossi, 1944; Piaget, Vinh-Bang, and Matalon, 1958; Vurpillot, 1959). Although

---

[4] The past tense may be advisable here, since the recent book on classification and seriation (Inhelder and Piaget, 1959)—an "intellectual development" book certainly—is considerably more quantitative than its predecessors.

Piaget's perception work can stand alone as a substantial body of research in its own right, there is no doubt that he conceives it in relation to the larger corpus of research in intellectual development (e.g., 1956-1957; Piaget and Morf, 1958a, 1958b).

The third major area of endeavor is Piaget's continuing development of a systematic theoretical and experimental attack on problems of genetic epistemology. In 1950 Piaget published a comprehensive three-volume work on this topic, focusing particular attention on the implications of his developmental findings for epistemological problems in mathematics, physics, biology, psychology, and sociology (1950). Five years later, aided by a grant from the Rockefeller Foundation, he established at Geneva the Centre International d'Epistémologie Génétique. Each year three distinguished scholars with epistemological interests are invited to the Centre for the academic year to collaborate with Genevan psychologists on certain delimited issues pertinent to genetic epistemology. Attempts are made to set forth problems which admit of experimental as well as theoretical study. At the year's end, findings and conclusions are presented at a symposium composed of these scholars plus eight or nine others invited to participate in critical discussions. The results of a given year's work are then published in a series of monographs, e.g., four for the academic year 1955-1956 (1957, Vols. I-IV). There are some 12 such monographs in print at this writing.

This completes the resumé of Piaget's life and work as of 1961. It is, however, possible to make reasonable predictions from past and present as to the shape of things to come. First of all, the perception studies show no signs of abating and are quite likely to continue on into the indefinite future, both the experimental investigations of new phenomena and accompanying refinements in the theory. As to the ontogenesis-of-intelligence research, several kinds of developments seem probable. One class of developments could bear the rubric "refinements of present work." These include psychometric standardization of various of the Piaget tasks on large samples (Tanner and Inhelder, 1956, pp. 87-89),[5] longitudinal investigations which follow developmental changes on these tasks in the same subjects over time (*ibid.*, p. 79), and cross-cultural studies, especially for the relatively more language-free problems (*ibid.*, pp. 93-94). The other class of developments might be called "extensions of present work." This subsumes, first of all, attempts at gap-filling—the study of problems and age groups as yet incompletely investigated. Just as the work on adolescent reasoning of a few years ago (Inhelder and Piaget, 1955) investigated a relatively neglected older group, so does the recent book on classification and seriation (Inhelder and Piaget, 1959) shed new light on the behavior of children in the pre-operational period (2 to 6 years). And of course the forthcoming work on imagery is

---

[5] Large-scale work of this genre is currently in progress in Montreal under the direction of Dr. Adrien Pinard.

intended as a research exploration of a hitherto understudied problem area. A second and different sort of extension concerns the application of Piaget's intellectual development theory and research to practical problems of education. As mentioned earlier, he has been active in the field of education for many years and finds it natural to discover in his own system implications for pedagogic methods (e.g., 1951). The most ambitious attempts to relate his ideas to educational problems have been made by one of his co-workers (Aebli, 1951), and others seem likely to follow.

There are also portents in Piaget's treatment of cognitive structure. The most important recent development here (although, like all of Piaget's theorizing, it has a long history) is an attempt to specify a general equilibration model of development, both intellectual and perceptual (e.g., 1957a). This endeavor, the viewing of developmental stages in terms of successive equilibrium states or moments within a continuous equilibration process, has really just begun and further work on it seems a future certainty. Secondly, Piaget has long been interested in the possibility of discovering the neuro-physiological substrate of the psychological structures he has described (e.g., 1949a). Finally, the institution of the Centre International d'Epistémologie Génétique has been, and will doubtless continue to be, the fulfillment of Piaget's lifelong interests in epistemology. The pattern of work in the Centre seems to be a recurrent one, to define a set of epistemological problems and then to bring to bear upon them conceptual and empirical ammunition from developmental psychology.

PIAGET AND PSYCHOLOGY

Parallel to the chronology of Piaget's professional achievements is another history which, like the first, is not yet ended—the impact of his work on the larger field of psychology of which it is a part. There appears to be here an interesting and perhaps informative vignette in the history of science —one worth a brief recounting. We shall begin with a short description of the apparent pattern of assimilation from the 1920's up to the present and then attempt an analysis of some of the causal factors which may underlie this pattern.

The pattern of response to Piaget's work over the last 40 years has been one of marked underassimilation. However, the pattern is not a regular and even one, either with respect to historical time or to the portion of Piaget's work assimilated. Most of his early work in psychology—the "famous five" books on language, judgment and reasoning, moral judgment, etc.—had a happier fate than was to be the norm. These books were quickly translated into English and many other languages, and the research they contained has stimulated a spate of experimental work by others, beginning in the late 1920's and continuing at a steady pace well into the present. It is a fair guess that the average psychologist today is still likely to respond "animism" to the stimulus word "Piaget" (it would be interesting to see how many could respond with "grouping"!).

However, the assimilation of subsequent research and theoretical productions has been well-nigh glacial in tempo. The important investigations of infants, the numerous studies of number, quantity, space, and so on, the perception work, and above all, perhaps, the developmental theory itself (groupings as cognitive models, the equilibration theory, and so on)—most of this is still not well known in the English-speaking psychological world. Indices of low assimilation are everywhere apparent. For instance, if speed of translation is taken as a partial index of demand, one finds that, to take but two examples, the basic work on infancy was published in French in 1936 and translated into English in 1952 (1936); the studies of measurement appeared in French in 1948 and in English in 1960 (Piaget, Inhelder, and Szeminska, 1948), and, needless to say, there are many books, even early ones (Piaget and Inhelder, 1941), which have never been translated. Similarly, Carmichael's 1295-page manual of child psychology (Carmichael, 1954) cites only the aforementioned first five books, Jersild's child psychology text cites just three of these five (Jersild, 1954), and his more recent book on adolescence cites no Piaget work at all (Jersild, 1957).

However, unless all signs are amiss, there seem to be definite indications of something like a "Piaget revival" which has been gaining momentum over the last five years or so. First of all, there is a small but growing number of research papers which treat of Piaget's post-1920's work; one good example is Braine's monograph (Braine, 1959). Secondly, the pace of translation seems definitely to have accelerated; there were no Piaget books translated into English between 1933 and 1949, but there have been some nine or more since 1950, with several others said to be on the way. Third, there are alleged to be at least three independent books on Piaget's system currently in preparation; this is surely the workings of the Zeitgeist with a vengeance! And there are other, miscellaneous undertones—a seminar on Piaget here or there, a growing number of references to his work in recent articles and books, and, of course, the conference from which the present monograph stemmed.

In summary, then, the pattern over the past 40 years seems to have been an early (and one-course) breakfast, almost no lunch, and at least what looks like the promise of a late but perhaps full-course dinner. How to account for this pattern? It is probably easier to explain the over-all low nutritional level than the feasts and famines. The first obstacle to adequate assimilation is the sheer size of Piaget's output: with his various collaborators he has written some 25 books and over 160 articles; these latter range from brief notes to book-length monographs and include many papers in obscure journals. This is a discouragingly large bibliography for the student of Piaget. Although there have been two summary books (1946c, 1953) and a number of quasi-summary articles, these are not obviously helpful to the neophyte, especially one in search of the total system. Similarly, even the better summary papers by others (e.g., Berlyne, 1957) can give only the bare bones of a system of this magnitude and complexity. A second obstacle is of course the fact that many of the books and almost all of the papers and monographs are still available only in French; it is probably true, Ph.D. language examinations notwithstanding, that many psychologists cannot read French easily.

Assuming that these obstacles can be overcome, however, there are further problems. Piaget generally makes difficult reading, in either French or English, for several reasons. There are many unfamiliar and poorly-defined concepts in the system which interlock into a very complex, hard-to-grasp theoretical matrix. The research methods and manner of reporting data are also unfamiliar. Much of the work is saturated with mathematical-logical and epistemological concerns foreign to the experience of the average American psychologist. These difficulties all arise from the fact that Piaget does not approach psychological subject matter in ways familiar to most of us. He sees problems we would not be likely to see, he attacks these problems with methods different from those we would espouse, and he often theorizes about his results in ways which would seem esoteric and even incomprehensible to us. For better or worse, it seems to be true that anything like an adequate understanding of Piaget's system (especially the less straightforwardly empirical aspects of it) demands a certain reorientation and acclimatization—a certain holding in abeyance of habitual ways of looking at things, at least until it all starts to come clear.

Although these reasons may account for the low level of assimilation, they scarcely account for the apparent peaks and troughs of the historical curve. This is a much more uncertain matter but at least a few tentative speculations can be advanced. One fact in need of explanation is the quick assimilation of the early work (much of its reception was highly critical, as is well known, but at least there was a reception). It may be that two forces working in union were partly responsible. First of all, the content of the early books, especially that of the experiments themselves, is fairly straightforward and easy to grasp. Although there is considerable theorizing, the concepts are framed in words rather than logico-mathematical symbols, and many of them had led previous lives in the writing of earlier scholars and hence were not totally new and unfamiliar. But more than this, developmental study of children's cognition was already in vogue,[6] both *per se* and within the context of the intelligence test movement, and Piaget's highly original experiments may have found ready acceptance as fodder for an already going concern.

---

[6] Note—and this is important—that what was in vogue was the classical age-as-independent-variable *developmental* study of the kind Piaget has always done, not the *antecedent-consequent* design which occupies so prominent a place in child psychology today, e.g., the work of Sears and his associates.

The most plausible explanation for the many lean years that followed relates to changes in the psychological surround in which Piaget's system was growing and developing—changes in the field as a whole which naturally radiated into the subfield of child psychology. Koch expresses these changes in the following words:

> It is hardly necessary to reconstruct the atmosphere of the Age of Theory, particularly that of its classical interval, say, from the mid-thirties to the mid-forties. The regulation of systematic work by the directives and imagery of hypothetico-deduction, the sub-culture surrounding operational definition, the lore concerning the intervening variable, the belief in the imminence (if not achievement) of precisely quantitative behavioral theory of comprehensive scope . . . —all of these are easily recalled, if indeed recall is necessary. The rather stable geography of dominating theoretical positions and the standard contexts of apposition and opposition will also come easily to mind. These scattered fragments define an ideology not discontinuous with that of the present period (Koch, 1959, p. 732).

Add to this, for the field of child psychology especially, a shift towards personality versus cognitive development, antecedent-consequent versus straightforward developmental design, a learning-theoretical orientation and, in keeping with the atmosphere Koch describes, a great emphasis on precise quantitative methods in the study of children. One can scarcely conceive of a system more orthogonal to such a Zeitgeist than Piaget's, and it should perhaps come as no surprise that it received little attention during these tough-minded years.

And finally, why the recent advent of what we called a "Piaget revival"? Again, the principal motive force is probably another shift in the tenor of the field. There is good reason to believe that the frozen canons of what Koch calls the Age of Theory are beginning to thaw.

> There is a new contextualism abroad, a new readiness to consider problem-centered curiosity a sufficient justification of inquiry. . . . Schedules have been re-defined; systematic claims localized or, if general, made more modest; pre-theoretical knowledge has found a higher priority in the economy; a wider range of subject matters has begun to assert the right to autonomous systematic development; and a wider variety of formulations has been granted "theoretical" citizenship (ibid., pp. 784-785).

One gets the impression that psychology, and this of course includes child psychology, has become more modest in its self-demands and in its aims and, with this, simply a little less fussy about where and how it obtains interesting information about human behavior. Needless to say, and Koch makes this clear, this sort of change occurs in pockets rather than of a piece throughout the field and is often a furtive thing which intrudes unbidden and in stealth amid the blare of Age of Theory trumpets. Such a climate would be much more salubrious for Piaget than its predecessors. Whatever its shortcomings, Piaget's system is surely the source *par excellence* for offbeat experiments—just the sort to pique the interest of psychologists chafing under Age of Theory constraints.

There may be other more specific reasons for the revival—these also perhaps deriving their existence from the larger change of Zeitgeist. One might be a simple resurgence of interest in developmental theory; witness, for example, the recent publication of a book on this topic (Harris, 1957). The work, especially the recent work, of Heinz Werner and his students in this country has shown that a developmental theory of the straightaway, nonantecedent-consequent variety can be experimentally fruitful, and there is a decided similarity between his style of experimenting and theorizing and that of Piaget. Another reason for the revival might be a growing general interest in cognition and, particularly, in theories of cognitive structure; there is a remarkable communality of emphasis in the theorizing of Heider, Newcomb, Festinger, Abelson and Rosenberg, Peak, and Simon. Piaget also has a theory of cognitive structure and, unlike the others, this theory purports to provide information about developmental *changes* in structure. As such, it lies at the intersection of both recent trends—developmental theory and theory of cognitive structure—and this may draw increased attention to it, continuing a trend that seems well under weigh.

2

SOME ASPECTS OF PIAGET'S GENETIC APPROACH
TO COGNITION

BÄRBEL INHELDER[1]

University of Geneva, Switzerland

POINT OF VIEW, METHODS, AND MODELS

Jean Piaget's work must be both baffling and intriguing to Anglo-Saxon psychologists, particularly to those of the younger generation who have been brought up in S-R theory and in logical empiricism. In fact, it goes beyond experimental psychology. Piaget poses his questions from the point of view of psycho-epistemology; his methods, in the realm of cognition, are exploratory and flexible; and his methods of analysis are those of logical symbolism. But the experts in each of these disciplines tend to consider him as too eclectic and as something of an interloper. And yet the interest which has been shown in the Genevan researches seems to suggest that the facts brought out by this particular approach shed a new light on the intellectual development of the child.

By way of introduction I would like to outline briefly first, the point of view of genetic epistemology which orients our researches, second, the methods, and third, the models used.

The Point of View of Genetic Epistemology

Piaget has, from the very beginning of his career, constantly posed questions of genetic epistemology. It is true that, in their most general terms, such questions as: "What is knowledge?" can give rise only to speculative controversy; but, if formulated in more restricted terms and in terms of genesis, questions such as "Under what laws does knowledge develop and change?" can be dealt with scientifically. Research work in genetic epistemology seeks to analyze the mechanisms of the growth of knowledge insofar as it pertains to scientific thought and to discover the passage from states of least knowledge to those of the most advanced knowledge. To this end the categories and concepts of established science, such as those of space,

---

[1] The author wishes to acknowledge gratefully the kind assistance of Dr. G. Seagrim and Dr. M. J. Aschner in the translation and editing of this paper.

time, causality, number, and logical classes, have been studied as they develop in the life of the child.

Before undergoing formal tuition, the young child progressively elaborates his first logical and mathematical constants, such as logical classes, and the principles of conservation of numerical correspondences, of spatial dimensions, and of physical matter. These constants allow him to handle the transformations of the physical world in reality and in thought. The laws of this elaboration, while allowing us on the one hand to throw light on epistemological problems, allow us at the same time to analyze more appropriately the active part played by the child in the development of his knowledge of the world. For it does not seem—and I am here anticipating the interpretation of the facts—as if the growth of knowledge in the child were due exclusively to a cumulative stockpiling of information received or exclusively to the emergence of a sudden "insight" independent of preliminary preparation. Rather the development of knowledge seems to be the result of a process of elaboration that is based essentially on the activity of the child. In effect, two types of activity can be distinguished: firstly, a logico-mathematical type of activity, the activity in bringing together, of dissociating, of ordering, of counting, and so on—any activity for which objects are no more than a support; and secondly, an activity of a physical type, an activity of exploration aimed at extracting information from objects themselves, such as their colors, form, weight, and so on. It is thus in acting on the external world that, according to Piaget, the child elaborates a more and more adequate knowledge of reality. It is precisely the successive forms of his activity in the course of his development that determine his modes of knowledge.

One is often puzzled about where to place such an epistemological interpretation in the theory of ideas. Konrad Lorenz, with whom Piaget and I had the privilege of partaking for several years in succession in a seminar on the psychobiological development of the child, expressed, at the end of the third year, his astonished recognition of Piaget's place in the epistemological spectrum: "All along I have thought that Piaget was one of those tiresome empiricists and only now, after studying Piaget's work on the genesis of the categories of thought, I have come to realize that he is really not so far removed from Kant." On the other hand, some Russian colleagues, who believed Piaget to be an idealist because he did not admit that knowledge of the external world is simply a reflection of the objects in it, posed to him the following leading question: "Do you think an object exists prior to any knowledge of it?" Piaget replied. "As a psychologist, I have no idea; I only know an object to the extent that I act upon it; I can affirm nothing about it prior to such an action." Then someone offered a more conciliatory formulation: "For us an object is part of the world. Can *the external world* exist independently of and prior to our knowledge of it?" To this, Piaget replied: "The instruments of our knowl-

edge form part of our organism, which forms part of the external world."
Later Piaget overheard a conversation between these colleagues in which he
was able to distinguish the following statement: "Piaget is not an idealist."
In effect, Piaget is quite willing to label himself a "relativist," in the non-
skeptical sense of the term, because, for him, that which is knowable and
that which changes during the genesis of knowledge is the relation between
the knowing subject and the object known. Some commentators go further
and refer to him as an "activist," reflecting Goethe's assertion that "In the
beginning was the deed."

The Method

In studying the formation of concepts and of intellectual operations, we
have made use of experimental materials and methods which differ somewhat from the classical ones of child psychology. In associationist or Gestalt-
inspired investigations, the child is presented with elements or configurations; in our investigations designed to lay bare the operational mechanisms
of thought, he is brought to grips with physical or spatial transformation
of the materials. For instance, he deals with problems related to the pouring
of liquids from one container to another or with the spatial displacement
of rods. We then observe the manner in which, throughout the course of
his development, the child overcomes the conflict presented by the variations
and constancies involved.

Since we wish to avoid imposing any preconceived notions on our data,
our investigations of the child's thought are always initiated by an exploratory method that is adapted to the child's level of comprehension, both in
respect to the nature of the questions and to the order of their presentation.
The experimenter does not merely take account of the child's responses but
asks also for the child's explanation of them. And, by modifying the questions and the experimental conditions, the investigator seeks to test the
genuineness and the consistency of the child's responses. Proceeding cau-
tiously, one attempts to avoid two evils—one of imposing on the child
a point of view which is foreign to him, and the other, of accepting as pure
currency each of his responses. By means of this exploratory method—one
which calls for both imagination and critical sense—we believe we obtain
a truer picture of the child's thought than we would by the use of standardized tests which involve the risk of missing unexpected and often essential
aspects of his thought.

It goes without saying that results obtained by such a flexible procedure
do not lend themselves to statistical treatment. Because of this we have
undertaken, with M. Bang, the standardization of some of our procedures,
adapting them to the diagnosis of the reasoning process. When we have
once explored the whole range of reasoning exhibited by children of different ages, we then standardize the procedure of investigation. While standardized procedures increase precision, this method loses, of course, some

of the plasticity of the exploratory technique. The analysis of our observations then proceeds by the following steps: (a) a qualitative classification of the different types of reasoning; (b) an analysis in terms of logical models; (c) an analysis of frequencies of responses and dispersions by ages; (d) an hierarchical analysis by means of ordinal scales.

It is noteworthy and reassuring that this hierarchical and statistical analysis lends broad confirmation to the succession of stages of reasoning which had been established in a preliminary form by qualitative and logical methods.

The Models

For the analysis of the operations of thought processes, Piaget has borrowed models from modern mathematics, such as Klein's "four group" (*Vierergruppe*) and the lattices and structures of Bourbaki (algebraic structures, structures of order, and topological structures). He has himself constructed weaker structures, called *groupements,* which are comparable to semilattices. The use of such models in no way implies that the psychologist has succumbed to logicism, that is, has decided in advance that the real thought of the child should conform to the laws which govern logical and mathematical structures. Only the facts can decide whether or not it does so conform, in exactly the same way that facts decide whether a statistical distribution obeys one law or another. These models represent the ideal system of all possible operations, while actual thought makes but one choice amongst them. More than 20 years of research have shown that cognitive development approximates these models without attaining them completely.

The effective operations of the child's concrete thinking and of the formal thinking of the adolescent constitute among themselves closed systems of which the most important characteristic is their reversibility. An operation can be defined psychologically as an action which can be internalized and which is reversible—capable of taking place in both directions. Piaget distinguishes two forms of reversibility: inversion (negation) and reciprocity. At the level of concrete logical thought, negation applies to the classificatory operations, and reciprocity to those involving relations. While the thinking of a child of less than 6 years (in Switzerland at least) is still characterized by the absence of the reversibility, from 6 to 11 years the child can already achieve, in given situations, one or the other, but not both, of these forms of reversibility. Those more able adolescents who come to handle formal and propositional operations use the two forms of reversibility simultaneously. These two sets of operations form a unitary system which corresponds to the model of the four transformations (IRNC) described by Piaget.[2] This double reversibility confers a higher degree of mobility and coherence upon formal thought.

------

[2] I = Identity; R = Reciprocity; N = Negation; C = Correlate; NR = C; CR = N; CN = R; NRC = I.

COGNITIVE DEVELOPMENT

Definitions, Criteria of Stages, and Working Hypothesis

Like many other authors, Piaget describes cognitive development in terms of stages. Whereas somatic and perceptual development seem to be continuous, intellectual development seems to take place in stages, the criteria of which can be defined as follows:

1. Each stage involves a period of formation (genesis) and a period of attainment. Attainment is characterized by the progressive organization of a composite structure of mental operations.

2. Each structure constitutes at the same time the attainment of one stage and the starting point of the next stage, of a new evolutionary process.

3. The order of succession of the stages is constant. Ages of attainment can vary within certain limits as a function of factors of motivation, exercise, cultural milieu, and so forth.

4. The transition from an earlier to a later stage follows a law of implication analogous to the process of integration, preceding structures becoming a part of later structures.

Some of these hypotheses, advanced in connection with our previous research, have already found confirmation in the two-year longitudinal study which we have conducted. As we have outlined earlier, on the basis of having seen each child on only one occasion and at a definite moment of his development, the different types of reasoning seem to recur in a stable order of developmental stages.

In other respects we have noted certain differences between the "longitudinal" results now obtained and those obtained by former methods. The elaboration of certain notions and of methods of reasoning was found to be slightly accelerated in the subjects of the longitudinal study as compared to those of the control (cross-sectional) groups. This acceleration, probably resulting from practice, does not seem the same at all levels. When the child is given a series of reasoning procedures, we notice a tendency to homogeneity and generalization in his reasoning behavior which, though slight in the course of the formation of a structure, manifests itself more clearly once the structure has been achieved.

In certain areas, it now seems possible to separate some relatively constant evolutionary processes. For example, at regular intervals, the experimenter confronts the child with the problem of the conservation of a given physical quantity. A liquid is poured from one container into another of a different size. In early trials the child is impressed by the change in one of the dimensions of the liquid, neglecting others. With naive commitment to his position, he refuses to admit any conservation of the liquid quantity. Some months later, however, the same child is beginning to doubt his earlier stand. He tries to put the different changes into perspective, without, however, attaining an understanding of their compensation or inversion. One frequently observes a whole series of attempts to establish relationships, from the simplest to the most complex. Still later, the child finally affirms the constancy of the liquid quantity: "There is the same amount of liquid to drink." His justifications become more and more coherent; they indicate that he is beginning to comprehend the changes in the liquid as a reversible system of operations in which the modifications compensate each other. Strangely enough, not only does the child seem to have forgotten his own trials and errors, but he considers their possibility quite absurd. The events seem to suggest that a mental structure is prepared by a continuous series of trials, but that once it is established it becomes relatively independent of the process involved in its formation.

A theory of stages remains incomplete, however, as long as it does not clarify the contradiction between two concepts of development—the one stressing the complete continuity, and the other the absolute discontinuity, of stages. It seems to us, however, that this contradiction is more apparent than real. Our first longitudinal investigations led us to a third notion (as a hypothesis); namely, that in the development of intellectual operations, phases of continuity alternate with phases of discontinuity. Continuity and discontinuity would have to be defined by the relative dependence or independence of new behavior with respect to previously established behavior. Indeed, it seems as if during the formation of a structure of reasoning (characteristic of stage A) each new procedure depends on those the child has just acquired. Once achieved, this structure serves as a starting point for new acquisitions (characteristic of stage B). The latter will then be relatively independent of the formative process of the former structure. It is only in this sense that there would be discontinuity in passing from one stage to another.

If this working hypothesis were confirmed, the theory of developmental stages would take on a new meaning. We would then be inclined to regard it as more than a methodological tool. Rather, it would seem to offer a true picture of the formation of the child's intellectual processes.

Stages of Cognitive Development in Terms of Their Genesis and Structures

Three operational structures can be distinguished in the cognitive development of the child; each one characterizes the attainment of a major stage of development and, within each one, substages can be distinguished.

Stage I. Sensory-motor operations. The first major stage occupies approximately the first 18 months. It is characterized by the progressive formation of the schema of the permanent object and by the sensory-motor structuration of one's immediate spatial surroundings. The observations and longitudinal studies carried out by Piaget on his own children indicate that this progression originates in the functional exercising of mechanisms that are reflexive in origin, and leads gradually to a system of movements and of displacements. In this way the child's conception of the permanence of objects is brought about. This sensory-motor system is made up of displacements which, although they are not reversible in the mathematical sense, they are nonetheless amenable to inversion (*renversables*). The displacements made in one direction can be made in the inverse direction; the child can return to his starting point; he can attain the same goal by different routes. In the coordination of these movements into a system, the child comes to realize that objects have permanence; they can be found again, whatever their displacements (even if these be out of the field of vision). Piaget has compared this system, which has the characteristics of a group structure, to the structure of Poincaré's model of the geometric "group of displacements."

One can distinguish six substages in the course of this first major stage of development; their continuity is assured by "schemata" of action. The schemata are transposable or generalizable actions. The child establishes relations between similar objects or between objects which are increasingly dissimilar, including relations between those objects and his own body (for instance the extension of the schema of graspable objects to that of invisible objects). Thus, a schema can be defined as the structure common to all those acts which—from the subject's point of view—are equivalent.

The development of sensory-motor schemata is distinguished from habit-family hierarchies by the fact that a new acquisition does not consist merely in the association of a new stimulus or a new movement-response to already existing stimuli or movements. Instead, each fresh acquisition consists in the assimilation of a new object or situation to an existing schema, thus enlarging the latter and coordinating it with other schemata. On the other hand, a schema is more than a Gestalt in that it results simultaneously from the action of the subject and from his prior experience of accommodation to the object. The schema is thus the result of a process of assimilation which, at the level of psychological behavior, is a continuation of biological assimilation.

Stage II. Concrete thinking operations. The second developmental stage extends from the middle of the second year until the eleventh or twelfth year. It is characterized by a long process of elaboration of mental operations. The process is completed by about the age of 7 and is then followed by an equally long process of structuration. During their elaboration, concrete thought processes are irreversible. We observe how they gradually become reversible. With reversibility, they form a system of concrete operations. For example, we can establish that although a 5-year-old has long since grasped the permanence of objects, he has by no means yet any notion of the elementary physical principle of the conservation of matter.

Let us consider one of the many possible examples: Given two equal balls of plasticene, the child is asked to roll one of them into a long sausage form, to flatten it into a pancake, or to break it into small pieces. He is then asked, in terms adapted to his understanding, whether the quantity of matter has increased, decreased, or remained the same. This experiment and others similar to it have shown that most 5- or 6-year-olds assert without hesitation that each change in form involves a change in the amount of matter. Influenced sometimes by the increase in one dimension, sometimes by the decrease in the other, the child seems uncritically to accept the dictates of whatever aspect of change he happens to perceive. Errors decrease gradually, as the older child becomes more and more inclined to relate different aspects or dimensions to one another, until we finally come to a principle of invariance, which may be formulated somewhat as follows: "There must be the same amount of plasticene all the time. You only have to make the sausage into a ball again and you can see right away that nothing is added and nothing is taken away."

After a period of gradual construction, and at about 7 years of age, a thought structure is formed; as a structure, it is not yet separated from its concrete content. In contrast with the sensory-motor actions of the first stage—which were executed only in succession—the various thought operations of the second stage are carried out simultaneously, thus forming systems of operations. These systems, however, are still incomplete. They are characterized by two forms of reversibility: (a) negation, as expressed in the plasticene experiment, in which a perceived change in form is canceled by its corresponding negative thought operation; and (b) reciprocity, as expressed in the child's discovery that "being a foreigner" is a reciprocal relationship, or that left-right, before-behind spatial relationships are relative. At the concrete level, these forms of reversibility are used independently of one another; in formal thought, they will form one unified system of operations.

The gradual formation of this system of reciprocal relations can be observed most easily in an experiment concerning the relativity of points of view in a system of perspectives. The material for such an experiment—conducted by Piaget and Meyer-Taylor—consists of a landscape of three cardboard mountains, and a series of pictures of landscapes drawn from different points of view. The child remains at a given position, while the experimenter moves from one to another. For each position taken by the experimenter, the child is asked to select the picture which represents what the experimenter sees. It is difficult for 5-year-olds to realize that another person may see something different from what he (the child) sees. However, during the following years, the increasingly operational character of the child's thought leads to a definite progress in his choice of pictures, until finally he solves the problem.

Thus, during the course of this second period of development, we can follow the genesis of thought processes which—at about 7 years of age—issues in the elementary logicomathematical thought structures. Nevertheless, it still requires years before these structures are brought to bear on all possible concrete contents. It can be shown, for example, that the principle of invariance (constancy, conservation) is applied to the quantity of matter earlier than to weight, and to volume still later. In every case, as earlier schemas are integrated into later ones, they are altered in the process. Thus, the process seems indeed to be one of genetic construction—a gradual process of equilibration within a limited system of concrete operations. Equilibrium within this system is attained at about 11 or 12 years of age. This operational structure, in turn, forms the basis of the development of the formal thinking operations.

Stage III. Formal thinking operations. The third stage of intellectual development begins, on the average, at about 11 or 12 years of age and is characterized by the development of formal, abstract thought operations. In a rich cultural environment, these operations come to form a stable system of thought structures at about 14 or 15 years of age.

In contrast to the child in stage II, whose thought is still bound to the concrete here and now, the adolescent is capable of forming hypotheses and of deducing possible consequences from them. This hypotheticodeductive level of thought expresses itself in linguistic formulations containing propositions and logical constructions (implication, disjunction, etc.). It is also evident in the manner in which experiments are carried out, and proofs provided. The adolescent organizes his experimental procedure in a way that indicates a new sort of thought structure.

The following are two of many possible examples of formal thinking, one concerning combinatorial or formal logic, and the other, proportionality. In the experiment on combinatorial logic, the child is presented with five bottles of colorless liquid. The first, third, and fifth bottles, combined together, will produce a brownish color; the fourth contains a color-reducing solution, and the second bottle is neutral. The child's problem is to find out how to produce a colored solution. The adolescent in this third stage of development gradually discovers the combinatorial method. This method consists in the construction of a table of all the possible combinations and of determining the effectiveness or the ineffectiveness of each factor.

In experiments on proportionality the adolescent is given a candle, a projection screen, and a series of rings of different diameters; each ring is on a stick which can be stuck into a board with evenly spaced holes. The instructions are to place all the rings between the candle and the screen in such a way that they will produce only a single "unbroken" shadow on the screen—the shadow of "a ring." Gradually, the adolescent discovers that "there must be some relationship," and he tries to find out what relationship it is by systematic attempts, until finally he becomes aware that it is a matter of proportionality. As one bright 15-year-old said, "The thing is to keep the same proportion between the size of the ring and the distance from the candle; the absolute distance doesn't matter."

These experimental methods of procedure were not "taught" in our Geneva schools when our subjects were at this age level. Our subjects, at the

point of departure for the formal thought structures, discovered these procedures without specific tuition.

In analyzing these thought structures, Piaget found that they come
more and more to approximate formal models as the subject's experimental
procedures become more and more effective. The combinatorial method, for
example, corresponds to a lattice structure and the method of proportionality
to the structure of a group. Above all, the formal thought structure, as compared to the concrete, is marked by a higher degree of reversibility. And,
in this case, the two forms of reversibility already constituted—negation and
reciprocity—are now united in a completely operational system. We can say
that the new operational abilities formed during this third period are the
abilities that open up unlimited possibilities for the youth to participate
constructively in the development of scientific knowledge—provided that
his setting offers him a suitable practice-ground and a favorable intellectual
atmosphere.

An Hypothesis Concerning Factors of
Cognitive Development

According to Piaget the genesis of the mechanisms of knowledge cannot
be explained by any of the classical factors of developmental theory; it is
not due solely to maturation (we observe only phenotypes, never genotypes);
it does not result solely from learning on the basis of experience (the capacity
to learn is itself tied to development); and it does not result solely from
social transmissions (a child transforms the elements received while assimilating them). Piaget advances the hypothesis that another factor must be
put into play with those above. This is the factor of equilibration. It operates
in the sense which von Bertalanffy (e.g., Tanner and Inhelder, 1960) speaks
of in referring to "a steady state of an open system."

Piaget postulates that each organism is an open, active, self-regulating
system. Mental development would then be characterized by progressive
changes in the processes of active adaptation. The fact that, in healthy
children and adolescents in our civilization, this continual mental transformation tends nonetheless toward order and not toward chaos would indicate
—according to this hypothesis—the influence of self-regulating processes
such as those involved in a principle of equilibrium. Operational structures
—both concrete and formal—are a special case of this principle of equilibrium. A change in perception, for instance, can be seen as a disturbance of
the equilibrium; operations can restore by compensating or canceling the
change.

The states of intellectual development thus represent a constant progression from a less to a more complete equilibrium and manifest therein the
organism's steady tendency toward a dynamic integration. This equilibrium
is not a static state, but an active system of compensations—not a final conclusion, but a new starting point to higher forms of mental development.

The Formation of Spatial Operations in the Child

According to a current opinion, spatial notions—particularly the constants of Euclidean metrics (the conservation of dimensions, of distances, and of systems of coordinates)—are a direct extension of perception. It is as if the representation of space (which is commonly called geometric intuition) were no more than a mere "cognition" of perceptual data. But a series of investigations on the child's representation of space and on his spontaneous geometry have indicated to us that spatial notions do not derive directly from perception. On the contrary, they imply a truly operational construction. However, the genetic order of this construction does not follow the historical order of discoveries in geometry; it appears to be more closely related to the system of axioms ordered in terms of complexity. Whereas Euclidean geometry was developed several centuries before projective geometry, and topology (analysis situs) has more recently become an independent mathematical discipline, the child's conception of spatial relations begins with the abstraction of certain topological relations, such as homeomorphs, which are then integrated into more specific operations and notions of both Euclidean and projective geometry.

By way of example, here are some illustrations of the transition from topological to Euclidean "space":

1. *Homeomorphs.* When the child has passed the scribbling stage (at about $3\frac{1}{2}$), he is able, both in his drawings and by haptic recognition, to establish the distinction between open and closed figures. A cross and a semicircle are represented as open figures while, at the same ages, squares, triangles, and diamonds are still drawn as closed and not clearly distinguishable figures. Before the child is able, in his copies, to distinguish between different geometrical forms he is able to draw a figure that is connected with or separated from another closed figure.

2. *The formation of Euclidean invariants.* One of the most striking characteristics of the stage of topological representation (from about 3 to about 7 years) is the absence of principles of invariance, or constancies, regarding the dimensions of objects when the latter are displaced, for distances between fixed objects, and for the employment of systems of coordinates. For the child at the preoperational stage, it is as if empty space as well as occupied space possessed elastic dimensions. And it is as a result of the development of his operational activity that he gradually comes to endow his conception of space with an Euclidean structure.

a. For a young child, dimensions or objects change with their displacement. It two equal-length rods are placed congruently and one of them is then displaced in a direction parallel to the other so that their extremities are out of line, we found that 75 per cent of our 5-year-old subjects maintained that the one which "has moved" or which "passes" the other has changed in length relative to the other. From the age of 8, however, 85 per cent of the children maintained with conviction that the dimensions have not changed in spite of the displacement, thus annulling this displacement by means of the reversibility of their thoughts. Their arguments are more or less as follows: "The rods are still the same length, we have only moved them; what a rod has gained at one end, it has lost at the other—which leaves it the same." But it is interesting to note that this phenomenon of nonconservation or of conservation of length in face of displacement appears to be independent of a perceptual estimation of length. According to Piaget and Taponier (1956), the perceptual estimation of the length of two equal-length but offset lines is clearly better at the age of five than eight, showing that different mechanisms seem to be involved in perceptual estimates and in conceptual judgments.

b. For a young child, the distance between two fixed objects appears to alter when a third object is inserted between them. In contrast to the well known perceptual illusion, two dolls are estimated as being closer together when a screen is inserted between them because "the screen takes up some of the room; if there was an opening in it, the distance between the two dolls would be the same as it was before." Thus, the notion of distance seems to be applied at first only to empty space and the pre-operational child appears to experience difficulty in combining partly filled and partly empty spaces into one over-all space.

At first, the represented dimensions of space exhibit "privileged" aspects; they are not isotropic. The pre-operational child readily asserts that the distance to be traversed by an elevator is greater when it is ascending than when it is descending: "It takes more effort to look or to climb up than down." Spatial representations seem thus to be formed more on the basis of subjective motor experience than of perception, with the result that there is initial nonequivalence in the relation of distances. From the age of 7, in contrast, spatial relations are gradually transformed into a system of symmetrical and reversible relations which insure the invariance of distance, an invariance which the child expresses as follows: "The dolls have not moved, they are always the same distance apart," or again: "The room taken up by the screen counts just as much as the empty space does."

c. The use of a coordinate system is initially blocked by the child's inability to abstract horizontal and vertical coordinates when they are at variance with other indices—this in spite of the fact that the very young child possesses an adequate kinesthetic knowledge of the orientation of his own body in space (*Lagebewusstsein*). If the child of from 4 to 7 years of age is asked to represent and to draw the level of water hidden in a container which is tipped at different angles, he at first represents it as parallel to the base of the container, whatever its position, or even in one corner of the container. It is only after the age of 8 that the child discovers the constant horizontality of the water level. He does so by the use of a system of coordinates which permit him to place objects and their inclinations into mutual relationships. Once spatial representation meets these Euclidean (and Cartesian) requirements the operation of measurement becomes possible.

The Operations of Classification in the Formation of Concepts

Contrary to the generally accepted hypothesis that sociolinguistic transmission is the primary mechanism of concept formation, the facts disclosed through our research compel us to conclude that language plays a necessary but not sufficient part in concept formation. It is clear, of course, that language is essential to the subject's attainment of conceptual systems that involve the manipulation of symbols. Nevertheless, language still seems insufficient. This seems due to the fact that the component operations constituting logical classes—as a conceptual system—show evidence of being linked by a markedly continuous progression through such elementary behaviors as "to bring together," "to take apart," to anticipatory and retrospective processes that precede and go beyond the use of linguistic associations or connections.

The children whose classification behaviors we studied ranged from 3 to 11 years in age. Employing a wide variety of techniques, we engaged them in tasks requiring them to classify objects and pictures. After analyzing the protocols of over 2000 children, we are led to the following conclusions:

1. The operations of classification originate in essentially active behavior. In their primitive stages they are framed in the sensory-motor schemata concerned with noting and acting upon resemblances and differences. Long before they are able to handle the verbal counterparts of these concepts, children of 2 or 3 years succeed in bringing objects together in terms of their resemblances—sometimes shouting with the glee of the true classifier, "Oh—the same! The same!" When small children attempt to classify objects, they tend to construct spatial or figural collections. These figural collections seem to show the child's thinking to lie midway between his notion of the object and that of the class.

2. At first, children are unable to distinguish between the two criteria of all logical "classes"—comprehension and extension. *Comprehension* can be defined in the following way: all those essential and distinguishing properties which must be possessed by *any* item to be counted as a member of a given class or genus. The comprehension, thus, consists in general and specific properties. *Extension* can be defined as the sum-total of all those items which are members of a given class. In other words, the extension is "the population" of the class. The earliest glimmers of the child's grasp of "comprehension" are seen in his progressive tendency to assimilate—put together—elements (objects, pictures, etc.) on the basis of their resemblances

and differences. The child's first notion of "extension" appears in the way he begins to make particular spatial arrangements among objects.

Here is an example. When the child of 3 or 4 years is required to classify counters or tokens of different forms, colors, and sizes—to put together those which are alike—he tends to put them together, one after the other, on the basis of their resemblances. He seems to have no immediate recognition of the whole set of those tokens or objects which are alike, say in form or color or size. And his successive assimilations of objects into a group seems to be effected in the basis of their spatial proximity and *in terms* of this proximity. Similar objects are placed next to each other in either linear or two-dimensional arrangements. These resemblance relationships, however, are still extremely unstable. At the earliest level of classification procedure, the child loses sight of his criterion—the one with which he began—and ends up, instead, with a complex kind of "object"; he might call is a "train" or a "house." However, it is the composition of elements—chosen by successive assimilation—into a spatial whole which seems to foreshadow the child's eventual grasp of the notion of the extension of a class.

3. The child's ability to coordinate "comprehension" and "extension"— hence truly to classify—depends upon his control of the logical quantifiers "one," "some," and "all." Such control depends in its own turn upon a progressive elaboration of logical activities of the type: All A's are B's but only B's are A's. To put this in formal terms: $A + A' = B$, provided that A' is not an empty class.

An illustration of how this behavior progresses is seen in the following example. A row of counters is placed in front of the child. The counters consist of a series of blue and red squares, with a few blue circles among them. The child is asked questions phrased carefully so as to omit the ambiguous word "some." We ask him to consider a proposition coming from some other child—say, Tony: "Tony said all the circles were blue. Now, what do you think? Was Tony right?" A mistaken reply typical among our 5-year-olds would be like this: "No, Tony was wrong, because there are also blue squares." In fact, the child reasons as if the question has been: "Are all the A's also all the B's?" Among the correct answers,[3] arguments appear which show the child's understanding of the fact that the A's are some of the B's. "Yes, Tony is right—all the circles are blue, but not all the blue ones are circles; there are blue squares, too."

4. The quantitative aspect of the logical concept of class inclusion, in which, if all A is B, then B includes A ($B > A$), depends upon the prior formation—full of snares and pitfalls—of a hierarchical system of classes. And the logic of inclusion arises, moreover, out of the psychological elaboration of two types of operations: (a) the inverse relationship of logical addition and subtraction (different from our conventional arithmetical no-

---

[3] Twenty per cent of the responses among 6-year-olds were correct, 50 per cent at 7 years, 50 per cent at 8 years, and 80 per cent at the age of 9.

tions of these operations) is represented as follows: If $(A + A' = B)$, then $(A = B - A')$; and (b) the complementarity of A and A' with respect to B is expressed in this way: All A's are B's, and all A''s included all those B's which are not A's.

Although the notion of the inclusion of members in a class is foreshadowed in the child's early semantic frame of reference and is learned along with his learning of language, something more is needed before the child masters the operation of logical inclusion. In our experiments with children around 6 years of age, it has often happened that children who already understand that all ducks are birds will yet maintain that you could take all the birds away and still there would be ducks. Moreover, while some children maintain that not all birds are ducks, they may go on still to say something like this: "You can't tell which kind there are more of in the world. There are too many to count."

Some children show signs of transition to a higher level, during which the classes A and B are thought to have the same extension: "Ducks are birds; it's the same thing," says the child, "so there are the same number of both." Everything seems to show that a young child can compare A and A' only while neglecting B. Or else he can only compare A and B while neglecting the complementarity of A and A'. In the end—some years later— the child finally understands that $B > A$. And he expresses his logical reasoning in such statements as: "There must be more birds than ducks. All those which aren't ducks are birds, and they have to be counted along with them." The above experiments and many others confirm our hypothesis that operational behavior and activity make possible and extend beyond the eventual use of linguistic and other forms of symbolic manipulation.

5. The psychological development of such conceptual systems as those of logical addition and multiplication of classes is synchronized and proceeds all of a piece. It is during the same period that two other signs of progress appear. On the one hand, the child overcomes the obstacles which block his understanding of the fact that classes can be ordered into a system of hierarchies. On the other hand, he gradually learns to classify elements according to two or three criteria at once. And he can be observed to do this in experiments dealing with matrices or class intersection—in which the common element in a given row and a given column must be found.

6. The ability to "shift" criteria, once achieved, allows the subject to consider a collection of objects from several points of view—either in succession or simultaneously. This is a characteristically conceptual activity rather than a perceptual one. The early interplay of the processes of anticipation and retrospection lay the groundwork for this later ability to "shift." When the child is able to predict several possible ways in which objects might be classified (at about 7 to 8 years or older), his mode of expressing anticipation gives evidence of his retrospective processes. For example, he will say: "Must I first classify them by color and then by shape or size?"

This indicates the child's inclination to reconsider—to look back—and choose a criterion which he had earlier considered only as a possibility. And, as we have pointed out before, this process of anticipation and retrospection have their roots in sensory-motor activity and leads up to operational activity. And it is the essential mobility of operational behavior—both mental and physical—which allows for every transformation to be canceled or compensated for by its inverse. And this latter characteristic we believe to be one of the main underlying mechanisms forming the systems of logical classification.

3

PIAGET ON REASONING: A METHODOLOGICAL CRITIQUE AND ALTERNATIVE PROPOSALS

Martin D. S. Braine

Walter Reed Army Institute of Research

Introduction and Prospect

Piaget's study of intellectual processes has led him to conclude that, at around 7 years of age, the average child reaches a stage of development marked by the ability to use certain logical operations in his thinking. In this paper, I shall discuss Piaget's findings and his methods in this area and shall present for consideration an alternative view of the facts.

Piaget's comments on this stage are presented in his book on the development of intelligence (1946c); his position is set forth in more detail in his studies of the development of concepts of quantity, time, movement, and speed (1946a, 1946b; Piaget and Inhelder, 1941), of operations of measurement and of geometric concepts and relations (Piaget, Inhelder, and Szeminska, 1948; Piaget and Inhelder, 1948), and of concepts of number and of class (Piaget and Szeminska, 1941; Inhelder and Piaget, 1959). These studies, of course, comprise only a part of Piaget's work. The present discussion will not be relevant to his ideas about development in the first two years of life (1936, 1937a, 1945) nor to his many experiments on perception in children. Although parts of this treatment are relevant to his work on adolescent reasoning (Piaget and Inhelder, 1953; Inhelder and Piaget (1955), none of the special problems raised by this work will be discussed.

While the segment of Piaget's work under consideration is almost always concerned with fundamental, and usually neglected, problems, his methodology is vulnerable from several points of view, and its flaws often serve to prevent a clear formulation of his research problems. My primary purpose in examining Piaget's methods is to achieve a clear restatement of the basic problems in a manner which does not presuppose Piaget's *Weltanschauung*.

In the pages to follow, I shall address a number of questions of method. At the most general level I shall compare certain elements of Piaget's theory and research strategy with those of modern behavior theory. At a somewhat more specific level, I shall question the adequacy of verbal methods in investigating the processes Piaget has treated. Third, I shall be concerned with

Piaget's approach to the development of the concept of class, in the light of certain logical distinctions. And finally, I shall consider how, in one instance, the content of his theory determines his methods and his formulation of research problems.

PIAGET'S CONCEPTION OF A PSYCHOLOGICAL PROCESS

There are two criticisms which have often been made of Piaget's work: that he never reports his data fully, but rather illustrates his data with samples; and that he does not maintain a constant procedure from subject to subject, but rather uses an interview technique in which questions are tailored to the responses obtained.

To a large degree these failures to follow the usual canons of research design and reporting derive from his particular conception of a psychological process. His theory contains statements that certain intellectual processes develop at different ages. In seeking to determine whether a given child has developed some process, he treats the child as he would a clinical patient (cf. his discussion of his *methode clinique* [1923]); for Piaget the goal is to *diagnose* the intellectual processes available to the subject. Flexibility in the experimental procedure facilitates the diagnosis by permitting an inquiry into the reasons for the response, an inquiry taboo in a standardized procedure. Similarly, a diagnosis is more easily and more vividly supported with detailed illustrations than with statistical data and norms.

In contrast to Piaget's approach, modern behavioral theory accords intellectual processes the status of hypothetical constructs that are not directly observable. A hypothetical construct needs to be specified in two ways—in terms of its relations to other constructs of the system (here Piaget's theory is well developed) and in terms of a carefully designed set of experimental operations through which the process may be elicited and, given these experimental operations, the responses which testify to its presence. It is at this point that Piaget's theory is weak. Instead of specifying his constructs in terms of evidence, he illustrates them with a wealth of suggestive observations. For Piaget a psychological process seems not to be a theoretical construct; rather it is something which can be apprehended directly through acute observation of a subject's behavior and language. It may be that Piaget's failure to respond to persistent criticism of his research methods is largely due to this conception of an intellectual process as something to be diagnosed intuitively, rather than to be related to experimental operations. Piaget may feel that, if he modified his methods, he would only make the diagnosis more difficult, and he would therefore lose contact with the processes he wants to study. As he himself remarks, "Statistical precision could no doubt easily be obtained, but at the cost of no longer knowing exactly what was being measured" (Piaget and Szeminska, 1941 [1952, p. 149]). And for his own formulation of his research goals,

Piaget is probably right; a mere standardization of his tasks would lose the flexibility which is one of their virtues.

An Alternative Conception

If we do not wish to view intellectual processes as intuitively evident, but rather to treat them as theoretical constructs, we have two main avenues of approach—we can try to tie them either to stimulus events or to responses.

By "tying the process to stimulus events," I have in mind the following kind of research approach. Experiments may be designed in which the evidence for a change in psychological process from one age to another is a change with age in the ability to respond to different types of discriminanda or a change with age in parameters of stimulus generalization. For example, there is evidence (Braine, 1959) that all children taught to choose the longer, rather than the shorter, of two upright sticks (clearly different in height) do not generalize this discrimination with equal facility. If the stimuli are suddenly made nearly equal in height, many 6-year-olds disregard the apparent equality, make a careful visual comparison of the stimuli, and find the longer one more often than expected by chance. Most 3- and 4-year-olds, however, make no effort to seek the real differences—they behave as if the notion that things can *look* the same, yet *be* different, were beyond them. Children of different ages thus seem to adopt a different "set" toward a task, and the change in set from one age to the other may be indicated by a change in the parameters of stimulus generalization. The older children generalize to the situation where there is phenomenal equality under casual inspection; the younger ones do not.

Psychological processes are "tied to responses" in experiments which involve "strategies." In such experiments the subject is usually presented with a constant series of stimuli and a goal; the series of responses he makes defines the strategy (e.g., Bruner, Goodnow, and Austin, 1956). The subject, so to speak, chooses the information that he wants to receive in order to solve the problem. Although it would be amazing if there were not differences in strategy between age groups, there have been few attempts to discover them. A possible exception to this neglect is Inhelder and Piaget's work on adolescent thinking (1955).

It would be striking if intellectual processes specified in the first instance in terms of the discriminanda to which a child is capable of responding, or in terms of change in parameters of stimulus generalization, should ultimately turn out to be identifiable with processes specified as strategies in other experiments.

On Not Losing the Baby with the Bathwater

In trying to take a new look at Piaget's experiments, it is necessary to decide which of the two above conceptions of psychological process one is going to adopt; they do not mix well. The easiest reformulation of Piaget's experiments would keep his experimental task, but standardize the procedure and quantify the results. While the experiment will then conform to the usual canons of research design, the departure from Piaget's methodology may not be sufficiently radical. Standardization of procedure does not of itself presuppose a conception of intellectual process different from Piaget's, and, from the standpoint of Piaget's approach, it may merely make the "diagnostic problem" more difficult. There is a danger of falling between two methodological stools with the result that Piaget's research goals—the study of developing intellectual processes—may be cast out along with some of his methods. Such experiments can even end in a spurious, though apparently convincing, refutation of Piaget.

I would like to try to demonstrate this last point by caricature. Let us suppose a graduate student called Peabody decides to "test" Piaget for his doctoral thesis. His point of departure is an experiment in which Piaget presented the child with two "roads" composed of match sticks of unequal length placed end to end. These two sets of sticks were initially presented in parallel, and without overlap, to form two equally long lines. The subject was asked whether or not the roads were the same length. Even the youngest subjects were able to respond "Yes." One line of sticks was then altered so that the road was no longer straight but formed a "zigzag." The subject observed the alteration and then was asked again whether or not the roads were the same length. The youngest children did not consider the lines the same length after the rearrangement; either they considered the straight line longer because it extended beyond the other or they thought the zigzag line longer because of the turns. There was an intermediate stage in which children thought some arrangements altered the length while others did not. Finally, the older children knew that the lines were the same length irrespective of the rearrangements of parts in the zigzag line (Piaget, Inhelder, and Szeminska, 1948).

Peabody's revision of this experiment employs a procedure similar to Piaget's, but with a fixed questionnaire and without any spur-of-the-moment variations in procedure from one child to another. He tries several different pairs of roads, and there are hundreds of subjects divided equally into age groups. One thing he wants to find out is whether the young children are consistent in their "mistakes"; he finds, let us say, that a child tends to be consistent in calling the straight or the zigzag line longer. He also finds that the stages of development are not clearly delineated and that there is a steady increase in the Mean Number of Correct Responses with age. When he writes his experiment up, he claims that Piaget is incorrect in calling the young child illogical. Peabody argues that the child is being perfectly logical if one understands him in his own terms; he is just inexperienced and hasn't yet acquired the usual adult usage of "longer." Moreover, Peabody suggests, the adult concept is acquired slowly and without any abrupt transitions, no doubt by casual reinforcement over the years.

The data Peabody obtains may well be of interest, but unfortunately Peabody has misunderstood the purpose of Piaget's experiment. Piaget was trying to investigate the development of children's understanding of a fact basic to measurement—the additive nature of length—i.e., that any length can be regarded as composed of shorter lengths added together. By virtue of this additive character of length one can talk of the length of a zigzag line as the sum of the lengths of its straight parts. By standardizing the procedure, Peabody eliminates whatever information Piaget obtains through his inquiry and substitutes a statistic, Number of Correct Responses, which of course increases with age. There is not much to say about correct responses except that they are correct; so Peabody is obliged to turn away from the question of what processes may have developed in the older children, and he naturally focuses on the younger children's mistakes. The logic of his procedure thus distracts him from the main problem (i.e., what has developed that determines the correct responses of the older children) to one which is not central for Piaget (i.e., what determines the wrong responses of the younger children). The question of whether the young child's behavior can be made to appear reasonable is tangential. Peabody's "disproof" of Piaget is thus beside the point; he has not been investigating Piaget.

Having thus criticized Peabody, it seems only fair that I should suggest a way in which one might investigate the development of an understanding of the additive nature of length. The task could be set up initially as a length-discrimination task in which selection of the longer of two straight sticks (clearly different in length) led to, say, a candy reward. When this initial length discrimination problem had been learned to a criterion, the stimuli would be changed so that one of the sticks would be bent to form a zigzag on each trial. On these generalization trials the true difference in length between the straight and zigzag lines would be of such an order that no adult would have any hesitation in saying which one was longer. A child who understands the additive nature of length should then generalize from the initial learning trials to these generalization trials. That is, a child who has learned the relation "longer than" between straight lines should respond, if he understands the additive nature of length, to this same relation when it is presented between bent lines. If the experiment is conducted in this manner, the "psychological process" is made manifest as a change with age in one of the parameters of stimulus generalization. This process could then be studied by systematic variation of the learning and generalization stimuli in different age groups.

VERBAL AND NONVERBAL METHODS

One difference between Peabody's technique and the proposed alternative is that the former involved verbal questions and answers and the latter did not. Piaget has often been criticized for the verbal nature of the problems he poses his subjects and for his reliance upon interpretation of their verbal responses. When the experimenter makes frequent use of verbal stimuli, he introduces into the experimental procedure factors which are difficult to evaluate. The child presumably responds to the "meanings" he attributes to the experimenter's words. What these "meanings" are we do not know; we know only that they are intimately related to the events and circumstances surrounding the child's original learning of these words. The verbal method may, therefore, serve only to conceal the effective stimulus for the subject's response.

Criticism of the verbal method can be carried even further. It would seem to be intrinsically impossible to study how a concept *develops* with methods which employ verbal cues to evoke the concept. For, if the child understands the verbal cue, he must already have developed the concept. Suppose, to take a simplified example, that we wished to explore how the concept "table" develops. We might conduct subjects of various ages around the laboratory and ask them to point out the tables and only the tables; alternatively, we might indicate various objects "Is that a table or not?" To throw light on the subject's response we might ask him "Why?" or "What makes you call that a table?" These methods are verbal in the sense that the use by experimenter or subject of the usual verbal cue to the concept— the word "table"—is an integral part of the procedure. Such methods are admirably suited to uncovering the connotation of the word "table" in a subject who already has some understanding of the word; we can find out whether he accepts desks or endtables as tables and test him on all sorts of curious objects we may sketch or construct. But where the subject does not understand the word "table," the method clearly breaks down. That is, if the subject responds more or less appropriately, we can be sure he has the concept; but, if he fails to do so, we learn very little. The course of development of the concept remains obscure, and no light is thrown on the variation with age in the learning and generalization processes upon which the development of the concept depends. In part, this is because our verbal method takes for granted the child's original learning of the word "table."

Now suppose we attack the same problem another way. We tell the subject (or we let him discover by experience) that we are going to place objects one by one in front of him and that each time he is to make, or refrain from making, a certain response. Sometimes he will get a reward for making this response, sometimes for refraining from making it. We arrange matters in such a way that he gets rewarded only for making the response when there is a table in front of him. When he has learned to make the response only to tables, we test him out with generalization stimuli, which might be, e.g., desks, endtables, sideboards, cocktail tables, and so forth, and we find out how he classifies these. Such a method is nonverbal because, while some words may pass between experimenter and subject, there is no systematic association between any word and the cue stimuli to which response is rewarded, i.e., no verbal stimulus is used which might evoke the concept to be studied. The procedure, therefore, does not depend on whether the subject has learned the culturally appropriate verbal symbol before the experiment. By using the method with subjects of various ages, the development of the concept can be studied systematically. Moreover, the variation with age in the generalization processes that enter into the learning of the concept may be investigated by parametric variation of the learning and generalization stimuli. We can find out, for example, whether subjects who have learned to respond to (say) kitchen tables, spontaneously generalize to cocktail and endtables and whether the degree of such generalization is a function of age. With the nonverbal method, therefore, developmental phenomena not open to investigation with verbal methods can be studied.[1]

The concepts studied by Piaget are more complex and of greater interest than the concept "table," but the argument that their development cannot be investigated adequately with verbal methods applies even more strongly. Piaget's experiments are particularly vulnerable to criticism on this ground, since he has used verbal methods almost exclusively. For example, in a study of the development of a concept of order (Piaget and Inhelder, 1948), seven to nine beads of different colors threaded on a wire served as a model which the subject had to copy by choosing similar colored beads and threading them in the same order on another wire. If verbal instructions are used, the child need not interpret the word "same" to mean "same order," and any instruction which contains the word "order" presumably will be understood only by a child who already possesses a concept of order to which he can assimilate this word. One clearly cannot discover how a concept of order develops if one employs a method which presupposes its presence. It is noteworthy that Piaget does not seem to take cognizance of this problem; for instance, in reporting this experiment he does not discuss how he conveyed the instructions to the subjects!

An obvious further advantage of nonverbal methods for this area of research is that they make comparative study possible. Many of the complex nonverbal tasks that have been used with children were developed first in animal laboratories. Traffic in the other direction might also bring important theoretical and empirical enrichment to comparative psychology.

Additional criticisms of some of Piaget's experiments on the development of measurement and order concepts have been made elsewhere in the context of a partial evaluation of his theory with nonverbal methods (Braine, 1959) and will not be repeated here. Instead, I shall now turn to a detailed consideration of perhaps the most important single segment of Piaget's investigation of the development of reasoning—his work on the development of a concept of class.

---

[1] Conversely, of course, there are research goals which require verbal methods—the argument is not intended as a denial that verbal methods are ever useful.

PIAGET ON CLASSES

Piaget's work on the development of a concept of class relates closely to his theory that "concrete operations" develop at 6 to 7 years of age. The theory of concrete operations is pivotal in Piaget's system since these operations provide the foundation for the development of reasoning about class membership, number concepts, and the combinatorial logic of the adolescent. Quite apart from Piaget's particular viewpoint, however, an account of the development of a concept of class must occupy a central position in any theory of the ontogeny of reasoning since so much of the verbal behavior often vaguely called "abstract thinking" appears to consist of reasoning about classes and class membership (including all of mathematical reasoning —since numbers are classes of classes). The section to follow will approach, through the distinctions of logic, certain theoretical questions concerning the concept of class and will trace out the implications of these questions for that part of Piaget's work that treats of classification.

Levels of Abstraction

Logic treats of two kinds of terms—singular and general. Singular terms purport to apply to only one object (e.g., "Prof. Jones," "The White House"); they occur as the logical subject of a sentence. General terms may apply to many objects and are always predicates in the language of the logician, although colloquially they may often appear to be part of the subject.

The distinction between levels of abstraction is independent of this dichotomy; singular terms may be either concrete or abstract, as can general terms. It is simplest to discuss the notion of levels of abstraction first for general terms and then to apply it derivatively to the logical subject.

The most concrete general term is a predicate of objects. Object-predicates include most ordinary nouns, adjectives, and verbs (e.g., "round," "dog," "car," "runs") and relational phrases (e.g., "father of," "taller than"). In the remainder of this paper these will be referred to as *concrete general* terms or concepts.

The first level of abstraction among general terms contains predicates of classes and of attributes. Such words as "type," "sort," "class," "two," "three" are typically predicates of classes. Also this level of abstraction contains relational phrases like ". . . is a type of ——," ". . . is a characteristic of ——," ". . . is an instance of ——," ". . . is a way of ——," ". . . are more (numerous) than ——." Whereas predicates of objects can all be used to characterize individual physical objects in the environment, this is never true of class-predicates. For example, in the sentence frame ". . . is the father of ——" both spaces are appropriately filled with names of individual objects (e.g., Jones, Sr. and Jones, Jr.), whereas this is not true of the spaces in frames containing class-predicates. I shall subsequently refer to predicates

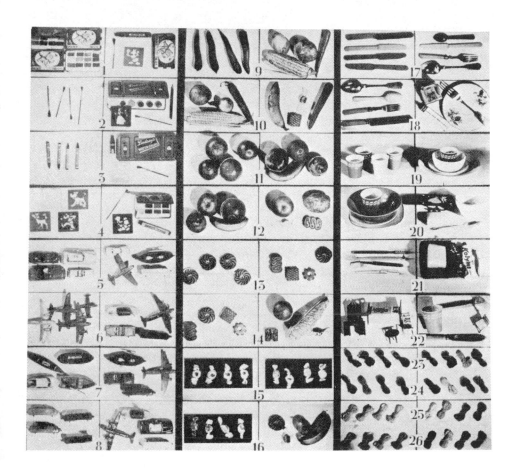

FIGURE 1—The attribute-inclusion problems.

of classes and of attributes as *abstract general* terms or concepts. Second and higher levels of abstraction among general terms (e.g., predicates of classes of classes) do not seem to be very common in nontechnical speech and will be ignored here.

Discussion of the logical subject is made somewhat technical by the fact that the subject may be either a singular term or a logical variable. Moreover, it is not terms which are concrete or abstract, but the designata of these terms—the entities to which reference is made, i.e., the designatum of a singular term or the values of the variables in a quantified sentence (Quine, 1953). These entities are hierarchized into (a) physical objects, (b) classes[2] and attributes, designated by so-called abstract singular terms, e.g., the Chevrolet (i.e., the make), *macaca mulatta,* roundness, circularity, (c) classes of classes and higher-order universals.

In assessing level of abstraction, the distinction between general terms and singular terms must be observed as the level of abstraction of a word will often depend on whether it is used as a singular or general term. "Man," for example, is usually a concrete general term applying to sundry individuals. Occasionally, however, it is used to designate the "generic" man, and on these occasions it is being used as an abstract singular, and an abstract general term will be predicted of it. Similarly, abstract general terms (especially numbers) are sometimes used as singular terms designating classes of classes. Since it requires the recognition of logical subject and predicate, it can be seen that level of abstraction is a function of sentence structure as well as vocabulary. For our present purposes, however, the distinction between concrete and abstract general terms will suffice.[3]

---

[2] Classes should be distinguished from mere collections or aggregates. Quine (1951) illustrates the difference as follows: "The . . . phrase 'mere aggregates' must be received warily as a description of classes. . . . Continental United States is an extensive physical body having the several states as parts; at the same time it is a physical body having the several counties as parts. It is the same concrete object, regardless of the conceptual dissections imposed; the heap of states and the heap of counties are identical. The class of states, however, cannot be identified with the class of counties; for there is much that we want to affirm of the one class and deny of the other. We want to say e.g. that the one class has exactly 48 members, while the other has 3075. We want to say that Delaware is a member of the first class and not of the second, and that the Nantucket is a member of the second class and not of the first. These classes, unlike the single concrete heaps which their members compose, must be accepted as two entities of a non-spatial and abstract kind" (p. 120).

[3] In the psychological literature, concrete general terms are often misinterpreted as class names and are thus treated as abstract singular terms. This is particularly likely to happen if the general term happens to be in the grammatical plural. Thus, in a sentence like "Cats are furry," the word "cats" may be described as the name of a class of animals to which "furriness" is attributed. The verbal behavior represented by the above sentence is better construed as the normal colloquial rendition that the logician would write formally as "Anything that is a cat is furry." In the logician's form of the sentence, "cat" and "furry" are both clearly concrete general terms, the "things" referred to are ordinary objects, and there is not a glimmer of an abstraction around. If the sentence were uttered by a preschool child, to interpret "cats" as a class name referring to the generic cat would probably overestimate the intellectual sophistication of the subject. Plural nouns need not be interpreted as class names unless an abstract general term is predicated of them. The presence or absence of the abstract general term is usually diagnostic.

There is a frequent usage of the term *abstract* in psychology, according to which "vehicles" (say) is considered more abstract than "cars," and "things" more abstract than either. To avoid confusion, I think it would be preferable in such cases to use the adjective *general* instead of *abstract*. The dimension *concrete-abstract* would properly apply to sequences like "Fido-Dog-Species" (treating these as singular terms designating an object, a class, and a class of classes, respectively), or "Jones' car—The Chevrolet—Make of car," or "Tom, Dick, and Harry—Trio—Three." Such sequences should be sharply distinguished from hierarchies like "Dogs—housepets—animals . . ." or "Chevrolets—cars—vehicles . . .," where all the terms are at the same level of abstraction and differ only in generality. I would suggest the label *specific-general* for this dimension.

An additional difference between generality and abstraction lies in the fact that the relation between degrees of generality is transitive; if Chevrolets are cars, and cars are vehicles, then Chevrolets are vehicles. But the "membership" relation between levels of abstraction is *not* transitive: If Fido is an instance of Dog, and Dog is an instance of Species, it does not follow that Fido is a species.

A clear recognition of the distinction between concrete and abstract general terms or concepts, or between an object, a class, and a class of classes, is, I think, vital to an understanding of the research problem that Piaget is trying to attack in his work on children's ability to handle classes. Consider, for example, the distinction between the meanings of the words "class," "type," "sort," "kind" and the meanings of words like "table," "furniture," "spoon," "vehicle," etc. The latter are concrete general terms applying to individual objects—the table in my living-room, my office chair, the spoon used to stir my coffee at breakfast, the 6:10 to Peekskill from Grand Central Station, and so on. The words "class" and "type," on the other hand, do not apply to individual objects, but rather to the class of tables, of furniture, of spoons, of vehicles, and so on. Procedurally, it would be comparatively simple to teach a monkey the concept associated with the word "spoon." One has only to place a spoon in front of him next to something that is not a spoon and let him find a raisin if he dislodges the spoon. In successive presentations he will quickly learn to dislodge only spoons. But to teach him the concept associated with the word "class" would be much more difficult because he would have to learn to dislodge classes of objects rather than individual objects. Similarly, it is not difficult to teach a monkey relations like "bigger," "darker," "more triangular," etc., since these relations hold between individual stimuli; but the relation associated with ". . . type of ——" (as in "Cars are a type of vehicle") would again require him to dislodge classes of objects.

Examination of Techniques for Eliciting Abstract Concepts

The distinction in logic between abstract and concrete general terms corresponds fairly closely (differing primarily in precision) to one of the

customary usages of "abstract" and "concrete" in the psychological literature. Although Goldstein and Scheerer (1941) nowhere define "abstract"
and "concrete" precisely, their illustrations and their tests suggest that they
are essentially trying to convey the distinction between abstract and concrete general terms. One of the explicit purposes of the sorting test, for
instance, is not to determine whether the patient can distinguish red from
not-red, round from not-round, and so forth, but to determine whether he
interprets the instruction "Put those things together that belong together"
to mean "Form a class." In terms of the discussion above, the purpose of
the sorting test is to discover whether the patient possesses the concept associated with words like "type" or "kind."

Inhelder and Piaget (1959) have employed a type of sorting test in a
manner similar to Goldstein. The test is, in fact, the principal technique
that they have used to study the development of "concrete operations." As
used by Inhelder and Piaget, the test material has consisted either of geometric forms or of socially meaningful material (animals, people, kitchen
equipment, furniture). The subject was instructed either to "Put those
things together which belong together," or "Put together those things
which are alike," or he was simply asked to arrange the material (*"mettre
de l'ordre"*). Although the results are often very suggestive and persuasive
the sorting test has several disadvantages when used in this way.

1. It is not a learning task, but a sort of intellectual projective technique.
The child is given a deliberately vague instruction, and the experimenter
watches to see how this instruction is interpreted spontaneously. The subject
may, or may not, indicate by his sortings that he has interpreted it as meaning "Show me those things that are members of the same class as this." If
the subject does give several "correct" sortings, it is probably safe to conclude
that the abstract concept associated with expressions like "same kind" is
available to him. The difficulty in interpretation arises when the subject does
not sort satisfactorily. In using the sorting test, most examiners claim that
subjects spontaneously interpret the instruction in the most sophisticated
manner of which they are capable. "... *Sans pouvoir encore comprendre
ce qu'est une classification . . ., l'enfant de 2–5 ans interprète nos consignes
selon la signification qui . . . se rapproche le plus de ce qu'il saisit de cette
structure operatoire"* (Inhelder and Piaget, 1959, p. 26). However, we lack
adequate evidence for this claim. Thus, in the case of an inadequate response,
one has much less confidence that the child's optimal response has been
elicited than one has in a learning task where correct responses are reinforced.

2. Response criteria are inevitably vague; only a fairly general definition
of what constitutes a "good" sorting can be given in advance. For example,
Inhelder and Piaget report that one of their subjects (Chri, 4 years, 10
months, *op. cit.*, p. 31) began by lining up five rectangles, of which the fifth
was yellow; this called forth four yellow triangles followed by two yellow

semicircles, which in turn provoked five other semicircles of various colors. Chri's sorting is considered immature because he is not sorting into distinct classes, but matching each piece chosen with the immediately preceding one without regard to the earlier choices of the series, so that his sorting criteria change fluidly from form to color and then back to form. Reliability is likely to be difficult to achieve in classifying complex responses of this sort. Moreover, in assessing a subject's sorting one usually relies partially on his verbal explanation of it. For example, a grouping of a man and a dog would be interpreted differently if it were explained as "both alive" than if it were explained as "The man takes the dog for a walk." However, young children may not always be aware of the reasons for their sorting behavior.

Another technique that Piaget has used to study the development of abstract concepts is also subject to criticism. This technique was utilized in an instance where the relation studied was the class-inclusion relation (i.e., the relation involved in sentences like "The Chevrolet is a type of car"). Piaget and Szeminska (1941) showed children a picture containing a number of flowers most of which were poppies and a few of which were bluebells. The subjects were asked, "Are there more poppies or more flowers?" The younger children (until about 6 years of age) always said that there were more poppies. The protocols make it clear that, when the children were asked to point out the flowers, they indicated all of them; yet immediately afterwards, when asked whether there were more poppies or more flowers, they said that there were more poppies. Piaget attributes this response to a difficulty in handling the inclusion relation between poppies and flowers; the subjects were unable to think of a poppy as being simultaneously an instance of poppies and of flowers.

While this experiment certainly demonstrates a mysterious deficit on the part of the child, it does little to clarify the nature of this deficit. First, it is not clear whether the child's difficulty is one of verbal formulation or whether he does not perceive the quantitative relation between the poppies and the flowers in the picture. For example, it is not certain that there would have been errors if, instead of using the words "poppies" and "flowers," Piaget had asked "Are there more of these (pointing to the poppies) or more of these (pointing to all the flowers)?" thus indicating the class-members ostensively rather than by name. Second, the nature of the quantitative relation is poorly defined since the picture presented confounds a class-inclusion relation with a spatial part-whole relation—the space occupied by the poppies being part of that occupied by the flowers. Thus, the question "Is this part (outlining poppies) larger or smaller than this part (outlining flowers)?" might or might not be interpreted by the child in the same way as the question Piaget actually asked. The distinction between "more" and "larger" is, after all, subtle. In any case, Piaget has elsewhere demonstrated that preschool children have difficulty with numerical concepts and relations, so it is not clear exactly what "... more ... more ..." would mean to a child of this age.[4]

Here, as in the sorting situation, one can be reasonably sure that the relation studied is understood by the child if he answers the question correctly (although in this experiment the possibility is not controlled that he might answer correctly by treating the question as a spatial part-whole problem, rather than in terms of class-inclusion.) But, if the child fails, very little information is obtained—in particular, very little is discovered about how well he is capable of responding to tasks involving this relation. Little light is thrown on the crucial ability that he lacks and the dimensions along which development occurs.

In both the procedures discussed above, the difficulty of interpreting results arises largely because an essential element in the stimulus situation is verbal in nature. The experimenter emits a noise ("belong together" or "more") which he hopes will mediate a complex generalization process in the child. If it does, well and good; if it does not, one learns only that it does not. A technique is needed which will bring this generalization process more clearly into focus so that it can be investigated; and, moreover, one needs to study this process while it is developing and not merely as a finished product.

Beyond Piaget's Techniques

It is easier to criticize than to improve upon Piaget's studies of the development of a concept of class. Any attempt to use nonverbal methods (such as were proposed earlier in this paper for investigating the development of measurement or of concepts of order or other complex spatial relations) at once meets the problem that levels of abstraction were defined above in linguistic terms. That is, abstract general *terms,* rather than abstract general *concepts,* were defined. Once abstraction is defined in this way, the question of the ontogeny of abstraction necessarily becomes a question of the ontogeny of a certain kind of verbal behavior—verbal behavior which employs abstract general terms such as "type." As the problem has been posed, there are obvious limits to the scope of study with nonverbal tasks. Let us, however, look at the matter more closely.

---

[4] These objections notwithstanding, Piaget's conclusion about the age of development are broadly confirmed (with a verbal form of presentation) in a study by Schooley and Hartman (1937). The child's task was to discover the meaning of the word "species" when presented with a series of examples of the form: "Dogs are a species of . . . (animal)," "Oranges are a species of . . . (fruit)," etc., the child's familiarity with the class names having been established previously. Correct anticipation of the supraordinate class name was used as the index of learning. There were over one hundred children systematically divided into age intervals and it was concluded that a grasp of the relation developed rather abruptly at about 6 years of age.

It is, I think, instructive that even a neat verbal method like this one throws little light on what processes are involved in learning the relation.

Many psychologists, myself included, assume that *terms* are usually associated with *concepts* and are connected with distinctions that the organism has learned to make. Abstract general terms presumably do not arise in the child *ex nihilo,* and the question therefore becomes, what kinds of distinctions are associated with the learning of abstract general terms, and how are these distinctions learned?

In answering this question, the logician can be of little assistance. In the logician's language "class" and other abstract general terms emerge completely *ex nihilo.* To include such terms in his language, the logician has to select at least one such term (usually "ε"—"is an instance of") as a primitive which he leaves undefined. Indeed, many of this century's major controversies in the foundations of mathematics arise from the logician's misgivings over this fact—he cannot do without abstractions and yet cannot explicate them (Quine, 1953). Thus, while the logician can help the psychologist by giving such terms as *abstraction* and *abstract reasoning* clarity of definition, he can do little else. How then are we to approach the study of the development of class concepts?

The first and most obvious line of approach would study directly the development of the logical structure of language during the first few years of life. From the work in semantics one can clearly infer that there should be changes in syntactic structure which correspond functionally to the changes that occur in the logician's language when the class primitive is introduced. From Piaget's work it is reasonable to assume that these language changes should appear clearly around the time that he claims that the "concrete operations" develop. There is no reason to assume that the language changes do not take place quite gradually. Unfortunately, to pursue this line of approach involves considerable technical difficulties since the investigator must possess a knowledge of linguistics and logic (especially the latter) as well as of psychology. To date, work along these lines has consisted exclusively of the speculations of philosophers. Quine (1960), for example, has discussed the development of logical structure in language instructively and in some detail, but his remarks are reconstructions of what he infers must be the course of development. No observations of children are made, and ontogeny is made to recapitulate a logical sequence of progressive complexity. Such work, however, in its analysis of the problems that language structure poses the young child, may provide a useful prelude to empirical observations.

While the information obtained from this approach is essential to an account of the genesis of abstract thinking, it cannot of itself tell the whole story. From the standpoint of philosophical empiricism, it must be argued that the developmental changes in language associated with the use of abstract general terms cannot arise *ex nihilo* and must ultimately be determined by some change in the response to sensory input. That is, the child learns to make distinctions of a kind he did not previously make, or there is some sort of change in parameters of stimulus generalization, or some change in strategy of processing the sensory input. Hypotheses about these changes can probably be investigated most adequately by nonverbal methods. However, if nonverbal tasks are to be relevant, i.e., if they are to elicit just those processes which are important in the ontogeny of abstract thinking, they will have to be derived from a close study of language structures employed in this kind of reasoning. A reasonably complete picture of the development of abstraction will be obtained only when an account of the development of the verbal behavior can be juxtaposed with information obtained from nonverbal tasks derived from language structures. Unfortunately, little is now known of the characteristic language structures that children actually use at any age.

Since the idea of a nonverbal task derived from a consideration of language structures may not be clear, I should like to illustrate what I have in mind with an exploratory experiment. This experiment is doubly relevant in the present context, since it was originally designed to develop a method with which one might explore Piaget's view that "concrete operations" develop in the average child rather abruptly at around 6 or 7 years of age. It was felt that, if a relevant nonverbal task could be designed, the results might indicate a gradual change in parameters of stimulus generalization over the course of development. If such a change were discovered, the relatively sudden emergence of abstract general concepts found by Piaget, and by Schooley and Hartmann, might then be interpreted as a product of using verbal methods.

An Illustrative Experiment

Consider a language structure frequently encountered in talk about classes and class-membership, phrases of the form:

"Chevrolets are a type of car,"
"Oranges are a type of fruit,"
"Cups are a type of dishware."

The general form of such phrases is

"P's are a type of Q."

The relation expressed in this sentence form has two properties: (a) Considering the sets of objects subsumed under "P" and "Q," the sentence form expresses a relation similar to the part-whole relation—the objects indicated by the first noun "P" are always a subgroup of the objects indicated by the second noun "Q." Since, in nature, both sets are usually of unknown, often infinite, size, it is difficult to see how this quantitative aspect of the relation could be learned directly either in nature or in a nonverbal task. (b) Considering the intensions, or attributes, associated with "P" and "Q," the sentence form expresses a relation which I shall call attribute-inclusion— the objects indicated by "P," always share all the properties shared by those indicated by "Q" and others besides. In usual parlance, the P's are always more alike than the Q's.

Since attributes can be specified without presenting the entire membership of a class, there exists a possible basis for a nonverbal task, which might be set up somewhat as follows. The task would consist of a series of discrimination problems, the discriminanda consisting of groups of objects. The relation between the two groups of objects used in every problem would have the property (b) above. For example, in one problem, one group might consist of a small number of oranges, and the other of an orange, a banana, an apple, and a pear. Or, in another problem, a rowboat, a sailboat, a battleship, and an ocean liner might comprise one set of stimuli; and a boat, a car, a plane, and a train, the other. In a third problem, a group of red wool skeins might be set against a group of wool skeins differing in color. Each of a large number of such problems would be presented in turn, with the anticipation that the subject would eventually achieve first-trial solutions of new problems.

When I attempted to design a usable set of problems, it became apparent that some problems that meet the above logical requirements would probably be more difficult than others for the average preschool child. The series of problems described below was finally selected and organized to permit exploration of a possible factor affecting problem difficulty.

Description of procedure. The entire task comprised 52 discrimination problems, in each of which two stimulus-sets were presented.

The first 26 problems, termed sameness-difference problems, were used for training. Each stimulus-set consisted of two colored paper figures (geometric forms) pasted on a white card 4 in. by 6 in. Two identical figures were presented on one card, and on the other there were two dissimilar figures, differing either in color or form, e.g., two red crosses vs. a red square and a red circle, or, two green diamonds vs. a green and a yellow diamond. No given pair of figures was presented in more than one problem.

The critical attribute-inclusion problems were the last 26 problems, shown in Figure 1. Both stimulus-sets consisted of four objects on a tray, e.g., four cars vs. four vehicles (a car, a boat, a plane, and a train). In each problem, the attributes presented by the objects of one set included those presented by the objects of other set. These problems were organized into two hierarchical groups which it was thought might differ in difficulty; 17 were "species-genus" discriminations (problems 1 to 9, 11, 13, 15, 17, 19, 21, 23, 25 in Figure 1), and the remaining nine were "genus-family" discriminations.

The subjects were children, 12 girls and 8 boys, attending a day nursery in New York City. They ranged from 43 to 76 months in age.

The stimulus-sets were presented on a table about 2½ ft. from the subject, and a piece of candy was hidden beneath, or behind, the correct card. On each trial the subject was asked "Do you remember (know) which one gives the candy?" He responded by pointing to one of the stimulus-sets, which was then raised by the experimenter to reveal the presence or absence of the candy.

For 11 subjects, the reward was always placed under the stimulus-set whose members were most homogeneous, i.e., under the two identical figures in the sameness-difference problems and under the subordinate "class" in the inclusion problems. For nine subjects, comparable in age to the first group, the correct stimulus-set was always the more heterogeneous: the two unlike figures in the sameness-difference problems and the supraordinate "class" in the inclusion problems.

The first problem was taught to a criterion of six consecutive correct responses, and thereafter a problem was changed after two consecutive correct responses. A grasp of the relation was demonstrated by interproblem transfer, leading to correct first-trial solution of problems.

TABLE I

PERCENTAGE OF SUBJECTS ACHIEVING A SIGNIFICANT* NUMBER OF FIRST-TRIAL SOLUTIONS OF SAMENESS-DIFFERENCE (S-D) (FINAL TWELVE PROBLEMS), SPECIES-GENUS (S-G), AND GENUS-FAMILY (G-F) PROBLEMS

		Type of Problem		
Group	N	S-D	S-G	G-F
A. Reinforced for S in S-D, S in S-G, and G in G-F	11	82	73	18
B. Reinforced for D in S-D, G in S-G, and F in G-F	9	33	(33)	(22)

* Correct first-trial solutions of 10 of the 12 S-D problems, of 13 of the 17 S-G problems, and of 8 of the 9 G-F problems would be achieved by a subject responding randomly on less than 5 per cent of occasions.

Results and Discussion. The percentage of subjects in the two groups who grasped the relation in each type of problem is shown in Table 1. The group difference on the sameness-difference problems was quite unexpected and, in the present context, is somewhat embarrassing since it introduces a complication of unknown import into what would otherwise be reasonably straightforward results.[5] Since the group for whom difference was rein-

[5] The difference is significant—$\chi^2 = 5.07$, $p < .05$ (the computation including three extra subjects who completed the sameness-difference problems and then inconveniently went on vacation). Incidentally, a sameness-difference problem, similar to the one reported here, has been presented to chimpanzees and solved by them (Robinson, 1955)—unfortunately response to difference was not investigated.

Exactly why difference should be more difficult to respond to is unclear, though this is probably an important finding. It may be pertinent that two subjects trained to respond to difference paradoxically showed unusually long sequences of *wrong* first-trial responses. Conceivably, response to difference is more difficult because it entails first, distinguishing identity, and second, learning to avoid it.

forced failed to solve the training (S-D) problems, it is perhaps not surprising that they failed also to grasp the relation involved in the later problems. Subsequent discussion will therefore ignore this group and relate to the subjects for whom sameness was reinforced.

In this group, most subjects readily generalized to the relation between the stimuli in the "species-genus" problems (usually from the first of these problems), but found the "genus-family" problems more difficult.[6] It appears therefore that the degree of generality of the relation learned can vary. Having learned the sameness-difference relation, some children generalize only to the species-genus problems: they reinterpret, as it were, "same" to mean "similar" to only a limited degree. Other children, among the older ones, generalize to the genus-family problems as well: they interpret "same" as "similar" more broadly, and even include within this category similarities which are purely functional (e.g., problems 10, 12, 20, and 22).[7] The results suggest a change in parameters of stimulus generalization, probably related to age.

The precise nature of the parameters that change is unclear in this experiment, but various possibilities can readily be explored by systematically varying the generalization problems. Two plausible parameters are the following: (a) Some subjects may generalize from identity to similarity only when the similarity is "perceptually given" (e.g., the similarity between four oranges may be said to be "perceptually given," whereas the properties held in common by a chair, a table, a bed, and a chest are functional—they do not *look* similar). (b) Older subjects may be more able than younger ones to transpose the relation between levels of a class hierarchy; perhaps a set Q is less readily grasped as more homogeneous than a set R, if Q has previously been seen to be more heterogeneous than P. That is, many subjects may have failed to respond to the relation between (say) fruits and foods only because they had previously perceived it in oranges vs. fruits.

The data obtained suggest that the second hypothesis was more influential in this experiment: species-genus problems in which the similarities were predominantly functional proved quite simple (e.g., problems 5, 7), whereas genus-family problems in which the instances of the genus had obvious sensory properties in common (e.g., problems 14, 16, 24, 26) did not seem easier than the other genus-family problems.

The question whether or not this change in parameters of stimulus generalization underlies the more dramatic changes postulated by Piaget

---

[6] Significantly more subjects achieved a better-than-chance performance on the species-genus than on the genus-family problems (χ^2, correlated proportions, Yates' correction $= 4.2$, $p < .05$), despite the small size of the group.

[7] The relationship to age is, of course, not established within this small exploratory preschool group; but it seems a safe assumption that the addition of a group of older children will result in frequent solution of the genus-family problems. Adults are uniformly successful with them.

cannot be answered at this point. One would need to know more about the parameters themselves and about the language changes with which they might be associated. However, the apparent connection between the relation presented in the task described here and that in the language structure ("P's are a type of Q") from which it was derived makes it likely that the developing abilities which determine the extent of generalization in this and similar tasks are related to the development of a concept of class.

It may be added that the task used in this experiment is only one of a number of possible nonverbal tasks in which relations of similarity, difference, and so forth are presented as stimuli and in which more or less complex relations between attributes are learned—relations which would be expressed verbally through abstract general terms. It can reasonably be anticipated that the parameters of stimulus generalization on such tasks will be found to vary with age.

A GENERAL FORMULATION OF PIAGET'S RESEARCH PROBLEMS

An Epistemological Confusion in Piaget's Theory

So far, some of Piaget's experimental work has been criticized on a number of grounds, and one large segment of it has been examined in detail. This critique indicated that the vulnerability of many of his research methods derives, in large part, from his particular conception of a psychological process. I believe that this conception comes, in turn, from a philosophical error in his theory. I have not discussed this philosophical confusion until now because I do not think it seriously reduces the interest of Piaget's work. It does, however, determine the way in which research problems are formulated by him, and the discussion to follow will suggest ways in which they might be reformulated somewhat more clearly.

Piaget's theory holds that certain psychological processes develop in the child at certain ages. These psychological processes are logical operations, e.g., "addition" or "multiplication" of lengths or regions of space in his work on the ontogeny of measurement and geometric concepts, or again, "addition" (disjunction) and "multiplication" (conjunction) of classes in his work on the development of concepts of class and number.

The treatment of logical operations as psychological processes seems to rest on the following line of thought. For example, suppose two sticks of wood, A and B, are placed end to end. One would normally regard the expression $(A + B)$ as a composite expression referring to the larger stick formed by joining A and B. However, one might conceivably choose to regard it instead as a record of the behavior of some subject: "S picks up B and places it end to end with A." Construed this way, the "$+$" sign has acquired psychological significance; it has been used to indicate the act of picking-up-and-placing-end-to-end-with. If, further, the subject does not displace B physically but only "in his imagination," then the " + " sign comes to indicate a psychological process which is the internalized act of displacement.

When the A and B are *objects* like blocks of wood, this line of thought might be admitted to have some plausibility; the situation is considerably less clear when the A and B are not objects but *lengths* of objects, as in some parts of the logic of measurement. When the A and B are *classes* or *numbers,* all plausibility seems to me to disappear, since it is difficult to see what kind of act, overt or internalized, might be represented by the " + " sign.

In making this equation of logical operation with reasoning process, Piaget makes an epistemological error very similar to that of Boole (1854 [1951]). Boole, it will be remembered, thought he was writing the laws of thought when he formulated the rules of his class algebra, thereby treating the psychology of reasoning as a branch of mathematics. Piaget is, of course, aware of Boole's error and claims he is not making it; but his defense is vulnerable. He seems to assert that the relation between reasoning process and logical operation is not so much one of identity as of correspondence; it is supposedly similar to the relation of physical geometry to pure geometry or of mathematics to mathematical physics (Piaget, 1949b, 1953). A weakness in his argument is suggested by a comparison with Carnap, who has discussed some of the same material. Carnap (1939) develops the position that a calculus, like "pure" geometry, is itself without meaning, being simply a system of rules for manipulating contentless symbols. A calculus (physical calculus) acquires significance only when relations between characteristics of the world appear to "fit" the relations between symbols in the calculus, thereby permitting an "interpretation" of the calculus. Thus, "pure" geometry—itself meaningless—becomes, when interpreted, "physical" geometry, a system of significant and testable statements about the world. In this view, the process of interpreting a calculus consists of assigning referents to the descriptive signs (thus assigning values to the variables) and of assigning conditions of use to the logical signs. Thus, when the values of the x and y of pure geometry are specified as being physical regions of space, the system is transformed into physical geometry.

But Piaget does not interpret his *"groupements"* by assigning physical values to the variables; rather, he attaches psychological significance to some of the logical constants—in particular to the relational signs " + ," " $\times$," " $<$ " and so forth. This seems to be just what Boole did, and to be quite different from Carnap's procedure. The relation between logical operation and reasoning process in Piaget's theory does not seem, therefore, to be similar to the relation between pure and physical geometry, but rather it seems to embody an epistemological confusion of the *products* of reasoning (e.g., sentences containing signs of operation) with the *process* (unknown) through which the products are brought about.

Concluding Remarks

This epistemological confusion—as I believe it to be—is the source of almost all my criticisms of Piaget's methodology. As a result of it, research problems are formulated as inquiries into when and how particular (psycho-) logical processes develop in the average child. With the problems formulated in this manner, the experimenter's task becomes one of diagnosis: If the answer to the question "What develops?" is largely predetermined as a logical operation of some sort, the question as to when and how becomes a diagnostic problem. And certainly in conducting this "diagnostic" task, Piaget has exhibited a unique combination of experimental ingenuity and clinical acumen.

It is a measure of the vitality of Piaget's work that it often gains rather than loses cogency when the research problems are reformulated without this epistemological confusion. In the case of his studies of the development of measurement and geometric concepts, the research questions can be reformulated straightforwardly as questions of how the child comes to understand certain facts of great generality or to distinguish certain relations. Thus, in studying the development of measurement, instead of asking how the "additive operation" develops, one can simply ask how the child comes to grasp the empirical fact that length is additive. The resulting experiments will not be very different because the problem is formulated in this way; for example, tasks in which the child is required to compare the lengths of straight and zigzag lines will remain highly useful. The main advantage of reformulation lies in the fact that the additive operation is not seen as a process whose development underlies the correct response. Instead, a grasp of additivity is seen as the product of the development of unknown factors or processes which now become the focus of inquiry.

However, in the case of Piaget's studies of the development of a concept of class, the research problems cannot be reformulated quite so simply. Here, the "facts" are peculiar ones which seem inseparable from certain sentence forms containing abstractions. It is therefore preferable, as was argued earlier, to pose the question about the language forms themselves —to inquire how they develop and to ask what factors determine their development.

4

"STAGE" AND "STRUCTURE" IN THE STUDY OF CHILDREN

William Kessen
Yale University

INTRODUCTION

Men seem always to have felt a need to impose segmentation on the complicated course of human development. Although it has usually been argued that development is "continuous" and without discrete shifts, more often than not the arguer has early called on the notion of "stage" or "level" to help him understand the speed and fluidity of change in children.

Two events in the history of modern science seem to have given systematic status to the ancient tendency to see human change as saltatory— Goethe's invention of morphology, with its sequels in the search for form, and the revolution of thought in which Darwin offered the ontogeneticist the entire animal kingdom as possible models for the stages of man. The offer was freely accepted; textbooks about children published near the turn of the century are crowded with putative parallels between the child and animals—witness the "chimpanzee stage"—or between the child and uncivilized man—witness the "pastoral stage" or the "hunting stage." Moreover, the morphological and evolutionary innovations brought forth one clearly reputable and productive scientific discipline—embryology—and the success of the embryologists also supported the child psychologist's search for the rules of segmentation or "stagification" that would permit him to describe and to predict the appearance and behavior of the growing child.

The problems posed by the search for stages cannot be evaded, either in the flight-by-redefinition so dear to contemporary psychologists and expressed in sentences like " 'Stage' is only a word, a verbal tic," or by poking fun at the excesses of the men who, subscribing to the dictum "Ontogeny recapitulates phylogeny," managed to see fish and fowl, ape and savage, in their children. The need for, and the difficulty of achieving, classification or segmentation of behavior are present throughout psychology; and the problem can be seen in the animal investigator's attempts to establish a workable definition of "response" and in the clinical psychologist's attention to diagnostic "indices" and "signs." Whatever his school or specialty, the psychologist must address the problem of fracturing—of segmenting—the undifferentiated clay of behavior into pieces that are suitable for precise description and sound prediction. The child psychologist may protest that his problems with response-segmentation are greater than anyone else's, including as they do all of the general psychologist's puzzles as well as the taxing issue of temporal organization; but in any case we cannot, with the pseudosophistication that comes from learning about operationalism early in life, dismiss out of hand the problems of description and explanation represented by "stage."

Two theories of human development demand and receive wide attention —the speculations of Piaget and of Freud—and both make use of the "stage" construct in ways that are certainly nontrivial and that may be crucial. It is not necessary to stipulate the usefulness or adequacy of these formulations; their very visibility requires that we attend to their devices of segmentation.[1]

The pages to follow present in some detail a critical examination of the "stage" construct, not chiefly from a historical or a textual-analytic basis, but rather in exploration of the theoretical range of the notion. What burden of theory is carried by statements about stages? Are there variations in use of the term which stand in need of separation? What formulations are available as alternatives to segmentation by stages? Discussion of these and related questions will uncover many traditional puzzles in the study of development; in fact, the ubiquity of the segmentation issue is well demonstrated by the variety of problems with which it is linked. One in particular—the theoretical status of statements about mental structure—is particularly relevant to the work of Jean Piaget and will be examined later in this paper.

The Several Uses of "Stage"

A systematic analysis of the "stage" construct is blocked at the outset by the variety of ways it is used in writings about children. Although no claim can be made for completeness, it will help in clarification of the segmentation issue if the several usages of "stage" are laid out in a compressed way.

Literary-Evocative

Unhappily, one common use of "stage" carries no more weight than a metaphor. To speak of children as being in the chimpanzee stage is to achieve a joke at best; there are no known and expressable relations between phylogenesis and the behavior of children that advance our understanding.

---

[1] The use of the "stage" notion is not confined to Freud and Piaget; on the contrary, there seems to be only one school of thought about development which does not use it—the group of child psychologists who have ancestral links with learning theory. This omission will be treated later. The notion of "stage," in child development and in other theories, bears some resemblance to the older and much-debated notion of "ideal type."

It would doubtless be much too hard-nosed to demand the excision of liter-ary-evocative descriptions of children, but it is worth our while to recognize that the game is limited in its usefulness. Nor is the metaphorical classifica-tion of children's behavior restricted to zoological comparisons; one may reasonably ask of any scheme of developmental segmentation—and particu-larly of the more plausible ones, such as those of Erikson[2] (1950; Tanner and Inhelder, 1960)—whether it depends for its convincingness more on poetical suggestion than on accurate and useful description.

"Stage" as a Paraphrase for Age and as a Paraphrase for Observation

Can we substitute for an expression "The child is in stage x" the alterna-tive expression "The child is y years old"? To the degree that such a sub-stitution is appropriate, the forms are redundant and the "stage" usage unnecessary. By and large, it has been the view of the child psychologists who use the constructions of learning theory that the notion of stage can be dispensed with on exactly these grounds of redundancy with age. The argu-ment runs in the following form: There are responses, complex or simple, which interest the child psychologist; he observes them and applies some measurement operation to his protocols; if he wants to show the develop-ment of this behavior, he plots the outcome of his measurement operations against chronological age. Here are the results; where is the need for talk about "stages"? A somewhat more sophisticated version of the same general argument goes: Age, as a major factor in learning, may have to enter as a parameter to many of our fundamental equations, but this does not justify the invocation of a superfluous and probably empty theoretical term. We must return to this argument later, but there should be noted in it one of the truisms of behavior study, a platitude we forget. Segmentational terms, whether on the model of "response" or on the model of "stage," are not observation words like "black" and "blue," or even easily determined vari-ables like age; they are theoretical terms and, like other theoretical terms, do not name things or events, but take their meaning from the context of theory in which they appear. Briefly then, when the language of stages is used merely as a paraphrase for age variation, it is not useful—particularly if such a substitution affords either the psychologist or his audience no more than the satisfaction of apparent new knowledge.

A closely related paraphrastic device, which occurs frequently in parental or natural child psychology and altogether too commonly among profes-sionals as well, consists in using the language of stages to describe observa-tions. The sequence

Q: Why did Johnny say "no" to me?
A: Because he's in the negativistic stage.

---

[2] This is not an assertion that Erikson's description is purely literary-evocative. As will be seen later, theories of segmentation do not fall conveniently into a single classificatory pouch.

is formally parallel with the well-rubbed example of the child who fights because of his pugnacity instinct. It should be added, however, that explanations of this order are not necessarily, or even usually, vacuous and meaningless; they fulfill an important function that some writers on method have missed. When we say that a child said "No" because he is in negativistic stage, we are saying something about what explanations will not work (e.g., it is not the case that he said "No" because his Uncle John gives him a dollar for each negation), usually suggesting that our knowledge of the antecedent events that could explain the behavior is incomplete. We also express the fact that there were times in Johnny's life when he did not say "No" so frequently; that is, his no-saying is not universally the case. But it is easy to transmute this device into a mere professional spasm when "He's at the teething age" can be translated as "He's teething" or when "Children at age x enter a tool-using stage" can be translated as "Children at age x begin to use tools."

An exception to the foregoing argument, and one not without interest, can be seen in the use of the "stage" construct to represent *sequence*. The knowledge, for instance, that the stage of tertiary circular reactions (Piaget) occurs after the stage of secondary circular reactions helps us to think coherently about the course of development and, of vastly more consequence, it suggests to us the descriptive or theoretical basis on which the behavior is seen as segmented and developing. For example, Piaget's treatment of changes in the response of the young child to inanimate objects (Piaget, 1937a) presents a description of sequence which suggests the operation of organizing—i.e., theoretical—principles. Take another example. A statement about "the stages of locomotor development" is, first of all, an abstracted and highly compressed *description* of a limited aspect of infantile behavior, but it also expresses the proposition that there is some nontrivial reason—some theoretical justification—for collecting these segments together in a chronological line. In the best case for sequential statement, there may be underlying regularities (e.g., cephalocaudal progression) which are demonstrated or suggested by the expression of sequence.

Reference to locomotor development leads to another use of the "stage" notion which, though it expresses sequence, aims at being more than a paraphrase for age or observation—the developmental norm or ideal. When it is said that a child is at such-and-such a stage on a normative basis—whether in a relatively primitive way such as "He's a typical 3-year-old" or in the highly sophisticated fashion of intelligence-test mental age scores—more is meant than the statement of succession of behaviors. The scope of the discourse is about differences among children of the same chronological placement (e.g., the typical 3-year-old) and not about inevitable and synchronous succession in all children. This is not an appropriate place to open a discussion of the meaning of intelligence-test norms, but it is appropriate to emphasize that the normative use of "stage" is different from the use of the stage construct in a general developmental theory.[3] Only when we have discussed "stage" as a theoretical construct can we return to a treatment of its proper relevance to the determination of individual differences.

Piaget (*passim*; esp. 1956b) and Inhelder (1962) have paid close attention to the uses of "stage" to encompass regular sequencing, and Inhelder (Tanner and Inhelder, 1956) has made what is probably the strongest available defense of the Genevan methods of stage description.

Description of the Environment

The typical occurrence of "stage" has dealt with some unfolding of behavior in the child more or less without reference to his surround, but there are relatively frequent occasions in which the notion has to do with the environment as much as with the child. Thus, when Erikson speaks of "crises in development," his emphasis is often on what is happening *to* the child as much as on what is happening *in* the child—witness the case of "trust vs. mistrust" and its relation to the mother's giving and withholding. Similarly, when there is mention of the "school-age child," we normally mean not merely an elliptical specification of age, but the presence of a typical environment—i.e., school—in which the child behaves. The list of examples can be extended almost indefinitely; what bears noting is that the characterization of stage is rarely, if ever, free of the environment in which the child acts, though there may be no explicit treatment of the dimensions of significant variation in behavior ascribable to environmental variations. Perhaps under lead of the ethologists, there is abroad in child psychology a renewed emphasis on the stimulus; that is, on the specification of environmental events antecedent to behavior which shows "maturational" change.

Specification of the Parameters of Variation

In the dissection of the construct "stage," a dramatic shift in generality and scope is seen when stages are taken as parametric variations of a fundamental set of theoretical statements. Before examining this species of stage in psychological usage, let us distort theoretical mechanics to provide a clear, even if absurd, analogous example. An object propelled upward within the earth's atmosphere will, at the top of its trajectory, begin to fall. Now, it would be possible to speak of its "upward-moving stage" and its "downward-moving stage," but this formulation would be favored by relatively few physicists, largely because the formulas for computing position and velocity are the same whether the object is going up or down. Once we know its initial velocity and direction, we can solve the problem. It is toward this use of the construct "stage" that general theorists of development tend—to

---

[3] "Stage" and "individual difference" share their isolation from the main lines of theoretical development in American psychology; there is little sign of a conceptual reconciliation of the study of variables with the study of people, in spite of warm protest by some psychologists—William Stephenson (e.g., 1961), for instance.

develop general and inclusive formulas about changes in behavior which are operative across the entire course of human development and, further, to reduce the notion of "stage" to parametric variation in these formulas.

There seems little doubt that much of Freud's developmental theory can be put in this form of general formulations combined with parametric variation. The pleasure principle is invariably relevant to behavior; there is a general pattern of reaction to danger, the occurrence of anxiety, and the elaboration of defenses; there are "standard" regularities in gratification and in object relations; all of these are conceptually independent of the specific stage of psychosexual development. The statement, then, that a child is in the oral or the phallic stage is a theoretical instruction to change the parameters of the fundamental equations in a specified way. Noteworthy too is the great economy of this use of the "stage" idea; there is no question that when we say that a child is in the oral stage we mean more than "He is x years old" or "He sucks." Translated in the fashion proposed here, the specification of stage makes a statement based on a theory about the child's behavior in diverse settings, relating the special and particular facts about orality to the general theoretical formulations applicable to any phase of development. Psychoanalysis is liable to the charge of imprecision and irregularity in the "fundamental equations" of its descriptive schemes, and this looseness seriously prejudices the usefulness of the theory. But in idealized form, at any rate, psychoanalysis presents "stages" as relatively complicated sets of theoretical statements.

A second example of this more fruitful way of conceiving developmental phasing has been mentioned earlier. Although largely programmatic in its applications to child psychology, the approach of the learning theorists has been of this order. In brief, there are postulated a set of general principles which apply to all ages of man (and, incidentally, of all other mammalian species as well); yet there are clear differences in behavior that can be related to age; therefore, if a theorist aims at a fully generalizable theory of behavior, it will be necessary to make changes in the generalized constants of the fundamental equations in order to predict variation with age.[4] At the empirical level, a good deal of work has been done on age-related variations in behavior having to do with amount, delay, and schedule of reinforcement, generalization and discrimination, responses to changes in drive, and so on; but there remains an obvious gap in the pattern—there is no clear sign of a theory of developmental change derived from the associationistic or more narrowly stimulus-response schools.

---

[4] Once more, it must be emphasized that this is a highly refined version of a possible strategy in psychology. It will be difficult in many instances to determine the difference between a change in a generalized constant and a change in a functional variable. Note too the illuminating difference between "oral-anal-phallic-latent-genital" as a dimension of parametric variation and age as such a variation.

General parametric formulations play an important part in Piaget's developmental theories. More specifically than either psychoanalysis or learning theory, Piaget states that there are ubiquitous processes—the functional invariants—which exert their effect throughout the course of development. The stages of Piaget's formulation are explicitly said to vary with variation in mental structure, and it is on mental structures that these unyielding and unvarying processes work. The introduction of "mental structure" prepares the ground for a later discussion of the place of structural notions in the understanding of children's thinking; it is sufficient here to remark that Piaget's general theoretical formulations are equally as general as those of the learning theorists and that he probably intends a wider coverage for his basic theoretical umbrella than did Freud. In truth, he maintains that at least an analogy is present between the action of assimilation and accommodation in the cognitive behavior of the child and their action in more restricted systems such as digestion.

In his recent work with Inhelder on the growth of logical thinking (Inhelder and Piaget, 1955) Piaget asserts again that the child's striking and often saltatory increases in skill at problem-solving, particularly problem-solving of a kind that involves the application of physical principles, can be organized around the development of an understanding of logical operations. The stages of the child's mental development, then, are determined by the elegance and advance of his comprehension of negation, reciprocity, and so on. The similarity to the Freudian schema is clear: To say that a child is in a pre-operational stage is to say much more than that he is such and such an age or that he can solve such and such a problem. There is included the statement, based on theory, that his approach to, and competence with, all problems demanding abstract operations will be of a particular and specific kind.

What a curious bag of tricks this is! Under one rubric can be found (or, to the methodological skeptic, can be forced) the diverse speculations of Freud, Hull, and Piaget. Nonetheless, the similarities are present and they deserve our closer examination, but there is one last and closely related use of the notion of stage which must be mentioned to complete the categorical arrangement.

The Operation of Different Rule-Systems

Suppose that one is studying some aspect of behavior in which there is good control over the input of stimulation and with which a fairly simple index or measure of responding is used—the case of probability learning or, more generally, of concept formation may serve as examples. Under some circumstances, it is possible to express the observations in a highly condensed and regular set of rules; that is, a group of equations that contain terms dealing with variation in stimulus input and which lead to prediction of certain response-outcomes. Suppose further that this set of equations or operations is so precise that we can write a computer program containing them and that, by acute selection of steps, we can simulate with fair accuracy the performance of human subjects. This is precisely the goal of some recent work in computer simulation (Simon and Newell, 1962), work which has gone far beyond such simplicities as concept formation and which approaches *tours de force* like the playing of chess or of Go. Take the suppositional game one step further, and the relevance to development will become manifest. If, as a function of age or of correlated change in the development of the child, different programs must be written for the simulation of his behavior, then the notion of "stage" can be given very exact definition. A "stage," under this dispensation, would be a simulation program different from the one which was adequate for the younger child. It may be a matter of some murkiness to decide how much of a change in the program will be called a change in "stage," and it may very well be that this approach to the problem of cognitive development will obliterate the theoretical need for the construct.

In the simple statement given here,[5] there are several differences between the interpretation of stage as a rule-system and the earlier treatment of stage as parametric variation of general principles. Perhaps the most important of these is the highly empirical character of the rule-system idea, for all its precision. Given a set of circumstances and a set of responses, the problem of the simulator is to write a machine program which will give him the answers the human being gave. In devising a program he may be neutral with respect to general psychological theory, however unlikely this case is in fact, and he may, if he chooses, ignore the problem of transition from one stage to another or the problem of differences among species or other sub-populations. His task is to make guesses about the functioning of the "black box" and then, in imitation of Providence, to build it.[6]

Stages, States, and Transitions

With some of the theoretical uses of "stage" outlined, and with the purely literary or paraphrastic uses put to one side, it is possible to make a generalized statement of the problem of stages. From this base, we can move to a discussion of problems and policies in the segmentation of development.

---

[5] The statement is artificially simple. Very complex processes can be simulated, and it would doubtless be an error for the psychologist to believe that there is any inherent limit to the flexibility and generality of the computer simulation program. The limits are largely human rather than electronic or mechanical (*see* Hovland and Hunt, 1960).

[6] Computers, as presently designed, cannot provide us with a theory of development *de novo*; they serve to remind us, however, that if a theory of development is not precisely enough stated to be susceptible to programming, then it probably is not an explicit theory at all.

Understanding the problem of segmentation entails remembering some primitive facts about the history of psychology, facts that would have only esoteric and antiquarian interest were it not true that these primitive facts demark continuing rifts among psychologists. Put in briefest compass, and largely to jog memories of old arguments, the divisive dimensions of child psychology (and perhaps of the field at large) can be stated in the following ways.

The psychologist may study *states* of the organism, in a sense catching the bird at the moment in flight and saying, "At this moment, the organism has such and such characteristics." In the language of contemporary psychology, the psychologist of states would, for example, speak of "anxiety state," "defensive structure," or "MMPI profile"; much closer to an interest in children's thinking, he would speak of "mental structure," "levels of cognitive development," and so on.

A colleague of the state-psychologist, and very often a colleague sharing the same skin, is concerned with stable *differences among people* in state-characteristics. This is the traditional view of the clinical psychologist and the psychologist of personality; his central task is in making meaningful segregations of people in terms of state-characteristics. This permits him, at least in program, to make predictions about the behavior of this or that particular person.

Still a third member of our little academic faculty is often out of agreement with his fellows about strategy. He sees the basic psychological problem to be the formulation of general rules for *transition* from one stage or state to another, and his concentration on understanding how the organism gets from one condition to another often makes him less than sympathetic with the psychologist of stage and psychologist of individual differences.

The sketches in Figure 1 tabulate this division. The sets are meant to represent stages or states, with "Th" representing the theoretical characterization of the stage; the letters "A," "B," "a," and "b" are diagnostic categories or levels within a state—the clinician's armory; the "x's" are persons (thus, "x_{12}" represents the second measure on person 1); the connecting lines with "f" for "function" represent the work of the psychologist of transitions—the learning theorist, the developmental theorist. Against this generalized pattern, let us put specific examples from developmental speculation and research, in order to see the dimensions of the problem of "stage."

Case I

For the child psychologist, characterizations of *state* are typically related to age. For a simple description of a narrowly circumscribed system—e.g., locomotion—the governing theoretical propositions "Th" of a stage may be as simply stated as "rests weight on hands and knees." This example, by the way, can be extended to case II (individual differences) by setting up

Case I. *The Psychology of State*

$$\text{Th}_k \left\{ \begin{matrix} x_{11}, & x_{12}, & \cdots \\ x_{21}, & x_{22}, & \cdots \\ \cdot & \cdot & \cdots \\ \cdot & \cdot & \cdots \end{matrix} \right\}$$

Case II. *The Psychology of Individual Differences in Stage*

$$\text{Th}_k \left\{ \begin{matrix} A & \left\{ \begin{matrix} x_{11}, & x_{12}, & \cdots \\ x_{21}, & x_{22}, & \cdots \end{matrix} \right\} \\ B & \left\{ \begin{matrix} x_{31}, & x_{32}, & \cdots \\ x_{41}, & x_{42}, & \cdots \end{matrix} \right\} \\ \cdot & \\ \cdot & \end{matrix} \right\}$$

Case III. *The Psychology of Transitions*

$$\left\{ \begin{matrix} x_{11}, & x_{12}, & \cdots \\ x_{21}, & x_{22}, & \cdots \\ \cdot & \cdot & \cdots \\ \cdot & \cdot & \cdots \end{matrix} \right\} \quad \text{---} f_k \text{---} \quad \left\{ \begin{matrix} x_{11}, & x_{12}, & \cdots \\ x_{21}, & x_{22}, & \cdots \\ \cdot & \cdot & \cdots \\ \cdot & \cdot & \cdots \end{matrix} \right\}$$

Case IV. *The Full Statement*

$$\text{Th}_k \left\{ \begin{matrix} A & \left\{ \begin{matrix} x_{11}, & x_{12}, & \cdots \\ x_{21}, & x_{22}, & \cdots \end{matrix} \right\} \\ B & \left\{ \begin{matrix} x_{31}, & x_{32}, & \cdots \\ x_{41}, & x_{42}, & \cdots \end{matrix} \right\} \end{matrix} \right\} - f_k - \text{Th}_o \left\{ \begin{matrix} a & \left\{ \begin{matrix} x_{11}, & x_{12}, & \cdots \\ x_{21}, & x_{22}, & \cdots \end{matrix} \right\} \\ b & \left\{ \begin{matrix} x_{31}, & x_{32}, & \cdots \\ x_{41}, & x_{42}, & \cdots \end{matrix} \right\} \end{matrix} \right\} - \cdots$$

FIGURE 1—Schematic representations of "stage."

the operator A as "achieves early" and B as "achieves late." Similarly, it can be extended to case III (transition rule) by introducing the transition function "gets older" or "undergoes neurological maturation."

Another quite common case I instance of the stage notion is seen in the use of norms of achievement or intelligence. The "Th" in this case would be expressed by an enumeration of the test items appropriate to a particular age.

A more complicated example of case I would be represented by the statement of the system of English grammar used by the 2-year-old child. Here the "Th" will turn out to be very intricate indeed and will be in a form that could hardly be called simply descriptive. Similarly, complex and extra-observational uses of case I can be found in psychoanalytic treatments of (say) orality or in Piaget's characterization of the sensory-motor stage of intellectual development.

Case II

In this transformation of the "stage" problem, interest centers not so much on the generalization across all x's as in case I, but rather on making statements about packets of people—presumably in support of the more accurate prediction of the behavior of the single person. Thus, the psychologist of case II may be interested in the differences in the use of grammar in 2-year-olds between anxious and nonanxious, or dependent and nondependent, children. Correspondingly, psychologists of the Freudian bent may wish to determine differences in the handling of orality by boys and girls, or by children in one-parent and two-parent families. Oftentimes, the concentration on individual differences may not warrant the suggestion of different stages (that is, in the language used here, different theoretical operators "A"), but there are instances—the Lewin-Kounin (Zigler, 1962) proposals about the rigidity of the feebleminded, for example, or more commonly, in the specification of sex differences—where segregation on individual differences requires marked change in the application of the more general "Th" operators.

Case III

For the psychologist who is primarily interested in the mechanics of behavioral change, the differentiations made earlier about state and individual differences are not crucial. Take the case of learning in children. Most of the emphasis for case III interpretation would be placed on transition-rules, on "f's," which would have to do with such constructs as reinforcement, discrimination, and so on. Although, as has been mentioned earlier, there is some tendency among experimental child psychologists to introduce both state variation and individual differences into their formulations by changing the constants in their functional generalizations, by and large there exists little vocabulary in contemporary learning theory for dealing with state-variation. The typical assumption of the theorist of children's learning is that his functions are not affected by initial variation among his subjects.[7]

A commitment to learning-theory analysis is not a prerequisite for interest in transition rules. As Piaget has pointed out, "It is not only in the correspondence of the stages, or perhaps not even in such correspondence, that one can hope to find the convergences [among different theorists and researchers] sought for. It is, perhaps, rather in the mechanism of the transition from one stage to the following, i.e., in certain characteristic processes of the actual mechanism of development" (Tanner and Inhelder, 1960, p. 15). This statement, made as Piaget discussed his own proposal for a major transition rule, is convincing evidence that transition by reinforcement does not hold the field entire. From the central transition rule of classical developmental psychology—aging—to the subtleties of transition rules in psychoanalysis—conflict (?)—there is a range of choice available for study of this most important issue in developmental psychology.

Piaget, and to some degree Freud, have tried to deal with the disjunction in attack presented by the psychologists of state on one side and the researchers of transition on the other. Piaget has specified, at least for the very young child, certain functional generalizations which govern the transition from one stage to another. These are apparently held to be invariant across development and have differential effect at different points in the development of the child only because they operate on a different initial point. For this reason, it is critical to Piaget's model that an accurate description of stages be possible; assimilation and accommodation lead to widely separated ends if they begin at different stages. Perhaps it is for this reason that Piaget is sometimes seen as using the traditional techniques of merely listing the behavior of the child as it changes with age; paradoxically, the "stage" notion is *formally* relatively unimportant for Piaget. But in order to explain how the child arrived at point t_k in his development by means of the general transitional principles, Piaget has to make a very accurate statement of where the child was at t_0. In a rapidly changing system like the child, this expository task is made easier by slicing the developmental loaf at intervals and exposing the resulting slice to view; an almost exact analog is the dis-

---

[7] It is for this last reason that no "Th" operator is shown for case III; it normally is no more than an expression of an averaging operation across all subjects. However, just as there is no necessary objection to the inclusion of more sophisticated transitional rules in the psychologies of state, so there is no necessary obstacle to the consideration of state-variation in learning theory. The fact of the matter is that both expansions are rare.

It is also the case that the differences in point of attack presented in this simplified way are sociological or idiosyncratic in origin, and it is difficult to see any metatheoretical rule that would tell us which approach is more likely to pay off in the study of children. The differences in strategy are there, nonetheless, and supported by a complicated and rather rigid institutional framework. Moreover, many of the vigorous, if not satisfying, arguments among psychologists of children stem from a failure to keep these divisions clear. Arguments are not likely to be fruitful if the contestants are not talking about the same thing.

section of embryological specimens to provide a developmental series on (say) changes in long bones.[8] In this regard, it should be noted that Piaget has little interest in individual variation among children in the rate at which they achieve a stage or in their over-all capacity during it; he is a student of the development of thinking more than he is a student of children.

In brief, the problems of the child psychologist in his search for segmentational systems can be seen from three points of view—the description of states or stages, the specification of stable individual variation, and the formulation of rules for transition from one state to another. Even though these ways of approaching the problem are apparently interrelated, and very closely so, theorists of child behavior have only occasionally made it their business to include all three in their purview. One of Piaget's important incidental achievements has been to demonstrate the necessary interrelation of stage and transition in the investigation of children's thought.

Tactical Problems in the Use of "Stage"

Let us stipulate for the moment that a complete treatment of the development of thinking will have in it some way of describing "stages." For the moment, it is unimportant what particular theoretical scaffold is used to hold this weight; because of its simplicity, it may be easiest to think of the "stage" as a miniature theory of input-output relations, i.e., *l'enfant machine*. A new stage is a different miniature theory linked to the preceding one by a set of transition rules. What will be the tactical problems in the use of the construct "stage"?

Implicit in much of the earlier discussion is a problem which we can only state and then move away from—the selection of observations. It has become increasingly clear over the recent history of psychology that the fundamental *tactical* decision in the building of a research program or of a theory is the decision about what to observe. Once this option is in force —to study problem-solving, or to study probability learning, or to study cognitive style—there follows almost without explicit notation a train of consesequences. If the decision is for problem-solving, then the machinery of the research will be in the line of Duncker or Bartlett, and there will be an almost inevitable affiliation for the theories of Piaget or Wertheimer; if the decision about what protocols to collect leads to the study of probability learning, the apparatus will look much like a complex lever-box, and the theory invoked will be drawn from behavior theory, e.g., Spence or Estes;

---

[8] This comparison is accurate when made about the Piaget of the trilogy on the first triennium; in the recent work on logical development, the rules for transition from one stage to another are less clearly seen. The recent emphasis by the Genevans on "equilibration" remains still in a trial form. Incidentally, the foregoing remarks are neutral with regard to the accuracy or usefulness of Piaget's theory of cognitive development; he may have grasped the central issues in the problem of segmenting development and still be wrong in his proposals for the solution of that problem.

if cognitive style is chosen as the center of interest, then materials akin to the clinician's diagnostic devices will be used to collect data, and the theoretical rationale will be in the terms of the personality theorists. This is not to say that the decision may not go the other way—an interest in Piaget may lead to a particular kind of research—but this does not weaken the point made here. When, for whatever reason, a child psychologist decides to make observations of a particular kind, he is then in a tradition of research design and of "canonical" theory from which he will find it extremely difficult to escape.

Recognition of these disjunctions may save time and wear-and-tear on our tempers; tactics and theories of the stages of intellective development are not so much right or wrong as different from one another. Piaget has no theoretical apparatus for handling probability learning; Hull has no theoretical apparatus for handling differences in cognitive style. It is credible that we will move more quickly to the systematic collection of relevant data about children's thinking if we do not worry overmuch about denying the chasms and if we do not use them merely to shout epithets across.

Once more, it can be seen that "stage" is a theoretical notion, a device for segmentation of behavior much like the more widespread "response," and the notions share a need to be specified within the context of research or theory. Thus, Piaget states that the range of his discourse will be (let us take *Construction of reality* [1937a] as example) the young child's behavior with regard to object, time, space, and causality; he writes of how he uses the notions of assimilation and accommodation as transition rules; he specifies—perhaps with debatable precision but nonetheless with a keen understanding of the problems involved—what will characterize the behavior of a child in each stage. It is incumbent on other theorists of development to take the same *formal* steps—the delineation of a range of discourse (i.e., a statement of the behavior he wants to account for, the results he wants to explain), including segmentation techniques, whether or not they involve the notion of stage explicitly; the character of transition rules from one condition or stage to another; and finally—of particular importance for the student of individual variation—the summarizing formulas used in determining placement in a particular stage of development.

The results of this program will probably not include an early and acquiescent feast of *agape* among developmental theorists with a decision about the True Way. It may, however, divert the energy uselessly given to debates about grand strategy and concentrate our efforts on finding out what other students of children's thought are doing and how their work, distant as it may continue to be from our own, advances us toward an understanding of thinking.

The choice of problem-focus once made, further issues arise for consideration in the tactics of studying developmental segmentation. Two of them concern chiefly the postulation of an invariable and universal occurrence of particular stages—e.g., Freud's Oedipal stage or Piaget's sensory-motor stage. These issues are the absence of the negative case and the related problem of manipulative experimentation.

In critiques of the psychoanalytic theory of psychosexual development, and the argument applies as well to other theories of universal pattern, philosophers of science have maintained that the absence of a negative instance—someone who did not pass through Oedipal conflict or did not experience the sensory-motor stage of his development—makes the construct "Oedipal phase" or "sensory-motor stage" theoretically meaningless. If you cannot compare people who had Oedipal conflict with the people who did not, then you cannot determine the effects of Oedipal conflict. It is well to be clear on the character of this attack. It does not argue against descriptions of regularities in the tradition of natural history—otherwise, a true statement like "human beings have two eyes" would be meaningless. Thus, it is appropriate—though subject to the usual scientific requirements for regularity of occurrence and reliability of demonstration—for psychoanalysts to maintain that at a certain point in the child's development he behaves in a way toward his parents and toward his own impulses that would warrant calling this an Oedipal structure or an Oedipal stage. Similarly, it does no disservice to the established rules of inquiry for Piaget to maintain that the child in the first days of life shows a pattern of behavior which can appropriately be labeled "the stage of the use of reflexes." Arguments about the absence of a negative case are directed against the use of a universal to account for (i.e., explain) some subsequent event. To return to the earlier example, to say that a child enters latency because of, or as a result of, Oedipal resolution is to make an untestable and thereby meaningless statement. In analogous fashion, to say that a child enters the stage of primary circular reactions because he has completed the stage of the use of reflexes is vacuous.[9] Only with a negative case—a non-Oedipal child or a "skipper" of reflex practice —can we determine whether subsequent events are determined by the positive instance.

There are three positions that may be taken in the face of this objection. One is to agree with the objection and to say that our interest is in reliably obtained description of sequences, and if we can find some way of simplifying the descriptive task—as Piaget has done in building his description around changes in comprehension of logic—so much the better. This answer abandons any attempt at a causal (i.e., general theoretical) handling of the data of development. The second answer is the more usual one, but it carries the burden of not always being implemented. This is to say that it is not the occurrence of the stage that matters, but rather the time it occurs, or the particular way in which it is introduced, and so on. Thus, the psycho-

---

[9] Piaget is careful to avoid statements of this order. His theory is weakest in the discussion of the particular variables involved in transitions.

analytic theorist might postulate that the male child of a weak father and weak mother will show behavior at age 4 or 5 or 6 quite different from the behavior shown by a male child of weak father and strong mother. The analogous transformation for a theory like Piaget's is obvious.[10] Still a third reply to the problem of the absent negative instance is to find the negative instance; that is, to modify the statement of the theory to make negative instances available. To illustrate this tactic with the present examples is difficult, but bear with the following distortions for the sake of the point. If the Oedipal stage were said to be absent in cases of children raised from birth in a many-caretaker orphanage, then presumably the objection is answered. And in parallel, if Piaget were to maintain that the absence of tuition in language prevents the achievement of operational-stage thinking, he would have a testable proposition involving a negative instance.

This last answer leads to another problem which any theory of development based on stage-succession (and that presumably includes all of them) must face—the problem of the manipulative experiment. The students of transition-rules in behavior, particularly the learning theorists, have argued from a strong position because they could freely use the sharpest instrument in the demonstration of knowledge—the controlled experiment. If the goal of scientific knowledge is the reliable statement of necessary and sufficient conditions for the occurrence of an event, then only the random-assignment manipulative experiment provides such scientific knowledge. It is difficult at first glance to see how the psychologist of state or the psychologist of individual differences can counter the demand for rigorous, i.e., experimental, verification of their hypotheses and general principles. It is possible that some of the interesting problems posed by the psychologists of state, particularly in the theories of Freud and Piaget, can be subjected to experimental examination. The advances of experimental embryology are a neat object-lesson in what can be done in the manipulative examination of development. The theories contain suggestions for experimental manipulations which have led to controlled study and which clearly warrant further investigation, e.g., the role of specific tuition in the stage-sequencing Piaget describes. Even beyond these possibilities of experimentation with children in laboratory settings, there exists the range of animal research which may prove quite useful in the experimental test of developmental hypotheses. It is reasonable to believe that, by one or another of these techniques, some of the problems of stages may be laid open to examination in a controlled setting.

But there is another comment appropriate to the question of manipulative experimentation and that is, briefly, that some of the problems of child development research are simply and ultimately unsuited to experimental

---

[10] If these changes are made, it may come out that the language of stages is no longer necessary to the theory (or that part of it) and can be substituted for by the variables used to demonstrate differences in outcome.

study. For better or worse, the development of the child is an aspect of the world which deserves careful and extensive study, whether or not it provides us with generalizable functional statements. Each child is an important particular, in the way that the Sun is an important particular in astronomical observation, and children will be studied regardless of the fact that we will accumulate bundles of descriptive data and build a group of developmental theories for which there is no adequate experimental test.

Such is the condition of the child psychologist who is not chiefly concerned with transition rules but rather wants to know as much as possible about that group of important particulars—children. The outcome of this ultimately refined concentration on the nonmanipulative study of a single species will not provide us with a general theory of behavior in the traditions of American psychology; but it accomplishes nothing to kick against this prick. If we are to study the child in his changes over age, we will have to study him, at least in part, in the Linnean rather than in the Galilean mode.

A NOTE ON "STRUCTURE"

The notion of structure or organization has played an important part in the history of psychology, usually dividing the associationistic schools, which maintain that organizational constructs are redundant, from the schools of Gestalt and its allies, which maintain that the organizational constructs are essential. It is not appropriate to enter here on an extended treatment of the terrain separating these camps; but it may be fitting to suggest a use for the term "structure" which relates to the foregoing discussion. A mental structure can profitably be considered as a minature theory of a stage—i.e., the "Th"-statements of the figure presented earlier. To say that a particular mental structure was operative would be to say that a set of transformation rules—a theory—exists which permits the prediction of outcome on the presentation of certain information or stimulation. This formulation of "structure" seems isomorphic with Piaget's use and can best be illustrated from his treatment of problem-solving "structures" in the child as systems of rules of logic (1953). Such a specification is a remarkable advance on the use of "structure" or "organization" pejoratively. What we need in the study of children's thinking is not so much a decision for or against structural theories as a statement of theories of thought precise enough to guide our observation and to stimulate our own invention.

SUMMARY

The child psychologist, like his colleague in other specialized study of behavior, faces the problem of segmentation—the decision about how to slice the developmental course. This has typically involved the student of children in a discussion of "stages." Although the term has had a checkered career, the optimal theoretical use of it appears to be as a link in a more general statement of the problems of the child psychologist. It was noted that the three goals of study—the description of states, the specification of individual differences, and the statement of transition rules—are often not aimed for simultaneously or brought into the range of interest of a single psychologist or a single school of psychologists.

Problems of tactics and of theory in the use of "stage" were discussed. It was concluded that "stage" is a descriptive-theoretical term in the Linnean mode of science and that "structure" may fruitfully be considered an expression for the theory of stages.

5

FROM PERCEPTION TO INFERENCE: A DIMENSION OF COGNITIVE DEVELOPMENT

Joachim F. Wohlwill

Clark University

Introduction

How shall we conceptualize the changes which the child's mental processes undergo during the course of development? This question has been answered most frequently in terms that emphasize an increase in powers of abstraction or an increased intervention of symbolic processes. More generally, one might say that there is a decreasing dependence of behavior on information in the immediate stimulus field. For instance, in the delayed reaction experiment we find that the maximum delay that may intervene between the presentation of a stimulus and a discriminatory response increases with age (Munn, 1955, pp. 306ff.). Similarly, much of Piaget's work on the development of concepts—particularly that on the conservation of length, weight, volume, number, and so forth—is interpretable in terms of the increasing stability of concepts in the face of (irrelevant) changes in the stimulus field.

We have here, then, the makings of a significant dimension along which to analyze the course of cognitive development. The eventual aim of this paper is to suggest a more systematic approach for such an analysis, based on certain principles relating to the ways in which the organism utilizes sensory information. However, the realization of this aim presupposes an adequate understanding of the interrelation between perception and thinking; it should therefore prove valuable to undertake a prior examination, in some detail, of the various ways in which this relation has been conceptualized, and more particularly of the developmental aspects of this problem.

A prefatory note of caution—given the notoriously elusive and ill-defined nature of such concepts as perception and thinking, no single, uniformly acceptable characterization of their relation is to be expected. For the same reason, the analysis of the developmental changes in the relationship between these two functions is beset with obvious difficulties. Nevertheless, we shall find that the alternative formulations that have been proposed to deal with this problem, and especially Piaget's illuminating comparison between perceptual and conceptual development, are not only of great interest in their own right, but contribute materially to the dimensional analysis of mental development.

THREE VIEWS OF THE PERCEPTION-CONCEPTION RELATION

Let us start by reviewing three different ways in which theorists have conceptualized the relationship between perception and conception. These three clearly do not exhaust all of the different positions that have been taken on this question, but they probably represent the major trends of thought; of greater importance, they define three sharply differentiated foci from which this problem may be approached, so that their consideration should bring out some major theoretical issues. It should be noted at the outset that all three of these viewpoints are essentially nongenetic, at least insofar as any explicit treatment of development is concerned.

The Gestalt Position

One of the solutions to the problem at hand is to take a model of perception and to attempt to fit it intact to the area of thinking, thus reducing these two functions to a common set of basic processes. This appears to be in large measure the course followed by the Gestalt school in its efforts to interpret phenomena in the field of the thought processes—as seen in Köhler's classical work (1925) on the problem solving behavior of his chimpanzees or Wertheimer's analysis of "productive thinking" (1959) in the solution of mathematical and other conceptual problems. In these works we find a heavy emphasis on such quasiperceptual terms as "insight," "restructuring of the field," "closure," and the like, which seem to represent the sum, if not the substance, of the repertoire of concepts used by the Gestaltists to handle the processes of human reasoning. This point is expressed quite explicitly by Koffka in *The Growth of the Mind*. After paying lip service to the increasing importance in the development of thinking of psychological processes affecting a delay between a stimulus and a consequent reaction of the individual, Koffka, states that

> . . . the ideational field depends most intimately upon the sensory, and any means that enable us to become independent of immediate perception are rooted in perception, and, in truth, only lead us from one perception to another (1924, p. 49).

This formulation, quite apart from its rather meager empirical yield, does not seem to have proved overly successful in its theoretical power. Not only has a major portion of problems in the field of thinking been left aside (e.g., concept formation, the nature of symbolic processes, and so forth), but even when applied to the situations with which the Gestaltists have concerned themselves, the explanatory worth of their concepts appears quite limited.[1] Thus, interpretations of problem solving in terms of restructuring of the field have a somewhat hollow ring in the absence of attention to the question of how a Gestalt may be restructured and of what keeps it from being appropriately structured at the outset. In fact, the whole problem of the ways in which conceptual activity may *transform* an immediate percept is ignored. Paraphrasing Guthrie's dictum about Tolman, whom he accused of "leaving the rat buried in thought," one might therefore be justified in criticizing the Gestaltists for leaving the organism too readily short-circuited in closure to permit him to think.

Last, but by no means least, the a prioristic and thus inherently non-genetic bias of the Gestalt school should be noted. In their work, even when it deals with the behavior of children, as in the books by Koffka and Wertheimer cited earlier, there is little interest in matters relating to developmental changes underlying such behavior—a limitation for which Piaget (1946c, 1954), among others, has repeatedly taken them to task.

Bruner's Position

Let us examine next a point of view diametrically opposed to the Gestaltists, one which regards perception as basically an inferential process, in which the perceiver plays a maximal—and maximally idiosyncratic—role in interpreting, categorizing, or transforming the stimulus input. This view is represented generally by the latter-day functionalist school of perception, particularly that of the transactionalist variety. Its most explicit statement has, however, come from Bruner (1957), according to whom

> Perception involves an act of categorization . . . the nature of the inference from cue to identity in perception is . . . in no sense different from other kinds of categorical inferences based on defining attributes . . . there is no reason to assume that the laws governing inferences . . . are discontinuous as one moves from perceptual to more conceptual activities (1957, pp. 123f.).

While Bruner claims neither that all perception processes can be encompassed in such a theory nor that it precludes a distinction between perceptual and conceptual inference, he does argue that the theory covers a wide variety of perceptual phenomena which conform in many essential respects to principles akin to those observed in the conceptual sphere.

Bruner's formulation raises a number of difficult questions. What is the implicit definition of perception on which it is based? What is the role assigned to structural aspects of the stimulus in such a model of perception? Most importantly, perhaps, to what extent does the operation of conceptual mechanisms in perception depend on conditions of inadequate or impov-

---

[1] The work of such investigators as Duncker and Maier might be cited in refutation of this statement. But these psychologists really fall outside the classical Gestalt tradition, utilizing concepts that bear little direct relationship to the principles of this school of thought—cf. Maier's "functional fixedness" and the general attention given to problems of set.

erished stimulation? Bruner has not ignored this latter problem, but he is inclined to dismiss its importance; for example, he reduces the difference between ordinary and tachistoscopic perception to a matter of degree— inferential mechanisms are always at work, but categorizations vary in the univocality of their coding of stimulus cues in proportion to the amount of stimulus information provided. Thus, for Bruner, veridical perception is a joint function of redundancy in the stimulus and the accessibility of appropriate categorizing systems, in the following sense:

> Where accessibility of categories reflects environmental probabilities, the organism is in the position of requiring less stimulus input, less redundancy of cues for the appropriate categorization of objects . . . the more inappropriate the readiness, the greater the input or redundancy of cues required for appropriate categorization to occur (1957, p 133).

We will find this notion of some interest in connection with one of the dimensions to be proposed later for tracing the development from a perceptual to an inferential level of cognitive functioning. For the present, it may suffice to point out, as Piaget and Morf (1958a) have, that Bruner's model of perception presupposes an adult perceiver; it would be difficult to apply it to the perceptions of a very young child, whose conceptual categories were still in the process of formation. Not surprisingly, under the circumstances, we find that Bruner has thus far failed, as much as the Gestaltists, to consider the developmental aspects of perception and thinking, either in the paper discussed here or in his monograph on thinking (Bruner, Goodnow, and Austin, 1956).

Brunswik's Position

The third viewpoint to be considered is that of Brunswik, who occupies a place somewhere between the two poles just discussed, emphasizing as he does the differences between perception and thinking, rather than attempting to explain one in terms of the other. While his untimely death kept him from pursuing this question beyond the sketchy treatment of it in his last work (Brunswik, 1956), his ideas still may contribute significantly to a workable distinction between perception and thinking—a point which we shall have occasion to acknowledge in the last portion of this paper.

Brunswik starts out by drawing a comparison—based on an actual empirical study—between the achievements of perceptual size judgments in a constancy situation and those of arithmetic reasoning where the equivalent task is presented in symbolic form. The perceptual task yielded the typical clustering of settings within a fairly narrow range of the point of objective equality; in contrast, a majority of the answers given to the arithmetic reasoning task coincided exactly with the correct value, but several subsidiary clusters of answers were found which were quite discretely separated from this mode and which corresponded to false solutions of the problem.

Generalizing from this example—the significance of which is obviously purely demonstrational—Brunswik contrasts the machinelike precision of the reasoning processes with the more approximate achievements of perception:

> The entire pattern of the reasoning solutions . . . resembles the switching of trains at a multiple junction, with each of the possible courses being well organized and of machinelike precision, yet leading to drastically different destinations . . . the combination of channelled mediation, on the one hand, with precision or else grotesquely scattered error in the results, on the other, may well be symptomatic of what appears to be the pure case of explicit intellectual fact-finding.
>
> On the other hand, . . . perception must simultaneously integrate many different avenues of approach, or cues. . . . The various rivalries and compromises that characterize the dynamics of check and balance in perception must be seen as chiefly responsible for the above noted relative infrequency of precision. On the other hand, the organic multiplicity of factors entering the process constitutes an effective safeguard against drastic error (1956, pp. 91f.).

This conception of the difference between perception and thinking, while hardly exhaustive, is a fairly intriguing as well as plausible one. It has, moreover, definite implications for the analysis of the development of reasoning, although Brunswik has not given these explicit consideration. It is pertinent, however, to note his suggestion in regard to the developmental changes in color and shape constancy which he studied in his early work; he attributed the decline in constancy found in adolescence to the intervention of cognitive mechanisms which lessened the *need* for precise veridical perceptual achievements (cf. Brunswik, 1956, p. 91).

DEVELOPMENTAL APPROACHES TO THE INTERRELATIONSHIP BETWEEN PERCEPTION AND CONCEPTION

The three contrasting positions just discussed serve to sketch out the boundaries within which one can trace the course of cognitive development from perception to thinking. As noted above, of the three positions, Brunswik's embodies the sharpest differentiation between these two functions and will be found the most useful for our purposes; in fact, we will presently see a striking similarity between Brunswik's view and Piaget's conception of this problem.

The Views of Piaget

The two Piagets. Let us turn, then, to the work of Piaget, who has given us by far the most explicit and formalized comparison between perception and thought and between their respective developmental patterns. We should note at the outset that there appear to be at least two altogether different Piagets. On the one hand, we have Piaget, the psychologist of the development of intelligence, author of a long and impressive series of books covering an array of cognitive functions (language, reasoning, judgment) and of dimensions of experience (time, number, quantity, space, and so forth). On the other hand, there is Piaget, the psychologist of perception, author or sponsor of an equally impressive and even longer series of studies on a variety of perceptual phenomena, published in the *Archives de Psychologie*.

To these two divergent areas of interest correspond two sharply differentiated modes of approach to research. The "clinical" method which Piaget has followed in his study of the development of intelligence, with its deliberate avoidance of standardized procedures and quantitative analysis, stands in marked contrast to the more traditional experimental approach which he has favored in his perception research. Furthermore, while Piaget's aim in his work on thinking is essentially a genetic one, his purpose in tracing developmental changes in perception appears to be rather different. The developmental dimension in the perception research represents primarily an additional variable, coordinate with other situational, experimentally manipulated variables through which basic perceptual processes are exhibited. In this connection it is worth pointing to Piaget's view that developmental stages exist in the realm of intellectual, but not of perceptual, development (1956b, p. 33). We will consider later the possible grounds for such a position.

In view of these various symptoms of a double personality, it is hardly surprising to find Piaget attempting to divorce thinking from perception and to minimize their mutual interrelatedness. Like East and West, "ne'er the twain shall meet"—or hardly ever. One of the very few instances where they do meet, i.e., where Piaget confronts perception and thinking in the context of the same experimental situation, provides an illuminating picture of his basic position. This is a study by Piaget and Taponier (1956), devoted in part to the investigation of a constant error arising in the comparison of the length of two parallel horizontal lines, drawn to form the top and bottom of a parallelogram (without the sides). In this situation the top line tends to be slightly overestimated; this illusion increases, however, from a zero-order effect at the age of 5 years to a maximum at about 8 years; for adults the extent of the error is intermediate. Piaget contrasts this developmental pattern with that obtained when the same judgment is made in the context of a cognitive task: The two equal lines are presented initially in direct visual superposition, so as to be perceived as equal; the top one is then displaced horizontally, the arrangement of the two lines corresponding to that of the previous problem. In this cognitive task, it is the 5-year-old children who show a pronounced bias in their judgment, which leads them to pronounce the two lines as unequal following the displacement. In other words, there is an absence of "conservation of length" in the face of configurational changes. By the age of 8, however, the equality of the lines is maintained fairly uniformly—conservation of length has been acquired. On the strength of these findings Piaget argues against a simple perceptual explanation for the young children's lack of conservation; since their error of perceptual judgment is at a minimum, their failure to maintain the equality of the two lines in the cognitive task must be due to other factors.

This example illustrates well the independence, in Piaget's thinking, between perception and conception or inference—even at the stage of "intuitive thought" where the child's responses appear to be governed by particular aspects of the stimulus field. In fact, as we shall note, Piaget has repeatedly stressed that these two functions follow very different paths and arrive at different ends during the course of development (1946c, 1957b). With Brunswik, although on somewhat different grounds, he has been impressed by the statistical, probabilistic nature of perceptual judgments, as opposed to the precise, determinate, and phenomenologically certain results achieved through conceptual inference.

The concept of "partial isomorphisms." Piaget's most recent and most systematic treatment of this question is contained in an article (Piaget and Morf, 1958a) the title of which states his position succinctly: "The partial isomorphisms between logical structures and perceptual structures." In spite of his characteristic reification of such concepts as "structures" and "schemata," Piaget is concerned here with the correspondence between the achievements or end products of perceptual as against conceptual mechanisms, the mechanisms themselves being left largely out of the picture.

In this paper Piaget and Morf discuss a number of phenomena which Werner (1957) has considered as illustrative of "analogous functions," i.e., functions serving similar ends but operating at different levels of cognitive organization. Like Werner, Piaget and Morf draw parallels between perceptual groupings and conceptual classes, between invariance in perception (the constancies) and in conception (the conservations); between the perception of stimulus relationships and the conceptual representation of relationships at the symbolic level. For these authors however, these analogies, or isomorphisms, are only partial; they emphasize, rather, the ways in which perceptual mechanisms differ from the corresponding inferential ones. They point out that perceptual phenomena generally do not meet the requirements of the fundamental operations of logic (reversibility, additivity, transitivity, inversion) except in a limited and approximate sense. For example, with respect to additivity, a line divided into a number of equal segments is actually perceived as slightly longer than its undivided counterpart (the Oppel-Kundt illusion); similarly, in the case of figure-ground reversals the perceptual inversion fails to satisfy the logical criterion of inversion insofar as the boundary line always remains part of the figure. To these examples relating to the logic of classes are added several others involving the logic of relationships. Thus, lack of additivity is illustrated in threshold phenomena, where two subthreshold differences when added together may yield a suprathreshold difference (i.e., $= + = \rightarrow \neq$ is possible in perception).

Again, a person's difficulty in judging projective size is considered a case of lack of inversion of the relationship between retinal size, distance and perceived size ($r \times d = p$): given r and d jointly, the subject may "solve" for p, but he cannot obtain r by "dividing through" by d—i.e., by abstracting size from distance.

Finally, Piaget and Morf argue that there are "pre-inferences" in perception which are partially isomorphic to the inferential mechanisms of logical reasoning. Indeed, all perceptual judgment *qua* judgment is thought to involve a decision-process partaking to a greater or lesser extent of the character of an inference from the sensory information given. The extent to which it does so depends on the level of complexity (mediation?) of the judgment, ranging from the simple, direct judgments found in psychophysical thresholds to judgments dependent on "perceptual activity" as in size constancy. Here the difference between these perceptual pre-inferences and conceptual inferences can be found not only in the certainty or univocality of the outcome of the conceptual inference, but also in the subjects' lack of awareness of the separate steps in the inferential chain in the perceptual pre-inferences.[2]

The perception-conception relationship in the development of the child. Despite the semblance of a link between perception and inference represented in Piaget's concept of "perceptual pre-inferences," the over-all impression one obtains from his treatment of partial isomorphisms, as well as from other discussions of the differences between these two functions, is of a parallelistic conception—perception and thinking represent two sharply differentiated processes which display certain structural similarities, but even more important differences. Developmentally, too, he considers perception and thinking as following two separate and independent courses, as may be seen in his comparison of the development of the "conservations" from the conceptual realm with that of the perceptual constancies (1957b).

Conservation may be exemplified by the invariance of the volume of a liquid under changes in its container, as when water is poured from a narrow glass into a shallow bowl. Piaget invokes here a gradual process of "equilibration," leading the child from an initial stage at which he focuses only on one biasing aspect of the stimulus (e.g., the height of the container) through an oscillatory stage where he shifts back and forth between this aspect and a competing one (here the width of the container), to a third stage in which the compensatory role of these two aspects begins to be suspected, and then to the final realization, with perfect certitude on the part of the child, of absolute, exact conservation, despite the perceptual changes. In the perceptual constancies, on the other hand, all aspects of the stimulus

---

[2] This specification of lack of awareness as a characteristic of pre-inferential processes in perception clearly brings to mind Helmholtz's "unconscious inference." Piaget is careful, however, to dissociate himself from those (e.g., Cassirer) who have read into this concept implications of a ratiomorphic process.

field, and notably the two stimuli to be compared, are always included in the individual's perceptual exploration of the situation, at least from a very early level of development. The only developmental change is in the extent and efficacy of this exploration or, conversely, in the potency of distorting factors present in this situation. These factors (e.g., a favored attention to the near object) bring about a relative lack of constancy in younger children, which is reduced in later childhood due to more intensive and complete perceptual exploration of the stimuli. But in the domain of perception the exact compensations achieved in the fourth stage of the development of conservation are not realized; instead, the compensations either fall short, as in most illusions, or actually lead to overcompensation, as in size constancy where overconstancy is the rule for adults.

We are now in a position to appreciate the reasons that probably motivated Piaget's denial of the existence of stages in perception, while affirming it for mental development. This distinction would be warranted, not in the sense that ontogenetic change in perception is necessarily more gradual, but rather in the sense that no meaningful structural criteria can be found in the area of quantitative perceptual judgments for distinguishing among different stages. The differences between successive perceptual achievements are necessarily only quantitative, whereas structural differences of a qualitative type, as in the above-mentioned sequence of stages, can be specified for conceptual development.

Some Critical Comments on Piaget's Views

The foregoing presentation is a highly condensed distillation of Piaget's ideas in which many and frequently subtle lines of reasoning—not to mention a number of obscure points—have been omitted. It would therefore be somewhat inappropriate to base an evaluation of the merits of his argument on the picture of it given here. Nevertheless there are several criticisms of Piaget which can safely be anticipated; let us consider three of these points in particular. This will lead us to a somewhat more general question regarding Piaget's approach and will pave the way to a reformulation in the final portion of this paper.

The first objection that is bound to be raised concerns the nonoperational, and at times frankly mentalistic, terms used by Piaget which may seem to leave his analysis devoid of empirical, and perhaps even of theoretical, significance. For example, the criteria which he proposes for a diagnosis of inferential and pre-inferential processes are anything but unambiguous; indeed, his whole conceptual apparatus of schemata, operations, centrations, and so forth appears to lack direct empirical reference. Admittedly, Piaget does little to dispel this impression; concrete illustrations or applications are at best sporadic, and rigorous, systematic efforts at tying the empirical phenomena to his constructs are generally eschewed in favor of ad-hoc and post-hoc arguments.

It is important to remember, however, that Piaget's ideas on the inter-relation between perceptual and conceptual development are not in themselves intended as a theoretical system; they serve rather to explicate, in formal terms, the different models underlying Piaget's theories of perception and intelligence, respectively. Furthermore, a few empirical studies relevant to this discussion can actually be cited (e.g., Piaget and Lambercier, 1946; Piaget and Taponier, 1956; Piaget and Morf, 1958b), and, while the first two of these are mainly demonstrational in character, Piaget and Morf's investigation of "perceptual pre-inferences" represents a step toward a more systematic empirical approach in this area through the manipulation of stimulus cues which change the nature of the task from a perceptual to a more nearly judgmental one. Unfortunately, the experimental design of this study leaves much to be desired, and the rather elaborate interpretations of the results seem unconvincing, if not unwarranted.

A second criticism might well be directed at Piaget's highly idealized conception of adult thought and, at the same time, at his insistence on the distorting and probabilistic character of the processes of immediate perception. In regard to the first point, Piaget has of course been repeatedly taken to task for his inclination to see nothing but perfect logic and rationality in adult intelligence. His reliance on the principles of abstract logic as a model for human thinking has blinded him to the question of the breadth and stability of logic as *used* by the individual. In actual fact, of course, it is little more than a truism that logical principles understood in the abstract may not be applied in particular contexts (as in the atmosphere effects in syllogistic reasoning); likewise, even in the thinking of adults we find frequent instances of failures to apply or generalize a concept or principle when it is presented in unfamiliar ways or extended to novel situations. Differential generalization in the realm of thinking, furthermore, may have all the earmarks of the generalization *gradient* familiar from sensory phenomena.

Conversely, one may argue that Piaget overstates the case for the statistical, approximative, and generally biasing aspects of perceptual achievements. For quantitative judgments, to be sure, Piaget's probabilistic model seems quite appropriate and, indeed, seductively appealing in its simplicity and generality (cf. 1955a).[3] If we deal, on the other hand, with qualitative judgments and more particularly with judgments of identity or difference among discrete categories of stimuli, we typically find something closely approaching the reliability and specificity of conceptual classifications. Paren-

---

[3] An interesting feature of this model is its ability to account for the instances of non-deforming shape perception represented by the Gestaltists' "good figures" as a special case in which the relationships among the component parts are such as to yield, on the average, zero-order errors due to complete mutual compensation among the various possible distortions arising in such stimuli.

thetically, it may be noted that for Bruner it is precisely this type of perceptual judgment which serves as his model of perception, a fact which presumably accounts for some of the ratiomorphic flavor of this model.

If Piaget, then, even more than Brunswik, overestimates the discrepancy between the respective achievements of perception and thinking, he seems also to exaggerate their functional independence. The very fact that the conceptual processes of adults can be characterized along such dimensions as concrete-abstract testifies to the continual interplay between these two functions in much of conceptual activity. Pointing in the same direction are the results from one of Piaget's own experiments (Piaget and Lambercier, 1946) involving size-at-a-distance judgments in which the correct matches could be arrived at inferentially by the intermediary of a reference stimulus. At a certain age level (in middle childhood) there is clear evidence of a "perceptual compromise," showing the mutual interaction, rather than absolute separation, between perception and thinking. We shall attempt to show below how the conceptualization of the development of the symbolic processes in general can be furthered by assigning to perception a differential role in conceptual tasks at different age levels.

Piaget's structural approach. If one examines Piaget's thinking further in order to account for his espousal of some of the views just discussed, as well as for the somewhat unsatisfactory explanatory status of the constructs of his system, one finds a ready answer in the structural approach which he has consistently favored in his theory of intelligence. What he seems in fact to have done is to specify the *formal* properties of the products of the thought processes at different stages of development. This has led him inescapably to a picture of successive metamorphoses in the mental development of the child. From this structural point of view, the differences between the reasoning processes of a child lacking "reversibility" and "conservation" and an adult whose thinking does conform to these principles will in fact appear comparable to the differences between a caterpillar and a butterfly—or, to suggest a rather more pertinent analogy, between the pattern of locomotion of the 6-month infant and that of the child who has learned to walk. At the same time, this process of conceptual development will emerge as quite incommensurate with the much less dramatic and seemingly more continuous changes in the area of perception. However, it may be that the structural differences between the *products* of perceptual and conceptual processes obscure the continual interplay between the two in most, if not all, cognitive activity and therefore detract from a true appreciation of the differential involvement of perception in conceptual activity at varying developmental levels.

This interdependence between perception and thinking is the major premise for an alternative conception of intellectual development to be offered presently—a conception built around the person's dependence on various aspects of the information contained in the stimulus field. Such a conception, it is hoped, will contribute to a more truly experimental attack on the phenomena of mental development and their determinants, and thereby serve to supplement the structural analysis which Piaget has given us.

THREE DIMENSIONS OF THE TRANSITION FROM PERCEPTION TO CONCEPTION

If we ask ourselves how one might operationally distinguish between a purely perceptual and a purely inferential task, one criterion for inference would be the opportunity for the subject to supplement or replace the sensory data with information or knowledge not contained in the immediate stimulus field. As a matter of fact, this criterion differentiates the two portions of the study by Piaget and Taponier (1956) referred to earlier in which perception was contrasted to conception within the same stimulus context. The only difference between the two tasks was that in the conservation task the subjects were in effect informed beforehand of the equality of the two lines; this knowledge could take precedence over the lines themselves, and provide a basis for the subsequent judgment under altered stimulus conditions.

It seems possible, however, to formulate this criterion in quantitative, rather than all-or-none terms; that is, the relative amount of information which the subject needs from the stimulus field in order to make the judgment may vary over a wide range. The precise sense in which this quantitative criterion permits us to place perception and conception at opposite ends of a single dimension will be more fully explained below. For the moment, let us simply grant the possibility of doing so and propose this dimension, along with two others that are closely related, as a skeleton for the construction of an experimentally useful conceptual framework within which the cognitive development of the child may be traced.

The three dimensions along which perception and conception can be related may be specified as follows:

1. *Redundancy:* As one proceeds from perception to conception, the amount of redundant information required decreases.

2. *Selectivity:* As one proceeds from perception to conception, the amount of irrelevant information that can be tolerated without affecting the response increases.

3. *Contiguity:* As one proceeds from perception to conception, the spatial and temporal separation over which the total information contained in the stimulus field can be integrated increases.

It should be noted that these dimensions are stated in such a way as to be applicable either to intertask differences or to intersubject differences. Let us examine these three dimensions in some detail from the double standpoint of their relevance to the differentiation of perceptual from conceptual tasks on the one hand and to the analysis of changes during the course of development from a perceptual level of functioning to a conceptual level on the other hand—bearing in mind that these two terms are to be regarded as the poles of a continuum.

The Dimension of Redundancy

The dependence of perceptual functions on a high degree of redundancy in the stimulus input is rather easily demonstrated. Redundancy is basic to the differentiation of figure from ground; similarly it is a requisite for shape perception, the perception of speech, and to some extent for perceptual constancy (as shown in the multiplicity of overlapping cues involved in size constancy). In contrast, at the conceptual end we find redundancy reduced to an absolute minimum—typically zero—in the symbolic representation of mathematical or logical relationships. Whether the average adult is capable of operating consistently at this rarefied level is another question; the difficulty which most people experience in dealing with such nonredundant material, and the fact that a considerable amount of redundancy is built into our language, suggests that there are definite limitations in this respect. This conclusion is supported by work on concept formation, such as that of Bruner, Goodnow, and Austin (1956).

A developmental trend in the direction of decreasing reliance on redundant stimulation can be found in a variety of contexts. First of all, within the area of perception as such, the writer found considerable relevant evidence in a recent survey of the literature on perceptual development (Wohlwill, 1960). The clearest example of this point comes from studies on the identification of geometric or familiar-object stimuli on the basis of partial cues (e.g., Gollin, 1956), where the degree of completion of the figure necessary for its identification gradually decreases during the course of development. It seems justifiable, in fact, to regard such a task as becoming increasingly inferential as the amount of information which the subject has to "fill in" increases.[4] Indeed, this appears to be in part the import of Piaget and Morf's study of "perceptual pre-inference," in which the importance of continuity of lines serving as cues in a perceptual judgment was found to decrease with age.

Looking at redundancy in temporal sequences of events, furthermore, one might conceptualize the formation of Harlow's learning sets in terms of the reduction of redundant information to a minimum; it is of interest, therefore, that the rapidity of formation of such learning sets is strongly correlated with mental age (cf. Stevenson and Swartz, 1958).

---

[4] The view proposed here offers a resolution to a rather ticklish question which confronted Attneave (1954) in his attempt to analyze form perception in informational terms. Should a task in which the subject has to predict the "state" of a visual field at a point, on the basis of information obtained at preceding points of a contour, be considered a perceptual or a conceptual one?

This conception is relevant, incidentally, to Bruner's (1957) view of perception as an "act of categorization"; as we noted earlier, he has postulated that the amount of redundant information required for veridical identification is inversely proportional to the availability or accessibility of the particular category in the individual's repertoire of perceptual categories. While the intervention of a specific perceptual category cannot be equated to the operation of general symbolic processes, the fact that the action of both can in some sense compensate for lack of redundancy in the stimulus suggests that Bruner, too, is dealing essentially with a dimension running from immediate perception to conceptually mediated judgment.

The Dimension of Selectivity

The ubiquitous interaction between sensory dimensions in virtually every area of perception (psychophysical judgments and illusions, for example) bears ample testimony to the organism's very limited ability to dissociate relevant from irrelevant information at the perceptual level. At the level of thinking, on the other hand, this dissociation represents a *sine qua non* of conceptual functions; the formation of conceptual classes clearly requires the systematic, selective abstraction of relevant (i.e., criterial) from irrelevant information. The same is true in the realm of logical inference, deductive reasoning, mathematical problem solving, and other such manifestations of symbolically mediated behavior.

It is thus noteworthy that one of the major developmental changes that seems to take place in the development of abstract concepts is precisely the differentiation of relevant from irrelevant, but more readily discriminable, attributes. This development is shown in various studies of concept formation (e.g., Vurpillot, 1960); it may also lie at the heart of a problem which Piaget has studied intensively—the development of conservation. Here one aspect of the stimulus, such as number, weight, volume, or quantity, has to be conceived as invariant, in the face of highly visible changes in some other irrelevant attribute with which it is typically correlated. Similar phenomena are involved in the development of the concepts of time, velocity, and movement, as studied by Piaget.

The Dimension of Contiguity

The third dimension is perhaps the most obvious one. Indeed, the major role which spatial and temporal contiguity plays in perception hardly needs detailed discussion. Spatially, we find it illustrated in the Gestalt law of proximity, as well as in the variation of illusions, figural aftereffects, and other perceptual phenomena as a function of the distance between the central stimulus and contextual portions of a field; similarly, figural aftereffects, among other phenomena, demonstrate the relatively limited temporal span over which two stimulus events separated in time interact.

It is characteristic of conceptual processes, on the other hand, that they enable the individual to deal with stimulus information whose components are widely separated in space or time. To give just one example, conceptual groupings can be achieved where the objects to be grouped are not in close spatial relationship and may not even be exposed simultaneously. Here again absolute independence of contiguity represents an ideal which is scarcely, if ever, realized even by adults. Thus, Davidon (1952) has shown that the opportunity for the subject to manipulate the stimulus materials in an object-classification task so as to provide spatial contiguity for the groupings made improves performance significantly; yet the results are perhaps more remarkable for the small size of the effect which manipulation produced.

Davidon's problem would be an ideal one in which to explore developmental changes; it would be hypothesized that with increasing age this factor of spatial proximity in conceptual grouping would steadily decrease in importance. While there is no evidence on this specific point, a variety of related findings can be mentioned. In the realm of perception, first of all, the writer's review of the literature on perceptual development (Wohlwill, 1960) uncovered various examples of developmental changes in the direction of an increasing ability or tendency to relate objects in the stimulus field, independently of their spatial or temporal contiguity. Such a trend appeared, for instance, in studies of size constancy, which for young children deteriorates much more rapidly with increasing distance between the stimuli than for adults, and in the perception of causality, which for children, but not for adults, requires a perceived contact between the objects in order for them to appear as causally related. With increasing age, furthermore, relatively remote visual frameworks exert an increasing influence on perception in diverse situations.[5]

With respect to tasks of reasoning or concept formation, we unfortunately have much less direct evidence of developmental changes indicating a decrease in the role of this factor of contiguity, although what we know of the thinking and problem solving behavior of children is consistent with the assumption of such an age trend. One experimental study that might be mentioned in this connection is that by Kendler and Kendler (1956), who found that the ability of 3- to 4-year-old children to respond inferentially in a Maier-type reasoning task was closely dependent on the temporal sequence in which the steps in the inferential chain were presented. Thus, if children were shown that A leads to B, X leads to Y and B leads to G (the main goal object), and if they were then presented with a choice of A or X, the frequency of inferential responses (choice of A) was considerably higher

---

[5] Certain perceptual phenomena appear, however, to be exceptions to this developmental trend, notably the role played by the factor of proximity in grouping and the role of spatial and temporal separation between stimuli in apparent movement. Thus, there appear to be definite limitations to the applicability of the principles outlined here.

if the *B-G* experience had immediately followed or preceded the *A-B* experience, than it was where the *X-Y* experience intervened between these two. Inferential choices likewise depended on the *direction* of the temporal sequence, being significantly more frequent when *B-G* followed *A-B* than when it preceded it—pointing to a rather obvious fact—that the temporal order between two events is of importance quite independently of the interval separating them. It would be of interest to determine whether this ordinal factor also decreases in importance with age.

The Resultant of the Three Dimensions: Specificity

Taken together, these three dimensions yield responses of varying specificity, ranging from those of perceptual judgment, in which accuracy is always relative and error is the rule, to the absolute precision and accuracy of the products of conceptual processes. To this extent they do not represent a departure from Brunswik's and Piaget's conceptions of the problem but rather an extension in the direction of continuity of process from perception to conception.

To illustrate the relevance of our dimensions to this specificity criterion, let us compare the assessment of the relative size of two objects through direct perceptual judgment with that achieved by the conceptual process of measurement, i.e., by the intermediary of a ruler. In the former case, the results will be affected by spatial or temporal separation, by variation in irrelevant aspects, and by lack of redundancy, i.e., one-dimensional stimuli yield larger thresholds than two- or three-dimensional ones (Werner, 1957, p. 118)—all of these factors interfering with accuracy and precision of judgment. None of these aspects, on the other hand, influences the results obtained through measurement, the precision of which is limited only by the accuracy of the instrument and the observer's visual acuity in reading it. A very similar kind of comparison could have been made between the assessment of quantity by estimation and by counting. It is thus of no little significance that, in the case of length and in the case of number, perceptual discrimination and conceptual measurement appear to develop in close interdependence (Braine, 1959; Long and Welch, 1941).

CONCLUSIONS

Granting for the moment the validity of the dimensions suggested earlier for the representation of important components of developmental change in cognitive functioning,[6] the question of their conceptual fruitfulness arises. Insofar as they do appear to encompass a wide array of phenomena, their status presumably transcends the level of pure description. It is suggested, moreover, that they provide the basis for the construction of a

---

[6] For an empirical demonstration of the heuristic value of these dimensions in the study of abstraction see the Appendix to this paper.

higher-order theoretical framework within which a more systematic and a more generalized approach to problems in this area may be realized.

The major argument in support of this seemingly pious hope is the built-in potential of these dimensions for leading to a set of constructs which can be securely anchored on the stimulus and response sides and which will also facilitate the integration of developmental changes with principles derived from the experimental study of perception and thinking. To give just one example, the conception should prove of heuristic value in the analysis of the perceptual constancies in terms of the role of stimulus variables such as amount of surplus cues, or redundant information, in interaction with organismic variables such as age.

Admittedly, the actual mechanisms mediating the effects of our dimensions of cognitive activity remain quite obscure as yet. Possibly, neurophysiological or cybernetic models of cognitive activity related to the internal activity of the organism in transforming the stimulus input so as to allow for varying degrees of stimulus determination of behavior may provide us with fruitful leads in our quest for such mechanisms. Thus, one might suggest the operation of scanning mechanisms as characteristic of perception, as against digital mechanisms intervening in reasoning. The process of developmental change could then be conceptualized in terms of varying forms of interaction between these two.

It would undoubtedly be sheer pretentiousness to elaborate further upon these highly speculative questions at this point, but one may point to certain empirical hypotheses that appear to be implicit in the postulated dimensions of developmental change themselves. For instance, in the previous discussion of selectivity, it was suggested that the problem of the development of conservation might be handled in terms of the dissociation of a particular concept (e.g., number) from irrelevant, though typically correlated and highly visible, perceptual cues (e.g., length over which a row of elements extends). If this dissociation does in fact represent a factor relevant to the psychological process involved in the development of conservation (as opposed to a mere description of the results of this process), it seems to follow that systematically arranged experiences aimed at untying these two variables for the child should at least facilitate the appearance of conservation.[7]

_____

[7] With respect to the development of number conservation, the writer is currently investigating the role of such experience experimentally, alongside other experiential effects pertinent to the alternative theoretical formulations of Piaget (involving the activation of relevant mental operations, e.g., those of addition and subtraction) and of learning theory (focusing on the role of reinforcement, through direct confrontation with the *fact* of number invariance).

A very similar research project, dealing with experiential effects in the realm of the conservation of weight (under changes in shape) is being conducted in Norway by Smedslund (1959). As regards the effects of dissociating irrelevant perceptual cues, the preliminary report of this author indicates mainly negative results thus far.

This brings us, lastly, to the more general question of the bearing of the formulation outlined in this paper on Piaget's work in this area. At first sight, it may seem that the two are at variance in several respects, notably in our postulation of essentially continuous dimensions, as opposed to Piaget's discontinuous stages of development, and in the emphasis here on modes of utilizing stimulus information as against Piaget's system of internal structures, operations, and mental actions. Much of this apparent contradiction disappears, however, if one recognizes that Piaget's concern is with changes in the structural characteristics of the products of intellectual activity, whereas the interest here is in the specification of the dimensions and processes of developmental change.

The distinction between these two essentially complementary approaches may be clarified by reference to their respective handling of the role of external environmental factors. Piaget, as is well known, tends to ignore the effects of antecedent conditions and environmental variables in development, relegating them to a place definitely subsidiary in importance to the unfolding of internal structures. This does not mean that he advocates a strict nativist position, for he has frequently emphasized the continual interaction between external and internal forces. Nevertheless, his biological orientation and interest in structure leads him to take external factors for granted and to regard the form which this interaction takes as largely predetermined from the start. The only problem, then, is that of specifying the successive stages through which the organism passes; little leeway is left for differential manifestations of external conditions. It is not surprising therefore that his treatment of learning effects in the development of logical processes (1959a) is limited almost exclusively to the activation of previously formed structures bearing a logical relationship to the particular structure under investigation. In comparison, the approach advocated here probably is less adequate to the task of analyzing the structural complexities of intellectual activity and its development; in compensation, however, it allows for a more thorough exploration of functional relationships between antecedent condition and developmental change and should contribute thereby to a more explicit understanding of the processes at work in the interaction between environmental and organismic forces.

APPENDIX

An Illustrative Experiment

By way of introducing some substance into the argument developed in this paper, let us consider an experiment specifically designed to show the applicability and usefulness of the first two of the dimensions discussed, namely, redundancy and selectivity. Since the purpose of this study is primarily illustrative, it should not be surprising if the results appear to some extent trivial.

The task was a very simple one—to pick out the odd one from among three stimuli. The stimuli were simple geometric figrues, varying along one or more of the following four attributes: shape (square, triangle, pentagon); color (red, green, blue); shading (outline, dotted, solid), and size (large, medium, small). Five different sheets, each containing eight such triplets of figures, were constructed, according to the design outlined in Table 1 (the terminology in this table is taken from Bruner *et al.*, 1956). Samples of each type of stimulus set are shown in Figure 1 and the appropriate colors are indicated under each stimulus.

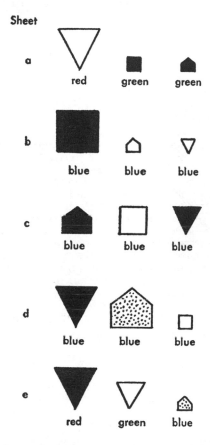

FIGURE 1—Sample stimulus sets used to represent different amounts of redundant and irrelevant information.

"Criterial" attributes in this study were those on which two of the three figures were alike, the third being the odd one. Where more than one attribute was criterial, they were perfectly correlated; thus, sheets *a* to *c* may be said to vary on the dimension of redundancy. Sheets *c* to *e,* on the the other hand, vary with respect to the amount of noise or irrelevant information contained, i.e., the number of attributes on which all three figures of a triplet differed. It will be noted

TABLE 1

SCHEMA FOR STUDY ON THE ROLE OF IRRELEVANT AND
REDUNDANT INFORMATION

Sheet	Number of Attributes that are:		
	Criterial	Quiet	Noisy
a	3	0	1
b	2	1	1
c	1	2	1
d	1	1	2
e	1	0	3

that redundancy was varied while keeping irrelevant information constant, and vice versa, this being accomplished by concomitant variation of number of "quiet" attributes—attributes on which all three figures of a triplet were identical. Each attribute was noisy twice on sheets *a* to *c* and criterial twice on sheets *c* to *e*, thus accounting for eight sets of triplets per sheet.

The hypothesis was that, as relevant information decreased or irrelevant information increased, there would be a gradual shift from a perceptual mode to a conceptual mode of functioning, reflected in three different ways. In children errors would increase, and younger subjects would show a larger effect in this respect than older subjects; for adults, time taken to complete each sheet would be directly related to degree of irrelevant or redundant information.

Table 2 presents the means for preliminary results obtained from 15 subjects from a third grade, 15 subjects from a fifth grade, and 15 college students.

TABLE 2

MEAN NUMBER OF ERRORS AND MEAN TIME (FOR ADULTS) PER SHEET

Sheet	MEAN NUMBER OF ERRORS			MEAN TIME
	3rd Grade	5th Grade	Adults	(Adults)
a	.6	.5	.1	17.0 sec.
b	.8	.3	.4	19.6
c	1.2	1.2	.4	19.5
d	3.4	3.0	1.2	32.2
e	3.8	3.9	1.9	31.0

Analysis of variance of the error scores discloses highly significant effects of age (third and fifth grades vs. adults), both as a main variable, and in interaction with the stimulus variable. In view of this interaction, which is in accordance with the second hypothesis, no test of the main effect of the stimulus variable was carried out, though the over-all trend is clearly as predicted. For the adults' time scores the effect of stimuli was likewise highly significant, although here, as in the case of the error scores as well, the major difference is between sheets *a, b,* and *c* on the one hand, as against *d* and *e* on the other.

This sharp rise in time and errors between sheets c and d suggests that the function relating the amount of *irrelevant* information to performance in this type of task differs considerably from that applying to amount of *redundant* information. This difference probably reflects the differences in the processes involved; whereas changes in the amount of redundancy affect primarily the perceptual differentiation of the odd from the even stimuli, changes in the amount of irrelevant information determine the extent to which the subject must try out successive hypotheses with regard to the criterial dimension.

As for the age variable, it is clearly represented in this study in only a very perfunctory fashion. It might be noted, incidentally, that for a small group of younger children (second graders), there was a strong indication that the amount of redundant information played a more important role than for the older subjects.[8]

6

PIAGET, BEHAVIOR THEORY, AND INTELLIGENCE

Harold W. Stevenson
University of Minnesota

Introduction

At first glance, the developmental psychologies of Jean Piaget and current American behavior theory appear to differ so much that an attempt to compare them would seem a strained and unproductive venture. It is difficult to find two points of view in psychology which have utilized more dissimilar methods, produced more disparate types of data, and developed more divergent conceptual systems. The workers in Geneva have concentrated primarily upon the accumulation of rich naturalistic observations concerning the cognitive life of children. Behavior theorists have been more concerned with the careful analysis of the development of simple nonverbal responses such as bar-pressing by children or running a straight alley by animals. The highly descriptive and wide-ranging theoretical formulations of Piaget form a striking contrast to the behavior theorists' attempts to present their systems in operationally well-defined and quantitative terms.

It is fair to say that most behavior theorists have no understanding of what Piaget has accomplished. Similarly, Piaget appears to have little knowledge of developments in American behavior theory since 1930. Although the two systems have developed simultaneously, behavior theorists have been totally uninfluenced by Piaget's thinking and Piaget has failed to be influenced by the methodological and conceptual developments of behavior theory. This lack of cross-stimulation is not difficult to understand when discussion centers on such topics as the development of causal thinking or the acquisition of mathematical concepts. Piaget and the workers at Geneva have been greatly interested in such topics and behavior theorists have generally avoided them. When the discussion concerns intellectual development during the first years of life, however, the lack of communication is surprising. Here, where relatively simple behavior is under consideration, both Piaget and the behavior theorists sometimes find themselves in the position of attempting to account for the development of the same forms of behavior.

Both theoretical approaches are faced with a number of similar problems. How is a stimulus to be defined? What is the relationship between stimulation and the modification of response? What changes occur in the stimulus after it has been responded to? What is the role of drive or need in the modification of behavior? To what degree is behavior modified without reinforcement? As we shall see, the two views have been forced to make many similar postulates in accounting for the development of simple forms of response.

Thus, although there may be reason for pessimism in attempting to relate the two approaches when more complex psychological processes are under consideration, Piaget's discussion of early cognitive development in *The Psychology of Intelligence* (1946c) and in *The Origins of Intelligence in Children* (1936) may be amenable to some type of integration with what behavior theorists have to say about learning. This paper discusses points of similarity and of difference between the two approaches and offers an account of the development of intelligence within the context of behavior theory.

PIAGET AND BEHAVIOR THEORY

Before attempting an integration of these two theoretical approaches to early development, it will be useful for us first to explore the major points of similarity and difference between the two positions.

Similarities between Piaget and Behavior Theorists

1. *Both are historical theories.* Behavior is seen by both as being progressively modified by experience. Piaget gives greater emphasis than the behavior theorists to the interaction between maturation and learning in his discussion of the development of behavior, but both reject the possibility of sudden changes in behavior independent of relevant prior experience.

2. *Both are reinforcement theories.* Piaget has criticized simple associationistic interpretations of classical conditioning in the following manner:

> When a response is associated with a perception, there is more in this connection than a passive association (i.e. becoming stamped in as a result of repetition alone); meanings also enter into it, since association occurs only in the presence of a need and its satisfaction. Everyone knows in practice, although we too often forget it in theory, that a conditioned reflex is stabilized only as long as it is confirmed or reinforced; a signal associated with food does not give rise to an enduring reaction if real food is not periodically presented together with the signal (1946c [1959, p. 91]).

Hull, on the basis of a similar argument, introduced into his system the notion that drive reduction constitutes a reinforcing state of affairs and that such drive reduction is necessary for learning to occur. Hull also postulated two other functions for drive: (a) an energizing function which activates the organism and (b) a behavior-directing function which occurs through the conditioning of overt responses to drive stimuli. Similarly,

Piaget assumes that behavior occurs as a consequence of a disturbance of the organism's state of equilibrium and that need directs response. Since both assume that responses gain strength through their occurrence and their relation to need, both Piaget and Hull may be classified as "reinforcement" or "confirmation" theorists.

3. *Both postulate some similar processes.* Several of Piaget's basic concepts (which will be discussed later in greater detail) do not differ greatly from concepts developed in reinforcement theory. The concepts of generalizing assimilation and recognitory assimilation have clear counterparts in the concepts of stimulus generalization and conditioned discrimination. A reinforced stimulus-response unit corresponds roughly to Piaget's concept of schema. Other apparent communalities in the two theories can be detected. Reproductive assimilation may be accounted for in reinforcement theory by assuming that the repetition of a response is due to the strengthening of a response through reinforcement, rather than to an innate need for repetition. Piaget's primary circular reaction can be accounted for quite simply through the behavior theorists' concept of secondary reinforcement. For example, sitmuli produced by sucking initially occur in the presence of primary drive reduction and thus acquire secondary reinforcing value. Hence, when the finger is sucked, this response gains strength through the reinforcing effect of stimulation of the mouth.

Differences between Piaget and Behavior Theorists

1. *The active-reactive problem.* Perhaps the major difference between the behavior theorists and Piaget is in the emphasis they place upon the individual's role in intelligent response. To Piaget, intelligence "does not consist—as accepted by reflexology entirely impregnated with empirical associationism—in an ensemble of responses mechanically determined by external stimuli and in a correlative ensemble of conditions connecting the new stimuli with old responses. On the contrary, it constitutes real activity, based upon an appropriate structure and assimilating to the latter a growing number of external objects" (1936 [1952, p. 409]). One of his objections to associationism, therefore, is that it views the world as independent of the subject and does not consider the active role that the subject plays in organizing his experience. Although the criticism made by Piaget of associationism is rather extreme and would not necessarily characterize behavior theory, behavior theory does in fact place a greater emphasis on the reactive aspects of the person's behavior than upon active seeking and directing of responses.

2. *The mechanical-dynamic problem.* Piaget rejects the principles employed by associationism because he considers them to be too mechanical and to place too much emphasis on the development of habits, which he considers random, passive, and nonreversible aspects of behavior. "Habit," writes Piaget, "has always seemed to some people to be the antithesis of intelligence. Where the second is active invention, the first remains passive repe-

tition; where the second is awareness of the problem and an attempt at comprehension, the first remains tainted with lack of awareness and inertia, etc." (1936, [1952, p. 409]). The core concept in most behavior theories is, of course, that of habit. Major interest has centered on developing a systematic framework to account for the modification of behavior without utilizing such concepts as "awareness," "invention," and "comprehension." The reluctance of behavior theorists to use such concepts or to view human behavior in dynamic terms contrasts greatly with Piaget's preference for these concepts and this view.

Although there are many specific differences between the theories, these two general points are those on which Piaget and behavior theorists differ most widely. The question of greatest interest to child psychologists, of course, is not whether differences can be found in the two theoretical approaches, but how well each can provide a satisfactory account for the emergence of behavior in the young human infant.

A SUMMARY OF PIAGET'S VIEWS

A brief summary of Piaget's views regarding the development of intelligence during the child's first five years is of value in providing the basis for further discussion. For Piaget, the function of behavior is to maintain a state of equilibrium between the individual and the environment. The occurrence of disequilibrium produces a state of need, and the person then attempts to reduce need and to reestablish a state of equilibrium. Both biological and psychological development show common "functionally invariant" processes which operate in morphological as well as in cognitive development. The most important of these processes are assimilation and accommodation. Assimilation involves the action of the person on objects and the changes produced in him as a consequence of his action; accommodation involves the action of the environment on the person. In the first case, the child assimilates objects of the environment into his psychic life; in the second, the child accommodates his behavior to the environment. Behavior is considered to be an historic process in which both perception and response are modified as a function of experience.

The primary difference between Piaget's ideas concerning adaptation and other views of adaptation or homeostasis is the introduction by Piaget of the concepts of accommodation and assimilation. Differentiation between these two processes during early phases of behavior is, practically speaking, impossible, and only in later development do the two processes become distinct. Accommodation seems to result from environmental changes or obstacles which force response from the person or guide his response. Assimilation, on the other hand, occurs whenever the individual makes a response. The action patterns become attached to objects and the objects become assimilated into these action patterns.

Intelligence is defined by Piaget as "the direction in which development evolves" from simple reflexes to novel responses. Intelligence is regarded as an organizing activity which extends biological organization and insures that the organism will be capable of more satisfactory adaptation. The development of intellectual processes makes it possible for equilibrium to continue as the environment becomes increasingly complex. Piaget has summarized his point of view in the following statement:

> Organic adaptation in fact only insures an immediate and consequently limited equilibrium between the individual and the present environment. Elementary cognitive functions, such as perception, habit and memory, extend it in the direction of present space (perceptual contact with distant objects) and of short-range reconstructions and anticipations. Only intelligence, capable of all its detours and reversals by action and by thought, tends towards an all-embracing equilibrium by aiming at the assimilation of the whole of reality and the accommodation to it of action, which it thereby frees from its dependence on the initial *hic* and *nunc* (1946c [1959, p. 9]).

Piaget's definition of intelligence is rather nebulous, but it gains in meaning from an examination of the stages through which the child passes in changing from a reflexive to a reflective organism. These stages produce changes whereby the response, which is initially reflexive and is made only to "immediate" objects, finally becomes inventive and goal-oriented and is made to "represented" objects. There are six stages through which the child passes. These encompass reflex behavior, the development of habits and associations, sensory-motor intelligence, and finally, cognition.

During the reflexive stage behavior is *elicited* by certain types of stimuli. Even at this stage, however, the organism is not passive, and, although it is difficult to separate the two functions at this age, both assimilation and accommodation occur. For example, the infant makes a sucking response and the schema (organized action) of sucking quickly develops. New objects are associated with the schema (generalizing assimilation); it is differentiated according to the object present (recognitory assimilation); and it tends to be repeated spontaneously for the sake of activity (reproductive assimilation). Experience thus modifies both perception and response, and current behavior can be evaluated only in light of its historical development. All aspects of assimilation—including the tendency for behavior to be repeated, for it to generalize to new objects, and for it to be different for different objects—are found in the simplest responses as well as in later, more complex types of behavior.

The second stage of development is marked by the first acquired adaptations (circular reactions). In this stage there is exercise of previous schemata, but the form of the exercise is determined by interaction with the environment. By chance, the infant performs an action which produces an effect that is interesting and satisfying, and the action is repeated in an endeavor to maintain the satisfying state of affairs. These actions are initially fortuitous, and they center upon the infant's own body rather than upon external objects. The repetitive nature of the responses leads Piaget to describe them as circular reactions; and, since they are the most primitive types of repetitive responses the infant performs, they are termed "primary circular reactions." Thumbsucking is a typical example of the types of reactions found in such "acquired adaptations." The pleasurable stimulation resulting from sucking leads the infant to attempt to repeat or to maintain this source of satsfaction.

Secondary circular reactions evolve in the third stage. Here, the infant by chance produced an effect in the environment and then strives to reproduce or maintain the effect. The infant strikes a rattle and it moves; he strikes at the rattle again and again. The secondary circular reaction involves some differentiation of means and ends; but this differentiation is not completely comprehended, and the infant will often attempt to utilize means which are ineffective in a given situation. This stage forms a transition between primary circular reactions and actions which are directed towards new combinations of schemata and actual inventions. The acquired associations occurring in secondary circular reactions constitute relations between things themselves—"objects" in the environment—and not just between different body movements.

In the fourth stage there is a clearer differentiation between the means and the ends. In approaching a problem in this stage, the infant tries means associated with other situations, but has the intention of effecting a certain type of consequence by his responses. The important aspect of development at this stage is that the infant keeps the goal in mind and tries different means of surmounting the obstacles. There is a coordination of previously acquired schemata with anticipation of the consequences of an act. For example, the infant appears to anticipate that he will be left alone, for he begins to cry when his parent gets up. This stage sees greater mobility and extension of the schemata in that response tendencies may be readily applied to a vast variety of objects. The infant begins to differentiate the environment from himself during this stage and begins the transition from the period when the environment is not differentiated from the self to the period when the two are clearly separated for the child (egocentrism to objectivity).

"Tertiary circular reactions" appear during the fifth stage. Whereas in the secondary circular reaction the child repeated the pattern of response to maintain a satisfying state of affairs, the child now varies the pattern of response to ascertain the different results which might be produced. There is, therefore, "empirical groping," in which the child discovers from experience the types of variations he can produce in the object by his responses. In other words, the characteristics of objects are now elaborated by the child. Earlier, his behavior changed only when accommodation to the environment was required; now the child actively searches for and creates situations in the environment to which he can react. The responses that the child makes

are directed by the goal and are not random, but they are not yet characterized by a sudden insightful process.

The sixth stage is marked by the invention of new means through
"mental combination" of schemata. It is no longer necessary for the child
to carry out acts in order to respond appropriately. There are now "interiorized actions" which make it possible for invention of new means to occur
and for symbolic functions to operate. Invention is contrasted with discovery; in invention the child produces a new type of response through mental
combination, while in discovery the child merely chances upon new procedures by active experimentation. There is "reasoned prevision" in that the
object does not need to be present for the child to make the response; thus,
representation as well as invention characterize this stage. Mental representation involves symbols; a word or image represents the object, and it has
meaning to the extent that the subject can apply prior assimilation patterns
to the object. As invention is contrasted with discovery, representation is
contrasted with groping.

With these developments, the origins of intelligence are established. The
child now has passed through the phase of sensory-motor intelligence, and
the development of mature, reflective intelligence can begin. With the further
acquisition of language and the assimilation of prior modes of response to
language, the child's cognitive development continues. The changes that
occur as the child moves from sensory-motor to reflective intelligence are
primarily changes in speed of responding, awareness of results, and increasing ability to operate at greater and more remote spatial and temporal distances. Piaget summarizes his view of the development of intelligence during
the first five years in the following words.

> Let us now recall how things occur in the course of our six stages from the
> point of view of this progressive accommodation with the external environ-
> ment. During the first stage there exists, of course, no direct contact with
> experience, since activity is simply reflex. Accommodation to things is there-
> fore confused with reflex use. During the second stage, new associations are
> formed and so the pressure of experience begins. But these associations are
> limited, at the beginning, to interconnecting two or more movements of the
> body or else a reaction of the subject to an external signal. That is certainly
> an acquisition due to experience. But this "experience" does not yet put the
> mind in the presence of "things" themselves; it places it exactly half-way
> between the external environment and the body itself. Hence accommoda-
> tion remains undissociated from the activity of repetition, the latter bearing
> simply on the results acquired fortuitously instead of being due to the devel-
> opment of reflex activity. In the third stage, the acquired associations consti-
> tute relations between different body movements. But these relations still
> remain dependent on the action, that is to say, the subject still does not ex-
> periment; his accommodation to things remains a simple attempt at repeti-
> tion, the results reproduced just being more complex than at the preceding
> stage. In the fourth stage, experience comes still closer to the "object," the
> coordinations between the schemata permitting the child to establish real
> relations between things (in contrast to practical, purely phenomenalistic

relationships). But it is only in the fifth stage that accommodation is definitely liberated and gives rise to true experience which still develops in the course of the sixth stage (1936 [1952, pp. 364-365]).

During the fifth stage, the utilization of experience spreads still more, since this period is characterized by the "tertiary circular reaction" or "experiment in order to see," and the coordination of schemata extends henceforth into "discoveries of new means through active experimentation."

Lastly, the sixth stage adds one more behavior pattern to the preceding ones: the invention of new means through deduction or mental combination. As with regard to the fourth stage, one can ask oneself if experience is not thereafter held in check by the work of the mind and if new connections, of *a priori* origin will not henceforth double the experimental relationships (1936 [1952, p. 361]).

A REINFORCEMENT VIEW OF INTELLECTIVE DEVELOPMENT

Although behavior theorists have not attempted to discuss the specific types of behavior with which Piaget is concerned, it would be of value to see whether a systematic use of concepts from behavior theory might not result in an adequate account of early intellective development. By using three assumptions within the context of general reinforcement theory, such an account will be attempted here. The three assumptions are as follows:

1. *For normal children, increased age is accompanied by the development of an increasing need for sensory stimulation.* This need is assumed to produce a primary drive of "stimulus hunger" which can be reduced by changes in the organism's sensory input. Other primary drives are assumed to restrict the opportunity for expression of stimulus hunger by increasing the organism's total stimulation to such a degree that further sensory stimulation is no longer reinforcing. Thus, we are concerned only with behavior which occurs when other drives have low strength. It is assumed that all but the most primitive forms of cognitive behavior are related to this need for sensory stimulation, rather than to needs of a more primary nature, such as hunger, thirst, and so forth.

2. *Repeated response to a reinforcing stimulus results in the reduction of the effectiveness of the stimulus as a reinforcing agent.* Any stimulus to which the subject is capable of responding may function as a reinforcing stimulus and reduce "stimulus hunger." Noxious stimuli are assumed to have limited capacity for the reduction of this drive because of their tendency to produce drive states linked to avoidance. For example, when drive states based on pain and fear are operative, "stimulus hunger" is assumed to contribute less to the total drive state of the organism, for fear and pain operate as strong drive states which increase the total amount of stimulation and reduce the effectiveness of other forms of sensory stimulation.

We assume that stimuli are not unitary but consist of a number of stimulus elements. Response may occur to different samples of stimulus elements—i.e., may be directed to various aspects of the stimulus. Response to each sample reduces the effectiveness of the elements in the sample as reinforcers. Repeated response is thus required before all elements of a given stimulus are sampled; hence a number of responses to the reinforcing stimulus may be made before its reinforcing effect is exhausted. It follows, therefore, that alternative modes of initial response (resulting in new samples of reinforcing stimuli) will eventually have to be introduced if response to the stimulus situation is to be maintained after the reinforcing effects of the consequences of initial responses are exhausted.

It should be emphasized that we are concerned with a double $S-R$ relationship: a stimulus (S) leads to a response (R); the response results in a change in the subject's sensory input (S_{re}); the response (R_{re}) to (awareness of) this new form of stimulation is reinforcing to the subject. The sequence of events with which we are concerned is, therefore, $S-R-S_{re}-R_{re}$. S_{re} will continue to be a potentially reinforcing stimulus until all elements of the stimulus have been responded to in the course of the subject's performance. As long as the stimulus maintains its reinforcing effects the $S-R$ relationship increases in strength. Eventually, S_{re} is no longer reinforcing and the $S-R$ relationship ceases to increase in strength. It is obvious that S and S_{re} may or may not be from the same stimulus universe. The baby may see a rattle (S) and strike it (R), resulting in a displacement of the rattle (S_{re}) which, if perceived (R_{re}), is assumed to be reinforcing. At the same time, the baby may see a rattle (S), shake it (R), and listen (R_{re}) to the noise (S_{re})which it makes.

3. *Intellectual level is negatively correlated with the number of stimulus elements required to produce a given response by the subject.* A given response is produced in subjects of higher intelligence by a smaller number of stimulus elements than is required for response by subjects of lower intelligence for the same response. As a consequence, the number of different responses which the subject will make within a constant period of time is directly related to his intellectual level. For the purposes of the present discussion, we will assume that the performance characteristic of children at higher chronological ages represents a higher level of cognitive development than the performance characteristic of children at lower chronological ages.

As can be seen in the following paragraphs, the use of such assumptions leads to quite different means of accounting for early behavior from those used by Piaget. The reflexes which exist at birth may be considered potential $S-R$ units. There are apparently differences among organisms in the degree to which experience is necessary to activate these potential $S-R$ units; in some cases frequent reinforced repetition is necessary to strengthen the response, while in others the response appears at high strength without experience. In the case of the sucking response, strengthening comes from the effectiveness of the response in reducing hunger. If the response does not lead to reinforcement, it will be extinguished. During the first few weeks, new stimuli may be associated with the reflex through the process of classical conditioning, in which a response made in the presence of new stimuli and accompanied by reinforcement becomes associated with the new stimuli.

During the first weeks after birth, the baby's behavior is primarily under control of hunger, thirst, and fatigue. By the end of this time, however, the infant becomes capable of satisfying hunger and thirst for longer periods and is less susceptible to fatigue. The baby is awake when primary drives are satisfied, and wakefulness makes it possible for a rapid development of behavior to occur. Sensory-motor activity increases during this period, and the primary function of experience is to organize and direct this activity rather than to initiate it.

The infant's first motor responses are directed to parts of his own body rather than to external objects. Because of the reinforcing value of somatic stimulation, the responses to his own body are reinforced and gain in strength. Gradually, the infant becomes able to initiate contact with external objects. These random and fortuitous responses tend to be reinforced by changes in the stimulus situation produced by the response. The very young infant is practically devoid of experience; thus all changes in the stimulus situation produced by a response maintain their reinforcing effect for long periods (under assumptions 1 and 2). During this time, therefore, there may be far greater repetition of a response than will occur later in the child's development. As time passes, some aspects of the stimulus situation produced by a response tend to be the same as those produced earlier, and the reinforcing effect of such stimulus changes are thereby reduced. At this point, old responses are sustained only on the basis of past reinforcement and no longer gain in strength. New responses, which produce more complex stimulus changes, emerge to replace the child's older, more simple responses. Thus, the type of stimuli which are reinforcing change as the child's behavior develops; at each stage there is exhaustion of the reinforcing effects of the stimuli to which the child has already responded. Initially, sounds, displacements of objects, bright images, and so forth may be reinforcing; later the reinforcing effect of such simple stimulus changes is decreased.

Repeated response to an object is made by the young infant because a great many repetitions are required before the reinforcing effect of the changes produced by the response is depleted. Even relatively simple objects are capable of producing a large variety of stimulus changes. After the reinforcing effect is depleted, responses which produce repetitive consequences will be replaced by responses which produce variable consequences. For example, the infant may at first hit a rattle because it always makes a noise; but later the infant will continue to hit the rattle only if it changes in color or position or makes different types of noises. As the reinforcing value of the consequences of simple responses become exhausted, more complex responses emerge. With complex responses, there is a greater likelihood that variable consequences of the responses will be produced. The fact that babies initially may show perseverative behavior, while later they show variable behavior, is consistent with the notion that only variable responses eventually produce consequences which are reinforcing. The child does not "try" to produce variation in the consequences of an act; behavior simply will not develop unless variable consequences are produced.

As the infant grows older, behavior is increasingly reinforced by sensory stimulation. Examination and manipulation of objects and persons is continued by the infant until their reinforcing effects have been exhausted. The range of stimuli to which the infant responds and the complexity of the responses made increase with experience. Stimuli immediately related to the child, such as his crib and his rattle, are frequently encountered. Repeated responses to these immediate stimuli decreases the reinforcing value of these stimuli, and distal stimuli then tend to become more reinforcing. The range of the child's perceptual experience is thereby increased. More and more complex types of responses are developed, since such responses produce different types of sensory stimulation and are reinforced.

Even though particular responses are replaced by other responses whose consequences produce novel changes in the environment, the responses that were made originally will have been learned and may recur when the stimuli are presented again, depending on whether or not alternative responses have been developed which have greater strength. Thus, although the old responses may no longer produce consequences which are reinforcing, the stimuli to which they have been conditioned remain capable of eliciting them.

With the development of language, the opportunity for stimuli to elicit more and more complex types of response is possible. The word "mama," for example, will have a variety of responses conditioned to it, and the word may now substitute for the physical presence of the mother. Language allows the response to be made despite greater and greater physical and temporal separation from the object represented. Some object in the environment may elicit the verbalization, and then a variety of responses conditioned to the verbalization may be made. Gradually, the verbalization may be interiorized, so that the actual activation of the vocal apparatus is unnecessary. Thus, operation of the organism independent of objects is assumed to be dependent upon the development of language.

As the population of S–R units increases, it is possible for the child to perform novel responses in a new situation. A novel response is assumed to consist of a combination of old responses; it is novel in its organization and not in its components. Novel responses may occur when a variety of responses has been conditioned to a single stimulus, enabling the stimulus to elicit a series of responses. Sudden production of a novel, correct response is due to a high degree of transfer; typically, modification of the novel response will occur before it is appropriate in producing the change in the situation demanded by the task facing the child.

The development of concepts in children occurs only after they have developed a large number of responses to a large number of stimuli. A concept is assumed to emerge when certain types of stimuli contain enough common elements that a common response is elicited by each stimulus or when each stimulus has conditioned to it a common mediating response. The mediating response may be a series of movements or a verbalization. Some types of stimuli contain communalities of stimulus elements, and the degree to which such communalities are responded to determines the level of the child's conceptual development. The concept is represented independent of the physical presence of the stimuli if verbal labels have been attached to the common elements the stimuli possess. The problem of meaning may be handled in an *S–R* framework by assuming that stimuli have meaning to the degree that the child has learned that certain responses to the stimuli will produce certain types of changes in the stimulus situation.

The preceding discussion is primarily a translation from one system to another in an attempt to cover the topics discussed in *The Origins of Intelligence* as these were summarized earlier. The test of the value of the alternative view is whether it is capable of generating any new predictions. The purpose of the following section is to discuss some of the types of predictions that may be made on the basis of the assumptions regarding the operation of sensory stimulation as a reinforcing agent and the differentiation of intelligence according to the number of stimulus elements required to elicit a response.

In applying these assumptions to a particular example, it will be assumed that differences in level of cognitive development can be discerned in children of the same chronological age and that our understanding of cognitive development will be advanced by a systematic comparison of bright and dull children.

PREDICTIONS ABOUT INTELLECTIVE DEVELOPMENT

It is assumed that there are differences among children at birth in intellectual capacity and that the number of stimulus elements required to produce response is negatively correlated with intellectual level. The opportunity for experience is necessary for these differences to become manifest, and development of behavior may be hindered if the environment does not provide opportunities for experience. From an early age, however, it should be possible to determine something about the nature of the relations between stimulus and response that will have value in predicting later intellectual level.

The fact that different numbers of stimulus elements are required to produce a response should not be interpreted as indicating that the brighter subject is more sensitive to simple stimulus qualities than is the duller subject. The discussion concerns objects which differ in more than one sensory dimension; hence we will consider the detail to which the subject responds and not his sensitivity to stimulation.

There are several ways in which such differences among subjects could be tested. The bright subject should respond to minimal cues, and extended presentation of an object should not be so necessary for response to be elicited. It may be predicted that conditioned responses in young infants (or of older children) will be established more quickly in brighter subjects than in duller subjects with rapid presentation of the conditioned stimulus, even though differences in rate of conditioning may be found with longer presentation intervals. The rate of development of anticipatory responses should also differ for bright and dull subjects. A response is anticipatory if it occurs when all of the cues to which it has been conditioned are not present. Bright subjects should make such responses at a younger age, and to fewer cues, than the dull subject. If a complex stimulus is used in conditioning, it would be possible during test trials to vary systematically the aspects of the stimulus which are presented. Differences should appear among bright and dull subjects in the number of cues that are necessary to elicit the response. Or, if minimal cues are presented during the conditioning trials, the conditioned response should develop more rapidly in brighter subjects.

Another factor which may have predictive value for later intellectual level is the reactivity of the subject. If it is assumed that fewer stimulus elements are required to produce response, the bright subject should make a greater number of responses to a stimulus in a given period of time than a dull subject. In other words, the bright subject should show more "curiosity" and manipulative behavior. For example, if an object is presented for a constant period of time, more aspects of the objects should be described by brighter subjects. In the terms of our theory fewer cues are required for bright subjects to elicit response both to the external stimulus and to the stimulus change produced by response. But fewer repetitions of a response will be required for bright subjects before the reinforcing effects of the stimulus change lose their reinforcing power. Thus, the bright subject will be forced to vary his behavior more frequently than the dull subject, and the incidence of variable response to an object in a given period of time should be related to intellectual level.

The dull subjects should show greater stereotypy of response. If a response produces a certain consequence, it should take the dull subject longer to exhaust the reinforcing value of the stimulus change, and a particular response will therefore gain greater strength in these subjects. Consequently, the response will be repeated more often during the subject's initial experience with the stimuli and will be more likely to reappear upon later presentation of these stimuli.

It is surprising that there have been so few studies in which the relationship between ease of learning has been related to intellectual level. Since most intelligence tests are used to determine the ease with which the subject will learn new responses, it seems reasonable that one of the best ways to assess intellectual level is in terms of the ease with which the subject learns at a particular age. The rapidity of learning should be positively correlated with intellectual level for tasks which are appropriate for the developmental level of the subject. In a simple situation with a dominant correct response, the response should be conditioned to more aspects of the stimulus situation in the bright subject; hence on later trials there should be a greater likelihood that the response will be elicited in the bright subject. In complex situations, the bright subject should make more responses, and, therefore, the likelihood that the correct response will be elicited is increased. In addition, the response will be conditioned to more stimulus elements and will therefore be more likely to recur on later trials. Such a prediction would not hold if the task is below the subject's developmental level. In problems which are too easy for the subject, the bright subject may, because of interference from more "advanced" responses, show slower learning than the dull subject. More complex responses may be made by the bright subject, and these responses may interfere with the emergence of the simple, but appropriate, response.

Differences in performance related to differences in intellectual level should also appear in transfer problems. Such problems should be especially sensitive measures of differences in intellectual level. Ease of positive transfer should be positively correlated with intellectual level. Dull subjects require more of the elements which were present in the earlier stimulus situation in order to make the earlier responses and should show poorer transfer than brighter subjects.

Differentiation of intellectual level should also be possible by determining the rapidity with which subjects show satiation to particular changes in the stimulus situation produced by their response. If a fixed, rigid consequent is produced, brighter subjects should cease responding sooner than dull subjects, since the brighter subjects will exhaust the reinforcing value of the stimulus change more rapidly. If variable consequents are produced by response, the number of trials which the bright subject will perform should be increased. One test of intellectual level may be the degree to which the subject chooses to respond to a stimulus with variable consequences rather than a stimulus with constant consequences.

Intellective development during the early years may be mirrored, therefore, in the ease with which subjects respond to partial or minimal cues, in the frequency with which responses are made and are repeated, in the ease with which behavior can be modified and can be transferred to new situations, and in the rapidity with which subjects show satiation for particular types of stimulation.

COMMENTS ON RELATIONS BETWEEN PIAGET'S THEORY AND S-R THEORY [1]

DANIEL E. BERLYNE
University of Toronto

Various views of the relations between Piaget's work and S-R behavior theory are possible. On the one hand, there are some who believe that there is no important common ground between them, holding that the former should be rejected in favor of the latter, that the latter should be rejected in favor of the former, or that they should both be accepted as applicable to areas with little overlap. The opposite extreme is represented by the important article of Apostel (1959) in which he argues that all the principal characteristics of logical thought, including those studied by Piaget, can be deduced from the core of principles common to all current learning theories.

I should like to suggest a third and intermediate point of view, according to which the essential parts of what Piaget has to say can be translated into S-R language, but the process of translation reveals some important innovations, extensions, and modifications that must be made in S-R theory, especially as applied to intellectual processes, if it is to assimilate the phennomena studied by Piaget. In particular, four lines of modification and extension recommend themselves.

1. Piaget claims that intellectual development cannot be ascribed to maturation and learning alone but requires the recognition of a third kind of process, which he calls "disequilibrium," making for change. His view of "learning" is, however, a highly limited one, approximating the 18th or 19th century associationist notion of a passive registering of sensory impressions which become associated through contiguity and similarity. Recently, however, he has begun to speak of a "learning *sensu largo*" to cover what the modern learning theorist means by "learning."

Rather than invoking a new principle to account for change, it would seem that the principles of maturation and learning may suffice if we recognize *new sources of motivation and reward* to which learning is susceptible. These proposed forms of motivation stem, not from visceral discomfort nor from the impact of noxious external agents, but from uncomfortable relations between the organism's own reactions. Similarly, the restoration of harmonious relations between the organism's own reactions would provide new forms of reward or reinforcement.

These new drives and rewards, which appear to correspond to what Piaget calls "disequilibrium" and "equilibrium," will depend on factors

---

[1] These notes are based on Berlyne (1960).

like novelty, complexity, surprise, uncertainty, and conflict. They are also forced on our consideration by recent work on exploratory behavior, as well as by recent neurophysiological discoveries concerning the "arousal system" and the "orientation reaction."

2. In his *Principles of Behavior* (1943), Hull suggested that there may be three kinds of generalization resulting from the establishment of a bond or association between stimulus *1* and response *A*, namely (a) stimulus generalization such that other stimuli resembling stimulus *1* become associated with response *A*, (b) response generalization such that other responses resembling response *A* become associated with stimulus *1*, and (c) stimulus-response generalization such that other stimuli resembling stimulus *1* become associated with other responses resembling response *A*. Of these, the first kind of generalization has received a vast amount of study, the second much less, and the third almost none at all.

The "operations" that figure in Piaget's work on thinking are highly abstract, generalized habits, applicable to a wide variety of situations with differing concrete content. Apostel (1959) compares them to "learning sets"; but I would suggest that they should be regarded as habits subject to great *stimulus-response generalization*. The use of the term "stimulus-response generalization" does not solve many problems by itself; indeed, it raises many. Nevertheless, something like stimulus-response generalization is necessary to cover Gestalt work on "transposition" of insightful problem solutions to new situations with different content but involving the same "principles." It is even more indisputably required by the facts of language learning in which a grammatical "rule" is grasped and prompts the generation of linguistic forms that the subject has never encountered (e.g., mistakes among children, like "I ment" as preterite of "I mend," or "I seed").

3. For many years, psychologists have wrestled with the differences between "directed thought," aimed at the solution of problems, and "autistic thought," which occurs in free association and in reverie. Attempts to explain the differences by assuming that directed thought is subject to more discipline—in the sense that fewer alternative thoughts are admissible at any particular juncture—have been inadequate.

The S–R type of theory of thinking is exemplified by Hull's article on "Knowledge and purpose as habit-mechanisms" (1930) and by Dollard and Miller's treatment (1950). These writers assume, roughly speaking, that thinking about a sequence of states of affairs consists in entertaining a sequence of implicit symbolic responses representing the states of affairs. Internal motivational stimuli are invoked to impose the discipline essential to directed thought.

Piaget's work implies, on the other hand, that thought should be conceived differently—that between the symbolic responses representing two consecutive states of affairs must come another kind of symbolic response representing a *transformation* that would turn the first state of affairs into the second.

The unit of thought would thus be "s_1–r_i–s_2," where s_1 and s_2 are implicit responses representing stimulus situations and r_i is an implicit response representing a transformation. A train of thought would then consist of an alternating sequence—s_1–r_i–s_2–r_{ii}–s_3 . . . etc. It must be noted that, although the letters s and r are used for convenience, all the elements, whether representations of stimulus situations or representations of transformations, function both as stimuli and as responses.

At first, the r_i will no doubt consist of fractional versions of the child's own instrumental responses, which transform one external stimulus situation into another. But later, he will acquire a stock of implicit responses representing physicochemical processes which change one external situation into another or logicomathematical operations which change one formula into another in accordance with rules of inference. The use of these operations would distinguish directed thought—thought that is capable of producing a course of action to compass a desired practical aim or a proof that would licitly lead from axioms to conclusion.

The transformation-responses would be transformations in the mathematical sense, i.e., they would associate a given member of a set of stimulus situations s_1 with another member of the set s_2 which may then be referred to as the "image of s_1 under transformation r_i," or as "$r_i(s_1)$."

The use of these implicit transformation-responses would require the possession of two kinds of habits—(a) one, to be indicated as $(s_1, r_i) \rightarrow s_2$, that enables the subject, when confronted with the representations of a stimulus-situation and a transformation, to apply the transformation to this stimulus-situation and obtain a representation of a second stimulus-situation, and (b) one, to be indicated as $(s_1, s_2) \rightarrow r_i$, that would enable the subject, when confronted with representations of two stimulus situations, to supply the representation of a transformation that would lead from the first to the second stimulus situation.

Ideas having much in common with these are found in the writings of Spearman, Selz, Bartlett, Tolman, and, interestingly enough, of Simon and others who have been simulating thinking on computers.

4. Quite early, Hull's notion of the *habit-family hierarchy* was deemed likely to prove fruitful for the study of thinking. The hierarchies considered by Hull and his immediate associates were, however, simple in structure, consisting of parallel strands united at the two ends (common initial stimulus and common goal situation). Maltzman (1955) has suggested that hierarchies with a somewhat more complicated structure, i.e., consisting of hierarchies of subhierarchies, must figure in the sort of reasoning exemplified by Maier's experiments. Much of what Piaget has to say about thinking can be translated into the language of habit-family hierarchies. But to take care of the experimental findings and theoretical ideas that he has furnished,

we must extend and complicate the notion of hierarchy. In particular, the hierarchies that make logical thinking possible (a) must be composed, not merely of chains of implicit, symbolic responses, but of implicit, symbolic responses representing alternately stimulus situations and transformations and (b) must have extremely complex structures.

These complex structures call for mathematical language to describe them, and the languages of algebra and graph theory seem the most promising.

Piaget emphasizes that the growth of intelligence and the progress of adaptation involve more and more approximation to structures isomorphic with *groups of transformations*. At the sensory-motor level, the child has not mastered spatial relations until his movements in space are organized into a group. And, at the symbolic or "operational" level, the earliest forms of "intuitive thought" lack group structure; the acquisition of the stage of "concrete operations" have an imperfect group structure (depending on "groupings" [*groupements*]); and, finally, the highest forms of thought, characterizing the "formal-operations" stage in which logic and mathematics become possible, rely on the group structure of the number system, the propositional calculus, and so on.

It can be shown that properties corresponding to the defining characteristics of an algebraic group of transformations may be possessed by habit-family hierarchies. Piaget insists that "reversibility" (which is, of course, one of the properties of a group—the existence of an inverse for every transformation in the group) is the essential characteristic of the highest intellectual structures, leading to "conservations" of invariants (e.g., of quantity of liquid despite changes in shape) and to the flexible consistency of logical thinking. I suggest that it is not reversibility as such that matters, since recognition of inverse transformations can occur while "conservations" are absent, but that the most advanced thought structures are *transitive groups,* i.e., groups in which one can get from any element to any other element in a single transformation (corresponding to *complete* or *trivial* graphs).

At the cost of a little speculation, one can see reasons why such structures should possess advantages lacking in others and the senses in which, reinterpreting Piaget's descriptions, these structures should have more "equilibrium" than others. Furthermore, since one of the principal functions of thinking is the formation of equivalence classes of objects that were formerly not treated as equivalent (i.e, the selection of information to discard), we can see how transitive-group habit-family hierarchies will bestow acquired equivalences on stimulus situations. In particular, they open the way to an understanding of Piaget's "conservations," in which two stimulus-patterns are treated as equivalent, not because of physicochemical resemblances (as in standard concept-formation experiments), but because of a knowledge (symbolic representation) of the transformations that the patterns have undergone.

7

COMPUTER SIMULATION OF HUMAN THINKING AND PROBLEM SOLVING [1]

HERBERT A. SIMON

Carnegie Institute of Technology

and ALLEN NEWELL

The RAND Corporation

INTRODUCTION

It is no longer necessary to argue that computers can be used to simulate human thinking or to explain in general terms how such simulation can be carried out. A dozen or more computer programs have been written and tested that perform some of the interesting symbol-manipulating, problem-solving tasks that human beings can perform and that do so in a manner which simulates, at least in some general respects, the way in which humans do these tasks. Computer programs now play chess and checkers, find proofs for theorems in geometry and logic, compose music, balance assembly lines, design electric motors and generators, memorize nonsense syllables, form concepts, and learn to read.[2]

With the proof of possibility accomplished, we can turn to more substantive questions. We can ask what we have learned about human thinking and problem solving through computer simulation: to what extent we now have theories for these phenomena, and what the content of these theories is. Since we want to talk about these substantive matters, we shall simply make the following assertions, which are validated by existing computer programs.

1. Computers are quite general symbol-manipulating devices that can be programmed to perform nonnumerical as well as numerical symbol manipulation.

---

[1] This is an abridgment of a paper presented March 23, 1961 in the Massachusetts Institute of Technology Centennial Lecture Series on "Management and the Computer of the Future." It is reprinted here, with permission, from the collection of these lectures published by the Technology Press and John Wiley and Sons. We are grateful for the opportunity to substitute this paper for an earlier one, distributed to the participants of the Dedham Conference, that did not include any discussion of the origins of children's speech.

[2] For an excellent recent survey of heuristic programs, although with emphasis upon "artificial intelligence" rather than simulation of human thought, *see* Minsky (1961).

2. Computer programs can be written that use nonnumerical symbol manipulation processes to perform tasks which, in humans, require thinking and learning.

3. These programs can be regarded as theories, in a completely literal sense, of the corresponding human processes. These theories are testable in a number of ways, among them, by comparing the symbolic behavior of a computer so programmed with the symbolic behavior of a human subject when both are performing the same problem-solving or thinking tasks.

The General Problem Solver

The theory we shall have most to say about is a computer program called the General Problem Solver. It is not "general" in the sense that it will solve, or even try to solve, all problems—it obviously won't. It is called "general" because it will accept as tasks all problems that can be put in a specified, but fairly general, form and because the methods it employs make no specific reference to the subject matter of the particular problem it is solving. The General Problem Solver is a system of methods—believed to be those commonly possessed by intelligent college students—that turn out to be helpful in many situations where a person confronts problems for which he does not possess special methods of attack.

Before general methods can be applied to any particular class of problems, of course, the problem solver must also learn, or be taught, the rules that apply to that particular problem domain. The General Problem Solver will not prove theorems unless instructed in the rules of proof in the particular branch of mathematics to which the theorems belong. Thus, in any particular problem domain, the resources available to the General Problem Solver include information about the task environment as well as its own repertory of methods.

Missionaries and Cannibals

Let us introduce the General Problem Solver (which we shall call GPS) by means of a simple example. Many of you are familiar with the puzzle of the Missionaries and Cannibals, and some of you saw a young lady solving the puzzle in a recent CBS television program celebrating MIT's centenary. There are three missionaries and three cannibals on the bank of a wide river, wanting to cross. There is a boat on the bank, which will hold no more than two persons, and all six members of the party know how to paddle it. The only real difficulty is that the cannibals are partial to a diet of missionaries. If, even for a moment, one or more missionaries are left alone with a larger number of cannibals, the missionaries will be eaten. The problem is to find a sequence of boat trips that will get the entire party safely across the river—without the loss of any missionaries.

Suppose, now, we encounter this puzzle for the first time. We are endowed by nature and nurture with certain abilities that enable us to tackle the problem. We might or might not solve it, but we could at least *think* about it. In what would this thinking consist? In particular, how could we bring to bear our general problem-solving skills, which make no reference to missionaries and cannibals, in this particular situation?

Clearly, we have to form some kind of abstraction of the problem that will match the abstractness of our general methods: We have some people and a boat on *this* side of the river and we want them on *that* side of the river. Stated abstractly, we have a certain state of affairs, and we want a different state of affairs. Moreover, we can describe both states, and we can also describe what the differences are between them—between what we have and what we want.

In this case, the differences between the given and the desired are differences in physical location. Our men are on one side of the river; we want them on the other. But we have had vast experience with differences in location, and that experience (stored somehow in memory) tells us that boats are useful devices for reducing differences of location on water. So we begin to consider the possible sequences of boatloads that will get our party across the river without casualties.

It is clear from this formulation of the problem what part is played in its solution by our general problem-solving techniques and what part by our knowledge and experience of the particular problem domain in question. A general solution technique is to characterize the given and desired situations, to find the differences between them, and to search for means—implements or operators—that are relevant to removing differences of these kinds. Our knowledge of the task and our experience tell us what the given and desired situations are and what kinds of operators may be relevant for getting from here to there.

Structure of GPS

We can now characterize the program of the General Problem Solver more formally.[3] The program deals with symbolic *objects* that describe or characterize situations—the given situation, the desired situation, various intermediate possible situations. The program also deals with symbols representing *differences* between pairs of objects and with symbols representing *operators* that are capable of inducing changes in the objects to which they are applied. (*See* Figure 1, left-hand column.)

Goal types. The processes of GPS are organized around *goals* of three types:

1. *Transformation* goals: to transform object *a* into object *b*.

---

[3] For a fuller description, *see* Newell, Shaw, and Simon (1960a).

2. *Difference Reduction* goals: to eliminate or reduce difference *d* between objects *a* and *b*.

3. *Operator Application* goals: to apply operator *q* to object *a*.

GPS	LEARNING SPEECH	ADAPTING TO ENVIRONMENT
Objects	Perceptual symbols (audited phonemes)	AFFERENT
Differences	Comparison between adult-child phoneme images	State language
Relevant Operators	Changes in motor symbols (control of speech production)	EFFERENT Process language

FIGURE 1—Comparison of basic categories in GPS, speech learning, and organismic adaptation.

Methods. With each type of goal in GPS there is associated one or more methods, or processes, that may contribute to the attainment of the goal. The principal methods in the present version of GPS are three in number, one for each type of goal:

1. Method for transformation goals: to transform *a* into *b*,
   a. Notice a difference, *d*, between *a* and *b*;
   b. Establish the goal of reducing *d* between *a* and *b*;
   c. Try to attain this new goal;
   d. If successful, find a new difference and repeat.

2. Method for difference reduction goals: to reduce *d* between *a* and *b*,
   a. Recall an operator, *q*, that is relevant to differences of the type of *d*;
   b. Establish the goal of applying *q* to *a*;
   c. Try to attain this new goal;
   d. If successful, return to the previous transform goal.

3. Method for operator application goals: to apply operator *q* to *a*,
   a. Compare conditions for application of *q* with object *a*;
   b. If these are not satisfied, establish and try to attain the goal of transforming *a* into an object that meets these conditions;
   c. When the conditions are satisfied, apply *q* to *a*, and return to the previous difference reduction goal with the modified object, *a'*.

This is a rather simplified description of what goes on in GPS, but it gives the broad outline of the program. GPS, to put it simply, is a program that reasons about ends and means. It is capable of defining ends, seeking means to attain them, and, in the process of so doing, defining new subsidiary ends, or subgoals, to the original end.

As a theory of human problem solving, GPS asserts that college students solve problems—at least problems of the sort for which the program has been tested—by carrying out this kind of organized ends-means analysis. It does not assert that the process is carried out consciously—it is easy to show that many steps in the problem-solving process do not reach conscious awareness. Nor does the theory assert that the process will appear particularly orderly to an observer who does not know the program detail or, for that matter, to the problem solver himself. It does assert that, if we compare that part of the human subject's problem-solving behavior which we can observe—the steps he takes, his verbalizations—with the processes carried out by the computer, they will be substantially the same.

Abstracting and planning processes. Before we leave this description of GPS, we should like to mention one other kind of process that we are incorporating in the program and that certainly must be included if we are to explain and predict the behavior of our subjects—particularly the brighter ones. We call these additional methods *abstracting* and *planning* processes. Briefly, abstracting consists in replacing the objects, the differences, and the operators with new symbolic expressions that describe the situation in much more general terms, omitting the detail.[4] For example, we might ask GPS to prove a trigonometric identity: $\cos^2 x + \sin^2 x = \tan x \cot x$.

Here, GPS might take as *a* the expression, "$\cos^2 x + \sin^2 x$," and as *b* the expression, "$\tan x \cot x$." In using the planning method, these might be abstracted to: (a') "an expression containing cos and sin" and (b') "an expression containing tan and cot," respectively. Then, the methods of GPS could be applied to transforming the abstracted given object, a', into the abstracted desired object, b'. If this goal were attained, the steps employed for this transformation would generally provide a *plan* for transforming the original, detailed given object, *a*, into the original desired object, *b*. In the particular case illustrated, the plan might be something like: "First eliminate cos and sin from the expression, and then introduce tan and cot."

THE GENERALITY OF ENDS-MEANS ANALYSIS

The processes incorporated in GPS have actually been observed in the behavior of our human subjects solving problems in the laboratory. By

---

[4] *See* Newell, Shaw, and Simon (1960a, pp. 261-262) for a description of a specific planning method for GPS. In our subjects, abstraction often takes the form of simply ignoring some of the problem detail at certain stages of the solution process.

analyzing the tape-recorded protocols of their problem-solving efforts, we can identify the occurrences of the three goal types and the four methods. Moreover, the augmented GPS, containing the planning method, incorporates a substantially adequate set of processes to explain our subjects' behavior in some of these simple theorem-proving, puzzle-solving situations.[5] By the adequacy of GPS, we mean two things:

1. We do not find in the subjects' protocols evidence of processes quite different from those postulated in GPS. This may mean only that we don't know how to look for them; but,

2. When we have compared the trace of the GPS computer (or hand simulations of the computer program) with the protocols of a subject solving the same problem, we have found that the two often follow the same path—noticing the same things about the problem expressions, establishing the same subgoals, applying the same operators, running down the same blind alleys—over periods of time ranging up to several minutes. That is to say, the processes in GPS are sufficient to produce a stream of behavior in a given problem situation quite similar to that produced by the human subject.

These kinds of tests, even if broadened, would still not say much about the generality of GPS as a theory of human thinking and problem solving. It might turn out that, if we examined tasks quite different from those used in developing the program and made the same careful records of subjects' protocols, we would find many new processes exhibited that are not contained in GPS. However, extensions of GPS in fair detail to problem domains that were not considered when the program was developed indicate that its processes are adequate, at least to these other domains. For example, Missionaries and Cannibals, which was first suggested as a possible task by Mr. Thomas Wolf of the Columbia Broadcasting System, has been solved by the current version of GPS—not without some reorganization of the program, but without addition of new goal types or methods. Similarly, the applications to algebraic and trigonometric identities and to certain learning tasks appear to require no enlargement of the basic repertory of methods. Less detailed analysis of a variety of other tasks shows GPS to be adequate for these also.

Still, these additional tests do not carry GPS beyond a fairly limited range of formal problem-solving situations. It would be of considerable interest to explore, even qualitatively, the powers and limitations of GPS when it is confronted with a thinking or learning task of quite a different kind from any of these. We should like to carry out a reconnaissance along these lines. First, we will describe, on the basis of what is now known, the processes that humans use in a task that appears, superficially, to be quite different from problem solving. Then, we shall propose a framework which

---

[5] *See* Newell and Simon (1961).

shows that these processes can be subsumed under those already incorporated in the General Problem Solver.

THE ACQUISITION OF SPEECH

There are many human activities to which we would apply the term "thinking" but not the term "problem solving." There are also many activities we would usually call "learning" rather than "thinking." We would ordinarily call a child's acquisition of speech, "learning." We propose to consider the acquisition of speech as an example of human cognitive activity that is at something of an opposite pole from the rather highly verbalized, somewhat conscious, practiced problem solving of an intelligent and educated adult. We can then judge whether the processes at these two poles are quite different or basically the same.

Speech acquisition has been about as well studied as any nonlaboratory complex human activity, and a review of the literature indicates that there is general consensus about the particular facts we shall use.[6]

Central Representations

We consider an infant who has already learned the names of a few objects—as evidenced by the fact that he can point to them or fetch them when they are named by an adult—but who has not yet pronounced their names. From his behavior, we can infer that, when the child perceives the spoken word "ball," his perception has some kind of internal representation in the brain that permits it to be associated, through previous experience, with some internal representation of a visually perceived ball.

To *say* the word "ball," the child must, in addition, store some kind of program capable of energizing, through motor (efferent) channels, the muscles involved in speech production—in the production of the specific phonemes of that word. Let us call the "whatever-it-is" in the central nervous system that represents internally a perceived sensory stimulus an *afferent* or *perceptual symbol.* Let us call the "whatever-it-is" that represents the program for initiating the motor signals an *efferent* or *motor symbol.*

Learning to speak, in this formulation, means acquiring the motor symbols that correspond to perceptual (auditory) symbols of words already known and associating the former with the latter. Now the difficulty is that there is no way in which the corresponding perceptual and motor symbols can "resemble" each other—that is, can symbolize the appropriateness of their association by resemblance. The correspondence is purely arbitrary.[7] The infant is faced (if he only knew it!) with the immense inductive task

---

[6] *See,* for example, Osgood (1953, pp. 683-690) and Miller (1951a; 1951b, ch. 7).

[7] We shall have occasion to qualify the adverb "purely" when we come to consider the factorization of words into phonemes and phoneme components.

of discovering which motor symbols will cause speech production that, when he hears it, will produce, in turn, an appropriate auditory symbol to be perceived and recognized. And the task appears at first blush to have little structure that would permit it to be approached with some less arduous technique than trial-and-error search.

There is ample evidence that much trial-and-error search is indeed required before the infant acquires the skill of speaking. The child imitates the adults around him, and he imitates himself (echoic speech). Gradually, over many months, he acquires the motor symbols that enable him to produce sounds which he hears as the expected auditory symbols. In the early stages, the child's acquisition of a speaking vocabulary appears to be paced by the task of developing the new motor symbols. At later stages, he is able to produce a word relatively easily once he has learned to recognize the corresponding auditory symbol.

Factorization

A little reflection will persuade us that something more than trial and error is involved. If that were all, the three hundredth word would be no easier to pronounce than the first. The child learns to learn. In what does this consist?

Although the motor symbol cannot be compared with the perceptual symbol, the *correct* perceptual symbol for a word can be compared, through imitation, with the perceptual symbol produced by the attempt to pronounce the word. If these are different, modification of the motor symbol can be attempted until an auditory symbol resembling the correct one is perceived.

Thus far, we have been assuming that the units in terms of which these transactions take place are words. But there is no reason for this assumption —the child might well attend to particular syllables, phonemes, or even components of phonemes. The auditory symbols for words can be compound symbols or *expressions*—strings of phonemes, each phoneme itself encoded in terms of its component frequencies and other characteristics. It is even more plausible to suppose that the motor symbols would be constructed from smaller units, for each word involves a temporal succession of syllables, each syllable a temporal succession of phonemes, and each phoneme a whole set of signals to the several muscles involved in that part of the speech act. Thus, one of the many components of the motor symbol for the spoken word "dog" might be the signal that pushes the tongue against the palate in the initial "d" phoneme of this one-syllable word.

The Learning Process

There is considerable evidence today that this picture of the processes of word-recognition and word-production is correct, at least in broad outline. Many of the components involved in both auditory and motor symbols have been tentatively identified, and there is good experimental evidence for some of them.[8] But what does the picture, if true, contribute to our understanding of the child's acquisition of speech?

It means that the inductive learning need not be blind inductive learning —attempting to associate by pure trial and error each of a large number of words with an appropriate motor symbol chosen from the myriad of producible sequences of speech sounds. On the contrary, to the extent that specific factors in the auditory symbol vary with specific factors in the motor symbol (e.g., as one of the formant frequencies in vowel sounds varies with the size of the resonating mouth cavity), the search for the correct symbol can be very much restricted. Components can be corrected on a one-at-a-time basis. For example, the child trying to pronounce "dog" can at one time attend to the correctness of the vowel, at another time to the correctness of the initial consonant, or even to the aspect of the initial consonant associated with tongue position.

Thus, the hypothesis of factorization is supported both by experimental evidence that it does take place and by theoretical reasons why it "should" take place—why speech acquisition would be very much easier with it than without it. Trial-and-error acquisition of phonemes would require a search from among only a few hundred phonemes (many fewer are actually used, of course, in any single dialect). Trial-and-error search among phoneme *components* would be even more restricted—there are, for example, probably only a half dozen distinguishable tongue positions. Thus, by factorization of the total space of possibilities, a very limited trial-and-error search of the factors can be substituted for an immense search of the product space. Moreover, once the child has acquired motor symbols corresponding to the common phonemes, acquisition of new words (new combinations of these same phonemes) can be very rapid.

Summary: The Child's Acquisition of Speech

Let us now summarize our description, partly factual, partly hypothetical, of the speech acquisition process. The child acquires perceptual auditory symbols corresponding to words he has heard and has associated with visual symbols. He tries, on a trial-and-error basis, to produce words, he hears his productions, and he compares these auditory symbols with those already stored. When he detects differences, he varies the motor symbol to try to remove them. As he learns, he detects that changes in certain components of the motor symbols alter only certain components of the auditory symbols. Thus, he is able to factor the correction process and thereby accelerate it greatly.

---

[8] For a general introduction to these topics, *see* Miller (1951b, ch. 2). An excellent recent survey is Fatehchand (1960). *See also* Forgie (1959) and Liberman *et al.* (1959). The last three references cited illustrate, incidentally, the large role that computers are playing today in linguistic and phonetic research.

Acquisition of Speech by GPS

Now it is very easy, with a few changes in vocabulary, to translate this whole description back in terms of GPS. When the translation has been made, we shall see that the processes just described are the methods of GPS.

Let us, in this translation, call the auditory symbol *objects* (Figure 1, second column). We assume that there exist central processes that modify motor symbols—that change one or more of their components. We will call these processes *operators*. A change in motor symbol will, in turn, change the auditory symbol that is perceived when that motor symbol produces a sound.

The child detects *differences* between the object he has produced (i.e., his perception of the sound) and the correct object (his perception of the sound when produced by adults). He applies operators to the motor symbol to modify the sounds he produces, hence the object perceived; and he compares the latter again with the correct object. This search process continues until he can reproduce the perceived object.

But this does not account for the factorization, which we have argued is so crucial to the efficiency of the learning process. How will GPS learn (a) which differences in objects are associated with which operators upon the motor symbols and (b) how to factor objects and operators? Although the answers to these questions are far from certain, a scheme we have proposed elsewhere would enable GPS to handle these tasks also.[9] We will sketch it briefly:

1. Given a set of differences and a set of operators, GPS can, with modest amounts of trial and error, detect which operators are relevant to producing or eliminating which differences. To take a crude, but simple, example: it takes relatively little trial and error to discover what differences in the perceived sound are associated with changes in the rounding of the lips while producing a vowel. The factorization has already largely been carried out by nature, so to speak, because changes in only a few aspects of the motor signal will change only a few aspects of the perceptual symbol.

2. The GPS processes can themselves be employed to discover inductively a "good" factorization—a "good" set of differences. To do this, GPS must be supplied with some very general criteria as to what constitutes such a good set. The criteria would be of the following sorts:

   a. Only one or a few operators should be relevant to each difference (so that, given a difference, an appropriate operator can be found without too much search).

   b. Only one or a few differences should be associated with each operator (so that the sounds produced can be varied factor by factor).

and a few others of the same general kind.

---

[9] The full account of this learning scheme is given in Newell, Shaw, and Simon (1960b).

With such a set of criteria provided, finding a good set of differences simply becomes another kind of problem to which GPS can apply its problem-solving methods. What are the objects, differences, and operators in terms of which this new kind of problem is formulated? To avoid unnecessary confusion, we will capitalize the terms OBJECTS, DIFFERENCES, and OPERATORS in speaking of the new problem context in order to distinguish them from the objects (perceptual symbols), differences, and operators (changes in motor symbols) involved in the original task of acquiring speech.

The OBJECTS for the new problem-solving task are the *sets of differences* in the original task environment. The new DIFFERENCES designate to what extent particular sets of differences meet the *criteria* we have just listed. OPERATORS are processes for altering the set of differences under consideration by deleting differences from the set, adding differences, or generating new differences for possible inclusion. GPS then tests in what respects particular OBJECTS (sets of differences) are DIFFERENT from the desired OBJECT (as indicated by the criteria). It seeks to remove these DIFFERENCES (modify the set of differences) by applying OPERATORS (by adding, subtracting, or modifying differences).

Since this scheme has not been realized on a computer, we cannot tell how effective GPS would be in handling it. All we can say is that it is a problem whose solution can be attempted with the means at the disposal of GPS.

A due respect for parsimony would suggest, then, that, instead of postulating quite different processes for the acquisition of such skills as speaking from these postulated for adult problem solving, we embrace tentatively the hypothesis that the processes are in fact the same—that the General Problem Solver provides a description of both processes. This hypothesis would provide a sharp focus for empirical research into the early speech behavior of the child.

THE STATE-PROCESS DICHOTOMY

Let us accept this hypothesis for the moment: that the same system of ends-means processes is involved in learning speech and in problem solving. Can we explain why a system of ends-means analysis should provide the basis for adaptive behavior in both classes of situations? We shall try to provide an explanation for the generality of ends-means processes by showing how these arise quite naturally from the problem that any organism must solve if it is to use its sensory and motor apparatus effectively to survive.

Relation of Perceptual to Motor Symbols

The terms "perceptual" and "motor," or "afferent" and "efferent," reflect the dual relation that every adaptive organism has with its environment. It perceives aspects of the environment, and it acts upon the environment. It must be able, therefore, to transmit, store, and operate upon internal representations—perceptual symbols—that stand for its perceptions; and it must be able to transmit, store, and operate upon internal representations—efferent or motor symbols—that can serve as signals to its effectors. The organism survives by associating appropriate motor symbols with the perceptual symbols that stand for various classes of perceptions.[10]

In particular, the organism can perceive, at least grossly, its own behavior caused by its efferent signals. Hence, among the perceptual symbols that it can store are symbols that stand for the perception of corresponding motor signals. Languages are especially adapted to facilitate this correspondence. Language behavior, built from limited alphabets of unit behaviors, is highly stylized so that to each distinct language "act" will correspond an easily perceivable and distinguishable perceptual symbol.

Nevertheless, the relation of a particular language efferent—say that which energizes the word "dog"—to the corresponding perceptual symbol is arbitrary. There is no more resemblance between the auditory "dog" and the motor symbol which produces that word than between "dog" and "Hund." If it is to be learned, the correspondence must be learned as a pure fact. By building up a dictionary relating motor with perceptual symbols—including language symbols—the organism gains the ability to produce the actions it "intends." In the last section we explored how this ability could develop in the case of speech.

The duality of our relation with the environment reveals itself in the vocabulary of natural languages—particularly in the distinction between nouns and adjectives, on the one hand, and verbs, on the other. We have *clean* clothes (a perceptual symbol) because they have been *washed* (a motor symbol). It is a fact stored in our "table of connections" that when we wash clothes they become clean. As we build up our vocabulary, however, we pass more readily from the one mode of discourse to the other. Thus, the clothes, in the last example, might also have been *cleaned*. As we learn what actions have what effects, changes in objects are named by the processes that produce them, and processes by the effects they create.

The Problem of Translation

It is precisely this duality of language—or, more broadly, of the internal symbols employed in thought—that makes behavior problematic. The world as it is and as it is desired is described in a *state language,* a language of per-

---

10 We need hardly say that this description does not commit us to any oversimplified reflex-arc picture of the peripheral and central systems. GPS is a concrete example of a system of the sort we are describing. In it, the perceptual-motor associations are represented by the table of connections between differences and operators. The use it makes of these connections, and consequently the relation of response to stimulus, is highly complex.

ceptual symbols.[11] Possible actions are described in a *process language,* a language of motor symbols (Figure 1, third column). The problem of adapting is the problem of finding the statement in the process language that corresponds to the difference between existing and desired states of affairs in the state language.[12]

But the problems that GPS was designed to handle can be viewed in exactly the same way. What is involved in discovering a proof for the Pythagorean theorem? The *theorem* is a symbolic object in the state language: "The square on the hypotenuse of a right triangle is equal to the sum of the squares on the sides." By comparing this theorem, so stated, with the axioms and previously proved theorems, we detect differences between them. A *proof* of the theorem is a symbolic object in the process language. This object—the justification that we generally write down alongside the successively modified axioms and theorems—describes the sequence of operations that eliminates the differences between axioms and desired theorems. Given a set of axioms, for every theorem defined in the state language, the theorem can be represented in the process language by the sequence of operations that constitutes its proof.

Thus, mathematics, and problem-solving generally, is an imitation of life. Problem-solving activity uses the very fundamental processes that all adaptive organisms must have if they are to coordinate successfully their perceptual and motor pictures of the world.[13] Ends-means relations, far from being highly special, are reflections of the basic state-process dichotomy, the dichotomy between perceiving and acting.

The Difficulty of the Environment

How hard a problem will be depends on the simplicity or complexity of the rules that define the correspondence between the two languages. An example of a relatively simple correspondence is the relation between the decimal and octal representations of integers. There is a simple and direct algorithm that solves all problems of the form: if *a* is the decimal representation of a number, what is its octal representation?

---

[11] It should be observed that the body is part of the environment that is perceived. Hence, drives like hunger produce perceptual symbols just as external senses do. Or perhaps it would be better to say that the drive *is* the perceptual symbol produced by the perception of hunger.

[12] Other aspects of the state-process dichotomy are discussed in Newell, Shaw, and Simon (1958).

[13] We should like to call attention to the similarity, hardly accidental, between the translation problems we have been describing and some of the most striking results of modern mathematics—the undecidability theorems. Decision problems, in the Gödel sense, can always be represented as problems of finding in language B the representation of an object that is described in language A, where there are at least some objects that have names in both languages. If the rules of correspondence between the two languages are sufficiently complicated, this will be difficult, and, as the undecidability theorems show, it may be impossible.

At the other extreme, the correspondence between the vocabularies may be purely conventional or arbitrary. Then, rote learning is the only means for building up the translation dictionary, and, if the correct translations must also be discovered, immense amounts of trial-and-error search may be required.

The aspects of the environment with which we, as organisms, deal effectively reach neither of these two extremes. The translation between the state language that describes our perceptions of the world and the process language that describes our actions on the world is reducible to no simple rule, but it is not, on the other hand, arbitrary. Most of our skill in dealing with the environment is embodied in elaborate *heuristics,* or rules of thumb, that allow us to factor—approximately—the complex perceived world into highly simple components and to find—approximately and reasonably reliably —the correspondences that allow us to act on that world predictably. This is the skill that the adult businessman uses when he makes a decision, the skill of the scientist in his laboratory, the skill of the subject in a problem-solving experiment, the skill of a child learning to speak.

AN INFORMATION PROCESSING THEORY OF INTELLECTUAL DEVELOPMENT

HERBERT A. SIMON[1]
Carnegie Institute of Technology

In the paper, "Computer Simulation of Human Thinking and Problem Solving" (Simon and Newell, 1962), a method for studying human-thinking and other intellective processes is described, a theory of problem-solving processes is set forth, and the theory is applied to the question of how an organism can develop the capacity to use spoken language.

In this note, I should like to take two further steps toward applying the information-processing theory of cognition to the phenomena of child development. In the first section, I shall propose an interpretation of the "operational structures" of Piaget in information processing terms. In the second section, I shall use the information-processing theory to discuss the concept of "stages of development."

OPERATIONAL STRUCTURES

I should like to see if information-processing theory can throw light on Piaget's notion of "operational structures"—that is, whether it can help

---

[1] My colleagues, and particularly Lee Gregg, Kenneth Laughery, and Allen Newell, will recognize our joint endeavors as the source of most of the ideas in this note.

us to provide a more precise definition of that concept and perhaps point the way to a rigorous and objective identification of the operational structures that are employed in any particular example of a subject's thought processes.

An information-processing theory of thinking postulates that the behavior of the subject in the face of a problem-solving situation is governed by a "program"—quite similar in organization to a computer program. The program is comprised of an organized system of processes and of organizations of memory contents. Some of these are quite specific to particular problem areas; others are relatively general and independent of subject matter. The General Problem Solver, for example, contains some very nonspecific processes for solving problems (means-end analysis and planning) and some nonspecific schemes for organizing an associative memory (lists and list structures).

In the course of his intellective development, the child presumably acquires, on the one hand, knowledge, skills, and schemata that are specific to a subject matter (e.g., the addition and multiplication tables, skills of arithmetic manipulation, and schemes for storing arithmetic data in memory). On the other hand, he acquires knowledge, skills and schemata that are relatively general in application (e.g., those incorporated in GPS or general notions of causality, space-time relations, and so on).

My conjecture is that, if we succeed in finding an objective referent for Piaget's "operational structures," this referent will consist in some of the relatively general features of the processes and schemes for storing information that children in our society acquire for performing intellective tasks. I should like to buttress this conjecture by showing how the broad structural characteristics of programs like the General Problem Solver could produce phenomena like some of those that Piaget has tried to explain in terms of operational structures.

The General Problem Solver is an information-processing system—a system for manipulating symbols. It is built on a memory organization that permits symbols to be organized in lists (each item on a list being associated with the preceding one) and in list structures (lists of lists or hierarchies of symbols). It incorporates also a basic set of processes that enable it to store information in memory and (sometimes) to retrieve this information when it is relevant. These processes are matched to the memory organization— that is, they are implicitly adapted to the fact that information in memory is held in list structures. Thus, they include processes for putting symbols on lists, finding symbols on lists, comparing symbols, and so on. A different memory organization would call for a different set of basic manipulative processes, and a different set of processes would call for a different memory organization.

In a list system, one of the centrally important processes is FIND NEXT (FN); *see* Figure 1. Roughly speaking, this process brings into immediate memory the symbol that is associated with ("next to") a symbol on a list

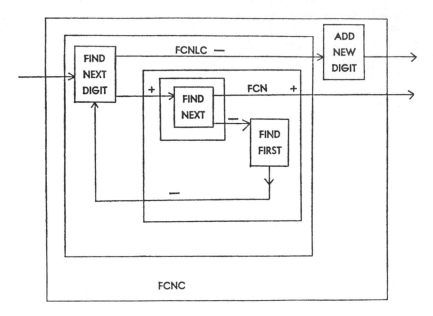

Figure 1—Processes for manipulating lists, periodic patterns, and hierarchical patterns.

that is already in immediate memory. Thus, if ABCDE . . . is a list and B is in immediate memory, execution of the process, FN, will bring C into immediate memory. One can see how some process like FN is involved in any serial performance: telling a story as a child tells it or memorizing nonsense syllables. It would appear to correspond to what Piaget calls "seriation."

Consider now the task of remembering and applying a repetitive pattern like: ABCABCABCABC. This task is part of certain standard concept-forming and pattern-recognizing situations. If the subject had in memory the list ABC, he could run through the pattern once, but how could he repeat it? Suppose he has acquired the process, FIND CIRCULAR NEXT (FCN). This process, like FN, courses down a list; but it holds in memory not only the current item but also the initial item of the list. When the end of the list is reached, it returns to the beginning. Thus, a subject could recite a periodic pattern by remembering: "Apply FCN to list ABC."

Consider next the task of writing the integers from 1 to 1,000. With the process, FCN, the subject could write: 1, 2, 3, 4, 5, 6, 7, 8, 9, 0, 1, 2, 3, 4, . . . ; but how could he go from 9 to 10? With a small modification, FCN becomes FIND CIRCULAR NEXT WITH CARRY (FCNC). The additional operations involved are to hold in memory the position on several lists (on the units lists, the tens lists, and so on), and, whenever FCN returns to the first item on any list, to use this as a cue to perform FCN on the list as well. Thus, after 9, the units list returns to the initial item, 0; and this signals a change in the tens item from 0 to 1—exactly as this is accomplished by a desk calculating machine.

Now my specific hypotheses are these: that in the course of his early intellective development, a child acquires the capacity to store symbols in lists (perhaps he is born with this capacity) and to perform the operation, FN. At some later time, he acquires the capacity to perform FCN, and, at a still later time, the capacity to perform FCNC.

Even supposing that this description of cognitive development turns out to be true, what is the virtue in stating it this way? First, it is specific. It states definitely what it is that the child has developed when he has acquired any of these processes; we can write a computer program that defines clearly and unequivocally the process and how it operates.

Second, the particular processes I have mentioned have extremely general utility in a variety of intellective tasks. I have already observed that FCN, or some equivalent process, is involved in handling any repetitive pattern—whether a double alternation maze or a simple musical round. The ubiquity of FCNC is even more remarkable. For a subject who can perform this process can perform what Piaget calls the "combinatorial operations" and those operations involved in the "multiplicative groupement." Let me illustrate. With FCNC, a subject would learn the sequence of 16 patterns: LLLL, LLLR, LLRL, LLRR, LRLL, etc., by memorizing simply: "Apply FCNC to the list, LL, LR, RL, RR duplicated"; or even more simply: "Apply FCNC to the list L, R quadruplicated." (We have found examples of subjects storing the solution in each of these modes.) But this sequence is precisely the sequence of all possible combinations of four classes.

A third advantage from this way of talking about "operational structures" derives from the two already mentioned. By the examination of thinking-aloud protocols, we can often identify precisely how the subject holds a particular pattern or concept in memory and precisely what processes are incorporated in his definition of it. Hence, we have here objective means for testing what processes are involved in particular intellective performances.

On the basis of our experiences to date in writing information-processing programs for human intellective processes, we are persuaded that the number of memory structures and associated processes that have relatively broad significance for adult performances, and hence for the theory of development, is not enormous. I have already mentioned a few that have been most prominent in the programs we have written.

I do not share Piaget's belief that information processes like those I have described are to be understood in terms of symbolic logic. The converse is more likely to be true: that formal logic will receive a more fundamental explication in terms of information processes. Certainly, this has been the trend of investigation in logic since Türing's classic paper, 25 years ago, which introduced what we now call the Türing Machine.

STAGES OF DEVELOPMENT

The concept of "stage" implies that we are dealing with a dynamic system that undergoes steady change through time. We select certain instants in the course of that dynamic change, take "snapshots" of the system at those instants, and use these snapshots as descriptions of the system at a particular stage of development.

As yet, we know very little about the kind of dynamic system with which we are dealing in the development of the child. In particular, we do not know whether the transition from one stage to the next is continous—as in the smooth, steady motion of a planetary system—or whether the transition between stages is abrupt—as in the development of the caterpillar into a pupa and then into a butterfly.

The distinction between smoothly and jumpily developing systems is important. It affects our strategy in selecting stages to examine. At what stages is there enough stability to permit static description? What vocabulary should we use in describing stages? How does the dynamic system make transitions from one stage to the next? Do we wish to describe the transitions or do we wish to describe the mechanisms producing them—for example, the events that have to occur in the environment for a given change to occur in the organism?

We gain hints of how to deal with these problems from the classical dynamic systems of the physical sciences. There, transition is dealt with by *differential equations* or *difference equations*. The equations answer the question, "As a function of what we had at time T_0, what will the system be like at time T_1?" In order to handle matters in this way, we must have T_0, or a way of describing the system at a particular time; and we need a set of differential and contingent rules—that describe the process of change.

In child development we are dealing with a system far more complex than the systems of physics. Our primary need is for an appropriate language, so that we can think clearly about this dynamic system. I have proposed the information-processing language as a good one for this purpose. In the discussion of the child's acquisition of speech, I have indicated why I think it is appropriate.

If we can construct an information-processing system with rules of behavior that lead it to behave like the dynamic system we are trying to describe, then this system is a theory of the child at one stage of development. Having described a particular stage by a program, we would then face the task of discovering what additional information-processing mechanisms are needed to simulate developmental change—the transition from one stage to the next. That is, would need to discover how the system could modify its own structure. Thus, the theory would have two parts—a program to describe performance at a particular stage and a learning program governing the transitions from stage to stage.

I do not want to gloss over the difficulties of this approach. It is not obvious, a priori, that a child is completely describable as an information processing system—that such a theory can deal with affect, for example. Perhaps we would settle for a theory of something less than the whole child—it would be extremely valuable to have a theory of cognitive development even if this did not handle affect well, or at all.

But why try this particular model? The strongest case for it is that it has already been tried for human behavior outside the sphere of child development. It has been quite successful in describing the performance of college sophomores in a limited range of problem-solving tasks and rote learning tasks. At the present time, the model must be judged by examining this experience and by assessing the plausibility of speculations such as the theory of speech acquisition that I have proposed above.

8

COMMENTS AND CONCLUSIONS

It is altogether fitting that a conference designed to discuss the work of Piaget should bring forth the variety of commentary and opinion that marks the foregoing papers. Unlike other scholars of great importance in behavioral science, Piaget has not had a gradual and cumulative impact on his American colleagues. Except for what Flavell has called the "famous five" books headed by *The Language and Thought of the Child,* Piaget's tower of books and articles has fallen almost pell-mell on American psychologists within the last decade. Nor does the pace slacken; the series *Études* alone presents a formidable demand on the investigator who "wants to know about Piaget," and the Genevan corpus, being translated into English at an accelerated pace, has produced quite diverse reactions among American psychologists.

Three loose clusters of opinion about Piaget's work can be detected. The first, and certainly the least likely to survive close enquiry, tends to dismiss Piaget's work with comments on the themes "speculative," "philosophical," and "lacking in proper research method." However relevant such comments may be, the position that Piaget's work can be ignored by conscientious students of child development is untenable. This curious attitude is reminiscent of Pillsbury's remark about psychoanalysis: "It stands as a strange episode in the history of psychology but one that has not been without many beneficial by-products" (Pillsbury, 1929, p. 268). A second attitude toward Piaget is the mirror-image of the first and is made up of equal parts of adulation and awe. Piaget is seen as the cognitive psychologist who has finally produced a viable theoretical alternative to the constrictions of associationism. In the face of his prodigious output (for example, the citations of Piaget in this monograph are drawn from roughly one-third of his full bibliography) and the provocative quality of much of it, the awe at any rate seems justified. The uncritical and all-accepting adulation, however, may be viewed with some reserve, and for the same reason that mars the arguments of Piaget's detractors—incomplete understanding of his work.

The third opinion of the Genevan work is not a synthesis of the first two but a compromise. Beguiled by some of Piaget's observations, irritated or

133

shaken by some of his theoretical postulations, overwhelmed by the reading task required to find the scattered arguments, many American psychologists have set about a critical examination of Piaget's work with the recognition that no simple, and no speedy, conclusions will be forthcoming (in spite of the question from colleagues "What do you think of Piaget?" Compare "What do you think of Freud?" or "What do you think of Skinner?").

During the course of the Dedham conference all three bands of opinion were expressed, though it is clear that the critical and open-minded attitude dominated. The result of the attempt to gain a hold on Piaget's work and to discuss it fruitfully in the course of a long weekend is the variety of commentary that characterizes this report. Piaget's work ranges widely; a serious student can only criticize in depth a small part of it; the variety is inevitable. For all of that, however, there were themes in the meetings and in the papers that formed their centers. In these last pages, the editors will try to bring some of the regularly occurring patterns into sharper focus. To do so will require distortion of the original material, at least by omission and possibly by restatement, but the aim is to suggest a series of enquiries that must be addressed in the pursuit of Piaget.

THE DIVERSITY OF PIAGET'S WORK

It is curious to call Piaget's many-sidedness a common theme of the conference, but the point requires emphasis specific to the Dedham meetings. Inhelder discussed genetic epistemological studies, as did Braine, though he confined himself to the problem of concrete operations; Wohlwill's emphasis was on the two Piagets of perception and thought; Stevenson, and this is the case for Wolff's monograph, was chiefly concerned with Piaget's theory of the (sensory-motor) origins of intelligence. Wohlwill's count of *two* Piagets seems to be an underestimate, and the discussions in Dedham pointed to the need to specify which aspect of the Genevan work is under critique at any moment. It may well be that the several parts of Piaget's work will have different effects on the study of children and different life spans in science.[1] The first question, then, to put to an attempted evaluation of Piaget is "Which Piaget is being evaluated?" It is paradoxical and perhaps uncongenial to Piaget to propose that he does not have a System in the classic sense, inclusive of all cognitive development, but rather, like most theorists, he has presented a map of a large country in which some areas are drawn with meticulous detail but there are as well great stretches of unknown territory and, if we may press the metaphor, the theory is often without clear roads from one well-mapped spot to another.

---

[1] Several of the ideas presented in these terminal notes derive from unpublished remarks by Flavell. He feels, on the point of scientific longevity, that Piaget's empiricodescriptive work will long outlast his treatment of genetic epistemology.

The "Projective Character" of Piaget's Constructs

It has been suggested, humorously but with serious implication, that the notions of "assimilation" and "accommodation" are projective devices, putting a demand on the reader to interpret them in terms of his own prejudices or to "translate" them into a better-comprehended theory. For reasons that are not unrelated to the diversity of Piaget's work remarked earlier, this "translation" can be made into almost any system of theoretical prejudices currently available in psychology. Several consequences of the ink-blot status of Piaget's postulations can be dimly detected even this early in the American renascence of interest in his writings. First, the attempted translations are often hasty and, thus far, always partial—hasty in that the implications of Piaget's theories are not worked over *in their own terms* before the translation is tried and partial in that only a segment of the available speculative sentences are attacked.[2] The apparent ubiquity of "assimilation," "accommodation," and "egocentricity" in Piaget's writings have made them the favorite targets of reformulation ("equilibration" is certain to join the group shortly), and it should be a matter of some concern among psychologists (the Piagetians in particular) that the constructs can be fit with more or less equivalent ease to the frames of Gestalttheorie, psychoanalysis, and S–R behavior theory. Again, it suggests that Piaget lacks a systematic, economical, and precise statement of his theory or theories— a statement that would permit a better evaluation of the several attempts at translation and incidentally of the theories themselves.

A second, less weighty, consequence of the ease with which Piaget's constructs can be appropriated to other positions is the development of something like a *mystique* of Essential Incomprehensibility. The chief propositions of this position can be stated with only slight exaggeration as "Nobody *really* understands Piaget" and "Let me tell you what I think he's saying, using my own words." It is probable that this aspect of Piaget's projective status indicates a general recognition of the importance of his speculations and, as well, the vague and scattered character of his writing style. It is also the attitude from which cults spring, and one of the reassuring by-products of the Dedham meetings was the absence of evidence that there is gathering around Piaget anything like the clouds of obscuring veneration that have shrouded Freud.

The projective character of Piaget's theoretical speculations will be likely to dissolve with recognition of the need first to understand what he is attempting within his own conceptual language and only then to attempt a

---

[2] Wolff's monograph (1960) is an exception to this general statement in that his study is truly comparative rather than translational, and Stevenson has attempted a more modest and reasonable goal than translation—the modification of an alternative theory to deal with some of Piaget's *observations*.

parallel formulation in the language of alternative theories. Inhelder's paper in this monograph is perhaps the best short fulfillment of the first requirement available; meeting the second will demand patience and ingenuity from child psychologists.

Problems of Stage and Problems of Transition

The first words spoken in discussion at Dedham had to do with a problem that never left the table—the problem of stating rules that govern the transition from one point or stage of development to another. Preoccupation with questions of this order is comprehensible if one remembers that that they are but specific statements of the most general problem of all, i.e., what is a proper theory of development? A clear division among the participants in the conference could be seen an the question of "stage." Those with an adherence to behavior-theory explanations, or even to a less demanding functional view of psychology, placed their emphasis in discussing developmental theory on rules of transition, on the process of getting from one condition to another, under the overriding premise that any treatment of "level" or "stage" was a shorthand and somewhat inaccurate index of a *point* or value of a function. On the other hand, there were several members of the group who held that the notion of stage was an essential characteristic of developmental theory; that, to put the argument briefly, transition had to be *from somewhere to somewhere*. It is of some interest that the two papers that treated of computer simulation, Simon's and Kessen's, mentioned specific analogs for the notion of "stage," suggesting that—rightly used or not— the construct is more than a way of speaking loosely. Although it is doubtful that those on either side were convinced of their error, it may be hoped that the problem of "stage" was clarified somewhat by the statement of questions to the two schools of thought. To the "pure transitionists," the central questions seemed to be, "How do you account for the apparent tendency for developmental changes (particularly cognitive changes) to take place over rather wide bands of behavior (as in the occurrence of reversibility)?" and "Do the transition rules not vary according to the character of the behavior on which they operate (i.e., according to the level of development)?" To the fanciers of the "stage" notion could be put the questions, "On what basis do you assign a particular response or class of responses to a particular stage?" and, relatedly, "What are the explicit criteria which determine the beginning, culmination, and termination of a stage or substage?"

On the other side of this area of enquiry—the problem of transition rules —many were proposed and none was chosen. "Maturation," "reinforcement," "equilibration," and "conflict" were explicitly discussed but without achievement of conviction about the precise conditions of their application to development. The interest of the conference expectedly turned to Piaget's proposals about equilibration, and rather spirited discussion failed to provide a specification of the notion adequate to serious critique. Readers who have the sense of unease about this proposed transition rule for development that was felt by several of the participants in the conference will want to see Piaget's extended treatment of the issue in the last volume of *Discussions on Child Development* (Tanner and Inhelder, 1960).

The paper by Stevenson and the notes by Berlyne in this monograph represent serious attempts to modify current S–R reinforcement theory to encompass developmental transitions in a way satisfactory to the facts. Even though their suggestions were recognized to be programmatic, there was some doubt expressed in discussion that the metatheory of stimulus-response associationism could deal with major issues of cognitive development, in part, because of the failure of associationism to deal with the notion of "structure" and, in part, because of the dependence on *reaction* as the central theoretical account of the child's response. On this last point, Inhelder in particular emphasized the difference between a theoretical attitude that sees the child as reactive and a theoretical attitude that sees the child as active. Although this disagreement did not receive in Dedham the attention it warranted, in retrospect it can be seen at the heart of several exchanges. The problem appears to have some immediate empirical implications—e.g., can one in fact detect the stimuli which are required by the reactionist position to get the child in motion in a particular direction—but far more the disagreement is at the metatheoretical level. It is a question of the kind of operating characteristics one will assign to the child or the kind of model of the child one chooses. Note, in this regard, that Simon's position is basically of the actionist stamp; once the computer is turned on, it runs, doing what it is programmed to do. The editors feel that this confrontation of opposing theoretical prejudices deserves close study and with particular attention to its relevance to theories of development.

There is one last issue under the cluster "transition and stage" or "What is a proper theory of development?"—the definition of the response. Raised in an abstract way by Kessen, the question was given flesh in several particulars. Brown presented a number of examples from language learning to indicate that a geographical or topographical delineation of response seems inadequate. Braine addressed the issue of variation in conclusions about cognitive development as related to the experimenter's use of verbal or non-verbal response criteria. Braine's paper, too, deals with a research problem at the crux of the difference between topographical and categorical modes of responding—the learning of classification. For Wohlwill and Simon, concerned more with the categories of perception and thought than with the shape of the indicator response, the problem of response definition can hardly be phrased in the usual way. On the contrary, their ability to treat of cognitive functions meaningfully without having to care overmuch about the specific shape of the output is an indication of the conceptual distance separating the several approaches to cognitive development represented at the conference.

The Relation between Process and Content

Piaget's work can be used as an anchor in the discrimination of a common characteristic of contemporary psychology—the gap between the abstract description of process and the concrete details of behavior. If we accept the evidence of his theoretical writing—notably in the first chapter of *The Origins of Intelligence*, the last chapter of *The Construction of Reality*, and all of *Logic and Psychology*, Piaget's conceptual goal is the statement of a theory of development (one may even say "of organic change") that will be relevant to biological as well as psychological phenomena, that will have implications for the construction of logic and of science, and ultimately that will be the framework for a rapprochement between psychology and philosophy. This is the setting and, considering the immensity of the proposal, it is remarkably well worked out in some aspects. But in front of this speculative construction appear particular children bent on the solution of very particular problems. What is striking in Piaget is not this disjunction—it is the rule in American psychology—but the facts that his particular observations are of great interest in their own right and that his theories stretch so far beyond the observations. There are not only two or more Piagets horizontally; there are at least two Piagets vertically—the one who tells us exciting new things about children, observations that can be duplicated in the laboratory, and the other Piaget who uses these observations in illustration of his systematic views of science at large and philosophy. Note the word "illustration." There is little evidence that Piaget is particularly interested in the hypotheticodeductive scheme with its routinely justifiable implications or that he is following a systematic inductive strategy in moving from the observations to the theory.[3] Rather, one may suggest that Piaget has built a normative theory of cognitive development which borders on classical epistemology; empirical evidence is relevant to it, but not decisive in any prescribable methodological sense. Instead, the observations of children can be seen as illustrations—or more bluntly, as demonstrations—of the appropriateness of his *Erkenntnistheorie*. For the greater number of American psychologists, the result has seemed to consist in a weak empirical base—e.g., the absence of standardization, the dependence on small numbers, and so on—and too flighty and elaborated a speculative superstructure. Piaget has not fallen between two stools in this view, but, with remarkable agility, on the far side of both. Inhelder's paper is a refreshing demonstra-

---

[3] This failure by Piaget to adopt either a "purely empirical" strategy or a strictly deductive one may account in part for the alien flavor of his work for American psychologists.

tion that the Genevan group is moving toward a more usual appreciation of the relation of data and theory and doing so without losing the power and breadth of Piaget's postulations.

Though the distinction between process and content can be seen in a somewhat exaggerated form in Piaget's work, it is, as noted, characteristic of other psychologists and important in an understanding of the Dedham proceedings. All of the papers which cited empirical findings or discussed specifically testable propositions—Inhelder's, Braine's, Wohlwill's, and Stevenson's—advanced different views of process and applied the proposals to different specific contents. If they are held to be general theories of cognitive development (even though the authors may not intend such generality), then it may be assumed that each process-explanation might appropriately be applied to every area of content. An intriguing exercise for the reader, and one likely to be rewarding as well, is to act as collative theorist, by applying one or another of the proposed explanatory schemes to someone else's empirical problem. But this is not the way of explanations. The description of process is, at some boundaries, constrained by the particular observations to be accounted for. The need is not for a statement of whether or not this is a "general" theory, but rather for a statement of the conditions of its application. American psychologists have shown a dialectical aversion to the notion that a number of theories—even contradictory ones—may be necessary to encompass the variety of empirical observations; but from examination of the foregoing papers, restricted as they are to a fraction of human behavior, it is difficult to escape the conclusion that, like it or not, psychological theories will be multiple and of partial truth. It goes without saying that a corresponding flexibility will be required in the choice of research methods for the study of cognitive development.

The Place of Piaget in Child Psychology

It is certainly too early to assess the ultimate impact of Piaget's work on the study of children, if only because that work is continuing and continually in modification. Nonetheless, there are clearly at least three ways in which his investigations have already changed the shape of child psychology. These are the obvious dimensions of impact—new observations, provoking theorizing, and a communication of attitude—but a brief rehearsal of them will summarize the gains of the Dedham meetings.

Forty years have passed since Piaget reported his first observations of the way in which children construct the world. Since that time, he has added to our knowledge more facts about cognitive development than any other investigator. Many of his observations have been called into question, with doubts expressed about the precision of his dating, the tendency to blink individual variation, and the casual attitude to normal research procedures. But when all the disclaimers and reservations are in, it remains the case that the Geneva school has told us more about the child's knowledge of the physical world than any other researcher or school. Putting aside for the moment Piaget's interpretations of his and his colleague's observations, child psychologists who propose general or comprehensive postulations to deal with the facts of children's behavior must take into account the enormous *empirical* literature which Piaget has contributed.

The place of his speculative or theoretical proposals is much more difficult to assess, save in the trivial way that, like all theoretical proposals, they will be supplanted. The obvious requirement for a more comprehensive and detailed critique than has been possible heretofore is a statement of theory—e.g., of equilibration or adaptation—satisfactory to Piaget and containing enough specificity to permit the making of discriminating predictions. One prophecy the editors are willing to make about Piaget's speculations: they will have in time a shattering impact on the development of philosophy. Unless all signs are amiss, Piaget is the chief bandit in the theft of epistemology from normative philosophical treatment and its transmutation into a psychological specialty. The implications of this transfer are too distant in time and too far from the present course of American psychology to be readily stated, but the development of a truly empirical approach to theory of human knowledge will owe an incalculable debt to Piaget.

The final contribution from Geneva that made itself clearly felt in Dedham is the communication of an attitude toward research and an attitude toward children which are substantially novel. Flavell has expressed this effect in the following way: "A child psychologist who has thoroughly assimilated Piaget's theoretical writings on intellectual development is likely to find himself looking at his own research problems and formulating his own theoretical explanations in ways somewhat different—the differences are never easy to specify—from those he would have used had the assimilation not taken place." The conference in Dedham probably represents a fair sample of what happens when a serious and intense attempt is made to comprehend Piaget's work; no one who was there is likely ever again to study cognitive development without reference, however modified by his own predilections, to the Genevan researches and theories.

REFERENCES

In referring to the works of Bärbel Inhelder and Jean Piaget, we have attempted to cite the first French edition and a recent American or English edition in preference to listing later French editions and the several American and English editions.

AEBLI, H. *Didactique psychologique; application à la didactique de la psychologie de Jean Piaget.* Neuchâtel: Delachaux et Niestlé, 1951.

ANTHONY, E. J. Six applications de la théorie génétique de Piaget à la théorie et à la pratique psychodynamique. *Schweiz. Z. Psychol. Anwend.,* 1956, 15, 269-277. (a)

ANTHONY, E. J. The significance of Jean Piaget for child psychiatry. *Brit. J. Med. Psychol.,* 1956, 29, 20-34. (b)

ANTHONY, E. J. The system makers: Piaget and Freud. *Brit. J. med. Psychol.,* 1957, 30, 255-269.

APOSTEL, L. Logique et apprentissage. In L. Apostel *et al., Logique, apprentissage, et probabilité* (Études d'epistémologie génétique, 8). Paris: Presses Univer. de France, 1959. Pp. 1-138.

ATTNEAVE, F. Some informational aspects of visual perception. *Psychol. Rev.,* 1954, 61, 183-193.

BERKO, J. The child's learning of English morphology. *Word,* 1958, 14, 150-177.

BERLYNE, D. E. Recent developments in Piaget's work. *Brit. J. educ. Psychol.,* 1957, 27, 1-12.

BERLYNE, D. E. Les équivalences psychologiques et les notions quantitatives. In D. E. Berlyne & J. Piaget, *Théorie du comportement et théorie des opérations* (Études d'epistémologie génétique, 12). Paris: Presses Univer. de France, 1960. Pp. 1-76.

BOOLE, G. *An investigation of the laws of thought.* [Reprint, Dover, 1951]

BRAINE, M. D. S. The ontogeny of certain logical operations: Piaget's formulation examined by nonverbal methods. *Psychol. Monogr.,* 1959, 73, No. 5 (Whole No. 475).

BROWN, R., & FRASER, C. The acquisition of syntax. Mimeographed paper, 1961.

BRUNER, J. S. On perceptual readiness. *Psychol. Rev.,* 1957, 64, 123-152.

BRUNER, J. S., GOODNOW, J., & AUSTIN, G. A. *A study of thinking.* Wiley, 1956.

BRUNSWIK, E. *Perception and the representative design of psychological experiments.* (2nd Ed.) Univer. of California Press, 1956.

CARMICHAEL, L. (Ed.) *Manual of child psychology.* (2nd Ed.) Wiley, 1954.

CARNAP, R. Foundations of logic and mathematics. *Int. Encycl. unified Sci.,* 1939, 1, No. 3. Univer. of Chicago Press.

CARNAP, R. The methodological character of theoretical concepts. In H. Feigl & M. Scriven (Eds.), *Minnesota studies in the philosophy of science.* Vol. 1. Univer. of Minnesota Press, 1956.

CHOMSKY, N. *Syntactic structures.* The Hague: Mouton, 1957.

DAVIDON, R. S. The effects of symbols, shift, and manipulation upon the number of concepts attained. *J. exp. Psychol.,* 1952, 44, 70-79.

DOLLARD, J., & MILLER, N. E. *Personality and psychotherapy.* McGraw-Hill, 1950.

ERIKSON, E. H. *Childhood and society.* Norton, 1950.

FATEHCHAND, R. Machine recognition of spoken words. In F. L. Alt *et al.* (Eds.), *Advances in computers.* Academic Press, 1960. Pp. 193-229.

FLOOD, M. M. Game learning theory and some decision-making experiments. In R. M. Thrall *et al.* (Eds.), *Decision processes.* Wiley, 1954. Pp. 139-158.

FORGIE, J. W., & FORGIE, C. D. Results obtained from a vowel recognition computer program. *J. acoust. Soc. Amer.,* 1959, 31, 1480-1489.

GELERNTER, H., & ROCHESTER, N. Intelligent behavior in problem-solving machines. *IBM J. Res. Develpm.,* 1958, 2, 336-345.

GOLDSTEIN, K., & SCHEERER, M. Abstract and concrete behavior; an experimental study with special tests. *Psychol. Monogr.,* 1941, 53, No. 2 (Whole No. 239).

GOLLIN, E. S. Some research problems for developmental psychology. *Child Develpm.,* 1956, 27, 223-235.

GOLLIN, E. S. Organizational characteristics of social judgment: a developmental investigation. *J. Pers.,* 1958, 26, 139-154.

HARLOW, H. F. The formation of learning sets. *Psychol. Rev.,* 1949, 56, 51-65.

HARLOW, H. F. The development of learning in the rhesus monkey. *Amer. Scient.,* 1959, 47, 459-479.

HARRIS, D. B. (Ed.) *The concept of development; an issue in the study of human behavior.* Univer. of Minnesota Press, 1957.

HEINICKE, C. M. Some effects of separating two-year-old children from their mothers—a comparative study. *Hum. Relat.,* 1956, 9, 102-176.

HILLER, L.A., JR., & ISAACSON, L. M. *Experimental music.* McGraw-Hill, 1959.

HOFSTAETTER, P. R. The changing composition of "intelligence": a study in T-technique. *J. genet. Psychol.,* 1954, 85, 159-164.

HOVLAND, C. I., & HUNT, E. B. Computer simulation of concept attainment. *Behavioral Sci.,* 1960, 5, 265-267.

HULL, C. L. Knowledge and purpose as habit mechanisms. *Psychol. Rev.,* 1930, 37, 511-525.

HULL, C. L. *Principles of behavior.* Appleton-Century-Crofts, 1943.

INHELDER, B. Observations sur le principe de conservation dans la physique de l'enfant. *Cah. Pédag. exp. Psychol. Enfant.,* 1936, No. 9, pp. 16.

INHELDER, B. *Le diagnostic du raisonnement chez les débiles mentaux.* Neuchâtel: Delachaux et Niestlé, 1943.

INHELDER, B. Some aspects of Piaget's genetic approach to cognition. This MONOGRAPH, pp. 19-34.

INHELDER, B., & PIAGET, J. De la logique de l'enfant à logique de l'adolescent. Paris: Presses Univer. de France, 1955. [*The growth of logical thinking from childhood to adolescence.* Basic Books, 1958.]

INHELDER, B., & PIAGET, J. *La genèse des structures logiques eléméntaires; classification et sériations.* Neuchâtel: Delachaux and Niestlé, 1959.

JERSILD, A. T. *Child psychology.* (4th Ed.) Prentice-Hall, 1954.

JERSILD, A. T. *The psychology of adolescence.* Macmillan, 1957.

KENDLER, H. H., & KENDLER, T. S. Inferential behavior in preschool children. *J. exp. Psychol.,* 1956, 51, 311-314.

KOCH, S. (Ed.) *Psychology: A study of a science.* Vol. 3. *Formulations of the person and the social context.* McGraw-Hill, 1959.

KOFFKA, K. *The growth of the mind.* Harcourt, Brace, 1924.

KÖHLER, W. *The mentality of apes.* Routledge, Kegan Paul, 1925.

KRAFFT, H., & PIAGET, J. La notion de l'ordre des événements et le test des images en désordre. *Arch. Psychol.,* Genève, 1926, 19, 306-349.

LAVOIE, G. Contribution à l'étude des relations entre la perception et l'intelligence. Unpublished L. Ps. Thesis, Université de Montreal, 1961.

LEVINE, M. A. A model of hypothesis behavior in discrimination learning set. *Psychol. Rev.,* 1959, 66, 353-366.

LIBERMAN, A. M., *et al.* Minimal rules for synthesizing speech. *J. acoust. Soc. Amer.,* 1959, 31, 1490-1499.

LONG, L., & WELCH, L. The development of the ability to discriminate and match numbers. *J. genet. Psychol.*, 1941, 59, 377-387.

MALTZMAN, I. Thinking: from a behavioristic point of view. *Psychol. Rev.*, 1955, 62, 272-286.

MARGAIRAZ, E. & PIAGET, J. La structure des récits et l'interprétation des images de Dawid chez l'enfant. *Arch. Psychol., Genève*, 1925, 19, 211-239.

MILLER, G. A. *Language and communication*. McGraw-Hill, 1951. (a)

MILLER, G. A. Speech and language. In S. S. Stevens (Ed.), *Handbook of experimental psychology*. Wiley, 1951, Pp. 789-810. (b)

MILLER, G. A., GALANTER, E., & PRIBRAM, K. *Plans and the structure of behavior*. Holt, 1960.

MINSKY, M. Steps toward artificial intelligence. *Proc. Inst. Radio Engrs.*, 1961, 49, 8-30.

MUNN, N. L. *The evolution and growth of human behavior*. Houghton Mifflin, 1955.

NEWELL, A., SHAW, J. C., & SIMON, H. A. The process of creative thinking. Paper read at a Symposium on Creativity, University of Colorado, May, 1958. [The RAND Corp., 1958, pp. 1320.]

NEWELL, A., SHAW, J. C., & SIMON, H. A. Report on a general problem-solving program. In *On information processing*. Paris: UNESCO, 1960. Pp. 256-264. (a)

NEWELL, A., SHAW, J. C., & SIMON, H. A. A variety of intelligent behavior in a General Problem Solver. In M. C. Yovits & S. Cameron (Eds.), *Self-organizing systems*. Permagon Press, 1960. Pp. 153-187. (b)

NEWELL, A., & SIMON, H. A. The simulation of human thought. In W. Dennis (Ed.), *Current trends in psychological theory*. Univer. of Pittsburgh Press, 1961.

ODIER, C. *Anxiety and magical thinking*. International Universities Press, 1956.

OSGOOD, C. E. *Method and theory in experimental psychology*. Oxford Univer. Press, 1953.

PIAGET, J. *Recherche*. Lausanne: Édition La Concorde, 1918.

PIAGET, J. Essai sur quelques aspects du développement de la notion de partie chez l'enfant. *J. Psychol. norm. path.*, 1921, 18, 449-480. (a)

PIAGET, J. Une forme verbale de la comparaison chez l'enfant. *Arch. Psychol., Genève*, 1921, 18, 141-172. (b)

PIAGET, J. Essai sur la multiplication logique et les débuts de la pensée formelle chez l'enfant. *J. Psychol. norm. path.*, 1922, 19, 222-261.

PIAGET, J. La pensée symbolique et la pensée de l'enfant. *Arch. Psychol., Genève*, 1923, 18, 273-304.

PIAGET, J. Étude critique: "L'expérience humaine et la causalité physique" de L. Brunschvicg. *J. Psychol. norm. path.*, 1924, 21, 586-607. (a)

PIAGET, J. *Le jugement et le raisonnement chez l'enfant*. Neuchâtel: Delachaux et Niestlé, 1924. [*Judgment and reasoning in the child*. Humanities Press, 1952.] (b)

PIAGET, J. *Le langage et la pensée chez l'enfant*. Neuchâtel: Delachaux et Niestlé, 1924. [*The language and thought of the child*. Humanities Press, 1959. Trans. from 3rd French Ed.] (c)

PIAGET, J. Les traits principaux de la logique de l'enfant. *J. Psychol. norm. path.*, 1924, 21, 48-101. (d)

PIAGET, J. De quelques formes primitives de causalité chez l'enfant. *Ann. psychol.*, 1925, 26, 31-71.

PIAGET, J. *La représentation du monde chez l'enfant*. Paris: Alcan, 1926. [*The child's conception of the world*. Humanities Press, 1951.]

PIAGET, J. La causalité chez l'enfant. *Brit. J. Psychol.*, 1927, 18, 276-301. (a)

PIAGET, J. *La causalité physique chez l'enfant*. Paris: Alcan, 1927. [*The child's conception of physical causality*. Littlefield, 1960.] (b)

PIAGET, J. La première année de l'enfant. *Brit. J. Psychol.*, 1927, 18, 97-120. (c)

PIAGET, J. Les deux directions de la pensée scientifique. *Arch. Sci. phys. nat.*, 1929, 11, 145-162. (a)

PIAGET, J. Le parallélisme entre la logique et la morale chez l'enfant. *Proc. 9th Int. Congr. Psychol.*, 1929, 339-340. (b)

PIAGET, J. Children's philosophies. In C. Murchison (Ed.), *Handbook of child psychology.* Clark Univer. Press, 1931. Pp. 377-391.

PIAGET, J. *Le jugement moral chez l'enfant.* Paris: Alcan, 1932. [*The moral judgment of the child.* Free Press, 1948.]

PIAGET, J. *La naissance de l'intelligence chez l'enfant.* Neuchâtel: Delachaux et Niestlé, 1936. [*The origin of intelligence in the child.* International Universities Press, 1952.]

PIAGET, J. *La construction du réel chez l'enfant.* Neuchâtel: Delachaux et Niestlé, 1937. [*The construction of reality in the child.* Basic Books, 1954.] (a)

PIAGET, J. Le problème de l'intelligence et de l'habitude: Réflexe conditionné, "Gestalt" ou assimilation. *Proc. 11th Int. Congr. Psychol.*, 1937, 170-183. (b)

PIAGET, J. Les relations d'égalité résultant de l'addition et de la soustraction logique constituent-elles un groupe? *L'enseign. math.*, 1937, 36, 99-108.

PIAGET, J. Remarques psychologiques sur les relations entre la classe logique et le nombre et sur les rapports d'inclusion. *Recueil travaux Univer. Lausanne*, 1937, 59-85. (d)

PIAGET, J. La réversibilité des opérations et l'importance de la notion de "group" pour la psychologie de la pensée. *Proc. 11the Int. Congr. Psychol.*, 1937, 433-434. (e)

PIAGET, J. *Classes, relations et nombres; essai sur les groupements de la logistique et sur la réversibilité de la pensée.* Paris: Vrin, 1942.

PIAGET, J. *La formation du symbole chez l'enfant.* Neuchâtel: Delachaux et Niestlé, 1945. [*Play, dreams, and imitation in childhood.* Norton, 1951.]

PIAGET, J. *Le développement de la notion de temps chez l'enfant.* Paris: Presses Univer. de France, 1946. (a)

PIAGET, J. *Les notions de mouvement et de vitesse chez l'enfant.* Paris: Presses Univer. de France, 1946. (b)

PIAGET, J. *La psychologie de l'intelligence.* Paris: Presses Univer. de France, 1946. [*The psychology of intelligence.* Routledge, Kegan Paul, 1950. Trans. from 2nd French Ed.] (c)

PIAGET, J. Du rapport des sciences avec la philosophie. *Synthese*, 1947, 6, 130-150.

PIAGET, J. Le problème neurologigue de l'intériorisation des actions en opérations réversibles. *Arch. Psychol.*, Genève, 1949, 32, 241-258. (a)

PIAGET, J. *Traité de logique.* Paris: Colin, 1949. (b)

PIAGET, J. *Introduction à l'epistémologie génétique.* Paris: Presses Univer. de France, 1950.

PIAGET, J. The right to education in the modern world. In UNESCO, *Freedom and culture.* Columbia Univer. Press, 1951. Pp. 67-116.

PIAGET, J. Autobiography. In E. G. Boring *et al.*, *History of psychology in autobiography.* Vol. 4. Clark Univer. Press, 1952. Pp. 237-256. (a)

PIAGET, J. *Essai sur les transformations des opérations logiques.* Paris: Presses Univer. de France, 1952. (b)

PIAGET, J. *Logic and psychology.* Manchester: Manchester Univer. Press, 1953. [Also Basic Books, 1957.]

PIAGET, J. Ce qui subsiste de la théorie de la Gestalt dans la psychologie contemporaine de l'intelligence et de la perception. *Schweiz. Z. Psychol. Anwend.*, 1954, 13, 72-83. [Also in J. de Ajuriaguerra *et al.*, *Aktuelle Probleme der Gestalttheorie.* Bern: Hans Huber, 1954. Pp. 72-83.]

PIAGET, J. Essai d'une nouvelle interprétation probabiliste des effets de centration, de la loi de Weber et de celle des centrations relatives. *Arch. Psychol.*, Genève, 1955, 35, 1-24. (a)

PIAGET, J. Rapport. In A. Michotte *et al.*, *La perception.* Paris: Presses Univer. de France, 1955. Pp. 17-30. (b)

PIAGET, J. La genèse du nombre chez l'enfant. In J. Piaget *et al.*, *Initiation au calcul.* Paris: Bourrelier, 1956. Pp. 5-28. (a)

PIAGET, J. Les stades du développement intellectual de l'enfant et de l'adolescent. In P. Osterrieth *et al.*, *Le probleme des stades en psychologie de l'enfant.* Paris: Presses Univer. de France, 1956. Pp. 33-49. (b)

PIAGET, J. (Gen. Ed.) *Études d'epistémologie génétique.* Paris: Presses Univer. de France, 1957, *et seq.* (a)

PIAGET, J. Logique et équilibre dans les comportements du sujet. In L. Apostel *et al.*, *Logique et équilibre* (Études d'epistémologie génétique, 2), Paris: Presses Univer. de France, 1957. Pp. 27-117. (b)

PIAGET, J. Les relations entre la perception et l'intelligence dans le développement de l'enfant. *Bull. Psychol., Paris,* 1957, 10, 376-381, 751-760. (c)

PIAGET, J. Apprentissage et connaissance. In M. Goustard *et al.*, *La logique des apprentissages* (Études d'epistémologie génétique, 10). Paris: Presses Univer. de France, 1959. Pp. 159-188. (a)

PIAGET, J. L'image mentale et la représentation imagée chez l'enfant. *Bull. Psychol., Paris,* 1959, 12, 538-540, 574-576, 724-727, 806-807, 857-860. (b)

PIAGET, J. *Le développement des perceptions.* Paris: Presses Univer. de France, 1960.

PIAGET, J., & INHELDER, B. *Le développement des quantités chez l'enfant.* Neuchâtel: Delachaux et Niestlé, 1941.

PIAGET, J., & INHELDER, B. *La représentation de l'espace chez l'enfant.* Paris: Presses Univer. de France, 1948. [*The child's conception of space.* Humanities Press, 1956.]

PIAGET, J., & INHELDER, B. *La genèse de l'idée de hasard chez l'enfant.* Paris: Presses Univer. de France, 1951.

PIAGET, J., INHELDER, B., & SZEMINSKA, A. *La géométrie spontanée chez l'enfant.* Paris: Presses Univer. de France, 1948. [*The child's conception of geometry.* Basic Books, 1960.]

PIAGET, J., & LAMBERCIER, M. Transpositions perceptives et transitivité opératoire dans les comparaisons en profondeur. *Arch. Psychol., Genève,* 1946, 31, 325-368.

PIAGET, J., & MORF, A. Les isomorphismes partiels entre les structures logiques et les structures perceptives. In J. S. Bruner *et al.*, *Logique et perception* (Études d'epistémologie génétique, 6). Paris: Presses Univer. de France, 1958. Pp. 49-116. (a)

PIAGET, J., & MORF, A. Les préinférences perceptives et leurs relations avec les schèmes sensorimoteurs et opératoires. In J. S. Bruner *et al.*, *Logique et perception* (Études d'epistémologie génétique, 6). Paris: Presses Univer. de France, 1958. Pp. 117-155. (b)

PIAGET, J., & ROSSELLÒ, P. Note sur les types de description d'images chez l'enfant. *Arch. Psychol., Genève,* 1921, 18, 208-234.

PIAGET, J., & SZEMINSKA, A. Quelques expériences sur la conservation des quantités continués chez l'enfant. *J. Psychol. norm. path.,* 1939, 36, 36-64.

PIAGET, J., & SZEMINSKA, A. *La genèse du nombre chez l'enfant.* Neuchâtel: Delachaux et Niestlé, 1941. [*The child's conception of number.* Routledge, Kegan Paul, 1952.]

PIAGET, J., & TAPONIER, S. L'estimation des longuers de deux droites horizontales et parallèles extrémités décalées. *Arch. Psychol., Genève,* 1956, 35, 369-400.

PIAGET, J., VINH-BANG, & MATALON, B. Note on the law of the temporal maximum of some optico-geometric illusions. *Amer. J. Psychol.,* 1958, 71, 277-282.

PIAGET, J., VON ALBERTINI, B., & ROSSI, M. Essai d'interprétation probabiliste de la loi de Weber et de celle des centrations relatives. *Arch. Psychol., Genève,* 1944, 30, 95-138.

QUINE, W. V. *Mathematical logic.* (Rev. Ed.) Harvard Univer. Press, 1951.

QUINE, W. V. *From a logical point of view.* Harvard Univer. Press, 1953.

QUINE, W. V. *Word and object.* Technology Press & Wiley, 1960.

ROBINSON, J. S. The sameness-difference discrimination problem in chimpanzee. *J. comp. physiol. Psychol.,* 1955, 48, 195-197.

SCHOOLEY, M., & HARTMANN, G. W. The role of insight in the learning of logical relations. *Amer. J. Psychol.,* 1937, 49, 287-292.

SIMON, H. A., & NEWELL, A. Computer simulation of human thinking and problem solving. In M. Greenberger (Ed.), *Management and the computer of the future.* Technology Press & Wiley, 1962. [Also this MONOGRAPH, pp. 137-150.]

SMEDSLUND, J. Learning and equilibration: a study of the acquisition of concrete logical structures. Pre-publication draft, Oslo, 1959.

STEPHENSON, W. Philosophy or statistics? A review of F. V. Smith, *Explanation of human behavior. Contemp. Psychol.*, 1961, 6, 46-47.

SZEMINSKA, A. Essai d'analyse psychologique du raisonnement mathématique. *Cah. Pédag. exp. Psychol. Enfant*, 1935, No. 7, Pp. 18.

TANNER, J. M., & INHELDER, B. *Discussions on child development.* Vol. 1. London: Tavistock Publications, 1956.

TANNER, J. M., & INHELDER, B. *Discussions on child development.* Vol. 4. London: Tavistock Publications, 1960.

VURPILLOT, E. Piaget's law of relative centrations. *Acta Psychol.*, 1959, 16, 403-430.

VURPILLOT, E. Étude génétique sur la formation d'un concept; role données perceptives. *Psychol. Franc.*, 1960, 5, 135-152.

WERNER, H. *Comparative psychology of mental developme.it.* (Rev. Ed.). International Universities Press, 1957.

WERTHEIMER, M. *Productive thinking.* (Enlarged Ed.) Harper, 1959.

WOHLWILL, J. G. Developmental studies of perception. *Psychol. Bull.*, 1960, 57, 249-288.

WOLFF, P. H. The developmental psychologies of Jean Piaget and psychoanalysis. *Psychol. Issues*, 1960, 2, No. 1 (Monogr. 5).

ZIGLER, E. Rigidity in the feebleminded. In E. P. Trapp & P. Himelstein (Eds.), *Research findings on the exceptional child.* Appleton-Century-Crofts, 1962.

II

BASIC COGNITIVE PROCESSES IN CHILDREN

Report of the Second Conference
Sponsored by the Committee
on Intellective Processes Research
of the Social Science Research Council

EDITED BY

JOHN C. WRIGHT
JEROME KAGAN

1

DEVELOPMENT OF PERCEPTION: DISCRIMINATION OF DEPTH COMPARED WITH DISCRIMINATION OF GRAPHIC SYMBOLS

ELEANOR J. GIBSON
Cornell University

The invitation to speak to this Conference on my work in the field of perceptual development came at a most welcome moment for me. For the past six years I have worked, with several colleagues, on developmental aspects of two radically different kinds of perception—the perception of *depth* and the perception of outline forms inscribed on a piece of paper—that is, *letters* and *words*. Here was the opportunity to compare the two and, hopefully, to synthesize them.

Interest in the development of perception (especially space perception) goes back as far as the philosophical beginnings of psychology. The empiricism of the British philosophers and the nativism of the Germans have always formed the core of courses in the history of psychology. Everyone takes a position in the controversy, usually on the side of empiricism in this country. Textbooks of child psychology reflect this fact; here is a typical quotation from a well-known one, Goodenough's *Developmental Psychology*: "Very early in life and without being aware that we are doing so, we learn to interpret this (binocular) difference in visual sensations in terms of tactual and muscular sensations we get from handling objects. . . . When we say the tree trunk *looks* rounded we mean only that the visual sensation has the qualities that from infancy on we have learned to associate with objects that *feel rounded*" (1934, p. 138). The current enthusiasm for experiments on "early experience" confirms the continued presence of the empiricist's bias.

On the other hand, we can find statements exhibiting the opposite bias, such as Pastore's that "All the significant aspects of perceiving are unlearned. These include pattern and depth perceptions, the so-called laws of organization, figure-ground relationship, solidity, the illusions, the constancies, the phi phenomenon, figural after-effects, and the perception of the world as upright" (1960, p. 93).

A recent criticism has been that the division of behavior into "innate" and "acquired" is an artificial dichotomy. Hebb, for instance, has said "I

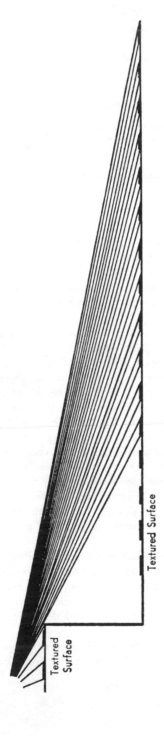

Textured Surface

Textured Surface

FIGURE 1—Schematic representation of the visual cliff.

urge that there are not two kinds of control of behavior and that the term 'instinct' implying a mechanism or neural process independent of environmental factors, and distinct from the processes into which learning enters, is a misleading term and should be abandoned" (1953, p. 46).

The dismissal of the problem as false is not very satisfying. It is too easy to find cases of behavior which seem primarily learned or primarily unlearned. There may even be mechanisms "different from the processes into which learning enters." A more appealing approach is to study the ontogenetic process, asking how learned and unlearned processes develop and interact.

We have at present many methods available for the study of perceptual development. The developmental testing program that characterized the early stages of child psychology in this country can be supplemented by comparative studies with different animal species and by controlled experiments. Experimental methods include control of early environment (the deprivation experiment and the enrichment technique); perceptual learning experiments such as Kohler's with distorting lenses; or others providing controlled practice under more normal conditions (our own scribble experiment). Besides these, there is the procedure of logical analysis with inference of what "must have" happened, and experimental test of the inference. This latter procedure may seem roundabout, but some very impressive work of this kind can be cited (for instance, that at the Haskins laboratory on "acquired distinctiveness" of phoneme features [Liberman *et al.*, 1957]).

My two cases have been or can be attacked by all these methods. But first they must be described in some detail. The potential information available in the stimuli for the two situations is the logical starting place.

Comparison of Stimuli

A standard situation for the study of depth discrimination was devised by Dr. Richard Walk and myself. We called this situation the "visual cliff." The important element of this situation is a drop-off downward, or depth-at-an-edge. The device consists essentially of a raised center runway with a sheet of strong glass extending outward on either side. Directly under the glass on one side is placed a textured pattern; farther below the glass on the other side, at any desired depth, is the same pattern. The simplest version of the stimulus situation might be conceived of as a platform with a drop-off to a floor below. Figure 1 shows the pattern of light rays projected to the subject's eye from the floor and from the platform on which he stands.

If the elements of the textured pattern are identical above and below, the light rays reaching the eye will differ in *density,* a finer density characterizing the surface farther below the eye. There is thus potential information in the light itself for the detection of the drop-off.

The same situation provides a second kind of differential stimulation if the animal moves. *Motion parallax* (differential velocity of elements in the stimulus array) will increase as the drop increases. There will be a velocity difference, therefore, between the projection of the floor under the animal's feet and that of the sunken surface below, which will characterize the amount of the drop-off.

Finally, the situation provides a third kind of differential stimulation, *binocular parallax,* if the animal has two eyes with overlapping fields and eye movements of convergence.

It could be said then that this stimulation literally specifies a drop-off. The proximal stimulus is unique and unequivocal. The information needed is present in the stimulation itself. If it is registered, the animal can make an appropriate response. Depending on the kind of organism it is, terrestrial, aquatic, or flying, it may avoid the deep side consistently, or not. A terrestrial animal would be expected to avoid it; an animal whose way of life includes diving into water from a height might approach it.

If the animal does not behave consistently and differentially, it may mean either that he does not "pick up" the stimulus difference, or else that the appropriate response has to be learned. But if he does respond differentially and consistently, it means that the difference is discriminated and that a response appropriate to his species can be made.

Now consider the kind of stimulation presented by graphic symbols. In the first place, the sources of the stimuli are marks on a piece of paper, not three-dimensional natural objects found in all men's environments. They are, in fact, man-made artifacts. The stimuli do not specify or refer to real objects or situations in space.

What they *do* specify is the sounds of speech. But notice that there is a *relayed* sequence involved. The light to the eyes specifies letters; the letters in turn specify speech sounds; the sounds in turn have morphic specificity relationships. Thus the graphic symbols have a *mediated* relationship with morphemes (referential meanings).

It is true that printed letters are unique, in the sense that one is discriminable from any other. But their meaning is not unequivocal, like that of a drop-off. The information for unequivocal specification of the appropriate speech sounds is *not* in the stimuli emanating from the letters; it is in a code characteristic of a given culture's writing system. Which mark or marks specify which sounds is arbitrary. A new code could be made up which would do as well or better (this, in fact, is often suggested by proponents of spelling reforms, speed writing, etc.).

It follows that at least two stages of development must be considered in the perception of graphic symbols: (1) the discrimination of the graphic symbols as unique items and (2) the mastery of the unequivocal specificity relations in the code.

Experiments on Discrimination of Depth

Our experiments with the visual cliff included comparative studies (both phylogenetic and ontogenetic) and experimental studies manipulating the environment during growth and some of the potentially available cues.

We built a small cliff first, tailored for rats, the most convenient and plentiful subjects. We provided a choice situation, a very shallow drop on one side of the runway and a deep drop on the other. The glass was at the same depth below the center runway on either side, as Figure 2 shows diagrammatically.

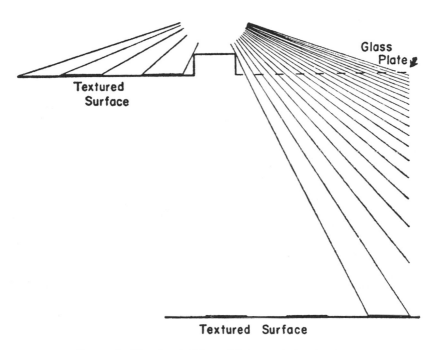

FIGURE 2—The visual cliff modified as a choice situation.

Pigmented adult rats, in a number of experiments, always descended from the center runway to the shallow side significantly more often than to the deep side. First choices, in all the experiments, ranged from 85 per cent to 100 per cent to the shallow side. The choice was significant with a wide variety of patterns. A 10-inch drop on the deep side was sufficient to demonstrate the preference. Control experiments with equal depths, graduated depths, and absence of texture are described in a forthcoming monograph. Rats as young as 30 days were as discriminating as adults.

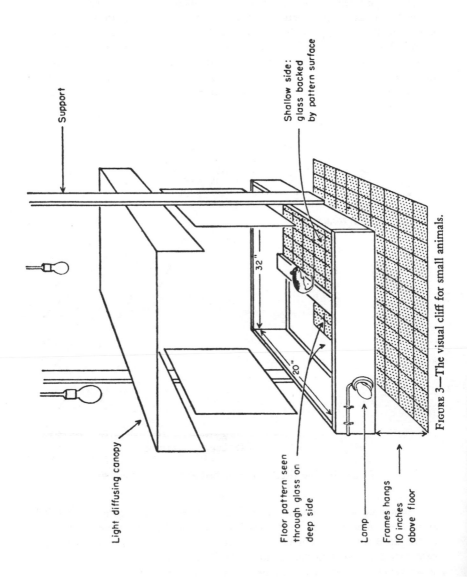

Support

Shallow side:
glass backed
by pattern surface

32"

20"

Light diffusing canopy

Floor pattern seen
through glass on
deep side

Lamp

Frames hangs
10 inches
above floor

Figure 3—The visual cliff for small animals.

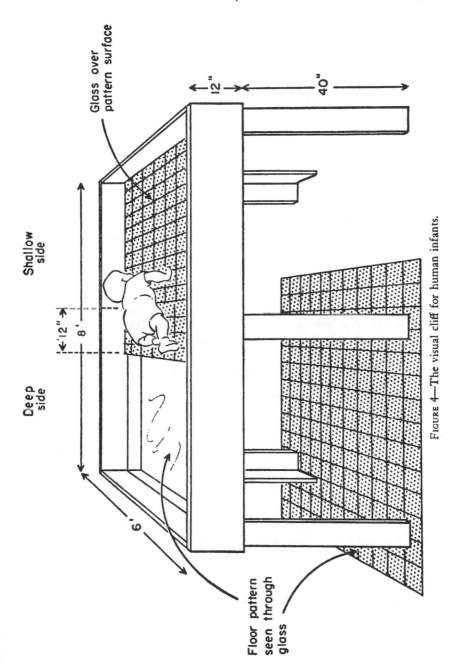

FIGURE 4—The visual cliff for human infants.

Comparative Studies

Experiments with cliffs constructed on the same plan, but adjusted to the size of the subject, were carried out on other animals as well: albino rats, baby chicks and adult chickens, lambs, kids, pigs, turtles, puppies, kittens, monkeys, and finally human infants (Figures 3 and 4). Many interesting species differences appear in these studies, but one generalization applies to all: all the animals that could locomote in any way at all avoided the deep side and descended to the shallow side in a significant majority of the trials. If aquatic animals had been included among the subjects, we might have found exceptions. The turtles (a semiaquatic species) showed the smallest preference for the shallow side.

There was a wide variety of ages in our subjects, for some of them could locomote immediately after birth; others could not do so until 8 months. Chicks and goats were tested before they were 24 hours old and showed as clear evidence of discrimination (100 per cent choice, in fact) as any adult animal.

The human infants could not be tested until they could crawl, so our subjects in this group ranged from 6½ to 12 months old. The great majority of them avoided the deep side, despite the entreaties of their mothers and tempting toys. We are ready to assert, therefore, that perception of depth has developed as soon as locomotion is possible in this young organism. The same assertion applies to other slow-maturing organisms, such as kittens. Development of this discrimination, therefore, is not dependent on stepping down, climbing up, or walking into things.

Dark-Rearing Experiments

The deprivation experiment is a technique which allows us to control some aspect of the animal's experience or practice during what is, normally, a developmental stage. Many groups of rats were reared in the dark, from birth to 90 days, or to 30 days, and compared with their litter-mates reared in the usual cages in the light. The dark-reared rats were tested on the cliff shortly after emergence from the dark-room, and they behaved as did their light-reared litter-mates, uniformly choosing the shallow side. Rats, therefore, although requiring maturation time after birth before locomotion is possible, discriminate depth *without any* previous visual experience.

Kittens were reared in the dark until 24 days of age, when their normal controls were walking and had good visual placing responses. When they were first put on the cliff, they presented the greatest contrast to their own controls and to the dark-reared rats. They crawled on their bellies, fell off the runway, and bumped into walls. Discrimination of drop-offs and even locomotion in the light were impaired. After some days in the light, the kittens had caught up and behaved normally. It seems clear that development in a lighted environment is required for this species. But learning the

difference between visually deep and shallow drops through external reinforcement (punishment from falling) was not the crucial factor, for the
kittens in the beginning fell equally either way to a glass surface at the same
depth below the center board on either side. Yet gradually, as Figure 5

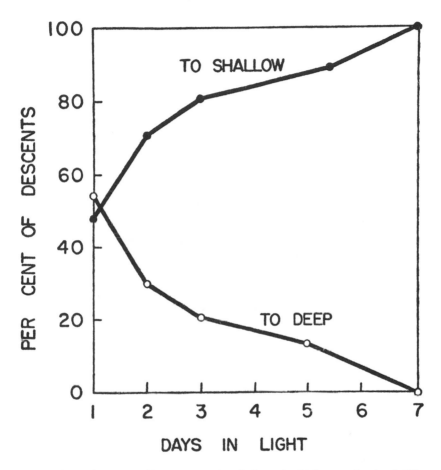

FIGURE 5—Performance of kittens, reared in darkness for 24 days, on the visual cliff.

shows, they began to avoid one side and choose the other, without reinforcement. Choices rose to 100 per cent by the seventh day.

Our conclusion is that discrimination of depth matures, when normal
conditions of development are provided, without benefit of reward or punishment or associative learning. Progress may indeed continue after birth,

through normal growth of organs. But early failure of discrimination is no reason to adopt the empiricist's bias. Differentiation of perception by developmental stages is characteristic of phylogenetic differences, and in the case we have just considered, of ontogenetic ones.

Enhancement Experiments

An interesting question arises at this point. Can we apply our generalization with respect to depth at an edge to discrimination of three-dimensional *objects* in the environment? If an object can be "seen around," conditions for parallax are present. It has, potentially, the attribute of depth and the possibility of being easily differentiated from the background.

We have a little evidence, from other experiments, that discrimination of objects having depth-at-an-edge occurs relatively early and is responsible for some *transfer* to two-dimensional pictured shapes.

Dr. Walk and I carried out a number of experiments of the "early experience" type, in which we hung cut-out triangles and circles on the walls of living cages of hooded rats from birth to 90 days. At 90 days these animals, as well as control litter-mates, learned a triangle-circle discrimination. For the discriminative learning, the figures were *painted* on flat surfaces (doors through which food was reached). In our first experiment, learning was significantly facilitated among the experimental animals.

In some further experiments, we painted the wall figures on a flat background, rather than cutting them out. To our chagrin, the transfer effect was no longer obtained. Our variables in these experiments were presence or absence of reinforcement, time of exposing the patterns, and so on. None of these seemed to make any difference; our original effect sometimes appeared and sometimes did not. We had decided that we were pursuing a will-o'-the-wisp until we noticed one factor which divided the results. Transfer occurred when the cage-hangings were cut-outs; it did not occur when they were painted on the flat surface that surrounded them.

Our interpretation of these facts is speculative, but rich in hypotheses. Objects having depth-at-an-edge are easily differentiated from their surroundings. They are therefore "noticed" by the animal. This noticeability, we guess, will transfer to similar pictured objects, thereby helping the animal to differentiate them from their surroundings when they must be isolated as cues for response.[1]

What transfers, exactly, is another question. For the rats, not dominantly "visual" animals, it may have been only differentiation of figure from background. It might also be features which serve to distinguish one object from another, such as curves opposed to corners, or openings (indentations)

---

[1] Harlow's discovery that stereometric (solid) objects, as contrasted with planometric (flat) patterns, are discriminated more easily by young monkeys is one confirmation of this hypothesis.

opposed to closure (smooth continuity). I should like to return to this possibility later, in the discussion of graphic symbols.

It should be apparent how different this view is from the traditional one that perception begins with something like a two-dimensional projection and progresses to appreciation of depth by associational meanings gained from experiences that are dependent on locomotion. The evidence suggests instead that discrimination of depth-at-an-edge is primitive, both phylogenetically and ontogenetically, and that development progresses toward discrimination of form in two-dimensional projections.

EXPERIMENTS WITH GRAPHIC FORMS

The jump from discrimination of depth-at-an-edge to discrimination of graphic symbols is a big one. The fact that only human subjects are appropriate for studying this case is an indication in itself. Furthermore, analysis of the situation made it clear that the stimuli provided by words and letters do not contain in themselves information that specifies unequivocally anything about the world. What they do specify can only be found in a code which varies from one language to another and therefore must be learned.

We have said that at least two stages of development need to be considered in this process. The first stage is the discrimination of the graphic symbols themselves as unique items. Our first question, therefore, was whether there is a developmental process involved in accomplishing the differentiation.

An old experiment performed by my husband and myself (Gibson and Gibson, 1955) suggested that there was. We presented subjects divided into three age groups (6 to 8, 8½ to 11, and adults) with drawn figures somewhat comparable to those of cursive writing. They were called "scribbles." The task was to recognize a presented figure when it was presented later in a series of similar figures. The standard to be recognized varied from the others along three dimensions (number of coils, horizontal compression, and right-left reversal). The subject looked at the standard and then went through a pack of cards on which the variants, some copies of the standard, and other quite different figures appeared (Figure 6). On the first run through the pack, the adults were already very accurate in their recognitions (a mean of only three errors), but the children confused many variants with the standard. The youngest group had a mean of more than 13 errors, and some of them did not achieve perfect recognition even after 10 repetitions of the whole procedure.

We have recently completed a large-scale comparison of the ability to discriminate graphic items in preschool and early grade-school children.[2] Our object this time was to study qualitative as well as quantitative differ-

---

[2] Anne Danielson and Harry Osser collaborated in this experiment.

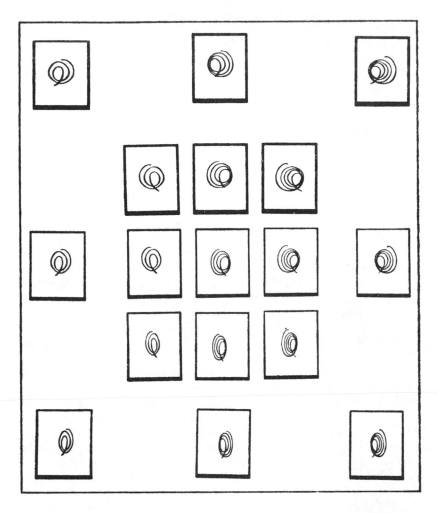

FIGURE 6—"Scribbles" used in the Gibson and Gibson experiment (1955).

ences. A set of letter-like forms, comparable to printed capitals, was constructed by the following method. The letters themselves were analyzed,
to yield a set of rules governing their formation. From these rules a population of new forms was generated, none of which violated the rules but
none of which were actual letters. From among these stimuli 12 were chosen
to serve as standards. Twelve variants were constructed from each standard
to yield transformations of the following kinds: three degrees of transforma-

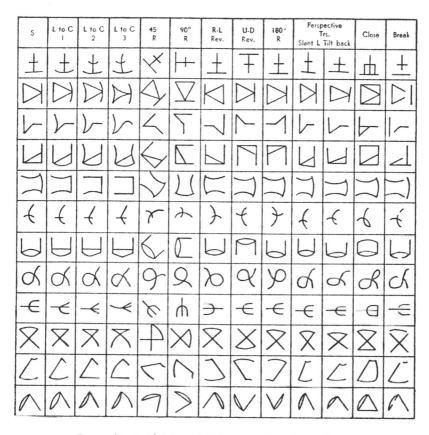

FIGURE 7—Artificial graphic forms and twelve variants.

tion of line to curve or curve to line; five transformations of rotation or
reversal; two perspective transformations (slant left and tilt back); and
two topological changes, a break and a close (Figure 7).

The master drawings were copied photographically on small cards, and
these were covered with plastic so that they could be handled without
marking. The task given the children was to *match* the standard with all its
variants and to select and hand to the experimenter only exact copies of it.
The cards were presented in a matrix board, with a standard centered in
the top row (Figure 8). All transformations of a particular standard were
assembled randomly in one row, accompanied by at least one identical copy.
When a child had finished matching for a given standard, it was removed
and another inserted in its place. Demonstration with corrected practice
was given before beginning, and then the child matched for all 12 forms.

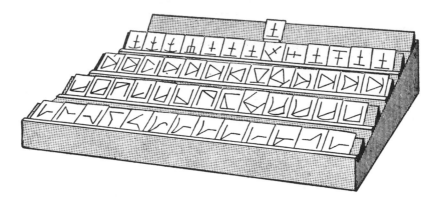

FIGURE 8—Matching board for studies of discrimination of graphic forms.

An error score (choosing as "same" an item that did not match the standard) was obtained for each child, and the errors classified according to type of transformation. The subjects were 165 children aged 4 to 8 years.

Errors decrease rapidly from ages 4 to 8. Furthermore, it is very clear that some transformations are harder to discriminate from the standard than others and that improvement occurs at different rates for different transformations.

Error curves for changes of break and close start low and drop almost to zero by 8 years. Error curves for perspective transformations start very high and errors are still numerous at 8 years. Error curves for rotations and reversals start high, but the curves drop to nearly zero by 8 years. Error curves for changes from line to curve start relatively high (depending on the number of changes) and show a rapid drop. The curves for two and three changes have dropped to the same low point as the curves for break and close by 8 years.

In Figure 9 the data have been combined for the four transformation groups. Our justification for doing so was twofold: one, the resemblances of the curves within transformation groups, but differences between groups (statistically significant, in fact); and two, the high correlations within transformation groups.

The experiment was replicated for the 5-year-old group with actual letters and the same transformational variants. Again, the correlations within transformation groups were very high.

Interpretation of Error Curves

The interpretation of the error curves for these transformation groups leads us to some interesting hypotheses about the development of discrimi-

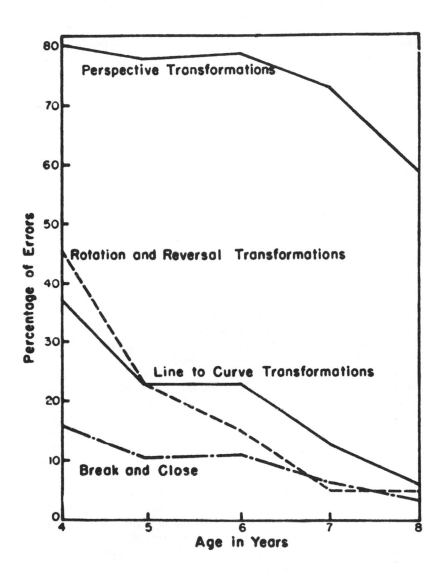

FIGURE 9—Errors in matching variants with standard graphic forms by type of
variant and age of S.

nation of letter forms. The concept of "distinctive features" is central to the argument. This term is borrowed from Roman Jakobson (Jakobson and Halle, 1956), who originated the concept of distinctive features of phonemes. Distinctive features are characteristics which a phoneme may or may not have; they are invariant; and they are critical for distinguishing one phoneme from another. "Bundles" of such features characterize any given phoneme. A child, presumably, learns to hear the distinctive features and can thereafter recognize phonemic patterns over a wide range of pitch and intensity variations (sung, whispered, shouted, and so on).[3]

Taking some license with Jakobson's term, we have assumed that the solid objects of the world, and also the set of graphemes, possess "distinctive features"—characteristics which are invariant and critical for distinguishability within the set.

An attempt to analyze all the objects of the world into a classification of distinctive features is not our purpose, but some progress has been made with letters. Suffice it to say here that breaks and closes (O vs. C), transformations from line to curve (U vs. V), rotations (M vs. W), and reversals (d vs. b) are all distinctive features with respect to which letters may differ. They often occur in some combination as bundles of distinctive features. For instance, A vs. V includes both rotation and closure as critical differences.[4] Perspective transformations are *not* distinctive features of letters. Changes of compression (such as would result from tilt or slant) often occur in handwriting but are never critical for differentiating letters. "Constancy" of the grapheme requires tolerance of such variance.

We assumed further (*see* p. 14) that there will be transfer from discriminating ordinary solid objects of the world to two-dimentional line drawings of the letter-like variety. *Positive* transfer should occur when the variable dimension distinguishing two line drawings is one which has been critical for discriminating one object from another in the past. *No* transfer should occur when the variable dimension has not been critical for object identification. Sometimes a variable aspect has not only been irrelevant, but has even been assimilated to a "concept" allowing free variation along this dimension. For instance, shape constancy occurs despite variation in orientation.

When transfer is possible from earlier object identification, errors should be few. When it is not, they will be numerous to begin with, but they will decrease with age if the dimension varied is a critical one (distinctive feature) for differentiating letters. The four transformation types should therefore show the following error trends with age.

1. Errors for differences of the break and close type should be few initially and show only a small drop (discrimination already being nearly

---

[3] *See also* Brown (1958, pp. 202 ff.).

[4] Note the comment of Deutsch's infant son (Deutsch [1960, p. 149]) when shown a "V": "Why isn't the A crossed?"

perfect). These changes are critical for object differentiation. There is no transition from break to close. Piaget (1956) has shown that such differences are discriminated very early with solid objects.

2. Initial errors for line to curve transformations will be higher than those for break and close but should drop rapidly. Line to curve differences are critical for distinguishing rigid objects, but not for live or plastic ones (e.g., the nonrigid transformations of facial expression). Since they *may* indicate different states of the same object, perfect transfer cannot be expected. Nevertheless, the error curve should drop rapidly because such differences are critical for letter discrimination.

3. Initial errors for reversals and rotations should be very high because transformations of this type are not critical for object identification. (Rotation is used in fact to study transposability of form;[5] it gives information of position of an object, such as leaning or fallen down.) But rotation is critical for letter discrimination, so the error curve should drop rapidly after school has begun.

4. Initial errors for perspective transformation should also be very high. They are not critical for object identification, indicating instead a change in orientation in the third dimension (slant or tilt). There is little reason to expect a drop in errors, for slant and tilt are not critical for letter identification.

The curves obtained do actually follow those expectations. There is, therefore, support for the view that there is perceptual learning of the distinctive features of letters in the stage of development before decoding to phonemes begins. The kind of learning is not associative; it is instead a process of isolating and focusing on those features of letters that are both invariant and critical for rendering each one unique.

Teaching is provided the child in this stage of learning, but it is not of the paired associates type. It is rather helping the child to "pay attention to" those features that are invariant and distinctive. Learning a name for each letter, on the other hand, is a case of association, but necessarily a secondary stage.

GRAPHEME-PHONEME CORRESPONDENCE

We have suggested that the development of discrimination of graphic symbols begins with the differentiation of letters, whose distinctive features must be learned, assisted by transfer from the earlier stage of object identification. Meanwhile the child has learned to recognize phonemes and to speak his language. But the final stage remains to be accomplished: the decoding of graphemic to phonemic units.

---

[5] The 2-year-old children tested by Gellerman (1933) responded to a form as equivalent after rotation. *See also* Deutsch (1960, p. 149).

It is not enough to describe this stage as merely associating grapheme with phoneme patterns. What are the units to be associated? In the English language, no single letter has an invariant phonemic equivalent. Words do, and this fact has led to teaching by the "whole word" method. This method, however, is both uneconomical and insufficient to generate the reading of new words.

An alternative to these two possibilities exists. Dr. Charles Hockett and his collaborators at Cornell have shown that rules for predicting pronunciation from spelling can be formulated, if the rules are stated in terms of vowel and consonant "clusters" and what comes before and after. Higher order invariant spelling patterns exist which can be mapped into correspondence with phonemic patterns. It is the grapheme-phoneme invariant correspondences that the skilled reader has learned. Letter-groups having such correspondence in the language come to have a high perceptibility, since they form units as stimuli; those lacking such correspondence are not equally perceptible because they are not effective units for pronunciation.

We have conducted several experiments with tachistoscopic viewing of pseudo words, some following the rules of correspondence (invariant spelling to sound correlation), some not.[6] Skilled adult readers are consistently more successful in perceiving correctly the letter groups which are "pronounceable," even though they have no referential meaning. These letter groups have a higher "visibility." Here we have a final case, at the top of the developmental ladder, of perceptual learning. What the reader has learned here (albeit unconsciously) is to perceive the higher order stimuli as units in reading. These stimuli are letter groups (ways of spelling) that exist in the language as invariants in the sense that they have a corresponding consistent pronunciation. The reader acquiring skill comes to perceive these as units by experiencing the heard and seen patterns together. He may or may not be taught them.

The letter or spelling units are constituted, formally and objectively, by the rules of correspondence in the language. They are a psychological reality as well, as we have demonstrated. The problem for perceptual learning is to determine *how* the unit is constituted. Whether the process of unit formation is an associative one or one of "discovery" of the invariant relationships is yet to be determined.

SUMMARY

From our comparison of the development of perception of depth and that of graphic symbols, several generalizations can be drawn. The first, stated below, is a conclusion. The others have the status of promising, partly substantiated hypotheses.

---

[6] Collaborators in this experiment were Anne Danielson, Harry Osser, and Marcia Hammond.

1. Perception of depth at an edge is primitive, both phylogenetically and ontogenetically. Some animals are fully mature in this accomplishment at birth. Animals which have a longer maturation time after birth (e.g., cats, human infants) discriminate depth at an edge as soon as locomotion is possible.

2. Solid objects, which possess depth at their edges, are discriminated earlier than two-dimentional pictures or line drawings. If perceptual learning occurs in the earlier phase, it involves a discovery of invariant properties of the object which the stimulation itself specifies and which are critical for distinguishing one object from another. What is learned is isolation from background or differentiation rather than an associative meaning for depth.

3. Ability to discriminate those features of objects which are critical for identification may transfer to outline drawings such as letters, but some critical features of letters remain to be discriminated after four years of age. This process is again one of differentiation rather than association.

4. Unequivocal referential meaning of letters must be learned; it is *not* given in the stimulation emanating from them. At this stage (following differentiation) an associative process may be involved.

5. Mere association of letter with phoneme, however, is an inadequate description of the process of learning meaning. Letter clusters from "higher order units" which are invariant for pronunciation and reading pass through a learning phase of integration so that they are actually perceived as wholes.

This paper raises more problems than it solves. It is my hope that stirring up these problems will create interest in a field which I have found fascinating and productive.

REFERENCES

Brown, R. *Words and things.* Free Press, 1958.

Deutsch, J. A. *The structural basis of behavior.* Univer. of Chicago Press, 1960.

Gellermann, L. W. Form discrimination in chimpanzees and two-year-old children: I. Form (triangularity) *per se. J. genet. Psychol.,* 1933, 42, 3-29.

Gibson, E. J., & Walk, R. D. The effect of prolonged exposure to visually presented patterns on learning to discriminate them. *J. comp. physiol. Psychol.,* 1956, 49, 239-241.

Gibson, E. J., & Walk, R. D. The "visual cliff." *Sci. Amer.,* 1960, 202, 2-9.

Gibson, E. J., Walk, R. D., & Tighe, T. J. Enhancement and deprivation of visual stimulation during rearing as factors in visual discrimination learning. *J. comp. physiol. Psychol.,* 1959, 52, 74-81.

Gibson, J. J., & Gibson, E. J. Perceptual learning: differentiation or enrichment? *Psychol. Rev.,* 1955, 62, 32-41.

Goodenough, F. *Developmental psychology.* Appleton-Century, 1934.

Harlow, H. F., & Warren, J. M. Formation and transfer of discrimination learning sets. *J. comp. physiol. Psychol.,* 1952, 45, 482-489.

HEBB, D. O. Heredity and environment in mammalian behavior. *Brit. J. Anim. Behav.*, 1953, 1, 43-47.

JAKOBSON, R., & HALLE, M. *Fundamentals of language.* The Hague: Morton, 1956.

LIBERMAN, A. M., HARRIS, K. S., HORRMAN, S. H., & GRIFFITH, B. C. The discrimination of speech sounds within and across phoneme boundaries. *J. exp. Psychol.*, 1957, 54, 358-368.

PASTORE, N. Perceiving as innately determined. *J. genet. Psychol.*, 1960, 96, 93-99.

PIAGET, J., & INHELDER, B. *The child's conception of space.* London: Humanities Press, 1956.

WALK, R. D., & GIBSON, E. J. A comparative and analytic study of depth perception. *Psychol. Monogr.*, in press.

WALK, R. D., GIBSON, E. J., PICK, H. L., JR., & TIGHE, T. J. The effectiveness of prolonged exposure to cutouts vs. painted patterns for facilitation of discrimination. *J. comp. physiol. Psychol.*, 1959, 52, 519-521.

2

DEVELOPMENT OF MEDIATING RESPONSES IN CHILDREN [1]

Tracy S. Kendler

Barnard College

Learning theory and general behavior theory have, for the most part, shown little concern with developmental research. This is not to be taken as reflecting a lack of interest in children. There is an honorable, but spotty, tradition of experimental studies that used children as subjects dating back to Watson and his famous Albert. But the use of children does not automatically make the research developmental, especially if the emphasis is on the generality of behavior principles across species or across age levels within any one species.

Perhaps this indifference arises because developmental research appears to be more concerned with finding *differences* between age groups than in finding general laws of behavior applicable to all age groups. Learning theory, on the other hand, commits the investigator to studying general processes that relate the organism to its environment through its past history. "The organism," which may range from amoeba to homo sapiens, is often either a white rat or a pigeon. The use of these animals is not due to any particular interest in the species but rather to some very important advantages they provide to the researcher. For example, their past histories and motivational states can be manipulated or controlled at will and there are few ethical limitations imposed on the tasks they may be required to perform. Though he may restrict his research to some convenient laboratory organism, the behavior theorist implicitly assumes that at least some aspect of his findings are common to a wide range of organisms, usually including mankind. Within this tradition investigators who use human beings as subjects, and are explicit about the species, are often more interested in demonstrating the universality of the behavioral laws derived from animal experiments than in obtaining differences that might appear to reduce their generality.

If a discipline like comparative or developmental psychology is as much interested in differences as in similarities, then its findings may supply the

[1] The research described in this paper is supported by a grant from the National Science Foundation.

ammunition for an attack on the vital assumption of the generality of behavioral laws. This is possible, but it is not necessarily so. If the principles generated by research with laboratory animals are applicable to higher level human behavior, then research directed at understanding the changes that take place with increasing maturity can extend the range and the vitality of behavior theory. If some of the knowledge derived from learning experiments can give direction to developmental research and can help to explain and organize its findings, behavior theorists may yet convert a potential enemy into a valuable ally.

It will come as no surprise to the reader that the developmental research to be described, which was conducted jointly with Howard H. Kendler and our colleagues, derives from an S-R learning theory pretheoretical framework. Among the reasons for this choice (besides the fact that we were trained in this discipline) are the substantial body of relevant knowledge and the well developed experimental techniques that can be adapted to the study of higher mental processes. Moreover, learning theory possesses a rigor that may help to tighten a field where the temptation to be vague is great.

The mediated response is one of the mechanisms most often used to find a common theme between simple and complex behavior within this theoretical framework. The mediator is a response, or series of responses, which intercede between the external stimulus and the overt response to provide stimulation that influences the eventual course of behavior. These responses may be overt, but they are usually presumed to be covert. The mediated response is not an original idea. All theories of thinking, motor or central, behaviorist or phenomenological, dealing in the second-signal system or using computer models, postulate internal processes that intervene between the presentation of the problem and its solution, between the input and output, or between the stimulus and the response. The differences arise in the model used to generate hypotheses about the nature of this internal process and in the methods used to validate these hypotheses. Watson, who coordinated thinking with subvocal talking, used conditioning as his model and sought verification by direct measurement of the muscles of speech. The contemporary behaviorist approach allows for a wider range of mediating responses and for the possibility of treating them as theoretical constructs rather than as directly observable behavior. The scheme is exemplified in the research to be described in this paper.

The research started with a general interest in the mediating process and has become more and more concerned with how the process develops in children. This development has been studied in two interrelated ways. One way is primarily comparative. It consists of presenting a similar experimental situation to different species and to different age levels to study the uncontrolled changes that occur as a function of the differences among subjects. The other way employs the experimental method to discover and manipulate the variables that appear to be related to these "natural" developmental changes in order to determine how they come about and consequently render them subject to experimental control.

We have experimented in two areas that are generally conceded to be part of that area variously called cognitive process, thinking, or problem solution. One of the areas is *concept formation* or *abstraction*. The other is *inference*, defined as the spontaneous integration of discretely acquired habits to solve a problem. These processes have been reduced to some very simple operations in order to study them at their inception in young children. The operations are so simple that there may be some disagreement about their continuity with the high level process that they presume to study. The prepared reply to such potential objection is that there is no known way of reliably determining, on an a priori basis, the proper level of analysis for scientific research. It is only by its fruits that we shall know it.

Concept Formation

The experimental paradigm used in the investigation of concept formation is based on procedures developed by Buss (1953) and Kendler and D'Amato (1955). It consists essentially of studying mediation by means of the transfer demonstrated from an initial to a subsequent discrimination. The initial discrimination presents stimuli that differ simultaneously on at least two dimensions, only one of which is relevant. After criterion is reached, another discrimination is presented that utilizes the same or similar stimuli but requires a shift in response. One type of shift, called a *reversal shift*, requires the subject to continue to respond to the previously relevant dimension but in an opposite way. In another type of shift, called a *nonreversal shift*, the subject is required to respond to the previously irrelevant dimension. For example, if a subject is initially trained on stimuli that differ simultaneously in brightness (black vs. white) and size (large vs. small) by being rewarded for responses to black regardless of size, a reversal shift would consist of learning to respond to white, and a nonreversal shift would consist of learning to respond to small. Comparisons between these two types of shifts are of particular interest because theories based on single-unit versus mediated S-R connections yield opposed predictions about their relative efficiency. A single-unit theory assumes a direct association between the external stimulus and the overt response and would predict a reversal shift to be more difficult than a nonreversal shift. This is because reversal shift requires the replacement of a response that has previously been consistently reinforced with a response that has previously been consistently extinguished. In a nonreversal shift previous training has reinforced responses to the newly positive and negative stimuli equally often. Strengthening one of these associations does not require as much extinction of its competitor as in a reversal shift and should, therefore, be acquired more easily. Kelleher (1956) confirmed the prediction that, for rats, a reversal shift was more difficult than a nonreversal shift.

A theory that includes a mediating link (or links) between the external stimulus and the overt response leads to a different prediction. The mediating link is conceived of as a perceptual or verbal response, often covert, to the relevant dimension, which produces cues that elicit the overt response. In a reversal shift, the initial dimension maintains its relevance, hence, so does the mediated response. Only the overt response needs to be changed, and since the experimental situation provides only one alternative overt response, the problem presents no great difficulty. In a nonreversal shift the previously acquired mediation is no longer relevant, consequently both the mediating and the overt response must be replaced, making the task more difficult than a reversal shift. It is therefore to be expected that for subjects who mediate, a reversal shift will be acquired more easily than a nonreversal shift. Experiments by Buss (1953), Kendler and D'Amato (1955), and Harrow and Friedman (1958), using a more complex variation of the reversal-nonreversal technique with college students, confirmed the prediction of the mediational analysis. Unlike rats, college students learn a reversal shift more easily than a nonreversal shift.

This discontinuity between rats and adult humans led to two investigations with young children to determine whether their behavior, in this type of situation, was more consistent with the single-unit or the mediational formulation. The results suggested that children between 3 and 4 years of age respond predominantly in the single unit manner (Kendler, Kendler and Wells [1960]) and that children between 5 and 7 years of age divide about evenly, with half mediating and half not (Kendler and Kendler [1959]). What seemed to be implied was a developmental process in which very young children's behavior is governed by a relatively primitive, single-unit S-R process. Increasing maturity leads to increases in the proportion of children whose performance is determined by some mediating system of responses.

A recent investigation of the shift behavior of children from five age levels (3, 4, 6, 8, and 10 years) provided a direct test of these developmental implications (Kendler et al. [1962]). Previous procedures were modified to allow each subject to choose whether or not he would behave mediationally. This was accomplished in the following way. For their initial discrimination (series I) the children were presented, in random alternation, with two pairs of stimulus cards. One pair consisted of a large black square (LB) and a small white square (SW). The other pair consisted of a large white square (LW) and a small black square (SB). Each concept (L, B, S, W) was correct for one fourth of the subjects.

For the purpose of illustration let us take a child for whom black was the correct concept and size was irrelevant. For him all responses to SB or

LB were rewarded with a marble. If he responded to SW or LW, he had to return a marble to the experimenter. After he reached the criterion of nine out of ten successive correct responses, a second discrimination (series II) was presented that involved only one of the stimulus pairs, e.g., LB and SW, and the reward pattern was reversed. Now only responses to SW were rewarded, and he was again run to a criterion of nine out of ten successive correct responses. The child could reach criterion in this series by responding to the whiteness, in which case he was categorized as a *reversal* subject since he was responding in a reverse way to the original concept. Such a child is, by virtue of the previous analysis, presumed to have made relevant mediating responses in the first discrimination which either led to other relevant mediators or continued to be relevant in the second discrimination, thus requiring a shift only in the overt response.

A child could also reach criterion in series II by responding to the smallness of SW. Such a choice would be expected from nonmediators since during Series I responses to small were rewarded half of the time, while responses to whiteness were never rewarded. Such a child would, therefore, respond more readily to a stimulus from the previously irrelevant dimension (S) than to the incorrect stimulus of the previously relevant dimension (W) and would consequently be categorized as a nonreversal subject.

The last possibility is that the child learned to respond to both the smallness and the whiteness. A single-unit analysis would predict this result for nonmediating children who take a relatively long time to learn series II since each reinforcement should increase the habit strength of both stimulus components. As the trials increase, the difference in the excitatory strengths of white and small should decrease and ultimately disappear. Such children, for reasons that will soon be clear, were categorized as *inconsistent*.

In order to determine on which of the three possible bases series II was learned, it was followed immediately by a third series. During this last series both pairs of stimuli were again shown in random alternation. The pair that had not been used in series II, which is LW and SB in our illustration, served as the test pair. With this pair the child could respond either to the whiteness or to the smallness but not to both simultaneously. The test pair was presented ten times and either choice was rewarded. On the basis of his choices to this pair the child was classified as one of the three categories just described. The function of the other pair, which maintained its previous reinforcement pattern, was to keep the child responding as he did in series II.

The results for each category are presented in Figure 1. The prediction, based on theoretical analysis and previous results, was that the percentage of children who reversed (mediated) would be below 50 between the ages of 3 and 4 (Kendler, Kendler, and Wells [1960]), rise to about 50 between 5 and 7 (Kendler and Kendler [1959]), and then continue to increase with increasing age until some relatively high asymptote was reached. The results,

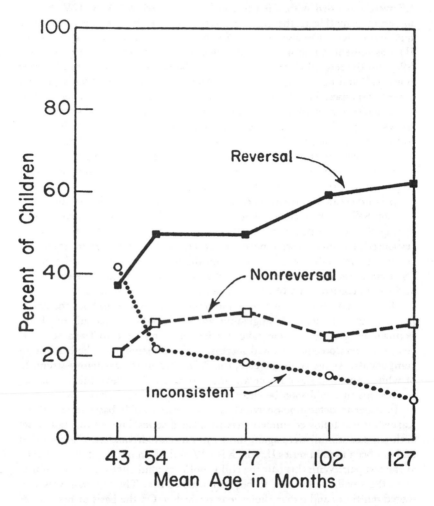

FIGURE 1—Percentage of children in each choice category as a function of chronological age.

which are in good agreement with the prediction, serve to confirm the general developmental implications of previous studies.

It was expected, of course, that the percentage of nonmediators would decrease with age. There seemed no a priori reason for making a discrimination between the nonreversal and inconsistent children, and so the decrease was expected in both categories. The results show a sharp and steady decrease for the inconsistent category. There was, however, no perceptible trend in the nonreversal group.

Despite the need for explanation of the performance of the nonreversal group, to which we shall return presently, it seems reasonable to conclude that the results of this experiment bear out the implication that there is a transition in the course of human development from unmediated, single-unit behavior to mediated behavior, at least with reference to size and brightness concepts. They also suggest that the proportion of children who have made this transition increases in a gradual and lawful manner. It remains for further research to determine whether the same or similar relationships will obtain with other concepts.

In addition to these results there were some *ad hoc* observations about the verbal behavior of the children that provide interesting suggestions about the nature of the mediation process and its development. These verbalizations should not be regarded as demonstrative of confirmed relationships. They should be regarded as empirically derived suggestions that require further experimental verification.

TABLE I

PERCENTAGE OF SUBJECTS GIVING VARIOUS DESCRIPTIONS AS A FUNCTION OF THEIR CHOICES IN SERIES III

Kind of Choice	Verbalized Correct Dimension	Verbalized Incorrect Dimension	No Relevant Verbalization
Reversal	84.8	7.6	7.6
Nonreversal	66.7	25.6	7.7
Inconsistent	57.7*		42.3

* If the behavior was categorized as inconsistent neither dimension could be considered correct. Therefore, mentions of either dimension were combined and placed between the two columns to indicate their special character.

After the children had completed series III, they were shown the stimulus pair used in series II and asked a series of questions to find out whether they could or would give a correct verbal report of what they had been doing and whether there would be any relationship between this after-the-act verbal behavior and mediated choices in series III. Table I presents these results arranged in three categories that are illustrated as follows. If a child had been responding to brightness in the test pair and described the "winner" as white (or black), he was grouped with those who *verbalized the correct dimension*. If he said "the square one" or "that one," or merely pointed without saying anything at all, he was placed with the *no relevant verbalization* group.

Despite the pressure on the child to respond generated by E's persistent questions, with the stimulus cards in full view, 42 per cent of the inconsistent children failed to produce any relevant verbalization. If verbalization is important for the mediating process, then it would follow that nonmediators would be relatively inarticulate. By the same token, mediating (reversal) children should produce a relatively large proportion of verbal comment that was relevant to their previous performance. The data in Table 1 support this expectation. If the pattern is clear for the reversal and inconsistent children, the nonreversal children present more complications. Two statements may be made about this group. First, an overwhelming proportion produced descriptions of the stimuli in terms of at least one of the manipulation dimensions. The proportion for the nonreversal group was just as large as that for the reversal group, suggesting that, under pressure to do so, the nonmediators could verbally describe the stimuli as well as the mediators. However, the verbalizations of nonreversal children were less frequently relevant to their previous behavior than were those of reversal children.

One tentative way to tie these observations together, and simultaneously throw further light on the fact that the proportion of nonreversal children did not decrease with age, is to propose that reversal, nonreversal, and inconsistent choice behavior represent a three-stage hierarchy of development. Reversal choice reflects the highest level where covert verbal responses occur during training and mediate choice behavior. Nonreversal choice constitutes an intermediate level, at which covert verbal responses can occur and sometimes do, but either occur rather late in the learning or they do not necessarily or readily mediate choice behavior. The most primitive level is characterized by little or no covert response and is manifested in inconsistent choice behavior. With increasing CA more and more children reach the highest level (i.e., reversal) and fewer and fewer are left at the lowest level (i.e., inconsistent), but at each age tested the proportion in transition between the two extreme levels (i.e., nonreversals) tends to be constant.

Such an analysis would lead to the expectation that the proportion of children who verbalized correctly would increase with age; the proportion of children whose verbalizations were absent or irrelevant would decrease with age; and the incorrect dimension category would not change. Figure 2 presents the verbalization data in terms of chronological age. The data demonstrate considerable correspondence between expectation and results and show a striking similarity to the choice behavior presented in Figure 1, a similarity that occurs despite the fact that the children who comprise each set of parallel developmental trends are not identical. For example, the "verbalized-correct-dimensions" results of Figure 2, which parallel the "reversal-choice" trend of Figure 1, included 67 per cent of the nonreversal children as well as 85 per cent of the reversal children. Thus, although these results do not point to a perfect relationship between verbal and choice

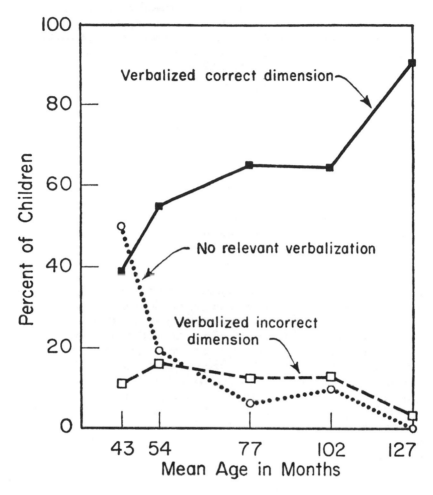

FIGURE 2—Percentage of children in each verbalization category as a function of chronological age.

behavior, the similarity of trends certainly suggests that the development of the mediational process is intimately related to the development of the ability to relate words to actions.

There is one more suggestive result yielded by the verbalization data that may help to explain (a) the high proportion of nonreversal children who verbalized correctly, (b) why the reversal results approached such a low asymptote, and (c) the lack of a decrease in the nonreversal category even at the ripe old age of 10. Some children described the "winner" accurately by mentioning both dimensions, e.g., "The big, white one." When this tendency was sorted out by age, it was found that the percentage of children who accurately described *both dimensions* was zero at age 3 and increased gradually to 25 at age 10, implying, reasonably enough, that there is a developmental aspect to the number of simultaneous mediating responses a child can handle. It also implies that at the upper age levels a nonreversal response to situations as simple as series II may not necessarily denote a primitive process. Instead it may represent the ability to integrate more than one mediating response. This is another way of saying that the task may have been too easy for the older children and that consequently they complicated it for themselves. It may be that the failure of the reversal curve to rise above 62 per cent and the nonreversal curve to drop below 28 per cent at age 10 is due to a perennial difficulty in developmental research: devising one task that is easy enough for the lower end of the scale and yet difficult enough to pose the proper challenge at the upper end. Although in the present instance the task was clearly capable of differentiating among the various age levels tested, it may be that the differences at the upper age levels were attenuated.

Thus far, the data derived from a comparative type of analysis show a measurable transition from a lower to a higher level behavioral process as a function of increasing chronological age. They also suggest that this development is somehow related to language. The relationship is probably not simple. Even the youngest children had a vocabulary sufficient for describing the simple concepts used. Moreover, one of the early experiments had demonstrated that with simple instructions all of the children could interpose relevant verbal comment between the presentation of the stimuli and their overt choice. It is clear that, if the overt behavior of the younger children is not influenced by mediating verbal discriminators, it is not because they are incapable of making these responses. This leaves two alternatives. One is that, although they are capable of doing to, they nevertheless do not, in the ordinary course of events, make such responses. The other is that they do make some verbal responses, but these responses, for some reason, do not serve as mediators. In order to explore some of these issues another experiment was performed which manipulated overt verbal mediation to ascertain its effect on the reversal shift behavior of 4- and 7-year-old children. Note that, while this study has developmental implications, it is more experimental in nature.

The same stimuli were used as in the study previously described, but they were presented differently. The initial discrimination used only one pair of discriminanda, thus rendering both stimulus dimensions relevant. Under these circumstances a child could be required to describe the correct stimulus according to either one of its two components. For example, if LB was correct, the child could be instructed to use either "large" or "black" to describe the correct stimulus. In the second discrimination both pair of stimuli were presented and all children learned a reversal shift. Only one dimension was relevant. For some children the reversal was on the size dimension, and for some it was on the brightness dimension. In this way the verbalization during the initial discrimination was rendered relevant or irrelevant according to the experimental group to which the child had been randomly assigned. For example, if the child had learned to describe the correct stimulus (LB) as "large," he would be rewarded in the second discrimination for response to SB and SW (small) if he was in the relevant group. If he was in the irrelevant group, he was rewarded for responses to SW and LW (white). A control group with no verbalization completed the design.

The first question to be asked is whether such overt verbalization, intervening between stimulus and response, affects the acquisition of the reversal shift. The answer is clear: it does. For both age groups relevant verbalization produced significantly faster shifts than irrelevant verbalization. These results add credence to the mediating response model used to explain reversal-nonreversal shift behavior. They also provide a technique for exploring the interaction between verbal and other developmental variables.

Another question this research was designed to answer was whether the utilization of verbal mediators differs with age as has been suggested by Luria (1957). That is, will the difference between the reversal shift behavior of younger and older children be reduced or eliminated when both are provided with the same verbal response, or is there another ingredient, associated with development, which is necessary before words exercise control over overt behavior?

TABLE 2

MEAN NUMBER OF TRIALS TO CRITERION ON REVERSAL SHIFT FOR EACH
VERBALIZATION CONDITION AT TWO AGE LEVELS

	VERBALIZATION CONDITION		
	Relevant	Irrelevant	None
4 years	16.1	30.4	22.2
7 years	8.3	35.6	8.8

Table 2 presents the results analyzed separately for each age group. It can be seen that the effects were somewhat different for the two age levels. As expected, when there was no verbalization the 4-year-olds took significantly more trials to reverse than the 7-year-olds. Relevant verbalization did not facilitate the shift for the older children, presumably because they did not require instruction about verbalization to supply relevant mediation.

They were able to supply it themselves. The responsiveness of the older children to verbal labels is seen, however, in the sharp increase in learning difficulty produced by irrelevant verbalization.

The 4-year-olds, on the other hand, profited from relevant verbalization and, like the older children, were hindered by irrelevant verbalization. This suggests that, although they are not likely to supply their own mediators, they can use their own words in this capacity when language responses are required. Although the results suggest an interesting interaction between verbalization and age, the implied interaction, as assessed by analysis of variance, fell short of statistical significance ($.10 > p > .05$). The definitive study of such interaction remains to be done.

Although it is clear that we have much to learn, some general conclusions can be drawn from these several studies. In this simple situation, which straddles the boundary between discrimination learning and concept formation, it seems that the single-unit S-R model adequately explains the behavior of the majority of children below 5 or 6 years of age. It does not explain the behavior of the majority of the older children. Invoking the theoretical construct of the mediating response can account for the more mature behavior within the S-R framework. This approach has the advantage of providing for continuity between the laws governing the behavior of younger and older children, since it attributes the observed developmental changes to a new and important system of responses, probably bound up with the development of language, rather than to a different set of behavioral laws. It is not sufficient, however, to point to an explanatory mechanism. After recognizing its potential it becomes necessary to show when and how it functions. The study of mediating responses in children can provide information about the nature and development of mediating processes at their source. Such information can serve to enlarge the scope of behavior theory until it can encompass human problem solving.

INFERENCE

Although it cannot be attributed to any preliminary strategy, our research on inference falls into a logical format resembling that of the research on concept formation. The phenomenon we have called *inference* bears considerable resemblance to Kohler's "insight" (1925) and Maier's "reasoning" (1929). Initially we sought to convert an experimental paradigm into a research vehicle for studying problem solving in very young children. The paradigm was adapted from that of Hull (1935, 1952) in his analysis of the behavior of Maier's reasoning rats. Subjects are trained on three separate behavior segments, each of which presents a distinctive stimulus, requires a different response, and yields a different reward. Two of these segments, designated as A-B and X-Y, lead to subgoals. The third segment,

B-G, leads to the major goal. After being trained on each of these segments individually, the subject is presented with a test trial in which only the A-B and X-Y segments are available to him and he is motivated to get the major goal. The solution to this problem is to link the behavior segments by responding to A to acquire B and then use B to get G. The X-Y segment serves as a control against which to assess the inferential behavior. For example, in our most recent study we used an apparatus with three horizontally arranged panels, one for each segment. For some children, the A-B segment consisted of pressing a button on the right hand panel to obtain a glass marble. The X-Y segment consisted of pressing a button on the left hand panel to obtain a steel ballbearing. The B-G segment consisted of dropping a marble into a hole in the center panel which yielded a fairy tale charm. During the preliminary training on B-G, the subject was provided with a marble and a ballbearing, but only the marble would work. In the test situation neither was provided; instead all of the panels were opened and the child was told that if he did what he was supposed to he could get the charm. Solution consisted of pressing *A* to get the marble and then dropping the marble into *B* to get the charm. For half of the children the A-B segment was on the right, and for half it was on the left. Similarly, for half of the children the marble was the B subgoal, and for half it was the ballbearing (in which case only the ballbearing would operate the B-G segment).

In a somewhat comparable but more loosely controlled experimental situation, Maier found that rats were capable of inference (1929). As far back as 1935, Hull, who accepted this datum, was so impressed with the necessity for a behavior theory to explain such a phenomenon that he set out to provide his own explanation. Hull suggested that during the acquisition of each segment of behavior, not only was the overt S-R connection strengthened, but the subject also acquired an anticipatory goal response (r_g) appropriate to the goal object. This r_g worked backward until stimuli that marked the beginning of the segment became capable of evoking it. The stimulus properties associated with the distinctive r_g for the major goal thus became connected with the A-B segment; they did not become associated with the X-Y segment. Since more connections have been associated with the response to A, and since these response tendencies summate, the subject should, when presented with a choice between A and X, while motivated for G, choose the former. Once A is responded to, it produces B, which in turn leads to the response necessary to produce G, by virtue of previous training. Thus, the habit segments were supposed to become linked to produce inferential behavior.

It is characteristic of Hull's explanations that they generate many deductions, several of which he made explicit. There was one readily testable and fundamental implication that he did not enumerate: inference should occur more readily when the order of training consists of presenting B-G before A-B, since this order maximizes the conditions for the associations between A and the r_g of the major goal.

The assembly of habit segments can also be viewed as an exercise in chaining. Skinner's formulation (1938) points out that in setting up a chain of behavior it is usually most efficient to start with the last link, in this case B-G. In that way the discriminative stimulus (B), through its association with the goal stimulus (G), acquires secondary reinforcing powers, which can serve to strengthen the A-B link. Since Y acquires no such additional secondary reinforcing capacity, the X-Y link should not be able to compete successfully with the A-B link. This analysis should engender the same prediction as was derived from Hull, namely that the optimum order would be that in which B-G precedes A-B.

Notice that both of these explanations are developed to account for the presumably demonstrated capacity of the rat to infer and consequently contain no response mechanism not available to that species.

Our initial interest in inferential behavior was to test the prediction about order using children as subjects. Before this could be done it was necessary to devise suitable experimental techniques. In the course of this search it was found that, given sufficiently simple segments, some nursery school children could infer (Kendler and Kendler [1956]) and this kind of inference was, like simple associative learning, influenced by reinforcement and motivation variables (Kendler et al. [1958]). More recently a study was completed that expressly tested the effect of order of presentation of the several segments on inferential behavior in preschool children (35 to 65 months) (Kendler and Kendler [1961]). The findings showed that there was *no order effect*. This study used a somewhat more complex procedure than the earlier ones and drew its sample from a lower socioeconomic level. Under these conditions, there was very little inferential behavior, and the little there was did not seem to be readily accounted for by the associative principles proposed by Hull.

The data were somewhat difficult to reconcile with the theoretical superstructure underlying the Hullian account and with Maier's data about the rat's capacity in this area. But after the study had been completed, an article by Koronakos (1959) appeared in the literature. He used the Hullian paradigm to study inferential behavior in rats. What he found began to help us see our results as part of a familiar pattern. After initial training when the rats were presented with the A or X choice, they chose one as often as the other. There was no evidence that rats could, in this carefully controlled situation, combine the habit segments spontaneously to attain the major goal.

It is now beginning to look as though inference, like reversal shift, may be a process that is not readily available to lower phylogenetic species and perhaps not to young children. Inference may be another developmental process with ontogenetic as well as phylogenetic implications. The last study to be described undertook to explore this possibility. All of the results have not yet been analyzed, and no statistical significances have yet been computed; nevertheless, some of the findings are sufficiently cogent to warrant presentation now.

This study compared the behavior of 64 kindergarten children (5 to 6 years old) with 64 third grade children (8 to 10 years old) on the inference task. When confronted with the test situation, only 50 per cent of the younger children as compared with 72 per cent of the older children chose to respond to A (the inferential choice). Furthermore, of the children who made the initial A choice only 12 per cent of the younger children and 67 per cent of the older children went on to complete the inferential sequence to obtain the major goal with no unnecessary steps.

This seems to be rather clear evidence that, in this situation, the capacity to combine independently acquired habit segments is present in very few youngsters below about 6 years of age. But among the third graders there were many more who plainly displayed such integrative capacity. Moreover, there is indication from other aspects of this experiment that the response of the two age levels to the connecting stimulus (B) is quite different. For the younger children it is necessary to have B in order to make the integrative response. For a substantial proportion of the older children the final integration is *more* dependent on self-produced cues than on the external stimulus B. Apparently the occurrence of inference, like the occurrence of reversal shift, is dependent on a system of covert mediating responses which occurs more readily in older than younger children. It seems that the experimental study of inferential behavior in children may provide another useful vehicle for examining the development of the covert response system underlying the higher mental processes.

CONCLUSIONS

Some interesting developmental changes occurring between early and middle childhood have emerged from applying an S-R learning theory approach to problem solving in children. Analyses of these changes in terms of a very broad conception of behavior theory has shown that the behavior of very young children is dependent on environmental cues, with which relatively simple S-R connections are formed and to which the laws of learning derived from simpler species are applicable. Older children's behavior, if it is to be dealt with in an S-R framework, must be conceptualized in terms of chains of responses in which some of the links are or become covert. It is proposed that a combined developmental-experimental approach can provide an understanding of how this transition occurs by studying it at its inception.

BASIC COGNITIVE PROCESSES

REFERENCES

Buss, A. H. Rigidity as a function of reversal and nonreversal shifts in the learning of successive descriminations. *J. exp. Psychol.*, 1953, 45, 75-81.

Harrow, M., & Friedman, G. B. Comparing reversal and nonreversal shifts in concept formation with partial reinforcement controlled. *J. exp. Psychol.*, 1958, 55, 592-597.

Hull, C. L. The mechanism of the assembly of behavior segments in novel combinations suitable for problem solution. *Psychol. Rev.*, 1935, 42, 219-245.

Hull, C. L. *A behavior system.* Yale Univer. Press, 1952.

Kelleher, R. T. Discrimination learning as a function of reversal and nonreversal shifts. *J. exp. Psychol.*, 1956, 51, 379-384.

Kendler, H. H., & D'Amato, M. F. A comparison of reversal shifts and nonreversal shifts in human concept formation behavior. *J. exp. Psychol.*, 1955, 49, 165-174.

Kendler, H. H., & Kendler, T. S. Inferential behavior in preschool children. *J. exp. Psychol.*, 1956, 51, 311-314.

Kendler, H. H., Kendler, T. S., Plisskoff, S. S., & D'Amato, M. F. Inferential behavior in children: I. The influence of reinforcement and incentive motivation. *J. exp. Psychol.*, 1958, 55, 207-212.

Kendler, T. S., & Kendler, H. H. Reversal and nonreversal shifts in kindergarten children. *J. exp. Psychol.*, 1959, 58, 56-60.

Kendler, T. S., & Kendler, H. H. Inferential behavior in children: II. The influence of order of presentation. *J. exp. Psychol.*, 1961, 61, 442-448.

Kendler, T. S., Kendler, H. H., & Learnard, B. Mediated responses to size and brightness as a function of age. *Amer. J. Psychol.*, 1962, 75, 571-586.

Kendler, T. S., Kendler, H. H., & Wells, D. Reversal and nonreversal shifts in nursery school children. *J. comp. physiol. Psychol.*, 1960, 53, 83-87.

Kohler, W. *The mentality of apes.* Harcourt, Brace, 1925.

Koronakos, C. Inferential learning in rats: the problem-solving assembly of behavior segments. *J. comp. physiol. Psychol.*, 1959, 52, 231-235.

Luria, A. R. The role of language in the formation of temporary connections. In B. Simon (Ed.), *Psychology in the Soviet Union.* Stanford Univer. Press, 1957.

Maier, N. R. F. Reasoning in white rats. *Comp. Psychol. Monogr.*, 1929, No. 9.

Skinner, B. F. *The behavior of organisms.* Appleton-Century, 1938.

3

VERBAL FACTORS IN THE DISCRIMINATION LEARNING OF CHILDREN

Charles C. Spiker

Iowa Child Welfare Research Station

Most so-called stimulus-response theories in psychology are based on principles established in research on conditioning. The last 25 years has witnessed an increasing influence of such theories on research programs dealing with discrimination learning. That is, conditioning principles have been applied to discrimination learning data in an attempt to explain or account for the phenomena discovered in the discrimination learning situation. The Spence theory, published in 1936, was the first systematic attempt to apply conditioning principles to discrimination learning. For the first 10 or 15 years of this quarter century, the application of such theories was largely restricted to the discrimination performance of infrahuman subjects. Recent years have seen a marked increase in the number of applications of stimulus-response theories to the discrimination learning of human subjects, and, in particular, to that of children.

Since even behavioristic psychologists do not ignore introspection as a potential source of information, it was inevitable that behavior theorists would make increasing use of the notion of response-produced stimulation in their attempts to apply conditioning principles to human learning. The logical or philosophical justification for the use of such concepts was laid many years ago in the writings of such people as Tolman and Hull. These writers, and others, rejected the Watsonian doctrine that mentalistic, or, more precisely, mentalistic-sounding concepts could not appear in the vocabulary of psychology. They insisted, however, that such concepts be introduced only after having been defined by means of terms which referred to public phenomena.

The empirical utility of such a view was demonstrated in several experiments conducted in the 1930's. Experiments by Leeper (1935) and Hull (1933) demonstrated that rats could discriminate on the basis of being hungry or being thirsty, which led to the notion of drive stimuli (S_D). Shipley (1933, 1935), in his research on mediated or secondary generalization, demonstrated that stimuli resulting from a subject's response can serve as a cue to which other responses can be conditioned. This led to the concept of the (implicit) response-produced cue. The well-known research by Mowrer and Miller on conditioned fear provides another example of the usefulness of the idea of responses and stimuli that are not directly observed by the experimenter.

There are still many psychologists who are quite uneasy about the use of implicit stimuli and responses. The objection appears to be essentially the same as that formulated by Watson in his rejection of such concepts as percepts, images, thoughts, and other introspective mainstays. At the other extreme are psychologists, presumably behavioristic, who use such concepts so freely that one is hard put to find any indication of research-grounded underpinnings. The present writer, hopefully, falls between these two extremes. On the one hand, he recognizes the theoretical utility of the notion of implicit responses and the stimuli associated with them. On the other hand, he is aware of the superficiality of theoretical explanations which make use of such notions without at the same time providing empirical criteria for their introduction.

It is no simple matter to specify satisfactory criteria for the theoretical use of implicit responses and their stimuli. It seems fair to say that the bulk

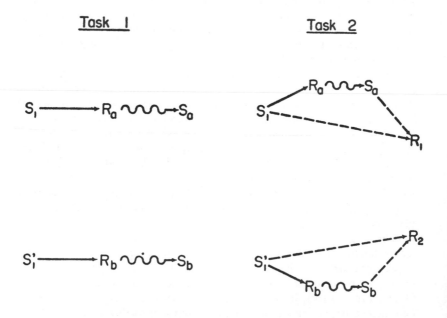

FIGURE 1—Schematic representation of the hypothesis of the acquired distinctiveness of cues.

of research conducted in this area has been concerned with determining the conditions under which it is useful to assume that such responses have occurred. The usefulness is evaluated in terms of an improvement in the theory's power to explain and predict behavior phenomena. The remainder of this paper is devoted to a summary of one research program concerned with testing the hypothesis of acquired distinctiveness of cues.

The acquired distinctiveness of cues hypothesis permits the prediction that, if an individual first learns to make discriminal responses to two or more similar stimuli, his subsequent learning to make different discriminal responses to these stimuli will be facilitated. The theoretical account offered by Miller (1948) for this type of transfer makes use of the concepts of mediating responses and response-produced stimuli. Miller's account is illustrated in Figure 1. During the first task, the individual learns to make distinctive responses (R_a and R_b) to the experimental stimuli (S_1 and S'_1). These responses produce distinctive stimuli (s_a and s_b). During the second (criterion) task, the experimental stimuli elicit the responses acquired in the first task. The stimulation produced by these responses thus forms a part of the total stimulus complexes to which the individual must learn new responses (R_1 and R_2). If the response produced stimuli are highly distinctive, the stimulus complexes of the second task will be distinctive, and, the more distinctive these complexes, the more readily the new set of responses will be acquired.

One of the frequently used experimental paradigms for testing the general hypothesis utilizes a relevant-stimulus group which is given preliminary training with the stimuli that appear in the criterion task and an irrelevant-stimulus group that is given similar preliminary training with a set of stimuli different from those used in the criterion task. In studies with human Ss, the preliminary training has typically involved the learning of different verbal responses to the stimuli, while the criterion task has required the S to learn different motor responses to the stimuli. Under certain conditions, investigators have reported verification of the hypothesis that relevant-stimulus pretraining results in facilitation in comparison to the irrelevant-stimulus pretraining. Some of the conditions indicated as necessary by presently available research include: (a) stimuli that are sufficiently similar that generalization among them occurs initially; (b) stimuli that do not readily elicit names or descriptive phrases in the control Ss; (c) sufficient preliminary training that the mediating responses are firmly established; (d) a criterion task that involves learning rather than simple psychophysical discriminations; (e) a criterion task for which the responses are discrete and not demanding of highly skilled performance.

The study of this type of transfer requires control over other sources of positive transfer, namely, warm-up and learning-to-learn. Research with human Ss in the transfer of learning has demonstrated that certain types of preliminary tasks serve to warm up S for subsequent tasks, even when the stimulus-response connections of the first task are unrelated to those of the second. The positive transfer resulting from these warm-up tasks has thus far been shown to be relatively transient, persisting for little more than a few hours, with most of the effects disappearing within a few minutes. Other research has shown that increasingly better performance on successive tasks results from the administration of a series of similar problems (e.g., a series of discrimination problems for either human or infrahuman Ss or a series of verbal learning tasks for human Ss). The results of facilitation from this source have been attributed to a response-set or learning-to-learn factor, and the facilitation has been shown to be relatively permanent.

The irrelevant stimulus group, mentioned before as the control group in the typical paradigm, has been used in order to control for both warm-up and learning-to-learn. Superior performance on the criterion task may thus be interpreted without reference to possible differences in warm-up or learning-to-learn.

Kurtz (1955) has suggested an interpretation of the facilitation occurring in such experiments which involves the notion of "observing responses." According to this view, if Ss are required to learn distinctive responses to the relevant stimuli during pretraining, they learn to make appropriate observing responses which transfer to the second task. An irrelevant-stimulus group, however, will not learn to make appropriate observing responses unless the irrelevant stimuli differ from each other with respect to the same dimensions as do the relevant stimuli. In effect, then, verbal pretraining is simply a convenient way to set up the observing responses, and it provides the experimenter with an objective criterion for determining when these observing responses have been firmly established. By this interpretation, the superior performance of the relevant stimulus groups may be attributed to the transfer of appropriate observing responses rather than to the benefits of the more distinctive response-produced stimulation.

A doctoral dissertation conducted in our laboratory by Gordon Cantor (1955) included an attempt to control for the differential perceptual experiences with the criterion task stimuli for Ss receiving relevant and irrelevant stimulus pretraining. The Ss for this experiment were preschool children. The criterion task was a simultaneous discrimination problem. The stimuli for the criterion task were a pair of pen-and-ink sketches of girls' faces. There were three groups of 20 Ss each, differing only in terms of the type of pretraining they received. A relevant-stimulus group learned the names "Jean" and "Peg" for the girls' faces. An irrelevant-stimulus group learned the names "Jack" and "Pete" for a pair of boys' faces. A third group, the "attention" group, was given approximately the same number of presentations of the relevant stimuli during pretraining, but they were simply asked to point to various features of the faces in order to assure "visual experience" with the stimuli. They were not required to learn names for the relevant stimuli.

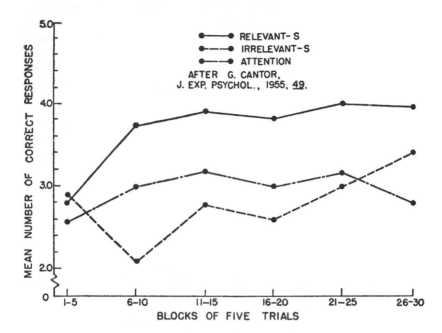

FIGURE 2—Mean number of correct responses as a function of trials and pretraining condition (Cantor).

All *S*s were given identical training in the criterion task, except for necessary counterbalancing of stimuli and stimulus order. They were given a marble for each choice of the rewarded face and were then allowed to exchange the accumulated marbles for a toy at the end of the experimental session. Figure 2 shows the number of correct choices in five-trial blocks for 30 trials of the criterion task. There it may be seen that the relevant-stimulus group performed better than either the irrelevant-stimulus or attention groups. This difference was statistically significant. Although the attention group performed somewhat better than the irrelevant group, the overall difference was not statistically reliable.

With respect to the Cantor experiment, it might be argued that, while the attention group had had visual experience with the relevant stimuli, they had not had such experience under a discrimination set as required by the Kurtz hypothesis. Thus, one might plausibly argue that the appropriate observing responses had not been established.

A subsequent experiment by Norcross and Spiker (1957) attempted to control for this possibility. The *S*s were again children of preschool age. The criterion task was a simultaneous discrimination problem and the stimuli were those developed by Cantor. The design included a relevant-stimulus and an irrelevant-stimulus group of 26 Ss each, and, to this extent, it represents a replication of the major features of the Cantor experiment. Instead of the Cantor "attention" group, however, a group of 18 Ss was substituted which received discriminative experience with the relevant stimuli, but which did not receive name-learning experience. This was accomplished by presenting the relevant stimuli in pairs and asking S to say "same" or "different" depending on whether duplicates of one member were presented or whether both members were jointly presented. This "discrimination" group was thus required to discriminate between the relevant stimuli in pretraining, but the Ss were not taught names for the pictures. Other procedures of the experiment were similar to those of Cantor.

TABLE 1

NUMBER OF CORRECT RESPONSES IN THIRTY TRANSFER TRIALS

| | GROUP R | | GROUP I | | GROUP D | |
Age	Mean	SD	Mean	SD	Mean	SD
Younger	19.5	6.0	15.9	3.7	17.1	5.0
Older	24.8	6.2	22.4	5.6	19.2	4.3

The results, shown in Table 1, in terms of the number of correct responses in 30 criterion task trials, demonstrated the relevant stimulus group to be superior to the irrelevant and discrimination groups, whereas the latter two did not differ significantly. Thus, although the superiority of the relevant stimulus group found by Cantor was confirmed, there was no evidence that the discrimination experience improved performance relative to the irrelevant stimulus pretraining.

The experiment by Kurtz (1955), the results of which he attributed to the role of observing responses, utilized the discrimination-type of pretraining, but the stimuli were presented one at a time in pretraining, and S was asked to judge whether the currently presented stimulus was the same as or different from the previous one. Conceivably, the successive method of presenting the relevant stimuli during discrimination pretraining might be more effective in eliciting the appropriate observing responses.

With this hypothesis in mind, the next experiment was designed (Spiker and Norcross, 1957). The Ss were again preschool children, the Cantor stimuli were used, and the criterion task was a simultaneous discrimination problem. The relevant-stimulus group of 18 Ss was included as in previous experiments. A discrimination group of 18 Ss like that of the previous experiment was used. A second discrimination group of 18 Ss was given successively presented stimuli during pretraining according to the Kurtz procedure. Neither discrimination group was required to learn names for the relevant stimuli during pretraining.

In Figure 3 are shown the results of this experiment in terms of the number of correct responses for each of the three groups on the criterion

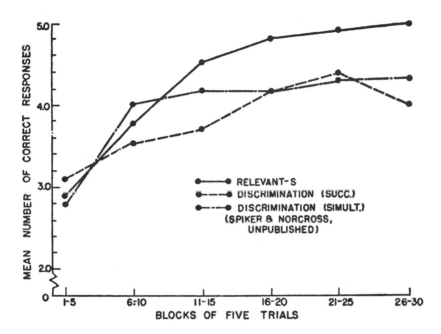

FIGURE 3—Mean number of correct responses as a function of trials and pretraining condition (Spiker and Norcross).

task, in blocks of five trials. The difference between the two discrimination groups was nonsignificant, while the relevant-stimulus group performed significantly better than either of the other two.

The results of these experiments suggest that there is facilitation resulting from prior learning of distinctive names for stimuli that cannot be attributed to warm-up, learning-to-learn, or observing responses. Apparently, there is something about the learning of names, *per se,* that results in the subsequent facilitation. To the extent that other implications of the acquired distinctiveness of cues hypothesis can be experimentally confirmed, the hypothesis may be used as a plausible explanation for these and similar findings.

The next two experiments were conducted in an attempt to confirm a further implication of the hypothesis. Taken jointly with other principles in learning theory, the hypothesis leads to the prediction that the amount of facilitation in such experiments will be an increasing function of the distinctiveness of the response-produced stimuli. On the assumption that the similarity of the responses is correlated with the similarity of the stimuli they produce, the stimulus complexes in the criterion task will be more distinctive the more dissimilar the responses learned in pretraining. More specifically, if the Ss learn similar names for the experimental stimuli, they should not do as well on the criterion task as Ss who learn distinctive names.

This deduction was tested by Norcross (1958) in her doctoral dissertation, which consisted of two separate experiments. In both experiments she made use of an intrasubject design, which, in addition to the statistical precision it permitted, also provided a convenient control over the warm-up and learning-to-learn factors. The Ss were kindergarten children. The criterion task consisted in the presentation, one at a time, of four faces, to each of which the child was to learn to push the appropriate one of four pushbutton switches. The stimuli were a pair of Indian girls' faces and a pair of Indian boys' faces. A correct response was designated by a bell, and S was allowed only one response per stimulus presentation.

TABLE 2

SCHEMATIC REPRESENTATION OF EXPERIMENTAL DESIGN
(Norcross [1958])

TASK 1		TASK 2
Subgroup 1	*Subgroup 2*	*Both Subgroups*
Boy 1 —— zim	Boy 1 —— wug	Boy 1 —— Button 1
Boy 2 —— zam	Boy 2 —— kos	Boy 2 —— Button 2
Girl 1 —— wug	Girl 1 —— zim	Girl 1 —— Button 3
Girl 2 —— kos	Girl 2 —— zam	Girl 2 —— Button 4

The design of both experiments is shown in Table 2. During pretraining, each S learned a pair of similar names (zim and zam) to one pair of faces and a pair of dissimilar names (wug and kos) to the other pair of faces. One-half the Ss learned similar names to the boys' faces and dissimilar names to the girls' faces, and vice versa for the other half. A total of 30 kindergarten children were used in the first experiment, with each S serving as his own control. In pretraining, the Ss learned the names to one perfect trial, where a trial consisted of the presentation of all four faces in some order. On the second day, the Ss were reviewed to the same criterion, and then 15 trials on the criterion task were administered immediately. During performance on the criterion task, the Ss were required to verbalize the names for the stimuli prior to responding with the buttons. The results of the experiment are given in Figure 4, in terms of the mean number of correct responses in blocks of three trials. It can be seen that Ss performed better on the dissimilarly named stimuli than they did on the similarly named. The difference is significant at the 1 per cent level of confidence.

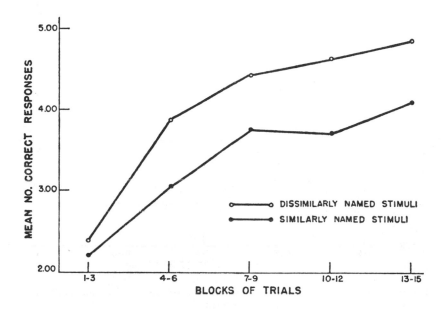

FIGURE 4—Mean number of correct responses as a function of trials and similarity of stimulus names (Norcross, Experiment 1).

In her first experiment, Norcross noted that the Ss, during the criterion task, misnamed the similarly-named stimuli more frequently than they did the dissimilarly-named stimuli, in spite of their having learned the names to the same criterion in pretraining. The E did not correct the Ss for errors in naming during the criterion task. Examination of the data suggested that Ss tended to make more button-pushing errors following misnaming than they did after correct naming. The second experiment was conducted to assure that the Ss made the correct naming responses immediately prior to responding during the criterion task. Twenty-six kindergarten children were used in this experiment which was identical to the first except that the experimenter corrected all misnaming during the criterion task and required S to verbalize the correct name prior to the button-pushing response. If the results of this experiment were to agree with those of the preceding experiment, it would appear that one can rule out the possible contribution of having the response-produced stimuli inconsistently associated with the experimental stimuli.

The results of this experiment are shown in Figure 5. Here it may be seen that the Ss again performed better on the dissimilarly- than on the

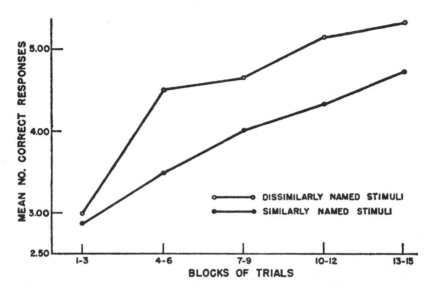

FIGURE 5—Mean number of correct responses as a function of trials and similarity of stimulus names (Norcross, Experiment II).

similarly-named stimuli. The difference was again significant. It will be recalled that in these two experiments each S served as his own control. This means that there are no differential effects of warm-up and learning-to-learn on the two experimental conditions. Furthermore, since each S learned in pretraining to respond differentially to the stimuli that subsequently appeared in the criterion task, the observing responses mentioned by Kurtz (1955) should have been set up during preliminary training and should have transferred to the second task equally for both pairs of stimuli. Thus, none of these three factors can be used to account for differences in performance for the two types of stimuli. These experiments are offered, then, as strong evidence for the importance of the verbal responses themselves, rather than of accidental concomitants, in determining the performance on the criterion task.

It will be noted that from neither of the Norcross experiments can we infer whether the transfer was negative, positive, or both. That is, we do not know whether the similar names resulted in interference, the distinctive names resulted in facilitation, or both interference and facilitation were involved. It should be noted that the hypothesis of acquired distinctiveness of cues will predict either facilitation or interference, depending on the similarity of the names relative to the similarity of the stimuli. If the verbal responses produce stimuli more similar than the external stimuli, there should be interference. If the response-produced stimuli are more distinctive than the experimental stimuli, there should be facilitation. What is required to determine the direction of the transfer is a control condition involving stimuli in the criterion task for which the subjects have not previously learned any names.

Such an experiment was subsequently conducted in our laboratory as a doctoral dissertation by Reese (1958). In addition to this hypothesis, Reese was also concerned with the hypothesis that the amount of verbal pretraining affects the performance on the second task, when such nonspecific factors as warm-up and learning-to-learn have been controlled. The design of Reese's experiment is shown in Table 3. Task 2 was a motor paired-associate task

TABLE 3

SCHEMA OF EXPERIMENTAL DESIGN
(Reese [1958])

Learning Criterion in Pretraining	Distinctive-Name Group (D)		Similar-Name Group (S)	
	Task 1	Task 2	Task 1	Task 2
High—two consecutive errorless blocks	$S_1 \rightarrow R_{v1}$	$S_1 \rightarrow R_{m1}$	$S_1 \rightarrow R_{v1}$	$S_1 \rightarrow R_{m1}$
	$S_1' \rightarrow R_{v2}$	$S_1' \rightarrow R_{m2}$	$S_1' \rightarrow R_{v}'_1$	$S_1' \rightarrow R_{m2}$
Low—one-third number of blocks for "high" ..	$S_2 \rightarrow R_{v3}$	$S_2 \rightarrow R_{m3}$	$S_2 \rightarrow R_{v2}$	$S_2 \rightarrow R_{m3}$
	$S_2' \rightarrow R_{v4}$	$S_2' \rightarrow R_{m4}$	$S_2' \rightarrow R_{v}'_2$	$S_2' \rightarrow R_{m4}$
None—		$S_3 \rightarrow R_{m5}$		$S_3 \rightarrow R_{m5}$
		$S_3' \rightarrow R_{m6}$		$S_3' \rightarrow R_{m6}$

in which colored lights were presented in a single aperture, one at a time, and S was to select one of six buttons arranged in a semicircle. This type of task has been analyzed as a successive discrimination problem. A stimulus light was presented, S was allowed 3 seconds to respond, and, at the end of 3 seconds, a small indicator light appeared beside the correct button, remaining on for a 2-second period. The first task involved the same presentation apparatus, but without the response unit present. In Table 3, the v and the m signify verbal and motor responses, respectively. Different numerical subscripts indicate different responses or different stimuli—that is, those which produce little or no generalization. A pair of stimuli or responses differentiated only by the presence or absence of the prime sign are similar —that is, generalization occurs between them. Thus, S_1 and S_1' are similar stimuli, whereas S_1 and S_2 are readily discriminable. R_{v1} and R_{v1}' are similar verbal responses; R_{m1} and R_{m2} are distinctive motor responses. Reese had two different groups of fourth, fifth, and sixth grade Ss, 36 per group. One of these groups learned similar names for similar pairs of stimuli in task 1 (group S), and the other learned distinctive names for similar pairs of stimuli in task 1 (group D).

Within each group, the names for one pair of similar stimuli were learned to a high criterion—two consecutive correct blocks of presentations, each block consisting of eight stimulus presentations. A second pair of similar stimuli was presented only one-third as frequently as the first pair. The third pair of stimuli was not presented at all during pretraining. In this way, Reese established three levels of first-task training which could then be compared on a within-subject basis. We shall refer to these three levels as "high," "low," and "none."

On the basis of some preliminary work, he selected three pairs of stimulus lights—a pair of reds, a pair of greens, and a pair of blues. From preliminary work, these were judged to be of approximately the same degree of difficulty, although the results of his experiment indicated that this judgment was not entirely correct. Similarly, two pairs of distinctive names (lev-mib and wug-zam) and two pairs of similar names (zim-zam and wug-wog) were selected. An elaborate counterbalancing system was utilized which will not be described here in detail. The counterbalancing was designed to control for possible differential difficulty of the light-button pairings, for the differential difficulty of the two pairs of distinctive names, and for the differential difficulty of the two pairs of similar names. Looking at Table 3 again, the reader will note that, as the design is schematized, R_{v1} and R_{v2} are shown as being given a high level of pretraining. Actually this was true for only half the Ss in group D; the other half received these names under the low level of pretraining. Similar counterbalancing was utilized for the similar names of group S. The stimuli and buttons were also counterbalanced with respect to the level of pretraining.

Immediately after S reached criterion in pretraining, the response unit was put in place for task 2. He was then given training until he had reached a criterion of four consecutive errorless trials, or until 20 trials had been administered, where a trial consisted of the presentation of all six stimuli in some order. Reese's basic response measure was the number of within-pair, generalized errors. That is, it was the number of times that S responded to S_1 in task 2 with the response that was correct for S_1', the number of times he responded to S_2 with the response that was correct for S_2', etc. The pretraining was designed to reduce the amount of generalization (or increase it for similar names) between pairs of similar stimuli. It was not designed to affect between-pair errors. This basic measure was then divided by the total number of errors occurring to each pair of stimuli, and this proportion was multiplied by 100 to obtain a percentage measure. Thus, the measure which he analyzed was the percentage of total errors for each pair of stimuli that were generalized, within-pair errors.

Analysis of the number of trials required to reach criterion in task 1 revealed a differential difficulty in the two pairs of similar names. The wug-wog pair required significantly more trials to learn. The zim-zam pair was intermediate in difficulty, and the two pairs of distinctive names were easiest and of approximately the same level of difficulty. On the assumption that the differential difficulty of learning in task 1 reflected differential similarity of the pairs of names, Reese concluded that he had three levels of similarity of names rather than the two levels that he had originally designed. There-fore, he analyzed his data from task 2 in terms of three levels of name similarity with three degrees of task 1 learning. Since the three groups did not receive exactly the same mean number of trials, Reese adjusted the scores

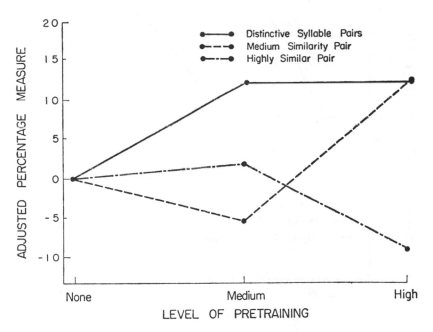

FIGURE 6—Facilitation and interference from stimulus pretraining as a function of level of pretraining and similarity of stimulus names (Reese).

for each group by subtracting each S's scores on the no-pretraining stimuli from his score on each of the other two levels of pretraining.

The results are shown in Figure 6 with signs changed so that a positive score represents facilitation and a negative score, interference. It can be seen that increasing amounts of first-task practice on the distinctive names produced increased facilitation in task 2. Increase in the amount of first-task practice with the names of intermediate similarity first brought about interference and then marked positive transfer. An increase in the amount of first-task practice with names of high similarity at first produced little or no effect, but then a large amount of negative transfer.

The statistical analysis of these results indicated that there is a significant interaction between the amount of first-task practice and the similarity of the names learned in task 1. Thus, whether verbal pretraining produces interference or facilitation on a subsequent discrimination task depends upon whether or not the pretraining is carried to a high enough level and also upon the degree of similarity of the names.

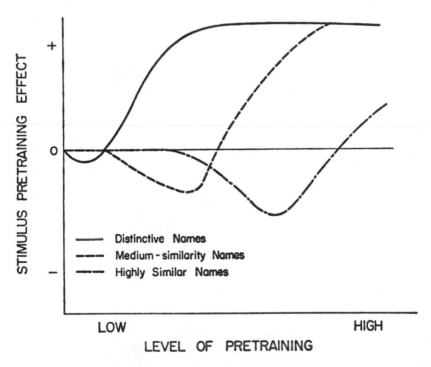

FIGURE 7—Theoretical generalized relationship between the effect of stimulus pretraining, level of pretraining, and similarity of stimulus names (Reese).

Reese suggested a generalization of these findings which is represented in Figure 7. Verbally stated, this generalization is that poorly learned names, whether distinctive or similar, will produce interference; well learned names, whether distinctive or similar, will produce facilitation. It takes account of the well-known fact in verbal learning that similar responses will generally be learned more slowly than distinctive ones and that retention will be poorer. This finding is particularly reliable when the responses have been learned as a list prior to the time that associative learning begins, a condition which obtained in both the Reese and Norcross experiments. Thus, according to this interpretation, if the names are highly distinctive, even a moderate number of pretraining trials may produce a high amount of positive transfer. With intermediate similarity of names, a moderate number of pretraining trials may produce interference, but a high amount of pretraining will produce facilitation.

This interpretation emphasizes the S's tendency to confuse the similar *responses* in the second task rather than his tendency to generalize on the basis of the response-produced stimuli. If the names are inadequately retained, so that they occur indifferently to the stimuli, then we would predict interference rather than facilitation. The interference is expected because each stimulus complex would frequently have elements (the response-produced stimuli) in common with every other stimulus. To the degree that this occurs, there should be an increase in generalization among the stimulus complexes of task 2 with a resultant confusion among the second-task responses.

Although most of the results that have been presented above are consistent with the hypothesis of acquired distinctiveness of cues, at least one alternative hypothesis should be considered. Theoretically speaking, this hypothesis is at an entirely different level. It was suggested some years ago in connection with an experiment involving verbal pretraining of preschool children with subsequent performance on a delayed reaction experiment (Spiker [1956]). It was found that Ss who had been taught the names for the stimuli used in the delayed reaction task performed better than those who had not been taught the names. It was also noted that many of the Ss who had been taught the names "bridged" the delay interval by saying aloud the name of the stimulus which they selected following the delay interval. It was suggested at that time that the verbal pretraining might produce more efficient verbal rehearsal or recitation during the intervals between presentations in the typical verbal pretraining study. It is of some interest to note, that to the writer's knowledge, no one has yet reported facilitation in a verbal pretraining study in which the responses of the transfer task could not be readily described or named verbally. On the contrary, several reports of no transfer have involved responses requiring considerable skill-learning on the part of the subject (e.g., responses in the Mashburn apparatus). In an experiment by the writer (Spiker [1960]), it was found that instructions to rehearse between presentations of items in a verbal paired-associate task produced marked improvement in the performance of fourth-, fifth-, and sixth-grade children. That verbal rehearsal is a potent factor in verbal learning studies has been known for a number of years. The role it plays in certain types of "motor" tasks has not received as careful attention.

From the research reported here, it seems justified to conclude that, under certain conditions, some of which can be specified, the possession by *S* of names for the stimuli he is subsequently to receive in a discrimination problem will affect his learning of that problem. If the discrimination stimuli are similar enough that generalization among them initially occurs, if the responses to be learned in the discrimination problem are discrete, if the names learned in pretraining are distinctive, and if the names have been learned to a high criterion, then the results tend to be facilitation. On the other hand, if the names learned in pretraining are similar and if they have not been learned to a high criterion, or are not adequately retained in the second task, the evidence suggests that the results will be interference. Indeed, there is some evidence that even distinctive names, if not learned to a high enough criterion, will produce interference (McCormack [1957]). And there is some evidence from the Reese experiment to indicate that even similar names, if learned to a high enough criterion, will produce facilitation in the second task.

These empirical facts can reasonably be explained, either by the hypothesis of acquired distinctiveness of cues or by the verbal recitation hypothesis. A significant contribution to this area would be made by a research project that demonstrated whether both of these explanations are required or whether one of them is entirely sufficient.

REFERENCES

CANTOR, G. N. The effects of three types of pretraining on discrimination learning in preschool children. *J. exp. Psychol.*, 1955, 49, 339-342.

HULL, C. L. Differential habituation to internal stimuli in the albino rat. *J. comp. Psychol.*, 1933, 16, 255-273.

KURTZ, K. H. Discrimination of complex stimuli: the relationship of training and test stimuli in transfer of discrimination. *J. exp. Psychol.*, 1955, 50, 283-292.

LEEPER, R. The role of motivation in learning: a study of the phenomenon of differential motivational control of the utilization of habits. *J. genet. Psychol.*, 1935, 46, 3-40.

McCORMACK, P. D. Negative transfer in motor performance following a critical amount of verbal pretraining. Unpublished doctoral dissertation, State Univer. of Iowa, 1957.

MILLER, N. E. Theory and experiment relating psychoanalytic displacement to stimulus-response generalization. *J. abnorm. soc. Psychol.*, 1948, 43, 155-178.

NORCROSS, K. J. The effects on discrimination performance of the similarity of previously acquired stimulus names. *J. exp. Psychol.*, 1958, 56, 305-309.

NORCROSS, K. J., & SPIKER, C. C. The effects of type of stimulus pretraining on discrimination performance in preschool children. *Child Develpm.*, 1957, 28, 79-84.

Reese, H. W. Transfer to a discrimination task as a function of amount of stimulus pretraining and similarity of stimulus names. Unpublished doctoral dissertation, State
Univer. of Iowa, 1958.

Shipley, W. C. An apparent transfer of conditioning. *J. gen. Psychol.*, 1933, 8, 382-391.

Shipley, W. C. Indirect conditioning. *J. gen. Psychol.*, 1935, 12, 337-357.

Spence, K. W. The nature of discrimination learning in animals. *Psychol. Rev.*, 1936,
43, 427-449.

Spiker, C. C. Stimulus pretraining and subsequent performance in the delayed reaction
experiment. *J. exp. Psychol.*, 1956, 52, 107-111.

Spiker, C. C. Associative transfer in verbal paired-associative learning. *Child Develpm.*,
1960, 31, 73-87.

Spiker, C. C., & Norcross, K. J. The effects of previously acquired stimulus names on
discrimination performance. Unpublished manuscript, State Univer. of Iowa, 1957.

4

PSYCHOLOGICAL SIGNIFICANCE OF STYLES
OF CONCEPTUALIZATION [1]

Jerome Kagan *and* Howard A. Moss[2]

Fels Research Institute

Irving E. Sigel

Merrill-Palmer Institute

Study of cognitive products during the last quarter century has been influenced by domestic theory and Gallic persuasion. The behavioral theorists have been concerned with the role of mediating symbols and motivational variables; whereas those who have been influenced by Piaget have turned their attention to the maturational stages of cognitive organization. However, the intimate interaction between perceptual organization and the conceptual process and the importance of stable individual differences in mode of cognitive functioning have not received as much systematic attention as they, perhaps, deserve.

Current theory holds that the child's initial perceptions of the world are global, but, with time, become more articulated and differentiated. The 4-year-old has a penchant for reacting to the stimulus-as-a-whole, whereas the 9-year-old is more likely to consider both the whole and the internal parts of a stimulus array. It is probable that this age difference is a matter of maturational capability as well as acquired habit.

Conceptualization passes through a similar developmental sequence. Concepts, which are labels for groups of similar things, are also global and overgeneralized initially, but they become specific and differentiated with age. However, there is a second maxim about conceptual growth that we teach our students. With age, the child becomes increasingly more capable of using abstract concepts. Thus, cognitive development is accompanied by more differentiated perceptions and the acquisition of *differentiated* as well as *abstract* concepts. To illustrate, the child initially labels all objects that have four feet and move "dogs." With increasing age, this label is applied selectively to objects with more discrete characteristics, and concurrently, the

---

[1] This research was supported, in part, by research grants M-4464 and M-1260 from the National Institute of Mental Health, United States Public Health Service.
[2] Now at the National Institute of Mental Health.

more abstract label "animal" or "mammal" becomes an active part of the child's language repertoire.

Thus, differentiation and abstraction proceed simultaneously, and Brown (1958) has suggested that the number of differentiated elements that belong to a category or class may be a more critical attribute of level of cognitive development than the broadness of the category. In effect, the child gradually comes to learn structured wholes or *"ensemble des parties,"* as Piaget phrases it.

Although the constructs of differentiation and abstraction help us understand the gross differences between the cognitive activity of preschool and school age children, they do not adequately account for the blatant individual differences in cognitive products among children of adequate IQ at any one age. Even the assumption that all children do not pass through the above states at the same rate is not strong enough to bear the burden of explaining the qualitative differences in intellective performance among school age children and adults who have no known organic deficit. Guilford (1956) has attempted to fill part of this theoretical void by postulating individual differences in the five basic cognitive processes of recognition, memory, convergent and divergent thinking, and evaluation.

There are additional classes of variables, however, that deserve attention in descriptions of cognitive activity. One of these classes has acquired the title of "cognitive style," a term that refers to stable individual preferences in mode of perceptual organization and conceptual categorization of the external environment. One particular style dimension involves the tendency to analyze and to differentiate the stimulus environment in contrast to categorizations that are based on the stimulus-as-a-whole.

Among children of adequate intelligence there are those who characteristically analyze and differentiate the stimulus field, applying labels to subelements of the whole. Others tend to categorize a relatively undifferentiated stimulus. Some children are splitters, others are lumpers. We have called the former response an analytic attitude and believe that it is related, in some degree, to Witkin's notion of field independence versus field dependence (1954).

Our present constructs are not the products of a' fanciful theoretical conception of human cognition. They began as accidental discoveries, and, as a result, the empirical work during the last few years contains a trial-and-error quality. Only recently have we gained some insight into the processes underlying an analytic attitude and devised some direct experimental tests of our hunches.

Initially, we found a strong association between the way adults sorted human figures and varied aspects of their behavior. Figure 1 illustrates one of the stimulus arrays that was presented to a group of 71 Fels adults (age range 20 to 29) who were being studied as part of a larger project. Each subject was asked to select out groups of figures that went together on a

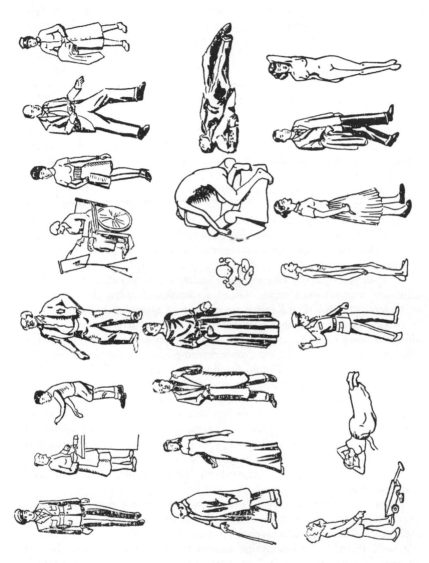

FIGURE 1—Stimulus array used with figure sorting task for adult Ss.

common basis, and a total of 32 conceptual responses was obtained with three different stimulus arrays. The concepts these individuals produced could be classified as belonging to one of two basic orientations and to one of three formal conceptual classes. The two basic orientations were *egocentric* vs. *stimulus centered,* and the three conceptual classes (*analytic-descriptive, relational,* and *inferential-categorical*) each had subcategories with denotative meaning. The two basic orientations were defined as follows:

Egocentric. This class refers to concepts which are based on the individual's personalized, affective classification of a group of stimuli and/or the inclusion of aspects of the subject as part of the conceptual grouping. That is, the individual uses his personal reactions to the stimuli or his personal characteristics in arriving at a basis for similarity among the stimuli. Examples of egocentric concepts with the stimuli in Figure 1 would be "People I like," "People who scare me," "People who like me," and "People wearing the same clothes I am wearing."

Stimulus centered. In this alternative orientation the concepts are based on aspects of the external stimulus; the individual's personal feelings are not part of the categorization. Examples are: "Men," "Soldiers," "Active children," "Happy people," and "Women with skirts on."

The three formal conceptual categories under each of these orientations follows:

Analytic-descriptive. This category includes concepts that are based on similarity in objective elements, within a stimulus complex, that were *part* of the total stimulus. The S selects an element of objective similarity shared by two or more figures that is a differentiated part of the total stimulus. Moreover, the conceptual label adopted by the S contains a reference to the objective attribute shared by the grouped stimuli. Some examples of analytic-descriptive concepts are: "People holding something," "People with their left arm up," "People with no shoes on," and "People holding weapons."

Inferential-categorical. This category includes concepts that are not directly based on a partial objective attribute of the stimuli, but involve an inference about the stimuli grouped together. Moreover, in an inferential concept, as in a descriptive one, any stimulus in the group is an independent instance of the conceptual label. Examples of inferential concepts are: "Professional men," "People who help others," "Poor people," "Soldiers," and "Medical people."

Relational. This category includes concepts that are based on a functional relationship between or among the stimuli grouped together. This functional relationship can involve temporal or spatial contiguity between objects or interobject relationships among the stimulus members. In this category no stimulus is an independent instance of the concept, and each stimulus depends for its membership on its relationship to other stimuli in the group. Examples of relational concepts are: "Murder scene—he shot this man." "A family," "A married couple," "People arguing with each other,"

"Stages in the life of a person," "Mother cutting cake for the child," and "Doctor and nurse take care of this crippled person."

We viewed the relational response as requiring the least amount of analysis of the stimulus array. Relational concepts differ from analytic-descriptive concepts with respect to the part-whole analysis of the stimulus. In a relational concept each stimulus in the group retains its complete identity and is classified as a whole. In an analytic-descriptive concept the S selects from each stimulus a specific subelement that is similar to a subelement within another stimulus. In effect, to form a descriptive concept, S usually separates figure (the element of similarity) from ground (the irrelevant aspects of the stimulus). In a relational concept the entire stimulus is figure, and there are no background elements. For example, in the descriptive concept, "People with shoes on," the crucial stimulus element is the presence of shoes, while the remaining aspects of the stimuli are disregarded. However, in the relational concept, "A family," all aspects of each stimulus member are relevant for the concept. Thus descriptive concepts involve an active conceptual analysis, while relational concepts seem to involve a passive acceptance of the entire stimulus. Moreover, production of relational concepts to these particular stimuli was often a reaction to their most obvious aspects, while descriptive concepts were often based on more subdued attributes.

The remainder of this paper summarizes our empirical work to date on the significance of a preference for analytic categorizations in both children and adults.

Study A

Correlates of a Descriptive Approach in Fels Adults

In our first study, 36 men and 35 women between 20 and 29 years of age were administered a lengthy assessment battery. The battery included five hours of interview, followed by eight hours of testing over five separate sessions. Following the interview, each S was rated on a seven-point scale for 36 variables related to varied aspects of personality. These ratings were made before the subjects were administered the sorting tasks, and the median interrater reliability for these variables was $+.80$. The figure-sorting tasks were administered during a three-hour session in which tests of tachistoscopic perception and intelligence were also administered.

The men who were above the median on analytic concepts, in contrast to those below the median, were rated significantly higher ($p < .05$) (all p values mentioned in this paper are for two tails) on the following interview derived variables: (a) reluctance to be dependent on their family or friends, (b) striving for social recognition, and (c) concern with intellectual mastery. These individuals also had slightly higher IQs than the other men in the sample. Since these Ss had been observed since birth, independent evaluations of their behavior during childhood were also available. These evaluations were based on ratings of prose material describing the child's behavior at home, at the Fels nursery school or day camp, and at his public school.

As children (age 6 to 14), the analytic men were rated as persistent in the face of problem situations, confident in their approach to challenging, intellectual tasks, and motivated to obtain achievement-related goals ($p <$ .05 for all three variables).

The men who were above the median on relational concepts, in contrast to those below the median, differed from the analytic men in many ways. These men were rated as more dependent on their family as adults ($p <$ .05) and less concerned with the acquisition of recognition goals ($p < .10$). As children, these men were rated as anxious in new social situations, and they behaved as if they expected rejection from peers and adults.

These conceptual preferences for analytic-descriptive or relational concepts were correlated with the S's autonomic reactivity at rest. The men who were both above the median on analytic-descriptive sorts and below the median on relational sorts had more frequent spontaneous PGR responses *at rest* (i.e., drops in palmar resistance of 600 ohms or more during a ten-minute rest period) than the men who were high on relational and low on analytic concepts ($p < .05$). Thus, analytic-descriptive men were ambitious, independent, and had relatively high levels of spontaneous sudomotor reactivity. Men who preferred relational concepts were dependent, not overly ambitious, and showed less labile sudomotor reactions. The relations between these conceptual variables and overt behavior were more equivocal for the adult women. Although the directions of the relations were similar, they were not as significant.

The differences between these behavior clusters suggested the usefulness of postulating a conceptual dimension of analytic versus nonanalytic that would be superordinate to the empirically derived constructs of analytic and relational sorting responses on this test. We assumed that analytic concepts required a careful and purposive analysis of the stimulus and a differentiation of relevant from irrelevant cues. The men who produced analytic concepts behaved as if the stimulus arrays were something to be objectively differentiated and unambiguously categorized. It seemed more than coincidence that their overt, interpersonal behavior reflected a similar orientation. The men who produced relational sorts were behaviorally more passive and dependent, and their conceptual approach to the figures lacked differentiation. These men grouped the figures on the basis of their obvious meanings. They would typically select a man with a gun, a wounded person, and a doctor and reply, "A murder scene." This appeared to be a response to the most salient cues of the stimuli, a response that did not require much analysis or differentiation. The different cognitive requirements for analytic vs. relational concepts, together with the negative correlation between these categories, suggested the reasonableness of assuming a preferred mode of conceptualization that ranged from analytic to nonanalytic.

As suggested earlier, the present descriptions of analytic versus non-analytic conceptual attitudes are somewhat similar to concepts used by other investigators. Witkin and his colleagues have used the Gottschaldt Embedded Figures and spatial orientation tests (e.g., rod and frame techniques) to assess field independence—the ability to select relevant stimuli that are embedded in a larger context and to resist the interfering effects of contextual stimuli (Witkin *et al.* [1954]). Moreover, Witkin has found behavioral correlates of field independence (using spatial orientation methods) that resemble in part the behavioral characteristics associated with production of analytic concepts. Field independent college men, in contrast to field dependent ones, were rated following an interview as more independent and self-reliant in problem situations, more insightful, and more self-confident. As in our work, the results were more striking for men than for women. Other investigations using one of Witkin's indexes of field independence (Embedded Figures Test) have indicated that field independent adults tend to differentiate experience more than field dependent subjects (Bieri *et al.* [1958], Gollin and Baron [1954]).

The Menninger and N.Y.U. groups have also studied cognitive styles in contexts that are closely related to perceptual functioning. Gardner (1953, 1959), Holzman (1954a, 1954b, 1959, 1960), and Klein (1954) have been concerned with preferential methods of organizing experience and have called these strategies perceptual attitudes, *Anschauungen,* or styles of cognitive control. In a recent monograph they postulated six types of cognitive styles, one of which is related to Witkin's dimension of field independence.

The research to date suggests that the preference or ability to analyze and to differentiate complex stimulus arrays may be involved in behaviors as diverse as memory organization, interpretation of ink blots, and psychophysical judgments. The material to be presented in the remainder of this paper suggests that an analytic attitude may influence the quality of many kinds of cognitive products (e.g., verbal content in an interview, projective test responses). Our current program is designed to test the stability and development of an analytic or nonanalytic attitude and the antecedent variables that are responsible for this predisposition.

Study B

Perceptual Vigilance and an Analytic Attitude

With the cooperation of Harry Jerison of Antioch College a human vigilance experiment was devised. A group of 16 male undergraduates were required to monitor a Mackworth clock on which signals, which were defined as 20 degree steps of the clock hand, were interposed between one-per-second ten degree steps. The signals were programmed at intersignal inter-

FIGURE 2 (part 1)—Sample stimuli used in conceptual style test for children.

FIGURE 2 (part 2)—Sample stimuli used in conceptual style test for children.

vals ranging from 52 to 203 seconds with an average intersignal interval of 138 seconds. These Ss monitored the clock during two uninterrupted 92-minute work sessions. During one of the sessions S had to press a button continually in order to keep the display illuminated. Each of the Ss was scheduled for three test sessions on alternate days. During the first session he was administered the two arrays of human figures described earlier and required to produce eight conceptual sorts to each array. He was also given a ten-minute familiarization period with the vigilance experiment and several TAT cards to assess production of achievement fantasy. The second and third sessions involved vigilance sessions with or without the requirement that S illuminate the display. These sessions were administered in counterbalanced order.

The rank order correlation between accurate detections during the 92 minute vigil in which the clock was illuminated and number of analytic conceptual responses was $+.54$ $(p < .05)$. The corresponding correlation between analytic concepts and accurate detections during the session in which the subject was required to illuminate the clock was also positive, but short of significance (rho $= +.36$). Thus, production of analytic concepts was associated with the ability to detect small changes in a monotonous but constantly changing perceptual field over a long period of time.

Correlates of an Analytic Style in Children

We have initiated investigations of a preference for analytic categorizations in children in order to gain more insight into the antecedent events that predispose a child to develop and maintain an analytic attitude. Our first task was to devise a special set of stimuli that might serve as a preliminary measure of this conceptual preference.

One of our tests included a set of stimuli, each containing three black-and-white drawings. For each stimulus, the child was required to select two of the figures that "were alike or went together in some way." For all stimuli, two, and sometimes three, types of conceptual responses were possible (e.g., an analytic and a relational response, an inferential and an analytic response, or an inferential and a relational response). There were 44 stimuli in the initial form of the test. We recently eliminated the 14 stimuli that were least discriminating, leaving a set of 30 cards. Figure 2 contains eight sample test stimuli.

Three points should be mentioned before we present the results of this study. First, the stimuli used with children are perceptually and conceptually simple and do *not* allow for highly inferential concepts. This was done purposely because we were primarily interested in the production of analytic and relational concepts. We attempted, therefore, to prevent the child from using inferential categorical responses, for these are typically more popular with both school age children and adults.

Second, in this type of task, the child's verbal label or reason for group-ing is the only behavior that can be coded. We are aware of the fact that one child may apply the label "animal" to a grouping of a dog and a cat as the result of a rote association to these specific objects. The same child might be unable to use this concept if zebra and elephant had been illus-trated. A second child may comprehend the abstract quality of the word "animal" and be capable of applying it to a broad class of relevant objects. The problem of what the child means when he uses a class name is an especially knotty one. However, the scoring of analytic or relational concepts is somewhat insulated from this problem.

Third, since the stimuli are simple and always allow for more than one conceptual grouping, we have assumed that the production of an analytic grouping is a result of a preference for this kind of concept and is not always due to the child's inability to produce other kinds of groupings. We have verified this assumption by performing inquiries after the initial administration of the test. Almost all children are capable of giving alterna-tive concepts easily.

Finally, since this task is different in many ways from the free sorting of human figures used with adults, it is probable that analytic responses on the two tests are not identical in meaning. However, in order to avoid the proliferation of terms, we shall continue to use the term "analytic" when referring to the results for children. The reader should bear in mind the potential difference in meaning between analytic responses to the two test arrays.

Study C

In this study a total of 38 boys and 39 girls from two sixth grades in different cities were administered the following battery, with male exam-iners for the boys and female examiners for the girls:

Conceptual style test (44 triads). The S was asked to select the two "things that are alike or go together in some way." The responses were scored for analytic, relational, and inferential concepts.

Word association test. The S was required to give his first association to each of 40 words (20 count nouns, 10 adjectives, and 10 transitive verbs). The associations to the nouns were scored for a variety of categories. We shall be concerned here with three major categories: (a) noun-noun sequences, (b) noun – not noun sequences, and (c) a subcategory of (b) in which nouns were followed by verbs that were phrase completions (e.g., dog-bark, baby-cries, moon-shines).

Serial learning. Three separate lists of 12 words each were devised, with two six-word groupings in each list. The groups of six words belonged to either an inferential or a relational concept. For example, the first list contained the words: thunder, dog, lightning, cat, rain, cow, puddle, horse, storm, pig, windy, chicken. We assumed that the words thunder, lightning, puddle, storm, rain, and windy were all *related* to each other in a functional way (i.e., they were contiguous events in the child's experience of a storm). The words dog, cat, cow, horse, pig, and chicken, on the other hand, had no functional interrelationship but belonged to the inferential category "animal."

Two of the lists contained six words whose parts had similar sounds. For example, list 2 contained the words: blind, black, blank, blow, bless, and bloom, each of the words having the initial *bl* sound in common. It was anticipated that the analytic children might be most sensitive to these similarities in sound and preferentially group these words together in the recall. The three lists used in the learning task appear in Table 1.

TABLE 1

LISTS USED IN SERIAL LEARNING TASK
(SIXTH GRADE CHILDREN, STUDY C)

List 1	List 2	List 3
Thunder	Blind	Mother
Dog	Shoes	Grill
Lightning	Black	Feed
Cat	Gloves	Grow
Rain	Blank	Bottle
Cow	Hat	Green
Puddle	Blow	Baby
Horse	Coat	Grip
Storm	Bless	Crib
Pig	Shirt	Grade
Windy	Bloom	Diaper
Chicken	Sweater	Group

For the serial learning, the child was told that E would read 12 words and that the child would be asked to recall as many of the words as he could following the reading. The E read the list three times, in a different order, and obtained a recall following each reading. The recall score was the number of words (classified, a priori, as relational, inferential, or analytic) under each of the three categories that were recalled contiguously. That is, if the child's recall for list 1 was "thunder, lightning, storm, cat, pig, windy," the contiguous recall score for the inferential concept would be "2" (i.e., cat and pig were recalled contiguously). For each recall trial the maximum score was "6"; the maximum for the three recall trials was "18."

Figure sorting test. The subjects were shown 22 human figures, similar to but not identical with those shown to the adults (see Figure 1) and were required to produce eight conceptual sorts. For the children, the figures that suggested nudity or sexuality were removed and several figures with blank faces were substituted. The sorts were scored for analytic, relational, and inferential concepts, but the distribution for relational sorts was asymmetrical. The statistical analyses will be presented only for analytic and inferential concepts.

For one of the sixth grades ($N = 23$ boys and 23 girls) mental test scores (California Test of Mental Maturity) were available.

The intratest consistency for the conceptual categories on the conceptual style test was satisfactory. The corrected odd-even reliabilities were .91 for analytic responses, .90 for relational responses, and .74 for inferential responses.

For boys, analytic and inferential concepts were negatively correlated with relational concepts ($r = -.57$ and $-.41$; $p < .001$, respectively). Analytic-descriptive and inferential sorts were independent of each other ($r = -.01$).

For girls, analytic and inferential responses were each inversely related to relational responses ($r = -.29$; $p < .10$) ($r = -.48$; $p < .01$), and analytic and inferential responses were negatively correlated ($r = -.48$; $p < .01$) rather than independent as found for boys. There were no significant sex differences in means of standard deviations for any of the variables described. Table 2 presents the correlations between the conceptual style categories and the memory, word association, and mental test scores. The term "nonanalytic" refers to relational concepts.

Results for boys were more consistent than those for girls. The boys who were analytic on the three-figures conceptual style test tended to be analytic in their sorts of the human figures ($r = +.37$; $p < .05$). Moreover, an analytic approach on either test was negatively correlated with the number of relational words contiguously recalled ($r = -.29$ and $-.28$; $p < .10$). Finally, an analytic approach on the three-figures conceptual style test was positively associated with production of noun-noun sequences on the word association test, in contrast to the production of verbs or adjectives to noun stimuli. It is interesting to note that the number of inferential responses on the conceptual style test was unrelated to noun-noun sequences on the word association test, despite the fact that the inferential score was correlated with IQ ($r = +.72$; $p < .001$). Thus, analytic boys avoided grouping words in the serial learning task on the basis of functional relationships and displayed a categorical, rather than a relational, approach in their spontaneous associations to nouns.

The boys who were nonanalytic on the conceptual style test performed in an opposite manner. They recalled more of the functionally related words on the serial learning task ($r = +.31$; $p < .05$) and produced more

TABLE 2

RELATIONSHIPS BETWEEN CONCEPTUAL STYLE AND OTHER COGNITIVE VARIABLES
(SIXTH GRADE CHILDREN, STUDY C)

| | CONCEPTUAL STYLE TEST | | | | | | FIGURE SORTING TEST | | | |
| | Analytic | | Nonanalytic | | Inferential | | Analytic | | Inferential | |
	Boys	Girls	Boys	Girls	Boys	Girls	Boys	Girls	Boys	Girls
Memory Score										
Contig. relational	$-.29^*$	.10	$.31^{**}$	$-.10$	$-.35^{**}$	$-.05$	$-.28^*$	$-.05$	.15	.05
Contig. inferential	.13	$-.19$	$-.03$	$-.12$	.13	.23	$-.06$	$-.21$	$-.07$	.05
Contig. analytic	.18	.00	$-.11$	.00	.17	.02	.04	.06	$-.16$	.02
Total recalled	.11	.03	.01	$-.05$	.13	$-.02$	$-.14$	$-.06$	.11	.00
Word Association										
Noun-verb phrase completion	$-.19$	.22	$.27^*$	$-.07$	.03	$-.03$	$-.09$	.03	.19	.19
Noun – not noun	$-.32^{**}$	$.29^*$	.22	$-.23$	$-.13$	$-.01$	$-.21$	$-.08$	.17	.17
Noun-noun	$.37^{**}$	$-.29^*$	$-.28^*$	.17	.12	.09	.24	.03	$-.03$	$-.03$
Intelligence										
VS IQ	.07	.20	$-.30$	$-.36^*$	$.57^{***}$	.31	$.38^*$	.00	$-.40^*$	$-.11$
PS IQ	$.42^{**}$	.26	$-.51^{**}$	$-.26$	$.47^{**}$	.25	.23	$-.15$	$-.22$	.23
FS IQ	.24	.14	$-.48^{**}$	$-.35^*$	$.72^{****}$	$.42^{**}$	.29	$-.10$	$-.23$	.01

* $p < .10$; two tails.
** $p < .05$; two tails.
*** $p < .01$; two tails.
**** $p < .001$; two tails.

noun-verb phrase completions on the word association test ($r = +.27$; $p < .10$).

The results for the girls were clearly less consistent and revealed no strong relationships between an analytic attitude and either memory performance or word-association categories. Moreover, girls displayed no consistency in analytic attitude between the two conceptual tests. The correlation between analytic responses on the conceptual style and figure sorting tests was .06. It would appear that analytic responses are of different significance for boys and girls and that analytic responses on the two tests are not measures of the same process.

The correlations between conceptual approach and scores on the California Test of Mental Maturity support the notion that an analytic attitude is more closely related to performance on items requiring perceptual differentiation than to facility on questions assessing language skills. There was no relation for boys between an analytic attitude on the conceptual style test and mental status on the verbal half of the California test ($r = +.07$). The items making up this score include vocabulary, verbal arithmetic problems, verbal reasoning, and memory for story elements. However, the nonlanguage score was moderately correlated with analytic concepts in boys ($r = +.42$; $p < .05$). This score is based on tests of comprehension of spatial relationships, mazes, and reasoning tests that involve visually presented materials rather than language. A nonanalytic approach was associated with poor performance on the nonlanguage scale ($r = -.51$; $p < .05$). Only inferential concepts showed a high, positive correlation with the language score ($r = +.57$; $p < .01$), supporting the popular opinion that verbal items on standard IQ tests assess, in large measure, the degree to which the child has acquired the conventional abstract labels of his language.

Study D

Some of the results of Study C on sixth graders were supported by an earlier study on 26 boys and 29 girls in the third grade with a female examiner for all children. The children were given the same conceptual style test described above, but slightly different lists of words to memorize in the serial learning task. Each of the lists contained, as before, 12 words, but the first and last words were buffer items, unrelated to the concepts in the lists. There were, therefore, five words belonging to each of two concepts in each list. For example, list 1 contained the words: clock, ocean, mother, sea, feed, lake, bottle, pool, baby, river, crib, and door. The words ocean, sea, lake, pool, and river belonged to the categorical concept "bodies of water"; the words mother, feed, bottle, baby, and crib belonged to a functionally related concept involving the mother-child interaction. The three lists are presented in Table 3.

TABLE 3

LISTS USED IN SERIAL LEARNING TASK
(THIRD GRADE CHILDREN, STUDY D)

List 1	List 2	List 3
Clock	Picture	Tree
Ocean	Dog	Bed
Mother	Nail	Pint
Sea	Cat	Sleep
Feed	Rail	Pirate
Lake	Cow	Sheet
Bottle	Sail	Pipe
Pool	Horse	Blanket
Baby	Trail	Pile
River	Goat	Dream
Crib	Mail	Pie
Door	Spoon	Boat

The word association list was also different and contained 22 count nouns and 8 adjectives, but was scored for the same categories described in the previous study. The measure of intelligence was the Pintner-Cunningham Scale which, unfortunately, does not allow for easy separation of language and nonlanguage scores. Table 4 presents the relations between the analytic, relational, and inferential responses and the memory, word association, and IQ scores.

The boys who were nonanalytic on the conceptual style test (high in relational concepts) recalled more of the functionally related words contiguously ($r = +.59$; $p < .01$) and gave more noun-verb phrase completions on the word association test ($r = +.44$; $p < .05$). These two results were also found with the sixth grade boys. For the girls, none of these relations was significant.

On separate groups of boys differing in age, community, and sex of the examiner, production of relational concepts was associated with the organization of words on the basis of their functional relationships to each other. The lack of relation between nonanalytic (i.e., relational) responses and IQ for the third grade boys ($r = -.05$) suggests that the younger the child, the greater the independence of this conceptual attitude from tested IQ score.

Stability of Conceptual Style

A group of 22 boys and 24 girls from the original sample of 55 third grade children utilized in Study D were retested one year later by a different female examiner. The conceptual style test and a 40-item word association

TABLE 4

RELATIONSHIPS BETWEEN CONCEPTUAL STYLE AND COGNITIVE VARIABLES
(THIRD GRADE CHILDREN, STUDY D)

| | CONCEPTUAL STYLE TEST | | | | | |
| | Analytic | | Nonanalytic | | Inferential | |
	Male	Female	Male	Female	Male	Female
Memory Score						
Contig. relational	—.11	.03	.59***	—.19	—.23	.27
Contig. inferential	.18	—.14	—.23	—.08	—.09	.22
Contig. analytic	.23	.06	—.24	—.02	—.08	—.04
Total recalled	.26	.03	.08	—.05	—.30	.16
Word Association						
Phrase completion	—.16	—.21	.44**	.17	—.08	.11
Noun – not noun	—.09	—.23	.29	.14	—.18	.13
Noun-noun	.05	.26	—.02	—.12	.06	—.15
Intelligence						
IQ (Pintner)	.09	—.29	—.05	.04	—.29	.28

** $p < .05$; two tails.
*** $p < .01$; two tails.

test were among the tests given to these children who were now in the fourth grade. Analytic responses showed remarkably high stability for girls, ($r = .70$; $p < .001$) and moderate stability for boys ($r = .43$; $p < .05$).[3] Nonanalytic relational responses showed parallel stability coefficients ($r = .64$; $p < .001$; $r = .40$; $p = .06$) for girls and boys, respectively. A majority of the boys (73 per cent) showed increases in number of analytic responses over the 12-month period. For the girls, however, only one half of the group showed a slight increase in analytic responses. The increase in analytic concepts for the boys over the one-year period was statistically significant ($t = 2.11$; $p < .05$).

The word association responses also showed moderate stability over this period despite the fact that the stimulus words differed between the two administrations. The distributions for noun-noun pairs, noun – not noun pairs, and noun-verb phrase completions were split at the median, and phi coefficients (with Yates' correction) were computed relating occurrence of these categories between the two tests. These three categories were highly

---

[3] Since the presentation of this paper a group of 52 boys (grades 1 and 2) have been administered the 30-item conceptual style test twice with a test-retest interval of one year. The stability coefficient for analytic responses was $+.47$ ($p < .001$).

stable for girls (phi = .67, .67, and .59; $p < .01$ for all three), whereas for boys they were positive but not significant (phi = .14, .32, and .23).

However, the positive association between production of nonanalytic concepts and noun-verb phrase completions on the word association test, which was significant for the third grade boys ($r = +.44$; $p < .05$), was still significant one year later ($r = +.43$; $p < .05$). The conceptual preferences as well as the word association categories appeared to be more stable for girls than for boys over this one-year period.

It has been reported previously that IQ scores during the early school years were more stable for girls than for boys (Sontag et al. [1958]), for twice as many boys as girls displayed large increases in IQ during the period 6 to 10 years of age.

These two sources of data suggest that the elements of cognitive organization may be less rigidly established in young boys than in young girls. Should future research demonstrate that cognitive organization becomes fixed earlier in girls than in boys, it would be reasonable to suppose that the

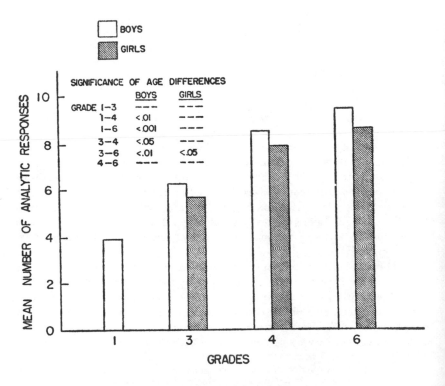

FIGURE 3—Age changes in analytic responses.

sex differences favoring adolescent and adult males on tests of creativity are due, in part, to the greater receptivity to change of the cognitive structure of boys than of girls.

Age Changes in Conceptual Approach

At the time of this writing several independent studies in progress include the administration of the 30-item conceptual style test to children in the first and fourth grades. Consideration of the protocols from these groups, together with the data on the third and sixth grade children previously described, provides a preliminary picture of age changes in analytic and nonanalytic concepts.

At present, we have data on 20 first grade boys, 38 boys and 38 girls in the third grade, 40 boys and 40 girls in the fourth grade, and 38 boys and 38 girls in the sixth grade. Figures 3 and 4 show the average number of analytic and nonanalytic responses as a function of grade level and the significance of the differences between grade levels. The age trends are linear

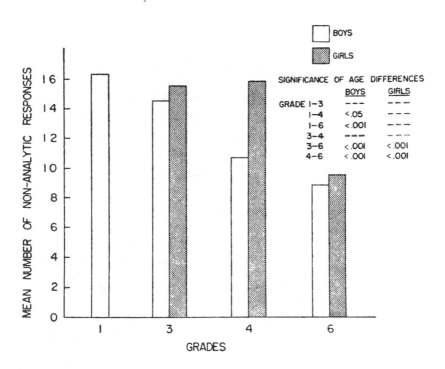

FIGURE 4—Age changes in nonanalytic (relational) responses.

and indicate that, with development, analytic responses increase and non-analytic responses decrease.[4]

These data are based on a 30-item test. Only one of the third grades and the two sixth grades received the original 44-item series. The 14 items that were eliminated from the original set typically elicited inferential responses from most children and infrequently pulled analytic or relational concepts. Thus, the distribution for inferential responses was only adequate for the longer series. When the responses of the third and sixth grade children who received the longer test were compared, inferential responses showed only a slight increase with age for boys, but a marked increase for girls ($t = 4.44$; $p < .001$).

In summary, analytic and nonanalytic responses are moderately stable over time, the former style gradually increasing and the latter decreasing during the early school years.

Let us now summarize some of the data on the relation of these attitudes to more complex aspects of the child's conceptual and overt behavior.

STUDY E

An Analytic Attitude and the Interpretation of Ambiguous Stimuli

The interpretation of an ink blot is a complex conceptual response and one that might be influenced by an analytic attitude. It might be hypothesized that an analytic approach would result in a differentiated perception of the ink blot, in contrast to a global or wholistic interpretation. That is, analytic children should be more likely than nonanalytic children to specify parts of their percepts, to avoid giving vague responses. For example, they should respond, "bird with *wings, feet,* and *head*" rather than merely reporting, "a bird." In a first analysis, the protocols of 21 Fels boys between 7 and 10 years of age were studied. These boys were administered the 44-item conceptual style test and, in a separate test session, a 32-item ink blot series which had been specially prepared by covering part of the standard Rorschach stimulus with templates. These 32 ink blot interpretations were scored for differentiated percepts: the number of responses in which an animal, person, or object together with *one or more differentiated* parts of the object were reported. Typical examples would be, "That's a butterfly and there are the wings and the feet," "That's a man with his legs, arms, and face," "That's the face of a beetle and here are his teeth and jaws." The conjunction of two discrete images was not regarded as differentiated (e.g., "There's a spider chasing a fly").

Although the distribution of analytic responses on the conceptual style test was symmetrical, one half of the boys gave no differentiated ink blot

_____

[4] Since the presentation of this paper, additional children in grades 2, 3, 4, and 7 (over 500 children in all) have been administered the conceptual style test. These data clearly indicate a linear increase in analytic responses with increasing age.

percepts while one half gave one or more. Both a phi coefficient and biserial r were computed relating number of analytic concepts (continuous variable) to the presence or absence of differentiated ink blot percepts (dichotomized variable). The phi coefficient was .50 ($p < .05$); the biserial r was $+.59$ ($p < .05$).

It also seemed reasonable to assume that the production of indistinct percepts (i.e., those with no definite outline) would be given infrequently by analytic children. Examples of such responses are "cloud," "paint," "design," "rock," or "map." These percepts have no definite form and involve minimal stimulus differentiation. The median number of such responses was 1, and chi square was used to relate the number of indistinct responses to number of analytic responses. The boys above the median on analytic concepts produced fewer indistinct percepts (chi square $= 6.82$; $p < .05$).

Study of the children's initial approach to the interpretation of TAT pictures suggested that analytic children were likely to mention objective parts of the stimulus before reporting a theme. The opening sentences of the TAT stories (on a 13-card protocol) for the 21 Fels boys between 7 and 10 years of age were scored for occurrence of (a) object naming (e.g., "That's a violin," "There's a gun," "The girl is holding a book"), (b) description of the posture of people (e.g., "He's standing," "The boy is lying down"), or (c) naming the sex of the figure illustrated (e.g., "That's a boy," "That's a girl," "That's a woman"). The use of words dealing with social roles (e.g., "That's a robber," "That's a father") were not scored as analytic.

The correlation between number of analytic responses on the conceptual style test and occurrence of these "picture naming" categories was .39 ($p < .10$). Thus, an analytic attitude had some degree of generality across ambiguous ink blots and pictures.

At a speculative level, it is possible that the content of a child's story productions is influenced by his initial labeling of a picture and, therefore, by his preferred conceptual approach. For example, card 3BM of the TAT illustrates a boy crouched over a couch and, in the background, is an ambiguous object that is infrequently mentioned by children. When a child does mention this object, it is usually perceived as a gun, knife, or dagger. If we assume that an analytic child is apt to attend to this indistinct object, and therefore is prone to incorporate it into his story, it is likely that he will tell an aggressive theme. Chris, who is a nonanalytic Fels child, did not notice the object and reported, "The fireman was dead because he got his shoe burned, because he didn't wear his boots—being careless." John, who is an extremely analytic Fels child, noticed the object and told a murder theme: "Well, it looks like some . . . I think that's a knife down on the floor. Some man was killed."

We are now studying the influence of an analytic style upon the motivational content of projective test responses. Preliminary data suggest that this influence may be considerable. If an analytic attitude predisposes the individual to differentiate the stimulus, he is, in effect, responding to a different stimulus.

Aggressive or sexual content in responses to ink blots or ambiguous pictures may be influenced, in part, by a preferred style of conceptualization, and *this style may be independent of motivational dispositions.*

This line of reasoning is supported by Baughman's (1954) work on stimulus factors in ink blot interpretations. Baughman has demonstrated that, when the figure-ground contrast between blot and card background is enhanced, human movement responses are more likely to occur. The production of motivational content (e.g., man being stabbed, person killing someone, snake eating a gopher, people kissing) is most likely to occur when the subject perceives people in action. A conceptual approach that emphasizes figure-ground differentiation of an ink blot would facilitate the reporting of human movement percepts and, consequently, more dynamic content. The hypothesis that the occurrence of motivational content in responses to ambiguous stimuli is related to the individual's conceptual style is both testable and persuasive. The question of whether the style is secondary to motivational variables or independent of them is, of course, a thornier problem.

Study F

An Analytic Style and the Question of "What Is Learned"

An analytic child presumably differentiates complex stimulus arrays to a greater degree than a nonanalytic child. That is, he applies labels to the whole stimulus, as well as to the parts. He reacts to a different immediate environment, if the environment is defined, in part, as that sector of the stimulus field that is labeled. One method of testing this hypothesis is to require the individual to learn a response to a complex stimulus and to assess subsequently the degree to which the response is transferred to discrete parts of the original stimulus. Preliminary results from a study of fourth grade children suggest that analytic children are more likely than nonanalytic ones to attach a verbal label to parts of an abstract geometric design.

The Ss were 25 boys and 25 girls who were tested by an adult of the same sex, while an adult of the opposite sex sat in back of the child recording his responses. Each S was administered the following tests:

   a. *Conceptual style test* (30 items).
   b. *Paired associate learning: task I (practice task).*

Each S was shown four life-like scenes (photographs) and required to learn nonsense syllables to these pictures. The syllables chosen (DEP, ROV, BUL, and FAS) have meaningfulness values of 90 to 100 per cent based on the figures reported by Glaze (1928) and Krueger (1934). After reaching a criterion of eight successive correct trials, the S was shown two versions of each of the four original stimuli. One contained a salient aspect of the

FIGURE 5—Stimuli used in paired associate learning task. The four stimuli to the left were used in the original learning; the four to the right were the corresponding "figures" presented during the transfer trials.

original stimulus (the figure); the other the original minus the figure (i.e., the ground). These eight stimuli were randomly presented, and S was asked to report the nonsense syllable that was appropriate to the stimulus.

c. *Figure sorting.* The S was shown 22 figures similar to those described in Study B and asked to produce five conceptual sorts.

d. *Transfer trial 2 for learning task I.* S was again shown the eight figure-ground stimuli for the paired associate task and asked to report the correct syllable.

e. *Paired associate learning task II.* A second paired associate learning task was administered, but this time the stimuli were geometric forms containing a background and a figure. Reproductions of these stimuli appear in Figure 5. The S was required to learn a nonsense syllable to each design (DAR, JUS, LIF, BEV); the syllables had association values of 90 to 100 per cent. After reaching a criterion of eight successive correct responses, S was shown the figure and ground separately and asked to repeat the correct syllables.

f. *Figure sorting.* The S produced five additional conceptual sorts from the array of human figures.

g. *Transfer trial 2 for task II.* The S was again shown the eight figure or ground stimuli in a different order and asked to report the correct syllables.

The first learning task was easy for most children, and few errors were made on the two transfer trials (i.e., failure to apply appropriate nonsense syllable). The second learning task, using the geometric stimuli, was more difficult, and the results to be reported here deal only with the errors made on the two transfer trials for the second learning task.

Girls made significantly more errors than boys when the figure was presented alone on the two transfer trials (means of 3.0 versus 1.7). This sex difference was statistically significant ($p < .01$; Mann-Whitney U test). The difference in number of errors to the background stimuli (mean of 2.3 for girls and 1.9 for boys) was in the same direction, but not significant.

Moreover, the children who were highly analytic on the conceptual style test made fewer errors when the figure was presented alone than did the nonanalytic children. Two related measures of analytic attitude were used: number of analytic concepts and the number of analytic concepts minus the number of relational concepts. Both measures were inversely associated with number of figure errors, with the former being more sensitive for the girls ($p < .05$) and the latter being more sensitive for the boys ($p < .01$). When the data for the sexes were combined, the product-moment correlation between number of analytic descriptive concepts and number of figure errors was $-.32$ ($p < .05$).[5] There was no significant relation be-

---

[5] Since the presentation of this paper, this result has been replicated on an independent group of 57 fourth grade boys. The boys who were highly analytic on the conceptual style

tween number of analytic concepts on the figure sorting task and figure errors, but the result was in the expected direction.

This finding is not due to the analytic children having a greater exposure to the original stimuli. In fact, the children who made more figure errors on the transfer trials tended to take slightly longer to learn the original task and, therefore, had more exposure to the original stimulus. The correlation between trial of attainment and total errors during the two transfer trials was — .04. Analytic children apparently had a greater tendency to associate the nonsense syllable to differentiated parts of the original stimulus. The greater number of figure errors for girls, in contrast to boys, is concordant with their tendency to give fewer analytic responses on our tests and with Witkin's findings that girls are more field-dependent than boys.

TABLE 5

MEAN SCORES FOR MALES AND FEMALES ON WAIS SUBTESTS
(Ages 16 to 64) (Wechsler, 1958, p. 147)

Subtest	N = 850 Male	N = 850 Female	C.R.	p
Information	10.2	9.6	3.72	.0001
Comprehension	10.0	9.7	2.20	.01
Arithmetic	10.4	9.3	7.28	.0001
Picture Completion	9.7	9.0	4.93	.0001
Block Design	9.5	9.1	2.75	.01
Digit Span	9.4	9.4	.00	....
Picture Arrangement	9.2(1)	9.2(2)	.07	....
Object Assembly	9.4	9.3	.47	....
Similarities	9.3	9.7	2.21	.02
Vocabulary	9.7	10.0	2.42	.01
Digit Symbol	8.3	9.4	7.42	.0001

Additional evidence for a stronger analytic attitude in males comes from Wechsler's normative data on sex differences in average scores on the ten

test, in contrast to those who were nonanalytic, made fewer errors when the geometric figure was presented alone ($p < .05$). In a separate investigation (Lee, Kagan, and Rabson [1963]) designed to test a similar hypothesis, 30 third grade boys were divided into analytic and nonanalytic groups on the basis of their responses to the conceptual style test. Each S was then required to learn six concepts (two of which required analysis of the stimulus) in a standard concept formation situation. The analytic boys learned the two analytic concepts (objects with black bands and objects with a missing leg) significantly earlier than the nonanalytic boys, but had greater difficulty than the nonanalytic boys acquiring the four concepts that did not require an analytic categorization (e.g., three of a kind, wearing apparel, objects related to school, objects related to a baby).

subtests of the recent form of the Wechsler Adult Intelligence Scale (Wechsler, 1958). Table 5 presents these data as reported by Wechsler.

The males performed better on picture completion and block design tests, tasks that require an analytic orientation. The females performed better on tests tapping acquisition of conventional linguistic concepts (vocabulary and similarities).

STUDY G

Conceptual Style and Behavior Plasticity

The data summarized thus far suggest that analytic children differentiate the stimulus environment; they tend to separate relevant from irrelevant cues. Witkin suggests that field-independent individuals resist the effects of interfering stimuli. The behavior of nonanalytic individuals, therefore, should be more susceptible to modification by immediate perceptual experience, for these *S*s may have difficulty inhibiting reactions to task-irrelevant cues. In effect, their behavior should be more malleable in the face of continual changes in the stimulus field.

An experiment on 25 freshman college males supports this hypothesis. These men were first seen in the Lacey's laboratory of psychophysiology at Fels as part of a study relating reaction time to autonomic reactivity. A brief description of the experiment follows:

The *S* was told that this was an experiment on speed of responses in which he would be given a "get ready" signal (a light) which would be followed by a "go" signal (light of different color). At the onset of the "get ready" signal he was to place his finger on a telegraph key; at the onset of the "go" signal he was to remove his finger as fast as possible. The experimental variable was the time interval between the "get ready" and "go" signals—the foreperiod. It has been shown that the use of three foreperiods in a counterbalanced program results in fastest reaction times to the middle valued foreperiod. Thus, if the foreperiods are 3, 4, and 5 seconds, the fastest reaction times usually occur at the 4-second foreperiod. This has been interpreted as indicating that the *S* adjusts his expectancies to the average foreperiod.

Moreover, the reaction time on a trial is also influenced by the foreperiod on the preceding trial. If the foreperiod for trial $n-1$ was 5 seconds, the reaction time on trial n is generally longer than if the foreperiod on trial $n-1$ had been 3 seconds. This is a group result. But there are important individual differences in the degree to which an individual's reaction time on trial n is influenced by the length of the preceding foreperiod (i.e., trial $n-1$). For example, reaction times of *S*s with low heart rate variability were more influenced by the preceding foreperiod than the reaction times of subjects with high heart rate variability (i.e., the more stable the cardiac cycle, the more likely that S's reaction time would be correlated with the length of the preceding foreperiod).

These college students were first seen for a 30-minute session in the Lacey's laboratory during which heart rate, respiration, and palmar conductance were continuously measured during the reaction time experiment. The foreperiods (3, 4, and 5 seconds) were counterbalanced so that each trial was preceded an equal number of times by all three foreperiods. Following this session, they were taken to another part of the Institute and given a series of modified ink blot stimuli and a 40-item word association test by one of us (JK or HAM).

Four major variables were intercorrelated: (a) phrase completions (i.e., noun-verb or verb-noun sequences such as dog-bark or run-boy) on the word association test, (b) differentiated ink blot percepts (responses which included elaborations of the parts of an object, animal, or person), (c) heart rate variability, and (d) susceptibility to the length of the preceding foreperiod.

Heart rate variability at rest was obtained by casting the amplitudes of trough to peak changes in heart rate during a rest period into a frequency distribution and selecting the 75th percentile as a measure of variability. The higher this value, the greater the Ss spontaneous tendency to display large spontaneous changes (increases and decreases) in heart rate.

The S's susceptibility to the preceding foreperiod was obtained with the aid of regression analysis. A correlation was obtained between the subjects' reaction times to the trials following 3- and 5-second preceding foreperiods. This correlation for the group was used to predict each S's reaction time on trials that had been preceded by a 5-second foreperiod. The subject's deviation from this predicted value (in standard scores) was the measure of his susceptibility to having longer than average reaction times on trials preceded by foreperiods of 5-seconds (i.e., his reaction time on trial n was larger than expected when the foreperiod of the preceding trial was 5 seconds). Table 6 presents the intercorrelations among these four variables.

The results are in a direction that might be predicted from our earlier statements. The most significant finding was that Ss who gave phrase completions to nouns or verbs that matched language usage (i.e., verb-noun or noun-verb sequence) were most influenced by the length of the preceding foreperiod. These men might be regarded as easily swayed by incoming information since their behavior was continually influenced by changes in the length of the preceding foreperiod. It will be recalled that the young boys who gave noun-verb phrase completions on the word association test were nonanalytic on the conceptual style test. The correlation between production of nonanalytic concepts and phrase completions on the word association test was $+.44$ ($p < .05$) for the third grade boys; $+.43$ ($p < .05$) for the retest of these boys one year later and $+.27$ ($p < .10$) for the sixth

TABLE 6

RELATION BETWEEN REACTION TIMES AND CONCEPTUAL STYLES
(ADULT MALES, STUDY G)

	Word Associa-tion Phrase Completions	Heart Rate Variability	Susceptibility to Preceding Foreperiod
Analytic ink blot percepts	—.14	.33*	—.15
Word association phrase completions	. . . .	—.30	.47**
Heart rate variability		. . . .	—.29

* $p < .10$; two tails.
** $p < .05$; two tails.

grade boys. Thus, *phrase completions* were associated (a) with response modifiability to irrelevant cues in male adults and (b) with a nonanalytic conceptual attitude in young boys. Incidentally, phrase completions in children were relatively independent of IQ, the correlations being —.02 and —.23 for third and sixth grade boys, respectively.

STUDY H

Reaction Time and an Analytic Style

An analytic response should require more time for stimulus scanning than a less differentiated response. If an analytic response involves more scanning time, the average reaction time for analytic concepts should be longer than the time required for relational responses. The average reaction time for analytic responses on the conceptual style test for the sixth grade children was 5.4 seconds; the average reaction time for relational responses was 4.0 seconds ($t = 3.20$; $p < .01$), verifying this prediction. Unfortunately, we did not measure reaction time on the third grade children.

Since analytic responses were associated with longer response times, it was assumed that children who were analytic on the conceptual style test might be less impulsive in their responses in other test situations.

Data on both Fels children and adults indicate a relation between response time and conceptual approach. The Fels boys (age 7 to 10) who were analytic on the conceptual style test had slightly longer reaction times to TAT cards ($r = +.38$; $p < .10$) and to ink blots ($r = +.32$; $p < .15$). When the boys' reaction times to the TAT and ink blots were ranked separately and the ranks averaged, the correlation between analytic concepts and the pooled reaction time score increased to $+.46$ ($p < .05$). Thus, an analytic attitude was associated with a more *reflective* approach to conceptual tasks; a nonanalytic response associated with more impulsive responding.[6]

Behavioral Correlates of an Analytic Style

The longitudinal observations on our Fels children were studied in an attempt to obtain some clues to the antecedents and behavioral correlates of these conceptual variables. The children in the Fels longitudinal program are regularly observed from birth through adolescence in their homes and in the Fels nursery school. Detailed summaries of these observations furnish a rich and continuous picture of the child's behavior with peers and parents.

The results summarized thus far suggest that an analytic style is associated with a reflective attitude, a tendency to differentiate experience, the ability to resist the effects of distracting stimuli on ongoing behavior. The nonanalytic child tends to be impulsive, more reactive to external stimuli, and less likely to differentiate complex stimulus situations. Study of prose summaries of early observations of the 21 Fels boys who were recently administered the conceptual style test tends to support these conclusions. Nonanalytic children are apt to be more impulsively aggressive, less likely to withdraw from the group in order to work on a task, and more hyperkinetic than analytic children. We are in the process of quantifying these observations. However, for illustrative purposes, two pairs of boys have been selected. The pairs are matched on IQ and social class but differ in their conceptual approach. Verbatim excerpts from their longitudinal records reveal dramatic differences in the behavior of analytic and nonanalytic children. Both boys were given the conceptual style test when they were 7 years old.

John and Chris. John is a bright, analytic child (IQ 133) who produced 26 analytic and two relational concepts in the 44-item conceptual style test. In addition, he produced seven highly differentiated ink blot percepts. He is the third child in a family of four and has two older sisters. Both parents are college graduates. His Stanford-Binet IQ has risen steadily from 107 at 2½ years of age to 133 at 7 years and 3 months. During the first three years of life John was an affectionate, placid, and non-aggressive child. The mother described him as being "quiet, sensitive, affectionate and an essentially reasonable child." At 3 years of age, John made his first visit to the

---

[6] Since the presentation of this paper, this result has been partially replicated on a group of 60 boys in the first and second grades. When the children were divided into high and low groups on verbal facility (based on the average of Vocabulary and Information subtests of the Wechsler Intelligence Scale for Children), a positive relation between mean reaction time for 16 ink blot interpretations and number of analytic responses on the conceptual style test was obtained; but only for the boys above the median on verbal intelligence ($p = .06$; one tail). This relation did not occur for the boys below the median on verbal skills, perhaps because young boys with low verbal facility are apt to block and delay on tests calling for complex verbal interpretations.

Fels nursery school and the following summary was written after three weeks of observation:

> S was inactive quite a bit of the time. He played quietly with animals or crayons or sat looking at books. Sometimes he just watched the children or, more often, the teachers. Most of his play was solitary. He isolated himself from other children with his back to the activity going on in the room. However, he could play cooperatively and occasionally initiated games with the other children. He did what the teacher requested if she talked directly to him, but he ignored her if she gave a general order to clean up. In these cases he continued to do what he was doing. He seemed content to read or play alone, didn't strive for the children's approval, and did not act aggressively toward them. S often sat alone and read, turning the pages diligently, and ignoring the noises that were around him, for he had a very long attention span.

A year and one half later (age 4½) he again visited the nursery school and his behavior resembled that shown during his first visit:

> S's activities on the first day were similar to his behavior during most of the nursery school period. He examined the shelves, took out the vehicles, and played alone with the trucks, trains, and cars. He often sat on the window ledge, out of the way of traffic, and played contentedly without noticing the children who often milled around him. Sometimes John would watch or listen when another boy would ask him to do so, but sometimes he just ignored the boy's frequent show-off techniques. He showed obvious interest in the stories that the nursery school teacher read, asking questions about things and listening with rapt attention. The majority of John's nursery school time was spent alone. Not only did he choose solitary activities but he pursued them away from other children. While reading, he would talk to himself about the book, finger the illustrations, eat imaginary meals, etc. John could express himself well verbally. He told himself stories with lots of expression, exhibiting a highly varied vocabulary, and lively imagination.

At 5½ years of age, the following report was written:

> Although S was the youngest child, he seemed to be the most mature member of the group. His ways of using his time, his poised relationship with the children and adults, *his outstanding ability to concentrate, and his unusual skill in physical coordination* are examples of why he appeared more grown-up. His conversation was assured and interesting. He liked to sing and tell stories, and he was full of inventive play ideas. He was quick to retreat if the play got very rough; although, when he did go off by himself, it was always to do some constructive activity. He had little need to challenge rules and was usually helpful. Besides a wealth of play ideas and a sense of humor, he enjoyed other children's antics and liked to joke himself. S seemed to have a quiet competence and a friendly unaggressive manner. Whenever other boys got rough or aggressive, he would always withdraw, although there were times when he would wrestle playfully with some of the other children. *John was very aware of loud noises. He almost always blinked or looked startled at a sudden loud sound.* When the children crashed the symbols loudly in the rhythm band, John would put his hands over his ears and look uneasy. He stopped his clay work and watched uneasily when

there were several loud crashes of the big blocks. Outdoors John was active, free, and well coordinated. He enjoyed climbing, and he was not timid about jumping from high levels. Indoors he was less active than most of the boys. When he was working on a hard puzzle or intricate project, *he would frequently pay little attention to people near by and he only looked up when a loud noise occurred.* John was skilled and persistent at working hard puzzles. He stuck with them until they were done and rarely asked for help. He was inventive and capable with both paper and clay and made several very original designs with paper, paste, and crayons.

Finally, at 6½ years of age, six months before the conceptual style test, the following summary was written:

> Initially, John walked around cautiously watching the other children, worked quietly alone with a puzzle, or looked at a book. He looked serious and tense, but every once in a while, when he passed a friend or an adult, he would smile. He kept busy with his own ideas which were abundant and often quite original. He was very friendly to adults, but rarely asked for help. Outdoors *S* was graceful in his movements, running around freely, joining climbing games in the jungle gym, and going as high and jumping as far as anyone. John was an unaggressive member of the group. He did not pick fights and approached peers in a tentative manner. He rarely objected if another child took something with which he was playing. John very rarely gave up on a task until it was completed. One day he spent a long time sawing wood. Another day he spent at least half an hour making something out of tinker toys. Even when there was much noise and confusion in the room, *S* continued to work very hard at what he was doing. When a lot of wild activity or rough play started, he would withdraw.

These excerpts suggest that, as early as 2½ years of age, John showed a sensitivity to changes in the external environment and an ability to concentrate and focus on relevant tasks despite distracting stimuli. John was reflective, and rarely impulsive. However, he was not motorically inhibited and seemed capable of graceful and coordinated physical activity.

Let us contrast John with a boy from the same social class background and similar IQ level (IQ 130), whose conceptual style scores were the reverse of John's. Chris produced three analytic and 17 nonanalytic responses to the conceptual style test. In addition, he produced *no* analytic ink blot percepts and gave two indistinct percepts.

Chris was the fourth child of college educated parents. He has an older brother and two older sisters. His IQ score fluctuated over time: 130 at 2½ years of age, 114 at 3½, and 130 again at 5½ years of age. On the Gesell schedule, he was always two or three months advanced over his chronological age, in contrast to John, who was a month or two retarded. Thus, Chris's motor development during the first 18 months was precocious.

In contrast to John, Chris was hyperactive during the first year or two of life. He had a very short attention span, he was difficult to control, and he was easily angered by minor frustrations. When he came to the nursery school at 2 years of age, the following summary was written:

Chris is an exuberant child and rarely still. From the beginning he plunged into activity immediately and impulsively. He would run around, smile at everything, and seemed to be having a wonderful time. His play pattern seemed immature in comparison with other members of the group. He banged objects or crawled around picking things up and then throwing them down. When playing alone, he would look around often, smile and converse with children or teachers, and then wander off to a new activity. Chris often approached adults; he hugged them, conversed with them, momentarily, and then dashed off to his own activities. Often he grabbed another child's toy and rushed away. His attention span seemed short, and he played only with simple toys like peg-boards.

During a visit to the home when Chris was 3½ years of age, the observer noted that Chris was full of energy:

He is active, lively, full of enthusiasm, restless, and often unwilling to entertain himself. He shows very little interest in toys and would often follow his mother through the house bouncing on the bed as she made it or being mildly destructive. Chris is not interested in coloring or pasting and only did such things if someone did it with or for him. He expressed frustration and anger freely by kicking, screaming, and, occasionally, throwing things. He becomes angry when someone takes something from him or when he feels he is not being listened to.

At 3½ years of age, the following report was written following a nursery school session:

On the first morning, Chris tested limits more than once, which was typical of his behavior throughout the two-week period. When frustrated, Chris got angry and rebelled by continually doing something forbidden. *Chris seemed very impetuous and usually did whatever the spirit moved him to, regardless of the consequences.* For example, he often crashed into the furniture as he tore wildly across the room. He frequently climbed dangerously on fragile structures. While riding the tricycle, he was reckless and often took hard falls. He was always taking spills and bumps, and he had the highest accident rate of any child in the entire group. Chris often took other children's toys by grabbing them, but he did not accept such interference from other children. Chris rarely played alone, and he liked to be doing things with one or a group of children. He was restless and never stuck at one activity very long. He flitted from the blocks to the dolls, and then to converse with an adult, then stopping to listen to a story for a minute, and then racing about outside. He talked a lot using rather colorful words, and he loved to describe things that happened at home. If he suddenly got an idea, he would race off to tell someone about it, usually an adult, but sometimes other children. Chris gave up on tasks that were too difficult for him. Most of the time he wiggled on the rug, and he found it hard accepting motoric passivity.

At 4 years, 3 months of age his behavior had the same flavor:

S was the friendliest and the most affectionate member of the group. He often hugged his special pal and greeted everyone with enthusiastic friendliness. He often raced down the hall impetuously or grabbed forbidden things from the high cupboards. Occasionally he smashed someone's house with a wild stroke of the hammer. He rarely played by himself and was usually with other children. Chris didn't stick very long at any one activity and gave up quickly if a puzzle proved too difficult.

Finally, at 5½ years of age the following report was written:

> S was very active but also stood out as more babyish than the other children. He flitted from one activity to another and had the shortest attention span of the entire group. At times he was unusually impulsive, breaking other people's houses, chasing around the hall, running into bikes on the playground, and falling over things because he didn't notice them. Chris was physically and verbally aggressive. He would steal a ball from another child or annoy children who were playing in a group. He liked to kick objects around and tease the girls. He always ignored the teacher's directions to help in the clean-up, even when told directly. It seemed very important that he be playing with somebody, and he was constantly going to adults for attention and approval, showing them what he had brought from home or talking to them about something that had happened. S rarely stuck with an activity for any amount of time. He would try a puzzle for a minute and then race off. He never sat down and really worked on any puzzle. Occasionally he would dash off a picture, splattering the paint and then leaving it. Chris was facile in his use of language. He talked all of the time, chattering away about all sorts of things, the way he felt, what he had done at home, what he was going to do next.

The contrast between these two children is striking. They are of equal intelligence, and there is no difference in the frequency or quality of their language. The major dimensions that differentiate John and Chris involve hyperkinetic impulsive behavior, reflectiveness, withdrawal from social situations, and task involvement.

Twins A and B. The second pair of boys are dizygotic twins of average intelligence (IQs of 114 and 112). Twin A was analytic on the conceptual style test (12 analytic responses); twin B produced only five analytic responses. Moreover, twin A gave five differentiated and no indistinct ink blot percepts, whereas twin B gave no differentiated ink blot percepts and 15 indistinct ones. Let us now trace their behavioral development as contained in their longitudinal records.

When the twins were 10 months of age, the observer noted during a home visit that:

> Twin A is slow in his physical development. He can barely crawl, has no teeth and does less things than twin B. Twin B is lively and more advanced. He has several teeth, crawls effectively, and pulls himself to a standing position in his bed. B is the mischievous one, according to the mother. He takes the slats out of the play pen and throws them around, rattles the bed, and keeps the older child awake. I watched the twins being fed and they are used to having the bottle propped up. B is the one who can feed more effectively under these conditions. A often loses the bottle and has a hard time finding it again.

During a home visit when the twins were 2½ years of age, the visitor wrote:

Twin B had several scratches on his face, and the mother says that he falls often and frequently bumps his head against doors and walls. B plays primarily with the older boys in the vicinity and is preferred by the older brother. B also seems to be hyperactive and impulsive in contrast to twin A. The mother feels that twin A is immature, for he is slower in the acquisition of motor skills. Twin A not only eats with his hands but likes to feel food. He crumbles donuts or puts his hands into jello and plays with it. When there is fighting in which he may be involved, A usually walks away and wanders off by himself. Twin A is affectionate and friendly with anyone he meets.

At 3 years of age, both twins came to nursery school. The following summary was written:

Twin B cried periodically all morning. He ran into the hall, tried to open the outside door, and ignored prohibitive statements by the teachers. When he painted, his attention span seemed short and he often fought with others. Twin B took toys from twin A but seemed more concerned with exerting his influence over twin A than with utilizing the toys he took. He seemed disinterested in any type of play and spent most of his time wandering around the room. He cried intermittently one of the mornings, but did not succeed in communicating what he wanted to say to any of the adults.

Twin A, on the other hand, initially watched the other children and the teachers. When children attacked him or took something from him he usually did nothing. He was quiet, often played by himself, and ignored the activity around him.

At 3½ years of age:

Twin B flitted from one activity to another. He worked puzzles, looked at books with one of the observers, joined the girls for a tea party for a moment, or dashed off a painting. Out of doors he rode a tricycle and bumped into the girls. On the jungle gym he would rock wildly with the boys. He constantly approached the teacher for attention and called the teacher if he was losing a fight. B rarely played alone and usually tried to dominate the other children. He occasionally made the girls cry by hitting or pushing them.

Twin A usually played quiet sedentary games, rarely joining in the wild running or shouting. He frequently sat by himself and played contentedly, talking to himself as he looked at a book or arranged the dishes. He put puzzles together and fitted train tracks in a neat row. He seemed to enjoy coloring with a group of children and often joined peers at the craft table. When fitting the tracks together or working on a puzzle alone, he usually ignored everything else in the room. Sometimes he played in a corner with his back to the room or sang and talked quietly to himself while putting his teddy bear to bed. Twin A was never observed to interfere with another child's play or to make an unprovoked attack, and he often allowed other children to take his toys without objecting.

This excerpt clearly illustrates the same behavioral differences seen in John and Chris. The nonanalytic child is described as impulsive, unable to play alone, and unwilling to get involved in mastery tasks. The analytic child was more sedentary, less hyperkinetic, less impulsive, more apt to be-

come involved in tasks and able to become oblivious to the external surroundings.

B's tendency toward hyperkinesis continued for the next year or two. He
was constantly getting hurt through falls and his mother remarked, "He
flings himself around and doesn't watch where he is going."

A home visit was made when the twins were 4 years of age. The mother
reported that:

> Twin B was more of a problem. He was argumentative, aggressive, and
> didn't respond to any kind of punishment. He also developed a habit of butt-
> ing and tripping people and often wandered away from home.
>
> The contrast between their behavior was most striking when twin A
> turned on the TV and started to watch quietly. As twin B ran by him, B
> pulled A's hair and ran into another room. Twin A looked startled and un-
> happy and put his thumb into his mouth. After much darting back and forth,
> twin B finally brought out his shoes, sat down next to his mother and with
> some grumbling dressed himself. While this was going on, twin A went
> into another room, brought out a pencil, and stood quietly next to me, look-
> ing at my pad of paper. He finally asked me "Can I have one?" I handed
> him the paper and he started to draw. During the afternoon twin A often
> got involved in sedentary tasks, whereas twin B dashed through the house.

At 5 years, 8 months:

> Early in the nursery school session, twin A spent a good deal of his time
> alone, in quiet activity. He would work at puzzles, play with the clay, or
> set up the dishes. Although he seemed sociable, he rarely joined group ac-
> tivities such as block building projects or wild racing games. For the first
> few days A was more able to sustain an activity than later on in the period.
> He completed some rather hard puzzles and spent long periods of time
> drawing. He became engrossed during story telling time, for he would sit
> still, listen intently, and ask reasonable questions, even volunteering com-
> ments to the group.

In contrast, twin B was described as follows:

> B was an exceptionally *keyed-up* child. He was very stubborn and aggres-
> sive. He tested limits constantly and was least likely to do what the teacher
> asked. He seemed to be unable to inhibit immediate urges to action. He
> found it especially difficult to stay in the room, and liked nothing better than
> to race around the halls.

Finally, when the twins were 7 years of age, they were seen in the Fels
day camps:

> A was rather sedentary for most of the time. He seemed easy and relaxed
> while at the day camp. He wandered around, going from one group of chil-
> dren to another, talking to them in an easy, friendly way. He seemed to
> enjoy physical games as well as sedentary ones. He always seemed in a happy
> frame of mind, friendly, affectionate, and talkative with the other children.
> A didn't express much aggression to the other children. He seemed good
> natured and got along peacefully with others. A was not dependent on any-
> one. A painted, worked with wood, did some puzzles, and played basketball.

Once he became very interested in a book on *rockets* and spent a long time looking at it. *On another occasion he found a book on animals and became very interested in it. In fact, he sat for almost 20 minutes looking at each page and each animal in an absorbed manner.* A was verbal, and there was an imaginative quality to his speech. Sometimes he acted immature, slurring his words, as if on purpose to show off; but usually his speech was clear and he had a good vocabulary.

On the first morning, B came running in with the other children from his car and immediately went around the room looking eagerly at all the toys and talking to the adults and children. He was unusually active and friendly, and perhaps more adult oriented than the other members of the group. His body was stiff and he seemed to be hyperactive and jumpy. He found it very hard to sit still. Although he showed little aggression and hostility to the other children, he would not let other children take things with which he was playing. He was the most adult oriented child in the group. He seemed to enjoy discussing things with adults and was highly affectionate. He would lean on adults, stand near them for a long time, smile at them, and almost climb upon their laps. One time he ran to the observer, threw his arms around her, and gave her a kiss. He was the only child in the group to behave in this fashion. He rarely spent much time at a task. If he began to draw, he would slap off anything that entered his mind and then leave the paint area.

It was difficult for B to learn to roller skate because of his stiff and uncoordinated body movements. Most of the time he flitted from one thing to another, talking to people, throwing things, climbing, and running. This behavior seemed like activity for the sake of activity, rather than for the sake of mastery.

These two pairs of cases provide provocative clues to some of the potentially significant behavioral correlates of an analytic style. The longitudinal observations corroborate the data on the relation between fast reaction times and a nonanalytic style and suggest that a nonanalytic child is more impulsive, less able to inhibit urges to action, more distractible, and less capable of intense involvement in intellectual tasks requiring concentration and motoric passivity.[7]

---

[7] Since the presentation of this paper, we have collected more systematic data suggesting a negative relation between analytic responses and hyperkinetic and impulsive tendencies. In one investigation, 16 Fels boys (age 7 to 8) were observed in a group play setting at the Institute for five consecutive half-day (three-hour) sessions. Their behavior was observed by two independent observers using a time-sample procedure. One of the variables rated at the end of the session assessed tendencies toward uncontrolled motoricity (inter-rater reliability was +.84). The rank-order correlation between number of analytic responses and this rating was −.49 ($p < .05$; one tail).

In another study, pairs of second grade children ($N = 120$ in all) were matched on sex, education of parents, and reading ability. One member of the pair was given the conceptual style test with the instruction "to respond as quickly as you can, to get the answer as fast as you can." The other member of the pair was told to "take your time and think about your answer before telling it." The children instructed to delay before answering reported significantly more analytic responses than those told to respond without reflection. This finding suggests that an impulsive categorization of stimuli interferes with the production of analytic concepts.

In a study in progress, 35 second and third grade boys have been observed continually for two hours in their classrooms. The observer noted every 10 seconds whether the child was attending to the task before him (e.g., reading, coloring, arithmetic, etc.) or attend-

Additional data from a much larger project strongly suggest that serious inability to inhibit motoricity (i.e., hyperkinesis) during early childhood is inimical to the development of an involvement in intellectual skills and activities. As part of a comprehensive follow-up investigation of 71 Fels subjects who had reached adulthood (the Ss in Study A), Howard Moss evaluated the childhood observations of these children. The observations were similar to those reported for John, Chris, and the twins. One of the variables rated by Moss (on a seven-point scale) was hyperkinesis, the tendency toward restless and uncontrolled activity in contrast to motoric placidity. Each child was given separate ratings from ages 3 to 6 and 6 to 10. The senior author (JK) interviewed each of these adults but had no knowledge of their childhood information during the interview. One of the variables rated following the five-hour interview was called, "Involvement in intellectual mastery." The interrater reliabilities for both of Moss's childhood ratings and Kagan's adult interview ratings were satisfactory ($r = .52$, .80, and .98).

The correlation between hyperkinesis for ages 6 to 10 and involvement in intellectual mastery in adulthood was $-.37$ ($p < .05$) for men and .16 for females. When the rating of hyperkinesis for ages 3 to 6 was correlated with adult intellectual mastery the correlations were $-.27$ for boys, $-.36$ for girls ($p < .05$), and $-.32$ ($p < .05$) for the entire sample.

Thus, an inability to inhibit motoric discharge during the childhood years was predictive of future avoidance of intellectual activities.

A final piece of supportive data comes from behavioral ratings of attention span on the 46 fourth grade children described in Study D who were retested a year after the initial administration of the conceptual style test. Following the 40-minute test session, the examiner rated each child (five-point scale) on degree of continued attention to the tasks, in contrast to the ease with which he became distracted. The correlations between analytic responses and attention span for boys was $+.39$ ($p < .10$). This result did not occur for girls. Thus, several sources of information point to the relevance of *impulsivity and capacity for sustained attention* as possible antecedents to an analytic style in young boys. The significance of an analytic attitude in girls is not so clear.

SUMMARY AND IMPLICATIONS

The results of our preliminary investigations are encouraging and suggest that an individual's preferred conceptual strategy is implicated in a wide variety of behaviors—be it associations to words, organization of words for commitment to memory, interpretation of ink blots or pictures, or speed with which a subject lifts his hand from a telegraph key.

---

ing to irrelevant events around him (i.e., showed frequent distractibility). The ratio of time attending to task over time distracted was positively correlated with the production of analytic concepts.

The tendency to be analytic shows some degree of consistency, for boys at least, across different stimulus situations, (e.g., sorting of human figures, interpretation of ink blots and TAT pictures). Finally, this response disposition shows unusually high stability, considering the fact that the test we have used is probably not the final instrument that will be used as an index of this variable. We regard the 30-item conceptual style test as a much better measure of an analytic attitude in children than the free sorting of human figures.

Theoretical Significance of an Analytic Attitude

The notion of a preference for analytic conceptualizations is closely related to constructs used by other investigators. It is encouraging to note that, although Witkin uses spatial orientation techniques, the behaviors associated with an analytic performance on these methods are similar to those we have found with our conceptual tasks. It would appear that there may be some communality in process across these manifestly different task requirements.

The relation between motive and conceptual attitude poses a critical question for future research. At present, it is difficult to determine whether preferred conceptual strategies are developed in the service of, or secondary to motives or conflicts, or whether these attitudes develop independently of the popular motivational variables of aggression, dependency, mastery, or sexuality.

We believe that study of conceptual preferences in young children is likely to contribute relevant information to this problem, because the young child's motives are not yet crystallized. We would hazard the prediction, on the basis of our studies thus far, that an analytic attitude is not completely a by-product of popular motivational variables. One of the possible antecedents of an analytic attitude is the ability to inhibit motor discharge; the ability to modulate behavior in the face of irrelevant stimulation that tempts reactivity; the ability to reflect in situations that elicit alternative response tendencies.

These hypotheses suggest directions in which we might search for the antecedents of analytic style. Hyperkinesis is one class of behavior that might have a constitutional foundation, and biological processes linked to activity may influence analytic responding. It is also possible that those classes of parent-child interactions that lead to conflict and tension in the child would interfere with the ability to be reflective. Witkin has found that boys whose mothers are restrictive and reluctant to give them autonomy are more field-dependent than boys whose mothers allow the child freedom of action. Thus, early signs of motoric control and placidity, as well as maternal granting of autonomy, might be antecedent to the acquisition of an analytic orientation.

Implications for Reading Skills

Close observation of children who are beginning to learn to read suggests that an analytic attitude may facilitate early mastery of this critical developmental task. To notice the differences between "cat" and "bat" and "dog" and "bag" requires differentiation and analysis of the stimulus. Those who work with children with reading difficulties often note that boys of normal IQ with reading problems are restless and impulsive, unable to accept the sedentary and reflective requirements of the reading situation. Research in reading has had little theoretical direction, and the underlying processes involved in this developmental problem are enigmatic. The dimension of an analytic versus a nonanalytic conceptual preference may provide a clue to the etiology of this syndrome.

Sex Differences

The sex differences in the pattern of relationships among cognitive measures are not easy to explain. Other investigators have also reported them (Gardner *et al.* [1959]; Witkin *et al.* [1954]). Observations of preschool children suggest that a greater proportion of boys than girls are likely to show extreme degrees of motoricity and impulsive, disorganized behavioral outbursts.

It is possible that analytic and nonanalytic responses are the product of different causal agents in boys and girls. Specifically, motoric impulsivity may be one of the primary antecedents of nonanalytic, undifferentiated conceptual products for boys, but of less relevance for girls' conceptual responses.

One implication of these sex differences takes the form of a suggestion to investigators of cognitive processes to analyze their measures separately for the sexes and to pool data only when the directions of the relationships are similar for boys and girls.

Moreover, investigations of cognitive processes should perhaps begin to control for preferred conceptual attitudes, just as sex, IQ, and social class are controlled. It is reasonable to assume that matching subjects for analytic attitude would reduce the error variance in experimental investigations of paired associate or serial learning, concept formation, and perceptual phenomena.

We believe that future work on conceptual preferences will help to answer the question posed early in the paper—the reasons for the dramatic and consistent individual differences in the form and content of cognitive products among children, adolescents, and adults.

REFERENCES

BAUGHMAN, E. E. A comparative analysis of Rorschach forms with altered stimulus characteristics. *J. proj. Tech.*, 1954, 18, 151-164.

BIERI, J., BRADBURN, W. M., & GALINSKY, M. D. Sex differences in perceptual behavior. *J. Pers.*, 1958, 26, 1-12.

BROWN, R. W. *Words and things.* Free Press, 1958.

BRUNER, J., GOODNOW, J. J., & AUSTIN, G. A. *A study of thinking.* Wiley, 1956.

GARDNER, R. W. Cognitive styles in categorizing behavior. *J. Pers.*, 1953, 22, 214-233.

GARDNER, R. W., HOLZMAN, P. S., KLEIN, G. S., LINTON, H. B., & SPENCE, D. P. Cognitive control: a study of individual consistencies in cognitive behavior. *Psychol. Issues,* 1959, 1, No. 4.

GLAZE, J. A. The association value of nonsense syllables. *J. genet. Psychol.*, 1928, 35, 255-269.

GOLLIN, E. S., & BARON, A. Response consistency in perception and retention. *J. exp. Psychol.*, 1954, 47, 259-262.

GUILFORD, J. P. The structure of intellect. *Psychol. Bull.*, 1956, 53, 267-293.

HOLZMAN, P. S. The relation of assimilation tendencies in visual, auditory and kinesthetic time-error to cognitive attitudes of leveling and sharpening. *J. Pers.*, 1954, 22, 375-394. (a)

HOLZMAN, P. S., & KLEIN, G. S. Cognitive system principles of leveling and sharpening: individual differences in assimilation effects in visual time-error. *J. Psychol.*, 1954, 37, 105-122. (b)

HOLZMAN, P. S., & GARDNER, R. W. Leveling and repression. *J. abnorm. soc. Psychol.*, 1959, 59, 151-155.

HOLZMAN, P. S., & GARDNER, R. W. Leveling-sharpening and memory organization. *J. abnorm. soc. Psychol.*, 1960, 61, 176-180.

KLEIN, G. S. Need and regulation. In M. R. Jones (Ed.), *Nebraska symposium on motivation.* Univer. of Nebraska Press, 1954. Pp. 224-274.

KRUEGER, W. F. The relational difficulty of nonsense syllables. *J. exp. Psychol.*, 1934, 17, 145-153.

LEE, L. C., KAGAN, J., & RABSON, A. The influence of a preference for analytic categorization upon concept acquisition. *Child Develpm.*, 1963, in press.

SONTAG, L. W., NELSON, V. L., & BAKER, C. T. Mental growth and personality. *Monogr. Soc. Res. Child Develpm.*, 1958, 23, No. 2 (Serial No. 68).

VERNON, M. D. *A further study of perception.* Cambridge Univer. Press, 1954.

WECHSLER, D. *The measurement and appraisal of adult intelligence.* Williams & Wilkins, 1958.

WITKIN, H. A., LEWIS, H. G., HERTZMAN, M., MACHOVER, K., MEISSNER, P. B., & WAPNER, S. *Personality through perception.* Harper, 1954.

WOHLWILL, J. F. Developmental studies of perception. *Psychol. Bull.*, 1960, 57, 249-288.

5

DEVELOPMENT OF EQUIVALENCE TRANSFORMATIONS IN CHILDREN [1]

JEROME S. BRUNER *and* ROSE R. OLVER

Harvard University

I would like to devote my attention exclusively to the problem of what people do when they relate one thing to another, when they are faced with the problem of grouping two or more words, events, or objects, occurring either simultaneously or in succession. I shall purposely avoid the explicit form of grouping involved in the process we call sentence-making, for I am concerned with the more traditional type of associative grouping.

The usual approaches to the problem of association are two in number. In the first, one simply invokes what I would like to call the passive principle of association. The question of what happens in associative grouping is answered by saying, "It happens." The words, objects, or events are said to get linked, bonded, or hitched by virtue of the fact that they exhibit certain qualities of similarity, contiguity in space or time, or some other form of communality. Under this passive regimen associative clusters are alleged to form, much as concepts are formed. Indeed, once these clusters have formed, it is then possible for there to be mediated associations. Things get linked because they share membership in the same associative cluster.

It is all very neat and it is all very automatic, but the difficulty with the scheme is that it explains too many things that do not happen. One example is the contiguous association between the period at the end of a sentence and the word, "The," in that order. This is one of the most frequent juxtapositions in the English language. Thorndike attempted to handle this "exception" by invoking the principle of belongingness, implying, but never quite saying, that only those things are naturally associated by the proper associative laws that are seen as belonging together. His hope was that the property of belongingness could eventually be derived from the principles of association as well, like Bishop Berkeley's coach.

Mental development in the cognitive sense was assumed, in this rather old-fashioned view, to be the progressive forging of associations and associa-

[1] This investigation was supported in part by a United States Public Health Service Research Grant No. M-1324 from the National Institutes of Health and in part by a United States Public Health Service Predoctoral Fellowship Grant No. 10,975 from the National Institute of Mental Health.

tive clusters. Possibly, too, there was room in such a view for the bases of association to change as the child grew, but this was usually due to the intervention or mediation of newly formed associative clusters.

A second approach to the problem of association is sufficiently powerful to stand exaggeration and still seem reasonable. It is the grammatical approach. It holds that most grouping is determined by gradually emerging, learned *rules* of morphemic and syntactic ordering of the speech flow, aided and abetted by the formation of conceptual rules for grouping classes of objects in the world of experience and memory. A prediction of grouping could be made in this system from one's knowledge of the emerging conceptual geography.

The sequence of rule-learning under these circumstances could be variously put as to what kinds of rules are formed first and on the basis of what clues. For example, Piaget, (Inhelder and Piaget [1958]), who is an eminent example of this particular view of the development of associative grouping, assumes that at the earliest stage there is sensorimotor patterning based essentially on a rule of action, with the gradual development of representation and reversibility, the stage of concrete operations, and finally a set of rules having to do with the generation of the possible, when the child is capable of spinning out what Piaget calls "full combinatorial ensembles."

Other people have a different conception of the order of rule learning. Vygotsky, for example, in his "new" book, *Thought and Language* (1962) takes a quite different view from that of Piaget. Roger Brown (1958) has implicitly still a different view.

I happen to be of the school of thought that assumes that associations do not just happen, that they are governed by certain rules, and that these are the result of certain rather complex transformations imposed on data by active, collective, limit-bound, talking organisms. What in fact does happen when we observe association? Can we observe something that we could call transformational activity? Can this be observed to change in a systematic way with development? I do not mean the usual transformational activities of converting a set of unrelated words into sentences by grouping. Rather I am talking about a more primitive rule of transforming input that underlies what we refer to as association in our textbooks.

A disparate collection of words or objects, each discriminably different from the others, is presented to a person. It is not automatically the case that he will group or associate them. Whether he will or will not group a given set depends on a variety of circumstances. It will depend, if you will, on what he is up to. Indeed, it is a nice question as to what will lead an individual to group things, or to form an association. He may have to pack them in the same suitcase, for example. Or he may want to assemble them in order to build a shelter. Or he may want to warn somebody of their presence on the grounds that they are contaminating or dangerous. Or he may be a journalist or an anthropologist who plans to report that they were present at the same time and place. There may not, on the other hand, be any reason for him to group the disparate things, and, under these circumstances, there will be a very sharp and quick loss in the ability to report what things were conjointly present just a few minutes before.

Generally speaking, if there is arousal of a strategy or plan for grouping, granted that we know little about what arouses such behavior, it usually exhibits two features. The first is that, however the grouping proceeds, it usually achieves a reduction in load. The grouping rule is simpler than the elements in the collection that are grouped. That is to say, the grouping is less complex than the sum of all the distinguishable features of all the elements in the collection. In this sense, the group always has the property (if it is to achieve any economy at all) of being less than the sum of the elements that compose it. Such load reduction is achieved first by a selection of a fraction of the properties available for forming a group. If I group oranges, apples, bananas, pears, and grapes as fruit, I am ignoring a whole load of attributes having to do with color, skin texture, missile-worthiness, etc., and subordinating them to the function that could be served by all of the elements.

Secondly, the grouping rule always has the property of being a generalizing rule such that, if none of the instances in the group were known, knowledge of the grouping rule would permit one to regenerate the elements in excess of chance, defined as what would be predicted if one did not know the rule. Thus, the second feature of grouping, or of a grouping strategy, is that the grouping rule used usually relates to previous rules of grouping that the organism has used. That is to say that we place things in a context that has been established. Perhaps human beings learn to extend all groupings to new situations in the interest of maximizing connectivity and transfer, and perhaps for other reasons which do not concern us here. In any case, we know that, when people associate things with each other, they most often do it by the extension or combination of groupings previously formed.

In sum, it can be said that a grouping is always less than the sum of its discriminable elements. It can also be said that a grouping is more than the instances it is used to encompass here and now. The "more" represents not so much a content of things as a way in which things can be related to prior groupings. Let me emphasize again that I am referring to the forms of grouping that are not sentencial, in the sense that we may group "man," "bites," and "hat" into the grammatical form, "man bites hat," or "hat bites man." Rather, in discussing the set of experiments conducted by Rose Olver at the Harvard Center for Cognitive Studies, I shall limit myself to associations formed within collections in terms of their similarities.

One last point before turning to our data. Associating things according to their similarity involves, as we have said, some act of selection with respect to attributes. Most things are alike and different in more than a single way. In most real life situations the objective of the behavior in force will determine the basis of selection. Short of that, there may be tendencies of various kinds operating in the actual grammar of the grouping. We shall be concerned with these tendencies as they change with growth and development.

An Experiment on Associative Grouping

The experiment that I want to report is still in progress. Here the task set for the subjects was especially designed to measure the manner in which subjects of different ages impose a similarity transformation on a set of verbally presented materials and the way in which this transformation is conserved or altered in the face of difficulties. The materials used were made up of series of nine sequentially presented nouns, first spoken aloud and then laid out on cards on a table, one at a time. Two sequences were presented to three groups of young subjects made up of equal numbers of boys and girls, ten to a group. Subjects were drawn from a public school in the Boston area. The first grade had a mean age of 6 years, 3 months; a fourth grade group of 9 years, 6 months; and a sixth grade group of 11 years, 7 months. The same experimental procedure has been administered to an additional group of 62 sixth grade children to give us norms for comparing our more carefully matched groups of ten. The two lists used on the three smaller groups are shown in Table 1.

TABLE 1

LISTS OF WORDS USED IN THE STUDY

Banana—Peach	Bell-Horn
Potato	Telephone
Meat	Radio
Milk	Newspaper
Water	Book
Air	Painting
Germs	Education
Stones	Confusion

The first two words, bell and horn, for example, were presented together, and each child, tested individually, was asked in what way they were alike. He was then presented a third word, along with the first two, and asked in what way the third word differed from the first two and then how all three of them were alike. A fourth word was then added to the list, and the child was asked to tell how it differed from the first three and then how all four were alike. The experiment continued through the list until all nine words had been presented. The subjects were under no time pressure; they could take as long as they wanted. They were not pressed for further responses; and, if additional responses were given, they were excluded from the analysis. When the ninth word was given, they were asked only how it was different from the rest, not how it was similar. At best the last word served to crystallize their concept by contrast. At worst, it served as a negative instance of what might have been a concept if they had formed one.

By using the "difference" instruction as well as the "similarity" instruction, we sought to give them as much of a prod as possible toward seeing the likeness in the preceding groups. The use of contrast was intended to elicit their best possible grouping response. Note that the lists are made up of successively more distant items. In generating these logarithmically increasing disparities, we found that none of the lists generated by the mechanical procedures we tried yielded as good agreement among judges as those lists made up by our own intuition.

GROUPING STRATEGIES

I would like to describe some of the different forms of grouping that have nothing to do with the content used in the grouping.

I. *Superordinate Concept Formation*

The first form of grouping is called *superordination*. Items are grouped on the basis of one or more attributes common to them all. The basis is one of genuine conceptual grouping. The attributes can be functional properties, perceptible qualities, some common affective reaction, etc.

TABLE 2

GENERAL SUPERORDINATE

Grade I	"Both something that makes noise."
Grade IV	"You can get information from all of them."
Grade VI	"They all communicate ideas."

A. Table 2 shows the *general superordinate* grouping. For example, the bell and the horn are "Both things that make noises," or "You can get information from all of them," or "They all communicate ideas," a rather fancy sixth grade response. That is one type of superordinate concept formed for grouping the set.

B. Table 3 shows the *itemized superordinate* grouping, where the elements have a generalized property that ties them all together, but where

TABLE 3

ITEMIZED SUPERORDINATE

Grade I	"Bell makes noise; horn makes noise too—bell says ding ding; horn says doo doo."
Grade IV	"They're all alike because you learn something from each one of them—telephone you learn by talking, bell you learn, horn you learn how to use them, book you learn news from, newspaper you learn from."
Grade VI	"You hear things from them—bell, horn, telephone, radio hear things by doing something to them, newspaper you have to read."

there is explicitly stated the basis on which each term qualifies. "Bell makes noise; horn makes noise, too. Bell says ding ding; horn says doo doo." In short, itemization is added to superordinate grouping as a means of specifying communalities.

II. *Complex Formation*

The examples of superordination given are to be contrasted with a range of responses that I refer to as *complex formations*. The characteristic of complex formation as a general strategy is that the subject uses selected attributes of the array without subordinating the entire array to any one attribute or to any set of attributes. We have been able to distinguish five clearly discernible complex-forming maneuvers, and these five can be used with a wide range of filler content.

TABLE 4

ASSOCIATION COMPLEX

Grade I	"Bell and horn are music things, when you dial telephone it's music a little."
Grade IV	"Bell, horn, telephone, radio make sound you can hear, when a person talks from a newspaper it is actually a sound too."
Grade VI	"Bell, horn, telephone, radio all make noises, if you fold back a newspaper then it will crackle and make a noise."

A. The first one, shown in Table 4, is the *association complex*. What the subject does is to make an association between the first two elements. For example, "Bell and horn are music things." Then: "When you dial a telephone, it's music a little." The subject uses the bond between two elements as the nucleus to form a group. As can be seen from Table 4, they get more complicated. "Bell, horn, telephone, and radio make noises. If you fold back a newspaper, then it will crackle and make a noise."

B. The *key ring* complex (Table 5) consists of taking an element and ringing all of the others on it by choosing attributes that form relations between one item in the list and each of the others, in a special way. "Painting—well, one thing is a newspaper has got some painting in it, a book has got some black printing, a radio and a telephone have painting on them, and a horn—well, there's a little painting on it. And a bell is also the color of paints." The author of this example looked a little shamefaced, but also defiant as he gave the latter instances. Another example: "Germs are in banana, peach, potato, meat, milk, water, and air," which is another, but more sophisticated form of key ringing.

TABLE 5

KEY RING COMPLEX

Grade I	"Painting, one thing is book's got some painting in it, newspaper's got some black paintings—printings, radio's got painting on it, telephone's got painting on it, horn well there's a little painting on it, bell is also the color of paints."
Grade IV	"In an education you learn how to do painting, you read books and gradually you learn how to read newspaper, how to use radio, how to use telephone, and horn and bell the same way."
Grade VI	"Germs are in banana, peach, potato, meat, milk, water and air."

C. The *edge matching* complex (Table 6) is also an interesting one. I was surprised to discover that the patterning I call edge matching was reported in Hughlings-Jackson's (Head [1926]) description of sorting behavior in various kinds of brain-injured patients. It consists of forming associative links between neighboring items. "Banana and peach are both yellow. Peach and potato are both round. Potato and meat are served together. Meat and milk both come from cows." The associations pile up in linked pairs.

TABLE 6

EDGE MATCHING COMPLEX

Grade I	"Banana and peach look alike—yellow, potato and peach are round."
Grade IV	"Telephone is like a bell because telephone has bell inside it, it's like a horn because you put your mouth up to a telephone and you put your mouth up to a horn."
Grade VI	None

D. The *collection* (Table 7) consists essentially in finding complementary, contrasting, or otherwise related properties that all the things have,

TABLE 7

COLLECTION COMPLEX

Grade I	"Bell is black, horn is brown, telephone is sometimes blue, radio is red."
Grade IV	"Newspaper you can read, book you can read, telephone you get messages over, radio you get messages over, you can blow a horn and ring a bell."
Grade VI	None

but not quite tying them together in terms of the attributes that are shared by the form of complementarity. "Bell is black, horn is brown, telephone is blue, radio is red." Or "Newspaper you can read, book you can read, telephone you get messages over, radio you get messages over, and a horn you can blow." We failed to get this kind of complex from sixth graders, aged 11 to 12, in either of our samples. It is a sort of putative brand of concept in which they are exploring the specificity. They are providing the itemization, but they cannot quite bring off the superordinate concept.

TABLE 8

MULTIPLE GROUPING COMPLEX

Grade I	"Telephone is like a radio, I know that, bell is like a horn because they both make sounds, but I don't know about a newspaper."
Grade IV	"Newspaper, book, painting tell stories; bell, horn, telephone, radio make sounds."
Grade VI	"You eat banana, peach, meat; you drink milk."

E. Last is the *multiple grouping* complex (Table 8) where several sub-groupings are formed. "A telephone is like a radio—I know that. A horn and a ball both make sounds, but I don't know about a newspaper." Multiple groups are thus formed within the list. The child will draw the line at some point, forming two or more separate groups, but refusing to bridge the gap between them.

III. *Thematic Grouping*

The last form of grouping (Table 9) yields very beautiful structures, of course, that are about as uneconomical as anything the subject could do with the stimuli. The sequence, coat, sweater, umbrella, house, infection, yielded the following example of thematic grouping: "If you get an infection, you wouldn't go out of the house, but if you did, you'd take an umbrella if it were drizzling and wear a coat and sweater." The story, of course, can continue to incorporate almost any additional items that are provided on the list.

TABLE 9 THEMATIC	o o o o

Grade VI   "It all fits in with fabrics and cotton—if you got hit in the head by a rock you'd get a bandage."

"If you got an infection you wouldn't go out of the house, but if you did, you'd take an umbrella if it were drizzling and wear a coat and sweater."

"Earphones you can hear like when you land at an airport."

There are many things that can be said about the differences between the groupings, but I have time to mention only a few. In the first place, it is apparent that, if each were considered a rule for forming a group, the complexity of the instruction for forming the rule increases at a marked rate as one goes from superordinating strategies, through complex-forming strategies, to thematic strategies. Indeed, the number of attributes one needs for stating the rule of grouping or associating rises quite sharply as one goes from general to itemizing superordination, to the various maneuvers for forming complexes. Key ringing, for example, requires the use of at least $n-1$ different attributes, where n is the number of elements in the set. Edge matching similarly requires $n-1$ attributes at a minimum.

It can also be seen that to extend the groupings emerging from complex formation requires a steady increment of cognitive work, with the possibility of overload always present. In a sense, then, it is characteristic of groups formed by strategies other than superordination that they are often not much less than the sum of their parts in the sense of economy. Nor are they much more than the sum of their parts in the sense of generalization. In order to combine a grouping formed by a complexive strategy with another grouping already formed, a considerable amount of additional cognitive work is required. To join two key ring complexes, for example, means finding a way of relating the nucleus of one to the nucleus of another, which is quite a trick if one takes some of the key rings actually given and tries to link them. Contrast this with the logical addition and subtraction of classes that is possible in categories formed by superordination, that tremendous generator of the possible. One can create a group with superordinate concepts by logical addition no matter how complicated the concept. Female presidents of the United States under 40 with blonde curls and size eight shoes is an example, illustrating the great power of the superordinate concept.

Let me state a first developmental theorem, emerging from these investigations: The development of intelligence, given intervening opportunity for problem solving in the life of the growing organism, moves in the direction of reducing the strain of information processing by the growth of strategies of grouping that encode information in a manner (a) that chunks information in *simpler* form, (b) that gains *connectedness* with rules of grouping already formed, and (c) that is designed to *maximize the possibility of combinatorial operations* such that groupings already formed can be combined and detached from other forms of grouping. In a word then, what distinguishes the young child from the older child is the fact that the young one is more complicated than the older one, not the reverse. The effect of the complexity is not only to produce a cognitive overload, once the child attempts to operate effectively in settings of a type not familiar to him, but also to establish structures that are less amenable to change through experience and learning. Herein lies the significance of the distinction drawn by both Piaget and Vygotsky between spontaneous concepts and systematic concepts. The virtues inherent in replacing the former (complexes in our language) by the latter, or in supplementing the former with the latter, are that the child is able to use his intellectual resources over a wider range of events by mastering strategies that permit of generality, as well as economy of operations.

You will note that the point I am making here goes quite counter to the picture of development that grows out of association theories of the old kind, and even of the newer type of S-R theories, both of which regard growth as a matter of increasing complexity and range of associations, with various devices thrown in presumably to take care of clustering.

TABLE 10

FREQUENCIES OF GROUPING STRATEGIES BY GRADE LEVEL

	I	IV	VI
Superordinate			
itemized	12	7	8
general	53	96	113
Complex			
key ring	10	5	6
association	5	4	4
collection	15	5	0
edge matching	10	2	0
multiple grouping	17	14	8
No Grouping	18	7	1
Totals			
Superordinate	65	103	121
Complex	57	30	18
No Grouping	18	7	1

TABLE 11

FREQUENCIES OF GROUPING STRATEGIES BY GRADE LEVEL AND SEX

	B o y s			G i r l s		
	I	*IV*	*VI*	*I*	*IV*	*VI*
Superordinate						
itemized	6	6	5	6	1	3
general	13	44	57	40	52	56
Complex						
key ring	10	3	2	0	0	4
association	3	1	0	2	3	4
collection	4	5	0	11	0	0
edge matching	10	2	0	0	1	0
multiple grouping	11	5	5	6	10	3
No Grouping	13	4	1	5	3	0
Totals						
Superordinate	19	50	62	46	53	59
Complex	38	16	7	19	14	11
No Grouping	13	4	1	5	3	0

If we look at the chronological ages between 6 and 12, as the child is emerging from the final stages of preoperational thought and advancing to well-structured and formal operations, we note a steady change in behavior. Tables 10 and 11 show a steady increase in the use of general superordinate concepts with age. The complexes, however, all decline with age. These results for boys show the most striking changes. It is interesting to notice that the first grade girls are at about the level of fourth grade boys, and this is not surprising in view of various findings showing general age advantages for girls in many areas of performance. By the sixth grade, they are about at the same level.

Notice that the lists proceed from near to far items, from easily associated to almost unrelatable elements, and, incidentally, from more specific and concrete to more collective and abstract instances. In short, the second half of the list is more difficult than the first, and we have analyzed separately responses to the first three items in the list and the second four items. Table 12 shows the percentage of responses representing each of the different grouping strategies by sex, grade, and difficulty. Notice that superordinate responses decline as S proceeds from the first item in the list to the later and more difficult items, in each grade. The opposite occurs for the complexes and the failures.

TABLE 12

PERCENTAGE OF RESPONSES GOVERNED BY DIFFERENT GROUPING
STRATEGIES AS TASK GROWS IN DIFFICULTY

	GRADE I		GRADE IV		GRADE VI	
	1–3 (easy)	4–7 (hard)	1–3 (easy)	4–7 (hard)	1–3 (easy)	4–7 (hard)
Superordinate	67	31	83	66	100	76
Complexive	28	50	15	26	0	23
Failure	5	19	2	8	0	1
Total	100	100	100	100	100	100
No. of responses..	60	80	60	80	60	80

I would like to comment on the intrusion of action into the complex forming strategies we have discussed. Both Piaget and Vygotsky have noted that at the early stages a concept is essentially governed by the action appropriate to it. There is no "decentration" of the concept from the action and affect that go along with it. We became very interested in the extent to which subjects generated attributes for grouping based on action with respect to the object. An example from children's literature is, "A hole is to dig." Another from our data is, "A newspaper makes a noise when you crinkle it." Generating attributes by action is a tremendously complicated form of self-instruction. About half of the first grade children generate at least one instance of action-produced attributes, and the incidence drops very sharply to about 10 to 15 per cent in fourth grade children, though it never completely disappears, even in the few college students we have tested.

LANGUAGE FRAMEWORK

We have also analyzed the content or language frames of the strategies children use in carrying out these groupings. A language frame is defined as a sentence form appropriate to the answering of a particular question. The question, "Where are they?" is appropriately answered by the frame, "They are X—Y," where Y is a place, and X is a preposition of the class including at, by, in, near, on, etc. Table 13 is a list of the language frames we were able to distinguish in the responses of the children studied.

1. First, we have a set of *intrinsic perceptible* language frames. "They are X," where X has an adjectival quality of a kind that can be pointed to directly. Another example is, "They have Y," or "They are made of Y," where Y is usually a noun or noun phrase.

TABLE 13

LANGUAGE FRAMES

Perceptible
  Intrinsic
    They are ___. (X: adjective: ". . . both yellow.")
    They have ___. (X: noun: ". . . writing on them.")
    They are made of ___. (X: noun: ". . . paper.")
  Extrinsic
    They are (preposition) ___. (X: position in time or space: ". . . in a house.")

Functional
  Intrinsic
    They ___. (X: verb: ". . . make noise.")
  Extrinsic
    You ___ them. (X: verb: ". . . can turn them on.")

Affective
    You ___ them. (X: value or internal state: ". . . like them both.")

Linguistic Convention
  Positive
    They are ___. (X: noun: ". . . both fruit.")
  Negative
    They are not ___. (X: noun: ". . . food.")

Fiat Equivalence
  Positive
    "A" is ___ "B." (X: like, similar to, the same thing as: "They are the same
                      thing.")
  Negative
    "A" is not ___ "B." (X: like, the same as: "They are not alike.")

Defeat
    "I don't know."

---

2. Secondly, there are *extrinsic perceptible* language frames, such as, "They are X," where X is a position in time or space, where the items are commonly assembled.

3. A third frame is the *intrinsic functional.* "They X," is of this class if X is a verb phrase describing their general or intended purposes. An example is, "They are for sending messages."

4. A fourth frame, the *extrinsic functional,* is distinguished from the third in that the verb phrase has a subject. "You," or "We," or "People X them," is an example. Others are "You can eat them," or "We turn them on."

5. In the *affective* language frame, the operative phrase accomplishes a preference or value scaling of the items.

6. Sixth, there is a frame having to do with *linguistic convention,* in either positive or negative form. These frames are infrequent and sometimes involve vague usages having to do with mass, class, or collective nouns that are applied to a class. An example is, "They are (or are not) X," where X is a class noun such as "things," or "inventions," or "instruments," where because the grouping term exists "ready made" in the language, it is impossible to judge its attribute basis with any certainty.

7. The seventh frame involves equivalences essentially accomplished by fiat. For example, "They are alike," or are "essentially the same thing as X."

Finally, there are a series of statements that are equivalent to the *defeat reaction,* "I don't know," or "I can't tell," and the like, which conveys the signal that there is no further information forthcoming.

TABLE 14

PERCENTAGE OF RESPONSES IN DIFFERENT LANGUAGE FRAMES*

	Grade I	Grade IV	Grade VI
Intrinsic Perceptible	24	8	6
Extrinsic Perceptible	5	6	10
Functional	49	73	75
Affective	1	1	..
Failure	14	5	..
Other	11	13	11
No. of Responses	140	140	140

* Columns total to 100 per cent or greater since some double classifications of responses were made.

Table 14 shows the responses given by the three age groups in each language frame. The great bulk of the responses given was in the first four categories: the perceptible and the functional language frames. Of the 140 responses made by the children in each of the three age groups, 14 per cent were failures in the first grade, 5 per cent in the fourth grade, and virtually none in the sixth grade. There is a decline in the use of perceptible qualities of objects from grade 1 to 6. There is a rise in the use of functional grouping. In a word, growth brings a decline in the apparent qualities of objects as a basis for grouping and an increase in the use of functional bases for grouping.

One comment is in order here. The increase in the use of functional groupings, very marked in all of the groups we have studied, including the large sixth grade sample, indicates that the first major shift in the economy of grouping comes with the adoption of the use of functional techniques for combining or associating items. Perhaps it is American functionalism that is reflected here, but I doubt it. We lack cross-cultural data, but I would be surprised if the findings were culturally limited.

The surface qualities of things have, on the whole, begun to be abandoned as bases for grouping even before children reach the first grade. Is it not reasonable to suppose that functionalism is perhaps a first major step along the way toward being free of the diversity of impressions that the environment loads upon us? To deal with function is perhaps the first way of packaging properties into nonperceptible units of belonging. A coach with this chunking transformation of functions is a coach, and not the smell of the leather, the sound of the hooves, the rolling motion, etc., through the rest of Bishop Berkeley's catalog.

An interesting point can be made about the change in the use of language frames as a function of the difficulty of the task. Once more we can examine the change as the children go from the first three groupings to the much more difficult final four (Table 15).

TABLE 15

PERCENTAGE OF RESPONSES CAST IN DIFFERENT LANGUAGE FRAMES FOR GROUPING TASKS OF VARYING DIFFICULTY

	GRADE I		GRADE IV		GRADE VI	
	1–3 (easier)	*4–7* (harder)	*1–3* (easier)	*4–7* (harder)	*1–3* (easier)	*4–7* (harder)
Intrinsic perceptible	33	16	10	8	7	4
Extrinsic perceptible	2	8	2	10	. .	17
Intrinsic functional	32	15	30	16	45	38
Extrinsic functional	13	38	37	59	27	41
Affective	. .	3	. .	3	. .	. .
Linguistic convention . . .	17	4	22	6	22	3
Fiat equivalence	2	5	. .	3	. .	1
Failure	5	21	2	8	. .	1
No. of responses . . .	60	80	60	80	60	80

The contents of Table 15 can be summed up in this way: When the going gets rough, the young children shift from their preferred mode of dealing with the surface attributes as a basis of grouping and either fail to group or adopt the frame of extrinsic functional grouping. There also occurs a scattering of fiat equivalence and affective groupings. In the older children the shift with increasing difficulty seems to be from intrinsic functional to extrinsic functional. At all ages the use of linguistic convention occurs with moderate frequency when the going is easy, but drops to a negligible level when the more difficult items are presented. The only group in which intrinsic functional modes hold up under the more difficult items is the oldest class, the sixth graders.

Language and Strategy

Finally, I want to discuss the relationship between these two forms of analysis, the grouping strategies and the conceptual modes or language frames in terms of which groupings are made. In principle there is no reason to expect any canonical relationship at all, save in respect to the so-called failure categories. Complexes and superordination patterns can be constructed on any basis: locus, perceptible attributes, intrinsic or extrinsic functioning, affect, linguistic convention, even fiat. We consider now the linguistic mode in which complexes and superordinations are constructed (Table 16). The first and most striking finding is that for the youngest

Table 16

PERCENTAGE* OF EACH GROUPING TYPE STATED IN TERMS OF DIFFERENT LINGUISTIC FRAMES

	Superordinate Concept			Complexive Grouping		
	I	IV	VI	*I	IV	VI
Intrinsic perceptible	15	11	6	39	..	..
Extrinsic perceptible	..	3	8	13	16	29
Intrinsic functional	40	23	45	5	29	12
Extrinsic functional	29	50	32	36	55	59
Affective	..	2	..	4	..	..
Linguistic convention	18	18	12	2	..	..
Fiat equivalence	..	..	..	4	6	..
Failure	..	..	..	4	..	..
No. of responses	65	101	120	56	31	17

* Since double classification was necessary, columns total either 100 per cent or greater.

children, the 6-year-olds, the great majority of the superordinate groupings are constructed by means of the functional mode. Very few of these more efficient groupings are carried out in terms of perceptible attributes. When we examine the complexes formed by the younger children, however, we find that a considerable proportion of these less-efficient forms are constructed by reliance on the apparent or perceptible properties of objects. Indeed, nearly two thirds of the complexes produced by the youngest group are constructed on the basis of perceptible properties, locus, affect, or fiat declaration. Where superordinate groupings are concerned, the figure is less than two in ten formed on this basis.

In the older children there is an increasing tendency for both complexes and superordinate concepts to be formed by the use of the functional mode. In short, then, the functional mode of analyzing events seems to develop before there is a full development of the superordinate strategies, and one is tempted to speculate that the shift from the consideration of surface, perceptible properties to more embracing functional properties may be the vehicle that makes possible the development of efficient and simpler grouping strategies. Indeed, to go back to an earlier mention of Piaget's conception of decentration, one may argue that to consider objects in terms of their potential use represents a step away from immediate concentration upon the ego-object relation, expressed in terms of what I see when I examine this set of objects that is before me here and now.

In sum, then, our analysis of these far too scant data suggests that the development of a mode of functionally analyzing the world permits the child to be free of the myriad and changing appearances of things. It makes possible the development of more efficient modes of grouping, the emergence of true concepts rather than complexes. In turn, the child is equipped with simpler modes of grouping that fulfill the dual function of being less than the sum of the items grouped where economy is concerned and more than the sum of the elements grouped in terms of generalization value and combinatorial possibility. I could close by repeating the conjecture with which we started. May it not be the case that development consists of finding techniques for being simple with respect to information?

REFERENCES

BROWN, R. *Words and things.* Free Press, 1958.
HEAD, H. *Aphasia and kindred disorders of speech.* Macmillan, 1926.
INHELDER, B., & PIAGET, J. *The growth of logical thinking.* Basic Books, 1958.
VYGOTSKY, L. *Thought and language.* M.I.T. Press & Wiley, 1962.

6

MATHEMATICAL MODELS IN RESEARCH
WITH CHILDREN [1]

RICHARD C. ATKINSON

Stanford University

GENERAL COMMENTS

For the past few years part of my research has been directed toward evaluating a theory of discrimination learning that incorporates a perceptual-observing response process.[2] The experimental program has included a variety of tasks, and subjects have been selected from among rats, college students, graduate students in business administration, schizophrenic patients, and also grade-school children.[3] The research has not been comparative in nature, for we have made no attempt to construct comparable experimental procedures. We have simply selected subjects as a matter of convenience, with the hope that certain aspects of the theory could be more easily tested with one subject population than with another.

Thus, I want to make clear at the outset that my research is not directed at an analysis of developmental processes, and I have not had extensive experience in this area. Nevertheless, I feel that mathematical models have a role to play in this field of research, and to justify this assertion I shall describe some of our own work. The study to be reported analyzes the role of an observing response in discrimination learning by fifth and sixth graders. The reason for discussing this particular study is that it deals with a complex learning situation which can be analyzed in quantitative detail by an extremely simple set of learning axioms. In developing the theory that is needed to analyze the data, I hope to clarify the various functions of a formal model. A comparable experiment has also been conducted with adult subjects and will be referred to briefly.[4]

[1] This research was supported by the Office of Naval Research under Contract Nonr 233(58).

[2] For a detailed statement of the theory and relevant research, *see* Atkinson (1960).

[3] Several of the studies with children were performed in collaboration with G. R. Sommer at the Behavioral Development Laboratory of the Psychology Department, University of California, Los Angeles. We are indebted to Professor Wendell Jeffrey for making the facilities of the laboratory available to us.

[4] The study employing adult Ss is reported in Atkinson (1961).

261

Before turning to our experimental example, a few general comments on the use of the models seem in order. Perhaps the most important role of models in psychological research is that they provide a framework within which the sequential aspects of behavior can be analyzed. An experiment designed only to establish the existence of a relation between two variables, such as response-speed and amount of reward, ignores the many sequential properties of psychological phenomena. Examination of these properties is a significant step forward in the analysis of response data. Theories stated only in qualitative terms cannot provide an adequate detailed account of such sequential effects.

The use of mathematical models is virtually synonymous with the construction of a quantitative theory of behavior. From a mathematical standpoint it is logically possible to have a theory of behavior that leads only to qualitative predictions. However, in the history of science it is difficult to find theories of this sort that have had sustained empirical significance. From the systematic standpoint a theory based only on qualitative distinctions leads to a small number of testable predictions. Aristotle's physics and Lewin's topological field theory are good examples.

Further, the absence of precise systematization usually leads to pseudo-derivations from the theory—that is, derivations that require additional assumptions that are not part of the original theory. Some behavioral scientists claim not to be concerned with whether the predictions tested by an experiment follow in a strictly logical sense from the basic postulates. They maintain that the essential thing is the making of the prediction, not its derivation from fundamental theory. The reply to this argument appears obvious. The inability of a theory to yield significant predictions without additional *ad hoc* assumptions is an indication that the theory does not provide an objective analysis of behavior. An important function of the mathematical model is to clarify this aspect of a theory. Of course, many models can stem from the same fundamental theory. The important factor is whether the theory will yield at least one well-defined model in a nonarbitrary manner. The attempt to specify a model will in itself require an exact characterization of the theory and will frequently reveal unstated assumptions.

Thus, if a theory has systematic content and is not simply a vague collection of heuristic ideas, then there exist models that satisfy the theory, and it is up to the experimentalist to determine whether the model provides an adequate account of behavioral phenomena. Of course, the use of models in itself will not solve the significant problems of psychology. A quantitative model is defined by any numerical equation. Classical psychophysics is replete with numerical relationships, yet its limitations as a scientific discipline have been apparent for many years. What it lacks is a theory of the elementary process by which the organism makes psychophysical judgments.

Fortunately, in the recent work of Luce and others the elements of such a theory are being formulated.

Experimental Situation

To clarify some of these remarks we now examine an experiment conducted with fifth and sixth grade children. Our concern in this study is to analyze the role of an observing response in discrimination learning.

The experimental situation involves a sequence of 400 discrete trials. Each trial is described in terms of the following classifications:

T_1, T_2: *Trial type.* Each trial is either a T_1 or T_2. Trial type is set by the experimenter and determines *in part* the stimulus event occurring in that trial.

O_1, O_2: *Observing responses.* At the onset of each trial the subject makes either an O_1 or O_2 response. The particular observing response made determines in part the stimulus event for that trial.

s_1, s_c, s_2: *Stimulus events.* Following the observing response, one and only one of these stimulus events occurs. On a T_1 trial either s_1 or s_c can occur; on a T_2 trial either s_2 or s_c can occur.

A_1, A_2: *Discriminative responses.* On each trial the subject makes either an A_1 or A_2 response to the presentation of the stimulus event.

E_1, E_2: *Reinforcing events.* Each trial is terminated with the occurrence of one of these events. The subject is instructed that an E_1 indicates the A_1 response was the correct response for that trial and E_2 indicates A_2 was correct.

The sequence of events on a single trial is as follows: (1) Ready signal to which the subject makes either an O_1 or O_2. (2) Following the observing response, s_1, s_2, or s_c is presented. (3) To the onset of s_i ($i = 1, 2, c$) the subject makes either A_1 or A_2. (4) The trial is terminated with reinforcing event E_1 or E_2.

The trial type and reinforcing event are determined by the experimenter. The probability of an E_1 event on a T_1 trial is denoted by π_1, and the probability of an E_1 event on a T_2 trial is denoted by π_2. Consequently, the probability of an E_2 is $1 - \pi_1$ on a T_1 trial and $1 - \pi_2$ on a T_2 trial. The two types of trials were equiprobable in the present experiment.

The particular s_i event that is presented on any trial depends on the trial type and the observing response. Specifically:

If an O_1 is made then

(a) with probability α the s_1 event occurs on a T_1 trial and the s_2 event occurs on a T_2 trial, or

(b) with probability $1 - \alpha$ the s_c event occurs, regardless of the trial type.

If an O_2 is made then

(a) with probability α the s_c event occurs, regardless of the trial type, or

(b) with probability $1 - \alpha$ the s_1 event occurs on a T_1 trial and the s_2 event occurs on a T_2 trial.

To clarify the procedure, consider a case where $\alpha = 1$, $\pi_1 = 1$, and $\pi_2 = 0$. If the subject is to be correct on every trial, he must make an A_1 on a T_1 type trial and an A_2 on a T_2 trial. However, the subject can only determine the trial type by making the appropriate observing response. That is, O_1 must be made in order to identify the trial type; the occurrence of O_2 always leads to the presentation of s_c. Hence, for perfect responding in this case, the subject must make the O_1 response with probability 1 and then make A_1 to s_1 or A_2 to s_2.

The aim of this study is to investigate the effect of various event schedules on observing behavior. In particular, we are interested in the values of π_1, π_2, and α as determiners of the probability of an O_1 response. In our study with fifth and sixth grade children three groups were run. For all groups $\pi_1 = .9$, and $\alpha = 1$. The groups differed with respect to the experimental parameter π_2 which took the values .9 (group I), .5 (group II), and .1 (group III). The study with adults employed these same groups plus another three groups where $\alpha = .75$ instead of 1.

THEORY

The basic theory used to describe our experiment is a modification of stimulus-sampling concepts as originally formulated by Estes (1950). We begin the discussion of the theory by formulating (in a nontechnical manner) its fundamental axioms. A more general formulation, and applications to social-economic experiments, are to be found in *Markov Learning Models for Multiperson Interactions* (Suppes and Atkinson [1960]). The first group of axioms deals with the conditioning of sampled stimuli, the second group with the sampling of stimuli, and the third with responses.

Conditioning Axioms

C1. *On every trial each stimulus element is conditioned to exactly one response.*

C2. *If a stimulus element is sampled on a trial, it becomes conditioned with probability θ to the response (if any) that is reinforced on that trial; if it is already conditioned to that response, it remains so.*

C3. *Stimulus elements that are not sampled on a given trial do not change their conditioning on that trial.*

C4. *The probability θ that a sampled stimulus element will be conditioned to a reinforced response is independent of the trial number and the preceding pattern of events.*

Sampling Axioms

S1. *Exactly one stimulus element is sampled on each trial.*

S2. *Given the set of stimulus elements available for sampling on a trial, the probability of sampling a given element is independent of the trial number and the preceding pattern of events.*

Response Axiom

R1. *On any trial that response is made to which the sampled stimulus element is conditioned.*

In applying this set of axioms to our experiment we are faced with the problem of identifying both the stimuli and reinforcements in the situation. Clearly, an experimental test of the theory may fail for either of two reasons: the theory is wrong or the wrong identification of the basic concepts has been made. Some philosophers of science have been fond of emphasizing (particularly, in discussing the theory of relativity) that by sufficiently distorting the "natural" interpretation of concepts they may save any theory from failure. This viewpoint is referred to as the doctrine of conventionalism. It is not to the point to examine how psychologists apply this doctrine in practice, but in our opinion the issues of conventionalism are not particularly relevant to a newly developing theory. However beautiful the structure of the theory may be, if it does not yield stable, nonartificial, experimental interpretations leading to new predictions, it does not have empirical significance. The particular interpretation of stimulus-sampling theory that I shall give in this paper has such a stable character and is justified by much previous research.

We shall assume that associated with the ready signal (denoting the onset of each trial) is a set, S^*, of stimulus elements and that each element in S^* is conditioned to either the O_1 or O_2 response. Associated with stimulus events s_1, s_2, and s_c are sets of stimulus elements S_1, S_2, and S_c, respectively. Elements in these sets are conditioned to either the A_1 or A_2 response; for simplicity we assert that these three stimulus sets are pairwise disjoint. Thus, the sequence of stimulus events on a given trial is as follows: (1) A single element is sampled from S^* and, depending on the conditioning state of the sampled element, either an O_1 or O_2 occurs. (2) Following the observing response, one of the sets S_1, S_2, or S_c is made available for sampling. Again, a single element is sampled from the available set and an A_1 or A_2 occurs.

Given this interpretation of the stimulus situation, we now need only to provide rules specifying when a given response is reinforced in order to apply the axioms. We begin with the reinforcement rule for the discriminative responses since it is the simplest. Specifically, we assume that response A_i $(i = 1, 2)$ is reinforced on a trial if E_i occurs on that trial. Thus, if an element is sampled from S_i $(i = 1, 2, c)$ and an E_k $(k = 1, 2)$ occurs on the trial, then (by Axiom C2) at the start of the next trial that element will be conditioned to response A_k with probability θ.

The reinforcement rule for the observing responses is somewhat more complicated but the idea is straightforward. If an observing response occurs and is followed by a stimulus event which elicits a correct discrimination response (A_1–E_1 or A_2–E_2), then we assume that the observing response emitted on the trial is reinforced. However, if the observing response leads to a stimulus event which elicits an incorrect discrimination response (A_1–E_2 or A_2–E_1), then we assume that the other observing response (not emitted on the trial) is reinforced. Thus, if an element is sampled from S^* and is conditioned to O_i ($i = 1, 2$) and on that trial an A_1–E_1 or A_2–E_2 sequence occurs, then (by Axiom C2) on the next trial the element will remain conditioned to O_i; however, if an A_1–E_2 or A_2–E_1 sequence occurs, then on the next trial the element will be conditioned to the other observing response with probability θ.

In addition to these correspondence rules between theoretical constructs and observable events, we must also specify those parameters which characterize the stimulus sets. That is, for each set S^*, S_1, S_2, S_c we need to indicate the number of elements contained in the set—we denote these numbers as N^*, N_1, N_2, and N_c, respectively. Since the stimulus events s_1, s_2, and s_c are physically comparable in our experimental procedure, it is natural to assume that $N_1 = N_2 = N_c = N$. Hence, in applying the theory we require estimates of the parameters θ, N^*, and N. Once these parameters have been estimated for a subject, then predictions can be made for any aspect of that subject's protocol of responses.

EXPERIMENTAL METHOD

Experimental Parameter Values

Three groups of subjects were run. For all groups $\pi_1 = .9$ and $\alpha = 1$. The groups differed with respect to the value of π_2. For group I, $\pi_2 = .9$; for group II, $\pi_2 = .5$; and for group III, $\pi_2 = .1$.

Subjects

The subjects were 48 children randomly assigned to the three groups with 16 per group. The mean age was 10 years, 9 months, and all subjects were in the fifth and sixth grades.

Apparatus

The apparatus, viewed from within the subject's booth, consisted of a shelf at table level which was 30 in. wide and 13 in. deep. A panel 30 in. wide and 30 in. high was mounted vertically on the edge of the shelf furthest from the subject. Three red panel lights (the s_i stimuli) were in a column and centered on the vertical panel; the bottom light was 20 in. from the base of the panel; the others were spaced above each other at $1\frac{1}{4}$ in. intervals. Two silent operating keys (the A_1 and A_2 responses) were each mounted $1\frac{1}{2}$ in. in from the edge of the shelf facing the subject; these keys were 14 in. apart and centered on the column of red lights. On the shelf, 1 in. behind each of these keys, was a white panel light (E_1 and E_2 events). Two additional silent operating keys (the O_1 and O_2 responses) were each mounted 6 in. in from the rear edge of the shelf; these keys were 2 in. apart and also centered on the red lights. A green light (the signal) was centered 3 in. behind the observing response keys on the shelf. The presentation and duration of the lights were automatically controlled.

Procedure

Within each of the three experimental groups, four subgroups of four subjects were formed by counterbalancing right and left positions of the observing response and the discrimination response keys. For each subject one of the three red lights was randomly designated s_1, another s_c, and the remaining one s_2.

The subjects were read the following instructions:

> We want to find out how well you can do on a pattern recognition problem. The problem consists of a series of trials. The green light on your panel will go on to indicate the start of each trial. Some time later, one or the other of the two lower lights will go on. Your job is to guess on each trial which one of the two white lights will go on and to indicate your guess by pressing one of the two lower keys.
> However, before you make your guess you will receive more information. That is, as soon as the green light goes on, press one or the other of the two upper keys—which key you press is up to you. Shortly afterward, one of the three red lights will light. The red light which goes on will help you in making your guess as to which white light will come on. After you have seen one of the red lights go on, you will then guess which white light will go on by pressing the proper key. That is, if you expect the left white light to go on, press the left lower key, and if you expect the right white light to go on, press the right lower key. If the light above the key you pressed goes on, your guess was correct, but if the other white light goes on, you were incorrect and should have pressed the other key. So each time here is what will happen: (1) the green light goes on to signal the start of the trial, (2) you press one of the two upper keys, (3) one of the red lights will go on, (4) you press one of the two lower keys, (5) if the white light goes on above the key you pressed, your guess was correct; if the light above the other key goes on, you were incorrect and should have pressed the other key.

Questions were answered by paraphrasing the appropriate part of the instructions. Following the instructions, 200 trials were run in continuous sequence. This was followed by a 5-min. rest period. Following the rest, 200 additional trials were run. For each subject, random sequences of s_i and E_i events were generated in accordance with assigned values of π_1, π_2, α, and the observed sequence of observing responses.

On all trials, the signal light was lighted for 2 sec. The appropriate s_i stimulus light immediately followed the cessation of the signal light and remained on for 3 sec. After the offset of the s_i light, one of the reinforcing lights went on for 2 sec. The time between the offset of the reinforcing light and the onset of the signal light for the next trial was 3 sec.

As noted earlier, another study was carried out with adults using the same apparatus and procedure. The adult study, however, employed more subjects ($N = 240$) and had three additional groups (i.e., the parameter α was fixed at both 1 and .75).

ANALYSIS OF DATA AND DISCUSSION

As indicated earlier, once the parameters θ, N, and N^* have been estimated for a given subject, then predictions can be made for any feature of his response data. As the experimenter, we may be interested in generating predictions for gross learning functions (e.g., mean curves for observing and discrimination responses over trials) or we may direct our attention toward detailed sequential predictions (e.g., the probability of an O_i response on trial $n + k$, given an O_i–A_k response pair on trial n). Of course, not all predictions depend on having estimates for θ, N, and N^*. Some predictions involve only one of these parameters, and yet others are parameter-free in that they depend only on the experimentally specified numbers π_1 and π_2. An advantage of the parameter-free predictions is that they can be made before the study is run.

To avoid a technical discussion of the problems of parameter estimation and goodness-of-fit criteria, we shall restrict the data analysis in this paper to predictions that are parameter-free.[5]

The first set of predictions to be considered deals with the proportion of various responses at asymptote. I shall not display the derivation of these predictions from the theory, for the arguments are fairly long and involved. The reader interested in the mathematical development is referred to Atkinson (1960). We consider the following asymptotic predictions:

(1) $P(O_1)$:   the asymptotic probability of an O_1 response.

       $P(A_1 \mid T_i)$:   the asymptotic probability of an A_1 response on T_i
                              type trials ($i = 1, 2$).

       $P(O_i \cap A_1)$:   the joint asymptotic probability of an O_i response and
                              an A_1 response ($i = 1, 2$).

Table 1 gives the observed values for these proportions over the last 160 trials for both the child and adult study. Individual estimates were obtained

---

[5] For a discussion of problems of estimation and goodness-of-fit tests relevant to models of the type proposed here, *see* Suppes and Atkinson (1960, ch. 2).

TABLE I

PREDICTED ASYMPTOTIC VALUES AND OBSERVED PROPORTIONS OVER
THE LAST BLOCK OF 160 TRIALS

	$P(A_1 \mid T_1)$	$P(A_1 \mid T_2)$	$P(O_1)$	$P(O_1 \cap A_1)$	$P(O_2 \cap A_1)$
Group I					
Predicted	.90	.90	.50	.45	.45
Observed children	.89	.92	.50	.46	.44
Observed adults ..	.94	.94	.45	.43	.47
Group II					
Predicted	.81	.59	.55	.39	.31
Observed children	.82	.61	.56	.42	.29
Observed adults ..	.85	.61	.59	.42	.31
Group III					
Predicted	.70	.21	.73	.37	.13
Observed children	.76	.20	.77	.32	.16
Observed adults ..	.79	.23	.70	.36	.16

for each of these quantities and then averaged over all subjects in a group. The predicted values are also presented in Table 1. By presenting a single value for each theoretical quantity in Table 1, we imply that these predicted proportions are independent of θ, N, and N^*. Actually this is not always the case. However, for the event schedules employed in this experiment, the dependency of these particular theoretical proportions on θ, N, and N^* is negligible and only affects predictions in the third or fourth decimal place. It is for this reason that we present theoretical values to only two decimal places.

In view of these comments it should be clear that the predictions in Table 1 are based solely on the experimentally assigned values of π_1 and π_2. Thus, they are entirely *a priori*, and differences between subjects (that may be represented by intersubject variability in θ, N, and N^*) do not substantially affect these asymptotic predictions.

An inspection of Table 1 indicates no systematic differences between adults and children on any of the response measures. Further, the over-all agreement between predicted and observed values is remarkably good for such a large array of numbers.

Note that both $P(A_1 \mid T_1)$ and $P(A_1 \mid T_2)$ decrease from groups I to III. Thus, as we increase the frequency of reinforcing the A_2 response to T_2 trials, we not only observe an increment in $P(A_2 \mid T_2)$ but also a decrement in $P(A_1 \mid T_1)$. For $P(O_1)$, an increase occurs from groups I to III in accordance with predicted results. That is, the proportion of O_1 responses increases as a function of the difference between π_1 and π_2. This result would be expected in view of the fact that differential reinforcement for the observing response depends on the difference between the reinforcement schedules on T_1 and T_2 trials. It is surprising, however, that the observed value for $P(O_1)$ is only about .75 for group III; considering the large difference between π_1 and π_2, one might intuitively expect a value very close to 1.

The agreement between these observed and predicted asymptotic response probabilities provides considerable justification for the type of model construction considered in this paper. However, the model provides a much richer analysis of the experiment than the above results indicate. From the model we can predict not only average performance but also trial-to-trial increments and decrements in response probabilities. As noted earlier, one of the major contributions of quantitive learning theory has been to provide a framework within which the sequential aspects of learning can be scrutinized. Prior to the development of mathematical models relatively little attention was given to trial-to-trial phenomena; for many experimental problems such phenomena may be the most basic feature of the data.

To indicate the type of sequential analysis that can be carried out, we now proceed to examine restricted subsets of trials. In particular, consider that subsequence of trials on which s_1 occurs for a given subject. In terms of this subsequence we define the following events:

(2) $A_{i,n}^{(1)}$:   the occurrence of the A_i response on the nth presentation of s_1 (note that reference is not to the nth trial of the experiment but to the nth presentation of s_1).

$E_{j,n}^{(1)}$:   the occurrence of E_j on the nth presentation of s_1.

$C_{k,n}^{(1)}$:   the state of condition for set S_1 where k elements are conditioned to A_1 and $N-k$ to A_2 (again for the trial on which the nth presentation of s_1 occurs).

Given these definitions, consider the following probability:

(3) $P(A_{1,n+1}^{(1)}\ E_{1,n}^{(1)}\ A_{1,n}^{(1)}\ E_{2,n-1}^{(1)}\ A_{2,n-1}^{(1)})$.

That is, the joint probability of (1) an A_1 response on the $(n+1)$th presentation of s_1, (2) a reinforced A_1 response on nth presentation of s_1 and (3) a reinforced A_2 response on the $(n-1)$th presentation of s_1. To obtain this result note that

(4) $P(A_{1,n+1}^{(1)}\ E_{1,n}^{(1)}\ A_{1,n}^{(1)}\ E_{2,n-1}^{(1)}\ A_{2,n-1}^{(1)})$

$$= \sum_{i,j} P(A_{1,n+1}^{(1)}\ C_{i,n+1}^{(1)}\ E_{1,n}^{(1)}\ A_{1,n}^{(1)}\ E_{2,n-1}^{(1)}\ A_{2,n-1}^{(1)}$$
$C_{j,n-1}^{(1)})$.

In terms of our axioms we may rewrite the sum as

(5) $\quad \sum\limits_{i,j} P(A_{1,n+1}^{(1)} \mid C_{i,n+1}^{(1)})$

$\qquad \cdot P(C_{i,n+1}^{(1)} \mid E_{1,n}^{(1)} A_{1,n}^{(1)} E_{2,n-1}^{(1)} A_{2,n-1}^{(1)} C_{j,n-1}^{(1)})$

$\qquad \cdot \pi_1 P(A_{1,n}^{(1)} \mid E_{2,n-1}^{(1)} A_{2,n-1}^{(1)} C_{j,n-1}^{(1)})$

$\qquad \cdot (1 - \pi_1) P(A_{2,n-1}^{(1)} \mid C_{j,n-1}^{(1)}) \cdot P(C_{j,n-1}^{(1)}) .$

But again, by our axioms,

$\qquad P(A_{1,n}^{(1)} \mid C_{j,n}^{(1)}) = j/N \qquad$ and

$\qquad P(A_{1,n}^{(1)} \mid E_{2,n-1}^{(1)} A_{2,n-1}^{(1)} C_{j,n-1}^{(1)}) = j/N .$

Further by Axiom C2,

(6) $\quad P(C_{i,n+1}^{(1)} \mid E_{1,n}^{(1)} A_{1,n}^{(1)} E_{2,n-1}^{(1)} A_{2,n-1}^{(1)} C_{j,n-1}^{(1)})$

$\qquad = \begin{cases} 0, & \text{for } i \neq j \\ 1, & \text{for } i = j \end{cases}$

Carrying out the summation, we obtain

(7) $\quad P(A_{1,n+1}^{(1)} E_{1,n}^{(1)} A_{1,n}^{(1)} E_{2,n-1}^{(1)} A_{2,n-1}^{(1)})$

$\qquad = \pi_1 (1 - \pi_1) \sum\limits_{i=0}^{N} (i/N)^2 \, [(N-i)/N] \; P(C_{i,n-1}^{(1)}) .$

In order to evaluate this prediction we need to know $\dot{P}(C_{i,n-1}^{(1)})$ which depends on θ, N, and N^*. However, one interesting feature of our particular model which distinguishes it from many other classes of learning models (for example, linear models) is that yet another quite different sequential prediction yields precisely the same result. Namely, the expression for

(8) $\quad P(A_{1,n+1}^{(1)} E_{2,n}^{(1)} A_{2,n}^{(1)} E_{1,n-1}^{(1)} A_{1,n-1}^{(1)})$

is also given by (7). Note that the difference between (4) and (8) is in the order of the reinforced A_1 and A_2 responses. The fact that (4) and (8) yield identical predictions for this particular set of axioms, but not for other sets of learning axioms, makes these quantities particularly interesting.

Let

(9) $\chi_{12}^{(1)} = \sum_n P(A_{1,n+1}^{(1)} \, E_{1,n}^{(1)} \, A_{1,n}^{(1)} \, E_{2,n-1}^{(1)} \, A_{2,n-1}^{(1)})$

$\chi_{21}^{(1)} = \sum_n P(A_{1,n+1}^{(1)} \, E_{2,n}^{(1)} \, A_{2,n}^{(1)} \, E_{1,n-1}^{(1)} \, A_{1,n-1}^{(1)})$,

where the summation is over all s_1 trials. Then in terms of the identity
between (4) and (8) it is obvious that

(10) $\chi_{12}^{(1)} = \chi_{21}^{(1)}$

for any given subject independent of the values of π_1 and π_2. Of course, the
quantities in (10) are expectations, and for a given subject's protocol (i.e.,
a single realization of the experiment with a finite number of trials) we
expect, only on the average, that the observed values of $\chi_{12}^{(1)}$ and $\chi_{21}^{(1)}$
are equal.

For the child study we have tabulated for each subject the number of
$\langle A_{1,n+1}^{(1)} \, E_{1,n}^{(1)} \, A_{1,n}^{(1)} \, E_{2,n-1}^{(1)} \, A_{2,n-1}^{(1)} \rangle$ events that occurred over
the subsequence of s_1 trials as an estimate of $\chi_{12}^{(1)}$; comparable tabulations
were carried out to estimate $\chi_{21}^{(1)}$. Thus, for each of our 48 subjects we
have a pair of numbers: $\hat{\chi}_{12}^{(1)}$ and $\hat{\chi}_{21}^{(1)}$. When we compute the sign of
the difference between $\hat{\chi}_{12}^{(1)}$ and $\hat{\chi}_{21}^{(1)}$, we obtain 28 pluses and 20 negatives—in terms of this result there is no reason to reject the hypothesis that
$\chi_{12}^{(1)} = \chi_{21}^{(1)}$.

Similar compilations were carried out for the subsequence of s_2 trials.
If we define $\chi_{12}^{(2)}$ and $\chi_{21}^{(2)}$ analogous to (9), then, by the same arguments, it can be shown that $\chi_{12}^{(2)} = \chi_{21}^{(2)}$. For our data, taking the sign
of the difference, we obtain 27 pluses and 21 negatives on the s_2 subsequence
—again not significant in terms of a binomial test.

The absence of a difference between χ_{12} and χ_{21} is a rather striking
result and lends support to our particular formulation of stimulus-sampling
theory. Additional compilations on the child data are needed to check out
the detailed features of this finding and, as yet, these analyses have not
been completed. Also, similar computations are required for the adult data
to check the generality of this finding. However, independent of the final
outcome of these analyses, the above discussion exemplifies the role of a
model in the detailed analysis of sequential behavior.

At this point it would be nice if we could refer to a list of criteria and
a decision rule which would evaluate our approach to this problem and
tell us whether this specific development or related mathematical models
are of any genuine value in analyzing the phenomena of interest to psychologists. Of course, such decision procedures do not exist. Only the perspective gained by refinement and extension of these models with empirical

verification at critical stages will permit us to make such an evaluation. Certainly within the last decade almost all learning phenomena have been examined with reference to one or more mathematical models, and there is no doubt that these analyses have led to a deeper understanding of the empirical findings. In addition, many new lines of experimentation have come about directly from the work on mathematical models of learning. In spite of these developments, some behavioral scientists maintain that psychology has not yet reached a stage where mathematical analysis is appropriate; still others argue that the data of psychology are basically different from those of the natural sciences and defy any type of rigorous systematization. Of course, there is no definitive answer to these criticisms. Similar objections were raised against mathematical physics as recently as the late 19th century, and only the brilliant success of the approach silenced opposition. A convincing argument is yet to be made for the possibility that mathematical models in psychology will not enjoy similar success.

REFERENCES

ATKINSON, R. C. A theory of stimulus discrimination learning. In K. J. Arrow, S. Karlin, & P. Suppes (Eds.), *Mathematical models in the social sciences.* Stanford Univer. Press, 1960.

ATKINSON, R. C. The observing response in discrimination learning. *J. exp. Psychol.,* 1961, 62, 253-262.

ESTES, W. K. Toward a statistical theory of learning. *Psychol. Rev.,* 1950, 57, 94-107.

SUPPES, P., & ATKINSON, R. C. *Markov learning models for multiperson interaction.* Stanford Univer. Press, 1960.

7

SOVIET RESEARCH ON INTELLECTUAL PROCESSES IN CHILDREN [1]

Daniel E. Berlyne
University of Toronto

General Remarks

I shall attempt to outline some of the principal kinds of research with a bearing on intellectual processes in children that have been going on in the U.S.S.R., but before doing so a few general remarks may be in order.

First of all, this is an extremely serious matter. In many areas of psychology, 80 or 90 per cent of the important work is published in English, so that anybody who neglects the literature in foreign languages may be missing a few interesting studies, but will not be missing a great deal. In child psychology, however, this is not the case. There are in the world today three bodies of work on child psychology, each of about equal volume as far as empirical data and theoretical ideas are concerned. These are the literature in English, the literature in Russian, and the literature in French. The literature in French includes Piaget's work which, in sheer quantity, is about equal to all the English-language or all the Russian-language literature put together. In other words, if we confine ourselves to English-language literature in child psychology, we are confining ourselves to about a third of the literature of child psychology. If we further restrict ourselves to English-language literature on intellectual processes in children, we shall probably have access to considerably less than a third of the significant work.

It is generally realized that the boundaries between disciplines in the Soviet Union are not quite the same as the ones we have in the West. Certainly, a great deal of work that we should regard as psychology is carried out in the U.S.S.R. by people who call themselves physiologists. This includes not only work that we should classify as physiological psychology but also work on learning in human beings and animals. There is also a great deal of psychology carried on under the egis of philosophy, as in most continental European countries. In the middle, there is a considerable and influential group of people who are psychologists without being categorized

[1] The preparation of this paper was facilitated by Research Grant M-4495 from the United States Public Health Service.

as either philosophers or physiologists, and these people spend much of their time studying children. The child is, in other words, the rat of Russian psychology.

There are, however, some important differences between the Russians and Piaget. Apart from obvious differences in theoretical approach, Piaget holds himself aloof from what he calls "scholastic" questions, although he does not mind if others apply some of his ideas to practical educational problems. The Russians, on the other hand, are impelled by their official ideology to believe strongly in carrying on pure and applied research in conjunction with each other. So, while they do fundamental work on intellectual processes in children, they are at the same time looking out for ways of improving their educational techniques and of ameliorating handicaps due to brain injuries, mental deficiency, deafness, blindness, etc.—the study they call "defectology."

It is also necessary to say a word about the role of Pavlov in contemporary Russian physiology and psychology. Almost anything written in the Soviet Union in these fields is likely to be liberally larded with quotations from Pavlov and his predecessor, the 19th-century "father of Russian physiology," Sechenov. These references to Pavlov are, however, not nearly so numerous as they were several years ago, especially immediately after the famous joint meeting of the Academy of Sciences and the Academy of Medical Sciences in 1950, at which it was decreed that Pavlov's research techniques and theoretical formulations should be closely followed. There are actually some quite radical modifications and extensions of Pavlovian theory in contemporary Russian writing with differences of approach that, at times, parallel the divisions that marked American learning theory in the 1930's and 1940's. There is, moreover, much work in psychology that has actually very little in common with the Pavlovian tradition.

Pavlov was in many ways a highly useful man. He lived a long time, and he wrote prolifically, and it seems that, whatever point of view one wishes to espouse, one may find a quotation from Pavlov somewhere that makes it look as if he thought so too. It is, in fact, not uncommon for a writer who is offering a theoretical innovation to make it look as if he has put his finger on the very idea toward which Pavlov was groping.

The truth of the matter seems to be that, although Pavlov's influence, both in content and terminology, is universal, the Pavlovian tradition is only one of several traditions within Soviet psychology. It is certainly a major current in contemporary Soviet child psychology. The current stemming from Bekhterev has now more or less coalesced with it. Bekhterev's school was in official disfavor during the Stalin period, but its members continued to do their work. Now, there do not appear to be any great distinctions between the experimental and theoretical approaches of pupils of Pavlov and pupils of Bekhterev, although there are still slight differences in emphasis.

A second major trend in Soviet psychology, particularly child psychology, is the one that can be traced back to Vygotsky, several of whose pupils and close associates are still active. Those who are in this line of descent write as if they are making a synthesis between the ideas of Pavlov and the ideas of Vygotsky, and to some extent they are doing so. But Vygotsky was a very different kind of man from Pavlov. He was a psychologist, pure and simple, of a rather typical continental European type, being close to the German tradition in many respects. He is best known in this country for the Vygotsky concept-formation test, which was modified and applied to psychotics by Hanfmann and Kasanin. But that is only a very small part of what he did. His principal book, *Thought and Language* (1956) is now available in an English translation (1962).

There are some other currents in Russian psychology which have given rise to work with children, such as the one initiated by the Georgian psychologist, Uznadze (1958), and still enthusiastically pursued by his successors in Tbilisi. But in what follows I shall limit myself to the two major currents, namely, those stemming from the work of Pavlov and Vygotsky, respectively, and I shall take them up in turn.

PAVLOV AND THE SECOND SIGNAL SYSTEM

In Western countries, Pavlov's experiments on conditioned reflexes and the conclusions to which they led him are of course well known. But there are also some misunderstandings about his work. For example, Pavlov has often been represented, especially in the writings of persons sympathetic to the Gestalt school, as a man who believed that all behavior consists of simple, isolated, unitary reflexes, each of which is automatically set in motion by a stimulus and unaffected by anything else. This picture of Pavlov's position is, however, a mistaken one and almost an ironical one, because Pavlov became famous in the first place for taking exactly the opposite position.

Long before he did the work in neurophysiology for which he is most famous, he worked on circulatory and digestive processes, and, in fact, was awarded the Nobel Prize in 1904 for his work on gastric secretions. His principal contribution at that stage was his advocacy of what he called the "chronic" method. He held that it was a mistake to use the "acute" methods that were then current among physiologists (i.e., to dissect out the organs of interest and study them *in vitro*). In the chronic method, the organism is left as far as possible intact, and the only modifications of its normal condition consist of minor operations to gain access to the organs of interest. These organs are studied in the living animal, while their connections with the rest of the body are still functioning. Pavlov insisted that this was the method to use whenever possible, because he believed that any process going on in one part of the body is profoundly affected by what is going on in other parts of the body. He did not abandon his view when he took up the study of conditioned reflexes, since he found a great deal of evidence for interaction among reflexes, being influenced in this regard by some of the conclusions Sherrington had reached in the study of spinal reflexes. Pavlov likewise stressed the influence of the physiological state of the organism as a whole on the behavior elicited by particular stimuli.

Secondly, Pavlov is often represented as naively convinced that the principles he derived from his experiments on simple salivary conditioning in the dog will suffice to explain all the complexities of human behavior. This was simply not true of Pavlov, and it is not true for his followers today. The hope that findings from experiments on simple learning in animals can be extrapolated to account for more or less everything in human psychology has been taken more seriously and tried out more consistently by American learning theorists than by Russians, among whom "biologism" (i.e., overstressing similarities between animals and human beings) used to be condemned as a "deviation."

Toward the end of his life, Pavlov had reservations about the scope of his conditioning principles as applied to human beings. He certainly believed that the human nervous system exhibits all the phenomena that he discovered in the dog's nervous system, and this has, of course, been amply demonstrated. Nevertheless, he began to believe that a large part of human behavior, especially the intellectual part, differs in far-reaching respects from anything found elsewhere in the animal kingdom and that these differences reduce the scope of the laws that have emerged from experiments on salivary conditioning. These reservations resulted primarily from the recognition of what Pavlov called the "second signal system."

The "second signal system" is a term that occurs extremely often in contemporary Russian psychological and physiological literature, but, in such works of Pavlov as are available in English, there are, as far as I can ascertain, only two paragraphs (Pavlov [1941, pp. 113-114]) devoted to the concept. Put briefly, the second signal system is the portion of the nervous system that is concerned with verbal behavior. The first signal system is what Pavlov had been studying in the dog. Conditioned stimuli are generally, but of course not exclusively, stimuli that excite distance receptors. Sights and sounds do not have either beneficial or harmful effects on the tissues as such, except when they are exceptionally intense. But they can come to evoke vigorous responses if they signal events of biological importance. The second signal system, on the other hand, enables us to respond to words as "signals of signals." Just as a light, an initially indifferent stimulus, may act as a signal for the impending appearance of food, the word "light" becomes a signal for the light. Of course, a verbal stimulus affecting the second signal system does not, in general, stand for one particular stimulus of the first signal system; it stands for a whole class of nonverbal stimuli with a certain property, or set of properties, in common. The second signal system thus makes possible high levels of. abstraction.

And although in many ways the second signal system resembles the first signal system, some essential differences between them were evident from the start. For one thing, the second signal system seems to work according to something like the old principle of association by contiguity. If a word is frequently encountered together with an object that the word represents, the object will acquire an association with the word, and the word will evoke responses appropriate to the object. The presence of a stimulus eliciting a powerful overt response does not seem to be required to provide reinforcement, in contrast with classical conditioning.

Secondly, the associations on which the second signal system depends can be formed rapidly. One might, for example, meet a man once and be told that his name is "Jones." One might not see him again for the next 30 years, but "Jones" never loses its connection with this man. One-trial learning can be realized, as it is many times a day in ordinary life and can be remarkably stable. A continuing reinforcement in the Pavlovian sense (whether or not there may be a reinforcement in the sense in which the term is used in America) is not necessary. There need be no further pairings of the word with the original stimulus (i.e., the sight of the man).

Thirdly, despite its stability, the learning involved in the second signal system can be amazingly flexible. One might have learned to refer to a certain man as "Jones" for 30 years, but, if one is then informed that Jones has changed his name to "Smith," the word "Jones" immediately loses the meaning it has had for so long.

These are some of the properties of the second signal system that caused Pavlov to think that the human intellect complicates the study of "higher nervous activity" in the human being and sets severe limits to the analogies to be drawn between the behavior of lower animals and our own behavior. And that is about where Pavlov left things when he died in 1936, although several of his pupils had already begun to work on the second signal system.

Soviet work on conditioning in children began quite early. The first experiments on the conditioned reflex in dogs were done in 1899 (see Pavlov [1927, p. 42]). In 1907, Krasnogorski was already adapting Pavlov's technique for use with young children. He did not, of course, operate on the children to produce a fistula permitting saliva to be extracted through the cheek. Instead, he developed salivometers which were placed in the mouth and drew off the saliva that accumulated. In conjunction with these, he used a device for recording chewing movements. The child sat or lay down with this recording equipment attached to him and received various conditioned stimuli, each followed by the unconditioned stimulus, which consisted of something like cranberry sauce delivered by a chute into the mouth. School children were studied quite intensively by this method, and it turned out that, on the whole, the same phenomena appeared as had been observed in dogs, although there were some quantitative differences between children and dogs as well as differences among children of various ages (Krasnogorski [1958]).

Later, other investigators developed additional techniques for studying conditioned reflexes in infants. These included not only reflexes connected with feeding, but also defensive reflexes (originally evoked by noxious stimuli such as electric shock or a puff of air striking the eyeball) and orienting reflexes (turning the head towards a source of stimulation) (Elkonin [1960]; Kasatkin [1952]). By these methods, the development of classically conditioned responses, including both artificial ones which occur only in laboratory conditions and natural ones that occur in the normal infant's everyday experience, were traced back to the beginning of life.

Interestingly enough, the first experiment on instrumental conditioning appears to have been done with children. One can, of course, regard some of the early experiments on maze learning in the rat or Thorndike's experiments with puzzle boxes as instances of instrumental conditioning, if one chooses. But this is perhaps broadening the concept inordinately. Several workers in different countries appear to have hit upon experimental techniques that exhibited the instrumental conditioned response in situations enabling similarities and differences between it and the classical conditioned response to be seen clearly. There was Skinner (1935) in the United States, Grindley (1932) in England, and Miller and Konorski (1928) in Poland. All this work was done in the 1920's or early 1930's. But as far as I can tell, the earliest of all these experiments was that of Ivanov-Smolenski (1927), who used children. His subjects were rewarded with a bar of chocolate if they pressed a rubber bulb as soon as the chocolate became visible in a slot as it passed down a chute.

Work on the second signal system, for which children are particularly appropriate subjects, began largely with attempts to explore the extent and direction of generalization involving verbal stimuli (Ivanov-Smolenski [1949, 1951, 1956]), and it was found repeatedly from the start that there would be considerable generalization between a verbal stimulus and its corresponding nonverbal stimulus. For example, if a child were taught to perform a certain response on perceiving a bell, the word "bell" would be found, without further training, to evoke the same response. Similarly a response that had been established to the word would generalize to the corresponding nonverbal stimulus.

There were also studies of generalization between words. As is to be expected, a response will generalize from written to spoken versions of the same word. But particularly interesting were cases of what in Western countries is called "semantic generalization" (i.e., generalization depending on similarity in meaning). Many of the semantic relations familiar from free-association experiments were explored (i.e., subordination, supra-ordination, coordination), as well as forms of synonymy. In all cases, it was found that the degree of generalization corresponds to the closeness of these relations. There was also found to be generalization between a word and a phrase or sentence describing the referent of the word (e.g., between "Bird" and "It flies").

Perhaps the most remarkable of the multifarious studies of generalization between verbal stimuli are those reported by Volkova (1953, 1957) using the Krasnogorski technique. In one experiment, she established the word "ten" as a positive stimulus and the word "eight" as a negative or inhibitory stimulus. It was then found that such verbal patterns as "5 + 5" or "80/8" became positive stimuli, whereas "4 × 2" and "4 + 4" became inhibitory stimuli, through generalization. In another experiment, the positive stimulus was the word "correct" and the negative stimulus the word "mistake." Consequently, true sentences such as "The doctor cures sick people" became positive through generalization, whereas a sentence such as "At night the sun shines" became negative. The sentence "Today is the second of January" was a positive or negative in its effects according to the day on which the trial took place.

Various conditioning methods have been used to trace out these semantic links and the processes of generalization that followed them. Krasnogorski and his pupils used their accustomed secretory-motor method. Luria and Vinogradova (1950) have recently used the psychophysiological measures supplied by recent studies of the orientation reaction to ascertain the degree of affinity between the meanings of particular words. Ivanov-Smolenski and his associates, who did most of the work on these problems, used several methods of conditioning autonomic processes. But their favorite method was the "verbal method" (Ivanov-Smolenski [1922, 1936]), which raises some interesting questions. It has been criticized at times, and I understand that Pavlov himself had his doubts about it. Now that Ivanov-Smolenski himself has retired and his laboratory has been dissolved, it is still widely used in Russia as a convenient way of inducing a conditioned response in human subjects, but I do not know of anybody who has ever tried it out in the West.

The apparatus consists simply of a device for producing stimuli such as sounds or colored lights, a rubber bulb that can be held in the subject's hand, and a kymograph or some such equipment to record the duration of the stimuli and any pressure exerted by the subject's hand on the bulb. The experimenter produces the conditioned stimulus, say a red light. Then he says the word, "Press" (the unconditioned stimulus), and the child presses. After a few trials, a conditioned response develops: the child begins to press the bulb during the CS-US interval (i.e., when the red light alone comes on and before E has time to say, "Press").

One can also build up a discrimination by adding a negative CS, say a green light. When the green light comes on, E does not merely omit the reinforcement by not saying, "Press." Instead he provides negative reinforcement by saying, "Don't press." The child then learns to press on seeing a red light and not to press when a green light appears.

All of the standard Pavlovian phenomena have been demonstrated with this technique. Once the procedure is well under way, the technique changes somewhat, and I think this is extremely interesting in itself.[2] There are four possibilities: red light or green light in combination with press or no press. Following the response in each case E does something. If the child presses to the red light (positive) or does not press to the green light (negative), E says, "Correct" or some such phrase. If S presses when he is not supposed to press, then E says, "You shouldn't have pressed" or "You were not supposed to press." Similarly, if S fails to press within a decent interval after a red light, then E says, "You were supposed to press" or "You should have pressed." Essentially the technique involves changing from a classical to an instrumental procedure in midstream. The experimenter begins with classical conditioning by pairing the red light with the word "Press" and in later trials presents a reinforcement for a correct response by saying, "Correct" after the performance of the response.

Another question raised by the technique is how far it really produces something analogous to salivary conditioning in the dog. Suppose you are a child put into this situation as a subject. You are given a red light, and the man says, "Press." You are given a green light, and the man says, "Don't press." You would probably regard this as a sort of game. You can see that this fellow wants you to press sometimes and not at other times, and there is obviously supposed to be some way in which you can tell whether to press or not. What you do is to try to work out what is going on in his mind and do your best to conform. In other words, this would seem to be more an experiment on thinking than one on conditioning. It is a test of how well the child can figure out the rules of the game.

There are, however, marked differences between older and younger children, and that is why the technique is particularly instructive. Ivanov-Smolenski discovered differences between younger children and older children which have recently been verified by Paramanova (1956), one of the Moscow University group not connected with Ivanov-Smolenski. Paramanova finds striking differences between younger children of about 3 years and older children of 5 to 6 years. In older children, a discrimination of this kind is established very quickly. It may take a few trials, but, once they have had a little experience, they perform perfectly every time. If E changes the procedure (which we would call reversal training), by suddenly and without warning making the green light positive and the red light negative, the older children will again catch on very quickly. It will require perhaps a

---

[2] This modification of Ivanov-Smolenski's original technique was apparently introduced by Povorinski. *See* A. S. Dmitriev, "On a motor technique with verbal reinforcement," published in English in *Soviet Psychology and Psychiatry*, 1962, 1, 8-15.

trial or two, and then they will understand and reverse their responses without difficulty. Older children will remain remarkably stable, continuing to make correct responses every time, trial after trial. If the experimenter asks them what they are doing, they will explain by saying, "Obviously I'm supposed to press when there's a red light and not when there's a green light, and that's what I am doing."

Younger children behave quite differently. It takes 3-year-olds time to build up the discrimination. At first they respond to both lights, and then very gradually the response to the negative stimulus disappears, exactly as with salivary conditioning in the dog. Reversal training takes some time, and conditioning is very unstable. Now and then the younger children will miss a response just as a dog will.

The conclusion drawn is that, with an older child, the process is being controlled by the second signal system, while in the younger child it is not. This conclusion coincides with our assumption that the older child is thinking out the problem. The way Soviet investigators put it is that the younger child is responding directly to the lights in exactly the same way as a dog responds to the beats of the metronome. He is building up typical classically conditioned responses to the lights. The older child, on the other hand, is not responding directly to the lights at all. He is using what we call "mediating responses." He is reacting to the light with internal verbal responses that amount to self-instruction, and he is reacting to the self-instructions with a pressing response. Because this complicated learning involves the mediation of intellectual processes, it has the properties of flexibility and stability.

Another significant difference between older and younger children concerns whether or not, as the Russians put it, the "connection is reflected in the second signal system" (i.e., whether the child can verbalize what he is doing or, in other language, whether he is aware of it). This is one question to which Ivanov-Smolenski's group have devoted attention, and some of the phenomena that they found have been confirmed by other experimenters (Paramanova [1956]) in recent years. Whereas the 5- or 6-year old can report accurately what he did and what stimulus made him do it, the verbal reports of the younger subjects are defective. They may deny that they pressed the bulb when they did. Alternatively, they may say that they did not notice the conditioned stimulus, or they may report both their response and the conditioned stimulus correctly, but fail to recognize any connection between the two.

The early investigators of the second signal system, including the most active of them, Ivanov-Smolenski, tended to emphasize the differences between the first and second signal systems. It was evident to them that the second signal system is subject to "selective irradiation" (i.e., generalization confined to semantic relations built up by learning). In the first signal system, there was irradiation in all directions, reflecting any kind of similarity along any dimension. They seemed to think that these differences must depend on different ways in which the neural substrates of the two signal systems function.

Recently, however, there has been a trend in the opposite direction, exemplified by the work of Koltsova (1958). Since Pavlov recognized common principles uniting the two signal systems and distinctions between them, both trends can claim some authority from his writings.

Koltsova has been investigating the development of the child's responses to verbal stimuli and patterns of verbal stimuli from the earliest ages at which they appear. She uses verbal utterances as conditioned stimuli for an eye-blink response. She also studies the child's ability to obey simple verbal commands and tests his ability to pick out objects to which a particular word is appropriate from a pile of miscellaneous objects. Some of her experimental designs come near to those of Western concept-formation experiments, but she is eager to relate the establishment of a word as a label for a class of stimulus objects to the processes that underlie simple conditioning.

Her findings bring out the necessity of a training procedure that contrasts the objects or stimulus patterns to be covered by a word with other objects or patterns to which the word is not applicable. They also reveal the necessity of associating a definite common motor response with the former, while the inhibition of that response or the performance of an incompatible response is associated with the latter. In this way, it appears that the first and second signal systems do not obey discordant principles but that the differences between the effects of verbal and nonverbal stimuli are due to peculiarities of the circumstances in which verbal stimuli are generally encountered and accompanied by reinforcement.

VYGOTSKY AND THE RELATIONAL CONTROL OF BEHAVIOR

Vygotsky also was interested in the role of speech in controlling behavior, but he concentrated on variables different from those studied by the early followers of Pavlov. His pupils, however, particularly Leontiev, Luria, and Zaporozhets, have been trying to effect a synthesis between the two bodies of work.

Vygotsky (1930) distinguished the role of speech in affecting the behavior of other people from its role as a means of affecting one's own behavior. When one is using words to influence one's own responses, the words do not need to be pronounced out loud, and it is, of course, usually advantageous for many reasons to make the words subvocal. Vygotsky pointed to distinctions between the properties and structure of this inner speech and those of outer speech that is used to communicate with others. He said that thought and speech are not quite the same thing. Thought does not grow out of speech or vice versa, but obviously, once thought and speech have appeared, they interact and influence each other intimately, and speech becomes the principal vehicle of socialization. In fact, the child begins by allowing his behavior to be directed by speech coming from others, and he later uses speech to direct his own behavior as a by-product of his responsiveness to what others say to him. So, Vygotsky's work led to a large body of experimentation on relations between thought and language and on ways in which both thought and language regulate overt behavior.

Of those who belong to this school, Luria is the one whose work is best known in the West, because he has written articles in English (1959) or French (1958a) and he has been on lecture tours in Western countries during the last ten years. He has studied the ways in which linguistic processes produce voluntary control over behavior, but he has shown that there are very many facets to this control.

A similar theme was quite prominent in American psychology in the 1920's and the 1930's. Hudgins (1933) and others (Hilgard and Marquis [1940, ch. 11]) did experiments in which, for example, subjects learned to make their pupils contract at will, and this was accomplished by conditioning verbal responses. The Ss were trained to contract their pupils when they heard the word, "Contract." This generalized to hearing themselves say, "Contract," which in turn generalized to the feedback stimuli from thinking the word, "Contract."

The phenomenon led to some disputes. Skinner (1938), for one, claimed that it was not really voluntary control over behavior, but rather a substitute for voluntary control. Suppose that an actor has to weep in a certain scene. He might get himself to weep by thinking of his childhood home or some other poignant scene, just as he might place an irritating substance in contact with his eyeball. These devices would all produce the desired effect, but one could not really say that he established voluntary control over his tear glands.

Luria (1956, 1957, 1958b) carried the inquiry further by showing that words have a number of different ways of influencing behavior, which appear at different ages. For example, in the young child of 1½ to 2 years—about as young as one can get a child to respond to language at all—language does not have much effect other than the production of *orienting* responses. If E says something to the child, he may stop whatever he is doing and look at E, or he may look at the object E names, or he may look for the object E names if it is not immediately present, but he will not do what E tells him. If E says, "Give me the ball," the child will just look at the ball.

At a somewhat later stage, language has an *impulsive* or *releasing* function. The effect of a verbal instruction then seems to be to make the child do whatever he is ready to do. In other words, if the child is ready to give E the ball, and E says, "Give me the *doll*," he gives E the *ball*. That is what he was ready to do, and the language merely releases the response.

Subsequently, language acquires a *selective* function. *E* tells a child, "Press the bulb," and he does so here and now, showing that he can obey simple orders.

Finally, the most advanced and interesting function about language has is that of *preselection*, the same sort of function that language presumably fulfills in self-instruction. The experimenter tells the child, "A red light is going to come on. When there is a red light, press the bulb." (Note that Luria has inherited Ivanov-Smolenski's apparatus, which has come into wide use for varied purposes in Russia.) The situation may be more complicated and require a discrimination. The *E* may say, "Press the bulb if a red light comes on, but do not press if a green light comes on." Again, a child of about 2½ years cannot do this. If *E* says, "Press the bulb when the red light comes on," then *S* will start pressing right away, and, in fact, when the red light comes on, he will stop because of external inhibition. A child of about 3 years will solve the simple problem, but not the discrimination. If *E* says, "Press the bulb when the red light comes on," he will wait until the light comes on before pressing, but he will also press when the green light comes on, even if *E* has told him not to. Finally, at about 5½ or 6 years, a child can solve both parts of the discrimination. He can withhold a response, or he can perform a response where it is appropriate, in accordance with a set produced by previous instruction.

Luria also studied ways in which these deficiencies can be made up—ways in which the child can be given a crutch, as it were, to enable him to solve some of these problems at an earlier age (e.g., giving him feedback stimuli or making him give himself verbal or other response-produced cues). Luria's work shows the many-sidedness of the control that verbal processes can exert over behavior.

One final body of research that I should like to mention shows things to be more complicated still. This is the research carried out by Zaporozhets and his associates. Zaporozhet's book, *The Development of Voluntary Movements* (1960), seems to me to be one of the most important psychological books to have come out in any country within the last ten years.

Zaporozhets attacks the American S-R point of view, more in sorrow than in anger. (Before about 1953, Western "bourgeois" science was usually denounced more in anger than in sorrow.) Zaporozhets declares himself to be adopting the "reflex" point of view derived from Pavlov and Sechenov. But interestingly enough, this "reflex" point of view seems to be very much like what N. E. Miller (1950) has called "liberalized S-R theory." In general, the problems with which Zaporozhets and his colleagues are concerned and the solutions they propose are quite strikingly parallel to some of those favored by contemporary Western S-R theorists.

The point from which Zaporozhets starts is one that a number of Western psychologists also are beginning to take up: certain forms of human behavior are strikingly different from anything found in animals or even from some of the more automatic forms of behavior found in human beings. There are actions that are voluntary, and there are actions that are involuntary and automatic. Some actions appear to be conscious—the actor seems to be aware of what he is doing—while others do not. These distinctions used to be discussed in mentalistic terms, which has made some psychologists disinclined to recognize them at all, but we are now beginning to see that they can and must be faced and studied without abandoning the merits of an objective, operationist methodology.

To what extent are the same principles of learning applicable to both kinds of behavior? To what extent do the more complex kinds of behavior obey quite different principles? This is precisely the sort of question that Zaporozhets is trying to answer.

He comes to the conclusion that, without lapsing into mentalism or "idealism" as they call it in Russia, psychologists must discuss consciousness and accept its problems as legitimate. And this is what many Western psychologists in the behaviorist tradition have also been feeling. The early behaviorists paid some attention to these problems as Goss (1961) has reminded us, but in recent years, the feeling has become particularly widespread (cf. Dollard and Miller [1950]; Mowrer [1960]; Taylor [1962]).

Zaporozhets' way of going about the task is different from theirs in some respects, but it is similar in that it involves mediating processes. The idea of a mediating response as the unit of thinking and intellectual functioning seems to have appeared in several different places at once. The unit of thought is held to be an attenuated or curtailed version of an overt response. This idea was one of the pillars of behaviorism from the start, and it received, of course, some supporting evidence in Jacobson's (1937) data on electromyographic action currents. We find the same idea in Piaget's (1949) contention that the operations of thought are "internalized" actions. And in 19th-century Russia, Sechenov asserted very plainly that thinking consists of interrupted reflexes.

Although different kinds of mediating responses and different kinds of abbreviated, fractional responses have been recognized, each of the three countries has its favorite. In American the implicit *verbal* response has generally been accorded prime importance. For Piaget the most important mediating responses are implicit *executive* responses—responses that act to modify the environment. The Russians attribute a major role to verbal responses, largely through the influence of Pavlov's views on the second signal system, but they have been giving more prominence to another source of internal mediators, namely *orienting* responses.

The "orienting response" is a concept that has gone through several revisions in Russia. Pavlov used the term "orientational reflex" to refer to such phenomena as turning the head and the eyes toward a stimulus source, pricking up the ears, etc. (i.e., overt receptor-adjusting responses). About 1949-1950, the Russians became aware that these overt orienting responses are accompanied by other changes, which could not be detected at all without special instruments. Overt orienting responses are accompanied, for example, by EEG phenomena, physicochemical processes in the sense organs, changes in the visceral organs controlled by the autonomic nervous system, and rises in muscular tension. All of these are beginning to be called the "orientation reaction" (Sokolov [1958]; Berlyne [1960, ch. 4]). It is a complex of events that seems to have at least two groups of functions. First of all, it increases the organism's capacity to extract information from the environment. It is accompanied by increases in the sensitivity of the sensory equipment as a whole, demonstrated by reduced thresholds. Secondly, it consists of processes that prepare the organism to act rapidly and vigorously, which a novel stimulus might well require.

Lately, however, and especially in the Vygotsky-descended group, the orientation reaction seems to have acquired yet a third connotation embracing purely central attentive processes. For Zaporozhets, the objective equivalent of a conscious attentive process, and the object indicant of a conscious attentive process, is the occurrence of an orientation reaction. A conscious process is thus virtually defined operationally as a process that is accompanied by an orientation reaction.

He extends this reasoning to the analysis of voluntary behavior to suggest that the essence of voluntary behavior is in feedback. (The Russians have taken very eagerly to cybernetics and information theory.) He points out that there is a difference between primitive behavior and complex voluntary behavior with respect to how much feedback occurs and at what stages. If the organism is functioning at a primitive level, as is the case with most lower animals or with human beings at their more primitive moments, it has a stab at the problem and obtains feedback from the end product. It behaves like a rat indulging in trial-and-error learning. Having done something, it determines whether it has reached its goal or not. If so, all well and good; it continues to do more of the same. The response is learned and it is performed with greater strength on the next occasion. But if the goal has not been reached, the behavior is modified and another response is tried out.

Such all-or-none trial and error is, however, rather dangerous. Some actions have consequences that must be identified prior to performance if the organism is to survive. Gibson's visual cliff is an example.

Therefore, according to Zaporozhets, it is important to reach the stage of voluntary behavior, in which we receive feedback *en route*. In other words, we do not merely wait until we have completed an action to find out whether we have reached the desired end, but we continually monitor our behavior along the way and extrapolate from what has happened so far to anticipate the next move. To take an old example, if we go to pick up a piece of chalk, we do not just grab and then check to see whether we have the chalk. Rather, we utilize visual, proprioceptive, and other feedback stimuli throughout, to keep us on the right course. If we find that we are deviating from the right course and going in a direction that will obviously not bring the hand into contact with the chalk, then we have time to correct our motion and set a better course.

Feedback explains the flexibility of voluntary behavior. It explains why we can start or stop behavior at any point, why we can modify it to conform to changed external circumstances. If, while we are reaching for the chalk, somebody moves it, we can take account of that fact and change our action accordingly.

One series of experiments, illustrating the essential contribution of feedback to voluntary control, was performed by Lisina (1956). It is interesting to compare this work with the experiments of Hudgins. Lisina, like Hudgins, sought to make a normally involuntary response voluntary. The involuntary response on which she concentrated was vasodilation in the finger. Moreover she tried to produce vasodilation in the finger as a conditioned response to electric shock, running counter to the unconditioned response to electric shock, which is vasoconstriction. Thus the response was not merely doing something that is normally involuntary but doing something voluntarily that is the very opposite of the normal involuntary response.

She tried various procedures and found some that worked. Those that worked were of two kinds. One of them involved linking the vasomotor response with an external feedback stimulus, auditory, visual, or tactual. Let us take the auditory feedback condition as an example. Subjects heard a tone which went up in pitch when their blood vessels dilated and down in pitch when they constricted. They were not told this. They were told only that the tone represented something that was happening inside them. Nevertheless, they were rewarded whenever they made the tone go up (i.e., when dilation occurred), and this procedure was fairly successful.

The second technique, which worked still better, involved using the subjects' natural feedback. First, they were given a lecture about vasomotor responses. Then they were given training to recognize the sensations emanating directly from their own vasomotor responses. The technique is reminiscent of Jacobson's (1934) method of progressive relaxation, in which patients are trained to recognize their muscular kinesthetic feedback. After the training, when subjects could feel whether the blood vessels in their fingers were constricting or dilating, it took them practically no time at all for them to learn to perform the response whenever they liked. The finding is claimed by Zaporozhets as a vindication of his point of view. It certainly looks, from the incomplete accounts that are available, as if this control was rather more clearly voluntary than was that produced in Hudgin's experiments.

Zaporozhets combines these two emphases, the emphasis on orienting reactions and the emphasis on feedback, to work out a theory of the nature of voluntary action and the development of voluntary action in the child.

His experiments involve various motor tasks. He uses, for example, maze problems. Instead of a stylus maze, he uses a maze in which the child has to push a toy car around the correct path. There is also a task in which subjects have to push a sequence of buttons in response to a sequence of colored lights. He also uses knocking in a nail with a hammer and, finally, gymnastic exercises.

In some of these experiments, he employs children of different ages to find out what they will make of the problem when they are left to their own devices. They are, of course, given knowledge of results or some sort of reinforcement when they are right, but they solve the problem by trial and error. In other experiments, Zaporozhets tries to cut down the process of trial and error by verbal instruction. The child is told beforehand what he is supposed to do, and then he is free to try it. In still another set of experiments the child is allowed to learn by imitation. The teacher or experimenter demonstrates exactly what the child has to do, and then he does it.

Zaporozhets considers how competence develops with age. Needless to say, the child gets better at all of these tasks as he grows older, and he makes more and more effective use of imitation and of verbal instructions.

The interesting finding that emerges from these numerous experiments is that verbal instruction and imitation are much more effective if they are directed toward orienting responses as well as executive responses. In other words, in teaching a child how to carry out a complex task, one must make sure that he is also taught how to organize his orienting responses. He must learn what to look at; his attention must be directed to the right cues, both external and proprioceptive. He must make use of feedback from both the external situation and his own actions, and the experimenter must train him to do this. Several experiments show that the time to learn a task can be cut down if orienting behavior is specifically trained. This conclusion may well represent a fact that every teacher knows and puts into effect daily, but it is, at any rate, demonstrated clearly in these experiments.

Zaporozhets and his collaborators have shown how children of different ages spontaneously organize their orienting responses. The orienting responses of a young child are rather haphazard. As Piaget (1961) has shown, they are disorganized and not very efficient. Later on they become more organized and more useful, so that the child does not have to be told what cues to seek out and attend to; he can find out for himself.

Other interesting results were derived from studies of maze learning. When Zinchenko (1958) photographed the eye movements of a subject confronted with a maze, he found several distinct stages. First, there is a stage where the subject just looks over the maze randomly to get his bearings. Then there is a stage when he is obviously tracing out possible paths through the maze with his eyes, and, finally, when he has mastered the problem and performance becomes automatic, eye movements become abbreviated and their original exploratory function ceases.

Coming still nearer to intellectual processes, which are our main concern here, Zaporozhets has related this work to thinking. Voluntary behavior is, or can be, planned behavior. When a child has behavior under voluntary control (e.g., in the tasks that have just been described), he can plan ahead. For example, given a maze to learn, a younger child will immediately grasp the car and try to move it through the maze, going up blind alleys and eventually finding the correct route, but wasting considerable time in the process. An older child or an adult will look for a path first, and, if the maze is not too complex, he will either follow the correct path the first time or will, at least, require fewer trials for mastery.

Planning behavior in advance means being able to reason about it, being able to think it out, and that means building up an *image* of the activity. The subject must build up an image of the whole activity, which means he must construct an image of what he is going to do when he meets each of these cues. For example, I have to fly from Minneapolis to New York tomorrow, and I probably have a sufficient knowledge of the geography of the United States to be able to name the states that I shall be flying over. But I do not do this by a mechanical rote process, such that each named state brings to mind the name of the next, unless I have been given this task so many times in the past that it has become mechanical. On the other hand, I do not have in my mind's eye a patchwork map of the United States with all the 50 states in different colors, so that I can simply read off the states that I shall pass over as I might from a real map.

What probably happens is something like this. I have first of all an imaginary map of the United States with the area around Minnesota clearly in focus and the rest of the country rather hazy. This enables me to see that the next state to the east is Wisconsin. I then focus my attention on that part of the map so that I can identify the next state after that as Michigan, etc. After all, even when I look at a real map, I can fixate and derive information from only one part of it at a time, and this limitation must be still more severe when I am dealing with an image of a complex structure.

In other words, we must have responses that move us from one part of the cognitive map to the other. We must have a motor pattern of some kind as well as a perceptual pattern. And according to Zaporozhets, the devices that conduct us from one element of an elaborate image or thought structure to another are orienting responses in an implicit form.

REFERENCES

BERLYNE, D. E. *Conflict, arousal and curiosity.* McGraw-Hill, 1960.
DOLLARD, J., & MILLER, N. E. *Personality and psychotherapy.* McGraw-Hill, 1950.
ELKONIN, D. B. *Detskaia psikhologiia. (Child psychology.)* Moscow: Uchpedgiz, 1960.

Goss, A. E. Early behaviorism and verbal mediating responses. *Amer. Psychologist*, 1961, 16, 285-298.

Grindley, G. C. The formation of a simple habit in guinea-pigs. *Brit. J. Psychol.*, 1932, 23, 127-147.

Hilgard, E. R., & Marquis, D. G. *Conditioning and learning*. Appleton-Century, 1940.

Hudgins, C. V. Conditioning and the voluntary control of the pupillary light reflex. *J. gen. Psychol.*, 1933, 8, 3-51.

Ivanov-Smolenski, A. G. Biogenez rechevykh refleksov i osnovye printsipy metodiki ikh issledovaniia. (The biogenesis of speech reflexes and basic methodological principles for their investigation.) In *Psichiatriia, i eksperimental'naia psikhologiia (Psychiatry, neurology and experimental psychology)*, 1922, No. 2.

Ivanov-Smolenski, A. G. On the methods of examining the conditioned food reflexes in children and in mental disorders. *Brain*, 1927, 50, 138-151.

Ivanov-Smolenski, A. G. Na puti k izucheniiu vysshikh form neirodinamiki rebenka. (Towards the study of the higher forms of neurodynamics in the child.) *Trudy Lab. Fiz. i Pat. Vys. Nerv. Deiat. Renbenka*, 1934.

Ivanov-Smolenski, A. G. O vzaimodeistvii 1-oi i 2-oi signal'nyk sistem pri nekotorikh fiziologischeskikh i patologicheskikh usloviiakh. (On the interaction of the 1st and 2nd signal systems in certain physiological and pathological conditions.) *Fiz. Zh. SSSR*, 1949, 35, 271-281.

Ivanov-Smolenski, A. G. Ob izuchenii sovmestnoi raboti 1-oi i 2-oi signal'nykh sistem mozgovoi kori. (On the study of the joint action of the 1st and 2nd signal systems of the cortex.) *Zh. Vys. Nerv. Deiat.*, 1951, 1, 55-66.

Ivanov-Smolenski, A. G. Ways and perspectives of the development of the physiology and pathophysiology of the higher nervous activity of the child. (1956) In *The Central Nervous System and Behavior*. U.S. Public Health Service, 1960.

Jacobson, E. *You must relax*. Whittlesey House, 1934.

Jacobson, L. E. The electrophysiology of mental activities. *Amer. J. Physiol.*, 1932, 44, 677-694.

Kasatkin, N. I. Early conditioned reflexes in the child. (1952) In *The Central Nervous System and Behavior*. U.S. Public Health Service, 1960.

Koltsova, M. M. *O formirovanii vysshei nervoni deiatel'nosti rebenka. (On the formation of higher nervous activity in the child.)* Leningrad: Medgiz, 1958.

Krasnogorski, N. I. Opyt polucheniia uslovnykh refleksov u detei. (An attempt to obtain conditioned reflexes in children.) *Russk. Vrach.*, 1907, 36.

Krasnogorski, N. I. *Vysschaia nervnaia deiatel'nost' rebenka. (The higher nervous activity of the child.)* Leningrad: Medgiz, 1958.

Lisina, M. I. Rol' orientirovki v prevrashchenii reaktsii iz neproizvol'ykh v proizvolnye. (The role of orienting activity in the conversion of involuntary into voluntary reactions.) In L. G. Voronin *et al.* (Eds.), *Orientirovochny refleks i orientirovchno-issledovatel'skaia deiatel'nost'. (Orienting reflex and exploratory behavior.)* Moscow: Acad. Pedag. Sci., 1958.

Luria, A. R. O reguliriushchei roli rechi v formirivanii proizvol'nykh dvizhenii. (On the regulating role of speech in the formation of voluntary movements.) *Zh. Vys. Nerv. Deiat.*, 1956, 6, 645-661.

Luria, A. R. Experimental analysis of the development of voluntary action in children. Paper read to XV Int. Cong. Psychol., Montreal, 1957. Reprinted in *The Central Nervous System*. U.S. Public Health Service, 1960.

Luria, A. R. Le rôle du langage dans la formation des processus psychiques. *La Raison*, 1958, 22, 3-26. (a)

Luria, A. R. Rol' rechi v regulatsii normal'nogo i anomal'nogo pobedeniia. (The role of speech in regulation of normal and anomalous behavior.) In A. R. Luria (Ed.), *Problemy vyssei nervoni deiatel'nosti normal'nogo i anomal'nogo rebenka*. Vol. II, Moscow: Acad. Pedag. Sci., 1958. (b)

Luria, A. R. The directive function of speech in development and dissolution. *Word*, 1959, 15, 341-352; 453-464.

Luria, A. R., & Vinogradova, O. S. An objective investigation of the dynamics of semantic systems. *Brit. J. Psychol.*, 1959, 50, 89-105.

Miller, N. E. Liberalization of basic S-R concepts; extensions to conflict behavior, motivation and social learning. In S. Koch (Ed.), *Psychology—a study of a science.* Vol. 2. McGraw-Hill, 1959.

Miller, S., & Konorski, J. Sur une forme particulière des réflexes conditionnels. *C. R. Soc. Biol.*, 1928, 99, 1155-1157.

Mowrer, O. H. *Learning theory and the symbolic processes.* Wiley, 1960.

Paramanova, N. P. O formirovanii vzaimodeistvii dvukh signal'nykh sistem u normal' nogo rebenka. (On the formation of the interaction of the two signal systems in the normal child.) In A. R. Luria (Ed.), *Problemy vysshei nervnoi deiatel'nosti normal' nogo i anomal'nogo rebenka. (Problems of higher nervous activity of the normal and anomalous child.)* Vol. I. Moscow: Acad. Pedag. Sci., 1956.

Pavlov, I. P. *Conditioned reflexes.* Oxford: Clarendon Press, 1927.

Pavlov, I. P. *Conditioned reflexes and psychiatry.* International Publishers, 1941.

Piaget, J. Le problème neurologique de l'intériorisation des actions en opérations réversibles. *Arch. de Psychol.*, 1949, 32, 241-258.

Piaget, J. *Les mécanismes perceptifs.* Presses Universitaires de France, 1961.

Skinner, B. F. Two types of conditioned reflex and a pseudo type. *J. gen. Psychol.*, 1935, 12, 66-77.

Skinner, B. F. *Behavior of organisms.* Appleton-Century, 1938.

Sokolov, E. N. *Vospriiatie i uslovny refleks. (Perception and the conditioned reflex.)* Moscow: University Press, 1958.

Taylor, J. G. *The behavioral basis of perception.* Yale Univer. Press, 1962.

Uznadze, D. N. *Eksperimental'nye issledovaniia po psikhologii ustanovki. (Experimental investigations in the psychology of set.)* Tbilisi Acad. Sci. Georgian SSR, 1958.

Volkova, V. D. O nekotorykh osobennostiakh obrazovaniia uslovnykh refleksov na rechevye razdrazhiteli u detei. (On certain peculiarities in the formation of conditioned reflexes to verbal stimuli in children.) *Fiziol. Zh. SSSR*, 1953, 39, 540-548.

Volkova, V. D. O korrigiriushchem vliianii okriuzhaiushchei sredy pri obrazovanii uslovnykh refleksov na nekotorye rechevye razdrazhitelei. (On the corrective role of the environment in the formation of conditioned reflexes to several verbal stimuli.) *Zh. Vys. Nerv. Deiat.*, 1957, 7, 525-533.

Vygotsky, L. S. Thought and speech. *Psychiatry*, 1939, 2, 29-52.

Vygotsky, L. S. *Mishlenie i rech'. (Thought and language.)* Moscow: *Acad. Pedag. Sci.*, 1956. English translation. M.I.T. & Wiley, 1962.

Zaporozhets, A. V. *Razvitie proizvol' nykh dvizhenii. (The development of voluntary movements.)* Moscow: Acad. Pedag. Sci., 1960. (To be published in English)

Zinchenko, V. P. K voprosu o formirovanii orientiruiushchego obraza. (Concerning the formation of an orienting image.) In L. G. Voronin *et al.* (Eds.), *Orientirovochny refleks i orientiovochno-issledovatel'skaia deiatel'nost'. (The orienting reflex and exploratory behavior.)* Moscow: Acad. Pedag. Sci., 1958.

8

SOME SOVIET RESEARCH ON LEARNING AND PERCEPTION IN CHILDREN

Herbert Pick

University of Wisconsin

I shall first make a few comments on the historical trends in research relating motor movements to perception. Along with the Pavlovian physiological trend, there is a philosophical trend underlying this work. The philosophy is, of course, that of Marx as modified by Lenin. Although one might think upon first exposure to the Russian psychological literature that mere lip service is given to Marx, there is, in fact, a definite guiding influence of this philosophy on the directions taken in research. In particular, the materialism of Marx would suggest that there is a real world; we learn about this real world through the interaction of ourselves and our bodies with the objects in the real world. Lenin's modifications would suggest that, in perceiving the real world and getting information about it, we are coming into closer contact with what is really there. We are getting a real representation in the sense of a copy or image. This *obraz* is a copy in the sense of a photographic copy; it is not a coded copy, at least this is one current hypothesis in Soviet psychology. The reason that Soviet psychologists are not willing to accept a coded copy or the equivalent amount of information in some coded form, but instead prefer a more realistic representation of what is in the world, is that the coded aspect would represent the deviation of "idealism" that they reject. They accept neither idealism nor a logical positivism.

Since the material world is really out there and really exists, we must have a real copy of it. The way we develop this real copy is by combination of input through our receptors with feedback from our own motor movements. The orienting reflex enters this system in that, when we make an orienting response to the real object, it is purely reflexive. Our movements are guided by the real object, and the movements we make are important in the perception. If our movements are guided by this real object, then they will reproduce this real object, so that we generate an actual physical projection of some sort in the brain as a result of feedback from our eye movements around the physical contours of the real object. The model works very well for tactual perception. If we encounter a physical object, we explore it. The relation between our own bodies and the physical object is such that we move around the contours of the object. If we perceive these movements, we can get a representation of the real contours.

The problem is a little more difficult when we come to visual perception, because the eye movements (at least in the American literature on the subject) need not follow the contour of an object in order to perceive it adequately. By perception I mean successful performance in a recognition task, such as a "same-different" judgment of a pair of objects. There is, then, a discrepancy between the Russian philosophical and theoretical position and some of the empirical data. Although research on micromovements of the eye indicates that small movements as in mystagmus are important in perception, evidence was lacking for a necessary eye movement around the contour, almost in a Hebbian sense. Therefore, a group at the Institute of Psychology in Moscow followed several lines of investigation to find out whether movement was important in some respects, even though under the ordinary conditions of perception it is not critical. The topic was pursued along three lines:

1. Visual perception in the adult was studied under conditions where the visual stimulus was unfamiliar as opposed to familiar. When an unfamiliar figure was exposed at a high rate of speed, that is, tachistoscopically, it was found that Ss, even adults, could not recognize it without making eye movements. If, however, it was a familiar figure, then they could recognize it. It is not clear whether the experiment was controlled adequately for the amount of information in the stimulus.

2. Another direction pursued particularly by V. P. Zinchenko was an attempt to show that orienting eye movements in a new situation could be controlled by the stimulus, similar to the way in which the orienting reflex is controlled. That is, novel stimuli coming into view should attract eye movements. By using a screen where lights would flash on in succession, it was found that, initially, Ss who were given no instructions at all would gradually follow around as the lights came on. If there was any sequence to the presentation, very soon anticipatory eye movements became conditioned. That is, when one signal came on, the eye moved to the next light, and, as the second light came on, the eye moved to the third, etc. Gradually all eye movements dropped out. Apparently in this situation the orienting reflex was, in a way, extinguished. The orienting reflex could be revived again by giving S an instruction, such as to pay attention to the lights or to turn off a light as it came on. In this case the eye movements would again recur. Several variations on this sort of experiment were conducted to show the importance of eye movements under conditions of novel stimulation, and in executive tasks where stimuli were appearing and disappearing.

3. A third line of investigation attempted to determine the real significance of eye movements and the relation between eye movements and hand movements. A comparative study of eye movements and hand move-

ments was done jointly by Zinchenko and B. F. Lomov of the Department of Psychology at Leningrad University. A developmental study of eye movements and hand movements in the perception and recognition of form was carried on under the direction of A. V. Zaporozhets. I shall not consider the comparative study of eye and hand movements in detail, but in general it was found that, with respect to orientation, there is a strong common trend between what sorts of eye movements and what sorts of hand movements occur. If a novel stimulus is presented visually, there are wide, sweeping eye movements which seem at first to have the function of fixing the stimulus in space and then exploring around it. Finally a more detailed exploration by smaller movements around the contour and within the contour of the object occurs. The same sequence was found for hand movements when an object is presented to be explored tactually.

The developmental study of the tactual and visual recognition of form was interesting, but it is difficult to determine how well it was done. The procedure was to adapt some nonsense forms reported by Gaydos (1956) for the problem. Children ranging in age from 3 to 8 years examined a form either visually or tactually. Then they had to identify the form by picking it out of an array of three forms presented either visually or tactually, thus generating four conditions: visual or tactual exploration followed by visual or tactual recognition. In general, all the studies found that the amount of movement around the contour was related to the accuracy of recognition of the forms. This was true for both visual and tactual perception. There was a general developmental improvement in recognition. There were fewer errors as progressively older children were tested, but the trend was very uneven. There were interactions between the mode of exploration and recognition called for and the rate of developmental improvement. In every case where the rate of improvement was affected by perceptual mode, the investigators felt that the result could be explained by consideration of the actual movements that occurred during exploration or during the recognition task.

An initial finding that was instrumental in arousing interest in the problem was that children who were given a task of visual identification had to trace out the contours with their fingers in the air. That is, when a form was projected on a screen and they were to pick it out from an array of three figures placed in front of them, very young children would spontaneously trace the form with their finger and could succeed at the task only if they also traced the contours of the figures in front of them. The interpretation was that, for young children, feedback from exploratory movements is essential in a recognition task.

All the studies that I have referred to dealing with within-modality and across-modality perception used successive presentation of stimuli. That is, subjects were given the form; then it was taken away, and they were given the three recognition figures. The investigators suspected that the developmental trend was an artifact due to the memory factor, and so they repeated the experiment using simultaneous presentation of the recognition figure and the matching array. When they presented the visual form and the three-choice array simultaneously, all the children showed performance decrements, except the very oldest ones, and this was explained on the basis of a division of attention. The problem becomes too complicated when all the figures are presented at once—it confuses all but the older children, and it is claimed that the older children transform it into a successive recognition task by concentrating first on the one and then on the other and keeping the movements separate.

One other series of studies that I think are the most important and exciting that I saw while I was in the Soviet Union were attempts to adapt the *obraz* point of view to audition. These were done in the Department of Psychology at Moscow University under the direction of A. N. Leontiev. With touch, and to a lesser extent with vision, it is easy to see how a kind of reproduction of the physical stimulus could be important in perceptual recognition. In audition, however, we do not reproduce sounds by wiggling our ears, yet the investigators sought to adapt the reproduction and feedback model to auditory perception. Essentially their strategy was to replicate some of the classical studies in pitch perception. They obtained the classical results in terms of mean thresholds and variation in the population. Then they disrupted the correspondence between pitch and timbre. They repeated the threshold studies of pitch discrimination, but distorted the timbre so that a low pitch was paired with generally high timbre, and vice versa. Therefore, a subject who might be making the discrimination on the basis of timbre would be confused. In fact, they found that a large proportion of the population was confused—about 35 per cent showed tremendous increments in their discrimination thresholds as determined under this distorted condition.

Following the notion of the importance in perception of reproducing the physical stimulus, they asked Ss to intonate both tones before they made the judgment of which of the two tones was higher in pitch. It was found that, when subjects intonated, difference thresholds were considerably lower than when the judgments were made without intonation. If the same subjects were then instructed to stop intonation, thresholds were again raised. This would suggest an important correspondence between vocalization of a note and discrimination of pitch. The investigators correlated the ability of subjects to vocalize a note accurately and their ability in terms of pitch discrimination and found a correlation of about .84. When a subject could vocalize a tone accurately, he was also able to discriminate accurately. Moreover, with people who had narrow zones of good vocalization, it was found that within this narrow zone the pitch thresholds were very low. Outside this zone, where a person could not vocalize accurately, pitch thresholds were again high.

Leontiev and his associates conceptualize the development of pitch discrimination as follows: If a child (or an adult, for that matter) hears a sound, reproduces this sound, and is reinforced for his reproduction, then a link in an S-S sense can be established between the feedback from the vocal muscles and the auditory input through the ear. Gradually a subject can come to identify a tone by vocalizing it after he hears it, discriminating it on the basis of his own muscle feedback or the combination of muscle feedback and auditory input. Obviously, we do not actually vocalize every time we make auditory pitch discriminations. With continued practice, these voice muscle movements drop out or become implicit just as eye movements drop out with increased familiarity of the stimulus. At this stage one would have to use electrical techniques to get at the movement of voice muscles, and in some cases even the electrical activity would be expected to drop out.

The hypothesis suggested further experiments. In languages such as Russian, English, etc., pitch is not a carrier of meaning, and, therefore, it is not important that the child (in learning the language) also learn to vocalize or discriminate pitch. There are, however, some languages, such as Vietnamese, where pitch does carry meaning, and in these languages children would have to learn to vocalize pitch in order to speak, and, of course, they would also have to learn to discriminate pitch. The experiment was performed on Vietnamese students to see if the same percentage of Vietnamese would display the sort of pitch deafness found in the Russian subjects (35 per cent). The Vietnamese subjects were essentially unaffected by the distortion of pitch and timbre.

It has been found that training facilitates discrimination, but only when it involves motor mediation. In one experiment, two tones were sounded, the subject made his guess, and then he was corrected as to whether he was right or wrong. When this training was accomplished using one or two timbres and pitches, Ss could learn, but the training did not generalize over the whole range of timbre and pitch. Another group received motor training, which did not involve any discrimination, but required Ss to match tones by intonation. The Ss were told when their matching was correct. The same tones were used as in the earlier psychophysical experiments. It was found that this motor-trained group could learn to match the tones and that the training generalized over the whole range of tones tested. Once they stopped the training and put the subjects in a test situation, the subjects could then discriminate tones in a psychophysical sense. Moreover, if they were told to sing a note, thus occupying their voice during the tests, then their pitch discrimination was disrupted. Watson would have thought this a very nice result indeed.

The last experiment in the series involved essentially the same sort of motor training, but, instead of using feedback from the voice muscles, Leontiev's group tried training with feedback from hand pressure. The S was told to press on a lever with intensity corresponding to the pitch of the note. Then on the basis of an arbitrary scale, he was told whether he was pressing with the right degree of force or not. These subjects learned, although very slowly, to press with a certain pressure when a certain note sounded, and then, when they were tested in a psychophysical situation, they were able to make proper pitch discriminations. Actually, I think this is a very ingenious experiment. On the other hand, it does depart from the original idea that you have to reproduce the original physical stimulus isomorphically. When the voice was the mediator, Ss were, in a sense, reproducing the physical stimulus, but later when hand pressing was the mediator, subjects were not reproducing the physical stimulus.[1]

In general, when Soviet investigators find a psychophysical property that seems to be dependent on past training and past experience, they are quite delighted—it fits in with that aspect of their philosophical tradition which emphasizes the influence of the social environment. However, in the case of audition, the *lack* of necessity to reproduce the stimulus does not fit in with their original hypothesis, which itself stems from another aspect of their philosophy. Perhaps any scalar response learned in correspondence to a stimulus will facilitate perceptual discrimination, and the fact that the most common of such responses bear either a linguistic or an isomorphic relationship to the stimulus is an incidental aspect of the natural circumstances of early learning, when orienting and labeling predominate.

REFERENCES

GAYDOS, H. F. Intersensory transfer in the discrimination of form. *Amer. J. Psychol.,* 1956, 69, 107-110.

---

[1] The scale relating pressure and frequency was an arbitrary linear one.

9

SUMMARY

If one reflects on the range of phenomena considered at the conference and the diversity of propositions designed to account for them, one cannot help but be struck by the theoretical immaturity of that sector of behavior we call "intellectual development." There are many promising variations more or less closely tied to empirical data, but there is no single firm theme. It is surprising, for example, that, despite the attention currently given to Piaget (this committee devoted its first conference to his work), mention of his name, his data, and his ideas occurred relatively infrequently during three days of almost continuous talking.

The reasons for this lack of a general structure can be specified only partially. Theoretical descriptions of processes such as classification, abstraction, and inference require constructs that deal with perceptions, motives, and responses different from those ordinarily studied by social scientists in the orthodox behaviorist tradition. Conventional responses and response measures (e.g., performance in mazes, on pursuit rotors, in bar pressing, or in probabilistic situations) are the end products of interaction among many component parts. Acquisition of habits typically involves the elimination of errors and the gradual strengthening of a large number of correct segments. The course of this learning seems to be best described by an incremental law—strength of habit gradually increases with frequency of reinforcement.

The learning of a linguistic label, on the other hand, seems to adhere on many occasions to an all-or-none law. Acquisition of a noun and its correct application to a class of relevant objects may be described more accurately by a sudden increase in response strength from zero to maximum than by the traditional negatively accelerated learning curve.

Moreover, the human motivations to be rational, to be correct, to structure information efficiently, and to avoid dissonance, uncertainty, and cognitive strain are always present. Unlike hunger, thirst, pain, or sex, these motives do not require deprivation operations or special external arousal to guarantee their maintenance. The praiseworthy attempt to make human cognition conform to the simple kinds of theoretical structure used to explain animal behavior and human motor learning leads to a neglect of vital issues that need careful attention and explanation in their own right.

An alternative position toward which we might turn, that of the Geneva group, is open enough to allow for optimism and is intuitively more appealing. But the critical missing feature in this obviously significant corpus of work is an hypothesis pertaining to the mechanisms of change from one cognitive stage to another.

We are faced with two interlocking questions that must be answered before a theory of cognitive development can be written: How does the child acquire conceptual structures; and what mechanisms must be invoked to explain the abandoning of one structure and the taking on of another? At present we are unable to offer elegant solutions to these problems. It seems clear that there are qualitative changes in the child's organization and classification of the environment at about 1 year, when the child becomes capable of elementary conceptual activity. By age 6 several other changes have occurred, including acquisition of the ability to produce the verbal cues that will serve most effectively to guide his own behavior. But the rules of classification and self-instruction that he uses are still a mystery, and we are as yet far from ascertaining the forces that determine which objects are initially categorized and what operations are first programmed.

No single theoretical position emerged from the presentation of findings and confrontations of viewpoints that occurred at the conference. However, several issues received such repeated emphasis that one feels certain of their continued relevance and value as guide lines.

THE GROWTH OF MEDIATIONAL SYSTEMS

If the child is impelled to organize stimuli for himself, then it is obvious that mediating responses—and linguistic labels, in particular—are the most important and effective means of doing so. While orienting reflexes and relevant attending responses are important, they can account for only a fraction of the power that generic labels and semantic mediations provide to the child as he uses language to order his world. It might be argued that the most central theme of the meetings was developmental changes in the role of language. Both Kendler and Spiker emphasized the increasing importance of implicit linguistic labels as mediating responses in learning. These papers reemphasized the point that two distinct and critical bonds are formed as a result of the child's commerce with his environment. One is the link between an external stimulus and a verbal label. The other is a subsequent bond between the label and an overt response.

Perhaps the most important difference between human and infrahuman learning is the preferential operation in humans of the bond between verbal label and response. Learning distinctive names for visually presented stimuli and learning them well aid subsequent discriminations. Learning to label compound stimuli as "black" or "white" or as "large" or "small" facilitates rapid reversal shifts. Acquisition of speech makes it possible for older children to accomplish permanent, one-trial learning in the second signal system, by means of sophisticated verbal mediating responses. Finally the child's tendency to label objects and events is so prepotent that he spontaneously invents and uses verbal mediators, even when the investigator seeks to prevent him from doing so.

A verbal mediator may remind S of what a stimulus is, but it may also tell him what he might or should do about it. Just as objects can be organized by labels, so operations can be organized by verbal propositions. A highway sign, such as "Railroad Crossing" may serve to make an object or event in the visual field distinctive and prepotent. In addition, a response rule or proposed operation may be specified, such as "Right Turn on Red Light Permitted Except 4-6 PM." Similarly, language may mediate discrimination in the form of a labeling response ("this face is a wug") or in the extended form of a self-instruction or proposition ("I need a marble, not a ballbearing, to put in the hole so that a charm will come out"). The propositional form of verbal mediating response has received less attention than the simple verbal label, but its potential value is clearly seen in Kendler's work on inferential behavior and in the functional classification of objects described by Bruner and Olver. The inclusion of "newspaper" in a group of objects tentatively labeled "noisemakers" and containing the stimuli, "bell" and "horn," requires an implicit functional test operation, "Will a newspaper make noise?" The ability to verbalize such branching or testing operations and the ability verbally to anticipate the consequences of such operations makes possible many kinds of abstract reasoning not accessible to the child whose mediational repertoire is limited to names and labels.

SELECTION OF DIMENSIONS AND STRATEGIES FOR STIMULUS ORGANIZATION

A second general issue pertained to preferred strategies for processing information. Cognitive activity typically consists of three processes that normally occur in sequence: the initial selection of the dimensions for categorizing stimuli, the sorting of this coded information, and the imposing of transformations upon the coded data. The storage and transformation stages are influenced by the availability of categories in which to sort the incoming information and the possession of rules and segments of knowledge that allow the individual to impose transformations upon coded categories.

The initial selection of dimensions on which categories are to be formed, that is, the salience or distinctiveness of stimuli, is a function of other processes and is characterized by age, sex, and intraindividual differences. Since every final cognitive product is a function of the dimensions initially selected for processing, it is important to ascertain those factors that govern selection of one aspect of a stimulus rather than another and to discover the existence of any unlearned or prepotent links between certain distal stimulus dimensions and specific behaviors. Children with equivalent ability and equivalent mediational structures might arrive at different end states in a problem situation as a result of differences in the initial processing of stimuli.

Gibson discussed two provocative aspects of the relation between specific stimuli and behavior. She suggested that perception of depth at any edge may be an unlearned characteristic of young human and infrahuman terrestrial organisms and that such a stimulus has an aversive quality. Young cats, rats, and infants avoid stimuli that we would regard as veridical with respect to depth. If such a link between perception and an avoidant response is an inherent structure of the central nervous system, it is not unlikely that other S-R couples are also part of the equipment with which children begin life. Gibson's paper adds incentive to a search for these regularities.

Gibson also reported on research with children suggesting some of the stimulus dimensions of graphic symbols that are preferentially selected for initial categorization. Children from 4 to 8 years of age are likely to attend to broken vs. closed lines and straight vs. curved lines in nonsense figures and to regard these features as distinctive. Changes in the perspective of figures, on the other hand, are less likely to be regarded as relevant distinctions.

Mastery of reading is preceded by a process of isolating and focusing on those features of graphemes that are distinctive; learning the name of a letter is a secondary stage. Gibson's work is relevant to current theorizing about the reading process, and concomitantly, the symptoms of reading retardation. Such retardation may be traceable, in some instances, to difficulties in apprehending the distinctiveness of letter symbols.

While Gibson emphasized preferential modes of organizing *visually presented* designs, Bruner and Olver emphasized differences in the selection of strategies for the conceptual grouping of *words*. Young children are more apt than older ones to group words together on the basis of concrete or irrelevant characteristics or, more importantly, on the basis of attributes that do not serve as efficient modes of storing information. The 7-year-old, for example, is likely to group the words, apple, pear, and peach, together under the rubric, "things to eat"; or stove, toaster, and radio as "things that do things for you." The 11-year-old uses abstract words and concepts to tie the diverse objects together more parsimoniously. He is more likely to group apple, pear, and peach together as "fruits"; stove, toaster, and radio as "electrical appliances." Such labels do not destroy the essential attributes of the grouping.

The paper by Kagan, Moss, and Sigel extended and reemphasized the importance of dimension selection in categorization behavior. Children appear to differ consistently in their tendency to analyse and to differentiate visually presented stimuli. The analytic tendency increases with age, is slightly stronger and more consistent in boys than in girls, and, at any age level, appears to be involved in many of the child's conceptual activities.

Study of individual differences in preferred modes of categorization is one area where research on cognition engages the work on individual differences in other domains, including motives, attitudes, conflicts, and constitutional parameters. There is, for example, some evidence that a tendency toward impulsive classifications—classifications that are given with little reflection—is an immediate and critical antecedent of a nonanalytic style. Therefore it becomes possible to consult the existing theoretical and research literature on "impulsivity" for fertile hypotheses about the antecedents of this response tendency. In summary, the way has been paved for initiating theoretically directed research on relationships between traditional personality constructs and individual cognitive processes.

Cognition as an Active Process

If cognitive functioning in humans requires the development of verbal mediators and selection of dimensions for stimulus categorization, then, in a broader sense, it must be seen as an active, rather than a reactive process. In one way or another every paper emphasized the active, questioning, testing, inventing, and generally information-producing behavior that is both typical of children and critical to our understanding of intellectual development. Beginning with Gibson's evidence that infants of several species can discriminate depth at an edge, primarily by means of parallax cues produced by the organism's own movements, we have seen how frequently the organism participates in the production of the stimuli to which it will respond. Somewhat older children learn or invent vocalizations which serve as stimuli for more complex kinds of responding. In Kendler's reversal studies the older and more successful children actively invent or discover dimensional organization in what is presented to them as a simple choice problem. The linkage of independently acquired responses in organized chains of apparently purposeful behavior, as seen in the studies of inference, is another example of active information processing in ways never explicitly taught to the child.

Similarly in Spiker's paradigm for the acquired distinctiveness of cues, it is not the pretraining with distinctive names that produces, strictly speaking, the improved discrimination. Rather it is the active and voluntary *use* of the names by the subject during the discrimination task that provides the facilitation. Spiker's paper is an impressive illustration of how effectively children can be induced to make relevant and useful cue-producing responses.

Bruner and Olver dealt with the active, spontaneous transformational behavior that children use in order to provide themselves with orderly systems for grouping words. Whenever possible, as a function of the age of the child and the difficulty of the problem, children invent grouping structures that (a) are as simple and economical as possible, (b) make it possible for them to go beyond the information given, and (c) serve to organize a given set of words in a useful, strainless, and reproducible fashion consistent with previously established groupings. Kagan, Moss, and Sigel considered groupings of visual representations of people and objects as a measure of preferred strategies of conceptualization. An analytic strategy requires both the inhibition of impulsive responding and the active imposition of an orderly, disciplined scanning strategy for differentiating the environment. Finally the "close hard look" and the "what is it?" response appear to play a major role in even the earliest and most primitive kinds of cognitive functioning. Atkinson's observing response, the orienting reaction described by Berlyne, and the stimulus-reproduction view of perceptual learning reported by Pick again serve to remind us that information-generating behavior is of the utmost importance to an information-processing organism.

MATHEMATICAL MODELS AS DESCRIPTIONS OF THE LEARNING PROCESS

As in 1960, the committee was encouraged by recent developments in formal, logical, and mathematical descriptions of the learning process. Atkinson presented an impressive demonstration of the potential power of a specific model to predict the course of learning in a discrimination problem. The predictions were not only verified by the empirical data, but offered as well an extension of learning models into the area of children's thinking that was congruent with other data and viewpoints. Since some of the assumptions made by the model do not correspond with those of more traditional theories of learning, we may expect that continued validation of the model, and others like it, may lead to new insights into the fundamental propositions necessary to explain the learning process.

We anticipate increased research emphasis on cognitive development in children, especially among psychologists who have been traditionally concerned with other issues. The frontiers of our knowledge are accessible, and, as we have seen in the papers presented here, diversity of theoretical orientation need not interfere with progress, and may substantially aid it. Contemporary psychology is fortunate to have escaped some of the strong behavioristic prejudices of the 1940's, and inquiry into the psychology of thought and its development may now be undertaken with objectivity and accepted as basic to a theory of behavior. The use of verbal labels and mediators, the selection of dimensions and strategies for organizing experience, and the active, information-producing behavior of children appear to be phenomena that will play a central role in a continuing investigation of cognitive functioning.

III

THE ACQUISITION OF LANGUAGE

Report of the Fourth Conference
Sponsored by the Committee
on Intellective Processes Research
of the Social Science Research Council

EDITED BY

URSULA BELLUGI
ROGER BROWN

1

THE DEVELOPMENT OF GRAMMAR IN CHILD LANGUAGE [1]

WICK MILLER *and* SUSAN ERVIN
University of California

Before describing the development of children's grammar, it is necessary to specify some of the properties of natural languages as used by adults. This is the model presented to the child and the eventual outcome of his development.

It is possible to analyze in all languages two types of constructs (or linguistic units): phonemes and morphemes. There are at least two corresponding systems which can be called the phonological and grammatical levels.[2] While this paper is concerned only with the grammatical level, certain properties of the phonological level will be briefly considered by way of contrast.

The phonetic substance, the raw material of language, can be analyzed into a finite set of mutually exclusive classes. The distinctive features by which the classes are contrasted are few in number. Each phonological system may be described in terms of different privileges of occurrence of the features or the sets of features called phonemes. Phonemes are grouped together into larger units in limited arrangements, and the groupings can be completely described by distributional statements. Thus it is possible to predict *all* possible phonemic shapes.[3] From the standpoint of the learner, the phonemic rules are given. Even nonsense words or coinages normally follow these rules. Imitation of sequences already heard is the normal mode of acquisition and use, and continues with the expansion of vocabulary.

---

[1] The project described in the paper is supported by a grant from the Department of Health, Education, and Welfare (M-3813) to the Institute of Human Development, University of California, Berkeley. Facilities have also been provided by the Center for Human Learning under support of the National Science Foundation.

[2] The term "level" has been used in a variety of ways in the linguistic literature. Our use of the term does not apply to the so-called levels within the syntactic system, or the distinction between morphology and syntax. As we use the term, the two levels correspond to what communication theorists call the channel and the message.

[3] Whorf (1940) has given a succinct statement for phonemic sequences in English monosyllables.

If we turn to the grammatical level, we see many differences. Morphemes, like phonemes, can be grouped into a number of classes, but the nature of the classes is different. The classes can be divided into two groups, which following Fries (1952) we can call lexical and function classes. Lexical classes are large and open and the number of classes is small. English lexical classes include nouns, verbs, and adjectives. A lexical class can normally be divided into subclasses, e.g., English mass nouns, count nouns, proper nouns. In contrast, function classes are small and closed and the number of classes is larger. English function classes include prepositions, conjunctions, interrogatives, noun determiners, and auxiliaries. It is more often possible to point to a simple referent for members of lexical classes than for members of function classes. The contrast between lexical and function classes is often only a relative one, which may mean that it is not always a useful distinction to make in organizing a grammar.

The grammatical productivity of a language is infinite. A speaker can produce utterances which he has never heard before. Unless the words are nonsense or the sentence semantically aberrant, such utterances will be understood by the hearer. This property of grammars is in contrast to the phonological system. Any novel recombination of phonemes, while it may follow phonological distribution rules, is nonsense until or unless conventional meaning is assigned.

Every language has a major predication type formed by placing together two constructions. The predication is *exocentric*—that is, the resulting construction does not belong to the same class as either of the two constituent constructions. In most languages at least one of the constituents of the predication is a member of a lexical class or an expansion of a lexical class, e.g., the English subject is composed of a noun or noun phrase. Most nonpredication constructions are *endocentric,* or expansions in which the head of the construction belongs to the same class as the resulting construction. An example is the noun phrase, *the three boys,* which is an expansion of the noun phrase, *three boys.*

The term *discourse agreement* is used to indicate formal relationships that cross sentence boundaries. They are of two kinds: (a) *class restrictions,* and (b) *verb restrictions.* The first occur in answers to questions. A question has a formal structure, which normally restricts the formal structure possible in the response, and also a semantic content or a request for information. The comparison of two questions illustrates this point; on formal grounds we would expect the following answers:

A: *Where is Main Street?   I don't know.* or *Straight ahead.*
B: *Can you tell me where Main Street is?   No.* or *Yes.*

Obviously the responses to question B fail to meet the semantic requirements posed by the question. The two questions differ formally but are semantically equivalent.

In addition to "yes-no" questions, there are "or" questions and interrogative word questions. "Or" questions require a choice of an alternative if there is a falling intonation. The short response to interrogative word questions must be a word or phrase belonging to the same class as the interrogative word or words.

Verb restrictions involve the maintenance of tense or auxiliary features across sentence boundaries, and can be characterized as long components of a grammatical category. Compare the following set of sentences:

> A: *This ice cream is good.   Yes, it is.*
> B: *This ice cream tastes good.   Yes, it does.*

The initial sentences of A and B are semantically equivalent, but differ formally and require different responses. Verb restrictions can apply to successive utterances of the same or different speakers, but our attention will be focused on situations in which different speakers are involved, in particular when the second speaker is required to answer a "what—do" question.

In this paper we will distinguish three functional categories in the child's utterances. The first may be called *reference* (Skinner's *tacts*). It involves naming or describing and may be accompanied by pointing. Such behavior is initiated by the child and does not necessarily demand a response from another person. The second may be called *direction* (Skinner's *mands*) and demands verbal or active response from the hearer. Such utterances include commands and questions. It is often impossible to discriminate questions from reference utterances of the child. A third category may be called *responsive discourse* and includes informational responses. This category can be initiated by the interlocutor or the child, but we are primarily concerned with this category when initiated by the interlocutor.[4]

A person has two grammatical systems, one for encoding and another for decoding, or an active and passive grammatical system. For the adult, a single grammar can normally account for almost all of both systems. Quite clearly this is not the case with the child. We assume that a child must understand a grammatical pattern before he can produce it. Presumably the decoding and encoding systems at any point in time are not independent. It seems likely that rules could be found for the derivation of one from the other. Such a procedure might be a fruitful way to approach grammatical development. We have little evidence concerning the decoding system at this time.

THE RESEARCH PROJECT

The data mentioned in this paper were obtained in a project consisting of longitudinal testing of 25 children and more intensive text collection

---

[4] Linguists frequently distinguish three functions: referential, directive, and expressive; for a recent account see Hymes (in press), and Jakobson (1960).

from a subgroup of five. Texts for four of the children were collected beginning when the children were about 2. The fifth child, Susan, was added when she was 1.9. Text collection was scheduled to continue for two years. The standardized tests collected from the larger group consisted of three tests: a plural test, a pronoun test, and two forms of a discourse agreement test. The children in the smaller sample were older than the other children in the group.

The texts were at first collected weekly, in sessions of 45 minutes, because of rapid change. As the rate of change decreased and the fluency of the children increased, the frequency of text collection was gradually reduced, until texts were collected at two-month intervals, in two or three sets of closely spaced interviews totaling four or five hours.

The texts were all tape recorded. The transcription was at first phonetic, but later it was made in the normal orthography marked for stress and intonation, with a phonetic transcription only for ambiguous material. The texts also included utterances of the investigator and pertinent contextual information.

The earliest texts were collected in unstructured interviews. As techniques which elicited certain types of utterances were noted, the investigator increasingly structured the interviews. For example, attempts to elicit negatives were made by putting clothes on the wrong doll or puzzle pieces in the wrong place. Doll clothing was used for eliciting possessives. To elicit an interrogative sentence, two dolls were "fed," and the child was told to "ask Joe what he wants to eat." Plurals were produced for nonsense objects made of play-doh. If one of the dolls was left behind, "because he is sick," the child was asked to talk on the toy telephone to find out how "Joe" was, another device for eliciting questions. Telephone conversations with the child tested his reliance on verbal rather than gestural cues. Techniques that were discovered in this way were incorporated where appropriate into tests for the larger group.

The plural test consisted of 17 items. In each case a toy object or picture was shown, its name elicited, and then two were shown. "Here are two what?" Thus the test did not give the children the option of using a syntactical plural signal rather than a morphological one. The items included certain pairs in which nonsense items (wooden constructions) were given names which had the same final consonant as a familiar word (*boy-kigh*, *block-bik*, *bed-pud*, *horse-tass*, *orange-bunge*). Irregulars were *foot*, *man*, and *house*. The singular of the regular and nonsense words was offered by the investigator if it was not offered by the child. In the case of *foot* and *man*, however, the singular was not offered by the investigator. This procedure was followed in order to determine which form, e.g., *foot* or *feet*, was used by the child as the singular. Testing was stopped on items after they had been contrasted for several months.

On the pronoun test, the child was questioned about pictures, the questions being designed to elicit sentences containing possessives and nominative pronouns varying in number and gender. In the test of discourse agreement, questions tested the class of responses, verb restrictions, comprehension of subject-object distinctions ("Who is he feeding?" vs. "Who is feeding him?") and "why" questions. There were two matched forms alternated each month, using the same pictures.

THE FIRST GRAMMATICAL SYSTEM

The children in our project began forming primitive sentences of two or more words before their second birthday.[5] It is clear that the grammar of these sentences is not identical with the adult model. It is often striking that one can provide a translation of children's utterances into adult utterances by the addition of function words and inflectional affixes. It appears that the children select the stressed utterance segments, which usually carry the most information. Brown and Fraser have called this a "telegraphic" version of English.

Since children's language undergoes a constant process of change through imitation of adult models, it makes sense that it should be describable in terms of its relation to the adult model. There are, however, some utterances which cannot be described as telegraphic speech:

> At 2.3 Christy and her baby sister each had a balloon. The baby bit her balloon and broke it. Christy first said *Baby bite balloon,* then pointed to the unbroken balloon and said, *Baby other bite balloon no.*
>
> Between 2.1 and 2.4 Lisa had a particular kind of construction which often generated sentences that had no adult analogue, e.g., *all-gone puzzle.*
>
> A conversation between the investigator and Susan at 1.10:
>
> Susan: *Book read. Book read. Book read.*
> Inv: *You want me to read book? OK.*
> Susan: *Read book.*

The last example shows a correction by imitation in the direction of telegraphic speech. However, the child's original utterance either was an unpatterned error or represented a productive pattern that deviated from the model.

Is there any kind of system or pattern to the child's first sentences? In attempting to answer this question we will examine some of the text material of Susan (1.9 to 2.0) and Christy (2.0 to 2.3).

---

[5] We will use the term "word" rather than "morpheme" except when the distinction is necessary. A word class of the model language, as opposed to a word class of the child's language, is indicated by an abbreviation and a superscript "m," e.g., N^m and Adj^m indicate model language noun and adjective. Age is indicated by year and month, e.g., 2.4 indicates 2 years and 4 months old.

Susan

Susan, according to her parents, started putting words together at 1.8 to form multiword sentences. One-word sentences, however, predominated until 1.9½. Thus, the system to be described represents the very beginning of the development of the grammatical level.

During this period the most common words in Susan's vocabulary were *off* and *on*. A consistent pattern emerges when the preceding words, classified as to part of speech in the model language, are charted, as in Table 1.

TABLE 1

Antecedents of *off* and *on* (Susan 1.9–2.0)

	Noun	Verb	Other	Initial	Total
off	28	8	4	1	41
on	29	7	11	3	50

The figures in the chart represent text occurrences, excluding obvious imitations and chain repetitions.

The words that preceded *off* and *on* showed a large amount of overlap, and can be combined into one list, in Table 2. Words marked with an

TABLE 2

Antecedent Types for *off* and *on* (Susan 1.9–2.0)

back	dress	Liz	shoe	that
bandage	dusting	one*	sit*	them*
blanket	fall	pants	snap*	this*
button	fix	paper	sock	this-one
came	flower	piece*	sweater	(neck) tie
chair	hair	salt	take*	
coat*	hat	scarf	(scotch) tape	
diaper	hold*	shirt	tear	

* These words were found only in sentences of more than two words.

asterisk were found only in sentences of more than two words. Other words have been found in two-word sentences. *This-one* is assumed to have been a unit in Susan's speech.

Most of Susan's sentences with *on* and *off* reflected model sentences with two-word verbs, but a few reflected the prepositional use. Susan used *off* and *on* in a construction which had the shape W + I; W stands for any word(s) and I stands for *off* or *on*. We can call this the particle construction. The W will be defined as the complement, the I as the particle.

Most of the characteristics of the particle construction are illustrated in the following example taken from a text at 1.10:

> Susan: *Hat off, hat off.*
> Inv: *That's more than the hat off. The whole Santa's head* [of a toy Santa Claus] *came off.*
> Susan: *Santa head off.* (Pause.) *Head on. Fix on, fix on.*

Class I words had a verbal force. Most of the examples of imitations were imitations of two-word verbs. She was able to construct sentences of this pattern that had no direct adult analogue, e.g., *fix on*; the adult would normally say something like *fix it* or *put it on*. This example also shows that *off* and *on* were opposites for Susan; this may help explain why these two particles were used so much more than other particles.

The particle complement was usually a N^m or noun phrase of the model language, but V^m was not uncommon: *White sweater off*, said while taking her sweater off; *white sweater on*, a request directed to her mother to put her white sweater on her; *salt on*, pretending to salt food; *scarf off*, said while taking her scarf off. The model language provides analogues in which the noun is the object: *I took my sweater off; put my white sweater on! I put the salt on; I took my scarf off.* There are also analogues in which the noun is the subject, but these seem less likely to have been the model for the child: *my sweater is off; my white sweater should be on; the salt is on; my scarf is off.* The fact that there were no sentences like *Susan off* or *Mommy on*, that is, transitive two-word verb sentences of the model analogue with the verb and object deleted, strengthens the view that the N^m usually represents the object of action. There were exceptions to this pattern, such as *chair off*, said while taking a teddy bear off a chair.

There were 12 sentences in which the complement was a two-word phrase:

> White sweater on.
> Blue sweater on.
> Mommy sweater on.
> Susan sweater on.
> Susan coat on.
> Bonnie coat on.
> This dress off.
> Put that on.
> That came off.
> Miller take off shoe sock.
> Shouldn't take off shoe sock.
> Let's take off shoe sock.

It will be seen that there was evidence for distinguishing two-word classes that reflected N^m and V^m. It was not clear if Adj^m should be grouped with N^m or kept distinct. Therefore the formulas $N^m + N^m$, $N^m + V^m$, or $V^m + N^m$, and perhaps also $Adj^m + N^m$ can be used to form expansions of the particle complement. The phrases that reflected auxiliary + verb, however, cannot be accounted for in this fashion. *Susan sweater on* and *Mommy sweater on* were ambiguous. In the first sentence a possessive relation was intended and a model analogue would be *Susan's sweater is on* or *Susan has her sweater on*. The second sentence was a request directed to her mother and a model analogue would be *Mommy, put my sweater on me*.

A rather neat pattern was found for the core of Susan's particle construction. There were, however, loose ends. In some sentences the particle was medial, and in a few it was initial:

> *Take off me* (requesting help in taking her scarf off).
> *Sock off Liz* (in imitation of *Let's take the shoes and socks off of Liz*).
> *Snap on off* (said while playing with the snap of a doll's dress).
> *Want to hold on Liz.*
> *Liz her hat back on* (indicating she wanted to put Liz's hat on after it fell off).
> *This one blue one on.*
> *Susan blue one sweater on* (this and preceding sentence were used to indicate she wanted to wear her blue sweater).
> *On tight* (putting her doll more securely on her Kiddy Kar so it would not fall off again).
> *Off of me* (requesting help in taking her scarf off).

No recurrent pattern can be found for these sentences.

Other particles of the model language were common, but none were as common as *off* and *on*. *Up* occurred 15 times: three times after N^m, nine times after V^m, two times after other words, and once in initial position. There are a few examples that fit the pattern described for the particle construction: *sleeves up*, requesting the investigator to roll up her sleeves; *red shoe up*, leaning her shoes against the door sill, pointed up. *Up bed*, indicating she wanted the side of the crib raised, would be **bed up* if it followed the pattern of *off* and *on*. Several sentences were probably learned units, thus accounting for the larger number of V^m than N^m before the particle: *tear up; come up; Susan get up*.

The remaining model language particles were common as a whole, but no single particle was very frequent. A large number of the sentences followed the pattern of the particle construction, but there were a larger proportion of exceptions to the general pattern than were found with *off* and *on*. A good many exceptions seemed to reflect the prepositional uses of the words in the model language.

When Susan's linguistic system became more mature and more closely approximated the model, transitive sentences with two-word verbs were common. The elements that developed into the object and particle were represented at this stage. The verbs less frequently, and the subjects almost never were represented.

The words *this, this-one,* and *that* showed certain consistent features. We can designate these three words class II. In initial position they formed the demonstrative construction. *This-one* had the phonological shape /disn/ or /disən/, and appeared to be a unit for Susan. The sequence /-n/ or /-ən/ was distinct from the vocabulary item /wən/ *one.* The demonstrative construction had less semantic consistency than the particle construction. It was usually used to identify an item: *this-one yellow, this book, this-one Joe, that bead.* But it could also be used to indicate location and action or quality (the last two are difficult to separate in Susan's speech): *this on top; this-one on; this-one tear.* The word classes of the model language that followed an initial class II word were also more variable, as shown in Table 3.

TABLE 3

Susan's Demonstrative Constructions (Susan 1.9–2.0)

		S E C O N D	W O R D	
First Word	N^m	V^m	Adj^m	Class I	Other
this	9	1	1	3	2
this-one	3	3	2	3	4
that	9	1	1	6	6

Class II words were usually in initial position; class I words were usually in medial or final position. However the positional preference is more consistent for class I than for class II.

A third class, labeled class III, may be recognized, consisting of *a* (19 occurrences), *the* (nine occurrences), and *(an)other* (11 occurrences). Excluding some examples of *a* (discussed below), class III preceded a N^m or a noun phrase of the model language, except in: *a red* (in answer to *What kind of an apple is that?*); *is that the blue mine?; have another blue.* In addition *a* was found in a few sentences in medial position before words where *a* was inappropriate: *up bed, (side?) a bed,* requesting that the investigator raise the side of her crib; *this a Bonnie pants; have a pants; this-one a Joe?; I know a that; these a Liz pants; this a back on; this a Joe?; mine, all a mine.* Shortly before Susan said *have a pants,* she had said *here a lemon* in imitation of her mother's sentence *here's a lemon.* Sentences like *here's a lemon* and probably also phrases like *all of* (/ə/) *mine, piece of* (/ə/) *toast* provided the model for Susan's pattern. The *a* seemed to have the function of dividing the sentence into two parts. This function was restricted to a two-month period from 1.9½ to 1.11½.

Eight words have been assigned to three classes. The remaining words in Susan's vocabulary were either less frequent or less consistent and cannot realistically be assigned to classes by the methods used for setting up classes I, II, and III. Are we justified in lumping the remaining vocabulary items into one large undifferentiated class? If we group the remaining words into the word classes of the model language and examine only two-word sentences, we find that a certain pattern emerges. The results are given in Table 4. Sentences that included *I, me, my, mine* were excluded because

TABLE 4

Class Contingencies in Susan's Two-Word Sentences (1.9–2.0)

Second Word	I	F II	I R III	S A	T B	W C	O D	R E	D *it*	*more*	Total
I	..	10	..	6	45	..	..	1	..	..	62
II	..	..	..	6	1	..	1	..	..	1	9
III	..	..	..	..	..	..	..	..	..		..
A	..	3	..	1	26	..	1	..	..	..	31
B	..	10	8	18	26	4	6	1	..	3	76
C	..	3	1	..	4	..	..	2	..	..	10
D	..	1	..	4	5	1	..	7	..	..	18
E	..	4	..	12	10	1	..	..	..	1	28
it	..	..	..	6	..	..	..	..	..	..	6
more	..	..	..	..	..	..	..	..	..		..
Total	..	31	9	53	117	6	8	11	..	5	240

NOTE.—Thirty-seven sentences that include the following words have been excluded: *night-night, I, me, my, mine, he, you, her, them, one, two, no, what, now, too, please, bye, like,* and *right* (in *right here*).

these words came in late in the period and were replacing *Susan. What* is also excluded because it represented a late development. A number of other words were excluded either because they were rare and their class membership was difficult to assign, or because they appeared to belong to learned formulas. Prepositions and particles have been lumped into one class.

Class A reflected V^m. There was only one example of A + A (*want talk*). The most common patterns were A + B and B + A. There were only six examples of A + *it*, but these comprise all the examples of *it*. *It* seemed to function as a suffix for class A words, and perhaps marked a subclass of A, words that reflected transitive verbs in the model. Class B reflected N^m and was common before classes A, B, and I, and after class A. Class C, which reflected Adj^m, was not common. The words reflected a variety of subclasses in the model language. Classes B and C show similar patterns and we cannot be sure they represent two classes in Susan's speech. If N^m and Adj^m words belong to one class in Susan's linguistic system, we would expect to find examples of Adj^m + I, because the pattern N^m + I was so common. Class D represents locative adverbs, and class E prepositions and particles of the model. These two classes cannot be sustained by the evidence presented in the table. The words represented in D and E might be aligned in a different fashion but the evidence is too meager to group these words with confidence. There were not many examples of *more,* but the evidence seems to indicate that the word belongs to class III.

TABLE 5

Demonstrative Sentences for Christy (2.0–2.3)

that	*that's*	*this*	*thatsa*	*this a*	*thata*	*'sa*
blue					blue	
broken			broken			
chicken	chicken					
dolly	dolly					
eye	eye					
elephant			elephant			
go		go				
hat	hat					
Joe	Joe					
pants	pants					
pretty			pretty			
truck	truck		truck	truck		truck
yellow	yellow					
			cup		cup	
airplane	bus	one	car	A	doggy	arm
blocks	milk		coffee		horse	baby
bowl	quack-quack		girl			block
cat			owl			boy
Christy's			pig			ear
Daddy's			plane			lion
dolly's						rabbit
fish						Wick
horsie						
huke*						
kitty						
neck						
pin						
pink						
po*						
Sarah						
turn						
yellow						

* *Po* and *huke* were the names of two nonsense shapes of play-doh.

Christy

A somewhat different pattern is found in Christy's grammatical development. The following paragraphs are based primarily on two-word sentences collected during 12 hours of recorded texts. The most common type of sentence began with *that*. The various initial elements of these sentences along with the following words are listed in Table 5. The lists may be pooled into one in view of the similarity of the lists and gradation of phonetic shapes represented by each category: /dæ, dæʔ, dæt, dæ, da, dat, dɔ, as, dæs, dædæ, dæda, dæa, æta, dætsa, dæsa, dæza, zæza, æza, sa, za, sæ, tsa/.

This and *this a* (found before *a, go, one,* and *truck*) and the variants of *that* may be pooled as class I. The items in Table 5 and the items found after *this* (*a*) may be called class A. As a result of this classification, a construction can be identified which we may call the demonstrative construction: I + A ↓ / ↑ (the arrows indicate falling and rising intonation). There were 74 examples of such utterances.

Nineteen sentences began with *the* or *a*. The words which followed were *other*, or class A words. *The* and *a* never terminated a two-word sentence. These words have been designated class II.

The words *in, on, out, away, over,* and *under* appeared in 16 sentences. They both preceded and followed class A and preceded class I. There was one set which followed, but never preceded class A: *away, out;* others which preceded but never followed: *over, under;* and others of dual mem-

TABLE 6

Class Contingencies in Christy's Two-Word Sentences (2.0–2.3)

Second Word	First Word							where	what	(an)other	it	Total
	I	II	III	A	B	C	D					
I	..	..	..	..	2	..	1	..	1	1	..	5
II	..	..	..	..	..	..	..	..	..	..	..	...
III	..	..	..	3	5	..	5	..	..	..	..	13
A	74	18	9	41	5	..	3	10	..	8	..	168
B	2	..	..	10	2	..	..	1	..	..	..	15
C	..	..	..	4	2	..	..	..	..	..	..	6
D	..	..	..	..	..	..	..	..	..	..	..	...
where	..‚	..	..	..	..	..	..	..	..	..	..	...
what	..	..	..	..	..	..	..	..	..	..	..	...
(*an*) *other*	..	1	..	..	..	..	..	..	..	..	..	1
it	..	..	..	..	2	..	..	..	..	..	..	2
Total	76	19	9	58	18	..	9	11	1	9	..	210

NOTE.—Nineteen sentences were omitted because they contained words of ambiguous class membership from the standpoint of the two-word sentence corpus: *his, walk, oh, no, else, my, right* (*right here*), *more, don't, two, both.*

TABLE 7

Classes in Christy's Two-Word Sentences (2.0–2.3)

I	...	this, thisa, that, that's, that's a, 'sa, thata
II	...	a, the
III	...	here, there
A	...	arm, baby, bus, cat, Christy's, dolly, dolly's, fish, horsie, truck, pretty, yellow, etc.
B	...	come, doed, flying, go, goes, got, hold, see, sit, sleep, sleeping, turn, want, walking
C	...	away, in, on, out, way
D	...	in, on, over, under

bership: *in, on*. The words which occurred in first position have been designated class D, and those in second position as class C. The decision to split these words into two classes, in spite of the overlap in membership, is based on the presumed later evolution into prepositions and adverbs or two-word verb particles. The accent pattern for sentences containing these items was relatively consistent.[6] In 13 out of the 14 cases where the stress was recorded, it occurred on the second word, e.g., *on cóuch, clothes ón*.

In addition to preceding class I and class A, words in class C preceded *there* and *here*, e.g., *in thére* ↑. *There* and *here* may be designated as class III. The words *where* and *what* occurred only in initial position. *Where* only occurred in sentences with falling pitch.

Class A was by far the largest class, both in terms of frequency and variety. Included are items which are N^m, V^m, and Adj^m. We may subdivide this category on certain distributional grounds. The sentences *see this, hóld it, doed it*, and *óther this* were not paralleled by any instances in which N^m or Adj^m occurred in first position in the same frame, in spite of the fact that N^m was far more frequent than V^m. V^m never followed class II, III, or D. The pattern I + V^m was relatively infrequent compared to A + V^m. V^m is designated class B, and the occurrences are shown in Table 6. If only two-word sentences are considered, the separation of class A and B is based on weaker evidence than the other class criteria, but it is quite likely that the analysis of longer sentences would confirm this division. On Table 5 the overlap was greatest between *that* and *that's*. If the words ending in *a* are viewed as in fact two words (*this a, that's a*), so that the sequences form three-word sentences, it may be seen that there are no cases of V^m in the last four columns, though three appear with *this* and *that*. Such sentences as *you hold this, make apple there*, and *take it off* suggest that the analysis of long sequences will require a separate class of verbs. In all cases except *apple eat* the semantic object followed the

---

[6] An accented word, defined for Christy's speech in the section on Prosody, is indicated by a primary stress mark.

verb. The semantic actor normally preceded, except in *I carry Christy* which had two objects and *where go eye* and *where go toast, huh* which had an inversion regularly following *where*. There was insufficient evidence for further subdivision of class A.

Christy's grammar included an accentual system. The locative construction consisted of A + Á or A + IíI. Sentences based on the possessive or adjectival analogue of the model consisted of Á + A: *baby róom* (in answer to *Where's the baby?*); *báby book* (in answer to *Is that the baby's book?*); *bíg choochoo*. In a few cases, however, the second item was accented in sentences that had a possessive and adjectival analogue: *baby báll* (in answer to *Is that the baby's ball?*); *baby cár* (in answer to *Whose car is this?*); *a big wádi* (wadi = dog). The first example might reveal imitation of the investigator's stress. The accent pattern was not consistent in the possessive or adjectival construction, in contrast to the locative construction.

Discussion

The partial descriptions for Susan and Christy show that the two language systems were quite different in their details. Some of the differences could be ascribed to the age difference, but others were due to a difference in their language style. There were, however, certain characteristics that applied to the speech of all the children in the project except Harlan, who was beyond this phase of development from the beginning.

A few high frequency words tended to be restricted to a given position in the sentence and tended to define the meaning of the sentence as a whole. The use of these words marked the first step in developing the grammatical system of the model language. These words may be called operators. The classes of operators for Susan and Christy have been labeled with Roman numerals. The difference between operator classes and nonoperator classes is relative rather than absolute. The nonoperator words tend to be grouped into large classes, but the division between the classes is sometimes difficult to make. Part of this difficulty is probably the nature of the data. If a low frequency word does not occur in enough different contexts, class assignments are difficult to make. But part of the difficulty may be the nature of the linguistic system of the child. The instability of class assignment is especially probable in a system based on order and not on additional markers. If a child has only heard a word from adults a few times, his sense of the meaning and the appropriate verbal contexts for that word may be easily changed by new experience. Thus, even though some regularity in order for two classes may exist, vacillation with regard to certain specific items may obscure that regularity. The method of classifying the child's words in part by pure distribution and in part by the word classes of the model language will not adequately account for all of the child's vocabulary, or vacillation of specific items. But the regularity displayed in the tables shows that this method yields information about structure.[7]

Operators are defined as those words having high frequency and few members in a class. These properties are found, in adult speech, in function words. The children's operators tended to be derived from adult function words and to be precursors of the function words which characterized a later phase of their own development. The nonoperators were precursors of lexical words. There was some tendency for the most frequent models of operators to be words which could serve as substitutes for lexical classes and carry stress, i.e., pronouns (demonstratives) rather than pure noun determiners, particles of two-word verbs rather than pure prepositions.

If the child used the operators in constructions that had analogues in adult speech, adults reinforced the child's pattern and enabled him to approximate adult patterns more closely. If the operators or constructions did not reflect patterns in the model language, they dropped out. There was one clear example. From 2.1 to 2.4, Lisa used *byebye, no, all-gone, another,* and *please* as operators. These words were used in a construction which consisted of an accented operator plus N^m: *nó toy*, indicating she did not want a particular toy any longer (contrast *no tóy?*, asking if there were any more toys). Many of the sentences can be related to the model only by reversing the order. Thus *all-gone puzzle* (the puzzles had just been put away) would normally be said by the adult as *The puzzle is all gone*, or some such sentence in which the word order is the reverse of Lisa's. It is always possible to find analogues that preserve the child's order, e.g., *It's all gone, the puzzle is* or *That which is all gone is the puzzle*. These are sentences the child is not likely to hear. This construction became less frequent and eventually disappeared.

Most of our analysis has been limited to two-word sentences, and the distinction between endocentric and exocentric constructions cannot apply. It seems clear, however, that this distinction will be needed to account for longer sentences. Most of the child's early constructions have exocentric models, and are probably to be considered exocentric in the child's system also. In addition, many phrases in longer sentences can probably be treated as expansions of single word classes. A characteristic feature of the children's speech was to take a construction that could be a complete predication for them and treat it as an expansion of one part of another construction. Thus the possessive construction in Christy's speech, $\acute{A} + A$, can be used as the demonstrative complement: *that Christy rabbit*. This kind of expansion seems to be typical in the early phases, and endocentric features of the

---

[7] A grammar cannot be derived from the tables. The tables only show that the elements in the child's sentences are systematized. The best explanation for the systematization is that the child has word classes, classes that have at least some properties of word classes in adult speech. The tables do not tell what the classes are, but they do provide clues.

model language were weakly represented in the children's language. There are certain problems to this kind of an analysis, however. In Christy's sentence *that one Joe, that one* can probably be treated as an expansion of the demonstrative, but in *-'s a one two* Christy was counting and *one two* appears to be an expansion of the complement. In *that this shoe, that* may be treated as the demonstrative, *this shoe* as the complement, and the complement also as a demonstrative construction. It is not certain, however, that such analysis can be formally sustained.

It seems surprising that the children's relatively systematic arrangement of classes could be sustained with so few overt markers. One explanation may be the relative semantic consistency of English lexical classes for the words in young children's vocabulary, a fact pointed out by Brown (1958b, p. 247). He found experimentally that lexical items with class markers were systematically identified with certain types of referents (*ibid*, p. 251). Thus it may be that regularities of order are aided by the additional cue that is provided by semantic similarities between items in a class. We have very weak evidence on this point, from Harlan. The word *have* in English serves as a verb, but it does not have a meaning of action. Harlan had considerable difficulty in giving *have* the verb markers he used with other verbs. It might be objected that the difficulty stems from its use as an auxiliary, but this is a specialized use that had not yet (at 3.1) appeared in Harlan's speech. Further, *do,* which was used by Harlan both as an auxiliary and main verb, was marked appropriately when *have* was not. Thus we have examples of past tense markers for many verbs, including *do,* at least six months before the past tense was marked for *have,* although contexts in which the past tense would have been appropriate for this verb did occur before that time. At 2.7, after the regular testing of discourse agreement was begun, it was found that Harlan could answer a question about what someone was doing with an appropriate response. Notice that he did not say *having* in response to this question:

Inv: *What do you think Paul was doing with the hoe?*
Harlan: *Have.*
Inv: *Hm?*
Harlan: *Have it.*

This is not altogether a clear case, since the semantic peculiarity of *have* is reflected in its lower probability in the *-ing* form in adult usage.

The casual observer is often struck by what appears to be a complete lack of any system in the young child's first speech efforts. The composition of words into sentences appears to be random; any words can be juxtaposed. Our evidence shows this not to be the case. There was a complex system even at the earliest stages, even though it was a much simpler system than the extremely complex adult model. Are we justified in calling the kind of system that a young child has a formal grammar? This depends to a large extent on what a formal grammar is conceived to be.

From the standpoint of a linguist, a grammar can be conceived as a set of rules that will account for the sentences produced by the speaker and will not predict impossible sentences. Vocabulary items have to be assignable to word classes so that new sentences can be generated by operating with the grammar. Normally in natural languages many constructions have stateable and consistent semantic correlates, but it might be debated whether this is a necessary property.

It is obvious from the description of Susan's and Christy's speech that for most generalizations there were exceptions. Some sentences seemed to fall outside the system. Other sentences reversed the patterns that held in all other cases. It is sentences like *off of me; clean in, in clean* (in Susan's speech); and *I carry Christy; that one Joe; that one two* (counting); *where rattle Christy; big shoe red, red shoe big; apple more; more apple* (in Christy's speech) that cause problems. Almost any rule that allows these sequences allows others that seem impossible.

How shall we know what is impossible with a child? With adult informants, one can test a grammatical solution by eliciting paradigmatic material or by asking *Can you say . . .?* This implies that a speaker can distinguish the grammatically impossible from the improbable; Maclay and Sleator (1960) have presented evidence that college rhetoric students could not make the distinction. Yet we do know that adults can correct their own grammatical mistakes. Harlan corrected grammatical errors in his speech. Was this simply recognition that the utterances were improbable?

There seem to be a number of views which could be defended as to whether a formal system existed for Susan and Christy. There were a few generalizations which could be made without exceptions, but these were weak in that they also predicted many sentences that did not appear and were improbable. It might be said that they were formal systems, but that they were undergoing change.

Alternatively, it could be said that the statistical tendencies and preferences were precursors of more stable and clearly defined classes. It might be argued that grammatical systems arise first in the child's exposure to differing probabilities in adult substitutions and sequences, which are reflected in a system of regularities which cannot be expressed by exceptionless rules.

THE GRAMMATICAL SYSTEM WITH WORD CLASS MARKERS

Eventually lexical classes could be identified by markers and order, not simply order as in the earlier stage. Nouns were marked by the plural suffix and noun determiners, verbs by verbal suffixes and auxiliaries. At this time it is convenient to describe the child's grammatical system as a simplified grammar of the model, along with added grammatical rules to account for constructions that have no counterpart in the model language.

Most of the mistakes or deviations from the model can be classified as omissions (*I'll turn water off* for *I'll turn the water off*), overgeneralization of morphophonemic combinations (*foots* for *feet; a owl* for *an owl; breaked* for *broke*), the incorrect use of a function word with a subclass of a lexical class (using *a* with mass nouns and proper nouns), or doubly marked forms (adding the possessive suffix to a possessive pronoun, *mine's*). Except for the first kind, these mistakes point to the fact that classes were marked. The children seldom used a suffix or function word with the wrong lexical class, either at this stage or at the earlier stage when markers were not well developed; the only examples of this kind of mistake were provided by Susan: *I by-ed that* where the adult would say *I went by that,* and *stand up-ed* where the adult would say *stood up.* In the second example it could be argued that the *-ed* was not added to the wrong word class, but rather was added to the verb phrase instead of the verb.

Most of our discussion of this stage of development will be centered on the linguistic system of Harlan, who was at this stage of development at 2.2 when we started working with him (the remaining children in the project entered this stage at 2.6 or shortly thereafter).

At 2.2, verbs in Harlan's system could be marked by the past tense suffix *-ed*, the progressive suffix *-ing*, the positive auxiliaries *can, will, want, going,* and the negative auxiliaries *can't, won't, don't.* The sentence: *I pushed it, I can push it* was typical. The markers were not always used, however:

> Inv: *It popped.*
> Harlan: (To his mother) *My balloon pop.*
> Mother: *You popped it?*
> Harlan: *I pop it.*

Harlan's parents reported that he had the past tense suffix a few weeks before we began working with him. At 2.2 a few strong verbs were correctly used with the past tense: *My Daddy-O went to work; I made a somersault.* These forms varied with the base form:

> Harlan: *I go boom boom* (past tense context).
> Inv: *What'd you do?*
> Harlan: *I went boom.*

Normally strong verbs were unmarked. The *-ed* form of the past tense was not added to such verbs until 2.5: *I breaked that.*

At 2.2 the progressive was simply the suffix *-ing* with no form of the verb *to be: Man talking on the telephone.* Thus the suffix had the same, or a very similar, distribution as the *-ed* suffix. At 2.3, forms with *to be* were used sporadically: *Man's taking out the baloney. To be* was not consistently used until 2.8.

Harlan grouped his auxiliaries into two sets, positive and negative. This resulted from his lack of negative transformations. In addition, he had two auxiliaries that are not in the model language, *want* and *going.* These words are analyzed as auxiliaries because they came directly before the verb without the infinitive marker *to: I want make two bowls; I going make a pig.*

At 2.2 the most common noun markers were *the, a,* and the plural suffix *-s.* The markers were sometimes omitted in contexts where they should have been used: *I want the duck, I want the duck, I want duck.* Other words marked nouns, e.g., *some,* possessive pronouns, numerals, but they were less frequent.

At 2.2 Harlan indicated the negative with a negative auxiliary, *not* or *isn't: I can't see the pig; That not go right; Isn't a boy. Isn't* was used primarily in one-word negations. It was not treated as a negative transformation of *is* as can be seen in: *That piece* (puzzle piece) *go right over there.* (Harlan tried the puzzle piece over there, and found it did not fit.) *Isn't.* Unfortunately our material does not allow us to say when the negative was first treated as a transformation, but the transformation pattern was present by at least 2.8.

At 2.2 *yes-no* questions were marked by the rising intonation. The following example at 2.3 indicates that Harlan understood that some sort of inversion should take place:

> Harlan: *Want d'you policeman?* /wan ǰuw pliysmæn↑/
> Inv: *Hm?*
> Harlan: *Want . . . want d'you policeman?* /want | want ǰuw pliysmæn↑/

We have noted that *want* was interpreted by Harlan as an auxiliary, and this may have had some influence on the inversion. But it is clear that Harlan did not understand the function of *do.* The interrogative inversion was used sporadically after this time, and became a productive pattern at 2.8:

> Inv: *You ask Liz what she wants, OK?*
> Harlan: *D'you want honey, you do? OK.*

The elliptical transformation appeared quite suddenly at 2.7, and was common and productive at that time:

> Inv: *Where's the deer going?*
> Harlan: *Because he is.*

> Inv: *How old are you?*
> Harlan: *Because I am.*

Inv: *Why can't you do it with me?*
Harlan: *Because I can't.*

Inv: *When do you eat breakfast?*
Harlan: *Because I do.*

Inv: *How did the bird get there?*
Harlan: *Because he did.*

Inv: *You've seen this book before, Harlan.*
Harlan: *I have?*

Emphatic transformations occurred sporadically: *I did turn it off* (2.3); *I did wake up* (2.7).

The above paragraphs show that the verbal transformations involving *do* and other auxiliaries started to come in about 2.3, and became an established feature in Harlan's grammar by 2.8. (Transformations with interrogative words, not treated here, came in a little later; the sentences with interrogative words showed more complicated patterns of development.) The verb restrictions in discourse agreement patterns were fairly well controlled by 2.8.

There seemed to be a correlation between Harlan's grammatical development and the functional categories described in the introduction. After the development of the verbal transformations and the verb restrictions in discourse agreement, the functional category of responsive discourse was utilized. Since functional categories are more difficult to recognize than formal categories, and since most attention has been focused on the formal categories, this correlation may not be correct. It seems likely that language functions are correlated with grammatical development, whether or not the suggested correlation is correct.

The linguistic system of the child is very unstable. After the word classes are overtly marked, the instability is very noticeable, as the above sketch of Harlan's grammatical system shows. The formal patterns are not set, and the child frequently lapses back into older patterns. It takes a long time for the learned patterns to become automatic.

When the child is able to correct his mistakes, it indicates that he considers certain sentences to be ungrammatical. This is excellent proof that the child has a formal grammatical system. Harlan, the only child to exhibit this ability early, started correcting himself at 2.9, soon after the appearance of verbal transformations and the development of verb restriction in discourse agreement.

PROSODIC FEATURES

Children are good mimics of prosodic features, particularly pitch, and they can give the impression of having the pitch-stress system under control.

This may be true from a phonetic, perhaps even phonemic standpoint, but does not necessarily entail the use of the prosodic features in the grammatical system. The rising and falling intonations used to distinguish questions and statements were the only prosodic features consistently found in the linguistic system before the use of class markers. Even this contrast may be later than is generally recognized. The earliest and best record of this contrast is for Susan. In the early records for her at 1.9, many sentences that ended in a level or rising pitch were interpreted as questions. The lack of a falling pitch was often the only indication that the sentence might be a question, and sometimes the context suggested that it was a statement. The adult (parent or investigator) always interpreted the sentence as a question and gave Susan an answer. Susan was over 2 years old before the rising intonation consistently indicated a question. It may be that she learned the intonation by noting which sentences drew a response from the adult.

Prosodic features that had no analogue in the model language were sometimes used in the early period. Christy and Lisa had an accentual system based on pitch and stress. Each sentence had one accented word. The accented word received the last high pitch and/or strong stress. The pitch and stress of the preceding words were variable. Each construction in both children's linguistic system had a particular accent pattern, but the accent pattern was not always adhered to.

All of the children had primary and secondary stress, and a two-level pitch system at the time they developed a linguistic system with marked word classes. The two-level pitch system persisted well beyond this period, probably because two levels are sufficient to indicate most of the grammatical contrasts signaled by the English prosodic system.

INDIVIDUAL DIFFERENCES

We have noted that there were certain features common to the early development of the grammatical level for all the children. Each child had a set of operators, usually derived from function words of the model language, that served as a means of breaking into the model language system. The children did not have the same operators, however. These differences between the children in preferences were clear from the beginning and have persisted in differences in foci of development. It is possible that certain types of patterns or constructions are more compatible than others. Greenberg (1961) has pointed to correlated structures in languages and we might find some patterns in the individual differences between the children at various stages, but our evidence is scant at present.

Lisa had a particularly primitive phonological system. As a result, it was often difficult or impossible to understand her. In addition, final sibilants were absent for a considerable period and she was not able to mark the plural with the suffix -s. Instead she used a syntactic device: *one two shoe* meant *more than one shoe.* She later gave this up in favor of other number combinations. According to her mother, she would pick two numbers to indicate the plural, e.g., *eight four shoe,* and then after a few days she would pick another combination, e.g., *three five shoe.* She finally developed a final /θ/ and was able to say *shoeth.* There may be a relationship between Lisa's syntactic marking of the plural and her earlier use of an operator class which had no adult analogue. In addition, at a later stage of development Lisa seemed to develop some grammatical rules of her own, rules which had no counterpart in the model language.

There are some suggestions in our data that linguistic patterns correlate with some nonlinguistic behavior. Susan's favorite operators were *off* and *on.* Susan was a busy little girl who always taking things off and putting them back on. Christy's favorite operator was *that,* and was used in the demonstrative construction to identify things. When the investigator arrived at Christy's house, she would run into the living room, sit down, and wait to be entertained—wait for the investigator to take toys out of his bag. Most of the children had a favorite toy and a favorite activity. Harlan had no favorite toy, but he had a favorite activity: talking. We found that if we could keep a conversation going he was less apt to throw things. Harlan had the most developed linguistic system of any of the children. He talked early and often. He also made more expressive use of language than the other children: the diminutive baby talk suffix *-y* was productive by 2.5; the expressive pitch pattern /312↑/ was in common use by 2.2.

In the preceding sections we have described a technique in which the child develops the grammatical level by composing, by placing words together to form sentences. A less common technique consists of treating a polymorphemic sequence of the model language as a monomorphemic unit, and then at a later stage of development segmenting the sequence into its proper parts. It is our impression from parental reports that this is more common with second children than with the first born, but still never an important pattern; all of the children in the small group are first born. A third, closely allied technique is the learning, or imitating, of a sentence, understanding the meaning of most of the words and the meaning of the sentence as a whole, but not understanding the grammatical function of the elements. If a number of sentences of a similar pattern are learned, it might be possible for the child to come to recognize the grammatical function of the elements. This technique is rare, or perhaps nonexistent, because the child would probably have to learn by heart a large number of sentences before he happened to learn two that contrasted in the proper fashion. Christy had a number of sentences which appeared to have been memorized, e.g., *where are the shoe?* (2.3). At this time neither *are* nor *is* were productive elements in Christy's speech, and there is no evidence that this or similar sentences were instrumental in her learning the copulative pattern.

DEVELOPMENTAL SEQUENCE

One of the purposes of this study is to describe developmental sequences of linguistic features. While the features studied are those of English, it would be valuable to be able to consider features inherent in any linguistic system. This is difficult to do until more is known about language universals and the prerequisites of language.

The relation between the time of mastery of skills may consist of co-occurrence or of necessary sequence. Sequential orders may arise either because one skill is dependent on the prior acquisition of another, because one is less often practiced, or because they differ in difficulty though are practiced equally. Many of the sequential findings of a normative sort have the third property. They occur because, on the average, it takes a different amount of practice to accomplish one task than another. We would like to separate the logically sequential features. These could be found best in an experimental transfer design, but, wherever in our data there are individual differences in acquisition patterns, some information about sequential dependence can be obtained from studying changes in individual systems rather than group averages.

Viewing the acquisition of phonological contrasts in terms of learning to distinguish features or properties rather than classes, Jakobson (1941) has proposed a developmental order for the phonological system of children. He has suggested that the child successively elaborates a phonological system approaching the adult's by binary division. If he begins with one feature or bundle of features for contrast, he can only have two classes; with two sets of independent features he may have four classes. Within each class he may have sounds which are in many respects phonetically different from the adult model.

Does anything of this sort happen in grammar? We have indicated that grammatical classes and grammatical markers do not have the structural properties of a matrix of features which phonemes have. The classes that are identified in grammatical analysis are not usually marked by features that can then be recombined to define another class. However, at various points in the grammatical system there are differing degrees of generalization possible. Proper, mass, and count nouns are contrasted by their occurrence with noun determiners, a function class that is unique to this system of classes. The learning of the morphophonemic series in the contrast plural/singular has greater generality. It can also serve in marking possessive nouns, and in marking third person singular verbs. An analogous series marks the regular past tense. At the level of grammatical transformations, a very broad transfer of skills is possible. We may seek for correlations between these related series. For example, though the contrasts plural/singular and possessive/nonpossessive may be acquired at different times for reasons which are semantic or based on frequency, if the contrasts of one are mastered, the other should be too. We have so far only one instance—Harlan—of mastery of both by a child in our study. He gave as productive forms *po - poez* for singular/plural at 2.3 and *Joe - Joez* for possession at 2.4½. At the latter date we find *nizz - nizzez* for singular/plural. But we do not find the possessive *Liz - Lizez* until 2.7. *Joe* and *Liz* were the names of dolls which were used to elicit possession for body parts and clothing, so the opportunity for these contrasts was frequent. This slight evidence does not support the expectation that the morphophonemic contrasts would generalize.

If we turn back to the learning of division into word classes when it first appears, we are limited by the fact that we have only two types of information on which to base our judgment as to the productive operation of classes. One is rules of order with different words. The other is semantic consistency of constructions using these words. At the point at which we first analyzed the children's speech, there were already many classes discernible. Thus we cannot say that at the initial stage before word classes were defined by markers that there was evidence of a first division into two primordial classes which then were subdivided.

If the division into lexical classes is marked by affixes and function words later, then we may expect to find some of the divisions appearing only at the later stage. The division into mass, proper, and count nouns is possible at this point.

In addition to sequences that depend on the availability of markers, some depend on the availability of vocabulary. Thus the rules of order that apply to subclasses of adverbs only could appear after these words enter the vocabulary of children and co-occur in the same sentences.

The earliest forms of markers which we found were inconsistently used. They were the possessive suffix, the plural suffix, *the, and* and *-ing* which were used sporadically. If they were consistent as to class, though, even sporadic use could help identify a class. Thus the first use for these markers may be to identify lexical classes, rather than to distinguish subclasses within lexical classes or to identify constructions. *Want* and *going,* which were used by most of the children of the project as auxiliaries, marked verbs. On the whole, where suffixed and nonsuffixed forms existed, the children preferred the nonsuffixed forms rather than free variants. This was probably in part a phonological problem, since the children had less control of the final consonants than of the other parts of the phonological system.

At the point where subclasses begin to be distinguished so that markers are used as a consistent signal, it is possible to make some simple predictions. For cases with a semantic correlate, a child will first begin imitating forms correctly, and after using a certain number of contrasts correctly will generalize the contrast to new forms. Until enough instances are learned, there will presumably be a delay between these two points. Generalization to irregular cases should occur also; the preferred form for the singular of irregular nouns probably depends on the relative frequency of the singular and plural and relative ease of pronunciation of the two. We already know from Berko's work (1958) that the plural of nouns with final fricatives, sibilants, and affricates tends to be late.

We have tested 25 children with systematic tests of familiar words, irregulars, and nonsense words with a technique similar to Berko's. Nearly always the contrast with familiar forms preceded the contrast with nonsense forms. Naturally, the familiar forms chosen give a rough estimate only. We do not know whether it is the variety of types or the frequency of tokens showing contrasts which is crucial in determining the length of time before generalization occurs.

The average gap for *boy* vs. *kigh* was 2.4 months; for *ball* vs. *kigh* was the same; for *block* vs. *bik* the gap was 1.1 months; for *cup* vs. *bik* 1.5 months. The cases were too few to estimate the gaps for the other contrasts. Thus the child who calls one cup by a different term than two cups might do the same with the nonsense toy *bik* in a month and a half. This analysis was not specific as to the phonological nature of the contrast.

Does the "concept" of plurality generalize; i.e., when one contrast occurs do the others occur soon after? There are artifacts in the restriction on age range provided by the time at which we stopped testing for this paper. For all items except those with fricative, affricate, or sibilant finals, the range between the first contrast to appear and the last was quite short—averaging 2½ months including the nonsense items.

Two irregulars were used as tests for overextension: *foot* and *man*. Of the 15 children who produced a contrast, three said *feet-feets* and 11 said *foot-foots* about the same age as other stop plurals were produced. One child had *foot-footis* first. For 18 children, a contrast between *man* and a plural was offered. For all, the plural was at first *mans*. Two children showed irregular development that can be shown as follows:

Sarah

2.4	bik-biks	tass-tassez	bunge-bunge	man-manz	foot-foots	box-box
2.5	bik-biks	tass-tassez	bunge-bungez	man-manz	foot-footez	box-boxez
2.6	....	tass-tassez	bunge-bungez	man-manz	foot-foots	box-boxez
2.7	bik-biks	tass-tassez	bunge-bungez	man-man	foot-foots	box-bockez
2.9	bik-biks	tass-tass	bunge-bunge	man-man	feet-feets	box-box
2.10	bik-biks	tass-tass	bunge-bunge	man-man	foot-foots	box-box

Harlan

2.8	bik-biks	tass-tassez	bunge-bungez	man-manz	foot-footez	box-box
2.9	bik-biksez	tass-tassez	bunge-bungez	man-manzez	foot-footsez	box-boxez
2.10	bik-biks	tass-tassez	bunge-bungez	man-manz	foot-footsez	box-boxez
2.11	....	tath-tassez	bunge-bungez	man-men	foot-feet	box-boxez
3.1	bik-biks	tass-tassez	bunge-bungez	man-manz	foot-feet	box-boxez

The vacillation in these series illustrates instability, regression, boredom, or, clearly with Harlan at 2.9, playfulness. Harlan frequently invented games with language.

In sum, the acquisition of the plural contrast followed a simple pattern in most children from noncontrast to acquisition of particular instances of contrast, generalization several months after acquisition of particular instances, and finally, differentiation of irregular forms.

In addition to inflectional suffixes, certain derivational suffixes are used to mark classes. For example, the diminutive or baby talk *-y* was used widely by the children in naming animals—*doggy, horsey*—even when we tried to get them to use the nonsuffixed form for the purpose of testing plurality. However, the suffix was used productively by only one child, Harlan, who produced the following in an argument about a name at 2.5½:

> Inv: *Really. His name is Cootes. Bill Cootes.*
> Harlan: *Billzy the Coooootsy.* (singing)

Transformations were not found in the earliest linguistic systems. The first to appear were simple (nongeneralized) transformations, such as the progressive (*be . . . -ing*), inversion of word order for questions, and the use of auxiliaries with *not*. There were some early interrogative inversions by Christy:

> 2.0 *Where's the arm?*
> 2.1 *Where go toast, huh?*
> 2.4 *Where belong shoe?*
> 2.5 *Where go button, Chrity, huh?*

Soon afterwards the coordinative transformation with *and* appeared. The two-part coordinative transformations (e.g., *both . . . and . . .*) and subordinative transformations have not appeared in our data yet.

Preliminary evidence suggests that discourse agreement features are sequentially ordered. We would expect discourse agreement features involving class restrictions to parallel the sequential development of the classes themselves. Appropriate answers to simple "who/what" questions and "what . . . do" questions came early. Preliminary evidence indicates that the child's adverbs are learned in the order locative, temporal, manner; if true, it might be expected that discourse agreement would proceed in the order where, when, how. In a similar fashion the development of verb restrictions in discourse agreement should follow the development of verb structure.

2

THE ACQUISITION OF SYNTAX[1]

Roger Brown *and* Colin Fraser[2]
Harvard University

What is done in a developmental study of behavior depends upon the investigators' conception of the terminal state, the outcome of the development. Normal adults speaking their native language seem to us to possess a set of rules of word construction and sentence construction which enables them to go beyond the speech they have actually heard and practiced to the creation of lawful novelties. If new monosyllables are created, speakers of English will agree that *stug* is "better English" than *ftug*. Probably this is because they have a shared implicit knowledge of the initial consonant clusters that are acceptable in English. If this new word is to be pluralized, they will agree that *stug*/-z/ is better than *stug*/-s/. Probably this is because they have shared knowledge of a rule of regular English inflection. If the new word is first heard in the sentence: "Here is some stug" they will agree that a second sentence: "The stug is there" is more likely to be grammatical than a second sentence: "A stug is there." Probably this is because they have shared knowledge of the syntactic rules for the employment of mass nouns.

The construction rules of which speakers have implicit knowledge are, in their explicit form, the grammar of a language. As these rules have been written down in traditional grammars, they constitute a collection of largely unrelated statements about such matters as the parts-of-speech, paradigms of conjugation and declension, the marking of gender, and the agreement of adjectives and nouns. Chomsky (1957) has shown that it may be possible to systematize traditional grammar into a mechanism for the generation of all the sentences of a language that are grammatical and none that are ungrammatical. Grammar becomes a theory for a range of phenomena— the sentences of a language—and also a program for generating sentences— a program that might be followed by an electronic device (Yngve, 1961).

[1] The work described in this paper was supported by the National Science Foundation by a grant administered through the Center for Communication Sciences, Massachusetts Institute of Technology. From *Verbal behavior and learning: problems and processes*, edited by N. Cofer and B. S. Musgrave. Copyright, 1963. McGraw-Hill Book Company. Used by permission.

[2] Now at the University of Exeter, Exeter, England.

It is the development in children of this kind of sentence-generating grammar that we are trying to study.

The child growing up hears, from his family, his friends, and the television, a large sample of the sentences of a language, and we think that he induces from the regularities in this sample an implicit grammar. First-language learning, so conceived, reminds us of two other operations with language: that of the linguist in the field and that of the adult learning a second language. The descriptive linguist trying to work out the structure of an unfamiliar tongue begins by collecting a large set of utterances—his "corpus." From regularities in the corpus and from inquiries of a native informant, he induces rules that predict beyond what he has observed. One check on the adequacy of his rules is their ability correctly to anticipate new utterances. Another check is the ability of the rules to duplicate the distinctions made by a native informant who has been asked to judge of each of a collection of utterances whether it is or is not a well-formed sentence. It may be that the linguistic procedures for discovering syntax in distributional facts are a good model for the child's learning of his native language— with the difference that the linguist works deliberately and aims at explicit formulation whereas the child works unwittingly and arrives at implicit formulations. The child's syntax is made explicit for him in "grammar" school, but we suggest that he operates with syntax long before he is of school age.

In learning a second or foreign language, it does not seem to be possible to memorize a list of sentences that is long enough to provide the right one when you need it. Somehow the situation is never exactly right for any of the sayings one has rehearsed. To be effective in a second language, it is necessary to be able to "construct" sentences, and there are two techniques for giving the student this ability. The traditional method is explicit instruction in the rules of grammar. With these rules and a stock of words, one puts together the sentence to suit the occasion. A difficulty is that deliberate construction is a slow business, and the boat will have sunk before you can properly call for help. Some modern instruction treats the second-language learner like a child and has him practice again and again the same set of sentences. The sentences may be delivered to an entire group by film strip, or the student may pace himself with one of the Richards and Gibson pocketbooks. Eventually the student finds himself the creator of a new sentence—one not practiced but somehow implied by what has been practiced. Second-language learning by sentence rehearsal relies on this step into automatic construction, though nothing much seems to be known about how to contrive sets of examples that will facilitate its occurrence.

It has seemed to us, then, that first-language learning must have much in common with second-language learning and also with scientific techniques for the discovery of linguistic structure. The shared characteristic that is the ground of the analogy is the necessity in all three cases of inducing general construction rules from sets of sentences. Of course the analogy suppresses those features of first-language learning that are not to be found in the other two processes, and it has taken considerable pressure from reality to bring them to our attention.

This paper is divided into three sections. The first reviews some studies with invented linguistic materials which show that children do indeed have rules of word construction and of sentence construction. The second discusses techniques by which an investigator might induce a child's generative grammar from a large collection of the child's utterances and the, possibly parallel, techniques by which the child could have induced that grammar from a large set of parental utterances. Most of the discussion in this section makes use of materials from a record of four hours of speech from one child of 25½ months. The third section discusses some substantive results from the records of 13 children between 2 and 3 years of age; these are the results that forced us to recognize that there are differences between children and either linguistic scientists or adult students of a second language.

EVIDENCE THAT CHILDREN HAVE CONSTRUCTION RULES

In the natural situation of the child with his family the best evidence that he possesses construction rules is the occurrence of systematic errors. So long as a child speaks correctly, it is possible that he says only what he has heard. In general we cannot know what the total input has been and so cannot eliminate the possibility of an exact model for each sentence that is put out. However, when a small boy says "I digged in the yard" or "I saw some sheeps" or "Johnny hurt hisself," it is unlikely that he is imitating. Furthermore, his mistake is not a random one. We can see how he might have made it by overgeneralizing certain existent regularities. Many verbs ending in voiced consonants form the simple past with /-d/ and many nouns ending in voiceless consonants form the plural with /-s/. The set of forms *me, my, myself* and *you, your, yourself* strongly suggests *he, his, hisself*. As it happens, actual English usage breaks with these simple regularities and prefers *dug, sheep,* and *himself*. By smoothing the language into a simpler system than it is, the child reveals his tendency to induce rules. Guillaume made this point in 1927 and illustrated it with a rich collection of French children's systematic errors.

A Study of Morphological Rules

Although Smith (1933) attempted to do a study of the development of the rules of inflection by simply waiting for the emission of erroneous forms, it is more economical to invent nonsense syllables and try to elicit inflections. This is what Berko did for English in her doctoral research (1958).

This is a wug.

Now there is another one.

There are two of them.

There are two _____.

FIGURE 1—Illustration of Berko's method for eliciting inflections.

A child is shown the small animal of Figure 1 and told: "This is a wug. Now there are two of them. There are two ———." The experimenter holds her voice up to signal the child that he is to complete the sentence; he will usually supply *wug*/-z/. For a different animal the word is *bik* and the correct plural *bik*/s/. For a third animal it is *niss* and the plural *niss*/-əz/. Printed English uses the letter "s" for all of these endings, but, as the phonemic notation shows and as attention to your own pronunciation will reveal, the endings are distinct. The rule in English is: A word ending in a voiceless consonant forms its plural with the voiceless sibilant /-s/ as in *cats, cakes,* and *lips;* a word ending in either a vowel or a voiced consonant forms its plural with the voiced sibilant /-z/ as in *dogs, crows,* and *ribs;* a word ending in the singular with either /s/ or /z/ forms its plural with /-z/ plus an interpolated neutral vowel as in *classes* and *poses.* We all follow these rules and know at once that a new word like *bazooka* will have, as its plural, *bazooka*/-z/, even though most speakers of English will never know the rule in explicit form.

Berko invented a set of materials that provides a complete inventory of the English inflectional system: the plural and possessive endings on nouns;

the simple past, the 3rd person present indicative, and the progressive on verbs; the comparative and superlative on adjectives. She presented these materials as a picture-book game to children of preschool, first-, second-, and third-grade age levels and worked out the development of the rules with age.

The productivity of the regular inflections for children seems to be greater than it is for adults. Both kinds of subjects were shown a picture of a man swinging something about his head and told: "This is a man who knows how to gling. He glings every day. Today he glings. Yesterday he ———." Adults hang suspended between *gling, glang, glung,* and even *glought* but children promptly say *glinged.* Berko also tested to see whether children who generalize the regular inflection would correctly imitate irregular forms or would assimilate them to the rules. She showed a picture and said, for instance, "Here is a goose and here are two geese. There are two ———." Most of her subjects said *gooses* and performed similarly with other irregular forms. These observations suggest that rules of great generality may survive and override a number of counter instances.

Knowledge of the paradigms of inflection could take a child beyond his corpus to the correct construction of new forms. It will not be necessary to hear each new noun in its plural and possessive forms; these can be anticipated from the regular paradigm and, except for an occasional *sheep* and *alumni,* the anticipation will be correct. The rules of inflection are rules of morphology, i.e., rules of word construction rather than rules of syntax or sentence construction. In English, though not in Russian and many other languages, inflection is a rather trivial grammatical system and knowledge of inflection cannot take a child very far beyond his corpus. There is much greater power in syntax.

A Study of Syntactic Rules

The fundamental notion in linguistic syntax is that the words of any natural language can be grouped into classes which are defined by the fact that the members of a class have similar "privileges of occurrence" in sentences. Certain very large and rough syntactic classes are traditionally called the parts-of-speech. In English, count nouns like *house, barn, table,* and *fence* are words that can be plugged into such sentence contexts as: "See the ———"; "I own a ———"; "The ——— is new"; "This ——— is mine." If a child has learned to organize words into such classes, to enter them on mental lists of syntactic equivalents, he will have a very powerful means of getting beyond his corpus.

Hearing *car* as a new word in the sentence: "See the *car*" a child could use this context as a basis for listing *car* with count nouns and so be prepared to hear and say such additional sentences as: "I own a *car*"; "The *car* is new"; "This *car* is mine." And a multitude of others. Of course the particular sentence uttered on a given occasion would depend on semantic and motivational factors, but the population of sentences from which the particular could be drawn would be established by the syntactic kinship linking *car* with *house, barn, table,* and *fence.*

What evidence do we have that a child acquires, with increasing experience of his native language, implicit rules of syntax? Brown and Berko (1960) invented a game for children that utilizes nonsense syllables but not, as in the inflection game, for the purpose of eliciting endings. For one problem the child was asked: "Do you know what a *wug* is?" He was then shown a picture of a little girl and told: "This is a little girl thinking about a *wug.* Can you make up what that might mean?" The picture was included only to engage the child's attention—it did not portray the referent of the new word but only someone thinking about it. The new word, *wug,* had been introduced in two sentences. In both cases it was preceded by the indefinite article; it functioned once as a noun complement and once as the object of a preposition. The positions of *wug* in these two contexts serve to identify it as a singular count noun. An adult speaker of English would have expected such additional sentences as: "Wugs are good" and "That wug is new" to be grammatical. Brown and Berko were interested in seeing whether young children would answer the question: "Can you make up what that might mean?" with a flow of sentences employing *wug* as a count noun.

In the complete study 12 nonsense syllables were used and they were placed in sentences identifying them as belonging to one of six parts-of-speech. Where *wug* was to be identified as a transitive verb, the investigator said: "This is a little girl who wants to wug something." As an intransitive verb the same sentence was used with the omission of *something.* With *wug* as a mass noun the little girl would be "thinking about some wug." *Wug* became an adjective by having the girl think of "something wuggy" and an adverb by having her think of "doing something wuggily."

Children in the first, second, and third grades all went on to make up sentences using their new words, but they did not always use them correctly. They did better as they got older and better at all ages with the count noun, adjective, transitive and intransitive verbs than with the mass nouns and adverbs. For the purposes of the present argument[3] the important result is that children showed an ability, increasing with age, to construct grammatically correct sentences using new words.

---

[3] The same children were given a word-association test employing familiar English words belonging to the same six parts-of-speech involved in the nonsense syllable task. The principal finding was that the frequency of paradigmatic word associations (i.e., a response word that belongs to the same part-of-speech as the stimulus word: *house-barn; run-walk; milk-water*) was related, across the various parts-of-speech and age groups, to the tendency to make correct syntactic use of the nonsense syllables. This result was taken to mean that paradigmatic word associations reflect the developing organization of vocabulary into syntactic classes.

The eliciting of speech with standard invented materials brings some very desirable control to the study of grammar acquisition. It left us, however, with the suspicion that we had only been chipping at the problem. The things we thought of doing were largely suggested by fragmentary facts about adult grammar and guesses as to what children would have to learn. If we were to collect a large number of utterances from an individual child, would it be possible to subject this collection to the kind of distributional analysis that a linguist applies to an unfamiliar language and thereby to discover the child's total generative grammar? Could one write grammar programs for children at different ages and describe language development as a sequence of progressively complicating programs?

Inducing a Grammar from a Corpus

Before collecting any data, we studied English grammar in its more traditional forms (Jespersen, 1938; Smart, 1957) and also in the recent works of Francis (1958), Hockett (1958), Chomsky (1957), and Lees (1960). The traditional works supply most of the substantive knowledge about word classes—knowledge which has been reinterpreted and systematized in recent works. The substance is often more effectively taught by the earlier grammars since this is knowledge that contemporary theorists often take for granted. The generative grammar using constituent analysis and transformation rules has been worked out for a part of English, but there is not yet a complete grammar of this kind for any language.

Rules of grammar are cultural norms; like other norms they are descriptive of certain regularities of behavior within a community, and they also are prescriptive in recommending this behavior to new members of the community. In general, the student of culture can discover norms either by observing behavior and inducing regularities or by asking participants in the culture (informants) to tell him what kinds of behavior are "right" (proper, correct) and what kinds are "wrong" (improper, incorrect). For example, if we were interested in the rules of etiquette of the American middle class we might ask informants what a seated gentleman should do when a lady enters a room and what a hatted gentleman should do when a lady enters an elevator. In addition, we might observe the behavior of seated and hatted gentlemen in the two situations. When the cultural rules to be discovered are linguistic, the possible approaches are the same: direct inquiry of informants as to what it is proper to say and what it is not proper to say; direct study of what is, in fact, said. Students of grammar have varied in the degree to which they have relied on one procedure rather than another.

The partial generative grammars for adult speech that have thus far been written have been written to meet the test of the grammar writer's own delicate sense of what is and what is not a well-formed sentence in his native language. This is a special case of the technique of direct inquiry of a native informant concerning right and wrong behavior; in the present case the investigator is his own informant. Of course the linguist working out a generative grammar believes his personal judgments of the "grammaticality" of utterances represent a community consensus. The evidence so far reported for judgments made by informants who are not linguists (Hill, 1961; Maclay and Sleator, 1960) suggests that there is some consensus on grammaticality in English but that the consensus is not perfect.

While we have adopted the generative model for grammar, we have not been able to use the method of the linguists who have written generative grammars. Clearly we ought not to rely on our own sense of grammaticality in writing the grammars of very young children. In addition, however, we have not found a way to make direct inquiries of native informants between 24 and 36 months of age as to what they regard as well-formed sentences. For older children, judgments of grammaticality may possibly be elicited in terms of what it is "right" and "wrong" to say. For the younger children, we have so far worked entirely from obtained behavior: a sample or corpus of what has actually been said.

It is by no means certain that the direct study of obtained speech is an alternative and equivalent approach to the eliciting of judgments of grammaticality. Chomsky (1957) certainly does not suggest that the notion of the "well-formed" or "possible" sentence can be operationally translated into the "obtained" sentence. Common observation shows that adult speakers of English often produce verbal sequences that are not well-formed sentences. In the case of such another set of norms as the rules of etiquette, behavioral practice might depart rather radically from ideal recommendations. The truth is that the relation between grammatical norms and verbal behavior is quite unexplored both theoretically and empirically. Without waiting for clarification of this relation for adult speakers, we have proceeded to explore the possibility of writing rules for the actual verbal behavior of children. Chomsky (1957) has argued that there are no really adequate mechanical procedures for discovering an adequate grammar, and our experience causes us to agree with him. Still there are some helpful tips, and Harris (1951) is the best source of these. In addition to reading about grammars, we practiced working them out from a speech corpus long before we collected data of our own. As practice materials we used the records collected by Barker and Wright (1954) for their Midwest studies. If anyone has a taste for word games, the grammar discovery game is an engrossing one, and, not surprisingly, it yields more understanding than can be obtained from the reading of theoretical works.

We decided to begin work in the age range from 24 to 36 months. The younger age is the approximate time at which most children begin producing two-word utterances (McCarthy, 1954). Some preliminary work showed us that by 3 years many children had about as complex a grammar as we were able to describe. We located 13 children in this age range whose parents were willing to have us spend a large part of one day at their homes recording the child's speech. For the first seven cases our procedures varied from one to another, but for the last six they have been reasonably uniform.

The families were of the professional, college-educated class, and it is likely that the linguistic behavior of these children was "advanced" in terms of age norms for the American population. Only two of the 13 children were acquainted with one another and so, with the exception of these two, the speech of any one child in the sample could not have been directly affecting the speech of any other. Many of the families had first arrived in Boston just seven months earlier, and the speech of these parents had been learned in several different parts of the country.

We hoped to get as much speech as possible in as little time as possible and to have examples of the full variety of sentence types the child could produce. There were those who warned that the child would be shy and speechless in our presence; this was not the case. Mothers told their children that visitors were coming and, in general, we were eagerly welcomed, shown a parade of toys and games, and talked to rather steadily. It became clear that the child expected a guest to put in some time as a playmate, and so the recording was a two-man job with one of us taking data and the other prepared to play cowboy, horsie, blocks, coloring, trains, and the mule in "Kick the mule." Several of the early records were made by Fraser alone, but for the last six cases both of us were always there. We found that by about noon we needed a rest and so went away for lunch, returning about two; the child took his nap in the interval. About half of each record was made before lunch and about half after lunch.

Much of the time the child was occupied with his normal routine of play, talking with his mother, washing, and eating. So long as these activities involved a reasonable amount of speech, we took no active part beyond delivering signals of attention and approval. When the operant level was very low, we sometimes tried to raise it. In the first days we did the sort of verbal prompting that is anyone's first notion of a technique for eliciting speech from children. You ask what something is called and this brings out vocabulary items—which are not useful for a study of grammar. Or you ask a "yes-no" question such as: "Is that your horsie?" to which the answer is either "yes" or "no." We eventually learned that it is easier to "inspire" speech by doing something interesting than to elicit it with questions. If the adult "playmate" starts a game that is simple, repetitive, and destructive, the child will usually join him and start talking. A universal favorite is to build (painstakingly) an unsteady tower of blocks and register chagrin when the child sends it crashing down. A simple game involving implicit rules—such as the green blocks belong to me and the red ones to you—

creates a situation in which negative sentences can be elicited. If the adult playmate breaks the established rule and moves one of the child's blocks, he is usually told that he is *not* to do that.

How were the child's utterances recorded? After trying several different things, we found that it was not restrictive to ask the mother to limit activities to one floor of the house and a small number of adjoining rooms. Then with two Wollensak tape recorders and long extension cords we were able, in the last six cases, to get almost everything on tape. The machines were handled by the "playmate," and the other member of the team made a continuous transcript of the child's utterances. This on-the-spot transcript was later checked against the tape and corrected into a final best version. Going over the tape takes about four hours to each hour of recording time.

What is the level of detail in the transcription? It is neither phonetic nor phonemic but only morphemic. It is, in short, as if we were to write down in conventional English spelling what an adult seemed to be saying in an interview. Of course the intelligibility of speech in the youngest children was not very good. We found it helpful to do no writing for the first half hour and to have the mother interpret for us everything her child said in that period. In this time we learned to allow for the child's phonetic peculiarities and sometimes found an initial near-complete unintelligibility giving way to about 75 per cent intelligibilty. At grammatically crucial points our general rule was to credit the child with the regular adult contrast if he made any sort of appropriate phonetic distinction. For instance, the emergence of the modal auxiliary *will* in a sentence like *I will get my book* is not at first marked with a well articulated /wil/ but probably only with a shift of the vowel formants in the *I* toward a back vowel like /u/. If we could hear a difference between this *I* and the way *I* sounded in *I got my book,* the child was credited with *will.* For the last six cases we were ultimately able to transcribe fully an average of 78 per cent of the total utterances on the tapes; this is a degree of success quite similar to that reported in previous studies (McCarthy, 1954). Where we were uncertain about the accuracy of transcription, the material was placed in brackets. Utterances were also marked with the following symbols: I for a functional imperative; ? for an interrogative; M for an utterance that mimics an immediately preceding utterance from another person; R for an utterance that is a response to a question.

One difficulty we had anticipated did not materialize—only one. We had thought that division of the flow of speech into utterances might be an uncertain business. In fact, however, the usual criteria of either a prolonged pause or a shift of speakers worked very well. There were few instances of uncertain utterance division.

For the last six cases we aimed at and obtained a minimum of 500 different utterances from each child. Since the utterance rate of the younger children is lower than that of the older children, we spent more time with the younger ones.

Methods for Discovering a Provisional Grammar

The process of grammar discovery has two facets. It is, most immediately, the technique of the investigator who is trying to describe the grammatical apparatus of a particular child. The investigator induces from obtained utterances a probable generative mechanism. Since, however, the child is also presumed to have built this internal mechanism by processing obtained utterances, it follows that the investigator's procedure may be a good model of the child's learning. Of course the child has not induced his grammar from his own sentences but rather from the somewhat more varied and complex sentences heard from adult speakers. A comparison of the recorded speech of mother-to-child with the speech of child-to-mother shows that the grammars induced by children from adult speech are not identical with the adult grammars that produced the sentences. The investigator of a child's speech, on the other hand, hopes to find the very grammar that produced the original utterances. Even so the similarity in the tasks of investigator and child is very great—to get from sentences to a grammar—and so while acting as investigators we shall want to consider whether the child may have carried out operations similar to our own.

For the kind of grammar we are trying to write the fundamental problem is to discover the syntactic classes.[4] Members of a common class are supposed to have similar privileges of occurrence, and these privileges are supposed to be different from one class to another. In addition to syntactic classes our grammars will involve rules of combination describing the ways in which members of the various classes may be put in sequence. Generally the rules of combination will get simpler as the syntactic classes get larger and fewer. If *a* and *an* in English were words having identical privileges of occurrence, our grammar would be simpler than it is. As it stands, however, the two forms must be separated, and a rule of combination written that requires *an* before count nouns with an initial vowel and *a* before count nouns with an initial consonant.

As a basic technique for the discovery of syntactic classes we might undertake to record for each different word in the corpus all of the utterance contexts in which that word occurs; in short we might make a concordance. The contexts of each word could then be compared with the contexts of each

---

[4] The generative grammar, as Chomsky (1957) has described it, is more than a set of sequence rules for syntactic classes; it also provides several levels of appropriate constituent analysis. We have so far not accomplished this result for the speech of children because we have not been able to invent appropriate behavioral tests of the child's sense of constituent structure. The requirement that a grammar make appropriate structural analyses does of course help greatly in the evaluation of adult grammars, and it is desirable to meet this requirement wherever it is possible to do so.

TABLE I

Total Contexts of Four Words in the Record of Adam

Total Contexts of "Mum"

Here it is, Mum.	(The) pan, Mum.	Apple, Mum.
Here, Mum.	I want apple, Mum.	Again, Mum?
Here (the) coffee pot broken, Mum.	I want blanket, Mum.	Out, Mum?
	I want blanket now, Mum.	Salad, Mum?
More sugar, Mum.	I want juice, Mum.	See, Mum?*
There it is, Mum.	Mum, I want some, Mum.	Coffee, Mum?
What's that, Mum.		Turn, Mum?
Mum, (where is the cards)?	Popeye, Mum?	No, you see, Mum?
Mum, (where's the rags)?	I wanta do, Mum.	No help, Mum.
	I wanta help, Mum.	Won't help, Mum.
Want coffee, Mum.*	I found, Mum.	Coffee, Mum.
Want apple, Mum.	I do, Mum.	Hi, Mum.*
Want blanket, Mum.	I don't, Mum.	O.K., Mum.
Want more juice, Mum.	I get it, Mum.	Here, Mum.
I want blanket, Mum.	(Gonna) dump, Mum.	Over here, Mum.
I want (it), Mum.	Fall down, Mum.	Enough, Mum.
I want paper away, Mum.	Fall, Mum.	Silver spoons, Mum.
	An apple, Mum.	

Total Contexts of "Dad"

See paper, Dad.	See, Dad?*	Work, Dad?
Want coffee, Dad.*	Dad, want coffee?	Hi, Dad.*
I want cream, Dad.	Some more, Dad?	

Total Contexts of "Here"

Here (a car).	Here more bricks.	Here (we go).
Here all gone.	Here more blocks.	See the bolt here, see?
Here (block).	Here more firetruck.	That block here.
Here brick.	Here more toys.	That one here.
Here chairs.	Here more truck.†	That one right here.
Here coffee is.	Here Mum.†	I put bucket here.
Here comes Daddy.	Here Mummy.	Come here.
Here flowers.	Here my bricks.	Do here.
Here goes.†	Here not a house.	Leave that block here.
Here is.†	Here stars.	Put it here.
Here it goes.†	Here (the) coffee pot broken, Mum.	Here not a house.
Here it is.†		Right here.†
Here it is, Mum.†	Here the card.	Over here.
Here's it here.	Here the cards.	Over here, Mum.
Here light.	Here the cheese.	Now here.
Here (mail) more paper.	Here (the) flowers.	
Here more.	Here the paper.	

Total Contexts of "There"

There goes.†	There more block.	I wanta put (it) right there . . . (under) the couch.
There (he) goes.	There more truck.	
There is.†	There more nails.	
There it goes.†	There Mum.†	Me see (in there).
There it is.†	There my house.	Blanket in there.
There it is, Mum.†	There my nails.	In there.
There kitty.	There Noah.	Right there.†

* Identifies contexts common to "Mum" and "Dad."
† Identifies contexts common to "Here" and "There."

other word and tentative syntactic classes set up so as to put together words having many contexts in common and so as to separate words having few or no contexts in common.

To illustrate the method of shared contexts, we have taken from the record of Adam[5] (28½ months) the word: *here, there Mum,* and *Dad.* In adult English *here* and *there* are locative adverbials while *Mum* and *Dad* are animate nouns. Will the pattern of shared contexts taken from Adam's record suggest the assignment of *here* and *there* to one class and *Mum* and *Dad* to a different class? In Table 1 all of the utterances containing these four words are listed and the shared contexts indicated. The upper limit to the number of contexts that two words can share in a given record is set by the number of contexts obtained for the less frequent of the two. *Here* occurs in 48 different contexts and *there* in 19. It would be possible for the two words to share 19 different contexts; in fact they share eight or 42 per cent of the possible contexts. *Mum* occurs in 49 different contexts and *Dad* in eight; they share 38 per cent of the possible contexts. *Here* shares no contexts with *Mum* and none with *Dad,* and the same is true for *there.* The pattern of shared contexts suggests the class break that operates in adult English.

If one has read about the notion of syntactic equivalence but never actually lined up the contexts for sets of words, it is startling to find such small numbers of identical contexts; especially startling since *here-there* and *Mum-Dad* must be as near to perfect syntactic equivalence as any pairs of words in the language and, in addition, the short sentences and small vocabulary of a child maximize the probability of repetition. Is a 38 per cent overlap enough for us to assume that the members of a pair are interchangeable? It may be.

We have taken the word *here* alone and set down all its different contexts in the first half of Adam's record and also all of its different contexts in the second half of the record (Table 2). A context that has already appeared in the first half is listed again on its first appearance in the second half. *Here* in the first half is the same word as *here* in the second half, and so we know that these two *heres* are syntactic equivalents. In the first half the word occurs in 33 different contexts; in the second half in 19. There are four shared contexts or 21 per cent of the possible—a lower value than the value obtained for *here-there* and *Mum-Dad.*

Perhaps it would be possible to set an exact percentage-of-shared-contexts criterion for the assignment of two words to the same class, the criterion to be empirically determined from percentages of shared contexts of identical words at various levels of absolute and relative frequency in two time periods. Clearly, the obtained percentages will be very unstable for small numbers of occurrences. For less frequent words only a mammoth speech sample would serve and the whole thing becomes a job for a machine. The

---

[5] The names used in this report for identifying child subjects are not the actual names of the children who were studied.

Table 2

Contexts of "Here" in the First and Second Halves of the Record of Adam

First Half

Here all gone.	Here more.*	Here the cheese.
Here (block).	Here more bricks.	Here the paper.
Here brick.	Here more firetruck.	That block here.
Here chairs.	Here more toys.	That one here.
Here coffee is.	Here more truck.	That one right here.
Here comes Daddy.	Here Mum.	Come here.
Here is.*	Here my bricks.	Leave that block here.
Here it goes.*	Here not a house.	(Put it) here.
Here it is, Mum.	Here (the) coffee pot	Here not a house.
Here light.	broken, Mum.	Over here.*
Here (mail) more paper.	Here the card.	
Right here.	Here the cards.	

Second Half

Here (a car)	Here's it here.	In here?
Here flowers.	Here more.*	(Over here)?
Here goes.	Here more blocks.	Over here, Mum.
Here is.*	Here Mummy.	Over here.*
Here it goes.*	Here stars.	Now here.
Here it is.	Here (the) flowers.	
Here (we go).	See the bolt here, see.	

* Identifies contexts common to first and second halves of record.

basic problem of setting a criterion for that machine to use or of writing the program for working out a criterion may also be a problem in the child's learning of syntax.

Once the classes have been established by some shared-contexts criterion, some contexts will turn out to be more "criterial" or distinctive for a given class than will others. After *the* in English one can have count nouns in the singular, count nouns in the plural, and mass nouns (which are used in the singular only). After *a* one can have only count nouns in the singular, and so this context is, for singular count nouns, the more criterial of the two. The introduction of new words to a child in highly criterial "tracer" contexts (like "Hi ———" for personal names) should be the best guarantee of subsequent correct usage.

A corpus of 500 utterances is not large enough to take us very far with a mechanical shared-contexts procedure. However, a generally adequate mechanical procedure for the discovery of grammars has not been worked out in any case. Grammar writing is for the present like theory writing in science, an undertaking for which there are some guides, clues, and models but not a set of guaranteed procedures. Let us therefore take one record, the utterances of Eve (25½ months) and, allowing ourselves a very free use of inductive reasoning, see what we can make of it.

It is a useful first step to restrict ourselves to the simplest utterances in the record, those of just two words, and, among these, the utterances in which the initial word occurs at least twice. In Table 3 the recurrent initial

TABLE 3

Two-Word Utterances with Recurrent Initial Words from Eve

Second Word	A	Daddy	Mummy	's	See	That	The	There	Two
bear		+	+						
bird				+		+	+	+	
block	+								
boat						+		+	
Bobby									+
book	+	+				+	+	+	
bowl						+			
boy					+	+		+	
broken						+			
candle	+								
car						+			
carriage								+	
chair								+	+
cricket	+								
cookie						+			
cow						+			
Daddy				+		+		+	
dimple			+						
dirty						+			
do			+						
dog	+								
doggie						+			
doll								+	
dollie								+	
Dru								+	
eye					+				
fall	+								
fuzzy						+			
Gale									+
girl							+		
go			+						
goes								+	
going						+			
honey		+							
horsie						+	+		
is								+	
kitty	+					+	+	+	
man								+	
meatball	+								
men									+
mike							+		
Mummy					+	+		+	
nurse	+								
pea								+	

(Table continued on next page)

TABLE 3 (*continued*)

Two-Word Utterances with Recurrent Initial Words from Eve

Second Word	A	Daddy	Mummy	's	See	That	The	There	Two
		I N I T I A L				W O R D S			
peas							+		
Peter						+			
picture				+					
pillow	+								
potty								+	
pretty						+			
puff			+			+			
puppy							+		
radio					+			+	
Rayma							+		
reel	+						+	+	+
rocker					+	+			
rug							+		
sun						+			
that					+				
'tis								+	
whistle							+		
wire						+			

NOTE.—"+" indicates that utterances of this type occurred.

words are listed at the heads of columns, and each row represents a second word that occurs in at least one utterance after one of the recurrent first words. The second word is given a + in a column if it occurs after the word that heads the column, and so a filled square represents an obtained two-word utterance defined by the column and row headings.

Table 3 is simply a technique for making a first inquiry into shared contexts, an inquiry limited to the most frequently repeated and so most informative contexts. By comparing the filled slots for any two rows, one can determine the number of shared contexts for two second words. By comparing the filled slots for any two columns one can determine the number of shared contexts for two initial words.

Table 3 is itself a descriptive grammar for an obtained set of two-word sentences. The table is a description that is only very slightly more economical than actual listing of the sentences; the single slight economy is accomplished by writing the recurrent first words just once instead of repeating them on each appearance. The descriptive grammar of Table 3 can easily be turned into a generative grammar. Table 4 presents the generative version. It reads: "In order to form an utterance: select first one of the initial words; select, secondly, one from the class of words that are permitted to follow the initial you have chosen." A machine that can go through this program would produce all-and-only the obtained set of utterances.

TABLE 4

A Grammar Describing All and Only the 89 Utterances Obtained

$$
\text{Utterance} \rightarrow \left\{
\begin{array}{ll}
A & + \quad C_1 \\
Daddy & + \quad C_2 \\
Mummy & + \quad C_3 \\
's & + \quad C_4 \\
See & + \quad C_5 \\
That & + \quad C_6 \\
The & + \quad C_7 \\
There & + \quad C_8 \\
Two & + \quad C_9
\end{array}
\right\}
$$

$C_1 \rightarrow$ *block, book, candle, cricket, dog, fall, kitty, meatball, nurse, pillow, reel*

$C_2 \rightarrow$ *bear, book, honey*

$C_3 \rightarrow$ *bear, dimple, do, go, puff*

$C_4 \rightarrow$ *bird, Daddy, picture*

$C_5 \rightarrow$ *boy, eye, Mummy, radio, rocker, that*

$C_6 \rightarrow$ *bird, boat, book, bowl, boy, broken, car, cookie, cow, Daddy, dirty, doggie, fuzzy, going, horsie, kitty, Mummy, Peter, pretty, puff, Rayma, rocker, sun, wire*

$C_7 \rightarrow$ *bird, book, girl, horsie, kitty, mike, peas, puppy, reel, rug, whistle*

$C_8 \rightarrow$ *bird, boat, book, boy, carriage, chair, Daddy, doll, dollie, Dru, go, goes, is, kitty, man, Mummy, pea, potty, radio, reel, 'tis*

$C_9 \rightarrow$ *Bobby, chair, Gale, men, reel*

NOTE.—{ } means a choice of one of the contained sequences.

Table 3 constitutes a list of different utterances: each is listed just once. In the original record the utterances varied in their frequency of repetition. One could write a generative grammar that would do a better job of mimicking the original record by setting probabilities at the various choice-points: the route "That-broken," for instance, ought to be taken more often than the route "That-Rayma." A printed record turned out by this machine would be indistinguishable from actual obtained records, indistinguishable as a list of sentences but perfectly distinguishable in the life situation for the reason that the machine described takes no account of semantics. It is quite capable of greeting the appearance of Daddy with "That doggie" or "That cookie." We have a grammar machine, not a machine that is a complete model for human sentence production.

Now we want to go beyond the obtained sentences to the syntactic classes they suggest. Is there any ground for considering all of the initial words to be members of a single class? Consider first the possibility of a shared-contexts criterion, of the type discussed, with reference to *here-there* and *Mum-Dad*.

The previous discussion was greatly simplified by restricting the problem to single pairs of words. However, the number of candidates for membership in a common syntactic class is generally greater than two, and that is the case with the initial words of Table 3. Each single word that is a candidate for inclusion can be compared for shared-contexts with each other word in the presumptive class. The criteria for class identification must then prescribe minimal levels of overlap for the full set. This is a complicated problem for which many different solutions can be imagined.

In the present case the words *that* and *there* are the most frequent in the set. They share seven second word (*bird, boat, book, Daddy, kitty,* and *Mummy*) which is 33 per cent of the number of contexts that could be shared. Of the other words in the set *'s, see, the, a, Mummy,* and *Daddy* all share at least one context with both *that* and *there*, while *two* shares with *there* but not *that*. One might use the syntactically close pair *that* and *there* as touchstones and count as members any words that share at least one context with either critical word. That rule would put all of the initial words into the same syntactic class (class 1).

What evidence is there that the entries in the rows of Table 3 constitute a second syntactic class? The words *bird, book, kitty,* and *reel* are most frequent. Since the contexts are the words of class 1, and so are few, these frequent words have a high degree of mutual overlap. Using the four as touchstones, most of the words entered in rows could be entered in class 2 on the criterion of having at least one context in common with one of the touchstones. A few, such as *dimple* and *do,* would be left out. Most of the words in class 2 are count nouns, and if we had a larger corpus, we should probably find that *dimple* belongs here for Eve while *do* does not. Our criterion is probably not good enough to separate out just the few words that do not fit.

The members of a syntactic class are credited with identical privileges of occurrence. In Table 3, the initial words are far from having identical patterns of actual occurrence, and the second words are also far from this pattern. If the actual occurrences were identical in either set, then the assignment to a common class might be confidently made, but the assignment would not take us beyond what we have obtained. If we do go beyond what has been obtained in our description of privileges of occurrence, then, of course, we will not have "proved" our description. This is the familiar problem of the impossibility of proving a generalization that goes beyond what has been examined—the very sort of generalization that is most valuable and which the human mind is most bent on making. We are, in the setting up of syntactic classes, trying to move from a partial similarity of actual occurrence to an identity of potential occurrence. This is the process of induction—uncertain but powerful.

To hold that the members of each of our present classes have identical privileges of occurrence is to hold that all the empty positions in Table 3 may properly be filled—they are utterances we should expect to hear from Eve. The generative grammar changes to the form of Table 5. This grammar will turn out more sentences than Table 4, and it ought to be very much easier to remember since the sequential contingencies are greatly simplified.

TABLE 5

A Grammar that Results from Filling In the Blanks in Table 3

Utterance $\rightarrow$ $C_1 + C_2$

$C_1 \rightarrow$ *A, Daddy, Mummy, 's, See, That, The, There, Two*

$C_2 \rightarrow$ *bear, bird, block, boat, Bobby, book, bowl, boy, broken, candle, car, carriage, chair, cricket, cookie, cow, Daddy, dimple, dirty, do, dog, doggie, doll, dollie, Dru, eye, fall, fuzzy, Gale, girl, go, goes, going, honey, horsie, is, kitty, man, meatball, men, mike, Mummy, nurse, pea, peas, Peter, picture, pillow, potty, pretty, puff, puppy, radio, Rayma, reel, rocker, rug, sun, that, 'tis, whistle, wire*

NOTE.—This grammar predicts the 89 utterances obtained plus 469 others.

The utterances of Table 4 and Table 5, since they are two-word utterances, can very well be thought of as a set of paired associates. It is usually the case in paired-associate learning that initial words and second words occur always and only in their pair relation. In the present case some initial words and some second words occur in a variety of combinations. If these utterances were to be made up as experimental materials, what task could we set the subject? If he were simply asked to respond to each initial word with some one of the acceptable second words, then he could meet the requirements by learning single associates. Suppose, however, he is required to do what the grammar does—respond to each initial word with all acceptable second words. There could be two sets of materials: one made up on the model of Table 4 with only the obtained secondaries occurring and one on the model of Table 5 with any member of class 2 likely to occur after any initial word. I think we can foresee that for the first set of materials it would take a long time to learn the exact set of words that can go after each initial word. With the second set it should not take very long to learn the principle that any second word can follow any initial word, but it would take some time to memorize all of the second words. But after how many pairs, of what kinds, will subjects move to the generalization of Table 5? We think it would be interesting to try paired-associate learning of this kind.

Refinements on the provisional grammar. Turning to utterances of three or more words, we find evidence to indicate that not all of the members of class 1 have identical privileges. Consider first the words *the* and *a*. Table 7a presents a set of utterances in which *the* or *a* occurs after members of class 1 and before members of class 2. However, *the* and *a* do not occur after all members of class 1; they do not occur after *the, a, Mummy,* or *Daddy.* There are no utterances like "The the doggie" or "The a horsie." These facts suggest that *the* and *a* should be withdrawn from class 1 and set up as a new class 3. The grammar would then be rewritten as in Table 6a.

T<small>ABLE</small> 6

Grammars Suggested by Three-Word Utterances

---

a. Eve's Grammar with the Articles Separated Out

$$\text{Utterance} \rightarrow (C_1) + (C_3) + C_2$$

$C_1 \rightarrow$ *Daddy, Mummy, 's, See, That, There, Two*
$C_2 \rightarrow$ *bear, bird, block, boat,* etc.
$C_3 \rightarrow$ *a, the*

b. Eve's Grammar Allowing for Possessives

$$\text{Utterance} \rightarrow (C_1) + (C_3) + C_2$$

$C_1 \rightarrow$ *'s, See, That, There, Two*
$C_2 \rightarrow$ *bear, bird, block, boat,* etc.
$C_3 \rightarrow$ *a, the,* plus human terms

N<small>OTE</small>.—( ) means that selection of the enclosed is optional.

The optional markings in Table 6a indicate that a class can be completely bypassed. It is necessary to make class 3 optional so as to get sentences like "That bird" and "There boat." Making class 1 optional makes it possible to obtain "The boat," "A book," and the like. If neither optional class is bypassed we get such utterances as "That the cup" and "See the reel." If both optional classes are bypassed, we get such one-word utterances as "Dolly," "Book," "Reel," and utterances of this kind were very numerous in Eve's record. We cannot get from this grammar such utterances as "The the horsie," "The that bird," "A see that" and other radically un-English sequences.

The grammar of Table 6a does turn out some kinds of utterance for which Eve's record provides no models. It is possible, for instance, to obtain "Two the bear" or "Two a bird." Eve produced nothing like these, and for adults they are definitely ungrammatical. It is quite likely that *two* should go with *the* and *a* in class 3 so as to yield: "That two bear" and "See the bird." However, Eve's record gives us no utterances like these, and indeed no three-word utterances including *two,* and so we may as well leave *two* in class 1. We have identified a point at which more evidence is needed in order to choose between formulations.

There is another sort of utterance that the grammar of Table 6a will produce for which Eve's record provides no model: "Mummy the bird" or "Daddy a book." These sentences do not use *Mummy* and *Daddy* in the vocative; the vocative would involve a distinctive juncture (pause) and intonation which is suggested in print by a comma (e.g., "Mummy, the

TABLE 7

Three-Word Utterances that Refine the Original Grammar

a. Utterances with *the* or *a* in Middle Position

's a man	See the horsie	That the bowl
's a house	See the radio	That the cup
's a Daddy	See the reel	That a horsie
There the kitty	See a boat	

b. Utterances with Human Terms in Middle Position

See Evie car	That Daddy car	That Evie dish
See baby eyebrow	That Daddy honey	That Evie pillow
That Mummy book	That man car	That Evie spoon
That Mummy paper	That baby bed	There Evie car
That Mummy hair	That Evie book	There man coat
That Mummy spoon		

bird"). An adult might form the vocative version as a kind of ellipsis of "Mummy, see the bird," but he would not form the nonvocative utterance that the grammar of Table 6a produces.

Thus far, *Mummy* and *Daddy* are in the same limbo as *two;* there is reason for withdrawing them from class 1, but we do not yet know where to put them. Eve's record provides no three-word utterances with *two*, but it does provide such utterances with *Mummy* and *Daddy* and these are listed as Table 7b. We find *Mummy* and *Daddy* in middle position between *that* (a class 1 word) and the class 2 words: *book, hair, paper, spoon, car,* and *honey*. Furthermore, we find in this same position the words: *Evie, man,* and *baby*. All of these middle-position words are names of human beings, and so we may hypothesize that such terms constitute a syntactic class.

The difficulty now is that the middle position between class 1 and class 2 already belongs to class 3 which is composed of *the* and *a*. This means that there are three clear options: (a) to include the human terms with *the* and *a* in class 3; (b) to set up the human terms as a separate class 4 and put this class in the selection sequence ahead of class 3; (c) to put the independent class 4 in sequence after class 3. Here now are examples of utterances that are predicted by the three versions of the grammar: (a) "That Mummy book"; (b) "That Mummy the book"; (c) "That the

Mummy book." Our interim decision is fairly clear. Since the record provides instances of (a) but not of either (b) or (c), we will put the human terms in class 3 with *the* and *a* as indicated in Table 6b. However, if a larger corpus were drawn, we would have to be on the alert to correct this decision.

It may be worthwhile to consider the very complicated rules required for adult English at an analogous grammatical point. Utterances like "Mummy book" and "Man car" and "Evie dish" are, we know from the situational contexts, Eve's version of the possessive; she omits the inflection. In forming possessives with human terms, the adult speaker will use an article before such generic human terms as *man* ("the man's car"), and so these terms cannot be classified as alternatives to *the* and *a*. With personal names like *Evie* the adult will form possessives but, with personal names, articles are never used, and so we will say "Evie's dish" but neither "The Evie's dish" nor "Evie's the dish." This means that personal names cannot be classified as alternatives to either the articles or the generic human terms. A final exasperating fillip is provided by the fact that some morphemes, like *Mummy* and *Daddy*, can serve either as personal names ("Mother's purse") or as generic terms ("the mother's role") and so would have to be listed in two syntactic classes.

Even the simple grammar we have now produced for Eve involves double syntactic listing for some forms—the human terms. They must be in class 3 because of such utterances as "That Mummy book," but they must also remain in class 2 because of such utterances as "That Mummy." The combinational formula predicts "That Mummy Mummy" (Grandmummy?) which is reasonably probable but also "That Evie Evie" which would not

TABLE 8
Utterances with Recurrent Second Members

Initial Word	S E C O N D		W O R D	
Baby				tired
Bird*	all gone			
Carriage*		broken		
Chair*		broken	fall down	
Doggy*				tired
Dollie*		broken	fall down	
Eyebrow	all gone			
Kitty*	all gone		fall down	
Microphone	all gone			
Mummy*				tired
Reel*	all gone			
Rocker*		broken		
Something		broken		

* A word already identified as a member of C_2.

be produced by an adult. As to whether Eve would say it, we cannot tell from the present materials.

Expansion of Eve's grammar. Recurrence of a context is always what is needed for the identification of a syntactic class. We started with recurrence of initial members, but recurrence at the end of an utterance can be equally useful. In Eve's record there is a set of terminal recurrences (*all gone, broken, fall down, tired*) which appears in Table 8. The first thing to note is that most of the initial members of these utterances have already been identified as members of class 2. Their appearance here with overlapping privileges of occurrence before *all gone, broken, fall down,* and *tired* is a valuable confirmation of the preliminary analysis.

Since the initial terms are already regarded as one class, we are inclined to assume that they have identical privileges of occurrence which means that empty cells could be filled. This makes a new class 4 of *all gone, broken, fall down,* and *tired,* and we now have a second type of sentence. The full grammar (Table 9a) involves two major routes corresponding to the two kinds of sentences.

There is a slight addition to be made to the grammar of Table 9a. The addition is suggested by three sentences: "The chair broken"; "The baby tired"; and "The book fall down." The initial word *the* has already been placed in class 3, and so it is a good guess that any word from class 3 can appear in first position in this new sentence type, and Table 9b presents this version. Class 3 must be entered as optional in the grammar since most of the obtained sentences omit it. It is not certain that our analysis of the limited materials in Table 8 is correct. The word *tired,* for example, does not actually overlap in the obtained distribution with any of the other second members. Our analysis, relying on the prior identification of the first members as class 2, assumes that the overlap would occur if more sentences were gathered. However, it should be noted that *tired* occurs only after names of animate beings—*baby, doggy, Mummy*—whereas the other second members are not restricted in this way. This is a fragment of evidence pointing to the eventual separation of animate nouns from the general syntactic class of nominal expressions. This separation is a necessity for adult grammar; certain verbs can only take animate nouns as objects. We can say: "It surprised John" or "It surprised the dog" but not: "It surprised the chair." In our discussion of the possessive we considered the possibility of separating out a class of generic human terms. The distributional facts of adult English will show that this class has to be broadened into animate nouns (we can have "the dog's house" as well as "the man's car") and is the same class hinted at by the restrictions on *tired.* However, Eve's utterances are so few that we cannot be sure these restrictions would be maintained.

The reciprocal of *tired* in Table 8 is *broken,* for *broken* only occurs after inanimate nouns—*carriage, chair, dolly, rocker, something.* In adult English *broken* would be restricted in this way, but we cannot be sure that it will continue so for Eve. *All gone* is interesting because Eve uses this form where an adult speaker would not—after count nouns. We would not say "The microphone is all gone" or "A kitty is all gone." For us *all gone* goes after plural count nouns ("The microphones are all gone") or mass nouns ("The sand is all gone"). Eve does not give us any plural count nouns in this record and does not make a syntactic distinction between mass and count nouns, and she uses *all gone* without any discoverable restrictions.

TABLE 9

Grammars Suggested by the Terminal Recurrence of Table 8

a. Eve's Grammar with Two Basic Sentence-Types

$$\text{Utterance} \rightarrow \left\{ \begin{array}{c} (C_1) + (C_3) + C_2 \\ C_2 + C_4 \end{array} \right\}$$

$C_1 \rightarrow$ *'s, See, That, There, Two*
$C_2 \rightarrow$ *bear, bird, block, boat,* etc.
$C_3 \rightarrow$ *a, the,* plus human terms
$C_4 \rightarrow$ *all gone, broken, fall down, tired*

b. Eve's Grammar with Articles Added to the New Sentence-Type

$$\text{Utterance} \rightarrow \left\{ \begin{array}{c} (C_1) + (C_3) + C_2 \\ (C_3) + (C_2) + C_4 \end{array} \right\}$$

$C_1 \rightarrow$ *'s, See, That, There, Two*
$C_2 \rightarrow$ *bear, bird, block, boat,* etc.
$C_3 \rightarrow$ *a, the,* plus human terms
$C_4 \rightarrow$ *all gone, broken, fall down, tired*

NOTE.— { } means a choice of one of the contained sequences.

The grammar of Table 9b does not represent the distributional distinctions among the class 4 members for the reason that we have so very little evidence on this point. Still, as we shall see in the next section, there are reasons for preferring to represent the distinctions rather than to assume identical privileges. If we were forced to freeze the grammar on the present evidence, it would probably be better to write the more differentiated version.

The sentences we have been discussing all begin with a class 2 word (*bird, book,* etc.) with a prior class 3 (*the, a,* etc.) being optional. There are many other sentences answering this description in Eve's record, but they do not have the recurrence of second members that made the sentences in Table 8 useful. These additional sentences are all unique and they vary in length: "Daddy fix it"; "Eve listen to tick-tock"; "The reel go round and round"; etc. The best thing to do with these sentences, at present, is to make a cut after the class 2 words (*Daddy, Eve, reel*) and call all of the remainder second members. These second members are, from the point of view of adult English, complex predicates. With our present inadequate materials we can only add them to *all gone, broken, fall down,* and *tired* as additional members of class 4. There is not enough material for a finer breakdown. The fact that some of these complex predicates contain class 2 words and some do not hints at an eventual distinction between transitive and intransitive verbs.

TABLE 10

Utterances of Previously Identified Types with Interrogative Intonation Added

---

Utterances that Have Occurred in Declarative Form*

's Daddy,	Book?
That daddy?	Doggie?

Utterances that Have Been Predicted in Declarative Form but Have Not Occurred

Daddy fix this?	See baby eyebrow?
Daddy work?	See baby horsie?
's a Daddy?	See cow?
's cow?	That block?
's Mummy?	That Evie spoon?
	Daddy?

---

* Utterances that have occurred without rising interrogative intonation.

There remains a collection of utterances belonging to types already identified but modified by the addition of a rising interrogative intonation (?), and these appear in Table 10. Since instances of both kinds of utterances allowed by our grammar occur with the interrogative intonation, it seems reasonable to suppose that any sentence allowed by that grammar can be so modified. The result is the revised formula of Table 11 which at one swoop doubles the number of sentences the grammar can generate. Table 11 is the complete version of our provisional grammar.

There are several things worth noting about the grammar of Table 11. It will produce most of the 500 utterances actually obtained from Eve and will produce many thousands beyond the obtained. The only classes that are not optional in the grammar are the reference-making words of class 2 (*bear, bird,* etc.) and class 3 (*all gone, broken,* etc.). These are, by our observation, the forms that are used as single-word "mands" and "tacts" (Skinner, 1957) for some time before the two-word utterance begins.

The generative grammar written out as a formula suggests a distinction between lexical meanings and structural or syntactic meanings. The class

Complete Provisional Grammar for Eve

$$\text{Utterance} \rightarrow \left\{ \begin{array}{l} (C_1) + (C_3) + C_2 \\ (C_3) + (C_2) + C_4 \end{array} \right\} \quad (?)$$

$C_1 \rightarrow$ *'s, See, That, There, Two*

$C_2 \rightarrow$ *bear, bird, block, boat,* etc.

$C_3 \rightarrow$ *a, the,* plus human terms

$C_4 \rightarrow$ *all gone, broken, fall down, tired, fix it, listen to tick-tock,* etc.

listings are the lexicon, and an utterance involves a shift of lexical meaning whenever there is a change in the selection within a class (e.g., from "That bird" to "That bear"). Structural meanings may perhaps be defined as those that shift whenever there is a change in the selections within the formula. Thus if we shift from the first major sentence route to the second, there seems to be a shift from demonstrative naming ("There bird" or "See boat") to predication ("Bird all gone" or "Bear fall down"). If we shift from not selecting ? to selecting it, we shift from a declaration to an interrogation. It is more difficult to say what the changes of meaning could be that go with selecting or not selecting the various optional classes.

Testing the Adequacy of a Grammar

In our discussion of techniques for the discovery of a grammar we have repeatedly pointed to the existence of equally reasonable alternative decisions. The arbitrariness of choice could be somewhat reduced by taking a larger corpus. However, we are sure that the best-founded grammar will not be uniquely determined but will only be a good provisional try. The same thing is surely true for the rules a child induces from adult speech; they will be hypotheses about the form of future speech events. Is there any way to check such hypotheses?

Very roughly the test of a grammar must be the same as the test of any theory of empirical events—the ability to make correct predictions. In the present case this means the ability to anticipate sentences that have not entered into the construction of the grammar. One might, for example, have tested our grammar for Eve by taking a second large collection of utterances on the following day or days and seeing how many of those that occur were predicted.

Three different kinds of successful prediction may be distinguished. There is, in the first place, occurrence of an utterance that has already occurred in the corpus from which the grammar was induced. This sort of occurrence does not help to validate the grammar as a set of generalizations that go beyond the data; the occurrence of a familiar sentence could have been predicted from a simple list of sentences in the original corpus. There is, in the second place, the occurrence of an utterance not included in the original corpus but allowed for by the generalized rules. For example, Eve's record did not include the sentence "There horsie" though it did include "That horsie" and "The horsie." By adopting the general rule that any class 2 word can follow any class 1 word, the utterance "There horsie" is predicted. If it occurs, that fact would increase our confidence in the generalization.

Suppose that, in a second corpus collected from Eve, we obtained the utterance "That lion." The word *lion* did not occur in the original corpus, and so the utterance was not predicted. It is not to be expected that a speech sample of only 500 utterances would exhaust a lexicon, and it would be unreasonable to permit incompleteness of lexicon to discredit a grammar. It would be better to say that an utterance does not come within the province of a grammar unless all of its words are included in the lexicon of the grammar—the lexicon being the lists of forms belonging to each syntactic class. Therefore, the sentence "That lion" counts neither for nor against the grammar. However, the occurrence of this sentence enables us to add *lion* to the class 2 list since the criterion for inclusion is occurrence after a class 1 word and *that* is such a word. Subsequent utterances such as "There lion" and "The lion" could be counted as evidence for the grammar since they are predicted once *lion* has been added to the lexicon.

We cannot think of any way to set a definite criterion as to the number of sentences, out of a collection of obtained sentences, that must be predicted for a grammar to be judged acceptable. It is clear, however, that the number of successful predictions can be increased by simply writing the grammar in the most general terms possible. We found, you recall, that the forms *all gone, broken, fall down,* and *tired* all occurred after class 2 words (Table 8). Looking more closely at Table 8, we found that the word *broken* occurred only after the names of inanimate things and *tired* only after the names of animate things. This fraction of the grammar could have been written in either of the two forms presented in Table 12. The less general form predicts 39 utterances, and the more general predicts these 39 plus 13 others. The more general will make all of the successful predictions made by the less general and has the possibility of making some that the less general cannot make. The way to write a "successful" grammar, if "success" is simply measured by the prediction of obtained events, is to write a grammar that predicts every conceivable sequence of obtained forms.

The job of a grammar, however, is to predict sentences that are possible while *not predicting sentences that are impossible*. This second part of the job gives an additional criterion of evaluation that will prevent us from always preferring the most general grammar. That grammar is to be preferred which predicts what occurs while predicting as little as possible that

TABLE 12

Alternative Forms for a Fragment of Eve's Grammar

a. The More General Form

$$\text{Utterance} \rightarrow C_2 + C_4$$

$C_2 \rightarrow$ *baby, bird, carriage, chair, doggie, dollie, eyebrow, kitty, microphone, Mummy, reel, rocker, something*

$C_4 \rightarrow$ *all gone, broken, fall down, tired*

b. The More Restrictive Form

$$\text{Utterance} \rightarrow \left\{ \begin{array}{l} C_2 \quad\ + C_5 \\ C_{2\,an.} + tired \\ C_{2\,inan.} + broken \end{array} \right\}$$

$C_2 \qquad \rightarrow$ *baby, bird, carriage, chair, doggie, dollie, eyebrow, kitty, microphone, Mummy, reel, rocker, something*

$C_{2\,an.} \quad \rightarrow$ *baby, bird, doggie, dollie, kitty, mummy*

$C_{2\,inan.} \rightarrow$ *carriage, chair, eyebrow, microphone, reel, rocker, something*

$C_5 \qquad \rightarrow$ *all gone, fall down*

does not occur. Therefore, the less general grammar will be better than the more general if it is equally successful in predicting what happens. A grammar should stay as close to the obtained materials as is consistent with generalizing beyond the obtained materials so as to predict future events. Only by invoking both criteria can we hope to obtain distinct grammars representing a developmental sequence. Our next step in this research program will be an empirical and logical study of techniques for evaluating grammars in terms of their predictive powers. (See Brown, Fraser, and Bellugi.)

In sum, the most that we are now able to conceive by way of grammar-evaluating techniques is a set of rough criteria for preferring one version to another. This problem of evaluation probably exists in implicit form for the child learning to speak. How does he judge the adequacy of his inductions? He can see how well they anticipate what others say. He can construct new utterances and see whether others appear to find them acceptable and comprehensible. He can ask direct metalinguistic questions: "Mother, can one say 'The carriage is tired'?"

CHILD GRAMMAR AS A REDUCTION OF ADULT GRAMMAR

The provisional grammar we have written for Eve is not a grammar of adult English. Most of the utterances it generates are not, for us, grammatical sentences. We cannot accept "That horsie" or "Kitty all gone" or "There Mummy hair" or "Two chair." Words that seem to be syntactically equivalent for Eve are not so for us. For example, the words *see* and *that* are members of class 1 for Eve and equivalent in that they can precede class 2 words such as *doggie, dollie,* etc. For the adult who might say "That is a doggie" and "I see a doggie," *that* and *see* are syntactically unlike. For Eve the word *two* is roughly equivalent to *the* and *a,* but that is because she does not pluralize count nouns. It is clear that Eve does not speak adult English, and so we cannot use an adult English grammar to describe her speech. It would be quite misleading to list Eve's *that* as a demonstrative pronoun and her *see* as a transitive verb though that is a correct classification of these words in adult English.

Since the speech of the younger children in our set of 13 is clearly not English, it is necessary to "discover" the grammar that is implied by their utterances. We have not in this first try collected large enough corpuses to write convincing grammars. However, for the younger children it does look as if we might manage with about 1500 different utterances to get a good provisional grammar. The prospect of "discovering" grammars for the older children is not nearly so good. Since the older children have larger vocabularies and longer utterances, there is less of the recurrence that is the basis of a structural analysis. The anthropological linguist who wants to describe adult usage in an unfamiliar language is likely to try something like 1,000 hours of speech, and there are times when we fear that not very much less than this would suffice for children of about 3 years.

The speech of the children in our collection who are nearly 3 years old is mostly English. They produce acceptable simple sentences. Furthermore, these simple sentences correspond very well with the set of English sentences for which a satisfactory generative grammar has been written by Chomsky (1957) and Lees (1960). For these records, then, it does not seem necessary to "discover" the grammar; it is quite reasonable to analyze them in terms of the syntactic categories of the adult grammar. We have done this job, classifying utterances under headings: copular sentences, transitive verb sentences, intransitive verb sentences, sentences with modal auxiliaries, sentences with progressives, sentences with preliminary verbs, imperatives, negatives, Wh-interrogatives, Yes-No interrogatives, and unclassifiable fragments.

When this analysis in terms of an adult grammar had been done for the most advanced records, we realized that it could, with some additional assumptions, be extended to the records of all the other children. For the striking fact about the utterances of the younger children, when they are approached from the vantage point of adult grammar, is that they are almost all classifiable as grammatical sentences from which certain morphemes have been omitted. You may have noticed that while Eve's sentences are not grammatically "complete" they are somehow intelligible as abbreviated or telegraphic versions of familiar constructions. "Mummy hair" and "Daddy car" seem only to omit the possessive inflection. Both "Chair broken" and "That horsie" become acceptable copular sentences if we leave the word-order intact and fill in *is* and *a* or *the*. We have, therefore, analyzed all of the records in terms of English simple sentences by assigning each utterance to the sentence-type it most closely approximates.

We have not yet hit on any good techniques for summarizing our compendious data, but one illustrative table (Table 13) will make a few im-

TABLE 13

Estimates of Mean Utterance Length and Reports on Selected Grammatical Forms for 13 Children

Name of Child	Age in Months	Mean Number Morphemes*	*Be* in Progressive	Modal Auxiliaries *will* or *can*
Andy	26	2.0	no	no
Betty	31½	2.1	no	no
Charlie	22	2.2	no	no
Adam	28½	2.5	no	no
Eve	25½	2.6	no	no
Fanny	31½	3.2	yes	no
Grace	27	3.5	yes	yes
Helen	30	3.6	yes	yes
Ian	31½	3.8	yes	yes
June	35½	4.5	yes	yes
Kathy	30½	4.8	yes	yes
Larry	35½	4.8	yes	yes
Jimmy	32	4.9	yes	yes

* Mean count from 100 consecutive utterances.

portant points. For each child we made an estimate of the mean length of utterances by counting morphemes from 100 consecutive utterances occurring in midmorning. From this count we thought it wise to omit the single-word rejoinders and exclamations: *No, Ok, Yeah,* and *Oh* since these are sometimes emitted many times in succession by speakers of any age, and if the small utterance sample happened to include such a repeating circuit the estimate would be very unrepresentative. The estimates appear in Table 13, and the children's names appear in an order of increasing average utterance length. This order is related to the chronological age order but not identical with it. An age-related increase in the mean length of utterances is, of course, one of the best established facts in the study of child speech (McCarthy, 1954). There is, however, no reason to expect perfect correspondence with age. We conceive of developmental sequence as a Guttman scale with performances following an invariant order but not

TABLE 14

Imitations of Spoken Sentences

Model Sentence	Eve, 25½	Adam, 28½	Helen, 30	Ian, 31½	Jimmy, 32	June, 35½
1. I showed you the book.	I show book.	(I show) book.	C	I show you the book.	C	Show you the book.
2. I am very tall.	(My) tall.	I (very) tall.	I very tall.	I'm very tall.	Very tall.	I very tall.
3. It goes in a big box.	Big box.	Big box.	In big box.	It goes in the box.	C	C
4. Read the book.	Read book.	Read book.	—	Read (a) book.	Read a book.	C
5. I am drawing a dog.	Drawing dog.	I draw dog.	I drawing dog.	Dog.	C	C
6. I will read the book.	Read book.	I will read book.	I read the book.	I read the book.	C	C
7. I can see a cow.	See cow.	I want see cow.	C	Cow.	C	C
8. I will not do that again.	Do again.	I will that again.	I do that.	I again.	C	C
9. I do not want an apple.	I do apple.	I do a apple.	—	I do not want apple.	I don't want a apple.	I don't want apple.
10. Do I like to read books?	To read book?	I read books?	I read books?	I read book?	C	C
11. Is it a car?	't car?	Is it car?	Car?	That a car?	Is it car?	C
12. Where does it go?	Where go?	Go?	Does it go?	Where do it go?	C	C
13. Where shall I go?	Go?	—	—	C	C	C

NOTE.—C means imitation correct. —— indicates that no intelligible imitation was obtained. ( ) indicates that the transcription was uncertain.

pegged to particular ages. The sequence can be covered at varying rates of speed; the rate would be a function of intelligence and learning opportunities.

When the analyzed records are ordered by mean utterance length, it becomes apparent that children all "reduce" English sentences in similar fashion. If the utterances of one child are, on the average, shorter than the utterances of another child, then, of course, the first child will be omitting some morphemes that the second child is producing. However, utterances could be shortened by omitting any morphemes at all; there are many ways to abbreviate sentences, and it is perfectly conceivable that individual children would hit on different ways. They do not do so. We have checked all the records for progressive constructions (e.g., "I am going to town"). Without exception, children whose mean utterance length is below 3.2 form this construction by omitting the forms of the verb *to be* (e.g., "I going"). We have checked sentences in which the verb would, for an adult, ordinarily require such a modal auxiliary as *will* or *can* (e.g., "I will park the car"). Children whose mean utterance length is below 3.5 invariably form these sentences by omitting modals ("I park the car" or "I go outside" or "I make a tower"). In general, it appears that children whose speech is not yet English are using grammars which are systematic derivatives of adult grammar and that the particular features of the derivative grammar are predictable from the mean length of utterance.

The abbreviation effect can be more directly studied in the utterances a child produces when he is asked to repeat back a sentence said by an adult. For the last six cases we presented 13 simple sentences of various

TABLE 15

Summary of Results with Sentence Imitations

Name and Age of Child	Number of Morphemes Imitated Correctly in Each of Three Serial Positions			Mean Length of Imitations (in morphemes)
	Initial	Middle	Final	
Eve, 25½	4	5	12	2.2
Adam, 28½	9	3	12	3.1
Helen, 30	6	8	9	3.7
Ian, 31½	9	7	12	3.5
Jimmy, 32	12	11	13	5.0
June, 35½	12	13	13	4.9
Per cent correctly imitated	70%	64%	96%	
Mean length of model sentences ..				5.2

NOTE.—The difference between initial and final positions is significant by sign test (two-tailed) with $p = .032$; the difference between middle and final positions is significant with $p = .062$; the difference between initial and middle positions is not significant.

grammatical types and ask the subject to "Say what I say." Half of the sentences were presented at the end of the morning session and half at the end of the afternoon session. For each child a different random order was presented. The sentences were spoken slowly and carefully and always by the same investigator. The child had the microphone directly in front of him, and so good recordings were made. Table 14 presents the first efforts of each child, and Tables 15 and 16 a summary of the main results.

TABLE 16

Percentages Correctly Imitated of Morphemes in Various Syntactic Classes

Syntactic Class	Correctly Imitated
Classes Having Few Members in English	
Inflections	44%
Pronouns	72
Articles	39
Modal auxiliaries	56
Copular verbs (*to be*)...................................	33
Classes Having Many Members in English	
Nouns	100
Adjectives	92
Main verbs	85

NOTE.—Using tests for differences between two percentages, the percentage correct in each of the classes with many members is significantly greater than the percentage correct in any of the classes with few members ($p < .001$, 2-tailed test).

With increasing age, children produce more imitations that are morphemically identical with the original. With increasing age, the imitative utterances produced include larger numbers of morphemes—approaching the numbers in the model sentences. The morphemes produced are invariably in their original order. Omissions do not appear to be random or idiosyncratic. On the contrary, it looks as if, across children and across sentences, there is a consistent tendency to retain one kind of morpheme and drop another kind. The two sorts of morphemes contrast on several correlated dimensions. The morphemes most likely to be retained are: morphemes that occur in final position in the sentence; morphemes that are reference-making forms; morphemes that belong mainly to the large and expandable noun, verb, and adjective parts-of-speech;[6] morphemes that are relatively unpredictable from the context; and morphemes that receive the heavier stresses in ordinary English pronunciation. The morphemes least likely to

---

[6] Aborn and Rubenstein (1956) have published evidence that, in six-word sentences, nouns are most frequent in final sentence position whereas function words tend to be most frequent in the fourth and fifth positions. This tie between position and part-of-speech is found also, and not by our intention, in the sentences we provided for imitation.

be retained are: morphemes that occur in intermediate positions in the sentence; morphemes that are not reference-making forms; morphemes that belong to such small-sized grammatical categories as the articles, modal auxiliaries, and inflections; morphemes that are relatively predictable from context and so carry little information; and morphemes that receive the weaker stresses in ordinary English pronunciation. This does indeed seem to be telegraphic English. There is substantial support for our findings in the results with sentence repetition for 100 children at ages 2 and 3 obtained by Gesell and his associates (1940) and also in work of Stutsman (1926).

Let us suppose that very young children speak a rather uniform telegraphic English. How do they come by it? It is conceivable that they hear it from adults, that they are imitating a "baby talk" which is an adult invention. We have on our tapes a large quantity of speech from mother to child, and, while this material has not yet been transcribed or analyzed, it is quite clear that Eve's mother and the mothers of the other children do not usually use telegraphic English. The very young children are exposed to a much more complicated grammar than they use and the older children to a somewhat more complicated grammar than they use.

While it seems safe to say that children do not learn their telegraphic English from adults, it is probably also safe to say that the average adult can do a good job of producing telegraphic English if he is asked to talk like a baby. We have even heard a 3-year-old drop his more mature grammar in speaking to a 2-year-old and produce a very good version of the 2-year-old's speech. It is an old observation of linguists that the "baby talk" version of a language is very uniform from one adult to another. We can see good reasons why this should be so. If there is something about the operation of the child mind that causes each child to "reduce" English in a similar form, then adults everywhere could learn the same sort of baby talk from their own children. It is even possible, of course, that baby talk in all languages shows certain stable features, e.g., omission of low-information, predictable forms. If, in addition, baby talk is a systematic transformation of adult simple sentences accomplished by the omission of certain kinds of words, then an adult should be able to throw some simple mental switch that activates the baby grammar.

A basic factor causing the child's reduction of adult sentences is surely an upper limit on some kind of immediate memory span for the situation in which the child is imitating and a similar limit of programming span for the situation in which the child is constructing sentences. A comparison of the mean lengths of utterances produced as imitations (presented in Table 15) with the mean lengths of spontaneously produced utterances from the same children (presented in Table 13) shows that the paired values are very close and that neither is consistently higher. An increasing span for random digits is so reliably related to increasing age as to be a part of the Stanford-Binet test (e.g., a span of two digits at 30 months, three at 36, four at 54 months are the norms). Munn summarizes the results of many studies by saying: "That the memory span of children increases with age has been shown for all kinds of material investigated" (1954, p. 413). We know from Blankenship's review of memory span work (1938) and from Miller's discussion of "the magical number seven" (1956) that it is not yet possible to reduce the various measures of span to a common unit (bits) and thereby reconcile variations in the data. But there does seem to be ample indication that one-or-more memory spans show a steady increase in early childhood. It is this limitation of span in children for which the work of the descriptive linguist provided no parallel, and our obsession with linguistic technique long diverted us from recognizing the systematically derivative nature of child speech.

Span limitation is probably the factor compelling children to reduce adult sentences, but it does not, of course, account for the systematic tendency to drop one sort of morpheme and retain another sort. Because the two sorts of morphemes differ in numerous correlated respects, there are many conceivable explanations for the child's selective performance, and this will be so until the variables are experimentally separated. Here are a few of the many ways in which the story can now be put together. Perhaps the human mind operates on an unlearned "recency" principle, and English sentences (maybe also sentences in other languages) are nicely adapted to this principle in that the least predictable, most informative words fall usually into the final position. Perhaps, on the other hand, the "recency" effect in human serial learning is an acquired tendency to pay particular attention to material in final position, a tendency acquired from the fact that sentences are so constructed as to place in that position words carrying a lot of information. Perhaps it is differential stress that selects what the child will reproduce and sentences are nicely adapted to this predilection in that the heavier stresses fall on the less predictable forms. Or perhaps it is some combination of these ideas.

CONCLUSION

This paper began with an argument that the correct English sentences produced by a child are not good evidence that he possesses construction rules for the reason that we can never be sure that a correct sentence is not directly copied from a model. It seemed to us that systematic errors and manipulation of invented words were better evidence, as a child is not likely to have had exact models for these. In the second section of the paper we discussed techniques for inducing construction rules or a generative grammar from the child's natural speech. Since this speech, for Eve at least, is not good English, it can be argued that she had no models for it and so it is legitimate to infer rules from such data. In the third section, however, we have seen that child speech can be rather well characterized as a systematic reduction of adult speech, and so, after all, there were models for Eve's sentences. She could have learned most of them by selective imitation if not by imitation per se.

Eventually children must do more than imitate and memorize if only because there is not enough time for them to learn as particular verbal responses all the sentences they will be able as adults to produce and evaluate as to grammaticality. (For a detailed statement of this argument, see Bruner, 1957, p. 156; or Miller, Galanter, and Pribram, 1960, pp. 146-147.) In addition to the logical argument that children must learn construction rules in view of their terminal linguistic achievement, there is much empirical evidence that children older than Eve do, in fact, learn construction rules. Some of this evidence is available to every parent in a child's systematic errors (*sheeps, I bringed,* etc.), and some of it has been collected in a controlled fashion by Berko (1958) and by Brown and Berko (1960).

While children must and do eventually induce construction rules, it is not necessary that they do so from the very earliest age at which words are combined. Eve, after all, is not yet prepared to produce an infinite set of sentences, nor, so far as we know, is she able to distinguish all grammatical sequences from ungrammatical sequences. It is possible that for the earliest linguistic accomplishments one sort of learning theory will serve—a theory developed largely from the study of animal behavior—while for later accomplishments a completely different theory will be necessary—a theory permitting the inductive formation of syntactic classes that generalize far beyond obtained information. However, it is also possible that the induction of rules goes on from the very first. Eve, for example, produces such utterances as "Two chair" and "Kitty all gone" which could conceivably be either direct or selective imitations, but might very easily be constructions resulting from overgeneralized rules for the use of *two* and *all gone.* For a single example, we will show how Eve might be forming construction rules at the same time that she is practicing selective imitation without this construction process being clearly revealed in the present data.

Selective reduction might cause Eve to imitate "That is a doggie" as "That doggie"; "That is a horsie" as "That horsie"; and "See the doggie" as "See doggie." At this point induction could operate and she might, because the context "That ———" is shared by "doggie" and "horsie," assume that the other context "See ———" can be shared and so form the utterance "See horsie." It is quite possible that the child reduces first, then forms inductive generalizations, and makes new utterances on the model of his reductions.

It will often happen if the above suggestion is correct that a child will find forms syntactically equivalent that are not so for the adult. Suppose Eve heard the sentence "I see the man" and reduced it to "See man." The original demonstrates the nonequivalence of *see* and *that* since *see* occurs after a pronoun, and, in addition, the original version does not justify adding *man* to the list started with *doggie* and *horsie*. The reduced sentence, on the other hand, leaves *see* equivalent to *that* and suggests that *man* belongs with *doggie* and *horsie*. If a child induces a grammar from its own reduced sentences, it should generally lose the distributional detail provided by such morphemes as *an, the, will, do,* and */-z/*. The result would be syntactic classes not identical with those of adult speech, few in number and large in size. In addition there would be loss of numerous semantic distinctions, e.g., the difference between "See the man" and "I see the man." It is important to note, however, that the gross sense of a sentence will usually be retained; e.g., in "See man" as in "I see the man" it is clear that *man* is the object of seeing. The crude sense of the sentence is generally recoverable from the child's reduction for the reason that one profound dimension of English grammar is perfectly preserved in telegraphese, and that dimension is word order.

For the present, then, we are working with the hypothesis that child speech is a systematic reduction of adult speech largely accomplished by omitting function words that carry little information. From this corpus of reduced sentences we suggest that the child induces general rules which govern the construction of new utterances. As a child becomes capable (through maturation and the consolidation of frequently occurring sequences) of registering more of the detail of adult speech, his original rules will have to be revised and supplemented. As the generative grammar grows more complicated and more like the adult grammar, the child's speech will become capable of expressing a greater variety of meanings.

EXPLORATIONS IN GRAMMAR EVALUATION [1]

ROGER BROWN, COLIN FRASER,[2]
and URSULA BELLUGI
Harvard University

In the 1961 edition of Gleason's *An Introduction to Descriptive Linguistics* the following paragraph appears:

> The difference between a description of a corpus and of a language is partly a matter of scope. A corpus consists of a few thousand sentences. A language might be considered as consisting of a very large number of sentences—all those, either already spoken or not yet used, which would be ac-

[1] The work described in this paper was supported by the National Science Foundation by a grant administered through the Center for Communication Sciences, Massachusetts Institute of Technology.

[2] Now at the University of Exeter, Exeter, England.

cepted by native speakers as "belonging" to that language. Even the largest corpus can be only an infinitesimal portion of the language (pp. 196-197).[3]

In the summer of 1961 we collected 26 hours of speech in one week from a 24-month-old boy whom we are calling Abel. In 26 hours Abel produced 2,081 different utterances. These utterances are a corpus and Abel is a native speaker. The problem is to find Abel's *language*.

Here are fragments of two additional paragraphs from Gleason:

> A second corpus of roughly comparable scope should also exemplify a similarly high percentage of the pertinent constructional patterns. This being the case, the greater part of the grammatical features of either corpus should be shared by the other.
>
> This gives a test for a grammar. It is only necessary to elicit another sample, independent of the first. If the grammar fits the new corpus equally well, it is highly probable that it is correct (p. 201).

A grammar is a set of generalizations induced from given data but going beyond the given data. Consequently a grammar makes predictions. From things already said, a grammar predicts things likely to be said and things not likely to be said. For the linguist working with adults an important test of the grammar written from one corpus is its ability to anticipate the sentences of a new corpus. This test is also available to the student of child speech.

The prediction test has never been made precise. The linguist in the field does not write down alternative grammars, generate predictions, and keep track of outcomes. He works at a single grammar, revising it so as to accommodate new data, but never subjecting it to an explicit, comparative, quantitative evaluation. Is such an evaluation possible? We are able to imagine some relevant calculations, and, being empirical mathematicians who do not know what numbers will do until they do it, we decided to work through some exercises with Abel's utterances.

The transcribed utterances were divided into two sets: one consisted of the utterances produced in 15 hours (the 15-hour corpus) and the other of utterances produced in 11 hours (the 11-hour corpus). The division was made in such a way as to guarantee that the two sets were similar to one another in the proportions of speech taken from each day and from each time of day. It was our plan to study first the 15-hour corpus and, from this study, to write grammatically rules whose predictions would be tested against the utterances obtained in the 11-hour corpus.

We began with a restricted grammar written from a subset of the utterances in the 15-hour corpus. The subset consisted of all two-word utter-

---

[3] This statement does not represent Gleason's final opinion but is for him, as for us, the starting point of an extended argument. In chapter 13 of *An Introduction to Descriptive Linguistics* (1961) the reader will find Gleason's full discussion of the relation between language and grammars.

ances created from a list of 79 words which were selected because they occurred frequently and in a variety of contexts. The restricted grammar was written from and designed to generate all of the two-word utterances using the given lexicon of 79 words in the 15-hour corpus, and it was tested by its ability to anticipate such utterances in the 11-hour corpus. The subset of utterances was chosen so as to reveal with maximal clarity certain problems that arise in the evaluation of any grammars written from the speech of very young children.

TABLE I

The Sample Lexicon

a	blanket	cookie	George	need	shovel	this
Abel	block	cup	get	nice	sock	throw
all	boat	Da	glass	no	some	two
another	book	Daddy	hat	on	soup	up
away	box	down	here	one	sweep	want
Baby	bubble-drink	draw	in	orange	swim	water
ball	bye-bye	eat	jump	paper	table	where
bathtub	cake	eye	man	pencil	telephone	
bed	car	find	milk	penny	tiger	
bell	chair	firetruck	Mommie	pillow	that	
big	clean	for	more	ring	the	
bike	coffee	fork	my	see	there	

The lexicon of 79 words appears as Table 1. On the distributional evidence (see Brown and Fraser) of the 15-hour corpus the 79 words were placed in 13 syntactic classes. There were five residual words which had little in common with the members of any syntactic class or with one another, and these must be dealt with individually. Adult speakers of English use a terminal sibilant inflection to pluralize regular count nouns and to mark the third-person present indicative of regular verbs. Abel sometimes used such an inflection, but he would add it to mass nouns as well as to count nouns and to any verb in any person. We provided for these possibilities by allowing a terminal [s] to occur with any member of four syntactic classes: count nouns, mass nouns, transitive verbs, intransitive verbs. This rule has the effect of entering each noun and verb into a lexicon twice and so brings the total number of words to 128. The classified lexicon appears as Table 2.

In order to determine how Abel combined the lexical items to form two-word utterances, we constructed the matrix of Table 3 in which the 13 classes and 5 residual words are listed on each axis. The abscissa is the word in initial position, and the ordinate the word in second position. An "X" means that one or more combinations of the type indicated occurred

TABLE 2

The Lexicon Distributed among Word Classes

Word Class	Lexicon
Definite articles (Art$_d$)	*my, the, two*
Indefinite articles (Art$_i$)	*a, another*
Descriptive adjectives (Adj)	*big, nice*
Count nouns (N$_c$)	*ball, bathtub, bed, bell, bike, blanket, block, boat, book, box, cake, car, chair, cookie, cup, eye, fire-truck, fork, glass, hat, jump, man, orange, pencil, penny, pillow, ring, shovel, sock, table, telephone, tiger* (Plus *-s*)
Mass nouns (N$_m$)	*bubble-drink, coffee, milk, paper, soup, water* (Plus *-s*)
Proper nouns (N$_p$)	*Abel, George, Baby, Mommie, Daddy, Da*
Intransitive verbs (V$_{in}$)	*sweep, swim* (Plus *-s*)
Transitive verbs (V$_t$)	*clean, draw, eat, find, get, need, see, throw, want* (Plus *-s*)
Locatives (Loc)	*here, there*
Demonstrative pronouns (Pro$_d$) ...	*this, that*
Prepositions 1 (Pr$_1$)	*away, down, up*
Prepositions 2 (Pr$_2$)	*in, on*
Qualifiers	*all, more, some*
Others	*where, for, bye-bye, no, one*

(e.g., Art$_d$ + N$_c$), and a blank that no combinations of the type indicated occurred (e.g., N$_c$ + Art$_d$).

From this matrix it is possible to write a rule for each class and each residual word describing the classes and words that have followed it and those that have preceded it. These rules may be considered a two-word grammar which produces all of the 371 two-word combinations of the designated lexicon. In addition, of course, the grammar generalizes the distributional facts of the 371 utterances since it permits the formation of all utterances of a given type if at least one utterance of that type has actually occurred.

It was then possible to determine the total number of combinations predicted by the rules. For example: there are three definite articles (*my, the,* and *two*). The first rule says that each of these can occur with any count noun (32 in the singular and 32 in the plural, or 64). Multiplying 3 × 64 yields 192 possible combinations of the type: Art$_d$ + N$_c$. The three definite articles can also occur with all of the six mass nouns in either the singular or plural, and the result is 3 × 12, or 36 additional sentences. Finally, the

TABLE 3

The Matrix of Two-Word Combinations

Word	Art_d	Art_l	Adj	N_c	N_m	N_p	V_{in}	V_t	Loc	Pro_d	Pr_1	Pr_2	Qual	*Where*	*For*	*By-bye*	*No*	*One*
Art_d					X													
Art_l																		
Adj				X	X													
N_c	X	X	X	X	X	X		X	X	X	X	X	X	X		X	X	X
N_m	X		X	X	X	X		X	X	X	X	X	X			X	X	X
N_p	X		X			X	X	X	X	X	X	X	X	X			X	X
V_{in}		X	X	X	X	X		X		X								
V_t		X	X	X	X	X		X	X	X								
Loc			X	X							X	X						
Pro_d											X							
Pr_1		X	X	X		X				X						X	X	
Pr_2		X					X											
Qual		X	X	X	X	X	X	X			X	X				X	X	
Where										X								
For																		
Bye-bye																		
No																X		
One	X				X	X												

NOTE.—"X" indicates that utterances of this type occurred.

grammar says that the three articles can occur with the six proper nouns, which is 18 more. The total number of utterances predicted by the first rule is then: 192 + 36 + 18, or 246. Proceeding in this fashion through all the rules, we found that the grammar as a whole generates 13,154 different utterances.

We looked next at the utterances of the 11-hour corpus selecting out all of the two-word combinations made up from the original lexicon. There are 90 exact repetitions of utterances from the original 371; 105 utterances predicted by the grammar but not in the original set; eight not predicted by the grammar. Clearly this grammar predicts most of the events of the second set that fall within its purview. Is it then a good grammar? Is it a better description of Abel's behavior than some other possible description?

We decided first to compare the grammar with a maximally general and simple prediction, a prediction of all possible combinations of two forms drawn from the lexicon. The total number of possible combinations is 16,384, and this figure includes 3,230 combinations not predicted by the grammar. For the obtained utterances of the second set the total-combinations rule predicts all 203 whereas the grammar predicts 203 — 8, or 195.

As a third comparison we decided to consider the obtained 371 utterances of the first set as predictors of the second set. What happens if we simply say that Abel does with two-word combinations in one corpus what he does with such combinations in the other corpus. In the second set there are 90 exact repetitions of utterances in the first set, and these are the only utterances predicted; the remaining 113 are not predicted. The numbers for the various kinds of combinations appear in Table 4.

TABLE 4

Two-Word Combinations in the 15-Hour Corpus and in the 11-Hour Corpus

15-Hour Corpus

Number of forms in lexicon	128
Obtained combinations	371
Combinations grammar predicts	13,154
All possible combinations	16,384
Possible combinations not predicted by grammar	3,230

11-Hour Corpus

Number of forms in lexicon	128
Obtained combinations	203
Exact repetitions	90
Predicted by grammar but not repetitions	105
Not predicted by grammar but obtained	8

Clearly it is to the credit of a grammar if occurring utterances are predicted, and to its discredit if occurring utterances are not predicted. On first thought, then, we might express the value of a grammar as the ratio of occurrences predicted to occurrences not predicted. The three ratios for the grammar, the total-combinations rule, and the original list rule appear in Table 5 under the heading "Ratio A."

The total-combinations rule has the largest ratio, of course, since it predicts everything conceivable. The grammar is next best, and the first set of utterances is least good. This index alone must therefore be insufficient since it would always lead us to prefer the same description—all possible combinations of items. This first ratio (A) offers a translation of one requirement of a grammar—production of all grammatical sentences—which is rendered as prediction of all obtained utterances. However there is a second requirement of a grammar—production of no ungrammatical sentences. We will try rendering this second requirement as: prediction of no utterances that do not occur.

Clearly it is to the credit of a grammar if utterances not occurring are not predicted. But what is the number of utterances not occurring and not

TABLE 5

Possible Grammar-Evaluating Ratios

Ratio A—Prediction of All Grammatical Sentences

Value$_A$ of grammar	=	Occurrences predicted / Occurrences, not predicted		
Grammar	=	195 /	8	=	24.38
All possible combinations	=	203 /	0	=	∞
First set of utterances	=	90 /	113	=	.80

Ratio B—Prediction of No Ungrammatical Sentences

Value$_B$ of grammar	=	Nonoccurrences, not predicted / Nonoccurrences, predicted		
Grammar	=	3,222 / 12,959	=	.25
All possible combinations	=	0 / 16,181	=	0
First set of utterances	=	15,900 / 281	=	56.58

predicted? We decided to interpret this notion as utterances conceivable in terms of the designated lexicon and the limitation on length, but yet not predicted by the grammar and not occurring in the sample. In the present case there are 3,230 such conceivable utterances (predicted by the rule of total combinations) which were not predicted by the grammar. Of these 3,230, only eight were obtained, and so 3,230 — 8, or 3,222, is the number of utterances not predicted and not occurring. Because these utterances are to the credit of the grammar, we entered them as the numerator of ratio B.

Utterances not occurring but predicted are to the discredit of a grammar. The present grammar predicted a total of 13,154 combinations, and, of these, 195 occurred. This leaves 13,154 — 195, or 12,959 combinations that were predicted but failed to occur. Because this number tells against the grammar, it is entered as the denominator of the new ratio.

A ratio of this second kind was also calculated for the total-combinations rule. For this rule there are no nonoccurrences not predicted since all conceivable combinations are predicted. There are very many nonoccurrences that are predicted (16,181). The numerator, which expresses the fact that nonoccurrences cannot be to the credit of this rule, causes the ratio for the total-combinations rule to have a value of zero. The total-combinations rule which does a perfect job of producing all grammatical (obtained) sentences is no good at all when it comes to not producing ungrammatical sentences.

Consider now the same ratio B for the list of utterances from the first set. There are very many combinations which do not occur and are not predicted (15,900), and a relatively small number of predictions that fail (281). The first set of utterances which is not very good at producing all grammatical sentences is the best of the three at not predicting ungrammatical sentences. Note that if the ratios were calculated for the total corpus the value of ratio B for the list would be infinity, since there would be no non-occurrences predicted.

Ratios A and B operationalize the two requirements of a generative grammar, and the summary of Table 6 shows how the three descriptions stand with respect to both requirements. A grammar is good in the degree that it is able to generate all the utterances that occur without generating any that do not occur. The rule of total combinations perfectly satisfies the former requirement but completely fails to satisfy the latter. The first set of utterances perfectly satisfies the second requirement but completely fails to satisfy the first requirement. Only the grammar can, in some degree, meet both requirements, and that is a reason for preferring the grammar to either the rule of total combinations or the first set of utterances as a description of what Abel knows. However, from the 15-hour corpus one could write a large number of grammars alternative to the one presented here but equally well adapted to the data of that corpus. Let us see why this is so.

TABLE 6

Values of the Three Descriptions for the Two Ratios

Description	Ratio A	Ratio B
Grammar	24.38	.25
Total combinations	∞	0
First set of utterances	.80	56.58
		(∞ for total corpus)

Consider the grammatical rule: $N_c + N_c$. This rule permits any count noun to go with any count noun, and since there are 64 count nouns in the lexicon (including both singular and plural forms) the rule generates 64 × 64, or 4,096 combinations. The rule is a generalization of a small number of such actual occurrences as: "baby boat," "book bed," and "chair Mommie." What rules other than the rule $N_c + N_c$ will cover these occurrences? At one extreme there is the rule that simply summarizes the obtained utterances: Nouns-occurring-in-first-position (No_1) + Nouns-occurring-in-second-position (No_2). This rule exactly describes utterances of a certain type in the 15-hour corpus, but it does not generalize at all and so will fail to anticipate the utterances of the 11-hour corpus. What generalized rules other than $N_c + N_c$ might be written?

In principle one could write general rules in terms of any categories into which No_1 and No_2 can be placed. Suppose that all the No_1 happened to begin with the letter "p" and all of the No_2 with the letter "q." One could generalize the facts as: $N_p + N_q$. This degree of distributional consistency with regard to a grammatically irrelevant attribute is not likely to exist in any real corpus. However, there would always be some degree of consistency in terms of initial letters or final letters or length-of-word that could be generalized into a predictive rule.

In writing rules for Abel, we only consider word categories that had a grammatical function in adult English and count nouns are one such category. However there are other noun categories. The majority of the combinations $No_1 + No_2$ are made up of an initial noun naming some animate being (N_{an}) and a subsequent noun naming something inanimate (N_{inan}). It seems likely that these combinations are "telegraphic" versions of a possessive construction. In adult English it is necessary, for syntactic reasons, to distinguish N_{an} from other sorts of nouns. Suppose then that we were to drop the $N_c + N_c$ rule from Abel's grammar and replace it with the rule: $N_{an} + N_{inan}$.

Since N_{an} are much less numerous in Abel's lexicon than are N_c, the new rule would greatly reduce the number of predicted combinations. Since most of these predicted combinations did not occur in the 11-hour corpus, the denominator of ratio B would go down and the value of ratio B would go up. However, the new rule fails to generate a few of the utterances in the 15-hour corpus that are generated by the old rule. For example, "book bed" and "chair Mommie" are covered by $N_c + N_c$ but not by $N_{an} + N_{inan}$. In the 11-hour corpus, too, a few utterances occur which the old rule covered but which the new rule does not cover. These then become "occurrences, not predicted," and they must be added into the denominator of ratio A. The result is that this ratio goes down. In the above example, then, one cannot simultaneously maximize both ratios. The cost of making the grammar less general is to make it less adequate to the facts.

It is not logically necessary that a less general rule be less adequate to the facts. If all of the members of No_1 in both corpuses had been animate nouns and if all the members of No_2 had been inanimate nouns, then the rule $N_c + N_c$ and the rule $N_{an} + N_{inan}$ would have been equally adequate though unequally general. In such circumstances the choice is clear—the less general formulation is to be preferred. However these circumstances are rare with Abel's utterances. The usual case is that improving the value of the grammar in terms of one criterion entails a certain cost in terms of the other criterion.

We have explored these problems of evaluation for grammars written from all of Abel's utterances as well as for grammars written from only the subset of two-word utterances. When all the utterances of the 15-hour corpus are considered, the size of the lexicon increases and the range in utterance length is from one to four words. With these increases the number of possible combinations runs into billions. It is possible to write a grammar that will cover all of the obtained utterances and yet will fall far short of generating this set of possible combinations. But the least general grammar that is adequate to all the utterances generates many millions of possibilities.

If we insist on generating all utterances, on using only categories that are relevant to grammar, and on preferring the least general set of rules that will meet these conditions, the choice of a grammar becomes reasonably determinate. Perhaps this is what we should do. It would mean crediting Abel with a machinery for generating millions of utterances. He may have such machinery. However, it is not obvious that one should insist on covering every obtained utterance when the cost of doing so is to predict astronomically large numbers of utterances that have not been obtained.

Here is a final quotation from Gleason (1961). "The occurrence of a sentence in a carefully elicited corpus is prima-facie evidence that the sentence does 'belong' to the language, but nothing more. Informants do make mistakes. Occasionally very bad sentences will occur" (p. 197). The linguist in the field commonly exempts his grammar from the obligation to cover certain ones of the utterances that have actually been obtained. If we allow ourselves to exclude utterances from Abel's 15-hour corpus, we can write less general grammars. But by what criteria does one select the utterances to be excluded?

An utterance produced by a child may be either a construction or a repetition. Only constructions should be consulted in formulating grammatical rules since these rules are intended to model the construction process. However, Brown and Fraser have argued that in the normal case of the child at home one cannot usually determine whether an utterance is a construction or a repetition. The basic difficulty is that one never knows exactly what a child has heard, and so any utterance, except certain errors, might be a repetition. If we had a rule for distinguishing constructions from repetitions in spontaneous speech, we would exclude repetitions from the corpus but the rule is hard to find.

Some of Abel's utterances immediately followed adult utterances which they closely resembled. Such seeming imitations are almost certainly repetitions rather than constructions, and we have excluded them in writing grammars. However a repetition need not immediately follow its model. When an utterance does not resemble anything that has immediately preceded it in the speech of others, how can one tell whether it is a construction or a well-practiced repetition of some earlier model?

Suppose we have a set of two-word utterances such that all the members have one word in common and the remaining words, which are not identical across the utterances, are drawn from the same part-of-speech. Abel produced many such sets. One of them is: "Big blocks," "Big boat," "Big car," "Big cookie," "Big fish," "Big man," "Big pockets." It seems likely that at least some of these two-word utterances have been constructed. It seems likely because the set establishes a very simple and definite pattern (Big + Noun) which makes new constructions very easy. We do not find it difficult to believe that Abel has abstracted this pattern and can commute nouns in the open position.

Abel also produced the two-word utterance: "Coffee cup." There were no other utterances of the type: *Coffee* + Noun, and none of the type: Noun + *cup*. There were, however, utterances of the type: Noun + Noun. It is possible that Abel constructed "Coffee cup" on that abstract model, but we feel that it is more likely that he has learned "Coffee cup" as a prefabricated whole, a repetition of a common adult utterance.

Some utterances, then, can be assigned to a recurrent type such that the type is partially defined by a particular word or words. Other words can only be assigned to recurrent types which are defined entirely in terms of word classes. We have a hunch (it is no more) that utterances which fall into the narrower, more concrete patterns are more likely to be constructed than utterances which can only be placed in abstract patterns. This hunch ultimately concerns what we think it reasonable to suppose that a 24-month-old child has learned to do.

Using the narrow sort of recurrence as a ground for excluding material from the 15-hour corpus, we have found it possible to write grammars that generate these more regular utterances of the corpus and only predict some thousands of utterances beyond those obtained. Such grammars, of course, fail to generate the many less regular utterances.

Some of us believe that the grammars which exclude the more intractable utterances come nearer to describing Abel's actual constructional competence than do the grammars that generate everything. However the exclusion criterion was fixed by pure hunch. A case can be made that it is just the odd utterance, the one that does not fall into any narrow recurrent type, that is most likely to have been constructed. The grammar-evaluation problem has not been solved.

Perhaps our problem has begun to seem rather "scholastic"—in the medieval sense. Is it sensible to worry about whether a child who has produced 2,000 utterances has a rule system for producing 50,000 utterances or 50,000,000 utterances? This problem seems particularly "scholastic" when you consider that the rule system would be likely to change before the child had time to turn out more than a fractional part of the supposed possibilities. However, you will grant that it can be reasonable and even practically important to determine whether a child knows how to add numbers. Suppose that the child cannot tell us anything about the addition process— and most children cannot. All he can do is operate with numbers. How would we decide whether or not he knew how to add?

The operation of addition predicts an infinite set of occurrences and an infinite set of nonoccurrences. If a child knows how to add, he will be prepared to say: "2 plus 2 are 4"; "12 plus 83,120 are 83,132"; "750 plus 91 are 841"; etc., and not to say: "2 plus 5 are 6"; "15 plus 19 are 22"; etc. We never hear a child say more than a triflingly small number of the acceptable utterances; yet we do not hesitate, on the basis of such evidence, to credit him with knowledge of addition. Furthermore most children will occasionally make a mistake; they will occasionally produce an incorrect sum. When that happens we do not feel that we must adjust our conception of the rules in the child's head so as to generate the unpredicted occurrence. We confidently exclude the difficult case from the corpus and decide that he knows how to add but sometimes makes computational errors. How do we come to be so confident here and so uncertain in the case of grammar?

The addition rule predicts more precisely than does a grammar. Given the numbers to be summed it generates the particular outcome. The chances of doing that if you have not got the correct rule are small, and that may be why we feel confident that the rule is right. A grammar, given the words to be made into a sentence, would in some extremely simple cases predict a particular outcome. Usually, however, the grammar would only generate a set of possible outcomes. For the particular sentence one must go beyond grammar to meaning and the motivation of a speaker. One difference between addition and grammar, then, seems to be in the precision of prediction.

There are rules other than the grammatical which only generate possibilities, rules that do not generate particular outcomes. Consider the rules for bidding in contract bridge. These rules do not tell us what a particular player will bid on a particular occasion, but they do permit one set of bids and proscribe another set. The class of permitted bids narrows with the accumulation of prior bids; if someone has bid "three diamonds," it is no longer acceptable to bid "two diamonds." However there is always more than one acceptable response.

Of course there are guides to intelligent bidding which do prescribe particular bids. In the case of language the particular sentence can only be prescribed by considering semantics and motivation in addition to grammar. The particular bid in bridge can only be prescribed by considering the hand the player holds as well as the rules of the game. The rules of bidding in themselves do not require that a bid be sensible, only that it be drawn from the population of lawful bids.

Suppose a player had not told us the rules of bidding, and most players could not easily do so. The player can only play, and we must judge whether he possesses the rules we have in mind. Even though these rules do not predict the particular bid, if the player repeatedly drew his bids from the class of possibilities, we would come to believe that he possessed the rules. I think we would not be convinced quite so quickly as in the case of addition, but it would not take very many games to persuade us that the player had the rules. If he then made a mistake, perhaps bidding "two diamonds" when it is not permitted to do so, we would not revise our conception of his knowledge so as to incorporate this deviant case. We would instead decide that he knew the rules of proper bidding but had lost track of the prior bids. How so?

There is a critical difference between the adding child or the bridgeplayer and the sentence-producing child. The child who has mistakenly said "2 plus 5 are 6" will sometimes correct himself or will accept our correction and agree that 2 plus 5 are 7. The bridgeplayer, if he is told that someone has already bid "three diamonds," will apologize for his "two diamonds" and offer instead an acceptable bid. We can be confident that these actions must be excluded from the corpus because they elicit a characteristic reaction from the person producing them. They are judged to be incorrect and so are separated out from the other sums or bids. The rule system identifies certain behavior as unlawful and the subject also identifies it as unlawful. It is very improbable that this would happen if our formulation of his rules were mistaken. It is chiefly because of this coincidence between the boundaries defined by the rules and the boundaries marked out by the subject that we can be so confident in attributing to him knowledge of bridge or of addition.

The linguist working with an adult informant gets reactions to utterances as well as the utterances themselves. The informant will sometimes stop and strike out an utterance following it with a corrected version. The linguist can test his hypotheses about the grammatical system by constructing possibly acceptable sentences and asking for judgments of grammaticality. The linguist is able to get judgments of the acceptability of behavior, and this is the kind of data that is so decisive for the adding child and the bridgeplayer. Can such data be obtained from very young children?

With Abel we were not successful in eliciting judgments of grammaticality. Of course there was no point in asking him whether an utterance was "grammatical" or "well-formed." We experimented with some possible childhood equivalents. The first step was to formulate tentative grammatical rules, and the next to construct some utterances that ought to have been acceptable if the rules were correct and other utterances that ought not to have been acceptable. For Abel "The cake" should have been grammatical and "Cake the" ungrammatical. How to ask? The experimenter said: "Some of the things I will say are silly and some are not. You tell me when I say something silly." Abel would not. If Abel had a sense of grammaticality, we were unable to find the word that would engage it. When do children begin to make judgments of grammaticality? We plan to find out.

How stands the problem of evaluating grammars written for the speech of children? There are two basic criteria: the grammar should generate as many as possible of the utterances that will be produced while generating as few as possible of the utterances that will not be produced. It is ordinarily the case that changing the grammar so as to better its performance with respect to one criterion entails a cost in that the change worsens the performance of the grammar with respect to the other criterion. It is not ordinarily possible to optimize performance on both criteria at the same time. There is no good rationale for pursuing one criterion to the neglect of the other. We might aim at achieving some minimal excellence in terms of both criteria but the setting of the acceptable levels would be quite arbitrary. It would be as if we tried to decide how many addition problems a child must solve correctly and how few incorrectly if he is to be credited with a knowledge of addition. A decision would be arbitrary and unsatisfactory.

The way out of this dilemma in the case of addition and also in the case of the linguist writing a grammar for adult speech is to obtain *reactions* as well as *actions*, reactions which judge the acceptability of actions. With one 24-month-old boy we could not obtain such reactions. Perhaps they can be obtained from older children. Children who are first combining words may not have a sense of grammaticality, and it may never be possible to settle on the best general description of their speech output.

Judgments of grammaticality and nongrammaticality are data for a grammar to fit; data in addition to occurrence and nonoccurrence. These additional data greatly reduce the number of conceivable grammars and so increase our confidence in any one that fits. It may be possible to obtain from children other kinds of data that will help to select among grammars, possibly data on the perception or comprehension of speech or data on imitation.

The psychologist working on computer simulation of cognitive pocesses has the same problem we have. If he simulates some single simple problem-solving performance, he cannot feel very sure that his simulation is similar to the information-processing of the human being because there will be a large number of alternative equally-adequate simulations. If the simulator increases the range of data he can generate, the number of alternative simulations will decrease and confidence in any one that works will increase. Of course with a greater range of data it is more difficult to create satisfactory generative rules. For the grammars of children, we have been setting ourselves too easy a task. We have not required very much of these grammars, and so they have not been very difficult to invent. But, also, there have been too many alternatives and no clear ground for choosing among them.

3

THE DEVELOPMENT FROM VOCAL TO VERBAL
BEHAVIOR IN CHILDREN

Margaret Bullowa, Lawrence Gaylord Jones,
and Thomas G. Bever[1]
Massachusetts Mental Health Center and *Harvard University*

This paper consists of a description of the research design for the study of language development which we have adopted. Vocal development of presumably normal babies is followed from birth by nonparticipant observation. The observations are made in the babies' own homes. The behavioral context in which each of the babies' recorded vocalizations takes place is specified. Detailed study of each child's development by independent observers makes it possible to relate vocal development to other aspects of the child's development in terms of maturational and environmental influences.

This study has been initiated because of concern with the verbal aspects of communication in the pathology and psychotherapy of schizophrenia. The link between normal speech development and the communication difficulties of schizophrenics is supported by the widely held impression that many of the phenomena of schizophrenia may be understood in terms of regression to less mature stages of development (Freud, 1914). It is also possible that deviations occur in the early speech development of people who later become schizophrenic. Knowledge of the details of the normal course of speech development is essential to detecting any such abnormalities in maturation. Since most schizophrenics give the general impression of speaking with normal articulation, possible deviation would have to be explored at the microlinguistic level. Schizophrenic language has long been known to have peculiarities in the ways in which words are used. More recently, note has been taken of peculiarities in tone of voice and other paralinguistic features connected with the expression of affect. The elucidation of these aspects of the pathology of schizophrenia cannot take place until the normal process is clearly defined and understood. It was the need for this information, not currently available in sufficient detail, which led to the initiation of these investigations.

[1] Principal Investigator, Linguist, and Acoustic Assistant. Study titled as above at Massachusetts Mental Health Center and Harvard University, Department of Psychiatry, supported by NIMH Research Grant, M-4300.

The *aims* of this investigation may be summarized as follows:

1. To study in the vocal productions of children the natural stages of development of two separable characteristics: (a) patterns observable in the paralinguistic features such as tone of voice, loudness, and rhythms, and (b) patterns observable in the phonemic features, the sound units out of which words are built. Both of these developing vocal patterns are to be related to speech patterns in the child's environment.

2. To determine whether a definite order of development can be demonstrated in the emergence of the child's ability to babble, use and recognize the phonemic contrasts of vocalization, i.e., to test the hypothesis concerning the step by step acquisition of speech sounds in children as set forth by Grégoire (1937) and elaborated by Jakobson (1941).

3. To study the mutual influence of the mother's and the child's speech patterns in the course of the child's development from vocalization to verbalization, with attention to the speech patterns of other members of the family and other environmental sounds.

4. To determine whether there is any consistent relationship between the child's development from vocal to verbal behavior patterns and the development of other behavior patterns.

METHOD

Subjects

The infants are selected before birth from an already well-studied population, the "Maternal-Infant Health Program" at the Boston Lying-In Hospital. This is a cooperating unit of the "Collaborative Study on Cerebral Palsy" under the National Institute for Nervous Diseases and Blindness. The use of this source provides normative data and protects us from unwittingly drawing conclusions from study of an unusual child. In order to obtain linguistically comparable data, the selection of subjects is controlled for certain characteristics. We have chosen to study first-born babies in families in which English has been the exclusive language used for three generations. We seek parents who are free from major physical and mental pathology. We prefer nonintellectual families to avoid undue concern with language development.

Developmental Observation

In order to be able to relate vocal development to maturational rather than chronological age, an independent team of observers assesses the progress of each child beginning at birth. The first examination is made immediately after delivery and includes specific tests of neurological adequacy and of sensory response to visual, auditory, tactile, and kinesthetic stimuli. These investigators hope to document individual differences in neonatal equipment. Two additional examinations are made during the lying-in period. The child is seen by this observation team in his own home at one week and three weeks after leaving the hospital and at four-week intervals thereafter throughout the study. Each observation is documented with about four minutes (100 feet) of black and white 16 mm film taken at 18 frames per second to show typical behavior and responses to tests. The findings are worked up independently by the child development observers, a psychiatrically trained pediatrician, and a senior child psychologist.[2]

This team is attempting to evaluate the impact of environmental influences on the innate equipment of each infant as it is reflected in all observable areas of his development. A prospective view of each child's personality and general development might lead to a better understanding of his use of speech as a specific response to his inner needs and his communication with his environment.

Vocal Observation

High fidelity tape recordings are taken weekly[3] during the first 30 months of life of four first-born infants. Each observation consists of one-half hour of tape and film of spontaneous activity of the child and any interaction in which she engages. Observations are made in the subjects' homes with the mothers usually present.

In order to enable us to study the vocal sounds in original context, a camera equipped with wide angle lens photographs the ongoing scene every half second. This includes the child and her environment, her mother when she is near enough, and the observer. Using a shielded microphone, the observer dictates details of behavior at a finer level than the camera records. The principal investigator, a psychiatrist experienced with both adults and children, serves as observer in all cases. A stereophonic tape recorder preserves these observations on a tape track parallel to the subjects' track. The audio and cinema records are coordinated by a timer (masked from the subjects) which gives a simultaneous coded audio and visual signal at five-second intervals. This makes it possible to resynchronize the three kinds of data.

We are using a field microphone masked by a "Hushaphone"[4] and find that the observer's whispered voice cannot be heard by the subjects. We have built a fairly compact and soundproof container for the camera and timing devices. The camera is re-aimed only when absolutely necessary to keep the child in view. The project is completely explained to the prospective parents. The mother is not expected to stage a performance but

---

[2] T. Berry Brazelton, M.D., and Mrs. Grace Young.

[3] The acoustic material from the first baby, born March 9, 1961, is augmented by a second half-hour tape recording obtained each week. By coincidence, all the study babies, chosen before birth, are girls.

[4] A device originally designed to mask telephones which we have now adapted to a tape recorder microphone.

rather to do and say whatever she feels like while with her child. Although the situation is somewhat artificial, we have found that repeated recording sessions in the same household become routine. With mother and child in their own home we automatically sample the sound environment to which the child is ordinarily exposed. Our records contain the father's and mother's customary voices as well as other voices and noises which the child hears, e.g., pets, musical instruments, radio, TV, traffic noises, etc.

Under ordinary circumstances the observer and technician go to a subject's home as soon after nine A.M. as possible. The field equipment consists of a Tandberg 6 tape recorder and a Kodak Ciné Special camera packaged with timing and signalling devices. A tubular aluminum frame with pan-head for mounting camera box and lower rungs to support tape recorder allows some flexibility in the field. While the equipment is being set up, the observer takes the opportunity to inquire of the mother about recent events in the household and about the baby's condition. The observation is started with the camera set up and the high fidelity microphone (Electro Voice 664) in operation. During the observation the technician keeps the camera pointed in the general direction of the baby, depending on the wide angle lens to catch the action, and monitors the tape tracks. The observer remains as near the subjects as possible without moving more than necessary so as to be able to report in detail items which the wide angle lens might miss or the film lose or distort, especially gaze, facial expression, and small movements at the extremities. The observer, while avoiding initiating action during the observation, is accessible to interaction initiated by the subjects. The film keeps track of the extent of participation of and in relation to the observer during the half hour's activity.

Each standard vocal observation produces three kinds of data: (a) 30 minutes of magnetic recording tape with audio material (taken at 7½ inches per second) from the subjects and environment, (b) 30 minutes of recording tape with dictated description, and (c) 90 feet (3600 frames) of 16 mm film of the observation (taken at two frames per second). Before the data from the standard session can be finally processed as a unit, each of these records undergoes individual processing and indexing.

Circumstantial information related to each observation is systematically recorded in two ways: (a) the technician makes notes on the time, temperature, equipment, and people present, and (b) after each session the observer dictates notes giving a general description of the observation, anything she considers important which might have been missed by the tape recorder or camera, and her general impression of the interpersonal situation.

Data Indexing and Processing

Whenever possible we index all three kinds of data from each standard observation within the day it was taken in order to keep track concurrently of significant changes in the babies' vocalizations so that we may be in a position to gather more data and test hypotheses when indicated. Furthermore, this enables us to reconstruct the situation while the experience is still fresh.

The audio track is audited and indexed by the technician, who enters on a worksheet items occurring within each five-second segment. These entries indicate source of the sounds: mother, baby, observers, objects, etc. Baby vocalizations are noted by a check mark corresponding to the appropriate time segment except in certain cases on nonlinguistic use of the vocal tract: cough, hiccough, etc. The descriptive tape track is transcribed by the typist and segmentation is indicated. The typescript is checked by the observer while auditing the tape. No further audit of this track is needed except to use the segmenting signals for orientation in detailed study of the audio track and resynthesis of the observations.

The film is viewed rapidly to review the events and activity occurring during the observation. A frame counter and visual signals on the film make it possible to analyze the subject's behavior in terms of observed motility. This specifies extent and direction of motion and distance between people, observer included. We hope to analyze the films in much greater detail when an analyzing projector becomes available to the project.

The behavioral data recorded during standard vocal observations on the film and on the observer's sound track will be coded in terms of categories describing gross neuromuscular patterns, facial expression, activity, and interaction with others.

INTERPRETATION

The audio material is studied in greatest detail.[5] A copy of the tape goes to the linguist for analysis. He is devising his own notation for infant vocal sounds and attempting to avoid the use of conventional phonetic transcription where it is obviously inappropriate, especially in the vocalizations produced during the first several months after birth. Several categories of vocalization are noted for these early months: "Whimper," "Tremble," "Cry," "Scream," which can be defined and contrasted in terms of duration, intensity, and pitch variation. These terms are given symbols (W, T, C, S) and noted on the data sheet at the appropriate time segments along with whatever diacritic additions are felt to be necessary. It is planned to attempt an acoustic definition of these terms and the additional terms which will become necessary for the analysis of later tapes, such as $<$ "opening," $B<$ "labial opening," $G<$ "velar opening," $>$ "closure," $>B$ "labial closure," etc.

---

[5] Since our oldest baby has only just passed her six months birthday at the time of writing, we are still concerned only with very early problems.

At the present time the tapes are being analyzed in roughly chronological order. Later they will be reviewed in reverse chronological order and compared in various ways in order to test the relevance of these categories to the development of the acquisition of distinctive speech units. Since the linguistic analysis is made mainly by the techniques of "impressionistic phonetics" (as opposed to instrumental techniques), it is planned to invite another linguist to review the data independently at the termination of the project.

RELATING METHOD TO AIMS

The work of the linguist brings out the natural development of vocal and verbal patterns. We plan to utilize acoustic analytic techniques when relevant as the project develops.

Emergence of the phonemic contrasts is studied by dividing the child's use and understanding of phonemic contrasts into three categories: (a) babbling, (b) purposeful use, and (c) discriminative comprehension. By being able to determine the situation in which the child uttered each vocalization, we expect to be able to follow in detail the progress from babbling to full command of language. We will attempt to relate the phonetic system which the linguist is developing for child vocalization to the phonetics and distinctive features of adult speech and also study these relationships by acoustic analysis.

Attention has been called to the observation that not only does the mother's vocalization influence the child's, but also the child's "baby-talk" influences the mother's speech. The vocalization of the child and the environmental speakers shall be related on two levels: (a) with reference to the habitual speech patterns of the children, and (b) in specific instances, closely neighboring vocalizations in the interaction. The acoustic record of the child's and the mother's vocalizations will be studied for evidence of imitation by listening and possibly by searching spectrograms. This information should enable us to study systematically the mutual effects at levels of magnification ranging from the level of fundamental pitch and distinctive features to that of content. Evidence of developmental achievement from examinations by our child development observation team (pediatrician and psychologist) and from MIH Study[6] examinations will be interpolated in the sequence and taken into consideration. The data on verbal development will be searched for evidence of consistent relationships with behavioral development in other areas. If any such recurring relationships occur in our limited series, it will be possible to test hypotheses on the vocal patterns accompanying specific developmental stages using a larger sample from the Collaborative Study.

---

[6] This is the local designation for the Collaborative Study.

Conclusion

For the field of linguistics, the introduction of modern technology and nonparticipant observation into the study of speech acquisition under essentially ordinary circumstances could contribute objectivity to an area still somewhat obscure. In the past, published reports have been based on studies of children within the investigator's own family, and, more recently, on institutionalized children. The main systematic studies by linguist fathers have started at an age when the child had already started to learn the language. This study is designed to use observers not otherwise involved in the child's language acquisition and to study the child's prelinguistic vocalizations in his natural habitat beginning at birth. By relating language development to the precise emotional and purposive situations in which it arises, we hope to understand the ways in which the utilitarian and affective aspects of speech become integrated. We expect that our study will test the hypotheses concerning the orderly acquisition of the distinctive features of the phonemes and other aspects of linguistic maturation.

While the order in which the distinctive features, phonemic patterns, and prosodic patterns are acquired is of importance to the linguist, the way in which they are learned could interest the psychologist, especially in regard to perception and category formation. If the normal order and patterning of verbal development can be established (and confirmed by later comparison with material from children developing in different language environments), the information could have application in other fields in which the knowledge of the structure of language is significant.

And finally in regard to the original purpose of our investigation of speech development, it is, of course, too early to make direct application to psychiatric problems. In the meantime we are collecting tape recordings of interviews with schizophrenic patients as a start toward developing a method of intensive study of their verbal communication.

4

SPEECH AS A MOTOR SKILL WITH SPECIAL REFERENCE TO NONAPHASIC DISORDERS [1]

Eric H. Lenneberg

Harvard University and *Children's Hospital Medical Center*

Investigations of speech as a motor skill are relevant to a wide spectrum of interests. Speech, as much as ambulation and posture, is a synergism with central nervous system correlates. Clinicians have noticed for many years that certain mesencephalic and diencephalic lesions can produce disturbances in these mechanisms which are highly characteristic of certain diseases or insults to the nervous system. However, physiologists have not been able so far to describe the neurophysiological events that either lead to such disturbances or are responsible for the normal operation of the healthy mechanisms. On the behavioral side of the ledger our state of ignorance is well matched to that of the neurological side. It is relatively easy to classify disorders of speech or gait into vague groups such as "Cerebellar Speech" or "Tabetic Gait." However, objective description of symptomatology is totally lacking to date. Since we cannot review here the literature on efforts to describe gait (Drillis, 1958), it will have to be sufficient to state that, despite modern advances in electrophysiological and cinematographic technology, so far no important gains have been made towards interesting or revealing descriptions.

Speech, which may well be more complicated in some respects than gait, has an invaluable advantage over the study of gait in that it has acoustic correlates which today can be studied accurately. Since every acoustic modulation is directly related to some motor event, acoustic analysis is quite likely to lead to descriptions in which the temporal relationship of different events can be viewed easily and thus contribute to our knowledge of synergisms. The study of speech, then, is of fairly general interest and is thought here to be in some sense ancillary to neurophysiological investigations of highly complex coordinating patterns. Some 13 years ago Lashley

[1] Research carried out while the author was a USPHS Career Investigator in Mental Health. Grateful acknowledgment is made for financial support from the National Institutes of Health, Grants M-2921 and M-5268.

Research assistance of Freda Gould Rebelsky, Irene Nichols, Eleanor F. Rosenberger, and M. A. Whelan has been a valuable aid in this study.

(1951) discussed problems of what he called "serial behavior," and at that time he pointed out that we might speak of a syntax of motor patterns and that this would not be merely a metaphor but that there might be an essential (though not causal) relationship between grammatical syntax and motor syntax. The research reported here (still in its infancy) has been largely influenced by Lashley's reasoning.

The study of motor speech skills affords a longitudinal view of the acquisition of a motor skill by a child, the potential accuracy of which is unparalleled by any other longitudinal study. Moreover, the investigations sketched out below will be found relevant to learning theoretical models for the acquisition of speech. I hope to elucidate in some, however modest, way the relationship between speech as motor events and speech as psychological processes. If nothing more, I might at least be able to justify such a dichotomy and show that the separation of motor from psychological processes is not a mere theoretical fiction.

The work reported here is carried out under the auspices of the Speech Research Laboratory at Children's Hospital Medical Center in Boston. Since the project is still in its initial phase, the material below must be considered as research in progress; theoretical formulations are strictly tentative and may well have to be revised as the work progresses.

ONTOGENESIS OF MOTOR SPEECH SKILLS

Data

Samples of infant's vocalizations were tape recorded by either one of two methods. The vocalizations of infants of 3 months of age or younger were collected by a 24-hour sampling method. The technique and the specially devised apparatus are described in the Lenneberg, Rebelsky, and Chan article. The vocalizations of older children were recorded in a sound treated room at Children's Hospital at the occasion of visits for speech research. Following is a short list of the most striking acoustic features of early vocalizations. Although I shall confine myself here to a qualitative description, most of the data gathered lends itself to frequency of occurrence statistics and distribution studies relative to the children's age as well as to their maturation level such as can be determined by motor indices.

Ill-defined Formant Structure or Absence
of Vowel Resonance

This is a constant feature in the vocalizations of the first three months. Figures 1 and 2a are examples. In the light of spectrographic evidence, it appears unjustified to speak of "frequency of occurrence of English vowels" at this age.[2]

_____

[2] The frequency of the laryngeal tone in infants is, generally, considerably higher (ca. 350 cps) than in adults (ca. 250 cps for female voice). The Kay Electronic Sona-Graph,

Absence of Glottal Stops before Vowel-like Sounds

The virtual absence of glottal stops preceding vocalic sounds is a striking feature of children's vocalizations throughout the prelanguage period. (See Figures 2a and b, 3, 4, and 5.) When glottal stops are present, they tend to be of an exaggerated nature in comparison to standard English. In the repertoire of babbling sounds one gains the impression that the glottal stop is as much an autonomous sound as labial or palatal stops.

Discoordination in the Initiation of Vocalic Sounds

Figure 4 is an example of this feature. Notice that during the first 100 msec. formants move almost randomly up and down but begin to assume a definable pattern at point A.

Non-English Formant Distribution

Between 2 and 4 months the infant emits an increasing number of sounds that have more definite vowel color, but the formant pattern is only rarely identifiable as any particular English vowel. (See Figures 2b, 3, and 4.)

English Formant Distribution with Un-English Features

Figure 5 does show a distribution of formants which one might transcribe as the glide "yiai," but anyone experienced in the reading of spectrograms readily identifies several features which do not occur in our language such as the excessive amount of nasality and the slope of the second formant.

In articulatory terms these features reflect two peculiarities: first, events in the glottis are not as yet correlated with events in the oral cavity; second, the resonance producing deformations of the cavities of the vocal tract have a random aspect and unsteadiness about them that betray a poorly developed mechanism for steady control which is likely to be related to imperfectly specialized reafferentation mechanisms at this age, a hypothesis which still needs empirical verification.

Two other features are of interest because of their more definite relationship to somatic maturation.

The "Accordion Effect"

Figures 1 and 3 are good examples of this phenomenon. Notice that in each case the initiation of phonation is characterized by a constantly changing frequency rate of cord vibrations (each vertical stria corresponds to one phase of cord vibration). In the mature healthy voice, the vertical striae are seen to be equidistant, i.e., the cords immediately vibrate at a characteristic frequency. (Variations in pitch are reflected in slight variations in

---

however, was constructed to produce optimal display for the average adult voice and may therefore slightly distort visual distinctiveness of certain acoustic patterns in the vocalization of infants. The logical argument in this paper is not affected by this instrumental shortcoming in that it merely emphasizes the fact that there are dramatic acoustic differences between children's vocal output and that of adults.

cord frequency, but close inspection shows that, graphically, the striae continue to be fairly equidistantly spaced. This indicates that change in pitch is produced under good muscular control of tension of the cords.) What is peculiar about the instances referred to here is that for periods as long as one to two tenths of a second there is a constant change of frequency, the striae being irregularly spaced, indicating poor muscular control over the voicing mechanism. This feature is not seen in the mature, normal voice and cannot be reproduced at will. This as well as the next feature is of special interest because it makes spectrograms resemble those of the voices of adult patients with adventitious central nervous system diseases. Compare, for instance, Figure 3 with Figure 6b. The latter represents attempts at initiation of voice by an 11-year-old child with lesions in the dentate nucleus of the cerebellum and degeneration of the putamen and globus palidus. A more detailed discussion of this and similar phenomena may be found elsewhere (Lenneberg, 1962). Suffice it to say here that the feedback mechanism which controls the tension of the muscles that stretch the vocal cords is affected in both cases, even though the history of these disturbances is somewhat different for the two subjects. Such parallelisms between extremely immature behavior and behavior states produced by central nervous system disease are not uncommon in neurology. As the neonate moves from maturational stage to maturational stage, primitive reflexes are modified by and integrated with new sets of reflexes so that early life is in many respects characterized by reflex motor events which in the adult only reappear under conditions of disease where the ontogenetically recent or adult inhibiting reflexes have been blocked pathologically, releasing more primitive "strata" of reactions. Grasping, rooting, and plantar reflexes are typical examples in case. The spectrographic reappearance, in neurological patients with dysarthria, of motor speech phenomena that are only seen normally in small infants lends credence to the notion of *physical maturation of speech coordinating mechanisms.*

Tremor and Unsteadiness

Figures 1 and 2b show a periodic unsteadiness in the regions marked A which proceeds at a rate of up to 40 cps. There are no coordinated movements under the control of the central nervous system known to proceed at this high rate except for pathological phenomena in the adult such as fasciculations or in the immature such as quivering of the soft palate and chin in the neonate (Ford, 1960, p. 214). Figure 7 was produced by a 26-year-old housewife with an unlocalized but supratentorial lesion which resulted in a tremor of the diaphragm and/or intercostal muscles which is well reflected in the grossly abnormal pattern of interruptions in the higher harmonics in this spectrogram. The spectrographic patterns of small formant waves in Figures 1 and 2a or marbling aspect of higher harmonics in Figure 2b may be seen in distressed crying of infants up to the age of approximately 6 months, but eventually these patterns disappear entirely and they only recur in later life in stages of pathological voice synergisms.

At present we are analyzing our entire tape material in order to determine the relative frequency of occurrence of the spectographic features mentioned above as well as other articulatory phenomena.

Another facet of our research on speech motor skills has to do with determination of typical rates of articulatory movements in an attempt at discovering inherent rhythms in speech activity. A method for the completely mechanical determination of rate and rhythm in adult speech has already been devised and will be put to test shortly. The aim is to obtain some norms on these parameters of motor speech skills so that it will be possible eventually to trace the origin or appearance of "normal values" ontogenetically and to study the earliest vocalizations in the light of these perhaps speech-specific aspects of motor activity.

A Note on Imitation and Similarity

The discussion so far has made it plain that infant vocalizations throughout the first year of life are acoustically very different from speech sounds. This raises an important theoretical question. If it is true that the infant's earliest motivation for speech development is due to his discovery of the similarity between his own sounds and those made by his mother while attending to his needs, we would expect that the mother could with special effort reproduce the baby's sounds faithfully. Figures 8a and 8b show that this is not the case. They were obtained in the following manner. The cooing sound of a 3-months-old baby was recorded on a continuous loop so that it could be played back indefinitely and without switching the tape recorder back and forth. The mother listened through ear phones to her own baby's tape recorded noise with the instruction to practice imitation. When she reported that she had learned to reproduce the sound accurately, her own version was tape recorded. When mother's and son's spectrograms are compared, the objective differences become visually obvious. Once alerted to the difference, the two tape recordings also begin to sound very unlike each other. The same experiment has been repeated with other mothers always with similar results. We must conclude either that sound imitation is a mere fiction or, if the infant should indeed strive for imitation, that he is innately equipped to hear similarities between his and his mother's vocalizations where, objectively, there are definite differences.

Prerequisites for Language Acquisition: The Role of Motor Skills

Above I have given a rough indication of how articulatory skills of normal babies may be studied and profitably compared with dysarthric phenomena in older subjects. Now I would like to illustrate how a systematic study of children with various kinds of deficits may give us important insight into the process of language acquisition. I shall confine my comments to a few simple observations on the development of congenitally deaf children and of children with mongolism. In addition I shall briefly discuss a case of a child with severe somatic speech disability (congenital anarthria).

Deaf Infants

Deaf babies have been followed in the Speech Research Laboratory with a view to recording the history of their sound development. The procedure here was essentially the same as that used in the study of normal children. In order to include in our sample some neonate congenitally deaf babies, the City of Boston was canvassed for young couples where both parents were deaf. By this method I was successful in securing at least one congenitally deaf baby and making recordings at regular intervals since birth throughout the first year of life. Other deaf children were seen periodically beginning at ages as young as 18 months and followed through to their entrance into schools for the deaf. This study has revealed the following important fact. Neither deafness nor deaf parents reduces the sound activity during the first six months to any appreciable extent. Qualitatively, the sounds of the first three months are virtually identical among deaf and hearing children. From the fourth to the twelfth month there can be no question that a great number of sounds emitted by deaf children are very much like the sounds of hearing children; however, after the sixth month of life the total range of babbling sounds heard in the deaf appeared to be somewhat more restricted than those of hearing children. (Unfortunately, at this point I have no formal statistic in support of these impressions. The assertions are made on the basis of listening to the actual tape recordings. Nor is the number of subjects studied so far sufficient to present conclusive frequency distribution data.)

The speech education of the hearing-handicapped in the course of their schooling is also interesting. It is generally agreed that a child who is profoundly deaf in both ears and whose loss is congenital has an extremely poor chance of learning to use his voice and speech organs in the same way as normally hearing people do. To the members of this conference, who are sophisticated in linguistic analysis and phonological research, this may not come as a surprise; yet there is one particular aspect of the vocalizations of these school children that is surprising. It is an unassailable fact that these individuals will laugh and may even emit certain babbling sounds in connection with emotional states, displaying a perfectly normal voice with good pitch and loudness control. Yet in the course of their efforts to speak the quality of their voices changes entirely, frequently resulting in some ugly low or high pitched tone, completely devoid of pleasing intonation patterns and obviously uncontrolled by appropriate feedback. In other

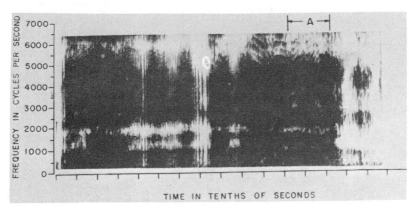

FIGURE 1—Spectrogram of 2-week-old boy, crying vigorously.

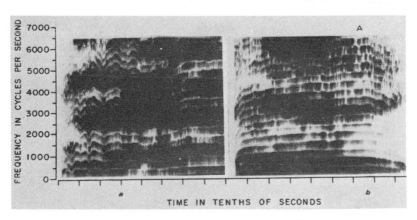

FIGURE 2a—Spectrogram of 6-week-old boy, crying vigorously.
Figure 2b—Spectrogram of 8-week-old boy, crying softly.

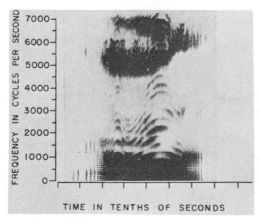

FIGURE 3—Spectrogram of
9-week-old girl, cooing.

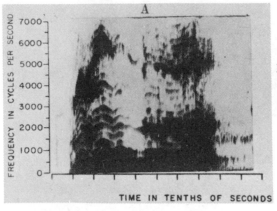

FIGURE 4—Spectrogram of 9-week-old boy, cooing in response to mother's talk (sounds like "ayeh").

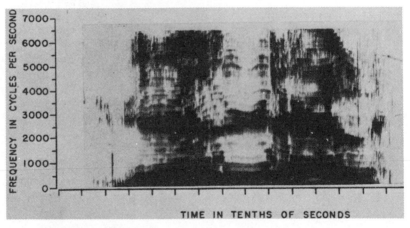

FIGURE 5—Spectrogram of 7-month-old girl, spontaneous cooing (sounds like "yiaiyai").

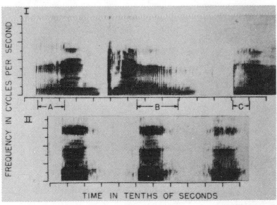

FIGURE 6a—Spectrogram of 11-year-old boy with Hepatolenticular Degeneration, saying "and cats get . . ." Bottom: Voice of healthy boy at same age.

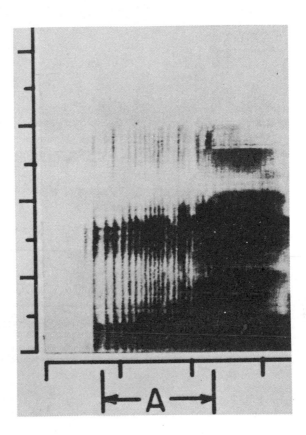

FIGURE 6b—Spectrogram of enlarged detail of 6a.

FIGURE 7—Spectrogram of 26-year-old woman with unlocalized supra-tentorial lesion, saying "aaah."

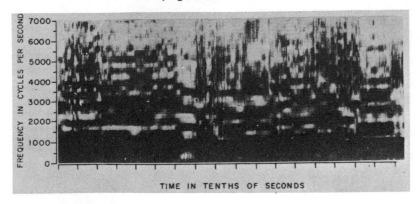

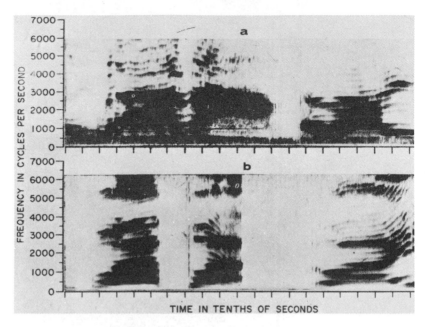

FIGURE 8a—Spectrogram of 3-month-old boy cooing.
FIGURE 8b—Spectrogram of mother imitating her child's cooing.

FIGURE 9—Spectrogram of 4-year-old boy with congenital anarthria; spontaneous sound "aaoo."

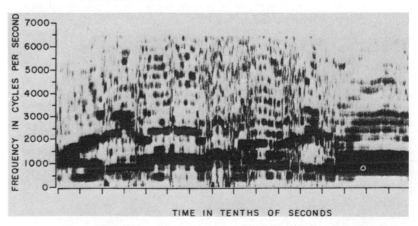

words, proprioception cannot take the place of auditory control, and no training procedures have been discovered as yet that would reinforce the use of normal voice and discourage the appearance of the abnormal-sounding pitch so frequently associated with deaf voices.

Language in Mongolism

A study of the language development of retarded children was undertaken in the hope that the retarded development would give us an opportunity to study the language acquisition process in slow motion. I had also hoped that this study would elucidate the question of the role of "biological intelligence" in the acquisition of language.

If it is true that there is a unique and orderly way of learning language, we would expect that certain stages of retardation are accompanied by certain definite stages of primitive language development and that each state should have some measure of consistency within itself. That is to say, there should be a correlation in the development of individual aspects of speech and language. For instance, we should not find a child who has learned to echo with great perfection but who is unable to generate grammatically correct sentences. Mongoloid children were chosen as subjects for this study because they offer a number of research advantages: the condition can be spotted at birth; and they constitute a relatively homogeneous test-population in that the condition produces a very consistent clinical picture which does not only extend over somatic symptoms, but also over behavioral ones. Thus, mongoloid children have typical mannerisms, typical ways of moving, typical ways of playing, and typical ways of communication.

For our study only children were chosen that are being raised by their parents at home. The vast majority of these children come from the middle income group, and the homes are frequently populated with other siblings. Since mongolism is not an inherited condition, these children come from normal stock which is further evidenced by the fact that their siblings have usually normal development.

My test population consists of roughly 60 children all of whom have been seen at least twice, most of them as often as three to six times. The research is observational and descriptive at the present stage. Tape recordings are made of spontaneous noises and speech; in addition a program of observations is followed which includes development of phonology (tested by the repetition method also used by Brown and Fraser), development of grammar with particular reference to the ability to concatenate individual words that are familiar to the subject, and syntactic development. Syntax is investigated both by the repetition method and by a scrutiny of the spontaneously emitted sentences. Further observations concern "semantic" development and the relative difficulties encountered by these children in learning the meaning of various types of words; we shall not concern ourselves at all in this paper with this last problem.

We have just finished making the first round of observations and are now in the process of analyzing the data; unfortunately, at the time of the present report final results are not yet available for this material. For the time being, the statements that follow can be corroborated only by playing typical tape recordings; the phenomena, however, are so dramatic that certain generalizations may be made with impunity about the over-all trend of the material. I shall confine myself to three important and obvious findings.

1. There is one stage—and some children's development is arrested at this stage—at which the subject is capable of repeating an English word only by rough approximation of the sound structure. When urged to repeat exactly what had been said to them, these subjects may, typically, improve the intonation and stress patterns of their response, but the articulatory skill remains consistently poor regardless of the number of repetitions. The disability has nothing to do with auditory preception of the word. In many instances it can even be shown that the subject is perfectly familiar with the word and knows its meaning. The deficit illustrates that a very special type of "understanding" is necessary in order to repeat the sequence of phonemes in a word following exactly the prototype. The understanding that I am referring to here has to do with understanding the *morphophonological structure* and rules. It can often be demonstrated that these children have imperfect acquisition of what Chomsky and Halle have called phonological syntax (unpublished seminar proceedings). Subjects may, for instance, have both a voiced and unvoiced interdental sibilant, but they may confuse these two sounds in the pluralization of nouns and not observe morphophonemic rules. Their utterances do allow of phonemecization; however, the phoneme structure is bound to be more primitive than the English paradigm, and, what is more important, the child will be consistent with himself in using the poorer phonemic system rather than having good enunciation of some, say, emotionally important words while using poorer enunciation for less important words. When we say glibly that learning to speak is "merely" learning to imitate, we forget that imitation actually implies the learning of analytic tools, namely grammatical and phonemic rules that can (and must) be applied to both the decoding and encoding of messages. This is even true on the level of so-called "simple phoneme sequences."

2. In a further stage of development some syntactic rules may have been acquired while others have not. At this stage children will repeat simple grammatical sentences corectly but make interesting mistakes in more complex ones even though the number of words remains the same as in the simpler constructions. A good example of this situation is the repetition of sentences in the active voice which for some children presents no difficulty, whereas to make them repeat similar sentences in the passive voice causes the child to make mistakes. Sometimes the mistakes indicate that

the child has not understood the sentence. At other times the child will produce a sentence that is grammatically correct but is put back in the active voice, often even preserving the original meaning. The same phenomenon occurs when these children are asked to repeat a question; they may repeat it with correct question intonation pattern yet without having performed the appropriate transformations. When we ask them to be very careful and repeat *exactly* what the experimenter has said, we find still the same failure prevailing and, even with the greatest effort, sentences will not be repeated correctly. The explanation for this extremely common phenomenon is quite simple. A sentence of 10 words contains an enormous amount of detail. It might consist of a sequences of some 60 phonemes, each one characterized by 9 to 12 distinctive features; each word in the sentence has well-defined intonation and stress characteristics; the sentence as a whole is the product of a male or female organ and bears acoustic peculiarities of age and idio-syncrasies of the speaker. "Blind" reproduction of all of this material, or even of the essentials, should be impossible, seeing that our memory is not even capable of reproducing a train of 10 random digits. Reproducing sen-tences in a totally unfamiliar language is difficult or even impossible because the sequence of phonemes strikes us as random. But when we understand a language, sequences of phonemes within words and sequences of words within sentences fall into familiar patterns that help to organize the stimuli and enable us to program the responses. The *sine qua non* for reproduction is, therefore, the ability to recognize the patterns—which is tantamount to saying the reproduction presupposes prior learning of grammar. When we are asked to repeat long sentences, we do not have to memorize the sequence of phonemes and their distinctive features, but as we receive the input signal we are capable of recoding the material in terms of a few principles, words, and their connections (Miller, 1956). We can now store this coded informa-tion which is simpler to do than storing the original, detailed information. When we are asked to reproduce the sentence, we reconstruct it by means of our knowledge of a few relevant rules. The output signal is now "our own way of saying what we heard" and is similar to the original only in terms of structural principles—not in individual phonological detail.

A child who has not acquired the complete grammar will fail to recog-nize the organization of symbols in a grammatically complicated sentence and is thus unable even to *store* the input signal without detrimental alter-ations. Apparently there are developmental stages at which recognition of certain grammatical patterns is possible without, however, being able to *use* the pertinent rules as yet. Thus a child may understand the meaning of a sentence couched in the passive voice, "The dog is fed by the boy," but, when asked to repeat it, the child will say "The boy feeds the dog."

(I may mention that my findings on the reproduction of syntactically complex sentences do, indeed, furnish some evidence in support of Chom-sky's notion of "understanding a sentence" and are practical evidence against the recent criticisms levelled against Chomsky by Reichling, 1961, who doubted that it is true that we understand a passive sentence on the grounds of its relationship to its underlying kernel sentence in the active voice.)

3. There are children with mongolism who do attain an excellent control of the English language. These are children with IQs of 50 or better. They will apply rules of grammar on most grammatical levels correctly even though the subject matter of their conversation may not be very bright.

I have mentioned these facts in order to indicate that there are some cases where the motor skill itself (which is thought to be a prerequisite for the "proper response-shaping" into language) is definitely present, yet language does not develop properly in spite of conducive environments, motivation, and all other variables commonly identified with the necessary reinforcing conditions in a learning situation.

One of the conclusions we must draw from the study of speech development in mongoloid children is that babbling and making noises approximating English are insufficient conditions for the complete acquisition of language skills. Some central element is also necessary. There is the temptation to label this element simply as *intelligence*. However, this is not saying much in the absence of good definitions of this concept. An IQ of 50 is deficient enough to keep a child from learning the most elementary concepts (counting, social distance, rules of kindergarten parlor games), yet it is high enough to use correctly plurals, tenses, question transformations, etc. The general problem that emerges from these considerations, and which is central to psychological theories at large, is: Why are certain tasks easier than others for a given species regardless of stimulus variables (recency, frequency, intensity) or motivational variables?

Before relating the findings of mongoloid speech with those of deaf children, I would like to present one other case of speech handicap of an entirely different nature.

The Acquisition of Language by a Speechless Child

A detailed report of this case may be found elsewhere (Lenneberg, 1962). In brief this is an 8-year-old child with a congenital neurological deficit for speech articulation. He can make sounds like Swiss yodelling, but he has never babbled or made any attempts at word imitation. He is mildly retarded (IQ in the 80 to 85 range). Psychiatric examination is negative. Family and social history are unremarkable. When this child was first seen at Children's Hospital at 3 years of age, it was at once obvious that his motor-speech handicap had not impaired his ability to learn to understand English. Since then he has been examined repeatedly, and his "passive language ability" has been investigated thoroughly. I have recently made a sound film of this patient which documents the ease with which he can execute commands, and it shows also other dimensions of his language comprehension. He understands prepositions, number concepts, and the meaning of color words. He fails in distinguishing right and left, but he can answer questions without "situational support." He can answer questions such as: "Does ice cream feel cold on your tongue?" "Is a spider a light animal?" and so on. He knows the meaning of such words as *now*, *later, always, yesterday,* and he can answer questions about a story even when they are put in the passive voice, thus demonstrating a complex analytic capacity for linguistic structure.

Figure 9 is a spectrogram of a typical example of this boy's vocalizations. It shows grossly abnormal control over voice and organs of articulation and there is evidence of a continuing tremor which closely resembles that of the patient whose voice and speech is reproduced in Figure 7.

Throughout the past 20 years traditional learning (conditioning) experiments have been performed on dogs treated with curare or similar drugs (Kimble, 1961, pp. 224f). The drugs render the animal totally paralyzed throughout the training period, and the objective has been to discover whether it could learn to adapt its motor behavior to certain new conditions even though it had been prevented from emitting motor responses during the training period. By and large the results of these experiments agree with each other and with a wealth of other data indicating that there is no need to assume an immediate and intimate relationship between a stimulus and a motor response in the course of the experimental acquisition of simple motor performances. In the light of these findings it is noteworthy that many learning theorists, when speculating about the acquisition of speech, either explicitly state or at least imply that this is a gradual process in which verbal responses of some primitive nature (e.g., babbling) are the essential prerequisites for language development. The difficulty (or actual impossibility) of teaching lower mammals to speak is attributed by these theoreticians to the animal's failure to babble.

The case reported here is evidence against this theoretical position. The learning situation here was very similar to that of the curarized animal, and the results of those experiments agree with the findings reported here. The case presented is an extreme example of a comparatively common clinical entity—severe congenital anarthria with unimpaired (or nearly unimpaired) intellect.

Conclusions

We have treated two distinct subjects: (a) the articulatory development of infant vocalizations and (b) the relation of speech as a motor skill to language as a psychological skill. We have briefly discussed the interdependence of these two skills during the acquisition of either. Table 1 sum-

TABLE I

Relationship of the Capacity for Making Speech Sounds to Understanding
Instructions as Illustrated by Children with Various Handicaps

UNDERSTANDING	MAKING SPEECH SOUNDS		
	Cannot	*Can but Does Not*	*Can and Does*
Does Not	Amented children (No language develops.)	Never observed	Feeble minded children (If IQ below 50, only primitive beginnings of language.)
Does	Congenital anarthria with normal cognitive development (Language can be acquired.)	Autistic and psychotic children (Some evidence for subclinical language acquisition is common.)	Normal children (Language is acquired spontaneously.)

NOTE.—The capacity for making speech sounds does not insure language development.

marizes the findings. It appears that understanding is more significant for
language development than the capacity for making speech sounds.

Spectrographic evidence was adduced in describing the gross acoustic
differences between the child's prelanguage vocalizations and mature language sounds occurring by the third year of life. The observations are of
interest to psychological theories because they throw considerable doubt on
the often heard assumption that the infant hearing himself babble notices
the similarity between his own noises and those of his parents and that this
similarity has the effect of secondary reinforcement, starting the child on
his long journey towards perfect acquisition of speech skills. Since his own
sounds are demonstrated to be objectively very different from those of the
adults, the child must have some peculiar way of determining or recognizing similarities in the presence of diversifications. The descriptions are also
of neurophysiological interest—even if only propaedeutic—in that relationships between immature motor coordination in the neonate on the one
hand and discoordination due to central nervous system lesions on the other
can be demonstrated.

A comparison of vocalization and speech behavior of deaf children, of
children with mongolism, and of one child with congenital anarthria revealed the following important points:

1. The voice, intonation pattern and large part of the phonological repertoire of the profoundly deaf cannot be shaped into normal standards,
despite the normal quality of these children's voices and sounds in their
earliest infancy. Thus, training is of no avail here because of a peripheral
interference with the nervous control mechanisms.

2. Mongoloid children with IQs of about 50 or less babble and produce approximations to English speech sounds but cannot be trained to develop full-fledged language because of a central deficit.

3. A child with congenital anarthria was described who has never been able to make normal babbling sounds and who has never acquired any motor speech skills, but who has perfect understanding of language.

From these observations we may conclude that motor speech skills are neither necessary nor sufficient prerequisites for the development of those psychological skills which seem to be an essential substrate for mature language. Certain aspects of motor speech development appear to be based on the innately given neurological mechanism controlling the voice box and vocal tract. Artificial shaping of random motor responses into controlled speech components meets—at least in the case of the deaf—with great difficulties.

SUMMARY

Sound spectrographic analysis of vocalizations during the first three months of life was presented and an automatic recording device for objective sampling was described. Language development was discussed in the light of these investigations and of studies of children with a variety of central nervous system deficits and peripheral deafness. It was found that language development may occur in the absence of motor speech skills and that the presence of motor speech skills is no insurance for language development.

APPARATUS FOR REDUCING PLAY-BACK TIME OF TAPE RECORDED, INTERMITTENT VOCALIZATION [1]

C. H. CHAN

Belmont, Massachusetts

ERIC H. LENNEBERG *and* FREDA GOULD REBELSKY

Harvard University and *Children's Hospital Medical Center*

Tape recording of verbal transactions is an increasingly used research tool. However, the problems of analyzing tapes are often enormous, and much time is wasted listening to recorded silence and timing taped sequences in order to get quantitative measures. The present apparatus was developed in order to reduce play-back time and to simplify quantitative

[1] Grateful acknowledgment is made for financial support from the National Institutes of Health, Grants M-2921 and M-5268.

analysis. It prevents the recording of silence but provides a graphic record of the distribution of noise over given periods.

The authors have used it successfully to investigate the vocalizations of human infants during 24-hour sample periods. Other uses for the apparatus will readily suggest themselves.

The equipment consists of an assembly of three units (Figure 1):

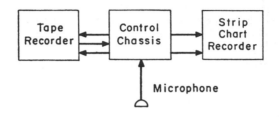

FIGURE 1—The equipment set-up.

1. A tape recorder with remote control transport (Uher model "Universal").

2. A control chassis (Figure 2) to operate the tape recorder and the strip-chart recorder.

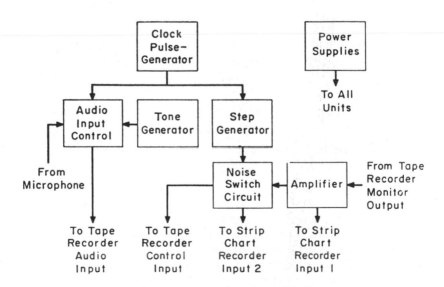

FIGURE 2—The control chassis.

3. A two channel ink writing strip-chart (polygraph) recorder (Brush Instruments Oscillograph model RD 2322 00) which registers the tape recording activities and time in hour-step signals.

The instruments are so connected that the tape recorder is turned on by any noise in the environment (with negligible delay) but shuts itself off after cessation of the disturbance. The strip-chart (polygraph) runs continuously, recording in one channel the time and the on-off activities of the tape and in the other channel the rectified acoustic input signal irrespective

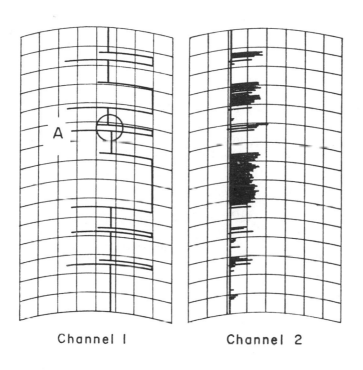

Channel I   Channel 2

Channel I. Record of off-on positions of tape recorder.

Channel 2. Record of noises in sound field of microphone.

A shows point at which baseline moves to indicate a new hour. Paper speed 6.5mm/min.

FIGURE 3—Sample of strip-chart recording.

of whether its volume is above or below the threshold for turning on the recorder. There is a time lapse between cessation of noise and stoppage of tape transport which can be varied manually from a short delay of .5 second to a maximum delay of 10 seconds. Periodically (for our study, every 60 minutes) a clock pulse-generator gates on a tone generator to produce a short beep signal of 1.5 seconds duration. This signal is recorded on the tape so that the final tape recording is segmented into periods marked by beeps to help orientation during play-back. The hour information is also clearly marked on the strip-chart as hour-step signals (see Figure 3).

Since the tape stands still during silence, it produces an economically "packed" tape. In the case of our research on baby-noise it was possible to reduce the 24-hour observation period to three to four hours play-back time. Yet the distribution of these noises over the baby's day are accurately preserved on the strip-chart which was left running continuously throughout the day. Synchronization of noises heard on the tape with signals seen on the strip-chart is easy because of the recurrent hour marks in both records.

The apparatus makes little noise and can be removed completely from sight and hearing range of subjects by using a microphone with a long cable.

5

MEDIATION PROCESSES AND THE ACQUISITION OF LINGUISTIC STRUCTURE [1]

JAMES J. JENKINS *and* DAVID S. PALERMO

University of Minnesota

> It is futile to inquire into the causation of verbal behavior until much more is known about the specific character of this behavior; and there is little point in speculating about the process of acquisition without much better understanding of what is acquired (Chomsky, 1959, p. 55).

When psychologists have addressed themselves to questions concerning mediation and language, they have dealt in the main with two general classes of problems: (a) language as a mediating behavior and (b) non-linguistic mediating responses as explicators of the meaning of lexical items. In the first case, exemplified by the work of Birge (1941), Kuenne (1946), Jeffrey (1953), Cantor (1955), Shepard (1956), Spiker (1956), Spiker, Gerjuoy, and Shepard (1956), Shepard and Schaeffer (1956), and Norcross and Spiker (1958), language is treated as of special importance because it furnishes a label, tag, or response which may be elicited in common by diverse members of some stimulus class.[2] Here it appears possible to show that such an intermediary response (whether overt or covert) serves an important role in the other, sometimes nonlinguistic, behaviors of the subjects.

In the second case, investigators such as Osgood (1953), Osgood, Suci, and Tannenbaum (1957), Bousfield (1961), and Staats and Staats (1957) have been concerned to show that "meanings" of items may be accounted

---

[1] This paper was prepared for the Conference on First-Language Acquisition sponsored by the Social Science Research Council, October 27-29, 1961. Dr. Jenkins' research in mediation processes is supported by the National Science Foundation. Dr. Palermo and Dr. Jenkins are jointly supported in their study "Word Associations: Grade School Through College" by Grant M-4286 from the National Institute of Mental Health, United States Public Health Service.

[2] It should be noted that some of these studies experimentally introduce and manipulate the mediator within the experimental setting while others infer the use of a verbal mediator on the basis of other data.

for by a theory which supposes that the occurrence of the item is accompanied by implicit, covert responses assumed to have been attached to the items by simple conditioning procedures earlier in the experience of the subject.

We feel that both of these areas of research are extremely important and need much further research and thought. In this paper, however, we would like to direct the reader's attention to a new area in which we think mediation theory has an important role to play: the area of linguistic *structure*. Strangely enough, this obvious aspect of language, the fact that it is structured, seems to have escaped psychological analysis to any appreciable degree.

In 1936, Kantor wrote *An Objective Psychology of Grammar* without more than casual reference to the facts of linguistic structure. One gathers, indeed, that he seems to have thought of "structure" as an insidious creation of the linguist to be abolished, along with other nonbehavioristic ghosts, rather than considered as a part of the description of behavior. The major point of the book seems to be that language behavior must be thought of as an adjustment of the organism, subject to the same laws as any other behavior. In the effort to make this laudible point clear, the description of language provided by grammar was to a great extent neglected.

In 1951 Lashley specifically pointed to the structured nature of speech as an example *par excellence* of the general problem of the serial ordering of behavior. He wrote, "In spite of the ubiquity of the problem, there have been almost no attempts to develop physiological theories to meet it. In fact, except among a relatively small group of students of aphasia who have had to face questions of agrammatism, the problem has been largely ignored" (1951, p. 113). Lashley pointed out that the phonetic elements were unpredictable at their own level, being determined by the words, and the words themselves were unpredictable in a left-to-right sequence since they were in turn determined by higher levels of organization. This led him to assert specifically that combinations of associations between words in sentences could not account for grammatical structure. He argued for a series of hierarchies of organization but confessed that he had not been able to systematize a set of assumptions concerning selective mechanisms which "was consistent with any large number of sentence structures" (1951, p. 130).

In 1953 a group of psychologists, linguists, and anthropologists met to discuss problems of psycholinguistics (see Osgood and Sebeok, 1954). This group explicitly recognized the problems faced in the area of grammatical structure but failed to deal with it effectively. The predominant approach of the entire section of the psycholinguistic monograph devoted to sequential organization seems to be built on the left-to-right assembly pattern or Markov process which Chomsky (1957) has since attacked with compelling success. The idea is presented that there need to be several levels of organization (skill level, integrational level, and representational level), and analysis by immediate constituents is introduced but no general fusion of the psychological theories and the linguistic analysis seems to have been achieved. Even in the analysis of word association phenomena where it was seen that the predominant organization of associative responses is in terms of agreement in form class with the stimulus, there is a vague suggestion that sentences are organized in terms of sequential associations (manifestly a contradiction of the first statement), and several research proposals related to that idea are offered.

Miller, Galanter, and Pribram (1960), in the main, avoid the problem of linguistic structure by accepting it as the *Plan* by which sentences are constructed. They take the grammatical model advanced by Chomsky and, approving of it, install it. Unfortunately, they do not tell us how Plans are acquired or how they are executed with the result that an independent explanation of grammar in terms of traditional psychological constructs is little advanced.

While other examples could be cited, the above are sufficient to indicate that psychologists have for the most part ignored, avoided, or mishandled the problem of accounting for grammar in particular or structure in language more generally.

The writers believe that it is clear to even a superficial analysis that the systematic nature of language is at the heart of its enormous utility. What it means to "understand" a sentence one has never heard before or to utter a sentence which is "novel but appropriate" (to borrow Brown's happy phrase) must rest on a psychological explication of the properties of *systems* in both stimulus and response roles. It will be the attempt of this paper to take a small step toward such an explication.

The reader should understand that the account to be given here is speculative in the extreme and little data are available which can be used to support it. The writers' apology is as simple as it is weak: the paper is premature. Our justification for presenting it at all is that research must begin somewhere and this is where we are beginning. Our current thinking and proposed research should both change and improve as our colleagues from several fields consider this material critically.

LANGUAGE IS STRUCTURED

What does it mean to say that language is structured? Most psychologists writing about language seem to feel that this can (and must) be said, but it is not quite clear what is meant by that sentence or what importance should be attached to it. A series of related quotations may provide certain guidance:

Dollard and Miller, *Personality and Psychotherapy* (1950):

> . . . a person can learn to respond to specific combinations of stimuli or relationships among them and to make different responses to the same cues in different contexts. This is called patterning. A person's responses to the words that he hears someone else speak obviously involve patterning. Thus a parent will respond quite differently to the following two reports containing the same words in different sequences: "Jim hit Mary" and "Mary hit Jim." . . . it is obvious that man's great innate capacity and rigorous social training have produced marvelously intricate and subtle patterning in his responses to spoken language (p. 100).

Carroll, *The Study of Language* (1953):

> The central concept in linguistic analysis is *structure* by which is meant the ordered or patterned set of contrasts or oppositions which are presumed to be discoverable in a language, whether in the units of sound, the grammatical inflections, the syntactical arrangements, or even the meanings of the linguistic forms (p. 14).

Hebb, *A Textbook of Psychology* (1958):

> What puts language on a higher level than the purposive communication of dog or chimpanzee is the *varied combination* of the same signs . . . for different purposes. The parrots and other talking birds can reproduce speech sounds very effectively—but without the slightest indication of transposing words, learned as part of one phrase or sentence, into a new order, or making new combinations of them (p. 209).
>
> The fundamental difference between man and chimpanzee in this respect seems to lie in man's capacity for having several sets of mediating processes at once, relatively independent of each other (pp. 209-210).

Brown, *Words and Things* (1958b):

> There is a refrain running through descriptive linguistics which goes like this: "Language is a system." . . . when someone knows a language he knows a set of rules: rules of phonology, morphology, reference, and syntax. These rules can generate an indefinite number of utterances. . . . The most important thing psychology is likely to get from linguistics is the reminder that human behavior includes the response that is novel but appropriate (p. viii).

From a set of statements like these it may be concluded that "language is structured" involves at least two ideas: (a) that structure has something to do with interrelated combinations and patterns which are differentially uttered and differentially responded to and (b) that language structure exists at several levels, at least at the levels of phonology, morphology, and syntax. What "structure" is, whether the same thing is meant by "structure" at each level, and whether there are general psychological explications of "structure" remain to be explored.

For our specific target we will take that aspect of structure which is called syntax or grammar. Within that area we will accept a phase structure grammar, such as the model given by Chomsky (1957), as our ultimate target, though we can make but the most meager beginning in this paper. For our mode of analysis we will take a simple notion of stimulus-response learning and the ramifications possible when one permits implicit responses having stimulus properties. To the elaboration of our simple tools we must next turn.

MEDIATIONAL PROCESSES

A decade ago it seemed to be the hope of the workers in the field that language assembly would turn out to be the general nature of the Markov chain model. For the S-R psychologist this would have been nearly perfect as far as explaining the formal system of language was concerned. Essentially, the cumulation of steps in the chain could account for the particular "state" of the speaker, and his behavior from that point on could be viewed as a probabilistic matter depending on habit strengths. Two difficulties which immediately arise (see Chomsky, 1957, and Miller, Galanter, and Pribram, 1960) are that this approach requires an enormous amount of learning on the part of the organism to acquire all the probabilities which would be needed to make even a small set of the sentences he would require in his daily life, and, secondly, it can be shown that many English sentences are made up of sets of "nested dependencies" rather than serial dependencies. Thus, in almost any English sentence one may find several places at which the sentence may be "opened up" and a whole new set of material introduced. Thus, "The boy runs" may be expanded almost without limit: "The boy . . . who lives in the big white house across the street from the curious looking bank that you saw when you first entered the town by the main highway . . ."

Some variety of phrase structure grammar seems to be required, and, as Chomsky points out, when one starts working with such a grammar, one finds lawful transformation rules from one basic set of kernel sentences to other sentence forms. These encouraging higher-order regularities make it all the more necessary that psychologists deal with phrase structure grammar seriously and attempt to explicate two problems: (a) how do verbal utterances become members of classes such as "noun phrase" and "verb phrase" (especially when the speakers may not be able to tell the investigator that there are such things as nouns and verbs) and (b) how can sequences be formed of materials in classes.

Before attempting to attack these two problems within a mediation framework, some minimal statements of operations which lead to mediational phenomena must be made. These may be much more elaborated, but for purposes of this paper they will be summarized briefly in the form of a few principles.

1. If there are two S-R contingencies such that the response to the first one is "the same" as the stimulus for the second one, then the first stimulus will acquire a tendency to elicit the second response.

That is:

Given that:	A elicits B;
and that:	B elicits C;
Then:	A will tend to elicit C.

This is the classic treatment of stimulus-response chaining and scarcely needs to be elaborated here. We know that it holds under a variety of conditions for men and lower animals. A very simple example is provided by "avoidance" conditioning with rats as in the classic experiment by May (1948). We can match the paradigm by letting A stand for a buzzer, B stand for a shock, and C stand for escape behavior. It is easy to establish a B-C connection, i.e., the animal readily learns to escape from shock. Now the animal may be penned and given the buzzer as a stimulus followed by shock where escape is impossible. Here the A-B connection is established. If the animal is put into the original situation, he will show escape behavior, C, when the buzzer, A, is presented. Similarly with children (see Norcross and Spiker, 1958), it has been shown that the verbal learning of a sequence such as *tree-pony* followed by the learning of *pony-doll* will facilitate the subsequent learning of *tree-doll*.

With respect to this paradigm we must add the caution that the chaining may not be wholly automatic (i.e., it can be inhibited, facilitated, or interfered with by various activities of the subject), and in the animal case at least (see Gough, 1961) the order in which the first two stages occur may be very important.

This paradigm is usually regarded as a *mediation* paradigm because the traditional S-R analysis assumes a mediating response in the last stage:

A-B learning;
B-C learning;
A-(B)-C.

The argument is that when A is presented in the last stage it is sufficient to elicit (B) as an implicit response. It is further argued that the stimulus consequences of (B) are sufficiently like the stimulus consequences of B presented as an explicit stimulus that C is elicited.

It is very important to notice that the outcome of this paradigm is a "chain" from A to C. This does not imply that a chain similarly exists from C to A. The association may be expected to be asymmetrical. (In many cases a reverse chain would be simply impossible. In the animal example given above we expect that the rat will run in the presence of the buzzer but not that he will buzz every time he runs.) While the human data are far from complete, there is a suggestion (Horton and Kjeldergaard, 1961) that real asymmetries may be observed even in the paired-associate situation in spite of the fact that the paired-associate situation probably maximizes the chance of observing reverse chaining (see Jenkins, 1961).

2. If a stimulus elicits two responses, the responses will acquire a tendency to elicit each other. That is:

> Given that: A elicits B;
> and that: A elicits C;
> Then: B will tend to elicit C and
>   C will tend to elicit B.

This may be called the "response equivalence" paradigm (see Jenkins, 1959). There is abundant evidence that this paradigm can achieve the equivalence result in laboratory experimentation with humans. (See Mink, 1957; Martin, 1960; Horton and Kjeldergaard, 1961.) There is little evidence that the paradigm may be found to be effective with lower animals, but this has not been systematically studied.

An example in the case of paired-associate learning would be the learning of *zug-dol* followed by the learning of *zug-gex* facilitating the learning of *dol-gex*. Using other materials, it has been possible to show that, if one has a strong A B association and learns an instrumental response C (such as a lever press) to A, the response will generalize to B (Mink, 1957).

Here again we must add the caution that the equivalence may not be automatic (it can be both facilitated and interfered with by various activities of the subject) and that it may have a directionality component in the association depending on the order in which the steps were learned and on the nature of the stimuli and responses involved. In general, however, if the order of the first two stages is mixed or alternated, we anticipate bidirectional associates if such would be compatible with the nature of the stimuli and responses.

We talk of this as a mediational paradigm because it too may be derived from simple S-R associations given the use of the implicit response:

> A-B learning;   A-C learning;
> A-(B)-C learning;   A-(C)-B learning;
> B-C results.   C-B results.

That is, over-all, with varying order of the first two stages: $B \leftrightarrow C$.

That is, if we sometimes have A-B followed by A-C and sometimes A-C followed by A-B, the terms C and B should come to elicit each other, $B \leftrightarrow C$. The key to this paradigm is of course in the second stage. It is assumed that A as a stimulus elicits (B) as a covert response. The stimulus consequences of (B) then have an opportunity to become attached to the response C. Similarly, in the other order of the first two stages, the stimulus consequences of (C) become attached to the response B. Thus, if both orders are experienced, B and C come to elicit each other.

(It is clear that this paradigm also offers an opportunity for [B] or [C] to become extinguished or inhibited which is an alternate possibility [see Jenkins, 1961]. We will assume, however, that the individual items are returned to full strength repeatedly so that B and C are held simultaneously and become associated.)

If B and C are two verbal responses to A, it can be argued that we may build up strong verbal associates, a class of responses, without ever practicing the elements together explicitly. As we shall attempt to demonstrate later, we feel this possible outcome to be of great importance in building classes which may enter into the syntax.

3. If two stimuli elicit the same response, they may be said to become "functionally equivalent" stimuli; i.e., if a new response is attached to one stimulus, the other stimulus will acquire a tendencey to elicit it. In diagram:

Given that: A elicits B;
and: C elicits B;
If learn: A-D;
Then: C will tend to elicit D.

This paradigm expresses the notion of "acquired stimulus equivalence" developed by Hull (1939) and exemplified in the experiments of Shipley (1935), Birge (1941), and Wickens and Briggs (1951).

This is regarded as a mediation paradigm because of the assumed mediating responses occurring in the third and fourth stages.

A-B;
C-B;
A-(B)-D.   A elicits the implicit (B) the stimulus properties of which become associated with the D response.
C-(B)-D.   C elicits (B) which in turn tends to elicit D via the presumed learning in the third stage.

An interesting characteristic of this model is that, as A and C function as equivalent stimuli, B and D become equivalent responses. Thus, this more elaborate paradigm contains the response equivalence paradigm within it.

Using both verbal and motor mediators, Birge (1941) has demonstrated the full stimulus equivalence paradigm using children as subjects. It should be noted that it was necessary for the mediating response to occur explicitly in the third and fourth stage to provide strong evidence for the phenomenon. (As was mentioned in the case of the response equivalence paradigm, the extinction of the mediator is a possible occurrence during the third stage of this paradigm resulting in a failure to obtain equivalence results.) By requiring the overt occurrence of the mediating response prior to the making of the new response, Birge obtained the expected results which were not apparent when the subjects were left to their own devices.

More recently, Greeno and Jenkins (unpublished research) have demonstrated with natural language materials the full stimulus equivalence paradigm. In this case, the subjects were presented with a paired-associate learning problem of exceptionally high difficulty unless use was made of common mediating associates of groups of stimulus words which required the same nonsense syllable response. Eighteen words used as stimuli were paired with six nonsense syllable responses in such a way that the three stimulus words paired with a particular response were related by a single word presumably used as a mediator, i.e., *iron, copper,* and *steel* were paired with one nonsense syllable with the expectation that the mediator would be *metal*. After learning was complete, it was demonstrated that excellent transfer could be obtained in new learning to other stimuli which called out the same mediator as the presumed one in the first learning or to stimuli which were the inferred mediating stimuli themselves. Thus, in the above example, regardless of whether *tin* or *metal* was used as a stimulus in the second task the transfer was very strong.

The general paradigm, of course, is the one ordinarily used for the explanation of concept formation via mediation.

APPLICATION

Now, given the processes of chaining, response equivalence, and stimulus equivalence, how are they to be applied? What constitutes a unit or element in one of the paradigms? Certainly we do not want to hold that the paradigms apply only to nonsense syllables or to discrete lever presses. Nor do we wish to limit ourselves to items taken two at a time. At the risk of making the processes inapplicable, we must say that they apply to any functional stimulus classes and any functional response classes at any level of complexity made up of any number of items and that all processes may operate on all levels at the same time. In essence we are saying that subjects have integrated both stimulus and response units at many levels and that these processes may apply to all of these units.

Let us look at some examples of application in limited domains to furnish illustrations of what we mean.

Application in Paired-Associate Learning

Following ordinary paired-associate learning, we observe that the subjects can give us the list of responses without having the individual stimuli present (Cunningham, Newman, and Gray, 1961). Their ability to do this much exceeds their ability to report the specific stimuli (in the experiment under discussion the advantage was of the order of 3.5 to 1.0). One wonders why this should be true. The subjects were not instructed to learn the responses as a group; on the contrary, they were required to learn the set of pairs a-b, c-d, e-f, etc.

We assert that this response-group learning behavior follows from the response equivalence paradigm. All of the response items in the paired-associate learning task were responses which had to be used in "situation X" (the complex of stimuli making up the entire learning situation); hence we have the X-B, X-C, X-D, etc. paradigm, and it follows that the responses should come to elicit each other, as they in fact do.

It can be seen that the most general order of learning in this experiment is to acquire the responses to "situation X." As the experiment proceeds and specific contingencies are built up, the responses become progressively more and more under the control of a particular element of "situation X"; that is, they will be controlled by the nominal stimulus and therefore "correctly" emitted. (See McGeoch and Irion, 1952, and Underwood and Schulz, 1960, on this point.)

We must also observe in this experiment that the learning of the so-called S-R pairs shows that the subject is capable of narrowing the range of stimulus conditions under which he will emit the response; i.e, he can select some aspect of the total stimulus situation. In this case, it is the one we want him to consider, the term (or picture, or color, etc.) presented on the left-hand window of the memory drum. Once one has accepted the notion that the subject may in some fashion select elements of the stimulus situation, it is easy to admit the converse of this; namely, the subject may not respond to all the stimuli presented to him. Thus, we may find that the subject is not responding to the left-hand term in its entirety but rather to some fraction of it. Underwood and Schulz (1960) report that their subjects often volunteer that they attend to only one letter of the stimulus cluster (when this is possible in an experiment). Recently, Jenkins and Allen (1963b) confirmed the Underwood and Schulz statement in paired-associate learning by using as stimuli triple consonants which were totally independent from one stimulus cluster to another. The responses were single digits from one to seven. Transfer tests showed that subjects tended to respond correctly to first letters of the triples, next best to the last letters, and poorly to the medial letters. In other words, selection of stimuli had taken place although all stimuli had been available all the time. Position of the letter was not, however, the only variable involved. In part, idiosyncratic relations of the particular stimulus-response pair appeared to be important; for instance, if the middle letter rhymed with the number (e.g., "q"-"two"), it was likely to have been selected for attention as the functional stimulus.

Recent work of Underwood and his students (see Underwood, 1961) showed that, given multiple stimuli, subjects tend to learn the response to the most "meaningful" aspect of the stimulus complex. When the stimuli are real words and colors, the response is learned to the words and not the colors; when the stimuli are difficult nonsense letters and colors, the responses are learned to the colors and not to the letters. Jenkins (1964) followed this with a replication of the second part of the study plus the use of the names of the colors as a test of mediation. In this experiment, although the subjects had been instructed to learn to respond to the letters and had, in fact, been required to read the stimulus letters aloud on every trial, the subjects learned to respond to the colors and not the letters as indicated by the fact that there was almost perfect transfer to the color *names* which up to that time had not appeared explicitly in the experiment. Thus, we have good evidence for the selection of aspects of the stimulus to be used as the functional stimulus and transfer to the name of that aspect of the stimulus.[3] Since this is a natural language case and we do not have the histories of the relations between the colors and their names, we cannot decide unambiguously which paradigms are operative here, but it is obvious that verbal mediation is enormously successful.

Just as the stimulus side of paired-associate learning may be separated into gross and specific stimuli and aspects of particular stimuli, so aspects of response structuring should be considered. If, in simple learning, the subject is asked to respond with the series of letters "w-a-t-c-h," he has a unitary response available from past learning, saying "watch." If he is required to spell it as a response, we have every reason to believe that he says it implicitly, and he runs off already-learned spelling habits. This is in marked contrast to his behavior when he is asked to respond with *hctaw*, which he cannot pronounce, cannot remember as a unit, and cannot run off from the usual letter contingencies in English writing. (We have in fact in our laboratories used pronounceable syllables as *volvap* and found them appreciably more difficult for psychology students to learn than the familiar *Pavlov* from which the nonsense term was derived.) To refer to this phenomenon, workers in verbal learning use the term *response integration*. Well-integrated responses are more easily learned than less well-integrated responses, presumably because they are single units and the subject needs to learn only when to emit the unit. Less well-integrated responses must first be "knit together" before they may be given in the presence of the correct stimuli.

It should be noted that we do *not* expect these processes to run off in an orderly fashion; i.e, first the subject integrates all the responses he is going to use, next he associates these with all the stimuli in the situation to form a response pool, next he selects what particular aspects of narrow stimuli he will respond to, and finally he "hooks up" the narrow stimuli to the particular responses. Instead, it is clear that for a given learning task some parts of the material may be at quite different stages of the various processes at the same time. In addition, the processes may overlap for a single item as in the case of a subject who is still mispronouncing a response but knows its appropriate stimulus. Now, if we further complicate this description by giving you the additional information that this learning task is the second

---

[3] To talk of the "functional stimulus" suggests that there will be a dangerous circularity and looseness in any subsequent formulation, but we think this constitutes no danger. It does mean that the search for the determinants of stimulus selection must be added to the task of the S-R psychologist, but even the early experiments seem to promise lawfulness and regularity.

stage of a mediation model and that the stimuli are eliciting implicit responses with their associated stimuli which are becoming associated simultaneously with responses which are evolving in the experiment (and that at the same time the implicit responses are probably being extinguished because they are not being specifically reinforced), you have some idea of the confusion which attends a mediational explication of almost anything.

Application to a Simple System

Let us become one step more specific. It seems to us that a good place to begin is with a simple system which has been studied experimentally in the hope that we can pull ourselves up by the bootstraps and improve our ideas of structure and our understanding of the psychology of structure as we go along. The simplest structure we know of is one studied by Esper, one of the first American psycholinguists. Esper's first experiment (1925) was as follows:

Three groups of subjects were given learning problems with the same objective reference matrix (four shapes in each of four different colors). Group I had "names" for the stimuli which were "structured"; the first syllable of the name was constant for a given color, and the second syllable was constant for a given shape. Group II had the same arrangement except that the color-shape order of the response was reversed and the division was no longer at the syllable boundary. Shape was denoted by the initial consonant and vowel while color was denoted by the medial consonants, second vowel, and final consonant, i.e., CV (shape) – CCVC (color) as contrasted with CVC (color) – CVC (shape) for group I (see Table 1 for the design). Group III received different names for each stimulus compound. In each

TABLE 1

First Esper Experiment (1925)

Color	Shape A	Shape B	Shape C	Shape D
Group I				
Red	nasling*	naschaw	nasdeg	——
Green	wechling	wechchaw	wechdeg	wechkop
Blue	shownling	shownchaw	showndeg	shownkop
Yellow	royling	——	roydeg	roykop
Group II				
Red	nulgan*	doylgan	pelgan	——
Green	nugdet	doygdet	pegdet	wigdet
Blue	nuzgub	doyzgub	pezgub	wizgub
Yellow	numbow	——	pembow	wimbow

* These are approximations of the Esper names.

group two of the 16 possible color-shape combinations were never given in the training trials but were presented on test trials to observe how the subjects extended the "language system" to deal with these "new" stimuli.

The results are intuitively predictable. Group I learned most rapidly; group II learned much more slowly and showed great interference between terms; and group III learned about as rapidly as group II but showed little interference. When the two stimulus combinations which had been withheld were presented for naming in the context of the other stimuli, the group I subjects named them correctly almost as frequently as they named the training stimuli correctly and in general *showed no awareness that the stimuli were new*. Group II subjects never did well on synthesizing the names for the new stimuli. Group III subjects tended to apply the name of a stimulus of the same color or the same shape (in this group, of course, there was no "correct" synthesis to score).

What descriptive generalizations seem to be justified here? First, with respect to group I it is clear that a "system" was learned. The order of elements (color referent-form referent) and the point of division of the element (by syllable) in the response agreed with the subjects' experience. We must assume that the subjects fractionated the stimulus and responded separately to its components, associating these components directly with the familiarly divided elements of the response. This may be argued from the grounds that they could not identify new combinations (though they responded to them correctly) and also from the fact that the number of color-shape terms correctly given in each learning trial is almost exactly predictable from the product of the proportion of correct color responses and the proportion of correct shape responses. It would appear here that we must be prepared to deal both with the matter of analysis of the stimulus and segmentation of the response as well as a combination rule. It is not implied that any of this is "naturally given," of course, since in this case both the stimulus divisions and the response divisions and ordering are in accordance with the natural language habits the subject brings to the experiment with him.

In the case of group II we must conclude that there is little evidence that the system was learned. The novel but appropriate response to the new stimuli failed to appear just as the learning of the rehearsed responses failed to exceed the learning of unsystematized responses in group III. The correct responding to individual color-form stimuli, trial by trial, steadily exceeds what would be predicted from the hypothesis of independent learning of the color and shape stimulus-response habits, indicating that individual responses were being slowly and tortuously memorized. Whether the system would have emerged had learning been carried to higher levels is unfortunately unknown (at the end the subjects were getting only about 50 per cent of the items correct as contrasted with 88 per cent correct responding being achieved midway through the experiment by group I). It is clear that the unusual segmentation of the response, or its unusual ordering, or both, seriously hampered the development of the linguistic system. A consideration of the very large number of errors made by the subjects suggests that they were "trying" to make an old familiar system work in an inappropriate place or, more simply, that old habits of response segmentation and ordering were interfering with the learning of the system. It is important to note that the semantic aspect of the system for group II is exactly the same as for group I. The stimuli may be fractionated in exactly the same manner, and each stimulus aspect may be unambiguously related to an aspect of the response. The difference is that one response is familiarly divided and ordered and one is not. The conclusion must be that the development or discovery of the system depends heavily on the active participation of the subject and his past learnings and habits with respect to his natural language system.

How shall we approach the Esper experiments? Let us start with group I. In this situation we have stimuli which are highly discriminable. Certainly the instructions[4] plus the visual presentation of the stimuli strengthen the responses of color and shape. We expect that the subjects would say (if asked to name the stimuli), "There's a red jagged one," "There's another jagged one and it's yellow," "There is a green lump with a square corner," etc. The responses which are provided to the subjects as auditory stimuli from the experimenter are familiar in structure and easily echoed. We assume that the subjects are well trained in English adjective-noun structures such as "red square," "green circle," etc., and that they expect (from both their experience and the instructions of the experiment) that stimuli of the same shape will be called by some common name and stimuli of the same color will be called by some common name. We further assume that they are actively trying to link their own linguistic responses (which are implicit here) to the artificial responses the experimenter requires. Simple contingencies of implicit and explicit responses will account for the remainder of the experiment. The diagram may be seen in Figure 1.

When any red figure is presented, we assume that the implicit naming response "red" is made by the subject. At the same time the experimenter says "nas ——" and the subject echoes "nas ——." This sequence sets up a virtually perfect chain from the color of the object to the implicit response and from the stimuli produced by the implicit response to the overt response itself. A similar argument may be made for any particular shape becoming associated with a particular second syllable through the implicit shape

---

4 "This is not an intelligence test. It is an experiment to determine how quickly you can learn the names of certain sacrificial objects in the Morgavian language, a language spoken on the northern slopes of the Himalayan Mountains. As each object is shown, I shall pronounce the name. You will immediately repeat the name after me aloud."

(Visually presented figure)   (Auditorially presented "name")

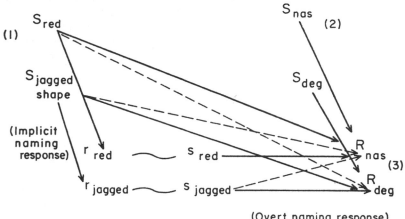

FIGURE 1—Mediational description of Esper experiment I (1925) for group I.

1. A complex visual stimulus. Color and shape are assumed to be two aspects of the stimulus which have high likelihood of eliciting naming responses.

2. Stimulus presented as one utterance. We assume that it is fractionated by the subject into two syllables as a result of his experience with English.

3. A complex response matching the auditory stimulus. We assume that it is fractionated as a result of the subject's experience with English.

4. Solid lines represent relationships which are assumed or observed to occur with very high probability, approaching $p = 1.00$. Dashed lines represent contingencies assumed or observed to occur approximately one quarter of the time, $p = .25$.

naming responses. It is clear then that for any color one nonsense syllable in one position will become overwhelmingly dominant, and that for any shape a nonsense syllable in the other position will become dominant. The dependencies between members (syllables) of "an utterance" will not be great because they will be essentially equal for all members of one class to all members of the other class. The classes formed, however, should be a considerable strength, e.g.,

Color$_1$-Shape$_1$	Color$_2$-Shape$_1$	Color$_3$-Shape$_1$	Color$_4$-Shape$_1$
Color$_1$-Shape$_2$	Color$_2$-Shape$_2$	Color$_3$-Shape$_2$	Color$_4$-Shape$_2$
Etc.	Etc.	Etc.	Etc.

This furnishes a sufficient condition to make the color names functionally equivalent responses to the total situation and functionally equivalent stimuli for the shape words. The shape words in turn become a functionally equivalent response class, both with respect to the total situation and with respect to the colors as immediately preceeding stimuli. Since the occurrence of the color class preceding the shape class has a probability of approximately 1.00, we may assume that this structure is virtually perfectly learned once the classes are established and serve as functional stimuli and responses.

Because the experimentally relevant classes are supported by the subject's language history, by the extra-experimental world, and by the semantic support they receive by correlation with physically different aspects of the experimental situation, everything leads to the formation of a strongly structured miniature linguistic system. When the new stimuli are presented, we can see that they conform perfectly to the system (i.e., the same shape and the same color have already been encoded) and hence are perfectly adequate stimuli to elicit the response. If a new member of either aspect were introduced to the experiment (either a new color or shape), we would expect an appropriate construction, a "something jagged" or a "red something." We would predict that the subject would never respond with a monosyllable.

The experience of group I overlaps so much with natural language that it is difficult to find much to explain that is not firmly rooted in habit already. The experience of group II, however, departs in two respects from English and does not permit us to assess unambiguously the "weight" of each deviation. Here the order of construction is violated (if the subjects do indeed think of the stimuli as colored things), and the response units are not those which the subject has integrated. We are virtually certain that the second alteration generated much more severe difficulty than the first.

Semantically the problems facing these subjects are the same as those facing the subjects in group I. However, when the subject begins forming associations between the implicit responses he is making (in English) and the echoes he is performing in the artificial language, he cannot achieve success. He has brought with him from English a set of well-integrated response units. He cannot even know that these units are inappropriate in the experiment. But even if he were to be given the "correct" responses for colors (e.g., *lgan, gdet, zgub, mbow*), he would find them unpronounceable and difficult to remember. The "units" cannot enter into the system because they are not units for the subject and would be extremely difficult to utter even if he were told that they were.

But the situation is even worse than it appears at first, for we may assume that the model for the color term would be much like the one given before, except that the order is incorrect and that the subject would not divide the response term properly.

Any Red Object

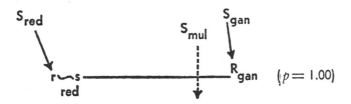

With the confirmed contingency for the R_{gan} syllable and "red," we would expect the subject to continue making this connection and direct his attention to the shape variable. What he is doing appears "correct" to him since the second syllable varies perfectly with the color. It will not be scored correctly, however, and he will not make correct total responses because the consonant preceeding the syllable will tend to be incorrect more times than it is correct.

With respect to shape, the subject will (both by elimination and by contingency) attempt to match the first syllable.

A Particular Shape (jagged):

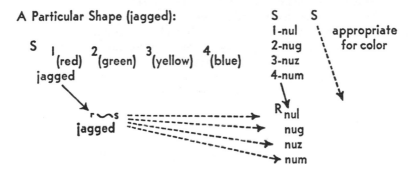

But note the conflict. The subject isolates *nul, nug, nuz,* and *num* for this shape. All will have some habit strength. Any one he says will be likely to be incorrect unless he also is using the color as a conditional stimulus. Thus the subject finds himself in doubt as to the first syllable which he is assigning to shape. As the experiment is scored, any response from this class will be scored as correct for shape but has three chances out of four of being wrong for color. If we examine the error list presented by Esper (which is not complete since he wished to illustrate only associative aspects of errors), we find that the last syllable in each of these "errors" is correct for the color in 40 of 54 cases and the initial consonant and vowel are correct for shape in 42 of 54 cases. The vast majority of the errors reported (even though they were selected to illustrate another point) are errors associated with the third consonant position.

We might argue that the strategy of the subjects was wrong. The fact is that they were probably (from their point of view) achieving almost complete success as to color names and coming very close (but missing for some mysterious reason) on the shape names, which from Esper's point of view was exactly the opposite of what was occurring. In the last analysis their learning was just as difficult as the learning of completely arbitrary names, because from the natural language syllable point of view the aberrant consonant at the end of the first syllable could only be given successfully when the color-shape pairing was used as the cue. This is apparently as difficult as learning a whole word for each color-shape pairing as the subjects in the third group were doing.

Finally, we should note that, despite the experimenter, the subjects in this portion of the experiment have learned a system. The syllables comprising the shape class have become functionally equivalent responses to the total situation and functionally equivalent stimuli for the color syllables. The color syllables, in turn, have become a functionally equivalent response class both with respect to the total situation and with respect to the shapes as immediately preceeding stimuli. The color syllables are appearing where they should and the shape syllables where they should although it is the reverse of the natural language. The only real difference in the systems of the experimenter and the subjects lies in the response unit being used.

Another experiment by Esper (1933) may also be fruitfully examined here. In this experiment a specific vocabulary was set up for a particular referential field, and then the referential field was enlarged. The experiment

TABLE 2

Diagram of Stimuli Presented in Esper (1933) Experiment

| Area of Figure | SHAPES OF FIGURES PRESENTED | | | |
	Shape A	Shape B	Shape C	Shape D
8 sq. cm.	——	B-1 (Name)	C-1 (Name)	D-1 (Name)
16 sq. cm.	A-2 (Name)	——	C-2 (Name)	D-2 (Name)
32 sq. cm.	A-3 (Name)	B-3 (Name)	——	D-3 (Name)
64 sq. cm.	A-4 (Name)	B-4 (Name)	C-4 (Name)	——

was designed to discover how the vocabulary would be shifted to cope with the larger referential system.

Sixteen stimuli were constructed. Four basic nonsense forms were chosen each of which was cut out in each of four sizes (8, 16, 32, and 64 sq. cm. in area). Four of the figures were removed from the set, and names were assigned to the remaining 12 figures. The names were nonsense monosyllables chosen so as to be easily discriminable. The experiment is diagrammed in Table 2. Appropriate names for the 12 figures were very thoroughly learned by the subjects over a period of months. An association test was given which included the names of the figures as well as English words. Test trials were given repeatedly over another period of months with all 16 figures present. Subjects were required to name all the figures which were presented four times each, three days a week, for approximately three months. No information was given as to correctness or incorrectness of their responses. At the end of this extensive testing period, stable naming systems had developed for the subjects.

Over all it was clear that the semantic system became stabilized by dividing the 12 terms among the 16 forms in such a way that there were individual names for each of the smallest and largest forms and a name in common for the two middle-sized forms in each shape series. The resolution and the shifts necessary for it are shown in Table 3.

TABLE 3

Resolution of Naming Problem When All Forms Were Present
(from Esper, 1933, Experiment)

| Area of Figure | SHAPES OF FIGURES PRESENTED | | | |
	Shape A	Shape B	Shape C	Shape D
8 sq. cm.	A-2 * ↑	B-1	C-1	D-1
16 sq. cm.	A-3 ↑	B-3 * ↑	C-2 ↓	D-2 ↓
32 sq. cm.	A-3	B-3	C-2 *	D-2 ↓
64 sq. cm.	A-4	B-4	C-4	D-3 *

NOTE.—Symbols * indicate name assigned in the final resolution. Arrows show source of name.

The study of the association pattern after initial learning showed that the names for forms of the same shape and adjacent size were most frequently associated. These, of course, were precisely the terms which had been hardest to learn and which had produced the most errors. After the new system had stabilized, the same finding was true, with the addition that now the terms for the middle-sized figures tended also to elicit one another across the shape categories. Esper was so impressed with the associative findings that he devoted considerable space to their discussion and formulated a series of principles which seemed to govern the establishment of verbal associations. Several of his conclusions bear directly on our equivalence paradigm:

> The greater the possibility of confusing an object, *a*, with a specific other object, *b*, and the less the possibility of confusing it with any other specific object, *c*, *d*, etc., the firmer and more universal does the verbal association between the names of objects *a* and *b* become (Esper, 1933, p. 359).

> When a given object is subject to confusion with a number of other objects, its name tends to become an alternative response to these other objects and an associative response to their names, and consequently to become the most frequently elicited name in the category (*ibid.*, p. 361).

Esper showed that subjects who responded very rapidly in the first period and made many errors, especially multiple errors (giving a wrong response and then rapidly correcting themselves and giving the correct response), tended to be fast in the association test and to give highly common responses to the nonsense stimuli. It also appears that subjects who were appreciably faster in their naming reaction times in the second period than in the first period were rapid on the association test, gave common responses in association, had little scatter on repeated association, and tended most markedly to shift the entire naming structure into the "small," "middle-sized," and "large" pattern.

Finally Esper foreshadowed the present paper with:

> . . . this readiness to respond to an object not only with a uniform verbal response but sometimes also with the responses usually made to somewhat similar objects, undoubtedly is the behavior tendency which has been responsible for most linguistic (and logical) organization. Its end-products in language are semantic and phonetic word groups. "Errors" of this type, particularly the semantic shifts which follow the introduction of the n-figures (new figures) . . . represent a progressive change in behavior and *interconnection of response units* which are to be regarded as a very important form of human learning (*ibid.*, p. 372).

This experiment fits easily into our framework of explanations and, in addition, provides supplementary data for our response equivalence paradigm. To begin with, we may assume that all responses in the experiment form an equivalence class of the broadest sort. That this is the case is shown by the fact that in the association test (where certainly other responses could have been made because all of the practice words and half of the test stimuli were meaningful English words) eight of the 12 subjects responded exclusively in the artificial language when the stimulus was in that language.

We would anticipate on grounds of primary stimulus generalization that the members of each stimulus form category would tend to elicit all the responses appropriate to the category and thus that these could form sub-classes. The more likely the stimuli were to elicit a particular pair of responses in a subclass (say, the next-to-smallest stimulus eliciting both the small and middle-sized names) the more these terms would become related. We would suppose, finally, to keep the stimuli distinct (acquired distinctiveness of cues), that the subjects would introduce implicit terms such as small, middle-sized, and large. When the shift in reference items occurs, we would expect the subjects to continue naming as before, but now the names would mediate the shift of responses to the new structure which finally becomes stable.

Example:

Period I			Period II		
A-2	(small ✕)	...... name 1	A-1	(small ✕)	...... name 1
A-3	(middle-sized ✕)	name 2	A-2	(middle-sized ✕)	name 2
A-4	(large ✕)	...... name 3	A-3	(middle-sized ✕)	name 2
			A-4	(large ✕)	.... name 3

Here the implicit responses, which may be presumed to have introduced order and clarity into the first system, are seen to mediate a change to a new but similarly structured system when the referential field is expanded. The specific changes are of course capricious, unless one views the system as a whole or studies the probable mediators. In essence, including the implicit response of the subject as a functional stimulus allows one to deal with the relations existing in the stimulus field, insofar as they are available to and responded to by the subject. (This is always of course subject to the proviso that one can show that the subject has such experience in his history and can make this response to the situation. As stated above, this extends the S-R researcher's task and responsibilities if he wishes to pursue such explanations.)

Application to Natural Language

The above examples have been simple exercises to warm up our tools, so to speak. Does the laboratory psychologist have anything to say about the acquisition of real language in all its complexity when it is first encountered? This is difficult to deal with for three reasons:

1. No one has provided us with the precise description of language acquisition that we need before we know what it is we are to explain. The material in McCarthy's (1954) excellent summary is of virtually no use if one wants to know the behaviors emitted by a child or the stimuli impinging on a child as he acquires language. The exciting work of Miller and Ervin and Brown and Fraser is just becoming available and is still far from complete even for one child. In a sense the Chomsky quotation which leads this paper is substantially correct.

2. Too much happens in genuine first-language learning, and it happens at all levels and all at the same time. To attempt to talk about first-language learning in all aspects is patently impossible.

3. Because we are dealing with first-language learning rather than the behavior of mature speakers of some language like first graders or college students, we lose our favorite salvaging device: the subject's talking to himself and providing just the stimulus we need at each crucial point.

The reader is reminded that the account is speculative, that we will attempt to speculate only about the formation of classes and the development of syntax, and we will have to do our best to defend the account without the self-stimulating verbalizations attributable to more advanced users of language.

How does language get under way? We think that children imitate the speech around them. They imitate because it is a functional property of the nervous system, because they are reinforced for imitating by other humans, because imitation is secondarily reinforcing, and because very soon the behaviors involved have functional properties for them as instrumental acts.

We believe that associative correlates between verbal behaviors and events in the world around the beginning speaker rapidly appear through simple S-R laws and that labeling or naming in its broadest sense ought to be one of the earliest forms to appear. (It will be understood that the label may be used descriptively, as in simple naming, or as a request, an announcement, a demand, etc.) It is clear that many general classes of behavior are present before the speaker learns labels for the salient objects and events involved, and we assume that the labels are readily used as instrumental acts within already-developed behavior repertoires. It seems reasonable to suppose that these early labels are attached to the functional properties of the situation which are of importance to the child as a result of his experience with the world or to properties which are "salient" in his stimulus field as a result of the way his nervous system is "wired." In other words S-R contingencies are developed where the functional stimulus is of the "acquired distinctiveness" sort, as well as where the functional stimulus is of the "figure-ground" sort.

We presume that at this early stage language behavior is too unstructured to speak of classes of utterances or of utterance units but that some contingencies would be observed (as a result of the groupings of stimuli in the external world if nothing else) which would form "proto-classes." One would merely expect that some elements are more likely to occur in the same time span than others.

When more than single word utterances appear, it is asserted that the development of classes begins in earnest. The simplest structure we have imagined (and, of course, the paper by Miller and Ervin reinforced this belief) would be some sort of "operator" plus the existing labels. Whether the operator precedes or follows the label makes little difference at this point; in either case the labels by our mediation principles will begin to form a class. Both reinforcement and primary stimulus generalization begin to play a part here as the grouping emerges. If the child makes a construction which is like the adult construction (within whatever weak limits we wish to specify "like"), we assume that this: (a) has a greater likelihood of being praised by others; (b) has a greater likelihood of inducing others to respond linguistically, which we presume is reinforcing; (c) has a greater likelihood of eliciting nonverbal behavior from the audience, if any; and (d) is secondarily reinforcing. All of this should lead to the greater selection of some sequences over others with this particular "operator" and, because of the semantic correlates probable in the successful utterances, to a semantic correlate of the class. It should be noted here that reference probably enters both in the original vocabulary development (the kinds of things talked about with children) and in the clarification and distillation of the class. One presumes that these dual determinants lead to the first class of this sort being "noun-like," although it is probably too gross to be given even that much of a name.

As utterances increase in length, the class formation process will continue to proceed to develop additional classes and finer and finer distinctions within classes. At this point a fairly complex phenomenon should begin to be manifest. Suppose that we are dealing with three-word utterances. Let us assume that we find a sequence A-B-C and also the sequence A-B-D. We conclude, of course, that C and D are members of the same class. Now we find E-B-C. We conclude that E and A are of the same class and predict the possibility of E-B-D. If we now find F-B-D, we would class it with A and E though in fact it has never appeared in the same specific context as E. If B has several equivalents, it is apparent that we may have many class members which have never appeared in the same context. It is clear, of course, that we are dealing with probabilities here. Not all words in a class will have equal probabilities of occurrence in a particular frame or sequence. We feel that behaviorally at this point we must go slowly. Our experience with laboratory learning leads us to at least two cautions here: first, it is probable that such classes develop quite slowly from the syntax base alone and require very high frequencies of occurrence to become firmly established; second, one must postulate varying degrees of strength of relationship between elements within classes, dependent on the number of contexts which they share and the degree of similarity of those contexts. It is clear that this is a potential source of trouble, because the "degree of similarity of contexts" will in turn depend on the degree of interchangeability of the words in the specific context with the other words in their respective classes. The difficulty here is expected to be great.

Basically the ideas we want to present here are of two sorts: *sequence* and *class*. We know that serial acts performed over and over become smooth, polished, easily performed, and integrated. This scarcely poses a problem for the specific act in question. The puzzling question is how a set of behaviors can become a smooth, polished performance when the entries in the behavior sequences are not the same specific entries from time to time. The appeal must clearly be made to a hierarchy notion. The sequences are the "same" because the entries are members of the "same" classes even though they may be different entries from time to time. Thus, a given sequence may begin with an *A*. Note that it is not A as a specific thing because A′, A″, A‴, etc. may be used. This is followed by a *B,* again, not B as a specific thing but B′, B″, B‴, etc. In this fashion a sequence may be developed and polished even though it appears to be different every time or nearly every time it is run off. But this creates two new responsibilities: (a) Can it be shown that classes really can be manipulated in this way? (b) How do members of the response community become organized into classes?

The first question is answered by language itself if we consider its entries as classes: "Colorless green ideas sleep furiously" is a sentence in English not because it is true, or sensible, or interpretable by the listener, but because it is a "correct" assembly of classes appropriately modulated, (i.e., they are the right general classes of entries properly modified to take their places in the particular sequence). If it is true, as Chomsky (1957) asserts, that such sequences are more easily spoken, recalled, learned, etc., than nongrammatical assemblies of words, then we have prima facie evidence that particular sequences, not previously experienced, are facilitated (polished, integrated, etc.) by practice of sequences of like classes. The critical question, then, is seen to be that of the organization of the elements into classes. For this question, we have proposed an answer from the point of view of the experimentalist interested in verbal behavior and mediation paradigms by outlining the three basic mediation processes we discussed earlier.

It should be clear, if our analysis is correct, that, in the natural language, class and sequential structure are learend simultaneously and interdependently. While this makes the detailed description of the process difficult and gives it the appearance of uncertainty, it is, nevertheless, our conviction that this is a valid contention.

Given that the child has a set of classes which he can arrange in functional sentences or utterances, all of the processes which led him to this point will similarly lead him to extend his behavior repertoire to other forms of ordering. Similarly, as he learns new sentence forms, he begins almost immediately on the learning of transformation rules. At this level of sophistication, we encounter trouble again. If the child were a complete grammarian, we could let him name the classes and proceed to learn the transformation rules by rote, but this is obviously ridiculous. Not only does he not have names for the categories he is supposed to label, but the linguists are still attempting to state explicitly the transformation rules he is supposed to learn.

At this point, at the risk of being regarded as hopelessly muddleheaded, we would like to reintroduce the notion of reference. We applaud and respect the efforts of grammarians to create a grammar without reference to meaning, and we feel that such proposals call attention to the syntactic contribution to the formation of classes which we feel is highly significant. We must, however, remember that there are semantic correlates of the major classses and that the main business of language is wrapped up in function and reference. From a psychological point of view it seems to us highly unlikely that transformations are generated without semantic support. We can facilitate the application of our mediation models by providing that the new forms (which are to be the transforms) are first learned instance by instance as independent constructions, and that the equivalences between such forms and the basic or kernel forms are identified and mediated semantically. It is our argument that the "thingness" of nouns is recognized and responded to as the implicit characteristic of the class; the "activeness" of verbs is similarly important, and the noun phrase, verb phrase, and even the sentence have semantic properties recognized, even though unverbalized, by the fledgling speaker of the language.

As the speaker becomes more and more practiced in the language, the precise semantic content may be supposed to recede in importance, and the (by this time) well-learned structural properties take over virtually unconscious control of the structure of the utterances.

In summary, we are suggesting that children's language begins with a form of imitation followed by the acquisition of a number of simple S-R connections between verbal labels and salient features of the environment to which they become attached. With a core of labels available, the child attaches words with other words in sequences, and the ordering or structuring begins. Particular structuring occurs more and more frequently because of the greater utility of some orders over others. With the development of particular structures, some words form classes in the sense that they take a particular position in an utterance which is different from the position which other words may take. Through the stimulus and response equivalence mechanisms, these classes of words become substitutable for each other in particular structural frames. Thus, new utterances may occur without prior training by the substitution of previously acquired equivalences. Transformations, initially learned independently, are facilitated by semantic mediation. Eventually the semantic basis of structure recedes, once the basic adult classes of structure have been acquired (more specific equivalences), and then structure is adhered to (within larger units) without conscious effort.

EVIDENCE

At the present time the evidence for the approach offered here is fragmentary and only suggestive; but we believe that it forms a pattern.

Werner and Kaplan (1950) imbedded nonsense words in sentences and invited children to give them meaning as in " A wet *corplum* will not burn." Young children gave contextual associations (i.e., sequences); older children gave potential substitutions (i.e., members of the implicit class). Werner and Kaplan report:

> . . . we should like to mention briefly that there are aspects of language development other than semantic, discussed in this paper, which showed similar abrupt changes at the same age levels. This is particularly true with respect to grammatical structure. The data indicate that there is a growing comprehension of the test sentence as a stable grammatical structure.
>
> The close correspondence of the developmental curves . . . between two seemingly independent aspects of language lends support to those theories that assume a genetic interdependence of meaning and structure (pp. 256-257).

In the gross sense we see this as supporting our general position that the items must first be learned in sequences (the sequences being reported as the "meaning" by the younger children), and after much sequence learning the emergence of classes and the identification of substitution with meaning occurs. This is also some evidence, we think, for the relatively slow development of complete systems.

In 1957, Brown reported evidence demonstrating that in children's speech the nouns are quite likely to be names of things and the verbs quite likely to be names of actions; furthermore, it was shown that children reliably respond to the semantic cues furnished by the parts of speech when nonsense entries are used for mass nouns, count nouns, and verb forms. This experiment indicates that the learning of structure and class membership may well be facilitated by semantic relations, as we suggested above, and that, once established, this relation may play a dual role: new entries may be classified semantically on the basis of syntactic cues, and new structures may be understood and related to old structures on the basis of semantic content.

Berko (1958) showed that the development of control over classes and their use is a continuous process with age. Extension to new cases of the "automatic" responses (such as pluralization) may be relatively late, with even the first graders having severe difficulty with some of the nonsense materials, though they were well able to handle most of the familiar material.

In addition, Brown and Berko (1960) have shown that, as the child grows older, the change in the form of word association responses is progressive toward "same class as the stimulus" responses (as Ervin, 1957, has also demonstrated) and that the change in word association is accompanied by the ability to make grammatical use of new words.

These findings give active support to the point of view we have endorsed concerning the shift from sequence to classes. It was a consideration of word association data, in fact, which led one of the writers of this paper to the exploration of the mediational models given above (see Jenkins, 1959). Saporta (1959) presented a paper containing material illustrating that subjects will often substitute an associate for a word in a sentence, if requested to strike out a single word and replace it. In a set of studies at Minnesota we have extended these findings with college students in the following respects: (a) On grammatically diverse sets of stimulus words, we have found that the part of speech of the stimulus word is most frequently matched by the popular response words. (b) We have found that, when one "sets" the subjects to give a response in the same class as the stimulus by giving a phrase stem for completion (e.g., table and ——, light or ——), one elicits most of the normal popular associates of the words. When one uses a sequential fragment (e.g., table is ——, or —— is heavy), one elicits the less frequent associative responses. (c) We have directed subjects to write sentences using selected stimuli, then directed them to strike out the key word and substitute another one. The substitute (as Saporta, 1959, suggested) is likely to be a high frequency associate. As an additional check on this line of thought, one more associative study has recently been performed. It was argued that in all probability a word must appear in several frames before it could gain effective class membership. An attack was made on this question by randomly choosing rare adjectives from the Thorndike Lorge list (1944) for use as associative stimuli. As was predicted, the associates to the rare adjectives turned out predominantly to be nouns. Apparently, such words do not appear in enough different sequences to attain strong relations to any other words of the same class. This suggests that the progressions observed by Brown, Berko, and Ervin are still proceeding (though at a very advanced level) with adult subjects.

A final piece of research with adults has greatly impressed us also with respect to the role of reference, as well as sequence, in the acquisition of language-like behaviors. Johnson, in his Ph.D. thesis at Minnesota (1961), attempted to teach a group of subjects a formal word ending for nouns and for adjectives in simple sentences of the form:

Article (adjective) (noun) verb.

Either the adjective or the noun was replaced by a nonsense form in a particular sentence. If the noun was replaced, the nonsense form appeared in the third position and ended in the syllable "pod"; if the adjective was replaced, the nonsense form appeared in the second position and ended in the syllable "lef." Sentences were then like the following:

> The green dupod rolled.
> The nolef ball bounced.

After intense training with many instances of this sort (which included, in some experiments, anticipation training so that the subject was forced to learn the nonsense syllable for each of several sentences), it was possible to obtain generalization to the extent that, given an "old" sentence (one used in the learning procedure), the subjects could pick out a correct filler from a choice of two new words (one a *pod* word and one a *lef* word). Similarly, given a pair of "old" words (words used in training), the subject could correctly pick the appropriate one for a new sentence requiring either an adjective or a noun. However, given both new words and a new sentence, the subjects did no better than chance.

This somewhat unbelievable finding was replicated on both general population adults and college students in several conditions. In addition, it was established that grammatical naiveté was enormous. Given an example of each kind of sentence and asked to sort a set of sentences into those of the same kinds, eight out of 10 subjects could correctly perform the task. Asked what characterized the two sets of sentences, only one out of these eight was able to give a specific reason for the separation.

Complete generalization was achieved (new words correctly chosen for new sentences) *only* when, prior to the training trials, the subjects were shown pictures of objects which were identified as being examples of particular "pod" words and squares of color identified as being "lef" words. Under these circumstances generalization was complete. As a control procedure the reference identification was given without the sentence training procedure. These subjects showed no generalization of the experimental words to appropriate sentences. At present it appears that, at least with an artificial and non-English procedure such as this, *both* semantic and syntactic cues are necessary to assign grammatical class to new instances of terms identified by formal characteristics.

Summary

This paper points out that the problems of grammar have rarely been made the subject of psychological analysis, although many psychologists have recognized the importance of such problems. Three general forms of mediational paradigms were advanced to be used as a basis for the explication of grammatical phenomena. These paradigms were applied in detail in explaining the behavior of subjects in two artificial language experiments.

General extension of this line of analysis to the question of the acquisition of grammar of natural first-language learning was attempted. Some experimental findings which seemed to be consistent with the approach offered here were briefly mentioned.

6

COMMENTS AND CONCLUSIONS

JAMES DEESE
Johns Hopkins University

I have been asked to comment on the proceedings of this conference as a representative from the field of learning and from the point of view of contemporary learning theory. This assignment is difficult for me because I had the conviction before the conference—and little has occurred to change that conviction—that contemporary learning theory has little to contribute to the problem of the analysis of language acquisition. There are, of course, some important exceptions to the extraordinary lack of concern with grammar and its acquisition, and I would like to mention at least one of these exceptions. I should also hasten to add that the lack of contribution from learning theory is not because of inherent weakness of current learning theory. It is, primarily, because the problems raised by the Ervin and Miller and the Brown, Fraser, and Bellugi papers have not been tackled by learning theorists.

There is a strong tradition in learning theory that language is somehow just like any other behavior. The classical attitude of many learning theorists towards the problem of language is that language learning is simply a matter of individual adjustment on the part of the organism. This belief provides the basis of most textbook accounts of language learning. The rules of the acquisition of linguistic responses are supposed to be not different from the rules of acquisition of any other kind of responses. From the 1920's on, there has been the feeling that one can deal with the acquisition of the individual elements of language by the principles of classical and/or instrumental conditioning. Such a view implies that one modifies and applies the apparatus of contemporary learning theory—stimulus generalization and the like—to the acquisition of language in general and grammar in particular.

However, the papers presented at this conference, particularly the two papers on grammar and the Jenkins and Palermo analysis of the Esper experiments, make it clear that we are dealing with systematic intraindividual organizations which require a different conceptual apparatus from that provided by traditional learning theory. The two papers on the development of grammar in children present for learning theorists a clarification of

439

the nature of the problem to which learning theory should address itself. This result may be one of the most important consequences of those papers. It may be indeed, as the linguists seem to assert, a virtually impossible task to write a grammar from the kinds of protocols or data presented in these papers; but the data presented there do provide the kinds of raw materials for inferences about the process of acquisition of learning of the kinds of structures apparent in the emitted verbal behavior of the child. These are the data to which one should address a theory, and the function of a theory so oriented is to recover the process—that is, to predict the sequences and the orders of emissions in the behavior under study.

Learning theorists, with a few exceptions, no longer regard the human organism as an indifferent, undifferentiated representative of all vertebrates so far as learning and conditioning are concerned. The notion of species-specific behavior has permeated modern learning theory. There are some species characteristics which have to do with the patterning of stimuli that impinge on the central nervous system, the organization of the central nervous system, maturational effects, and other special properties. Such a view, however, has not gone far enough in considering the special problems introduced by human language and particularly the grammar of human language.

One way in which an extension of modern learning theory has tried to deal with grammar is by mediation theory. Such a use of mediation theory is implicit in the classical treatment by Cofer and Foley (1942), and Jenkins and Palermo, in their paper presented here, make such a treatment quite explicit. The concept of mediation is built on the idea of stimulus-response units or contingencies between responses and events which precede them and which control their emission. Jenkins and Palermo make the assumption that these stimulus-response units can be chained together to form the flow of ordinary discourse, and they reduce the rules of such discourse to the stimulus equivalence and response equivalence paradigms of mediation theory.

The mediation model provides a very powerful tool of analysis, and it is a good beginning for the description of the emission of verbal behavior. It does come from learning theory and, so far as I know, is the most thorough contribution stemming from learning theory to the analysis of the acquisition of language. For this reason, if for no other, it deserves special attention.

The objection has been raised that the mediation model implies a left-to-right chaining of linguistic behavior. There are really two problems, however, in the implication of left-to-right chaining. One is simply the description of the order in which behavior occurs, and it is hard for me to imagine linguistic events in anything but a successive time order. The other problem, however, is more sophisticated, and it is the problem of how the rules constraining successive elements in an utterance are generated. Here we are dealing with such things as the possible nested properties of sentences. Yet, it seems to me, the question of a linguistic analysis of an utterance as a structural left-to-right unfolding, or as nested dependencies, may be irrelevant to the usefulness of the mediation model as a predictive device in describing the verbal behavior of children.

For one thing, we know that people can store words in their heads for short periods of time and react to these stored words as intraorganic events. Jenkins and Palermo give an example of a set of nested dependencies: "The boy . . . who lives in the big white house across the street from the curious looking bank. . . ." One can imagine such an utterance being generated in a time ordered way, but the order of generation is not necessarily the order of emission. "The boy" may be generated, and this set of elements in turn may generate the ultimate predicate phrase and then generate several dependent clauses. The predicate phrase is held in storage, however, until the long sequence in the middle is emitted. In fact, if it is held too long, it may be lost; such effects may be responsible for the evident disorganization of emitted speech seen in a literal transcription. There can be fairly complicated patterns built on temporary storage of material which has been generated but not emitted until some later time. Of course, what is stored may be altered by what is emitted in the meantime, which makes the problem of analysis of the emitted sequence even more difficult.

The mediation model, in the present context, can be taken as a notion as to how words become members of formal classes. It is also a model for the emission of verbal behavior, and because of its dual function it covers more ground than any comparable theory coming from the study of learning. Jenkins and Palermo are obviously interested in both aspects of mediation theory; though, in the present context, they are more concerned to show how the model describes the formation of verbal classes. It should be noted that the theory is built entirely upon the contingency rule. Classes or categories are derived from contingencies in perception and responding; the organism takes a kind of semirandom nature and organizes it into a highly structured intellectual system by a stimulus equivalence rule. Because of its dependence upon the contingency rule (contiguity), mediation theory ignores the possibility of innate intraindividual organizations. Gestalt psychologists, of course, have considered such organizations in a description of the perceptual world, but very little has been said about similar rules of organization in linguistic behavior. Despite the dependence of the Jenkins and Palermo mediation model upon stimulus-response contingencies, I do not think there is anything in the model which would preclude or deny innate organizations. Indeed, classical learning theory has one such innate organization in the form of stimulus generalization. Mediation may be viewed as an alternative to stimulus generalization, but it may also be viewed as something above and beyond primary stimulus generalization (such was the view of Cofer and Foley, 1942).

Mediation theory, at any rate, is one inheritance of learning theory in the study of language acquisition that is of potential importance. It may provide an extremely powerful tool for extending the experimental data on the acquisition of verbal behavior to the kinds of data observed by Ervin and Miller and Brown, Fraser, and Bellugi.

There is another side of modern learning theory that has received much attention lately in the study of verbal behavior, and a word should be said about it. This aspect of learning theory is not so concerned with description of the structure of verbal behavior (I view mediation theory as being so concerned) as with the incentive and motive conditions which control the production or emission of behavior. I am talking about the behaviorism of Skinner (1957). The essence of the Skinnerian analysis is concerned with incentive conditions. Skinnerian behaviorism is hardly at all concerned with learning—learning is early and easily dismissed. The Skinnerian, however, is concerned with describing the way in which environmental reinforcement contingencies and the like control the emission of behavior. The result of such an analysis is that one can write an historical account of how sequences of reinforcement contingencies produce particular outcomes in behavior.

Of recent years, this analysis has been applied to the emission of words, both in Skinner's own discursive treatment of verbal behavior and in a large number of experiments on the effects of reinforcement schedules on classes of verbal elements. The whole point of the application to verbal behavior is to show—and I am exaggerating only slightly—that verbal behavior is not different from any other class of operant or emitted behavior.

The Skinnerian analysis of the conditions controlling the emission of behavior is a very powerful one, and it is easy to be convinced that verbal behavior, along with other kinds of behavior, is under the control of reinforcement contingencies. Nevertheless, it is language which is central to a lot of the human being's specific characteristics, and we define language in such a way as to say precisely that it is not entirely under the control of reinforcement contingencies. It is, to a considerable measure, internally controlled by its own structural relations. That seems to be the point of a great deal of linguistic analysis. The human being is able to transcend the effects of a reinforcement schedule through his ability to store and internalize environment behavior and intrabehavioral relations through the mediation of language. Therefore, it is that aspect of language which makes it different from elements of behavior simply and entirely under the control of reinforcement contingencies, which makes language unique and worth studying in its own right.

All this has relevance to the study of language acquisition in children, for we must suppose that, as children acquire and use language, they divorce themselves in considerable measure from direct control through reinforcement contingencies. The internal events that can go on through the mediation of language take away some of the power of the environmental contingencies to control in a simple and direct way. Language must modify control exerted by external reinforcement. Thus, if we are to understand thoroughly the control exerted by reinforcement on the behavior of linguistically behaving children, we must find some way of externalizing (finding out about) the operations which the child performs upon his own behavior linguistically before we can make any real sense about the control of the behavior of children by reinforcement.

If we really want to have some leverage on the problem of the control of the emission of behavior in the young child, we must make usable some of the conceptual apparatus that is implied by the term "expectancy" and the like. We have little or no conceptual apparatus for dealing with such problems, but, if we are to appreciate the control exerted over the linguistically active child by his environment, we need some useful ideas about what goes on intraorganically, and specifically intralinguistically. Therefore, rather than using the data on reinforcement schedules to "explain" the acquisition of language, we need information about the acquisition of language in order to understand the effect of reinforcements upon the young child.

In this sense as well as others, the study of the nature or structure of language in children may well provide an important part of the information needed to control and predict the behavior of children. The structural study of children's language, then, may make as much of a contribution to the uses of learning theory as learning theory can make to an understanding of how those structures are acquired.

COMMENTS AND CONCLUSIONS

OMAR K. MOORE
Yale University

Deese's remarks will serve as a convenient starting point for my comments. First of all, I am less hopeful than he is about the possibility of successfully applying any of the current theories of learning to the acquisition of a first language; as a matter of fact, I do not think that they are adequate to explain the learning of anything very complex. There are many reasons why I am dissatisfied with contemporary learning theories: they tend to confound *learning* and *performance;* they tend to neglect the cue value of reinforcing agents; and they make the assumption that reinforcement is essential for learning, whereas I do not think that reinforcement is either necessary or sufficient for learning.

Today, however, I would like to draw your attention to the fact that learning theories fail to satisfy what is sometimes called the "sufficiency criterion." What do I mean by the "sufficiency criterion?" Imagine that we wish to evaluate some theory of learning; let us disregard the problem of whether human beings actually behave as the theory stipulates. Instead, let us ask whether *any* entity, which behaves as the theory prescribes, could learn the things which we know human beings do learn. If we find that no entity which behaves in strict accordance with the candidate theory of learning could learn what human beings obviously do learn, then the theory fails the sufficiency criterion. One practical way to test a theory for sufficiency is to construct a working model of the theory—give the working model appropriate inputs and see whether or not it does in fact learn. It is unnecessary to build a working model of most learning theories because it is obvious at first glance that these theories have almost nothing to say about what a working model should do with input data. A few researchers have made models of their own intuitive guesses about learning processes: for example, Newell, Shaw, and Simon (1958) have done this with the help of computers. And their research, unlike the work of most learning theorists, is at least relevant to the problem of constructing a theory of learning which would pass the sufficiency test.

My remarks up to this point may have been too general to convey clearly what I have in mind, so let me be more specific. We know that human beings frequently solve problems which have the following characteristics: (a) the likelihood of obtaining solutions by random, or quasi-random, trial and error is virtually zero; and (b) no practical algorithms exist for obtaining solutions (an algorithm is a method which guarantees a solution if one exists, or, in the case of a problem with no solution, will indicate that there is none). As I mentioned before, human beings frequently solve such problems, and, by definition, the learning process can neither be a purely random one nor a purely mechanical one. The question is, "How do human beings learn to solve such problems?" The most suggestive material that I have encountered for unraveling this mystery is contained in the writings of logicians on the topic of "natural deduction" (see, for example, Fitch, 1952). The various nonalgorithmic problem-solving schemata which logicians have developed in recent years as heuristic devices for approaching such problems—and which are very helpful, as a matter of fact—have certain features to which I would like to call attention. For the purposes of this discussion I will use Fitch's method of subordinate proof as an illustrative case.

Probably the most striking feature of Fitch's method is that the problem solver's attention is first directed to the goal, here, the theorem to be deduced. In brief, the learner is invited to behave in a goal-directed way. The first task of the learner is to work backward from the goal toward the initially given data. This process of working backward ordinarily requires the setting up of subgoals and of subsubgoals. From each subgoal the learner is enjoined to continue this backward working process. Of course, each subgoal must stand in some plausible relation to both superordinate and subordinate goals. Also, Fitch's method specifies ways of interrelating this hierarchy of proof sequences, and it also makes explicit provision for moving forward from the initial starting point to subgoal sequences. In sum, Fitch's method makes explicit provisions for working backward from a goal and working forward from some starting point, and also for the elaboration of an interlocking network of subgoals which are tied to both the goal and the starting position. Now the trouble with most learning theories is that they simply do not make provision within the structure of the theories themselves for any such system of goal-directed activity. I do not suggest that Fitch's system, or any other system of natural deduction, should be thought of as a learning theory, but I do say that learning theories should be at least as rich as the methods of natural deduction in specifying the procedures whereby learning could take place. And, since they are not adequate in this regard, I think it is obvious that they fail the sufficiency criterion.

From my point of view it is clear that the standard learning theories are not going to be of much help in understanding the acquisition of a natural language. After all, natural languages are much more complex than the simple, straightforward symbolic systems for which natural deduction is a useful tool. It is distressing to think that learning theories may well have to be recast at this late date, but perhaps we can begin in a more sophisticated way.

In our next attempts to construct theories of learning I think it would pay us to attend more closely to the formal disciplines, namely, mathematics and mathematical logic. For instance, it would seem wise to take into account the work of Church (1936). Prior to, say, 1930, I think that most researchers, certainly most logicians, would have thought it possible, in principle, to write a program which would constitute an effective method for solving any arbitrarily selected problem in any well specified class of problems. However, it is now clear that there are intrinsic limitations on the development of effective procedures; namely, in certain cases at least, the goals of achieving completeness and consistency are antithetical. From time to time during this conference we have talked about the possibility that there is a language generator within human beings which, granted certain inputs, would be capable of generating well-formed expressions in a natural language. It may be that such a language generator is impossible in principle. Perhaps there are formal arguments of the kind Church (1936) and Gödel (1931) have used which would make clear what some of the boundary conditions are for the development of adequate theories of learning. In any case, it would be worthwhile to give a great deal of thought to the problem of specifying what characteristics we might want in the way of a heuristic language generator.

Thus far I have talked almost exclusively about the inadequacies of learning theories. I would like now to make a few comments about the linguistic side of the problem of understanding language acquisition. We all recognize that linguists have made considerable headway in analyzing the structure of natural languages. The work on generative grammars is particularly clarifying. In my opinion, many of the empirical studies reported at this conference do not take account of the best that is known in linguistics. In particular, linguists are making it more and more evident that the structure of a language is best treated as a system—a system in which what were formerly thought of as more or less autonomous parts can now be seen to be only contingently autonomous. For example, it may be very misleading to think of language as consisting of a complex structure made up of elementary units, for example, built up out of phonemic classes— the status of a phoneme qua phoneme may well be dependent upon its relation to a complex set of formation and transformation rules. Now it seems to me that it would be most unfortunate if psychological research on language acquisition were to be carried out on the assumption that a language consists of a hierarchy of complex elements constructed out of elementary building blocks. If the "new look" in linguistics—by the "new look" I mean the work of Chomsky and his colleagues—is at all viable, it would be a serious mistake to conduct empirical studies of first language acquisition on the assumption that to master a language is to learn to handle the kind of linguistic entity posited by linguists in the 1930's and 1940's.

REFERENCES

ABORN, M., & RUBENSTEIN, H. Word-class distribution in sentences of fixed length. *Language*, 1956, 32, 666-674.

ADRIAN, E. D., & BUYTENDIJK, F. J. Potential changes in the isolated brain stem of the goldfish. *J. Physiol.*, 1931, 71, 121-135.

BARKER, R. G., & WRIGHT, H. F. *Midwest and its children.* Row, Peterson, 1954.

BATESON, G., JACKSON, D. D., HALEY, J., & WEEKLAND, J. Toward a theory of schizophrenia. *Behav. Sci.*, 1956, 1, 251-264.

BERKO, J. The child's learning of English morphology. *Word*, 1958, 14, 150-177.

BERNSTEIN, B. Aspects of language and learning in the genesis of the social process. *J. Child Psychol. Psychiat.*, 1961, 1, 313-324.

BIRGE, J. S. The role of verbal responses in transfer. Unpublished doctoral dissertation, Yale Univer., 1941.

BLANKENSHIP, A. B. Memory span: a review of the literature. *Psychol. Bull.*, 1938, 35, 1-25.

BOUSFIELD, W. A. The problem of meaning in verbal learning. In C. N. Cofer (Ed.), *Learning and verbal behavior.* McGraw-Hill, 1961.

BROWN, R. W. Linguistic determinism and the part of speech. *J. abnorm. soc. Psychol.*, 1957, 55, 1-5.

BROWN, R. W. How shall a thing be called? *Psychol. Rev.*, 1958, 65, 14-21. (a)

BROWN, R. W. *Words and things.* Free Press, 1958. (b)

BROWN, R. W., & BERKO, J. Word association and the acquisition of grammar. *Child Develpm.*, 1960, 31, 1-14.

BRUNER, J. S. Review of K. W. Spence, *Behavior theory and conditioning. Contemp. Psychol.*, 1957, 2, 155-157.

CANTOR, C. N. Effects of three types of pretraining on discrimination learning in preschool children. *J. exp. Psychol.*, 1955, 49, 339-342.

CARROLL, J. B. *The study of language.* Harvard Univer. Press, 1953.

CHOMSKY, N. *Syntactic structures.* The Hague: Mouton, 1957.

CHOMSKY, N. Review of B. F. Skinner, *Verbal behavior. Language*, 1959, 35, 26-58.

CHURCH, A. A note on the Entscheidungsproblem. *J. symbolic Logic*, 1936, 1, 40-41.

COFER, C. N., & FOLEY, J. P., JR. Mediated generalization and the interpretation of verbal behavior: I. Prolegomena. *Psychol. Rev.*, 1942, 49, 513-540.

CUNNINGHAM, J. W., NEWMAN, S. E., & GRAY, C. W. Stimulus-term and response-term recall as functions of number of paired-associate training trials. Paper presented at Midwest. Psychol. Ass., May, 1961.

DEGROOT, A. W. Structural linguistics and syntactic laws. *Word*, 1949, 5, 1-12.

DOLLARD, J., & MILLER, N. E. *Personality and psychotherapy.* McGraw-Hill, 1950.

DRILLIS, R. Objective recording and biomechanics of pathological gait. *Ann., N.Y. Acad. Sci.*, 1958, 74, 86-109.

ERVIN, S. M. Grammar and classification. Paper read at Amer. Psychol. Ass., 1957.

ESPER, E. A. A technique for the experimental investigation of associative interference in artificial linguistic material. *Language Monogr.*, 1925, No. 1.

ESPER, E. A. Studies in linguistic behavior organization: I. Characteristics of unstable verbal reactions. *J. genet. Psychol.*, 1933, 8, 346-379.

FITCH, F. B. *Symbolic logic.* Ronald, 1952.

FORD, F. R. *Diseases of the nervous system in infancy and childhood.* (4th ed.) Thomas, 1960.

FRANCIS, W. N. *The structure of American English.* Ronald, 1958.

FREUD, S. On narcissism: an introduction. In *Collected papers,* Vol. IV. London: Hogarth Press, 1914. Pp. 30-59.

FRIES, C. C. *The structure of English.* Harcourt, Brace, 1952.

GESELL, A., *et al. The first five years of life: a guide to the study of the preschool child.* Harper, 1940.

GLEASON, H. A. *An introduction to descriptive linguistics.* (2nd ed.) Holt, Rinehart & Winston, 1961.

GÖDEL, K. Über formal unentscheidbare Sätze der Principia Mathematica und verwandter Systeme I. *Monantshefte für Mathematik und Physik,* 1931, 37, 349-360.

GOUGH, P. B. The study of mediation in animals. Unpublished doctoral dissertation, Univer. of Minnesota, 1961.

GRAY, J., & LISSMAN, H. W. The coordination of limb movements in the amphibia. *J. exp. Biol.,* 1946-47, 22-23, 133-142.

GREENBERG, J. Some universals of grammar with particular reference to the order of meaningful elements. Paper for SSRC Conference on Language Universals, 1961.

GRÉGOIRE, A. *L'apprentissage du langage: les deux premières années.* Paris: Droz, 1937.

GROSSMAN, J. B. Trembling of the chin. *Pediatrics,* 1957, 19, 453.

GUILLAUME, P. Le développement des elements formels dans le langage de l'enfant. *J. Psychol. norm. path.,* 1927, 24, 203-229.

HARRIS, Z. S. *Methods in structural linguistics.* Univer. of Chicago Press, 1951.

HEBB, D. O. *The organization of behavior.* Wiley, 1949.

HEBB, D. O. *A textbook of psychology.* Saunders, 1958.

HELD, R. Exposure-history as a factor in maintaining stability of perception and coordination. *J. nerv. ment. Dis.,* 1961, 132, 26-32.

HILL, A. Grammaticality. *Word,* 1961, 17, 1-10.

HOCKETT, C. F. *A course in modern linguistics.* Macmillan, 1958.

HORTON, D. L., & KJELDERGAARD, P. M. An experimental analysis of associative factors in mediated generalizations. *Psychol. Monogr.,* 1961, 75, No. 11.

HULL, C. L. The problem of stimulus equivalence in behavior theory. *Psychol. Rev.,* 1939, 46, 9-30.

HYMES, D. H. Functions of speech: an evolutionary approach. In F. C. Gruber (Ed.), *Anthropology and education.* Univer. of Pennsylvania Press, 1961. Pp. 55-83. (a)

HYMES, D. H. Linguistic aspects of studying personality cross-culturally. In B. Kaplan (Ed.), *Studying personality cross-culturally.* Row, Peterson, 1961. Pp. 313-360. (b)

HYMES, D. H. The ethnography of speaking. In T. Gladwin & W. C. Sturtevant (Eds.), *Anthropology and human behavior.* Washington, D.C.: Anthropol. Soc., 1962. Pp. 13-53.

JAKOBSON, R. *Kindersprache, Aphasie, und allgemeine Lautgesetze.* Uppsala: Almqvist & Wiksell, 1941.

JAKOBSON, R. Linguistics and poetics. In T. A. Sebeok (Ed.), *Style in language.* Technology Press & Wiley, 1960. Pp. 350-377.

JEFFREY, W. E. The effects of verbal and nonverbal responses in mediating an instrumental act. *J. exp. Psychol.,* 1953, 45, 327-333.

JENKINS, J. J. A study of mediated association. Report No. 2. Studies in verbal behavior. N.S.F. Grant, Univer. of Minnesota, 1959.

JENKINS, J. J. Mediated associations: paradigms and situations. In C. N. Cofer & B. S. Musgrave (Eds.), *Verbal behavior and learning.* McGraw-Hill, 1963. Pp. 210-245. (a)

JENKINS, J. J. Stimulus "fractionation" in paired-associate learning. *Psychol. Rep.,* 1963, 13, 409-410. (b)

JENKINS, J. J., & BAILEY, V. B. Cue selection and mediated transfer in paired-associate learning. *J. exp. Psychol.,* 1964, 67, 101-102.

JESPERSEN, O. *Growth and structure of the English language.* (9th ed.). Doubleday, 1938.

JOHNSON, N. F. The cue value of sentence frames for the acquisition of speech categories. Unpublished doctoral dissertation, Univer. of Minnesota, 1961.

KAHANE, H., KAHANE, R., & SAPORTA, S. Development of verbal categories in child language. *Int. J. Amer. Linguistics,* 1958.

KANTOR, J. R. *An objective psychology of grammar.* Principia Press, 1936.

KIMBLE, G. A. *Hilgard and Marquis' conditioning and learning.* Appleton-Century-Crofts, 1961.

KLÜVER, H. *Behavior mechanisms in monkeys.* Univer. of Chicago Press, 1933.

KÖHLER, W. Aus der Anthropoidenstation auf Teneriffa: IV. Nachweis einfacher Strukturfunktionen beim Schimpansen und beim Haushuhn. *Abh. preuss. Akad. Wiss., phys.-math. Kl.,* 1918, 2, 3-101.

KUENNE, M. R. Experimental investigation of the relation of language to transposition behavior in young children. *J. exp. Psychol.,* 1946, 36, 471-490.

LASHLEY, K. S. The problem of serial order in behavior. In L. A. Jeffress (Ed.), *Cerebral mechanisms in behavior: the Hixon symposium.* Wiley, 1951. Pp. 112-136.

LEES, R. B. The grammar of English nominalizations. *Int. J. Amer. Linguistics,* 1960, 26, No. 3.

LENNEBERG, E. H. A laboratory for speech research at Children's Hospital Medical Center. *N.E.J. Med.,* 1962, 266, 385-392.

LENNEBERG, E. H. Understanding language without ability to speak: a case study. *J. abnorm. soc. Psychol.,* 1962, 65, 419-425.

LIBERMAN, A. Some results of research on speech perception. *J. acoust. Soc. Amer.,* 1957, 29, 117-123.

LURIA, A. R. The directive function of speech (I and II). *Word,* 1959, 15, 341-352 and 453-464.

MCCARTHY, D. Language development in children. In L. Carmichael (Ed.), *Manual of child psychology.* (2nd ed.) Wiley, 1954. Pp. 492-630.

MCGEOCH, J. A., & IRION, A. L. *The psychology of human learning.* Longmans, Green, 1952.

MACKAY, D. M. Towards an information-flow model of human behaviour. *Brit. J. Psychol.,* 1956, 47, 30-43.

MACLAY, H., & SLEATOR, M. Responses to language: judgments of grammaticalness. *Int. J. Amer. Ling.,* 1960, 26, 275-282.

MAGNI, F., MELZACK, R., MORUZZI, G., & SMITH, C. J. Direct pyramidal influences on the dorsal-column nuclei. *Arch. ital. Biol.,* 1959, 97, 357-377.

MARTIN, J. G. Mediated transfer in two verbal learning paradigms. Unpublished doctoral dissertation, Univer. of Minnesota, 1960.

MAY, M. A. Experimentally acquired drives. *J. exp. Psychol.,* 1948, 38, 66-77.

MILLER, G. A. The magical number seven, plus or minus two: some limits on our capacity for processing information. *Psychol. Rev.,* 1956, 63, 81-97.

MILLER, G. A., GALANTER, E., & PRIBRAM, K. H. *Plans and the structure of behavior.* Holt, 1960.

MINK, W. D. Semantic generalization as related to word association. Unpublished doctoral dissertation, Univer. of Minnesota, 1957.

MOTT, F. W., & SHERRINGTON, C. S. Experiments upon the influence of sensory nerves upon movement and nutrition of limbs. *Proc. royal Soc.,* 1895, 57, 481-488.

MUNN, N. L. Learning in children. In L. Carmichael (Ed.), *Manual of child psychology.* (2nd ed.) Wiley, 1954. Pp. 374-458.

NEWELL, A., SHAW, J. C., & SIMON, H. A. Elements of a theory of human problem solving. *Psychol. Rev.,* 1958, 65, 151-166.

NORCROSS, K., & SPIKER, C. C. Effects of mediated associations on transfer in paired-associate learning. *J. exp. Psychol.,* 1958, 55, 129-134.

Osgood, C. E. *Method and theory in experimental psychology.* Oxford Univer. Press, 1953.

Osgood, C. E., & Sebeok, T. A. Psycholinguistics: a survey of theory and research. *J. abnorm. soc. Psychol.,* 1954, 49, Supplement, Part 2.

Osgood, C. E., Suci, G. J., & Tannenbaum, P. *The measurement of meaning.* Univer. of Illinois Press, 1957.

Pike, K. *Language in relation to a unified theory of the structure of human behavior,* Part I. (prelim. ed.) Glendale: Summer Inst. Linguistics, 1954.

Probst, M. Über die anatomischen und physiologischen Folgen der Halbseitendurch-schneidung des Mittelhirns. *Jb. Psychiat. Neurol.,* 1903, 24, 219-325.

Reichling, A. J. B. N. Principles and methods of syntax: cryptanalytical formalism. *Lingua,* 1961, 10, 1-17.

Rudel, R. G. Transposition of response by children trained in intermediate-size problems. *J. comp. physiol. Psychol.,* 1957, 50, 292-295.

Rudel, R. G. Transposition of response to size in children. *J. comp. physiol. Psychol.,* 1958, 51, 386-390.

Rudel, R. G. The absolute response in tests of generalization in normal and retarded children. *Amer. J. Psychol.,* 1959, 72, 401-408.

Rudel, R. G. The transposition of intermediate size by brain-damaged and mongoloid children. *J. comp. physiol. Psychol.,* 1960, 53, 89-94.

Sapir, E. Communication. In D. Mandelbaum (Ed.), *Selected writings of Edward Sapir.* Univer. of California Press, 1949. Pp. 104-109.

Sapir, E. The psychological reality of phonemes. In D. Mandelbaum (Ed.), *Selected writings of Edward Sapir.* Univer. of California Press, 1949. Pp. 46-60.

Saporta, S. Linguistic structure as a factor and as a measure in word association. In J. J. Jenkins (Ed.), *Associative processes in verbal behavior: A report of the Minnesota conference,* 1959.

Shepard, W. O. The effect of verbal training on initial generalization tendencies. *Child Develpm.,* 1956, 27, 311-316.

Shepard, W. O., & Schaeffer, M. The effect of concept knowledge on discrimination learning. *Child Develpm.,* 1956, 27, 173-177.

Shipley, W. C. Indirect conditioning. *J. gen. Psychol.,* 1935, 12, 337-357.

Skinner, B. F. *Verbal behavior.* Appleton-Century-Crofts, 1957.

Smart, W. K. *English review grammar.* (4th ed.) Appleton-Century-Crofts, 1957.

Smith, M. E. Grammatical errors in the speech of preschool children. *Child Develpm.,* 1933, 4, 182-190.

Spence, K. W. The differential response in animals to stimuli varying within a single dimension. *Psychol. Rev.,* 1937, 44, 430-444.

Sperry, R. W. Neural basis of the spontaneous optokinetic response produced by visual inversion. *J. comp. physiol. Psychol.,* 1950, 43, 482-489.

Spiker, C. C. Stimulus pretraining and subsequent performance in the delayed reaction experiment. *J. exp. Psychol.,* 1956, 52, 107-111.

Spiker, C. C., Gerjuoy, I. R., & Shepard, W. O. Children's concept knowledge of middle-sizedness and performance on the intermediate size problem. *J. comp. physiol. Psychol.,* 1956, 49, 416-419.

Staats, C. K., & Staats, A. W. Meaning established by classical conditioning. *J. exp. Psychol.,* 1957, 54, 74-80.

Stutsman, R. Performance tests for preschool age. *Genet. Psychol. Monogr.,* 1926, 1, 1-67.

Teuber, H. -L. Perception. In J. Field, H. W. Magoun, & V. E. Hall (Eds.), *Handbook of physiology, Section 1. Neurophysiology,* Vol. 3. Washington, D.C.: Amer. Physiol. Soc., 1960. Pp. 1595-1668.

Teuber, H. -L. Sensory deprivation, sensory suppression and agnosia: notes for a neurologic theory. *J. nerv. ment. Dis.,* 1961, 132, 32-40. (a)

TEUBER, H. -L. Brain and behavior: summation. In M. A. B. Brasier (Ed.), *Brain and behavior*. Washington, D.C.: Amer. Inst. Biol. Sci., 1961. Pp. 393-420. (b)

THORNDIKE, E. L., & LORGE, I. *The teachers' word book of 30,000 words*. Teachers College, Columbia Univer., 1944.

TOWE, A., & JABBUR, S. J. Cortical inhibition of neurons in dorsal column nuclei of a cat. *J. Neurophysiol.*, 1961, 24, 488-498.

UNDERWOOD, B. J. Stimulus selection in verbal learning. In C. N. Cofer & B. S. Musgrave (Eds.), *Verbal behavior and learning*. McGraw-Hill, 1963. Pp. 33-48.

UNDERWOOD, B. J., & SCHULZ, R. W. *Meaningfulness and verbal learning*. Lippincott, 1960.

VON HOLST, E. Die relative Coordination als Phänomen und als Methode zentralnervöser Funktionanalyse. *Ergebn. Physiol.*, 1939, 42, 228-306.

VON HOLST, E., & MITTELSTAEDT, H. Das Reafferenzprinzip (Wechselwirkungen zwischen Zentralnervensystem und Peripherie). *Naturwiss.*, 1950, 37, 464-476.

VON SENDEN, M. *Raum- und Gestaltauffassung bei operierten Blindgeborenen vor und nach der Operation*. Leipzig: Barth, 1932.

WEISS, P. Self-differentiation of the basic patterns of coordination. *Comp. Psychol. Monogr.*, 1941, 17, No. 4 (Whole No. 88).

WERNER, H., & KAPLAN, E. Development of word meaning through verbal context: an experimental study. *J. Psychol.*, 1950, 29, 251-257.

WHORF, B. L. Linguistics as an exact science. Reprinted in J. B. Carroll (Ed.), *Language, thought and reality*. Technology Press & Wiley, 1956. Pp. 220-232.

WICKENS, D. D., & BRIGGS, G. E. Mediated stimulus generalization in sensory preconditioning. *J. exp. Psychol.*, 1951, 42, 197-200.

YNGVE, V. Random generation of English sentences. Mechanical Translation Group, M.I.T., (Memo 1961-4) 1961.

IV

MATHEMATICAL LEARNING

Report of a Conference
Sponsored by the
Committee on Intellective
Processes Research of the
Social Science Research Council

EDITED BY

LLOYD N. MORRISETT
JOHN VINSONHALER

1

LEARNING AND USING THE MATHEMATICAL
CONCEPT OF A FUNCTION[1]

MARSHALL H. STONE

University of Chicago

In choosing the subject to discuss at this conference, my aim was to emphasize a topic of commanding importance in modern mathematics. Any such topic obviously has a special claim upon the attention of individuals who are preoccupied with the mathematical, pedagogical, and psychological problems involved in modernizing the mathematical curriculum. Furthermore, because it is so close to the heart of mathematics any such topic is nearly certain to pose particularly subtle and complicated problems and, in a discussion of the kind we are engaged in here, to define the full scope of those problems and challenge to the limit the resolution and ingenuity of individuals coming to grips with them.

In the most varied situations, mathematicians recognize and identify entities that they call functions. These entities are also designated by many other names that are more or less specifically associated with different special branches of mathematics. The characteristic property of such an entity is that it acts upon (or combines with) certain objects converting each into (or producing from each) a *unique* object usually of the same, but not infrequently of a different, kind. In order to make effective use of these entities in all the different circumstances out of which they naturally emerge, mathematicians have developed an appropriate theory with its own special languages, both colloquial and symbolic, and its own special manipulative procedures. In the teaching of mathematics, it is essential to start at an early stage to lay the groundwork that will enable students, when they reach the stage between 15 and 18 years of age, to study this theory with understanding and master some of its numerous applications in arithmetic, algebra, geometry, and analysis.

---

[1] A discussion and development of the mathematics of the function concept, as presented at the Conference, appears in the Appendix, p. 143 ff.

HISTORY

The presence of the entities we call functions was first detected and explicitly, although somewhat vaguely, noted in the study of geometry. In order to treat the congruence of figures in plane geometry, Euclid had to think in terms of an act converting one (concrete) figure into another, point by point and part by part. It might be argued that functions were probably recognized even earlier in arithmetic, since addition and multiplication are particular functions converting an (ordered) pair of numbers into their sum and product, respectively. A careful study of languages, especially the primitive, might throw some light on this question. We must come down to quite recent times, however, before we can find any true comprehension of the nature, the ubiquitousness and the fundamental importance of functions in mathematics. Even as late as the end of the eighteenth century, such a great mathematician as Euler was far from understanding the true breadth of the function concept. In my own lifetime I have seen our mastery of the concept profoundly altered by the somewhat tardy realization that its arithmetic, algebraic, geometric, and analytic aspects do not have to be distinguished as essentially different but can be considered in a conceptual unity that is of the greatest value for our understanding of mathematics.

How can we explain the extreme slowness with which mathematicians penetrated to the common core of the different branches of their subject? It seems to me that we must note the historical fact that specific concrete examples of functions were accumulated only very gradually and did not become sufficiently numerous or variegated until something like a century ago. In other words, we appear to be in the presence of a well-known psychological phenomenon, that is, that a creative act of generalization or abstraction, whatever the psychomechanism underlying it, cannot take place without the accumulation and comparison of sufficiently numerous and variegated concrete experiences. At the same time, we may also recognize here an illustration of a basic principle of the economics of intellectual effort, that is, that generalization or abstraction from a very narrow or limited basis in experience rarely recommends itself as either necessary or useful to individuals actively preoccupied with particular problems. Parenthetically, it is worth noting that both these observations have a direct bearing on the problem of teaching the function concept to our students: they need, first of all, to be familiarized with many illustrative examples of different kinds from which the concept can eventually be educed or abstracted and its value made manifest.

Historically (*Encyclopedia Britannica*, 1964), it was in mathematical analysis and its applications to geometry and physics that the need for the function concept was first strongly felt. The term "function" was introduced by Leibnitz in 1694 and was then employed by James Bernoulli. In more general contexts, John Bernoulli and Euler used the term in the sense that became firmly established by the end of the eighteenth century. Euler, in 1734, introduced the notation that we still employ in mathematical writing. It was only around the middle of the nineteenth century, however, that Dirichlet formulated the concept of function in the full generality required in analysis. While the concept is just as useful in elementary geometry and elementary algebra, the most important functions occurring. there can be described in terms of a finite number of parameters. In analysis, on the contrary, an analytic function requires for its specification infinitely many parameters. This distinction almost certainly explains the historical role of the analyst in isolating and clarifying this central concept of modern mathematics and, also, the difficulty that was experienced at first in throwing off the tyranny exercised by explicit algebraic and analytic formulas over the mathematical thinking of the eighteenth and early nineteenth centuries. It would be too much to claim that the progress made by analysts during the nineteenth century had a specific influence on the parallel developments that were taking place in algebra and geometry. Certainly the standard use of the terms "operation" and "transformation," respectively, to describe the analogous entities that were recognized contemporaneously in these two fields suggests that the influence was, at best, a vague and subtle one exerted indirectly through the general mathematical spirit of the times. On the other hand, I believe it could be demonstrated that the further developments achieved during the present century are mainly the fruit of initiatives taken by analysts and logicians since 1890, or perhaps a little earlier. In particular, our understanding of the true generality of the function concept clearly grew out of now-classical studies in the theory of real functions, topology, set theory, and logic, dating from around the turn of the century.

THE CONCEPT OF A FUNCTION

Indeed, a discussion of the function concept adequate for our present purposes is impossible without some consideration, however summary and incomplete, of the light thrown upon it by modern studies in logic. The central point that needs to be appreciated is that the function concept is so intimately connected with primitive concepts of pure logic that it is nearly unanalyzable and must be grasped, like the primitive concepts of pure logic themselves, by a psychological act of direct perception. To put the matter very crudely, the concept of a function is included as a special case in the general concept of a relation which, from a psychological point of view, obviously has the character of a primitive and hence undefinable concept. To a very great extent, all language is concerned with the expression of relations through conventional devices of grammar and syntax which are often complex and sometimes inefficient. Thus the concept of relation, like other logical concepts, is built into colloquial speech and writing in such a way that from earliest childhood on it is a component of our thinking and is correspondingly difficult to isolate and analyse. The particular relations that are of the greatest concern in daily life are, for the most part, not functions; the relations of parenthood, friendship, ownership, partnership, and so on, do not fall within the definition of a function. On the other hand, the relations that seem most important to contemporary mathematicians are, in an overwhelming majority, functions—the principal exceptions are relations of equality or equivalence, relations of order and magnitude, and the membership relation that underlies the theory of classes and sets. Thus there is a contrast between general intellectual practices and mathematical practices which must be taken into account in training children and young people to pass from the familiar modes of thought of their daily speech to those characteristic of contemporary mathematics. At the same time, this passage need not appear forced or unnatural if proper use is made of the familiarity with the basic concepts of logic that are implicit in the ability to speak and write.

In the circle of concepts comprising those of relation, function, class, and set, many intimate connections of a technical nature are worthwhile noting. For example, associated with any relation involving two relata—a so-called binary relation—is the class of ordered pairs of relata that satisfy the relation. This class is called the graph of the relation. On the other hand, each class of ordered pairs defines a binary relation between the elements of the pair, that is, the relation of forming a pair in the given class. Thus, the consideration of relations can be reduced to the terms of the theory of classes. Many contemporary mathematicians like to define the general relation concept within the framework of the theory of classes. It should be observed that this does not eliminate the relation concept as a primitive because the theory of classes rests upon the relations of identity and membership or elementhood. Von Neumann's treatment of set theory in terms of the function concept, a much more profound insight into the connections among the concepts we are examining, shows that the concepts of class and set can be defined in terms of the function concept, and hence of the relation concept, as primitive. This point of view is beginning to prove its worth in the study of problems that arise from the theory of categories and its applications, and may very well prevail over others in a relatively short time. Another technical observation that may be appropriately mentioned here concerns the possibility of defining a general relation in terms of a function. The relevant device is to replace a binary relation by the function that converts the first element of a pair of relata into the class of all elements that form with it a pair satisfying the relation in question. This observation allows us to conclude that for all technical purposes the function concept can be given the central role in the logical foundations of mathematics. The more general relation concept, nevertheless, still must be considered to be primitive because it is indispensable to an axiomatic formulation of a theory of functions, such as von Neumann's.

TEACHING THE FUNCTION CONCEPT

From what has now been said, it should be possible to discern some basic pedagogical and psychological problems involved in the teaching of the function concept. They are necessarily similar to those involved in teaching set theory because of the obvious analogies and the intimate technical connections that have just been discussed. In each case we must deal with a spontaneous act of perception for which first an adequate background in experience must be prepared. Since the concepts that we wish our pupils to form in their minds are essentially primitive, we cannot explain the concepts in other terms that have already been mastered. It is true that we can expect pupils to have some kind of working familiarity with the concepts of class, relation, and function at the linguistic level, and that we can take advantage of this fact by acquainting ourselves in some detail with the nature and limitations of this familiarity. On the other hand, no matter how cleverly we build upon this foundation and provide our pupils with the broadened experience from which the concepts of class, relation, and function can naturally emerge, we still must await the spontaneous formation of these concepts in each individual mind. We are in much the same position, it seems to me, as if we were trying to teach golf or bicycle riding. After doing everything possible in the way of analyzing and explaining the elements of the skills, we shall not have taught a single pupil to swing his club effectively or ride his bicycle until some spontaneous and almost instantaneous realignment takes place within his organism—a realignment that is essentially irreversible and permanent because once it has occurred he will never be able under normal circumstances to forget what he has learned to do. Once the mind has learned to perceive, at the conscious level, classes, relations, and functions as entities, it will forever after see these entities in every kind of situation and, with a certain amount of systematic training, will become proficient in exploiting this intellectual capacity. What can the psychologists tell us about the mysterious processes involved here? Possibly, they can analyze them into components that are not obvious to a casual or untrained observer and thus can explain some of the difficulties we encounter as teachers. More certainly, they can give us valuable quantitative information on many aspects of the learning processes that confront us in teaching these fundamental mathematical and logical concepts. A very important area of study is the stage of maturity that the learner must attain before he is able to grasp these concepts, and the possibilities of displacing this stage through early enrichment of his background experience and thus creating conditions that enable him to grasp the concepts earlier. The study of the amount of exposure to such stimulus experiences needed to trigger the spontaneous act of perception that is the goal of our efforts as teachers has an obvious importance. So also does the study of individual differences, in relation to this particular situation. Much easier questions are posed by the teaching that follows this fundamental act of perception and aims at the development of technical proficiency in handling the concepts thus formed. These questions are not different in kind from those already familiar to us in the teaching of arithmetic or algebra. What we must do is introduce the relevant language and symbolism, develop certain manipulative skills and techniques, and give practice and self-confidence in dealing with the most useful patterns of thought that have been developed for treating the basic concepts. No doubt the psychologists can give us valuable guidance at this level, if they begin by paralleling for the theory of functions the investigations that were previously carried out in algebra and arithmetic. But, of course, further pioneering work needs to be done in those fields and, a fortiori, in the one that we are discussing here.

Let us now examine some of the ideas that should be emphasized in developing a theory based on the function concept. The introduction to this theory has been quite satisfactorily outlined for secondary-school presentation in the Dubrovnik Report, *Synopses for modern secondary school mathematics* (1961), so that only pertinent ideas need be given here.

The first step is to establish the basic definitions, terminology, and notation by using a wealth of illustrations. It would be tempting and quite worthwhile to digress here at some length upon the part played by symbolism in mathematics, but this would require more time than can be spared. It seems likely, however, that in elementary mathematical instruction more attention should be given to symbolism than has been given in the past. Once the basic definitions and accompanying symbolism have been introduced, illustrations should be drawn from the different branches of mathematics where a wealth of simple examples is available. With the help of these illustrations, it is then necessary to present and explain a rather long list of descriptive technical terms so that our initial explication of the function concept in colloquial terms can be tied in a fairly precise way to the theory of relations and to the basic formal definition of the term "function."

The concept of inverse functions, as exemplified by the exponential function and the logarithm in elementary mathematics, seems to be one with which students have considerable difficulty at first. It, therefore, should be given a very full and careful treatment in the classroom. The difficulty very likely has psychological roots that might be worth investigating.

In terms of the function concept, algebra can be characterized as the study of systems of functions or operations that convert ordered sets of objects, all of the same kind, into an object of that kind. In elementary arithmetic we deal with several different sets of numbers, all generated from the natural numbers, and the two basic operations of addition and multiplication, in terms of which other operations such as subtraction and division are defined. For some time it has seemed to me that a natural and relatively easy way to begin the study of modern abstract algebra would be to focus attention on the various addition and multiplication tables that occur in elementary arithmetic and generalize to the study of arbitrary functions of two variables. The analysis of such tables can even be made the basis for a first contact with the function concept and, once this concept is available, can rely heavily upon it. I have anonymously outlined such an analysis and the way in which it leads into modern algebra in the Dubrovnik Report and hope to carry it through in considerably more detail on some other occasion.

Turning now to geometry, I wish to touch upon a bit of mathematical theory that might very well serve as the kernel of a full-fledged axiomatic treatment of elementary geometry.[2] This theory depends upon the function concept and illustrates very nicely the techniques appropriate for dealing with it. The connections between geometry and algebra become apparent almost at the start, and the development leads very rapidly along paths pointed out by Artin (1957) to a framework within which affine geometry finds a natural place. Since, in the present state of mathematics, we have to consider the early introduction and adequate treatment of affine geometry as one of the principal objectives of our teaching, the theory has some pedagogical interest. The ease with which the transition from affine to Euclidean geometry can be made suggests also that a satisfactory approach to the axiomatics of Euclidean geometry can be found along this route. The basic pedagogical problem is the treating of physical or intuitive geometry in such a way as to draw out of classroom experiments and observations the concept of function or transformation, and some techniques for handling it. This means studying motions in space and arriving at a good intuitive understanding of the transformations that are designated as the euclidean motions. It is very fortunate that these motions can all be obtained by the composition of reflections in planes; in the case of the plane, reflections in lines; and in the case of the line, reflections in points. Thus, the simplest paper-folding games teach deep lessons in intuitive geometry. It seems fairly reasonable to hope that very young students can be led to a fairly good understanding on the intuitive level of the fundamental role of transformations, that is, functions, in geometry.

REFERENCES

Artin, E. *Geometric algebra.* London: Interscience Publishers, 1957.
Cartan, É. *Oeuvres complètes.* Paris, Gauthier-Villars, 1952-1955, 3 V. in 6.
Encyclopedia britannica. (14th ed.) Chicago: William Benton, 1946, 11, 915–921.
Piaget, J. *Introduction à l'epistémologie genétique.* Paris: Presses Univer. de France, 1950.
Piaget, J. *Logic and psychology.* Manchester: Manchester Univer. Press, 1953 (also Basic Books).
Synopses for modern secondary school mathematics. Washington, D. C.: Office of Scientific and Technical Personnel of the Organization for Economic Cooperation and Development, 1961.

---

[2] See the Appendix for details.

TOWARD AUTOTELIC LEARNING OF MATHEMATICAL LOGIC
BY THE WFF'N PROOF GAMES

LAYMAN E. ALLEN

Yale University

The efforts to devise the WFF 'N PROOF games are grounded in the belief that learning ought to be fun—a conviction that allowing youngsters to find joy in learning bears fruit throughout the rest of their lives. The primary goal in creating materials for such play activity is to encourage more favorable attitudes toward symbol-manipulating activities; a secondary goal is to teach something about mathematical logic and provide practice in abstract thinking.

Omar K. Moore's and Alan R. Anderson's approach to learning (Moore, 1959; Anderson & Moore, 1959; Moore & Anderson, 1961) has served as a guide in designing the WFF 'N PROOF games; learning by doing and a maximum of self-discovery by the learner are emphasized. Moore (1959) says: "Motivation is sustained throughout by seeing to it that the child is not robbed of the opportunity of making a series of interrelated discoveries leading to the acquisition of some basic intellectual skills."

Moore and Anderson seek to arrange a rather special kind of learning activity—something that will be done for its own sake, is self-motivating, and fun. They have coined a word to describe this kind of activity: "autotelic." By means of such autotelic activities, they have had unusual success in helping preschool three- and four-year-old children learn such basic symbol-manipulating skills as reading and writing. The part that requires some ingenuity is arranging the situation so that some fundamental intellectual skill is being rehearsed in the course of an activity that is being done simply because the participants enjoy it. The fundamental goal in designing

Research for the WFF 'N PROOF games has been supported by funds from the Carnegie Corporation of New York. The ALL Project—"ALL" is an acronym for "Accelerated Learning of Logic"—was established at Yale Law School in 1960 when a grant was received to develop games and other materials programmed for self-instruction to help teach mathematical logic to elementary-school students.

such autotelic activities is to encourage favorable attitudes toward symbol-manipulating activities. The intellectual skills or subject matter learned in the course of such activities are the useful by-products, rather than the primary aims, of what is being done.

Such an approach to learning encourages speculation on some interesting questions: How many beginners in our formal educational system in the United States come to kindergarten and first grade bursting with curiosity and filled with expectation that school *will* be fun? How long, however, does it take many of them—particularly the boys—to decide that the fun parts of school are recesses, weekends, holidays, and summer vacations, rather than what is going on in the classroom? Just how well does what is going on today in most of the elementary- and secondary-school classrooms throughout this country nourish and sustain motivation for engaging in intellectual activity?

In his important and provocative book James Coleman (1961) penetratingly diagnoses contemporary secondary education. His characterization seems apt for more than just secondary education.

> Modern adolescents are not content with a passive role. They exhibit this discontent by their involvement in positive activities, activities which they can call their own: athletics, school newspapers, drama clubs, social affairs and dates. But classroom activities are hardly of this sort. They are prescribed "exercises," "assignments," "tests," to be done and handed in at a teacher's command. They require not creativity but conformity, not originality and devotion, but attention and obedience. Because they are exercises prescribed for all, they do not allow the opportunity for passionate devotion, such as some teen-agers show to popular music, cars, or athletics [Coleman, 1961, p. 315].

Coleman devotes most of his concluding chapter to emphasizing the importance of developing gamelike activities to teach fundamental intellectual skills and enhance the prestige of those who master such skills. The same spirit that motivated construction of the WFF 'N PROOF games pervades Coleman's remedial prescriptions for secondary education.

> To put the matter briefly, if secondary education is to be successful, it must successfully compete with cars and sports and social activities for the adolescents' attention in an open market. The adolescent is no longer a child, but will spend his energy in the ways that he sees fit. It is up to adult society to so structure secondary education that it captures this energy [Coleman, 1961, p. 329].

The extent to which there is lack of enthusiasm for engaging in symbol-manipulating activities is perhaps most pointedly exemplified by the active antagonism and fear that many persons seem to have towards mathematics or anything that even looks like mathematical symbolism. Why is it that so many persons have such an unfavorable attitude toward this kind of symbol-manipulating activity, usually accompanied by an extraordinarily unrealistic underestimation of their own individual capabilities to engage in such activity? The hunch upon which the WFF 'N PROOF games are based is that we learn such negative attitudes and—what is more important—that it is possible to arrange experiences so that more favorable attitudes can be learned.

With this brief introduction, the rest of this report will present some general comment and background information about the WFF 'N PROOF games, and a highly condensed description of how the games are played.[1]

BACKGROUND INFORMATION ABOUT "WFF 'N PROOF"

Giving the name "WFF 'N PROOF" to a game that has been developed mainly at Yale, perhaps, deserves some explanation. Although some relation to the "Whiffenpoof Song" is a likely conjecture, the fact of the matter is that "WFF 'N PROOF" resulted from combining two prior sets of games —one set called "WFF" and the other, "PROOF." It happens that "WFF" and "PROOF" are technical terms in mathematical logic. They are also the terms used to express the first two ideas introduced in the WFF 'N PROOF games.

The expression "WFF" is the customary abbreviation for "well-formed formula." If mathematical logic is thought of as a set of carefully constructed and precise languages, then a WFF (or well-formed formula) can be thought of as an expression roughly equivalent to a sentence in English prose—that is, a unit that expresses a complete idea. Furthermore, just as certain sequences of sentences in English are valid arguments, similarly, certain sequences of WFFs in mathematical logic are PROOFs.

WFF 'N PROOF is a series of games— 21 in all—rather than a single game. They vary widely in complexity. Thus, they can be played by learners of widely varying ages and abilities. The first few games are quite simple and have been mastered by children as young as six, while the final games are sufficiently intricate to pose a genuine challenge to intelligent adults. One of the foremost considerations in designing the WFF'N PROOF games was to develop an activity that would be fun and challenging for teachers as well as students. The attitude of a teacher toward an activity is thus assumed to be an important ingredient in influencing the attitudes of the teacher's students toward the activity. The WFF 'N PROOF materials are recommended as enrichment materials to the regular mathematics program in grades 1–12 and to college courses in mathematical logic.

Thirteen ideas are introduced and used repeatedly in the play of the WFF 'N PROOF games: the definitions of WFF and PROOF, and eleven rules of inference (the Ko, Ki, Co, Ci, R, Ao, Ai, No, Ni, Eo, and Ei rules). These thirteen ideas, comprising one formulation of the system of logic called "propositional calculus" (sometimes abbreviated "PC"), are pre-

---

[1] The instruction manual for playing the 21 games in the revised WFF 'N PROOF kit (1962) is in the form of a 224-page programmed textbook containing 2,176 stimulus-response items.

sented very gradually as a learner proceeds through the series of 21 games. A learner moves on to the next idea in WFF 'N PROOF only after he has had considerable practice in using a given idea and has discovered many of the relations between that given idea and the other ideas that he has already learned. This gradual introduction of the ideas as a learner proceeds through the games is summarized in Table 1.

From Table 1 it can be seen that there are three kinds of games: WFF

TABLE 1

GAME[a]		IDEAS											
	WFF	Proof	Ko	Ki	Co	Ci	R & Rp	Ao	Ai	No	Ni	Eo	Ei
1. Shake-a-WFF......	Xi		.		.			.		.		.	
2. Count-a-WFF......	X		.		.			.		.		.	
3. Ko Practice	X	Xi	Xi	.				.		.		.	
4. Ki Practice.	X	X	X	Xi	.			.		.		.	
*5. Kio Proof..	X	X	X	X	.			.		.		.	
6. Co Practice.	X	X	X	X	Xi			.		.		.	
*7. Kio-Co Proof......	X	X	X	X	X	.		.		.		.	
8. Ci Practice.	X	X	X	X	X	Xi	.	.		.		.	
9. R Practice..	X	X	X	X	X	X	Xi	.		.		.	
*10. Kio-Cio-R Proof......	X	X	X	X	X	X	X	.		.		.	
11. Ao Practice.	X	X	X	X	X	X	X	Xi	.		.		.
12. Ai Practice.	X	X	X	X	X	X	X	X	Xi	.		.	
*13. Kio-Cio-R-Aio Proof...	X	X	X	X	X	X	X	X	X	.		.	
14. No Practice	X	X	X	X	X	X	X	X	X	Xi		.	
15. Ni Practice.	X	X	X	X	X	X	X	X	X	X	Xi	.	
*16. Kio-Cio-R-Aio-Nio Proof......	X	X	X	X	X	X	X	X	X	X	.		
17. Eo Practice.	X	X	X	X	X	X	X	X	X	X	X	Xi	
*18. Ei Practice.	X	X	X	X	X	X	X	X	X	X	X	X	Xi
*19. Kio-Cio-R-Aio-Nio-Eio Proof...	X	X	X	X	X	X	X	X	X	X	X	X	X
*20. PC Proof...	X	X	X	X	X	X	X	X	X	X	X	X	X+D
*21. Frantic WFF 'N Proof......	X	X	X	X	X	X	X	X	X	X	X	X	X+D

[a]Games marked with an asterisk (*) are proof games.
X indicates that the idea is or may be used in that game; Xi indicates that the idea is first introduced in that game.
+D indicates plus the derived rules.

games (1 and 2), rule-practice games (3, 4, 6, 8, 9, 11, 12, 14, 15, 17, and 18), and proof games (5, 7, 10, 13, 16, 19, 20, and 21).

In the presentation of the 21 WFF 'N PROOF games, propositional calculus is formulated in the notation of Jan Lukasiewicz (Prior, 1955, p.v.), using Frederick B. Fitch's technique of subordinate proofs (Fitch, 1952, chap. 2).

Beginners should not expect to learn to play the final game of WFF 'N PROOF in a single sitting. The games are organized so that players will learn in a systematic, step-by-step fashion the skills required to play the final game of WFF 'N PROOF. Thus, the learning proceeds in the programmed manner advocated by B. F. Skinner (1958). This systematic arrangement of the learning is one of the important characteristics that permits WFF 'N PROOF to be enjoyed by players of such widely ranging ages and abilities.

The instruction manual in the current WFF 'N PROOF kit is "programmed" for self-instruction and contains a total of 2,176 stimulus-response items. These items are used to provide the players with an introductory acquaintance with the 13 basic ideas dealt with in WFF 'N PROOF. Most of the interrelations between these ideas, however, are left for discovery during the course of playing the games. Much more is left to be discovered than is presented in the instruction manual. The number of stimulus-response items that can be generated in the course of playing the games runs into the millions.

It should be mentioned also that the instruction manual to the WFF 'N PROOF kit illustrates how programmed instructional materials can be incorporated into an ordinary textbook presentation. It may be least a partially self-fulfilling prediction to venture the hunch that in the future the art of programming self-instructional materials will veer more in this direction of incorporating programmed sections in regular textbooks.

The WFF 'N PROOF games are related to programmed instruction in another interesting way. They embody the important characteristics of active participation, immediate reinforcement of correct responses, and individual pacing of learners. At the same time, the WFF 'N PROOF games extend beyond what has been customary in programmed learning to date by incorporating a random element in the determination of what the actual stimulus item at a given time will be. In other types of so-called "branched" programming the actual stimuli that a learner is exposed to are determined by his competence in responding to past stimuli. In the WFF 'N PROOF games only the *degree of complexity* of many possible present stimuli is determined by the learner's response to past stimuli; the actual stimulus is determined in part by chance and, in part, by the plays of the other players. The WFF 'N PROOF games also extend customary programming techniques by taking advantage of interaction among the players, as well as between the programmer and individual learners, to provide reinforcement as part of the learning procedure.

In playing WFF 'N PROOF, students get practice in abstract thinking in a competitive and entertaining atmosphere; they learn symbol-manipulating skills in propositional calculus. The games are graduated in complexity so that the players first learn how to form sentences in a special language, that is, they learn to construct WFFs; next, they learn how to show that some of these special sentences can be deduced from others, that is, they learn how to construct proofs of theorems in this special language; and, finally, in the proof games the players learn how to construct logical systems. From various combinations of the 11 rules of inference that are learned in the rule-practice games, it is possible to construct a total of 2,047 logical systems, all subsystems of propositional calculus.

Evidence suggests that players become better problem-solvers by virtue of playing WFF 'N PROOF. The kinds of problems that they are able to do more effectively involve some logical reasoning.

The features of WFF 'N PROOF that seem to make the games especially suitable for teaching skills in logical reasoning and developing more favorable attitudes toward symbol-manipulating activities in general are the following:

1. The practice in logical reasoning is a by-product of an activity that is enjoyable in itself.
2. Although these games are enjoyed by young children, the more intricate ones pose a genuine challenge even for intelligent adults.
3. In the play of the games there is no waiting time. Each player proceeds at his own pace throughout the entire time of play. The more adept player is not delayed by those who play more slowly.
4. Everyone else in the games learns from the best player. His strategies are displayed openly so that all others may learn to adopt them. In effect, the best players act as teachers, although they are not formally assigned this role by the rules of the games.
5. In the play of the games, there is a built-in dampening effect that prevents any one player from getting too far ahead of the others in score. The better players are presented with more difficult problems to solve, while the slower players get relatively simpler problems.
6. The games are so ordered that each new game is slightly more intricate than the previous one and each later game uses the skills learned in earlier games.
7. The games emphasize individual, rather than collective, decision-making. Each player plans and executes his own strategy independently in order to achieve specified goals. Good players, however, in devising strategies take into account what other players are doing.
8. The games are flexible both in the number of persons who may play (two or more) and in the length of time of play (5 minutes or more).

From the use of the WFF 'N PROOF games experimentally in classrooms, there is impressionistic anecdotal evidence that the current version of the game is quite near the goal of being an autotelic activity enjoyable merely for its own sake. In classes in which the games were used in Orange, Connecticut, and in Burbank, California, some so-called "underachievers" performed much better in WFF 'N PROOF than in their other classroom work. One junior-high youngster in the Yale–North Haven summer school in North Haven, Connecticut, made a practice, until caught, of coming to school for the logic class first thing in the morning and playing hooky for the rest of the day. At the elementary school in Orange, Connecticut, parents of several boys with IQ's in the 80's remarked to the home-room teacher, at P.T.A. meetings, that their youngsters' attitudes toward school had noticeably changed. The parents indicated that they did not fully understand what this "logic stuff" was all about, but that "the kids sure liked it." One mother said that her son was no longer hard to awaken in the morning and that he had become quite concerned about not being late for school, because the logic class was scheduled for the first period. In Palo Alto, California, some elementary-school students voluntarily came to a half-hour game session before school began, giving up playground time to play WFF 'N PROOF; others in junior high schools in Palo Alto and Burbank, California, voluntarily stayed after school to learn to play WFF 'N PROOF and played it during their lunch hour. In one unsupervised session, two junior high participants became so deeply involved in a dispute that they adjourned to the hallway to settle matters with their fists. The amazed principal who halted the fracas reported that none of the 20-odd other players even came out to see the fight—they remained behind playing WFF 'N PROOF!

The number of games such as WFF 'N PROOF that can usefully be constructed and the range of subject matter that can be taught by means of them is an open question. It seems clear that any formal system of analysis can be presented in the form of such a game. The interesting empirical question that is yet to be answered is: How much of mathematics and logic is it useful to present this way? In other words, at what stage in learning by games is the attitude toward the activity sufficiently favorable so that it becomes more efficient and effective for a student to continue his learning of such material by the traditional method of reading books?

Some persons think the possibilities are good that such areas as the morphology of some foreign languages and the syntax of English and foreign languages can effectively be presented by means of such games. Others have suggested that some aspects of the legislative process and international relations can be taught this way. Efforts are under way, or soon will begin, by researchers at Harvard, the University of Rochester, and the University of Illinois to investigate such possibilities.

THE PLAYING OF "WFF 'N PROOF"

Turning now to a description of how to play some of the WFF 'N PROOF games, the first game to be considered is the one called "Shake-a-WFF." In order to play, the players must be able to construct expressions that are WFFs and they must be able to tell whether or not a given expression is a WFF. When the players can do so without error we say that they "understand" the definition of a WFF and are ready to go on to the next game.

The definition of a WFF is as follows:

A given expression is a WFF if, and only if, (1) it is a 'p', 'q', 'r', or 's';

or (2) it is the expression formed when an 'N' is immediately followed by exactly one WFF; or (3) it is the expression formed when a 'C', 'A', 'K', or 'E' is immediately followed by exactly two WFFs. Thus, by this definition, 'r' is a WFF by means of clause 1; 'Nq' is a WFF by means of clause 1 and clause 2 (an 'N' followed by exactly one WFF is a WFF).

'Nqr' is not a WFF, however; there is no clause in the definition of a WFF that says an 'N' immediately followed by two WFFs is a WFF. But 'Nqr' is a pair of WFFs'—the two-lettered WFF 'Nq' and the one-letter WFF 'r'.

If a 'C' is added to the left side of 'Nqr,' however, the resulting expression 'CNqr' is a four-lettered WFF by means of clause 3. 'CNqr' is a CAKE-letter (that is, a 'C', 'A', 'K', or 'E') immediately followed by the two WFFs 'Nq' and 'r'.

Similarly, the expression 'Asp' is a three-lettered WFF, because it is a CAKE-letter (namely, an 'A') immediately followed by exactly two WFFs.

The expression 'KCNqrAsp' is an eight-lettered WFF because it is a CAKE-letter followed by exactly two WFFs, namely, a 'K' followed by the four-lettered WFF 'CNqr', and the three-lettered WFF 'Asp'.

The expression 'NNs' is a WFF by means of clause 2 because it is an 'N' immediately followed by exactly one WFF, namely, the two-lettered WFF 'Ns'.

The expression 'KNNsKCNqrAsp' is a 12-lettered WFF; it is a CAKE-letter (namely, a 'K') immediately followed by exactly two WFFs (the three-lettered WFF 'NNs', and the eight-lettered WFF 'KCNqrAsp').

After gaining some acquaintance with the definition of a WFF, each player is given a playing mat upon which the definition of a WFF is written. In a game of Shake-a-WFF there may be two or more players each of whom is also given a set of seven logic cubes,[2] three capital-letter cubes and four small-letter cubes. Each capital-letter cube has a different one of the following capital letters on each of its six faces:

C   A   K   E   N   R

Each of the small-letter cubes has a different one of the following six lower-case letters on each of its six faces:

p   q   r   s   i   o

Each player then divides his set of seven cubes into a three-cube shaking set (containing one capital- and two small-letter cubes) and a four cube stockpile (containing two capital- and two small-letter cubes).

A coin is then placed in the center of the table as a device to terminate

---

[2] In the first class that played the games, these materials were very carefully called "logic cubes," but, the very first time the students saw them, they called them "dice," and they have been "dice" to the youngsters ever since—despite our fussiness.

each play of Shake-a-WFF. The first player done shouts WFF and grabs the coin. He is the WFFer for the play of the game.

Next, the players set their stockpiles aside and take the cubes in their shaking sets and simultaneously roll them on the table. Each player then tries as speedily as he can, to construct on his playing mat one of the longest WFFs possible from the letters facing upward on the cubes in his shaking set. Any cubes that cannot be used in constructing one of the longest WFFs possible is placed off the playing mat.

The first player done shouts "WFF" and grabs the coin in the center of the table to signal to the other players that the play is over and that it is time for them to evaluate the WFFer's play. The other players then examine the cubes that the WFFer has placed on the mat and those that he has left off and indicate their evaluation by saying "check" or "challenge."

If the WFFer has played correctly, he transfers one cube from his stockpile to his shaking set, thus getting four cubes in his shaking set for the next play while the other players continue to shake three. In this manner, if a player is competent and plays correctly, he gets a more complex problem to do on the next roll.

If the WFFer has played incorrectly, however, he transfers one cube in his shaking set to his stockpile. Thus, a player who makes a mistake gets a simpler problem to do on the next roll. This built-in dampening effect prevents any one player from getting too far ahead of the others. The faster players get more cubes and have more difficult problems to solve, while the slower players have relatively fewer cubes and simpler problems. In the play of Shake-a-WFF this results in the slower players becoming the WFFer more frequently, while the brighter players do more of the evaluating.

The goal of each player in Shake-a-WFF is to get all the cubes in his stockpile transferred to his shaking set. The first player to do so wins.

In playing Shake-a-WFF or any of the other games in WFF 'N PROOF, it is not necessary to tell the players what the signs are intended to mean. However, if students ask, it is explained:

—that a 'C' indicates implication (usually expressed in English by the words "if-then"),
—that an 'A' indicates disjunction (usually expressed by "or"),
—that a 'K' indicates conjunction (usually expressed by "and"),
—that an 'E' indicates equivalence (usually expressed by "if and only if"),
—that an 'N' indicates negation (usually expressed by "not"), and
—that 'p', 'q', 'r', and 's' are sentence variables that may assume the value of any sentence whatsoever—just as in algebra, x, y, and z are number variables that may assume the value of any number whatsoever.

The students are also told that other games can be played when they feel that they have mastered Shake-a-WFF. Each student moves on to the next game when he feels that he is ready and expresses his desire to do so.

The second game, Count-a-WFF, is a transition game between Shake-a-WFF and some of the later games in WFF 'N PROOF. In Count-a-WFF a slightly more difficult problem for the players is posed. Instead of *physically* manipulating the logic cubes to form WFFs, the players are required *mentally* to manipulate the letters appearing on the upward faces of a set of cubes and decide how many letters can be contained in one of the longest WFFs that can be formed from all the letters.

In Count-a-WFF there is only one shaking set of cubes. That set is rolled out in the center of the table where all the players can see the letters on the upward faces. Each player examines the letters and then, as speedily as he can, calls out a number, thus making a claim that he can build a WFF containing exactly that number of letters from the letters facing upward on the cubes in the shaking set. The first player to call out a number sets a timing device in motion. If a specified interval elapses before another player calls out a larger number, then the player who set the timing device in motion is the WFFer for that play. If another player calls out a larger number, however, before the specified time interval has elapsed, he restarts the timing device and the other players (including the first) seek to call out a still larger number before the specified interval elapses. The play continues in this manner and eventually one player becomes the WFFer and is called upon to prove his claim. If the WFFer can construct a WFF containing exactly the number of letters that he claimed from the letters facing upward on the cubes in the shaking set, his score is increased. If he cannot fulfil his claim, his score is reduced. The players play Count-a-WFF until they indicate their readiness for the next game.

The third game is the only one in WFF 'N PROOF in which two new ideas are introduced in one game. In general, only one new idea at most is introduced in each new game. In this third game, called "Ko Practice," the players are introduced to the Ko rule of inference and, also, to the definition of a proof.

The Ko rule of inference states that from Kw1w2 it is valid to infer w1 and it is valid to infer w2 (where w1 and w2 are the pair of WFFs that immediately follow the 'K' to make Kw1w2 a WFF). Thus, from 'Kpq' it is valid to infer 'p' by the Ko rule. Similarly, from 'KrNs', it is valid to infer 'Ns'; and from 'KsCrp', it is valid to infer 'Crp'.

The following sequence of three WFFs is an example of a proof:

KrKsp
Ksp
s

These three WFFs are a proof that from 'KrKsp', it is valid to infer 's'. This can be abbreviated by 'KrKsp→s'. In order for a sequence of WFFs to qualify as a proof in Ko Practice, three conditions must be fulfilled:

1. Each WFF must either be a supposition or else inferred from one or more of the preceding WFFs;
2. All WFFs that are suppositions must preceede all WFFs that are not suppositions; and

3. The last WFF in the sequence must not be a supposition.

P1 | KrKsp → s

1	KrKsp	s
2	Ksp	1, Ko
3	s	2, Ko

It is evident that the sequence of WFFs

KrKsp
Ksp
s

is a proof, because this sequence fulfills all three conditions:

1. Each WFF is either a supposition or else inferred from one or more of the preceding WFFs;
   a) 'KrKsp' is a supposition,
   b) 'Ksp' is inferred from item 1 by means of the Ko rule, and
   c) 's' is inferred from item 2 by means of the Ko rule;
2. 'KrKsp', the only supposition, precedes all of the non-suppositions;
3. 's', the last WFF in the sequence, is not a supposition; rather, it is inferred from a preceding WFF.

Ko Practice is played exactly like Count-a-WFF, except that instead of seeking to call out a number to indicate the maximum number of letters in a WFF that can be constructed, the players seek to call out a number to indicate the maximum number of WFFs in a proof that can be constructed.

In the fourth game, called Ki Practice, the players are introduced to the Ki rule of inference. The Ki rule states that from w1 and w2 it is valid to infer Kw1w2. Thus, from 's' and 'Nr', it is valid to infer 'KsNr' by means of the Ki rule. Similarly, from 'p' and 'Asr' it is valid to infer 'KpAsr'; and from 'Cpq' and 'Esp', it is valid to infer 'KCpqEsp'.

Ki Practice is played just like Ko Practice, except that with the added rule of inference additional sequences of WFFs qualify as proofs. For example, the following sequence indicating the symmetry of conjunction, now qualifies as a proof:

| Kpq → Kpq

1	Kpq	s
2	p	1, Ko
3	q	1, Ko
4	Kqp	3, 2, Ki

(1) 'Kpq' is a supposition,
(2) 'p' is inferred from item 1 by the Ko rule,

(3) 'q' is inferred from item 1 by the Ko rule, and
(4) 'Kqp' is inferred from item 3 and item 2 by the Ki rule.

The fifth game, called Kio Proof, is the first example of a proof game in WFF 'N PROOF. All the remaining 16 games in WFF 'N PROOF are either rule-practice games or proof games. The play becomes considerably more complex in the proof games and the incentive to play quickly is removed. The proof games are sequential, like chess and checkers in which one player makes a move and then it is the next player's turn. In brief outline, the proof games consist of a competition among players to be the first to construct both a logical system and a set of premisses, from which some specified conclusions can be inferred from the letters that have appeared on the upward faces of a relatively large shaking set of cubes.

The first player rolls out the cubes in the shaking set (18, 27, or 36 cubes, depending upon how complex the players wish to make the game) on the table. He then specifies a conclusion by constructing on one of the playing mats a WFF containing seven or less letters from the letters facing upward on the cubes in the shaking set. The conclusion must be one that can be deduced (1) from a set of premisses that can be constructed from the remaining letters facing upward on the cubes in the shaking set; and (2) within a logical system that can be constructed (by constructing the names of its rules of inference) from the remaining letters facing upward on the cubes in the shaking set; or else, the player who specified the conclusions has made a mistake and is subject to challenge by the other players in the game.

The players then take turns transferring one cube at a time from the shaking set to another pair of playing mats. Depending upon where on the playing mats he places a given cube, a player's move will have one of the following effects: it will (1) permit the letter on that cube to be used in constructing a premiss and prevent that letter from being used in constructing the name of a rule of inference, (2) permit the letter on that cube to be used in constructing the name of a rule of inference and prevent that letter from being used in constructing a premiss, (3) require the letter on that cube to be used in constructing either a premiss or the name of a rule of inference, or (4) prevent the letter on that cube from being used in constructing any expression at all—premiss or name of a rule of inference.

Even if the conclusion originally specified at the outset was an appropriate one (because it would have been possible by an appropriate sequence of plays to construct both a set of premisses and a logical system from the letters remaining in the shaking set), it is possible for a player to destroy (by making an inappropriate one of the four kinds of moves) this possibility of constructing an appropriate set of premisses and names of rules. If a player does so destroy the possibility of deducing the conclusion, then he has made a mistake and is subject to challenge by the other players.

Thus, in Kio Proof (and the other proof games) there are a variety of ways in which players can make mistakes. If another player detects that mistake and challenges before anyone else does, he wins that play of the game. This provides two different ways for a player to win: (1) by constructing an appropriate set of premises and names of rules and (2) by detecting a mistake that another player has made and challenging him before anyone else does. Because it is also a mistake to make a play and fail to challenge a prior mistake, some intricate strategies of bluffing and entrapment are possible in the proof games. These strategy features make the proof games probably the most fascinating ones in the WFF 'N PROOF kit. The final games—the ones that players are likely to continue to play as games even after they have learned all the others in the WFF 'N PROOF kit—are proof games.

CONCLUSION

A promising start has been made toward constructing game materials for encouraging favorable attitudes toward symbol-manipulating activities and teaching some mathematical logic.[3] Although the WFF 'N PROOF games are designed primarily to be fun—to be an autotelic activity that learners will voluntarily spend time doing for its own sake—they are also meant to provide practice in abstract thinking and teach some mathematical logic. To the extent that WFF 'N PROOF is autotelic, it will be played merely because it is fun to play, regardless of the fact that something useful is being learned in the process.

REFERENCES

Anderson, A. R., & Moore, O.K. Autotelic folk models. Tech. Rep. No. 8, Contract SAR/Nonr-609 (16), Office of Naval Research, Group Psychology Branch, 1959.

Coleman, J. S. *The adolescent society.* Glencoe, Ill.: Free Press, 1961.

Fitch, F. B. *Symbolic logic: An introduction.* New York: Ronald Press, 1952.

Moore, O. K. The motivation and training of students for intellectual pursuits: A new approach. Address given at the Tenth Thomas Alva Edison Foundation Institute, New York University, November 19, 1959.

Moore, O. K., & Anderson, A. R. Some puzzling aspects of social inter-action. Proceedings of Small Groups Symposium held at Stanford University, June 20–24, 1961.

Prior, A. N. *Formal logic.* London: Oxford University Press, 1955.

Skinner, B. F. Teaching machines. *Science,* 1958, 128, 969–977.

---

[3] The revised kit of the game materials is now available to teachers and others who may wish to experiment with the WFF 'N PROOF games. They can be obtained by writing to: WFF 'N PROOF, Box 71, New Haven, Conn. The description of the first five games—necessarily condensed in the presentation here —is elaborated in full detail in programmed form in the revised kit, as are the final 16 games of WFF 'N PROOF.

3

SOME FACTORS IN LEARNING
NON-METRIC GEOMETRY

ROBERT M. GAGNÉ

Princeton University

STAFF, UNIVERSITY OF MARYLAND MATHEMATICS PROJECT

University of Maryland

An experimental study was carried out to investigate the effects of some instructional variables on the acquisition of knowledge of elementary non-metric geometry. Specifically, the task was defined as "specifying sets, intersections of sets, and separations of sets, using points, lines and curves", and was taught by means of learning programs contained in looseleaf booklets. The purpose of the study was to test the effects on learning of the following variables: (*a*) amount of *variety* in problem examples used throughout the program to provide practice on each entity of subordinate knowledge; and (*b*) *time* introduced as an interval between the attainment of each subordinate knowledge and the introduction of the next. Following the general approach of previous studies, this experiment was designed in such a way that evidence could also be obtained on the effects of the attainment of subordinate knowledges themselves, as reflected in the *ordering of subtopics* within the learning program.

METHOD

Learning Materials

The initial step in designing the learning materials was to define a final task and then the subordinate knowledges that support the task. As de-

---

This study was supported in part by funds made available by the Carnegie Corporation of New York. The opinions expressed are those of the authors and do not necessarily reflect the views of that Corporation. John R. Mayor is the Director of the University of Maryland Mathematics Project and Helen L. Garstens its Associate Director. Other staff members who participated in the planning of the study and in the preparation of the materials are Noel E. Paradise, Mildred B. Cole, Elise B. Cussler, Otto C. Bassler, and William B. Moody. Dr. Gagné's present address is American Institute for Research, Pittsburgh, Pennsylvania.

scribed previously (Gagné & Paradise, 1961) the method employed was to ask the question of the final task, "What would the learner have to know how to do in order to attain this final performance when given only instructions?" In this case, the question applied to the final task yielded the identification of five subordinate knowledges. When applied in turn to these subordinate classes of tasks, and then successively to the additional tasks so identified, the analysis yielded a hierarchy of subordinate knowledges as shown in Figure 1.

As can be seen from an examination of the figure, each successive step in the analysis yielded one or more subordinate knowledge entities that are progressively simpler and more general as one proceeds downward in the hierarchy. The basic set of hypotheses generated by his "knowledge structure" is the following: (1) the attainment of each entity of knowledge (measurable in each case as a particular performance) is dependent upon positive transfer of training from the next lower subordinate knowledges connected to it by an arrow; and (2) such transfer requires the high recallability of all the next lower subordinate knowledges (connected to it by arrows).

The *topic order* of the learning program designed to establish competence in the final task was accordingly determined by the knowledge structure of Figure 1. The order represented a reasonable progression from subordinate knowledges to the next higher knowledge in all instances; the actual order was VIb, Va, IVa, IVc, IVd; VIa, IIIa, IIa; IIIb, IIId, IId; IVb, IIb, IIc, Ic, Ia, Ib, Id.

A systematic progression of frames was also employed in the learning program to advance the learner from one level of the hierarchy to the next. In approaching the attainment of each new knowledge entity, frames were designed to have the following functions in order: (1) inform the learner of the nature of the performance to be learned; (2) identify new symbols or terms (when necessary); (3) provide recognition of relevant subordinate knowledges previously learned; (4) guide the direction of thinking; and (5) require a response to a task example. In various forms, depending on the experimental conditions to be described, was the function, (6) repeat the task in other examples. These six functions were represented in each case by the number of frames required to keep the amount of printing on each frame reasonably short. In some cases, more than one function could be performed by a single frame while in others, two or three frames were required to fulfil one function. The order of presentation for the functions, however, was followed throughout.

The result of this development was a learning program consisting of 340 frames in its original form. They were divided into 11 roughly equal parts and made into looseleaf booklets, 5½ × 9½ in. in size. A numbered frame of the program appeared on each page, corresponding to a number of an answer sheet given to each learner, and the answer to each frame appeared on the back of the page. The booklets were concerned with these

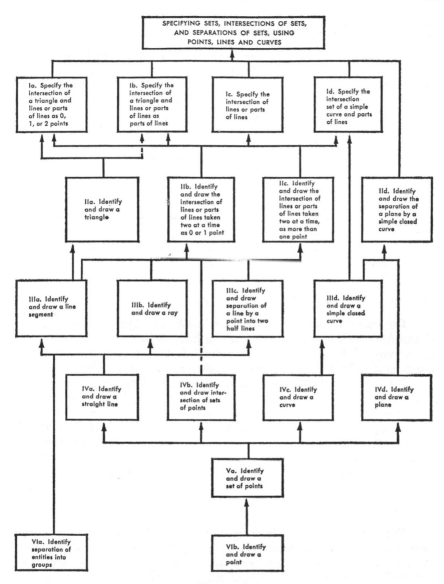

FIGURE 1

subordinate knowledges (see Fig. 1) intended to be used on successive class days: Day 1, VIb, Va, IVa; Day 2, IVc, IVd, VIa; Day 3, IIIc; Day 4, IIIa; Day 5, IIa, IIIb; Day 6, IIId, IId, IVd; Day 7, IIb; Day 8, IIc; Day 9, IIc; Day 10, Ic, Ia; Day 11, Ib, Id.

Experimental Forms of Learning Programs

In all, five different programs were developed. Program E1 contained examples in context minimally different from those of the frames used to induce the initial attainment of the task (minimal variety). Program E2 contained some of the E1 examples plus some that were of intermediate difference in context (intermediate variety). Program E3 contained E1 and E2 examples plus some that were of maximal contextual difference (maximal variety). The *number* of examples was the same in all these programs and ranged from 3 to 12 for each particular knowledge entity. Program E0 contained no examples (beyond the initial frame requiring completion of each subordinate task); its total number of frames was accordingly reduced to 216. Program EA was identical to E0 except that there was inserted, in place of the examples of the other programs, a set of arithmetic problems. These were designed to take approximately as much time to do as the examples of the other programs but otherwise were irrelevant to the learning being accomplished.

Subjects

The learners employed in the experiment were 116 sixth-graders, two classes from Walter Reed School and two from McKinley School, of Arlington County, Virginia. These classes contained students considered to be of intermediate ability and heterogeneously grouped within this category.

Students in each class were assigned to each of the five groups representing different experimental treatments. Those who, because of absence, missed one or more of the learning sessions were eliminated from the sample. Data analysis was carried out on a total N of 90, with 18 students in each group. A comparison of these groups in terms of their mathematics grades for the term up to the time of the experiment showed nonsignificant differences among them.

Procedure

The administration of learning programs and subsequent tests was carried out by the experimenter in each classroom. In all cases, the classroom teacher remained in the room during the experimental sessions. Before each session began, the teacher gave assignments for students to do, at their desks, after they had completed each booklet of the learning program and each of the tests.

In administering the learning program, the experimenter first read through with the students two sheets of mimeographed instructions. Examples were shown on the blackboard when appropriate. Students were instructed to write an answer to the question asked on each booklet page, then to turn over the page and compare their answers with the correct one printed on the back. If the answer was right they were to proceed; if wrong, they were to draw a line through it, turn the page back until they could see how the right answer was obtained, and then record the correct answer.

Since the length of the learning program was greatly reduced for experimental group E0, provisions were made for these students to begin their program on the fourth day, and assignments out of the classroom were given to them on the first three days.

Tests

On the class day following the administration of 11 booklets of the learning program (eight for group E0), a performance test was given. It contained a variety of problems requiring the specification of "sets, intersections of sets, and separations of sets, using points, lines and curves," and was scored for a total of 31 points.

On the subsequent class day a test of subordinate knowledges was administered to all students. It was designed to measure the performance of each subordinate knowledge of the hierarchy depicted in Figure 1, from Level III to the top. Further, each of these subordinate knowledges was measured by (1) an item minimally different from the context of the task in its initial attainment during learning; (2) an item of intermediate difference in context; and (3) an item maximally different in context. These three degrees of differences were comparable to those used in determining the degrees of variety in examples employed with groups E1, E2, and E3. For this test, scoring was pass or fail for each subordinate knowledge at each of these three "levels."

RATIONALE OF THE STUDY

Before presenting the results themselves, it will be useful to describe the specific experimental questions the study was designed to answer. Stated as hypotheses, these are as follows:

1. The attainment of each knowledge entity at progressively higher levels of the hierarchy (Fig. 1) is dependent upon the previous attainment of relevant subordinate knowledges at the next lower level. This hypothesis emphasizes the variables of *topic order* in that it predicts that learning will effectively cease at the point (in the hierarchy) at which any specific knowledge is failed of attainment.
2. Recall of subordinate knowledges, and therefore learning of the final task, is enhanced by greater amounts of *variety* in the repetition of task examples during learning. According to this hypothesis, E3 should achieve more than E2, and E2 more than E1.
3. A learning program containing *repeated* task examples is superior to one containing none (beyond the frame providing for initial attainment of each task). Thus E1, E2, and E3 should bring about greater achievement than E0.
4. Part of the advantage in presenting examples, as opposed to not presenting

them, resides in the interpolation of *time* between attainment of one sub-ordinate knowledge and the beginning of learning of the next. For this reason, group EA should show performance superior to group E0.

RESULTS

The pattern of positive transfer to each higher-level knowledge from the relevant lower-level knowledges is shown in Table 1. The basic data on which this table depends are pass-fail scores for the subordinate knowledges of "level 2" contextual variety. (Data for "levels" 1 and 3 yielded compara-able findings, although they are not shown here.)

TABLE 1

PASS-FAIL PATTERNS OF ACHIEVEMENT (ON LEVEL 2 TASKS) BETWEEN ADJACENT LOWER-AND HIGHER-LEVEL KNOWLEDGES IN NON-METRIC GEOMETRY, AND THE PROPORTION OF INSTANCES CONSISTENT WITH POSITIVE TRANSFER ($N = 90$)

TRANSFER TO KNOWLEDGE	FREQUENCY OF PASS-FAIL PATTERN— HIGHER : LOWER				TOTAL TESTABLE FREQUENCY	PROPORTION INSTANCES CONSISTENT WITH POSITIVE TRANSFER $\dfrac{(1) + (2)}{(1) + (2) + (3)}$
	(1) ++	(2) −−	(3) +−	(4) −+		
IIa from IIIa........	71	0	1	18	72	0.99
IIb from IIIa, b, c....	70	0	0	20	70	1.00
IIc from IIIa, b, d...	71	0	0	19	71	1.00
IId from IIId........	70	0	2	18	72	0.97
Ia from IIa, b, c.....	46	18	2	24	66	0.97
Ib from IIa, b, c.....	41	22	3	24	66	0.95
Ic from IIb, c........	38	23	1	28	62	0.98
Id from IIb, c; IIId..	37	24	3	26	64	0.95

The first column of the table lists the transfer relations tested; the Roman numerals are keyed to Figure 1. The next four columns indicate the frequency of pass-fail patterns obtained: under (1) + + is shown the number of individuals getting both higher- and lower-level knowledges correct; (2) − −, failing both; (3) +−, achieving the higher after failing the lower; and (4) − +, failing the higher after achieving the lower. Entries in the first two of these columns are consistent with the hypothesis that lower-level knowledges are *essential* for transfer; entries in the third column are not consistent with it. The small number of entries in this column, therefore, confirms the hypothesis, and the final column of the table expresses this confirmation as a proportion.

As will be apparent, the column − + indicates the number of students who failed to achieve a higher-level knowledge after having successfully at-tained lower-level ones. The number of such instances provides an index of the effectiveness of the learning program.

The evidence on the first hypothesis, then, is as clear as it has been in other studies (Gagné & Paradise, 1961; Gagné, Mayor, Garstens, & Paradise, 1962; Gagné, 1962). With few exceptions, it appears that the attainment of any entity of knowledge, as exhibited in Figure 1, depends upon the prior attainment of relevant subordinate knowledges.

TABLE 2

MEANS AND SD's FOR THE FIVE GROUPS OF THE EXPERIMENT ON THE FINAL PERFORMANCE TEST, AND ON NUMBER OF LEARNING SETS ACHIEVED AT LEVELS 1, 2, AND 3 OF CONTEXTUAL VARIETY ($N = 18$ IN EACH GROUP).

| | EXPERIMENTAL GROUPS | | | | | | | | | |
| | E1 | | E2 | | E3 | | E0 | | EA | |
MEASURES	M	SD	M	SD	M	SD	M	SD	M	SD
Final performance (total 31 points)..	18.2	2.7	18.6	3.8	18.0	4.5	17.9	5.2	17.2	5.3
No of subordinate knowledges achieved (total 12):										
Level 1........	8.9	3.4	8.8	2.9	9.4	2.7	9.4	3.0	9.3	2.8
Level 2........	8.8	3.3	8.4	3.0	9.2	2.9	8.9	3.3	9.2	3.0
Level 3........	8.4	3.2	8.1	2.8	8.8	3.0	8.6	3.5	8.5	2.8

Effects of Experimental Variables

The results exhibiting the effects of the number and variety of task examples and of the interspersion of time occupied with arithmetic problems are contained in Table 2. They can be readily summarized. None of the means of performance measures is significantly different from the others. In terms of the final performance test, or in terms of number of subordinate knowledges achieved, the variable of *task variety* has not been shown to have any effect on learning. As for the *time* factor, although the means for Group E0 (zero time between one stage of learning and the next) are consistently lower than those for Group EA (time between stages occupied by arithmetic problems), the differences are insignificant ones.

DISCUSSION

The importance of order of acquiring subordinate knowledges in a knowledge hierarchy has again been shown to be an important factor in mathematics learning. In one previous study (Gagné et al., 1962), evidence was obtained of the significant effect of the variable of number of repetitions of task examples. A similar finding, however, does not appear in the present study since groups that had no additional practice examples (E0 and EA) performed as well as groups that had a number of examples for each subordinate knowledge entity (E1, E2, and E3). The explanation of these different findings must be tentative at present, but the most obvious possibility is the dependence of such "repetition" effects on the nature of the material being learned. In a sense, the material of the present programs is relatively simple and "definitional," in contrast to that employed in the study previously mentioned. The difference in findings, however, needs further investigation.

The variable, amount of variety in task examples, is also not shown by our results to have a significant effect on the amount learned in the various groups. Similarly, the passage of time between stages of learning is not shown by these results to be a significant factor. These variables, also, are thought to be such that their effects may interact strongly with the nature of the material being learned. Consequently, generalizations from these findings should probably be made with considerable caution at the present time.

On the whole, it may be said that, if these results can be further confirmed with different learning materials, there is a strong suggestion that meaningful learning of this sort may be highly impervious to the effects of "method" variables. This may, in fact, turn out to be the case. The implication of such a finding is that one can affect the efficiency of the learning process quite readily by manipulating the *content* and *sequence* of material (Gagné & Paradise, 1961; Gagné et al., 1962; Gagné, 1962), but not at all readily by manipulating the repetitiveness and *temporal spacing* of this content, as these are reflected in the present experiment.

REFERENCES

Gagné, R. M. The acquisition of knowledge. *Psychol. Rev.*, 1962, **69**, 355–365.
Gagné, R. M., Mayor, J. R., Garstens, H. L., & Paradise, N. E. Factors in acquiring knowledge of a mathematical task. *Psychol. Monogr.*, 1962, **76**, No. 7 (Whole No. 526).
Gagné, R. M., and Paradise, N. E. Abilities and learning sets in knowledge acquisition. *Psychol. Monogr.*, 1961, **75**, No. 14 (Whole No. 518).

4

REPRESENTATION AND MATHEMATICS LEARNING

Jerome S. Bruner *and* Helen J. Kenney

Harvard University

The central concern of the present study is the psychological processes involved in the learning of mathematics by children who, in Piaget's sense, are in the stage of "concrete operations" and are not, presumably, yet able to deal readily with formal propositions. Better to understand how mathematics learning of a highly symbolized type might occur, we worked with a small number of children, observing them in minute detail to determine the steps involved in grasping mathematical ideas. Such an approach is, in our opinion, most pressingly needed at this stage of development of new mathematical instruction. It is closely akin to the detailed study of the naturalist and clinician. Perhaps such study can serve to aid more large-scale psychometric testing or, indeed, to elucidate the nature of instruction. It would be disingenuous to say that we (or any naturalist, for that matter) worked without due regard to some theory. Our theoretical predilections were, we should say, far clearer when we finished than when we started. They will also be plain to the reader as our account progresses.

The observations to be reported were made on four eight-year-old children, two boys and two girls, who were given an hour of daily instruction in mathematics four times a week for six weeks. The children were in the IQ range of 120–130 and were enrolled in the third grade of a private school that emphasized instruction designed to foster independent problem-solving. They were from middle-class professional homes. The "teacher" of the class was a well known research mathematician (Z. P. Dienes); his assistant was a professor of psychology at Harvard who has worked long and hard on human thought processes.

Each child worked at a corner table in a generously sized room. Next to each child sat a tutor-observer trained in psychology and with sufficient background in college mathematics to understand the underlying mathematics being taught. In the middle of the room was a large table with a

We are grateful to Dr. Z. P. Dienes, Mr. Samuel Anderson, Miss Eleanor Duckworth, and Miss Joan Rigney for their help in designing and carrying out this study. Dr. Dienes, particularly, formed our thinking about the mode of presenting the mathematical materials.

supply of the blocks and balance beams and cups and beans and chalk that served as instructional aids. In the course of the six weeks, the children were given instruction in factoring, the distributive and commutative properties of addition and multiplication, and, finally, in quadratic functions.

Each child had available a series of graded problem cards to go through at his own pace. The cards gave directions for different kinds of exercises, using the materials described above. The instructor and his assistant circulated from table to table, helping as needed, and each observer-tutor similarly assisted as needed. The problem sequences were designed to provide, first, an appreciation of mathematical ideas through concrete constructions using materials of various kinds for these constructions. From such constructions, the child was encouraged to form perceptual images of the mathematical idea in terms of the forms that had been constructed. The child was then further encouraged to develop or adopt a notation to describe his construction. After such a cycle, a child moved on to the construction of a further embodiment of the idea on which he was working, one that was mathematically isomorphic with what he had learned although expressed in different materials and with altered appearance. When such a new topic was introduced, the children were given a chance to discover its connection with what had gone before and were shown how to extend the notational system used before. Careful minute-by-minute records were kept of the proceedings, along with photographs of the children's constructions.

In no sense can the children, the teachers, the classroom, or the mathematics be said to be typical of what normally occurs in third grade. Four children rarely have six teachers nor do eight-year-olds ordinarily get into quadratic functions. But our concern is with the processes involved in mathematical learning and not with typicality. We would be foolish to claim that the achievements of the children were typical. But it seems quite reasonable to suppose that the thought processes going on in the children were quite ordinary among eight-year-old human beings.

As we have noted, the instruction emphasized concrete construction and embodiment of mathematical concepts. It could have been more axiomatic, less dependent upon visual intuition of forms. It is highly unlikely that there is one optimum procedure for teaching or learning mathematics. The observations obviously reflect the approach of the study as well as the nature of mathematical learning.

Four aspects of the learning seem worth special comment: the role of construction, the uses of notation, the place of contrast and variation, and the character of "insight."

THE ROLE OF CONSTRUCTION

In mathematical factoring, to start with an example, the concept of prime numbers appears to be more readily grasped when the child, through construction, discovers that certain handfuls of beans cannot be laid out in completed multiple rows and columns. Such quantities have either to be laid out in a single file or in an incomplete row-column design in which there is always extra or one too few to fill the pattern. These patterns, the child learns, happen to be called "prime" or they could be called "unarrangeable." It is easy for the child to go from this step to the recognition that a multiplication table, so called, is a record sheet of quantities in *completed* multiple rows and columns. Here is factoring, multiplication, and primes in a construction that can also be visualized. Take the matter of factoring in another physical embodiment: a balance beam with hooks placed equidistant from a central fulcrum is the construction vehicle this time (Fig. 1). Contrast this with factoring as the usual computational exercise—as in the problem, "what are the factors of 18?" Conventionally, the child parrots the

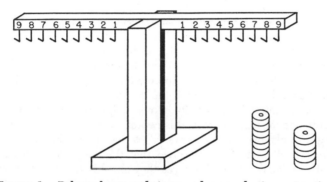

FIGURE 1.—Balance beam and rings used on quadratic construction.

correct set of factors with the usual uncertainty about whether 9 and 2 are different from 2 and 9, or 6 and 3 from 3 and 6. On the balance beam, we place 2 rings on hook 9; the child is encouraged to find and write down every combination of rings on hooks on the opposite side that will balance it. It is a beautiful discovery that 2 rings on hook 9 balances 9 rings on hook 2—and an introduction to the idea of commutativity. Note again that the construction produces a basis for imagery. And before long some startlingly abstract principles couched in elegant terms emerge: "You can exchange rings for hooks if you want." Factors are now events. When notation is applied now, there is a referent.

Note that constructions can be "unconstructed and reconstructed" even when the child does not yet have a ready symbol system for doing so abstractly. In short, construction, unconstruction, and reconstruction provides reversibility in *overt* operations until the child, in Piaget's sense, can internalize such operations in symbolized form.

Now consider quadratic functions. Each child was provided with building materials. These were large flat squares made of wood whose dimensions were unspecified and described simply as "unknown or x long and x wide" (Fig. 2). There were also a large number of strips of wood that were

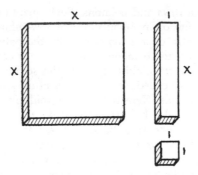

FIGURE 2.—Three components for quadratic constructions.

as long as the sides of the square and described arbitrarily as having a width of "1" or simply "1 by x." And there was a supply of little squares with sides equal to the width "1" of the strips, thus "1 by 1." The reader should be warned that the presentation of these materials is not as simple as all that. To begin with, it is necessary to convince the children that we really do not know and do not *care* what is the metric size of the big squares, that rulers are of no interest. A certain humor helps establish in the pupils a proper contempt for measuring in this context, and the snob appeal of simply calling an unknown by the name "x" is very great. From there on, the children readily discover for themselves that the long strips are x long—by correspondence. They take on faith (as they should) that the narrow dimension is "1," but that they grasp its arbitrariness is clear from one child's declaration of the number of such "1" lengths that make an x. As for "1 by 1" little squares, that too is established by simple correspondence with the narrow dimension of the "1 by x" strips. It is horseback method but quite good mathematics.

The child is asked whether he can make a square bigger than the x by x square, using the materials at hand. He very quickly builds squares with

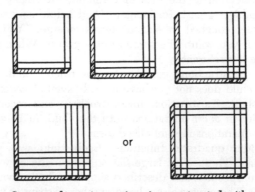

or

FIGURE 3.—Squares of ever increasing size constructed with components.

designs like those in Figure 3. We ask him to record how much wood is needed for each larger square and how long and wide each square is.

THE USE OF NOTATION

He describes one of his constructed squares; very concretely the pieces are counted out: "an x-square, two x-strips, and a one square" or, "an x-square, four x-strips, and four ones," or "an x-square, six x-strips and nine ones," etc. We help him with language and show him a way to write it down. The big square is an "$x^{\square}$", the long strips are "1 x" or simply "x," and the little squares are "one squares" or "one by one" or better still simply "1." And the expression "and" can be shortened to "+." And so he can write out the recipe for a constructed square as "$x^{\square} + 4x + 4$." At this stage, these are merely names put together in little sentences. How wide and long is the square in question? This the child can readily measure off —an x and 2 or $x + 2$—and so the whole thing is $(x + 2)^{\square}$. Brackets are not so easily grasped. And so the child is able to put down his first equality: $(x + 2)^{\square} = x^{\square} + 4x + 4$. Virtually everything has a referent that can be pointed to with a finger. He has a notational system into which he can translate the image he has constructed.

Now we go on to making bigger squares, and each square the child makes he describes in terms of what wood went into it and how wide and how long it is. It takes some ruled sheets to get the child to keep his record so that he can go back and inspect it for what it may reveal, and he is encouraged to go back and look at the record and at the constructions they stand for.

Imagine now a list such as the following, again a product of the child's own construction:

$$x \ + 2x + \ \ 1 \text{ is } x + 1 \text{ by } x + 1$$
$$x \ + 4x + \ \ 4 \text{ is } x + 2 \text{ by } x + 2$$
$$x \ + 6x + \ \ 9 \text{ is } x + 3 \text{ by } x + 3$$
$$x \ + 8x + 16 \text{ is } x + 4 \text{ by } x + 4$$

It is almost impossible for him not to make some discoveries about the numbers: that the x values go up 2, 4, 6, 8 . . . and the unit values go up 1, 4, 9, 16 . . . and the dimensions increase by additions to x of 1, 2, 3, 4 . . . . The syntactical insights about regularity in notation are matched by perceptual-manipulative insights about the material referents.

After a while, some new manipulations occur that provide the child with a further basis for notational progress. He takes the square, $(x + 2)^2$, and reconstructs it in a new way (Fig. 4). One may ask whether this is constructive manipulation or whether it is proper factoring. But the child is learning that the same amount of wood can build quite strikingly different patterns and remain the same amount of wood—although it also has a different notational expression. Where does the language begin and the manipulation of materials stop? The interplay is continuous. We shall return to this same example in a later section.

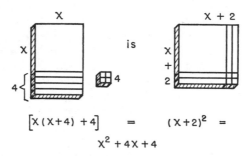

$$\left[X(X+4)+4\right] \quad = \quad (X+2)^2 \quad =$$

$$X^2 + 4X + 4$$

FIGURE 4.—Syntactic exercise supported by construction.

But the problem now is how to "detach" the notation that the child has learned from the concrete, visible, manipulable embodiment to which it refers—the wood. For if the child is to deal with mathematical properties he will have to deal with symbols *per se*, else he will be limited to the narrow and rather trivial range of symbolism that can be given direct (and only partial) visual embodiment. Concepts such as x^2 and x^3 may be given a visualizable referent, but what of x^n?

Why do children wean themselves from the perceptual embodiment to the symbolic notation? Perhaps it is partly explained in the nature of variation and contrast.

VARIATION AND CONTRAST

The child is shown the balance beam again and told, "Choose any hook on one side and put the same number of rings on it as the number the hook is away from the middle. Now balance it with rings placed on the other side. Keep a record." Recall that the balance beam is familiar from work on factoring and that the child knows that 2 rings on 9 balances 9 on 2 or m rings on n balances n on m. He is back to construction. Can anything be constructed on the balance beam that is like the squares? With little effort, the following translation is made. Suppose x is 5. Then 5 rings on hook 5 is x^2, five rings on hook 4 is $4x$, and 4 rings on hook 1 is 4: $x^2 + 4x + 4$. How can we find whether this is like a square that is $x + 2$ wide by $x + 2$ long as before? Well, if x is 5, then $x + 2$ is 7, and so 7 rings on hook 7. And nature obliges—the beam balances. One notation works for two strikingly different constructions and perceptual events. Notation, with its broader equivalency, is clearly more economical than reference to embodiments. There is little resistance to using this more convenient language. And now construction can begin—commutative and distributive properties of equations can be explored: $x(x + 4) + 4 = x^2 + 4x + 4$ or $x + 4$ rings on hook x and 4 rings on hook 1 will balance. The child, if he wishes, can also go back to the wood and find that the same materials can make the design in Figure 4.

Contrast is the vehicle by which the obvious that is too obvious to be appreciated can be made noticeable again. The discovery of an eight-year-old girl illustrates the matter. "Yes, 4×6 equals 6×4 in numbers, like in one way six eskimos in four igloos is the same as four in six igloos. But a venetian blind *isn't* the same as a blind Venetian." By recognizing the non-commutative property of ordinary language, the commutative property of a mathematical language can be partly grasped. But it is still only a partial insight into commutativity and noncommutativity. Had we wished to develop the distinction more deeply we might have proceeded concretely to a contrast between sets of operations that can be carried out in any sequence —like the order of eating courses at a dinner or of going to different movies —and operations that have a noncommutative order—like putting on shoes and socks—where one must precede the other. Then the child could be taken from there to a more general idea of commutative and noncommutative cases and ways of dealing with a notation, perhaps by identical sets and ordered identical sets.

INSIGHT AND DEVELOPMENT

What was so striking in the performance of the children was their *initial* inability to represent things to themselves in a way that transcended immediate perceptual grasp. The achievement of more comprehensive insight requires, we think, the building of a mediating representational structure that transcends such immediate imagery, that renders a *sequence* of acts and image unitary and simultaneous. The children always began by constructing an embodiment of some concept, building a concrete form of operational definition. The fruit of the construction was an image and some operations that "stood for" the concept. From there on, the task was to provide means of representation that were free of particular manipulations and specific images. Only symbolic operations provide the means of representing an idea in this way. But consider this matter for a moment.

We have already commented upon the fact that by giving the child multiple embodiments of the same general idea expressed in a common notation we lead him to "empty" the concept of specific sensory properties until he is able to grasp its abstract properties. But surely this is not the best way of describing the child's increasing development of insight. The growth of such abstractions is important. But what struck us about the children, as we observed them, is that they had not only understood the abstractions they had learned but also had a store of concrete images that served to exemplify the abstractions. When they searched for a way to deal with new problems, the task was usually carried out not simply by abstract means but also by "matching up" images. An example will help here. In going from the wood-blocks embodiment of the quadratic to the balance-beam embodiment, it was interesting that the children "equated" *concrete* features of one with *concrete* features of another. One side of the balance beam "stood for" the amount of wood, the other side for the sides of the square. These were important concrete props on which they leaned. We have been told by research mathematicians that the same use of props—heuristics—holds for them, that they have preferred ways of imagining certain problems while other problems are handled silently or in terms of an imagery of the symbolism on a page.

We reached the tentative conclusion that it was probably necessary for a child learning mathematics not only to have as firm a sense of the abstraction underlying what he was working on but, also, a good stock of visual images for embodying them. For without the latter, it is difficult to track correspondences and to check what one is doing symbolically. Here an example will help again. We had occasion, again with the help of Dr. Dienes, of teaching a group of 10 nine-year-olds the elements of group theory. To embody the idea of a mathematical group initially, we gave them the example of a four-group made up of the following four maneuvers (a book was the vehicle, a book with an arrow up the middle of its front cover): rotating the book a quarter turn to the left, rotating it a quarter turn to the right, rotating it a half-turn (without regard to direction of rotation), and letting it stay in the position it was in. They were quick to grasp the important property of such a mathematical group: that any sequence of maneuvers made could be reproduced from the starting position by a single move. This is not the usual way in which this property is described mathematically, but it served well for the children. We contrasted this elegant property with a series of our moves that did *not* constitute a mathematical group—indeed, they provided the counter-example themselves by proposing the one-third turn left, one-third turn right, half-turn either way, and stay. It was soon apparent that it did not work. We set the children the task of making games of four maneuvers, six maneuvers, etc., that had the property of a "closed" game, as we called it. They were, of course, highly ingenious. But what soon became apparent was that they needed some aid in imagery—in this case an imagery notation—that would allow them to keep track and then to discover whether some new game was an isomorph of one they had already developed. The prop in this case was, of course, the matrix, listing the moves possible across the top and then listing them down the side, thus making it easily possible to check whether each combination of pairs of moves could be reproduced by a single move. The matrix in this case is a crutch or heuristic and as such has nothing to do with the abstraction of the mathematical group, yet it was enormously useful to them not only for keeping track but also for comparing one group with another for correspondence. Thus the matrix with which they started had the property of

$$
\begin{array}{ccccc}
 & s & a & b & c \\
s & s & a & b & c \\
a & a & c & s & b \\
b & b & s & c & a \\
c & c & b & a & s.
\end{array}
$$

Are there any four groups with a different structure? It is extremely difficult to deal with such a question without the aid of this housekeeping matrix as a vehicle for spotting correspondence.

A still better example is provided by a colleague, pointing to the role of imagery in dealing with certain formal properties.[1] Suppose we specify the permissible moves in a finite state structure consisting of the states A, B, C, D, E. One may list the permissible transitions between states as follows:

$$
\begin{array}{c}
AB \\
AD \\
BC \\
BE \\
CE \\
DD \\
ED \\
EA
\end{array}
$$

Suppose we now ask of someone who has this set of rules for moving among the five states what is the shortest path from A to E that moves through C. Even with the ordered information in the list, it takes a moment to figure it out. How much easier the task becomes when one produces an image to carry the information, such as,

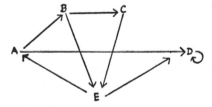

or better, the following:

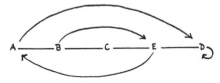

Much of mathematics is carried out with just such "less-than-rigorous" technique, and it is likely as important as abstraction in the actual *doing* of mathematical problems. One can use highly concrete embodiments to serve

---

[1] We are grateful for this example to Dr. Richard Hays.

such uses. The building blocks used in teaching quadratic functions can serve as a "source image" for checking and rethinking just as readily as the diagraming of finite state structures noted directly above.

In sum, then, while the development of insight into mathematics in our group of children depended upon their development of "example-free" abstractions, this did not lead them to give up their imagery. Quite to the contrary, we had the impression that their enriched imagery was very useful to them in dealing with new problems.

We would suggest that learning mathematics may be viewed as a microcosm of intellectual development. It begins with instrumental activity, a kind of definition of things by doing. Such operations become represented and summarized in the form of particular images. Finally, and with the help of a symbolic notation that remains invariant across transformations in imagery, the learner comes to grasp the formal or abstract properties of the things he is dealing with. But while, once abstraction is achieved, the learner becomes free in a certain measure of the surface appearance of things, he nonetheless continues to rely upon the stock of imagery he has built en route to abstract mastery. It is this stock of imagery that permits him to work at the level of heuristic, through convenient and non-rigorous, means of exploring problems and relating them to problems already mastered.

5

ON THE BEHAVIORAL FOUNDATIONS OF MATHEMATICAL CONCEPTS

Patrick Suppes

Stanford University

INTRODUCTION

The title of this paper will perhaps mean different things to different people. Philosophers and mathematicians interested in the foundations of mathematics and the philosophy of language may think I intend to pursue a systematic pragmatics built around such notions as Ajdukiewicz' concept of acceptance. Actually, I am going in a different direction. What I want to do is outline present applications of mathematical learning theory to mathematical concept formation. The aims of this paper are primarily constructive, that is, to contribute to the development of a scientific theory of concept formation. Before I turn to this subject, however, I want to comment on two general aspects of the teaching of mathematical concepts.

The first concerns the much-heard remark that the newer revisions of the mathematics curriculum are particularly significant because of the emphasis they place on *understanding* concepts as opposed to the perfection of *rote* skills. My point is not to disagree with this remark, but to urge its essential banality. To understand is a good thing; to possess mere rote skill is a bad thing. The banality arises from not knowing what we mean by *understanding*. This failure is not due to disagreement over whether the test of understanding should be a behavioral one. I am inclined to think that most people concerned with this matter would admit the central relevance of overt behavior as a measure of understanding. The difficulty is, rather, that no one seems to be very clear about the exact specification of the behavior required to exhibit understanding. Moreover, apart even from any behavioral questions, the very notion of understanding seems fundamentally vague and ill defined.

To illustrate what I mean, let us suppose that we can talk about understanding in some general way. Consider now the concept of triangularity.

This research has been supported by the U. S. Office of Education, Department of Health, Education, and Welfare, the National Science Foundation and the Carnegie Corporation of New York.

Does understanding this concept entail the understanding that the sum of the interior angles is 180°, or that triangles are rigid whereas quadrilaterals are not, or the ability to prove that if the bisectors of two angles of a triangle are equal then the triangle is isosceles? This example suggests one classical philosophical response to our query, that is, to understand a concept means, it is said, to know or believe as true a certain set of propositions that use the concept. Unfortunately, this set is badly defined. It is trivial to remark that along these lines we might work out a comparative notion of understanding that is a partial ordering defined in terms of the inclusion relation among sets of propositions that use the concept. Thus, one person understands the concept of triangularity better than a second if the set of propositions that uses the concept and is known to the first person includes the corresponding set for the second person. (Notice that it will not do to say simply that the first person knows more propositions using the concept, for the second person might know fewer propositions but among them might be some of the more profound propositions that are not known by the first person; this situation corresponds to the widely held and probably correct belief that the deepest mathematicians are not necessarily the best mathematical scholars.)

But this partial ordering does not take us very far. A more behavioral line of thought that, at first glance, may seem more promising is the response of the advocates of programmed learning to the charge that the learning of programmed material facilitates rote skills but not genuine understanding of concepts. They assert that if the critics will simply specify the behavior they regard as providing evidence of understanding, the programmers will guarantee to develop and perfect the appropriate repertory of responses. This approach has the practical virtue of sidestepping any complex discussion of understanding and supposes, with considerable correctness, no doubt, that without giving an intellectually exact analysis of what to understand a concept means, we still can obtain a rough consensus at any given time of what body of propositions we expect students to master about a given concept. This is the appropriate practical engineering approach, but it scarcely touches the scientific problem.

In this paper I do not pretend to offer any serious characterization of what it means to understand a concept. I do think that the most promising direction is to develop a psychological theory of concept transfer and generalization. The still relatively primitive state of the theory of the much simpler phenomena of stimulus transfer and generalization do not make me optimistic about the immediate future. For immediate purposes, however, let me sketch in a very rough way how the application of ideas of transfer and generalization can be used to attack the banality mentioned earlier in the standard dichotomy of understanding vs. rote skill.

We would all agree, I think, that such matters as learning to give the multiplication tables quickly and with accuracy are indeed rote skills. But there is also what I consider to be a mistaken tendency to extend the label "rote skill" to many parts of the traditional mathematics curriculum at all levels. The body of mathematical material tested, for example, by the British Sixth Form examinations is sometimes so labeled by advocates of the newer mathematics curriculum. In terms of the accepted notion of rote skill developed and studied by psychologists, this is a mistake, for the production of a correct response on these examinations cannot be explained by any simple principle of stimulus-response association. Moreover, the problems of transfer involved in solving typical British Sixth Form examination problems, in comparison with the kind of examination set by advocates of the newer mathematics curriculum may, in fact, require more transfer of concepts; at least, more transfer in one obvious way of measuring transfer, that is, in terms of the number of hours of training spent in relation to the ability to solve the problems by students matched for general background and ability. I recognize that these are complicated matters and I do not want to pursue them here. Also, I am fully in sympathy with the general objectives of the newer mathematics curriculum. I am simply protesting against some of the remarks about understanding and rote skills that occur in the pedagogical conversations and writings of mathematicians.

The second general point I want to mention briefly is of a similar sort. I have in mind the many current discussions of the efficacy of the discovery method of teaching. Such discussions seem to provide yet one more remarkable example, in the history of education, of a viewpoint achieving prominence without any serious body of empirical evidence to support or refute its advocates. From the standpoint of learning theory, I do not even know of a relatively systematic definition of the discovery method. I do not doubt that some of its advocates are themselves remarkably capable teachers and able to do unusual and startling things with classes of elementary-school children. The intellectual problem, however, is to separate the pedagogical virtuosities of these advocates' personalities from the systematic problem of analyzing the method itself. Workable hypotheses need to be formulated and tested. I know that a standard objection of some advocates of the discovery method is that any quick laboratory examination of this teaching method vs. a more standard immediate reinforcement method, particularly as applied to young children, is bound not to yield an unbiased test. The results and the implications of the methods, it is said, can only be properly evaluated after a long period. I rather doubt that this is the case but, if it is so, or if it is propounded as a working hypothesis by advocates of the method then, it seems to me, it is their intellectual responsibility to formulate proper tests of a sufficiently sustained sort.

I realize that my remarks on this subject have the character of *obiter dicta*. On the other hand, in a more complete treatment of mathematical concept formation in young children, I would consider it necessary to probe more deeply into the issues of motivation, reinforcement and concept formation that surround the controversy between the discovery method and other more classical methods of reinforcement. Some experimental results on methods of immediate reinforcement are reported in the section on "Some Concept Experiments with Children."

I turn now to the specific topics I would like to develop more systematically. In the next section, a version of stimulus-sampling learning theory is formulated that holds considerable promise for providing a detailed analysis of the behavioral processes involved in the formation of mathematical concepts. In the following section, I report in somewhat abbreviated form six experiments dealing with mathematical concept formation in young children. A particular emphasis is placed on whether the learning process in this context is represented better by all-or-none or incremental conditioning. The final section is concerned with behavioral aspects of logical inference and, in particular, of mathematical proofs.

FUNDAMENTAL THEORY

The fundamental theory I shall apply in later sections is a variant of stimulus-sampling theory first formulated by Estes (1960). The axioms given here are very similar to those found in Suppes and Atkinson (1960). I shall not discuss the significance of the individual axioms at length because this has been done in print by a number of people. The axioms I may mention, however, are based on the following postulated sequence of events occurring on a given trial of an experiment: The organism begins the trial in a certain state of conditioning. Among the available stimuli a certain set is sampled. On the basis of the sampled stimuli and their conditioning connections to the possible responses, a response is made. After the response is made, a reinforcement occurs that may change the conditioning of the sampled stimuli. The organism then enters a new state of conditioning ready for the next trial. The following axioms (divided into conditioning, sampling, and response axioms) attempt to make the assumptions underlying such a process precise (they are given in verbal form but it is a routine matter to translate them into an exact mathematical formulation):

Conditioning Axioms

C1. *On every trial each stimulus element is conditioned to at most one response.*

C2. *If a stimulus element is sampled on a trial, it becomes conditioned with probability c to the response (if any) that is reinforced on that trial; if it is already conditioned to that response, it remains so.*

C3. *If no reinforcement occurs on a trial, there is no change in conditioning on that trial.*

C4. *Stimulus elements that are not sampled on a given trial do not change their conditioning on that trial.*

C5. *The probability c that a sampled stimulus element will be conditioned to a reinforced response is independent of the trial number and the preceding pattern of events.*

Sampling Axioms

S1. *Exactly one stimulus element is sampled on each trial.*

S2. *Given the set of stimulus elements available for sampling on a trial, the probability of sampling a given element is independent of the trial number and the preceding pattern of events.*

Response Axioms

R1. *If the sampled stimulus element is conditioned to a response, then that response is made.*

R2. *If the sampled stimulus element is unconditioned, then there is a probability p_i that response i will occur.*

R3. *The guessing probability p_i of response i, when the sampled stimulus element is not conditioned, is independent of the trial number and the preceding pattern of events.*

Although not stated in the axioms, it is assumed that there is a fixed number of responses and reinforcements and a fixed set of stimulus elements for any specific experimental situation.

Axioms C5, S2, and R3 are often not explicitly formulated by learning theorists, but for the strict derivation of quantitative results they are necessary to guarantee the appropriate Markov character of the sequence of state-of-conditioning random variables. Axioms of this character are often called *independence-of-path assumptions*.

The theory formulated by these axioms would be more general if Axiom S1 were replaced by the postulate that a fixed number of stimuli is sampled on each trial or that stimuli are sampled with independent probabilities, and if Axiom R1 were changed to read that the probability of response is the proportion of sampled stimulus elements conditioned to that response, granted that some conditioned elements are sampled. For the experiments to be discussed in the next section this is not an important generalization and will not be pursued here. (From the historical standpoint the generalizations just mentioned actually were essentially Estes' original ones.) Nowadays, they are referred to as the assumptions of the component model of stimulus sampling. Axiom S1 as formulated here is said to formulate the pattern model, and the interpretation is that the organism is sampling on a given trial the pattern of the entire stimulating situation, at least the relevant pattern, so to speak. This pattern model has turned out to be remarkably effective in providing a relatively good, detailed analysis of a variety of learning experiments ranging from rats in T-mazes to two-person interaction experiments.

There is one other general remark I would like to make before turning to the discussion of particular experiments. The kind of stimulus-response theory just formulated is often objected to by psychologists interested in cognitive processes. I do not doubt that empirical objections can be found to stimulus-response theory when stated in too simple a form. I am prepared, however, to defend the proposition that, at the present time, no other theory in psychology can explain in the same kind of quantitative detail an equal variety of learning experiments, including concepts formation experiments. I should also add that I do not count as different, cognitive formulations that are formally isomorphic to stimulus-sampling theory. In our recent book Atkinson and I (Suppes & Atkinson, 1960) attempted to show how the hypothesis language favored by many people (e.g., Bruner, Goodnow, & Austin, 1956) can be formulated in stimulus-sampling terms. For example, a strategy in the technical sense corresponds precisely to a state of conditioning and a hypothesis to the conditioned stimulus sampled on a given trial, but details of this comparison are not pertinent here.

SOME CONCEPT EXPERIMENTS WITH CHILDREN

I now turn to the applications of the fundamental theory, stated in the preceding section, to a number of experiments that are concerned with concept formation in young children. It would be possible, first, to describe these experiments without any reference to the theory, but, in order to provide a focus for the limited amount of data it is feasible to give in this survey, it will be more expedient to specialize the theory initially to the restricted one-element model, and report on data relevant to the validity of this model.

We obtain the one-element model by extending the axioms given in the preceding section in the following respect: we simply postulate that there is exactly one stimulus element available for sampling on each trial and that at the beginning of the experiment this single element is unconditioned.

This special one-element model has been applied with considerable success by Bower (1961) and others to paired-associate experiments, that is, to experiments in which the subject must learn an arbitrary association established by the experimenter between, say, a nonsense syllable as single stimulus and a response, such as one of the numerals 1–8 or the pressing of one of three keys. The most important psychological implication of this one element model is that in the paired-associate situation the conditioning takes place on an all-or-none basis. This means that prior to conditioning the organism is simply guessing the correct response with the probability p_i mentioned in Axiom R3, and that the probability of conditioning on each trial in which the stimulus is presented is c. Once the stimulus is conditioned the correct response is made with probability one.

In an earlier paper Rose Ginsberg and I (Suppes & Ginsberg, 1963) analyzed a number of experiments, including some of those reported here, to exhibit a simple but fundamentally important fact about this all-or-none conditioning model. The assumptions of the model imply that the sequence of correct and incorrect responses prior to the last error form a binomial distribution of Bernoulli trials with parameter p. This null hypothesis of a fixed binomial distribution of responses prior to the last error admits, at once, the possibility of applying many powerful classical statistics that are not usually applicable to learning data. What is particularly important from a psychological standpoint is this hypothesis' implication that the mean learning curve, when estimated over responses prior to the last error, is a horizontal line. In other words, no effects of learning should be shown prior to conditioning. Ginsberg and I analyzed experiments concerned with children's concept formation, animal learning, and probability learning, and with paired-associate learning in adults from this standpoint. I shall not propose to give as extensive an analysis of data in the present paper as we attempted there, but I will attempt to cite some of the results on this question of stationarity because of its fundamental importance for any psychological evaluation of the kind of processes by which young children acquire concepts.

Other features of the experiments summarized below will be mentioned seriatim, particularly if they have some bearing on pedagogical questions. One general methodological point should be mentioned, however, before individual experiments are described. In many of the experiments, the stimulus displays were different on every trial so that there was no possibility of establishing a simple stimulus-response association. How is the one-element model to be applied to such data? The answer represents, I think, one of our more important general findings: *a very good account of much of the data may be obtained by treating the concept itself as the single element*. The schema, then, is that a simple concept-response association is established. With the single exception of Experiment I, we have applied this interpretation to the one-element model in our experiments.

Experiment I. Binary Numbers

This experiment is reported in detail in Suppes and Ginsberg (1962a). Five- and six-year-old subjects were required to learn the concepts of the numbers 4 and 5 in the binary number system, each concept being represented by three different stimuli; for example, if the stimuli had been chosen from the Roman alphabet, as in fact they were not, 4 could have been represented by abb, cdd, and eff, and 5 by aba, cdc, and efe. The child was required to respond by placing directly upon the stimulus one of two cards. On one card was inscribed a large Arabic numeral 4 and on the other a large Arabic numeral 5. All the children were told on each trial whether they made the correct or incorrect response, but half of them were also required to *correct* their wrong responses. Thus, in this experiment, in addition to testing the one-element model, we were concerned with examining the effect upon learning of requiring the subject to correct overtly a wrong response. There were 24 subjects in each of the two experimental groups. From test responses, after each experimental session, it seemed evident that whereas some subjects in both groups learned the concept as such, others learned only some of the specific stimuli representing the concepts so that, in effect, within each group there were two subgroups of subjects. It is interesting to note that this finding agrees with some similar results in lower organisms (Hull & Spence, 1938) but is contrary to results obtained with adult subjects for whom an overt correction response seems to have negligible behavioral effects (Burke, Estes, & Hellyer, 1954).

The data for both correction and non-correction groups are shown in Figure 1. It is apparent that there was a significant difference between the

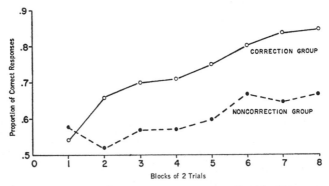

FIGURE 1.—Proportion of correct responses over all trials (binary-number experiment).

two groups in the rate of learning. The *t* of 4.00 computed between over-all responses of the two groups is significant at the .001 level.

For the analysis of paired associates and concept formation we restricted ourselves to the 24 subjects of the correction group. To begin with, we analyzed the data as if each of the six stimuli, three for each number, represented an independent paired-associate item. In accordance with this point of view, we have shown in Figure 2 the proportion of correct responses prior to the last error and the mean learning curve for all responses.

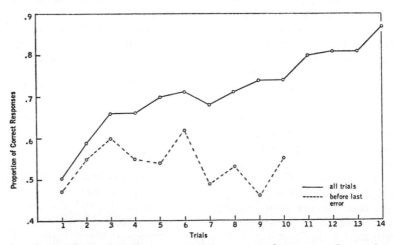

FIGURE 2.—Proportion of correct responses prior to last error and mean learning curve (binary-number experiment).

The data points are for individual trials. Because a total of only 16 trials were run on each stimulus we adopted a criterion of six successive correct responses, and thus the proportion of correct responses prior to the last error is shown only for the first 10 trials. A χ^2 test of stationarity over blocks of single trials supports the null hypothesis ($\chi^2 = 8.00$, $df = 9$, $P > .50$, $N = 844$).

Let us now turn to the question of concept formation. The identification we make has already been indicated. We treat the concept itself as the single stimulus, and in this case we regard the experiment as consisting of two concepts, one for the number 4 and one for the number 5. (It should be apparent that the identification in terms of the numbers 4 and 5 is not necessary; each concept can be viewed simply as an abstract pattern.)

The criterion for the learning of the concept was correct responses to the last three presentations of each stimuli. On this basis we divided the data into two parts. The data from the group meeting the criterion were arranged for concept-learning analysis—in this case a two-item learning task. The remaining data were assumed to represent paired-associate learning involving six independent stimulus items. For the paired-associate group over the first 10 trials we had 81 cases; for the concept-formation group we had 21 cases with 48 trials in each. The χ^2 test of stationarity was not significant for either group (for the concept subgroup $\chi^2 = 8.36$, $df = 9$, $P > .30$, $N = 357$; for the paired-associate subgroup $\chi^2 = 11.26$, $df = 8$, $P > .10$, $N = 570$).

To provide a more delicate analysis of this important question of stationarity we can construct Vincent curves in the following manner (cf. Suppes & Ginsberg, 1963). The proportion of correct responses prior to the last error may be tabulated for percentiles of trials instead of in terms of

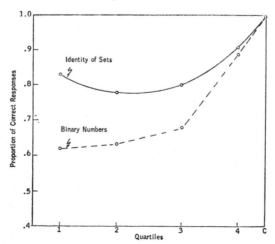

FIGURE 3.—Vincent learning curves in quartiles for proportion of correct responses prior to last error, binary numbers and identity of sets (Exps. I and II).

the usual blocks of trials. In Figure 3 the mean Vincent curve for the subjects in the binary-number experiment who met the concept criterion is shown. The curve is plotted in terms of quartiles. As the mean percentile of each of the four quartiles is 12.5 per cent, 37.5 per cent, 62.5 per cent, and 87.5 per cent, respectively, and C represents the 100 per cent point, the distance between 4, the fourth quartile, and C on the abscissa is one-half of that between the quartiles themselves. The evidence for nonstationarity in the final quartile will be discussed subsequently along with the other Vincent curve shown in this figure.

It should be noted, of course, that the subjects who take longer to meet the criterion are weighted more heavily in the Vincent curves. For example, suppose one subject has 16 responses prior to his last error whereas another subject has only 4. The first subject contributes 4 responses to each quartile whereas the second subject contributes only 1. This point will be discussed in more detail below. I turn now to the second experiment.

Experiment II. Equipollence and Identity of Sets

This experiment was performed with Rose Ginsberg and has been published in Suppes and Ginsberg (1963). The learning tasks involved in the experiment were equipollence of sets and the two related concepts of identity of sets and identity of ordered sets.

This subjects were 96 first-graders run in 4 groups of 24 each. In Group 1 the subjects were required to learn identity of sets for 56 trials and then equipollence for a further 56 trials. In Group 2 this order of presentation was reversed. In Group 3 the subjects learned first identity of ordered sets and then, identity of sets. In Group 4 identity of sets preceded identity of ordered sets. Following our findings in Experiment I, that is, that learning was more rapid when the child was required to make an overt correction response after an error, we included this requirement in Experiment II and most of the subsequent experiments reported below. Also, in this experiment and those reported below, no stimulus display on any trial was repeated for an individual subject. This was done in order to guarantee that the learning of the concept could not be explained by any simple principles of stimulus-response association, as was the case for Experiment I. For convenience of reference we termed concept experiments in which no stimulus display was repeated *pure* property of *pure* concept experiments.

The sets depicted by the stimulus displays consisted of one, two, or three elements. On each trial two of these sets were displayed. Minimal instructions were given the subjects to press one of two buttons when the stimulus pairs presented were "the same" and the alternative button when they were "not the same."

Our empirical aims in this experiment were several. First, we wanted to examine in detail if the learning of simple set concepts by children of this age took place on an all-or-none conditioning basis. Second, as the two sequences of learning trials on two different concepts for each group would indicate, we were interested in questions of transfer. Would the learning of one kind of concept facilitate the learning of another, and were there significant differences in the degree of this facilitation? Third, we were concerned with considering the question of finding the behavioral level at which the concepts could be most adequately defined. For example, in learning the identity of sets could the learning trials be satisfactorily analyzed from the standpoint of all trials falling under a single concept? Would it be better to separate the trials on which identical sets were presented from those on which nonidentical sets were presented in order to analyze

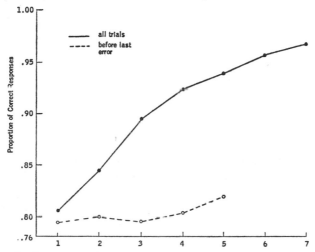

FIGURE 4.—Proportion of correct responses over all trials and before last error in blocks of eight trials, identity of sets, $N = 48$, Groups 1a and 4a (Exp. II).

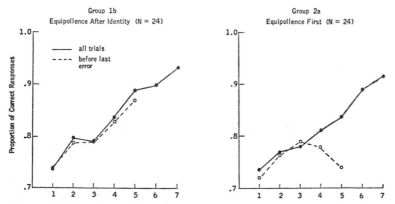

FIGURE 5.—Proportion of correct responses over all trials and before last error in blocks of eight trials, equipollence of sets, Groups 1b and 2a (Exp. II).

the data in terms of two concepts? Or would a still finer division of concepts in terms of sets identical in terms of order, sets identical as nonordered sets, equipollent sets and nonequipollent sets, be desirable?

In somewhat summary fashion the experimental results were as follows: The mean learning curves over all trials for all four groups are shown in Figures 4–7. As is evident from these curves the number of errors on the

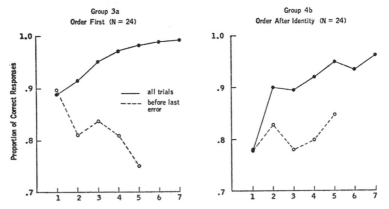

FIGURE 6.—Proportion of correct responses over all trials and before last error in blocks of eight trials, identity of ordered sets, Groups 3a and 4b (Exp. II).

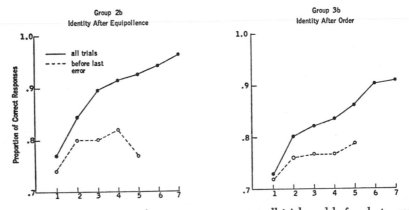

FIGURE 7.—Proportion of correct responses over all trials and before last error in blocks of eight trials, identity of sets, Groups 2b and 3b (Exp. II).

concept of identity of ordered sets was extremely small. From the high proportion of correct responses even in the first block of trials it is evident that this concept is a very natural and simple one for children. Learning curves for trials before the last error are also shown in these figures. To identify the last error prior to conditioning, we adopted a criterion of 16 successive correct responses. For this reason, these curves are only shown for the first 40 trials. The combined curve for Groups 1a and 4a is clearly stationary. This is also the case for 2b, 3a, 3b and 4b.[1] The results of the χ^2 test of stationarity for blocks of 4 trials are shown in Table 1 and confirm these graphic observations. Only the curve for 1b approaches significance. (No computation was made for 3a because of the small number of errors;

TABLE 1

STATIONARITY RESULTS FOR EQUIPOLLENCE AND
IDENTITY OF SETS EXPERIMENT (EXP. II)

Group	x^2	df	$p>$	Ss in last block
1a & 4a...	4.95	9	.80	9
1b...	16.69	9	.05	12
2a...	4.79	9	.80	11
3a...	—Too few errors—			1
4b...	4.89	9	.80	5
2b...	5.96	9	.70	5
3b...	3.49	9	.90	10

the number of subjects in the final block of 4 trials is shown in the right-hand column of the table.)

I shall restrict myself to one Vincent curve for this experiment. The 48 subjects of Groups 1 and 4 began with the concept of identity of sets. Of the 48 subjects, 38 met the criterion of 16 successive correct responses mentioned above. The Vincent curve for the criterion subjects is shown in Figure 3. Evidence of nonstationarity in the fourth quartile is present as in the case of Experiment I.

Examination of the mean learning curves over all trials apparently indicates little evidence of transfer. Somewhat surprisingly, the only definite evidence confirms the existence of negative transfer. In particular, it seems clear from Figure 6, there is negative transfer in learning the concept of identity of ordered sets after the concept of identity of unordered sets. Also, from Figures 4 and 7, it seems apparent that there is negative transfer in learning identity of sets after identity of ordered sets, but not after equipollence of sets.

The effects of transfer are actually more evident when we examine the data from the standpoint of two or four concepts. The mean learning curves over all 56 trials for the various concepts are shown in Figures 8-14. The data points are for blocks of 8 trials. The abbreviations used in the legends are nearly self-explanatory. For the learning curves shown at the right of each figure, the O curve is for pairs of sets identical in the sense of ordered sets, the IŌ curve for pairs of sets identical only in the sense of unordered sets, the EI curve for pairs of equipollent but not identical sets, and the Ē

---

[1] "Group 1a" refers to the performance of Group 1 subjects on the first of their two tasks, 1b to performance on the second task, and similarly for 2a, 2b, 3a, 3b, and 4b.

curve for pairs of nonequipollent sets. These four curves thus represent
all pairs of sets in four mutually exclusive and exhaustive classes. The
legend is the same for all figures. On the other hand, the curves for the
two-concept analysis shown at the left of each figure differ in definition
according to the problem being learned. In Figure 8 the dichotomy is

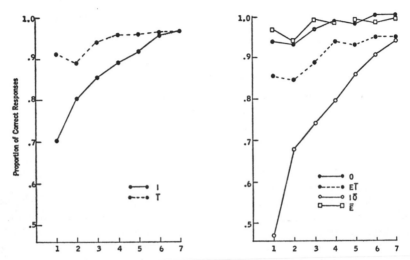

FIGURE 8.—Proportion of correct responses in blocks of eight trials for two
and four concepts, identity of sets ($N = 48$), Groups 1a and 4a (Exp. II).

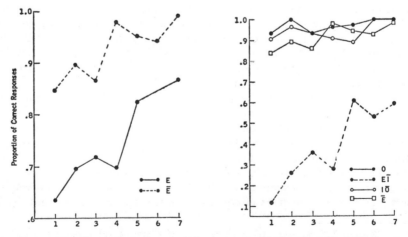

FIGURE 9.—Proportion of correct responses in blocks of eight trials for two
and four concepts, equipollence following identity of sets, Group 1b (Exp. II).

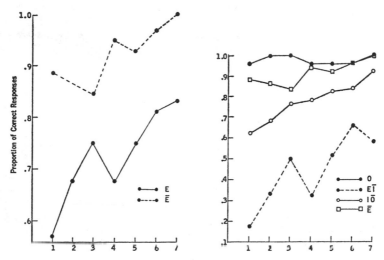

FIGURE 10.—Proportion of correct responses in blocks of eight trials for two and four concepts, equipollence, Group 2a (Exp. II).

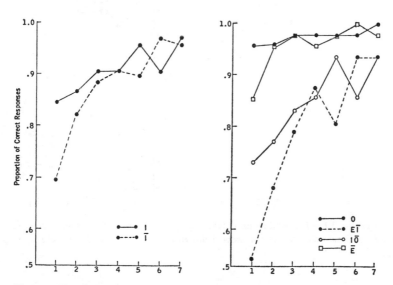

FIGURE 11.—Proportion of correct responses in blocks of eight trials for two and four concepts, identity following equipollence of sets, Group 2b (Exp. II).

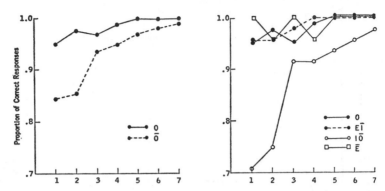

FIGURE 12.—Proportion of correct responses in blocks of eight trials for two and four concepts, identity of ordered sets, Group 3a (Exp. II).

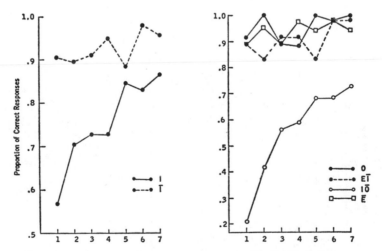

FIGURE 13.—Proportion of correct responses in blocks of eight trials for two and four concepts, identity of sets, following identity of ordered sets, Group 3b (Exp. II).

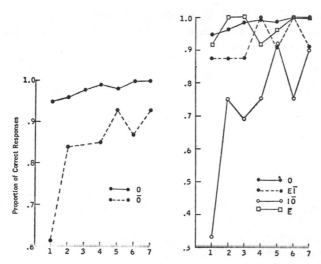

FIGURE 14.—Proportion of correct responses in blocks of eight trials for two and four concepts, identity of ordered sets following identity of sets, Group 4b (Exp. II).

identical and nonidentical sets (I and Ī); in Figure 9 it is equipollent and nonequipollent sets (E and Ē), and so forth for the other five figures.

Before considering questions of transfer, several observations should be made about the individual figures. First, for each of the eight subgroups (1a–4b) the learning curves for the two-concepts and the four-concepts are not homogeneous. A difference in difficulty at either level of analysis can be detected in all cases. Second, contrary to some experimental results in concept formation, the two-concept curves at the left of each figure show that the absence of identity or equipollence is often easier to detect than its presence. The dichotomy of O vs. Ō, that is, identity or nonidentity of ordered sets, is the natural one. When the "presence" of a concept disagrees with this natural dichotomy, as it does in the case of identity and equipollence of sets, it is more difficult to detect than the absence of the concept. This conclusion is borne out by Figures 8 and 10 for the groups beginning with identity and equipollence, respectively, as well as for Group 3b (Fig. 13), that was trained on ordered sets before identity of sets. This same conclusion even holds fairly well for the second sessions after training on some other concept (Figs. 9, 11, 12). Figure 14, that compares O and Ō after training on identity of sets, indicates, I think, the tentative conclusion to be drawn. *Whether the absence or presence of a concept is more difficult to learn depends much more on the previous training and experience of a subject than on the concept itself.* When we compare Figure 12 with Figure 14 we see that even the difference between O and Ō in Figure 12 is influenced by the prior training or identity, for the difference is greater in Figure 14, and surely this is so because the IŌ cases have to be reversed in going from sets to ordered sets.

Third, examination of the four-concept curves reveals a natural gradient of difficulty. We may apply something rather like Coombs's (1950) unfolding technique to develop an ordinal generalization gradient. The natural or objective order of the classes of pairs of sets is O, IŌ, EĪ, Ē. For any of the three concepts of sameness studied in the experiment, we may, without disturbing this objective ordering, characterize the classes exhibiting presence of the concept and those exhibiting its absence by cutting the ordering into two pieces. On a given *side* of the *cut,* as I shall call it, the nearer a class is to the cut the more difficult it is. Consider, to begin with, Figure 8. The task is identity of sets, and the cut is between IŌ and EĪ; we see that, on the one side IŌ is more difficult than O, and on the other side of the cut, EĪ is more difficult than Ē. Turning to Figure 9, the task is equipollence and thus the cut is between EĪ and Ē; of the three concepts on the EĪ side, EĪ is clearly the most difficult and IŌ is slightly more difficult than O, sustaining the hypothesis of an ordinal gradient. In Figure 10, the task is equipollence again, but in this case without prior training, and the results are as expected but more decisive than those shown in Figure 9. Figure 11, like Figure 8, sustains the hypothesis when the task is identity of sets. In the case of Figure 12, the task is identity of ordered sets and thus IŌ, EĪ and Ē occur on the same side of the cut. IŌ is clearly the most difficult, but it is not really possible clearly to distinguish EĪ and Ē in difficulty, for very few errors are made in either class. In Figure 13 the task is identity of sets again, but this time following identity of ordered sets. The proper order of difficulty is maintained but the distinction between EĪ and Ē is not as sharply defined as in Figure 8 or Figure 11. Finally, in Figure 14, the task is identity of ordered sets following identity of sets. The gradients are as predicted by the hypothesis and are better defined than in Figure 12—no doubt because of the prior training on identity of sets. The existence and detailed nature of these natural gradients of difficulty within a concept task are subjects that seem to be worth considerable further investigation.

I turn now to evidence of transfer in the four-concept analysis. From examination of the over-all, mean learning curves which, in the terminology of the present discussion, are the one-concept curves, we observed no positive transfer but two cases of negative transfer. As might be expected, the four-concept curves yield a richer body of results. I shall try to summarize only what appear to be the most important points. Comparing Figures 8 and 11, we see that for the learning of identity of sets, prior training on equipollence has positive transfer for class IŌ and negative transfer for EĪ. The qualitative explanation appears obvious: the initial natural dichotomy seems to be O, Ō, and for this dichotomy IŌ is a class of "different" pairs, but the task of equipollence reinforces the treatment of IŌ pairs as the "same"; the situation is reversed for the class EĪ, and thus the negative transfer, for under equipollence EĪ pairs are the "same," but under identity of sets they are "different."

Comparing now Figures 8 and 13 in which the task is again identity of sets but the prior training is on identity of ordered sets rather than equipollence, there is, as would be expected by the kind of argument just given, negative transfer for the class IŌ. There is also some slight evidence of positive transfer for EĪ.

Looking next at Figures 9 and 10, we observe positive transfer for the class IŌ when the task is equipollence and the prior training is on identity of sets. What is surprising is the relatively slight amount of negative transfer for the class EĪ.

Finally, we compare Figures 12 and 14, in which the task is identity of ordered sets; in the latter figure this task is preceded by identity of sets and we observe negative transfer for the class IŌ, as would be expected. The response curves for the other three classes are too close to probability 1 to make additional inferences, although there is a slight negative transfer for EĪ that cannot be explained by the principles stated above.

It seems apparent from these results that the analysis of transfer in the learning of mathematical concepts may often be facilitated if a fine-scale breakdown of the concepts in question into a number of subconcepts is possible. Needed most is a quantitative theory to guide a more detailed analysis of the transfer phenomena.

Experiment III. Polygons and Angles

This experiment is reported in detail in Stoll (1962), and some of the data is presented here with her permission. The subjects were 32 kindergarten children divided into two equal groups. For both groups the experiment was a successive discrimination, three-response situation, with one group discriminating between triangles, quadrilaterals, and pentagons, and the other group discriminating between acute, right, and obtuse angles. For all subjects a typical case of each form (that is, one of the three types of polygons or three types of angles) was shown immediately above the appropriate response key. As in the case of Experiment II, no single stimulus display was repeated for any one subject. Stimulus displays representing each form were randomized over experimental trials in blocks of nine, with three of each type appearing in each block. The subjects were run to a criterion of nine successively correct responses, but with not more than 54 trials in any one session.

For the quadrilaterals and pentagons, the guessing probability prior to the last error was essentially the same, $\hat{p} = .609$ and $\hat{p} = .600$, respectively. Consequently, the proportions of correct responses for the combined data are presented in blocks of six trials, together with the mean learning curve for all trials, in Figure 15. The corresponding data for the triangles are not

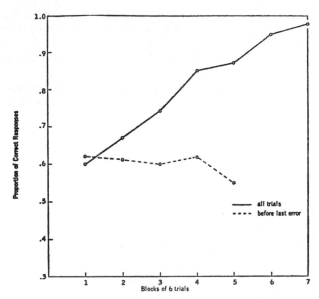

FIGURE 15.—Proportion of correct responses prior to last error and meaning learning curve (quadrilateral and pentagon concepts, Stoll experiment).

presented because the initial proportion of correct responses was quite high and the subjects learned to recognize triangles correctly very easily.

Fig. 16 presents the same curves for the combined data for the three types of angles, although the guessing probability varied between the

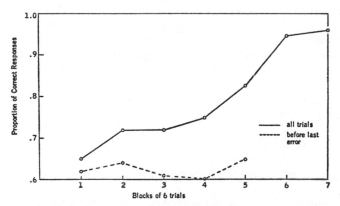

FIGURE 16.—Proportion of correct responses prior to last error and meaning learning curve (acute, right, and obtuse angle concepts, Stoll experiment).

angles. Both figures strongly support the hypothesis of a constant guessing probability prior to conditioning. In the case of the quadrilaterals and pentagons, $\chi^2 = 0.71$, $df = 4$, $P > .90$, $N = 548$. In the case of the combined data for the angles, $\chi^2 = 0.97$, $df = 4$, $P > .90$, $N = 919$.

The Vincent curves for each concept (except that of the triangle) are shown in Figure 17. The pentagons, quadrilaterals, and right angles have quite stationary Vincent curves, whereas there is a definite increase in the fourth quartile of the Vincent curves for the acute and obtuse angles, and

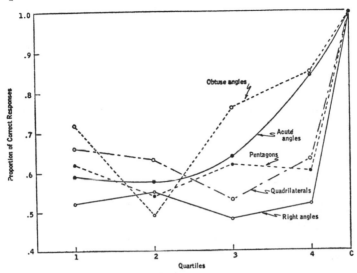

FIGURE 17.—Vincent learning curves in quartiles for proportion of correct responses prior to last error for Stoll experiment.

in the case of the obtuse angles there is, in fact, a significant increase in the third quartile. Statistical tests of stationarity of these Vincent curves support the results of visual inspection. Each test has 3 degrees of freedom because the analysis is based on the data for the four quartiles. In the case of the quadrilaterals, $\chi^2 = 1.75$; for the pentagons, $\chi^2 = 1.33$; for the right angles, $\chi^2 = 0.95$; for the obtuse angles, $\chi^2 = 12.63$; and for the acute angles, $\chi^2 = 16.43$. Only the last two values are significant.

Using responses before the last error, for all concepts except that of triangle, goodness-of-fit tests were performed for (1) stationarity in blocks of six trials, (2) binomial distribution of responses as correct or incorrect in blocks of four trials, and (3) independence of responses, the test made for zero-order vs. first-order dependence. The results of these tests are presented in Table 2. The results shown strongly support the adequacy of the one-element model for this experiment.

Experiment IV. Variation in Method of Stimulus Display

In this study conducted with Rose Ginsberg, we compared the rate of learning in two experimental situations, one in which stimulus displays were

TABLE 2
Stationarity, Order, and Binomial Distribution Results
(Stoll Experiment on Geometric Forms)

	X^2	df	$P>$
Quadrilateral, $p = .609$:			
Stationarity ($N = 273$)	1.68	4	.70
Order ($N = 262$)	0.65	1	.40
Binomial distribution ($N = 65$)	1.77	2	.40
Pentagon, $p = .600$:			
Stationarity ($N = 275$)	2.40	4	.60
Order ($N = 269$)	1.76	1	.15
Binomial distribution ($N = 65$)	2.07	2	.35
Acute angle, $p = .674$:			
Stationarity ($N = 338$)	7.96	4	.05
Order ($N = 348$)	3.17	1	.05
Binomial distribution ($N = 85$)	2.66	2	.25
Right angle, $p = .506$:			
Stationarity ($N = 313$)	6.34	4	.10
Order ($N = 326$)	2.41	1	.10
Binomial distribution ($N = 80$)	10.52	2	.001*
Obtuse angle, $p = .721$:			
Stationarity ($N = 268$)	1.10	4	.85
Order ($N = 256$)	7.32	1	.001*
Binomial distribution ($N = 63$)	2.90	2	.20
Quadrilateral and pentagon, $p = .604$:			
Stationarity ($N = 548$)	0.71	4	.90
Binomial distribution ($N = 130$)	1.77	2	.40
All angles, $p = .624$:			
Stationarity ($N = 919$)	0.97	4	.90

presented individually in the usual way, and the other in which the same stimulus displays were presented by means of colored slides, to groups of four children. The concept to be learned was identity of sets, and in both situations the children were required to respond by pressing one of two buttons, depending upon whether the stimulus display on that trial was identical or non-identical. Of the 64 subjects 32 were from first grade and 32 from kindergarten classes. For the children receiving individual displays the experimental situation was essentially identical with that of Experiment II.

Each group, however, was divided into two subgroups. One subgroup received the stimulus material in random order, and the other in an order based on anticipated difficulty; in particular, presentations of one-element sets came first, then two-element sets, and finally three-element sets.

The mean learning curves for the two subgroups with random presentation are shown in Figure 18. The results suggest that presentation by slides is a less effective learning device for younger children, and the younger the child, the more this finding seems to apply. At all levels of difficulty, the kindergarten children learned more efficiently when the stimuli were presented to them in individual sessions. With one- or two-

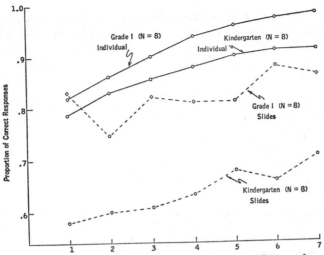

FIGURE 18.—Proportion of correct responses in blocks of 12 trials, subgroups with random presentation (Exp. IV).

element sets displayed, grade 1 subjects learned only slightly better in the individual session situation than in the slide situation, but when the task was more difficult (stimulus displays of three-element sets) the individual learning situation was clearly the most adequate. In interpreting these results it should be emphasized that the individual session was strictly experimental so that the amount of interaction between subject and experimenter was paralleled in both individual and slide situations.

Why these two experimental situations should produce different results in terms of learning efficiency is not yet clear to us. One possibility is the following: It has been shown, both with lower organisms (Murphy & Miller, 1955) and young children (Murphy & Miller, 1959), that the ideal situation for learning is the contiguity of stimulus, response and reinforcement. In the individual sessions these requirements were met, for the response buttons were 1.5 inches below the stimulus displays and the reinforcement lights were 1.0 inches from the stimuli. On the other hand, in the slide presentations, although the stimulus displays and reinforcements were immediately adjacent to each other, the response buttons were about 3 feet from the screen on which the stimulus display was projected. Experimentally, it has been shown (Murphy & Miller, 1959) that with children of this age group a separation of 6.0 inches is sufficient to interfere with efficient learning.

Experiment V. Incidental Learning

This experiment represents a joint study with Rose Ginsberg. Thirty-six kindergarten children, in 3 groups of 12 each, were run for 60 trials a day on 2 successive days of individual experimental sessions during which they were required to learn equipollence of sets. On the first day, the stimulus displays presented to the subjects on each trial differed in color among the three groups but otherwise were the same. In Group 1, all displays were in one color—black—and in Group 2, equipollent sets were red and nonequipollent sets, yellow. For the first 12 trials in Group 3, equipollent sets were red and nonequipollent sets, yellow; for the remaining 48 trials on that day the two colors were gradually fused until discrimination between them was not possible. On the second day, all sets were presented to all three groups in one color—black.

As is apparent from the brief description of the experimental design, Group 1 simply had two days' practice under the same conditions with the concept of equipollence. In Group 2, the child did not actually need to learn the concept of equipollence but could simply respond to the color difference on the first day. It is well known that such a color discrimination for young children is a simple task. If the child in this group learned anything about equipollence of sets the first day, therefore, we may assume it to have been a function of incidental learning. If incidental learning is effective, his performance on the second day, when the color cue is dropped, should have been at least better than the performance of children in Group 1 on the first day. In Group 3, where we gave the child the discriminative cue of color difference in the first trial and then very slowly withdrew that cue, the child should have continued to search the stimulus displays very closely for a color stimulus and thus have been obliged to pay close attention to the stimuli.

The mean learning curve for the three groups are shown in Figure 19.

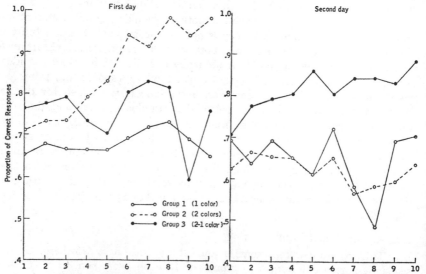

FIGURE 19.—Proportion of correct responses in blocks of six trials for both days (Exp. V).

Of the three groups only Group 2 approached perfect learning on the first day. In this group, of course, only color discrimination was necessary. Both the other groups did not improve over the first 60 trials, although Group 3 showed some initial improvement when the color cues remained discriminable. On the second day, Group 1 showed no improvement, and the learning curves for this group and Group 2 were practically identical. For Group 3, on the other hand, the results were conspicuously better on the second day than for those of any other group. It is apparent from these curves that the task chosen was relatively difficult for the age of the children because essentially no improvement was shown by Group 1 over the entire 120 trials. The conditions in Group 3, where the children were forced to pay very close attention to the stimuli, do seem to have significantly enhanced the learning.

Experiment VI. Variation of Response Methods

This study was made jointly with Rose Ginsberg. Its object was to study the behavioral effects of different methods of response. Specifically, 3 groups, each composed of 20 kindergarten children, were taken individually through a sequence of 60 trials on each of 2 successive days for a total of 120 trials. The task for all 3 groups was equipollence of sets.

In Group 1, the child was presented with pictures of two sets of objects and was to indicate, by pressing one of two buttons, whether the sets "went together" or did not "go together" (were equipollent or nonequipollent).

In Group 2, the child was presented with one display set and two "answer" sets and was required to choose the answer that "went together" with the display set.

In Group 3, the child was presented with one display set and three "answer" sets and was to make his choice from the three possible answers.

This situation has fairly direct reference to teaching methodology in the sense that Group 2 and Group 3 represent multiple-choice possibilities. In Group 1, where the child is required to identify either the presence of the concept or its absence on each trial, the situation is comparable to one in which the child must indicate whether an equation or statement is correct or incorrect.

On the first day, each group of children learned the task described above. On the second day, they were run on an alternative method. Specifically, Group 1 was run under Group 3 conditions and Groups 2 and 3 were run under Group 1 conditions.

The mean learning curves for all groups on both days are shown in Figure 20. It will be noticed that in Group 2, where the subjects were required to choose from one of two available responses, they learned slightly more quickly and to a slightly better level of achievement on the first day than the other groups but, on the second day, when the experimental conditions were shifted, Group 2 subjects did less well than the subjects in the other two groups. The clear superiority of Group 1 on the second day, when

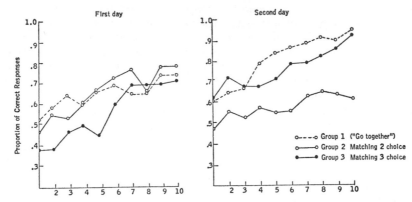

Figure 20.—Proportion of correct responses for two successive days in blocks of six trials for all subjects (Exp. VI).

they were transferred to Group 3 conditions, indicates some positive transfer from learning to judge whether or not a concept is present to the multiple-choice situation, whereas the results for Groups 2 and 3 on the second day indicate some negative transfer from the multiple-response methods to the presence-or-absence method.

These results are further supported when we examine separately the data from subjects achieving a criterion of 12 successive correct responses on the first day. The more successful method was clearly that used in Group I, as indicated by the curves in Figure 21. The subjects in this group were

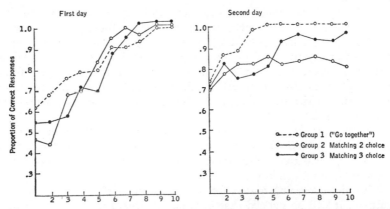

Figure 21.—Proportion of correct responses for two successive days in blocks of six trials for subjects achieving of 12 successive correct responses (Exp. VI).

conspicuously more successful than the other groups on the second day, making, in fact, no errors from Trial 30 to Trial 60. Group 3 achieved perfect scores on the second day only on the last six trials, and Group 2 never reached that level on the second day, although, like the other criterion subjects, they had achieved perfect learning on the first day.

It seems reasonable to conclude tentatively that the method used with Group 1, where subjects were required to recognize the presence or absence of some property on each trial, is the more successful method in establishing the understanding of a concept well enough to permit transfer to a different response method.

Support for the all-or-none model of conditioning is also to be found in this experiment. In Table 3, χ^2 goodness-of-fit tests of stationarity over trials before the final error for each group on each day are shown. The six values are all nonsignificant and thus support the basic assumption of the all-or-none models.

TABLE 3

TEST FOR STATIONARITY OVER TRIALS BEFORE THE FINAL ERROR (EXP. VI)

	Group 1		Group 2		Group 3	
	Day 1	Day 2	Day 1	Day 2	Day 1	Day 2
χ^2.........	4.97	2.41	10.76	4.255	16.07	2.87
df.........	8	1	9	8	9	7
$P >$........	.70	.10	.20	.80	.05	.80

Some Tentative Conclusions

On the basis of the six experiments just discussed I would like to draw some tentative conclusions, some of which are important for pedagogical procedures (cf. Suppes and Ginsberg, 1962b). I want to emphasize, however, that I do not wish to claim that the evidence from these experiments is conclusive enough to establish any one of the six conclusions in any final way, but what I do hope is that the attempt to summarize some of the implications of these experiments will stimulate other research workers to investigate these and related propositions in more adequate detail.

1. Formation of simple mathematical concepts in young children is approximately an all-or-none process. Evidence indicates, however, that significant deviations from the all-or-none model are present (see the discussion of the two-element model below).
2. Learning is more efficient if the child who makes an error is required to make an overt correction response in the presence of the stimulus to be learned (Exp. I).
3. Incidental learning does not appear to be an effective method of acquisition for young children. In Experiment IV the group of children that responded to a color discrimination did not subsequently give any indication of having learned the underlying concepts.
4. Contiguity of response, stimulus, and reinforcement enhances learning (Exp. V).
5. In the learning of related mathematical concepts the amount of over-all transfer from the learning of one concept to another is surprisingly small. However, considerable positive or negative transfer between specific subconcepts is often present (Exp. II).

6. Transfer of a concept is more effective if, in the learning situation, the subject is required to recognize the presence or absence of a concept in a number of stimulus displays, than if learning has involved matching from a number of possible responses (Exp. VI).

Several of these conclusions are at variance with generally accepted results for adult learning behavior. For example, the efficacy of an immediate overt correction response (see Burke et al., 1954, for negative results on this method in adults), the variation of response method, or the relative specificity of the learning of concepts with relatively little transfer. What is much needed is a wider range of systematic studies to isolate the factors of learning in young children which are particularly distinct from common features of adult learning behavior.

Two-Element Model

In the first conclusion mentioned above, we stated that the formation of concepts is approximately an all-or-none process in young children. On the other hand, the detailed analysis of responses prior to the last error indicates that, in many cases, there is an incremental effect appearing in the last quartile or even, sometimes, in the last two quartiles of the data. This matter is discussed in some detail in Suppes & Ginsberg (1963). I would simply like briefly to mention here what currently appears to be the best extension of the one-element model to account for these results.

The simplest alternative model is the linear incremental model with a single operator. The intuitive idea of this model is precisely the opposite of the all-or-none conditioning model. The supposition is that learning proceeds on an incremental basis. Let q_n be the probability of an error on trial n. Then the model is formulated by the following recursive equation:

$$q_{n+1} = (1-\theta)q_n, \tag{1}$$

where $0 < \theta \leq 1$. It is simple to show but somewhat surprising that this purely incremental model has precisely the same mean learning curve as the all-or-none model if we set $c = \theta$. (To obtain this identity of the learning curves we must, of course, consider all responses and not simply responses prior to the last error.) The incremental model differs sharply from the all-or-none model in the kind of learning curve predicted for responses prior to the last error, as is evident from equation (1). It may be shown, moreover, that the concave upward Vincent curves obtained in several of the experiments discussed above (see Figs. 3 and 17) cannot be accounted for by the linear incremental models.

The second simple alternative, that will account for these concave-upward Vincent curves, is a model that represents a kind of compromise between the all-or-none model and the incremental model. It results from a simple extension of the one-element model, that is, the assumption that associated with each situation are two stimulus elements and, therefore, learning proceeds in two stages of all-or-none conditioning. Each of the two elements is conditioned on an all-or-none basis but the two parameters of conditioning, one for each element, may be adjusted to produce various incremental effects on the response probabilities. Let σ and τ be the two elements. The basic learning process may be represented by the following four-state Markov process in which the four states (σ,τ), σ, τ, and O represent

	(σ, τ)	σ	τ	0
(σ, τ)	1	0	0	0
σ	$b'/2$	$1 - b'/2$	0	0
τ	$b'/2$	0	$1 - b'/2$	0
0	0	$a/2$	$a/2$	$1 - a$

the possible states of conditioning of the two- stimulus elements. Because we do not attempt experimentally to identify the stimuli σ and τ, this Markov process may be collapsed into a three-state process, in which the states are simply the *number* of stimuli conditioned to the correct response. In the matrix shown above a is the probability of conditioning at the first stage and b' is the probability of conditioning at the second stage. The division by ½ in the matrix simply represents the equal probability of sampling one of the two elements. If we consider only the number of stimuli, it is convenient to replace $b'/2$ by b and we obtain the transition matrix shown below:

	2	1	0
2	1	0	0
1	b	$1 - b$	0
0	0	a	$1 - a$

To complete the description of the process we associate with the sampling of each element σ and τ a guessing probability g_σ and g_τ when the elements are still unconditioned. For the states 0 and 1 of the second matrix shown we then have the guessing probabilities g_0 and g_1 defined in the obvious manner in terms of the sampling probabilities:

$$g_0 = \tfrac{1}{2} g_\sigma + \tfrac{1}{2} g_\tau,$$
$$g_1 = \tfrac{1}{4} g_\sigma + \tfrac{1}{4} g_\tau + \tfrac{1}{2} = \tfrac{1}{2} g_0 + \tfrac{1}{2}.$$

The probabilities g_σ and g_τ are not observable but g_0 is, and g_1 is a simple function of it. This means that we now have a process with three free parameters, the conditioning parameters a and b and the guessing probability g_0. I shall not attempt to report on the detailed application of this two-element model, but we are now in the process of applying it to a number of different experimental situations and hope to report in detail on its empirical validity in the near future. I would, however, like to remark that a very interesting interpretation of this kind of two-stage model has recently been given by Restle (1964), who interprets the two stages of learning as conditioning and discrimination. The model he proposes differs in detail from that given here, but for most observable response patterns the differences between the two will not be large.

Before turning to another topic, I would like to emphasize that I do not feel that the analysis of concept formation in terms of the simple one- and two-element models sketched here is fully satisfactory intellectually. It is apparent that these models must be regarded as schemata of the full process that is taking place in concept formation. What is surprising is that they are able to account for response data as well as they do. Theories that postulate more details about the learning process in concept formation are needed to go beyond the present analysis. This, I take it, will be particularly true as we proceed to the analysis of more complicated mathematical concepts, whose learning must rest upon the understanding of simpler concepts.

LOGIC AND MATHEMATICAL PROOFS

Together with several younger associates I have conducted, for several years, pedagogical and psychological experiments on the learning of mathematical logic with elementary-school children. Before turning to a relatively systematic statement of some of our results, I would like to survey briefly what we have attempted.

In the fall of 1956 I brought into my college logic course a selected group of sixth-, seventh-, and eighth-graders (they were, in fact, no more selected than the Stanford students in the course). Their demonstrated ability to master the course and perform at a level only slightly below that of the college students was the initial impetus for further work. The next important step was the extensive study by Shirley Hill of the reasoning abilities of first-, second-, and third-graders. This study was begun in 1959 and completed as her dissertation in 1961. I shall report briefly on this below. In 1960 Dr. Hill and I wrote a text and taught a pilot group of fifth-graders a year's course in mathematical logic. The course was structured very similarly to a college logic course except that material was presented more explicitly and at a much slower pace. Students were selected on the basis of ability and interest (the minimum IQ was 110), and again the positive results were an impetus to further work. Because of the success of this class, the text book was revised (Suppes & Hill, 1964) and, during the academic year (1962–63), was taught to approximately 300 selected fifth-graders in the Bay Area, with support for the project coming from the Office of Education and the National Science Foundation. These same classes were given a second year of instruction as sixth-graders and, in another year, we shall be able to report in detail on their level of achievement. We were also interested in seeing if we could train fifth-grade teachers to teach the course as part of their regular curriculum. To this end, we gave them a special course in logic in the summer of 1961 and all the classes but one were taught by the teachers.

We began experimental psychological studies of how and to what de-

gree children of still younger ages could learn the concepts of formal inference. I shall report briefly on a pilot study with first-graders. On the basis
of the experience of several of us with the teaching of logic to elementary-
school children, we conducted an extensive psychological experiment with
fourth-grade children to determine whether it was easier initially to learn
rules of sentential inference when the standard interpretations were given,
or whether it was easier simply to learn the rules as part of an uninterpreted
meaningless game. This last possibility was, of course, most disturbing for a
wide variety of mathematicians interested in the teaching of mathematics.
I shall not enter here into the many reasons why I think there are good
psychological arguments to believe that the initial teaching of inference
simply as a game will turn out to be the most effective approach. I am
frankly reluctant to formulate any very definite ideas about this highly
controversial matter until we have accumulated a much more substantial body of evidence.

I turn now to the two experiments mentioned above on which I want
to report briefly.

Experiment VII. Logical Abilities of Young Children

As already remarked, this extensive empirical study constituted Shirley Hill's doctoral dissertation (1961). Dr. Hill gave a test instrument consisting of 100 items to 270 children in the age group 6 through 8 years
(first, second, and third grades). Each of the 100 items consisted of 2 or 3
verbal premises plus a conclusion presented orally as a question. The subject was asked to affirm or deny the conclusion as presented. There were
two primary reasons for not asking the children to compose a conclusion: In
the first place, children of this age sometimes have difficulty formulating
sentences; this has sometimes been cited as the reason for inappropriate
measures of their reasoning abilities. The second reason is, simply, the
methodological difficulty of interpreting the correctness or incorrectness of
a conclusion given as a free response. The 100 items were equally divided
between positive and negative answers. The first part of the test consisted
of 60 items that were drawn from sentential logic. Every conclusion or its
negation followed from the given premises by the sentential theory of inference. The second part consisted of 40 items that were drawn from predicate logic, including 13 classical syllogisms. The predicate logic items,
however, also included inferences using two-place predicates together with
existential quantifiers.

Because it is easy for children to give the correct answer to a problem
in which the conclusion is generally true or false, every attempt was made
to construct the items in such a way that the omission of one premise would
make it impossible to draw the correct conclusion. To provide a behavioral
check on this aspect of the items a base-line group of 50 subjects was given
the test with the first premise of each item omitted. For instance, to quote

the illustration given by Dr. Hill (1961, p. 43), the original item might read:

> If that boy is John's brother, then he is ten years old.
> That boy is not ten years old.
> Is he John's brother?

For the base-line group the item would be presented:

> If that boy is not ten years old, is he John's brother?

An example of a badly constructed item would be the following:

> If boys are stronger than girls, then boys can run faster than girls.
> Boys are stronger than girls.
> Can boys run faster than girls?

Naturally almost all children gave the correct answer to this latter item, but their behavioral response actually told us little about their intuitive grasp of principles of logical inference. That Dr. Hill's items were well constructed are attested to by the fact that the base-line group averaged 52.02 per cent correct items, which does not significantly differ from chance. (Note that this percentage is based on 5,000 subject items.)

I shall not go into all the facets of Dr. Hill's study here. I mainly want to report on one or two of the most important conclusions. Let me first mention the results of the three standard groups of ages 6, 7, and 8 years. The 6-year-old group receiving the items described above got 71.18 per cent of the items correct. The 7-year-old group got 79.54 per cent of the items correct, and the 8-year old group got 85.58 per cent correct. These percentage figures indicate a steady increase with age in the ability to draw correct logical inferences from hypothetical premises. In addition to the fact of increase, it is just as important to note that the 6-year-old children performed at quite a high level, in contradiction to the view of Piaget and his followers that such young children are limited to concrete operations. Dr. Hill's study certainly provides substantial evidence to the contrary.

To avoid any possible confusion, it should be borne in mind that no claim is made that this study shows young children to be able explicitly to state formal principles of inference. What is claimed is that their grasp of the structure of ordinary language is sufficiently deep for them to be able to make *use* of standard principles of inference with considerable accuracy.

I would like to present just two other results of Dr. Hill's study. To avoid the conjecture that children aged six may be able to do the simpler forms of inference quite well but will do badly on the more difficult inferences involving two-place predicates, the percentage of correct responses for each age group on the 10 types of inferences appearing in the 100-item test are shown in Table 4. The last two categories entitled "Quantificational Logic—Universal Quantifiers" and "Quantificational Logic—Existential Quantifiers" refer to inferences that do not fall within the scheme of the classical syllogism. Although these last two categories are more difficult

TABLE 4

PERCENTAGE OF CORRECT RESPONSES FOR DIFFERENT PRINCIPLES
OF INFERENCE BY AGE LEVEL

PRINCIPLES OF INFERENCE	PERCENTAGE OF CORRECT RESPONSES		
	Age 6	Age 7	Age 8
Modus ponendo ponens	78	89	92
Modus tollendo ponens	82	84	90
Modus tollendo tollens	74	79	84
Law of hypothetical syllogism	78	86	88
Hypothetical syllogism and *tollendo tollens*	76	79	85
Tollendo tollens and *tollendo ponens*	65	77	81
Ponendo ponens and *tollendo tollens*	65	67	76
Classical syllogism	66	75	86
Quantificational logic—universal quantifiers	69	81	84
Quantificational logic—existential quantifiers	64	79	88

than the simplest *modus ponendo ponens* applications, the performance level of the children aged six is still well above chance, and it is interesting to note that the performance on universal quantifiers is actually slightly better than the performance on sentential inferences using both *ponendo ponens* and *tollendo ponens*.

The second result concerns the attempt to identify some of the more obvious sources of difficulty. The lack of a sharply defined gradient in Table 4 suggested further examination of individual items. What turned out to be a major source of difficulty was the inclusion of an additional negation in an inference. Two hypothetical items that illustrate this difference are the following: Consider first as a case of *modus ponendo ponens:*

If this is Room 7, then it is a first-grade room.
This is Room 7.
Is it a first-grade room?

Let us now modify this example, still making it an application of *modus ponendo ponens:*

If this is not Room 8, then it is not a first-grade room.
This is not Room 8.
Is it a first-grade room?

The additional negations in the second item are a source of considerable difficulty to the children. It might be thought that the negations simply cause difficulty because they represent an increase in general complexity. To examine this question Dr. Hill compared the cases using a single rule of inference in which negations occurred, with the use of combined implications involving more than one rule of inference. The results are shown in Table 5. It is clear from this table that an additional negation adds a greater factor of difficulty than the use of more than one principle of inference.

I have only presented here a few of the results of this important study. A complete statement of the results are included in Hill (1961).

TABLE 5
COMPARISON OF INCREASE IN ERROR ASSOCIATED WITH THE ADDITION
OF NEGATION AND WITH COMPOUND IMPLICATIONS

	PERCENTAGE OF ERROR OUT OF TOTAL POSSIBLE RESPONSES		
PRINCIPLES OF INFERENCE	Regular Form	Additional Negation	Combined Implication
Modus ponendo ponens.....................	.06	.19	.17
Modus tollendo tollens.....................	.12	.34	
Modus tollendo ponens.....................	.03	.25	.27
Modus tollendo tollens.....................	.12	.34	
Law of hypothetical syllogism.................	.08	.22	.16
Modus tollendo tollens.....................	.12	.34	

Experiment VIII. Pilot Study of Mathematical Proofs

The details of this pilot study are in Suppes (1962). The original study was conducted with the assistance of John M. Vickers, and we are now engaged in a larger study along the same lines. The primary objective of this pilot study was to determine if it is feasible to apply the one-element model, described earlier, to the behavior of young children by constructing proofs in the trivial mathematical system, described as follows: Any finite string of 1's is a well-formed formula of the system. The single axiom is the single symbol 1. The four rules of inference are:

$$R1. \quad S \to S11$$
$$R2. \quad S \to S00$$
$$R3. \quad S1 \to S$$
$$R4. \quad S0 \to S$$

where S is a non-empty string. A theorem of the system is, of course, either the axiom or a finite string that may be obtained from the axiom by a finite number of applications of the rules of inference. A general characterization of all theorems is immediate: any finite string is a theorem if and only if it begins with 1. A typical theorem in the system is the following one, which I have chosen because it uses all four rules of inference:

Theorem	101	
(1)	1	Axiom
(2)	100	R2
(3)	10	R4
(4)	1011	R1
(5)	101	R3

The proofs of minimal length in this system are easily found, and the correction procedure was always in terms of a proof of minimal length.

The stimulus discrimination facing the subject on each trial is simply described. He must compare the last line of proof in front of him with the theorem to be proved. This comparison immediately leads to a classification of each last line of proof into one of four categories: additional 1's need to be added to master the theorem (R1); additional 0's need to be added to master the theorem (R2); a 1 must be deleted to continue to master the theorem (R3); or a 0 must be deleted in order to master the theorem (R4). The rule in terms of whether the response should be made is shown in parentheses. When the subject is completely conditioned to all four stimulus discriminations, he will make a correct response corresponding to the application of a rule that will produce a part of a proof of minimal length. For each of the four discriminations with respect to which he is not yet conditioned, there is a guessing probability p_i, $i = 1, 2, 3,$ or 4, that he will guess the correct rule and thus the probability $1 - p_i$ that he will guess incorrectly. In the analysis of data it was assumed that four independent one-element models were applied, one for each stimulus discrimination. (It is a minor but not serious complication to take account of two possible responses, both correct, i.e., leading to a minimal proof; e.g., in the proof of 1111 we may apply R1 twice and then R3, or R1, R3, and then R1 again.)

The pilot study was conducted with a group of first-grade children from an elementary school near Stanford University. There were 18 subjects in all divided into 2 groups of 9 each. One group received the procedure just described, including a correction procedure in terms of which a correct response was always shown at the end of the trial. The other group used a discovery method of sorts and was not given a correction procedure on each trial but, at the end of each proof, the subjects were shown a minimal proof or, in the event the subject constructed a minimal proof, told that the proof constructed was correct.

The following criterion rule was used: A subject, according to the criterion, had learned how to give minimal proofs in the system when 4 correct theorems were proved in succession, provided the subject had proved at least 10 theorems. All subjects were given a maximum of 17 theorems to prove, and all subjects, except for 2 in the discovery group, satisfied this criterion by the time the seventeenth theorem was reached. The 17 theorems were selected according to some relatively definite criteria of structural simplicity from the set of theorems of which the length was greater than 1 and less than 7.

In Table 6, the mean proportion of errors prior to the last error, in blocks of 12 trials for each group and for the 2 groups combined, are summarized. A trial in this instance is defined as a step, or line, in the proof.

More than 60 trials were necessary in order to prove the 17 theorems, but because very few subjects needed the entire 17 theorems to reach criterion, the mean learning curves were terminated at Trial 60. From this table, it seems that the correction group did better than the discovery group, but I do not think the number of subjects or the total number of trials was adequate to draw any serious conclusions about comparison of the two methods. It is interesting to note that the discovery group had a

TABLE 6

OBSERVED PROPORTION OF ERRORS PRIOR TO LAST ERROR FOR THE
CORRECTION, DISCOVERY, AND COMBINED GROUPS (BLOCKS OF 12 TRIALS)

Group	Block				
	1	2	3	4	5
Correction..........	.28	.23	.15	.00	.10
Discovery..........	.23	.20	.40	.30	.33
Combined..........	.25	.21	.30	.18	.24

much more stationary mean learning curve than did the correction group, and in that sense satisfied the one-element model. Of course, these curves are obtained by summing over errors on all four rules. It is very possible that with a larger set of data, for which it would be feasible to separate out the individual rules as the application of the one-element model described above would require, the correction group also would have stationary mean learning curves for data prior to the last error on the basis of the individual rules.

REFERENCES

Bower, G. H. Application of a model to paired-associate learning. *Psychometrika,* 1961, **25,** 255–280.

Bruner, J. S., Goodnow, J. J., & Austin, G. A. *A study of thinking.* New York: John Wiley & Sons, 1956.

Burke, C. J., Estes, W. K., & Hellyer, S. Rate of verbal conditioning in relation to stimulus variability. *J. exp. Psychol.,* 1954, 48, 153–161.

Coombs, C. H. Psychological scaling without a unit of measurement. *Psychol. Rev.,* 1950, **57,** 145–158.

Estes, W. K. The statistical approach to learning theory. In S. Koch (Ed.), *Psychology: a study of a science.* Vol. 2. New York: McGraw-Hill, 1960. Pp. 380–491.

Hill, S. A study of the logical abilities of children. Unpublished Ph.D. dissertation, Stanford University, 1961.

Hull, C. L., & Spence, K. W. Correction vs. non-correction method of trial-and-error learning in rats. *J. comp. Psychol.,* 1938, 25, 127–145.

Murphy, J. V., & Miller, R. E. The effect of spatial contiguity of cue and reward in the object-quality learning of Rhesus monkeys. *J. comp. physiol. Psychol.,* 1955, 48, 221–229.

Murphy, J. V., & Miller, R. E. Spatial contiguity of cue, reward and response in discrimination learning by children. *J. exp. Psychol.,* 1959, 58, 485–489.

Restle, F. Sources of difficulty in learning paired-associates. *In* R. C. Atkinson (Ed.), *Studies in Mathematical Psychology.* Stanford, Calif.: Stanford University Press, 1964. Pp. 116–172.

Stoll, E. Geometric concept formation in kindergarten children. Unpublished Ph.D. dissertation, Stanford University, 1962.

Suppes, P. Towards a behavioral foundation of mathematical proofs. Technical Report No. 44, Psychology Series, Institute for Mathematical Studies in the Social Sciences, Stanford University, 1962.

Suppes, P., & Atkinson, R. C. *Markov learning models for multiperson interactions.* Stanford, Calif.: Stanford University Press, 1960.

Suppes, P., & Ginsberg, R. A fundamental property of all-or-none models, binomial distribution of responses prior to conditioning, with application to concept formation in children. *Psychol. Rev.*, 1963, **70**, 139–161.

Suppes, P., & Ginsberg, R. Application of a stimulus sampling model to children's concept formation with and without an overt correction response. *J. exp. Psychol.*, 1962, **63**, 330–336. (a)

Suppes, P., & Ginsberg, R. Experimental studies of mathematical concept formation in young children. *Sci. Educ.*, 1962, **46**, 230–240. (b)

Suppes, P., & Hill, S. *First Course in Mathematical Logic.* New York: Blaisdell Publishing Co., 1964.

6

ISSUES CURRENT IN EDUCATIONAL PSYCHOLOGY

Lee J. Cronbach

Stanford University

I was originally asked to describe the significance of the new curricular movements, particularly in mathematics, for educational psychology. As I wrote, however, I found myself approaching the theme from another angle, asking, what are the big open questions in educational psychology? The new curricula have had their part in opening up these questions. The reactionary critics of education and the new adventurers both talk of mental discipline, and psychologists are being forced to reconsider whether the concept has legitimate meaning or is only a haunting echo from an ancient fallacy. No one trained as a teacher to connect abstract knowledge with the "real problem" on which it bears can, without a shock, hear representatives of the Physical Science Study Committee state their conviction that the high-school physics course has no proper place for the mention of refrigerators and household wiring. The intelligence of the proponents and the obvious quality of their work requires us to give a respectful hearing when they challenge articles of the educational psychologist's faith. Frequent interchanges with curriculum developers in the last three years have helped me face psychological issues more squarely. Here I am going to discuss those issues, however, more than the curricula themselves.

EDUCATIONAL PSYCHOLOGY: DARK AGES AND RENAISSANCE

From 1940 to 1954 the educational psychology taught to teachers and considered in curriculum planning was almost static.[1] While not much new knowledge has been consolidated since 1954, a combination of influences— the new curricula, for one—has brought us a fresh perspective. The dates

---

[1] It is not that educational psychologists, as an isolated group, were failing to keep up with their science; the pertinent science itself was, on the surface, static. Neal Miller, an outstanding student of learning in the laboratory, was prevailed upon in 1954 to produce a book (Miller, 1957) spelling out the implications of learning theory for educational films and other "graphic communications." The concepts and principles that he used (very successfully) were those of a 1941 book (Miller & Dollard, 1941) only fleshed out by experience from wartime military applications.

1940 and 1954 are not precisely landmarks in educational psychology; 1940 marks only when I happened to complete my own doctoral work, and 1954 the appearance of my textbook in educational psychology (Cronbach, 1954), but, give or take a couple of years, this does mark off a significant period: the period in which commerce between academic psychology and educational psychology was cut off by a tacit embargo. Persons concerned with education found no nourishment in the systematic Hullian studies of T mazes and eyeblink conditioning that began to dominate experimental psychology in the late 1930's. Experimental psychologists were repelled by the educator's insistence on talking about "the whole child" in "real-life situations"—both being prescientific or even antiscientific phrases antithetical to the analytic, formal style that, for a time, was the ideal of American behavior theory. My colleague, J. McV. Hunt, tells me that the psychologist's aversion to educational entanglements was manifest even early in the century. Thorndike was respected in spite of rather than because of his concern with education. One eminent experimenter is reported as turning down a position, in 1921, that would have doubled his salary because it was connected with a School of Education. And Hunt recalls scornful discussion among the eminent Cornell staff of the 1930's about "the drag of education upon psychology with its demand for little steps for little feet."

The educational psychologist, during the years of estrangement, felt that the teachers he taught needed little from theoretical or laboratory psychology.[2] He worked hard and ingeniously to improve teachers' skills in analyzing the individual learner's aptitudes, emotional difficulties, and educational deficiencies. He extracted important educational implications from the burgeoning clinical and social psychologies. But he stopped doing research on intellectual learning or on "psychology of the school subjects," in part because these were not matters of live interest in educational circles. The wave of research into educational learning broke and drained away. Its last major manifestation, I suggest, was the 1936 book entitled *Education as the Cultivation of Higher Mental Processes*, by Judd (1936).[3] This book, with its out-of-fashion title and message, received little attention. Subsequent to 1940, only a few notable reports by such workers as Brownell dealt with intellectual learning. (Brownell concentrated on the development, through meaningful presentation and insightful practice, of skill in computation.)

---

[2] It was in 1937 that Geldard, an experimental psychologist, told teachers that "educational practices will have to be guided for some time to come by rules of thumb. . . . This is not to say that nothing of interest or importance has been done [concerning] learning. Our happy plight at present is that we have at hand far more laws of learning than can possibly be true" (Geldard, 1937). Such a view is occasionally echoed even today (Spence, 1959).

[3] About one-third of the book deals with mathematics. The argument closely matches Bruner's (1957), when he speaks of "the structure of knowledge," although it makes much less place for intuition than he.

We can pass over the 1940's, noting only that young experimenters blooded in the aviation research laboratories of the 1940's and early 1950's are taking over the front line in today's educational psychology. This is a new breed of educational psychologist, firmly grounded in theoretical psychology and technical research method, who did not, like earlier workers in the field, come up through public school teaching. (A representative list of these newcomers would include Crowder, Fleishman, Gagné, Glaser, Lumsdaine, and Stolurow.) These men might well have stayed in military training research, save for the coincidence that such programs were cut back just as national interest in education revived.

Today's work on intellectual processes is not merely a reaction to Russian spacemanship, although some pursestrings were loosened by it. Nor is it primarily a response to the curriculum programs. Movements within psychology emerged at a strategic time to offer new prototheories and new questions. Skinner's well-known 1954 paper on teaching machines was the by-product of 20 years of operant conditioning research. Perhaps more important as a foretunner of the new trend was Osgood's 1953 book, in which he elaborated a "mediation theory" to account for transfer of learning and thus made room within formal behavior theory for the internal verbal and conceptual processes that early behaviorism had tried to ignore. Subsequent work by other neo-Hullians (Berlyne, Lawrence, and Kendler, for example) brought problems into the laboratory that are not far removed from those of education; at the same time, the Russians, in a similar way, stretched Pavlovian theory to accommodate symbolic processes (Simon, 1957; Brozek, 1962). Two distinctive influences remain to be mentioned: Harlow and Piaget.

Harlow's (1949) striking paper on learning sets opened Americans' eyes to the fact that, in a certain reasonable interpretation of the phrase, intelligence is learned and, furthermore, that this learning can be cultivated under laboratory, experimental conditions. If you work with small rodents, you rear a litter in innocence, run them through your mazes for a week or so at the proper age, and then destroy them. But the primates with which Harlow worked are too expensive to use once and destroy. So Harlow had to study how one learning experience modifies the organism's approach to the next, and how these effects culminate over a long span.[4] Thus, the psychologist was forced to think like an educator.

The monkey acquired a learning set—presumably an awareness that

---

[4] Harlow confronted a monkey with three objects. On every trial a raisin was under the same object, say a blue cube. Only after many trials did the monkey always reach for the cube. Once this was mastered, the monkey had to solve a new problem with the same rule but a different object. Harlow found that in the course of 50 or so problems the monkey became efficient. On the first trial with new objects he had no recourse save trial and error. But the now-sophisticated monkey almost always made the right selection on the *second* trial. He had learned to extract information from experience.

there is a right answer to be looked for. Just such a learning set was formed, after countless trials, at that famous moment when Helen Keller learned that the tapping on her hand was connected with the water flowing over it, and so achieved the great insight that each thing has a name to be learned. In such teaching as David Page's, which seeks to convey to pupils that mathematics is a system of perceived regularities and that they can create mathematics rather than merely bow to it, the intended outcome is a learning set.

The notion that we learn to observe and to use information was not new; it was clearly present in Bartlett's concept of schemata and in Piaget's numerous observations of thinking in the child. But these transatlantic views, first encountered in the 1930's by Americans, did not fit into prevailing theories and methodologies; and so they were set aside until recent translations of the mature Piaget came to hand just as cognition came back in style.

There was no single reason for the revival of interest in cognition. Harlow's neat work contributed, and so did the engineering psychologist's flirtation with information theory. Investigators of human problem-solving, such as Bruner (1957), became concerned with the organization of ideas—a concept foreign to the old associative-learning theory. Among some specialists in education there was a matching return to questions about intellect, of which the notable example was the *Taxonomy of Educational Objectives* (Bloom, 1956) prepared by leaders in measurement. This recognized that disciplined relations between ideas is a type of learning to be investigated and encouraged in school. As a model for examination construction it departed radically both from the sampling of fragmentary "facts" and the pragmatic testing of the student's ability to apply isolated principles to concrete cases.

WHAT EDUCATIONAL PSYCHOLOGISTS HAVE BELIEVED

The issues I propose to discuss arise from re-examination of matters that were regarded for 20 years or so as settled, and, therefore, it will help to review those accepted beliefs. The chief "principles of learning" of the educational psychologist, vintage 1940, can be represented by the following statements. This list is not exhaustive, nor are the statements put in the sophisticated form that might have been in the professor's mind. More nearly, these are the simplfied views the educator remembers and which, therefore, influence him.

1. *Learning occurs through active practice.* This encouraged drill, but it has other implications when additional principles are brought into the picture.

2. *Pupils should not try tasks in which they are unlikely to succeed—* "for which they lack readiness." This led curriculum makers to postpone topics believed difficult.

3. *Transfer of a learned response is to be expected only if the later*

stimulus is much like that on which the person was trained. Corollary: classroom tasks and problems should be lifelike. Here is the origin of the "social arithmetic" of which mathematicians have been so critical.

4. *A response that leads to a desired goal will be easier taught than one motivated only by external incentives and compulsions.* Corollary: develop the topics for study out of the interests of each particular class.

5. *Learning is shown to be "meaningful" if the pupil can use his knowledge in new situations, particularly concrete situations.* This is the principle of applicational transfer, emphasized in the 1930's by Pressey and Tyler as a counteraction to Thorndike's early emphasis on drill in situations closely similar to that to be encountered later.

6. *Factual learning or learning not clearly understood is quickly forgotten.*

7. *A well-understood verbal generalization is remembered, and aids in adaptation to new conditions.* This favors the teaching of abstractions, but in close connection with their concrete referents.

All these principles are sensible and supported by some research. They contradict alternative views once accepted in educational theory and practice, that is, they are not truisms. All these statements deserve continued consideration by educators. Yet each statement or its corollary is partly false, open to dispute, or seriously incomplete, in the light of current research. We shall have to reconsider the evidence on which the statements rest, the value judgments they conceal, and their theoretical underpinnings. Ultimately, we may hope to distil out their essential truth and define the conditions in which they apply, and also learn the conditions under which some other generalization holds. The ensuing sections will discuss only a selected few of the searching questions or criticisms now in the air.

I feel constrained to put in a paragraph in defense of myself and my colleagues. This paper, written with the aim of stimulating argument at a conference, is an overdramatic report on the ignorance of educational psychologists, something like that fourth-grade version of history in which everybody before Columbus believed the world to be flat. Critical thinking about these issues is nothing new. The wisest educational psychologists among my seniors—Gates and Brownell are worthy examples—remained thoroughly aware of and explicit about most of the points that I shall make, and of the sound ones that Bruner (1960) and Judd have made. The difficulty in educational psychology is that in speaking to teachers one propagandizes for some worthy change and so emphasizes certain aspects of one's theory to the neglect of others. In fighting a battle against classroom authoritarianism, for example, one does not pause to spell out the legitimate case for the teacher as authority. I should add that this paper confines itself to the doubtful matters in educational psychology: it says nothing about the observations and interpretations that are beyond suspicion. Educational psychology has much to tell teachers that is worth telling.

PROMPTING VS. DISCOVERY

Of all the topics currently in the air, the sharpest split among psychologists is on the issue of prompting vs. discovery. We have, at the one extreme, the reinforcement theorists who follow Skinner's radical behaviorism. To them, a response is a response. Get clear in your mind what you want the pupil to *do* (mark that word well), construct a set of cues, or prompts, sufficient to provoke that response from him, and when he makes it, reinforce (reward) him at once. In time, he will have discriminated this from competing responses and will make it when only a few of the original cues are present. This theory is strongly reminiscent of the early Thorndike's which led teachers to use repetitious drill. Skinner's teaching machine, indeed, has been advocated primarily as a way of administering practice efficiently. Presentation of ready-made verbal generalizations is common in teaching of this type. Homme & Glaser (1961) advocate a "ruleg" system of programming in which you (1) give a verbal rule, (2) run application items to make sure the pupil knows what the words mean and how to use them, and (3) run verbal completion items to make sure the pupil has all the words in the right places. Other forms of teacher presentation and pupil practice have been the main standby in teaching science, English, and mathematics as well as in vocational training. The teacher who demonstrates an algorism—e.g., for division of decimals—first defines for himself the ideal overt response and then teaches directly to have the student execute it. In fancy language, he "exerts stimulus control to cause the pupil to emit the response."

The opposite extreme position holds that concepts, generalizations, and procedures ought to be created or discovered by the pupil. This position has been a dogma of the Illinois (UICSM) mathematics program and finds strong endorsement among some psychologists. Handing down a neatly packaged generalization, we are warned, stops the pupil from going through the preverbal adjustments of perceptions and trial actions that produce insight (Hendrix, 1961). Some persons (not in UICSM) argue that one should never lift the insight to the overt verbal level. Hendrix and Beberman, however, *lead the pupil* to construct the verbal statement after he has captured an idea in a preverbal way. In educational psychology, discovery and insight have been glorified since the work of Katona (1940) and other Gestalt psychologists in the 1930's, but we have never had a clear definition of the theoretical issues.

I am enthusiastic about teaching by discovery as a means of showing how knowledge originates. I do not want pupils to grow up slaves to formulas; I, like my colleagues in mathematics, want them to see knowledge as man-made and themselves as possible makers of it. I would like the girl to learn cooking in part by inventing new dishes. But once she has the basic concept of creativity in cooking I believe that she can follow a cookbook on most occasions without educational loss.

The questions are not about the motivational value of learning by discovery; it is its cognitive significance that concerns us. Must one discover a relation in order to understand it? Is discovery necessary to produce conviction rather than mere acquiescence? To begin with, let me try to skim off some of the irrelevancies and slogans that are tossed into the argument from both sides (Ausubel, 1961; Bruner, 1961; Hendrix, 1961),

1. "Discovery is democratic, didactic teaching is authoritarian."
   To be sure, the authoritarian is likely to be didactic. But reasoned presentation is consistent with democracy, most obviously so in mathematics, where dependence on authority is entirely unacceptable save in matters of convention.
2. "Discovered knowledge is meaningful, knowledge presented verbally is not."
   This is true only for stupid verbal presentation. Didactic teaching can be highly meaningful. That which is taught by discovery, moreover, is at best meaningful only to the student who discovers it, not to the many who fail to make the discovery.
3. "Discovery-before-words grounds the words in perceptions; giving words first does not."
   But words can certainly be presented in firm connection with their concrete referents.
4. "The student cannot discover Newtonian theory unless he is another Newton."
   This is no more than a debater's point. No teacher is truly teaching unless he is either arranging the conditions for discovery to occur, or explaining. A student, guided by a teacher who understands Newton, can reconstruct Newtonian principles.

The psychological truth has been obscured by partisan experimentation: technically unsound studies, studies that require "discovery" of arbitrary rules, studies that mislabel meaningful didactic teaching as "discovery," and so on. The fundamental questions are more subtle than is suggested by the proposition that learning by discovery is always best, or its opposite. The psychologist must identify the conditions under which induction or hypothesis-construction by the pupil is advisable, and he must learn the principles regulating the amount and timing of exposition by the teacher.

Ervin's (1960) recent study of third- and four-graders is an example of what is needed. She led pupils to discover the principle of reflection by means of experiments with a marble shot from a tube against a barrier. One group was given nonverbal aid in observing relevant facts: for example, the path of the marble was traced on the cloth and the equal angles were colored in. The other children were led by questions to work out the verbal principle from their observations. All instruction was individual. The most important result came from a transfer test in which a flashlight was to be aimed upward at a mirror with a back-to-front tilt so as to reflect on a target. Both groups improved, but there was no appreciable difference in their average scores. What is noteworthy is the result on the last, very difficult test item, in which the mirror was tipped sharply upward. On the earlier items, children could succeed by aiming about halfway between the vertical projection of the flashlight and that of the target onto the mirror, that is, by using an inexact, impressionistic principle. On the last item, the beam set in that manner would reflect onto the ceiling; only those who adjusted the angle of incidence could be right. Success on this problem was conspicuously greater among those who reached the correct verbal rule at the end of training, and this occurred most often in the verbally trained group. Moreover, the verbal training improved ability to formulate the rule for another problem. On the other hand, there were a fair number of pupils who attained the correct verbal rule on the marble problem and yet did not set the mirror properly. (Note that both groups here had guided discovery.)

In another well-designed study of discovery, Gagné & Brown (1961) prepared programs to teach high-school boys to develop a formula for the sum of a numerical series, e.g., arithmetic series. Instead of testing transfer by having subjects take the sums of other series of the same type, they tested *ability to construct new formulas* for series of unfamiliar types, e.g., of consecutive cubes. Three programs were prepared. One (RE) gave the formula—rule—for summing each training series and taught the pupil to apply it to examples. One demanded discovery (D) of the rule and gave a few hints as needed. The third broke the task into 40 steps of guided discovery (GD), each calling for analysis of a small bit of the series. All groups improved from one training series to another. On the test, they were asked to find the rule for a new series using hints as in the D training. Mean weighted time scores were: RE, 47; D, 28; GD, 23. Guided discovery was best. (It would be interesting to see comparable results on a program directly teaching rules for finding formulas, with examples. This would be rule-and-example teaching of a generalized procedure.)

We here observe, under experimental control, the teaching of a heuristic, a type of education not previously investigated formally. Even the most "meaningful" instruction in older mathematics curricula emphasized mastering certain theorems or models and applying them in appropriate specific situations. The new curricula, however, claim to be training the pupil to create new mathematical models or theorems, and Gagné is here showing how such learning can be demonstrated and investigated. The study also makes clear that the antithesis between discovery and programmed instruction is false. While Skinner does not favor the deliberate construction of a response by the subject, not all programmers are orthodox Skinnerians. Stolurow is directing an effort within UICSM to write a program that will elicit discovery of mathematical conclusions. This research will help to define the limits of programmed teaching.

It is premature to state firm general conclusions. Results will depend on the learner's maturity, his relevant concrete experience, and the symbolic systems he has at his command. The greater these are, the less I expect him to profit from the experience of discovery. We need to relate method to material to be mastered. Knowledge that can be verified experimentally or by its internal consistency is, I suspect, more appropriate for "discovery" than knowledge that is conventional (word meanings) or factual-descriptive. I think it pedantic to require children to "discover" that magnets attract iron, but they probably cannot comprehend the properties of a magnetic field save by exploratory investigation. We need experiments that carefully control the time allocated to discovery, to know how much slower that method is—for Gagné and Brown it was faster! And we need long extended, carefully observed educational studies to augment laboratory studies. I think we will find that a rich mixture of discovery-to-presentation is best to get the learner started, but that after he is well on the road, a leaner mixture will make for faster progress and greater economy.

IS PRACTICE REALLY NECESSARY?

No principle is so central to American psychology as learning through action. We have an array of sound experiments showing that answering questions imbedded in an educational film increases learning, reciting lessons to oneself improves study efficiency, and, in skill learning, more practice makes more perfect. This has led to recommendations for increased recitation, increased drill, more frequent tests, laboratory courses in science, activity programs—the whole range of "learning by doing." To be sure, someone satirically pointed out the oddity that, according to the psychological literature, "German rats sit and think, while American rats rush about making trials and errors." And a few of us heard Stoddard's protest to educators that "we learn not by doing, but by thinking about what we are doing." Nonetheless, we have remained action-oriented, right down to the teaching machine of the moment.

The Bruner-Miller nonbehaviorist faction of Harvard psychologists drew my attention to the fact that one sometimes learns best by *not* doing. They have a little experiment (Bruner, Wallach, & Galanter, 1959) in which the subject is to predict whether the left or right light in a display will go on next. If a regular series such as *RRRLLLRRRL* . . . is presented, an S allowed to watch for 20 trials before starting to predict will do significantly better than the S who is required to guess from the outset. Shortly after hearing this, I became aware of a stream of negative results coming from trials of programmed instruction. In several experiments (Silverman & Alter, 1960; Goldbeck & Campbell, 1962; Kieslar & McNeill, 1962; Krumboltz & Weisman, 1962) one group of students filled in the blanks in the statements of a programmed learning sequence and received immediate feedback of the correct answer; a second group read the same statements with the answers already filled in and underlined. The groups did equally well on posttests. This is a body blow to Skinner's rationale; it is a bit hard to see why the studies are reported so nonchalantly. Each study was done in a different laboratory; perhaps they are not impressive until one sees them all together. Explanations are seriously incomplete. George Miller suggests that, in information reception, guesses by the learner at the beginning introduce "noise" that impedes learning. This does not account for the results with teaching programs, for these are supposed to have an internal logic that eliminates noise.

I am inclined to the view that teaching machines are already obsolete. The machine rode in on the shoulders of reinforcement theory and automation, but Skinner's demand that the learner be led to the correct response on each trial quickly made the program central and the machine peripheral. The programming format has required unprecedented attention to the details of the stimulus series in teaching and to its internal logic.[5] The programmer is learning to write so that the learner always knows what he is about—an accomplishment beyond reach of the textbook writer, because he does not test comprehension after every sentence and so does not find out when he is confusing the pupil. But once the program approaches this perfection, the machine has done its part. Now the writing is so lucid and so well structured that the reader cannot escape the meaning even when it is presented in ordinary text form with the blanks filled in. Active-trial-and-reinforcement is most needed when lessons are nonsense, and become less and less necessary as presentations become clearer. If I am right, the machine will, in time, be relegated to its proper role as a proving ground for text materials in draft form and as a laboratory instrument helping us toward a science of clarity.

MEANING A PRODUCT OF CUMULATIVE EXPERIENCE

I turn now to a study with broad implications. In one of the best-executed of all educational experiments, Brownell & Moser (1949) set out to determine once and for all whether subtraction should be taught in terms of borrowing (decomposition) or equal additions. They sought also to produce evidence that the results depended on the meaningfulness of instruction.

$$\begin{array}{c} {}^{3}4^{1}2 \\ 2\,7 \\ \hline 1\,5 \end{array} \qquad\qquad \begin{array}{c} 4^{1}2 \\ {}^{3}2\,7 \\ \hline 1\,5 \end{array}$$

$$\text{Decomposition} \qquad\qquad\qquad \text{Equal addition}$$

Four groups, several hundred pupils in each, were taught to subtract two-digit numbers:

1. *D-M*—borrowing rationalized.
2. *D-A*—borrowing as a straight-forward algorism. "Follow these steps."
3. *EA-M*—equal additions explained.
4. *EA-A*—equal additions as an algorism.

Groups *D-A* and *EA-A*, taught mechanically, were nearly equal in performance. The *D-M* group did better than the other three on direct tests and very much better on subtraction with three-digit numbers—which had not been directly taught. The *EA-M* group was intermediate in performance;

---

[5] There is an intriguing parallel between programmed presentation and Socratic teaching. In the latter, questions are asked to which the student will give one of a limited set of answers. As in a branching program, the answer identifies which question should be asked next. But responses are constructed by the learner whereas, in most programming, the responses are explained or demonstrated to him.

none of the explanations given was well understood by the pupils. The conclusion was: teach subtraction by the *D* method for which an intuitively clear explanation can be given.

Now I am told that this recommendation is wrong. I have seen no evidence to support the claim, but the argument is plausible and merits a formal test. Richard Griggs, working in the Illinois Arithmetic Project, developed a new method of explaining *EA*. The child is asked to count steps along the number line: 27 + 5 steps gets us to 32 and one giant step of 10 units get us to 42: 5 + 10 = 15. This is readily comprehended and boils down to *EA*. Whether *this EA-M* method would work better or worse than Brownell's *D-M*, no one knows. But Griggs makes the point that his *EA* approach also neatly rationalizes subtraction of a negative number where borrowing cannot be used.

Griggs is concerned with broad transfer to subsequent mathematical topics rather than short-range transfer to a specific application or a slightly altered situation. This idea has been receiving greatly increased attention but is not new. Brownell and Moser had the same thing in mind when they pointed out that in schools where arithmetic had been taught mechanically in grades 1 and 2 pupils were unable to understand *any* explanation of subtraction. They had not learned how to use a rational or intuitive explanation. Such data

. . . expose "readiness" for what is, namely, the ability to take on new skills or ideas, that and nothing more. . . . Their readiness is determined, not by their age or by their grade, but by the kind of arithmetic they have had. . . . By manipulating their arithmetical backgrounds we may shift the placement of any arithmetical topic over a range of several years and several grades.

Readiness is cumulative. And it is specific: a function of both topic taught and teaching method. Griggs is right to see merit in the fact that his *EA-M* method will lay the groundwork for much later work in negative numbers. But it will do so only if the later teaching builds upon the number-line argument. Current theory strongly implies the desirability of a sequential curriculum in which topics and their formulations are chosen to fit into a logically and intuitively consistent scheme, as distinct from an episodic curriculum in which bits of coordinate geometry, permutations, etc., are sprinkled through the years.

The profound observations and theories of Piaget are a necessary point of departure for any attempt to design teaching methods that conform to and accelerate child development. I shall not attempt to review his position: not only would a cursory statement be a disservice, but the sponsoring Committee has already devoted one whole conference to his work (Kessen & Kuhlman, 1962). What emerges for education is the insistence that teaching methods must link new materials to the schemata that the child already has firmly in his grasp (Hunt, 1961). Just what these schemata are and how they can be catalogued is a complex question. The assumption is that if a pupil fails on a lesson or problem he lacks certain required schemata—discriminations, concepts, motor controls, or ways of organizing and transforming information. Under our older views, the child should practice on a task just like the ultimate criterion task; if a task is difficult for him, extended practice on it is considered wasteful. According to many studies, a little practice at a later age accomplishes as much or more than a lot of early practice and with less emotional hazard. But now we have to ask whether there is some altered form of the task or some propaedeutic task that will teach needed schemata earlier. This is the rationale of Moore's instruction in reading: the child who can control his fingers and his speech can be taught to type, and this slowly generates familiarity with visual forms that the young child normally finds quite hard, and pointless, to discriminate.

This is not to say that simplifying or breaking up the task is always the key to success. Greco (1959) offers this evidence (poorly controlled): The child, aged five is to learn that left-to-right order is reversed in a 180° rotation and conserved in a 360° rotation. The task can be simplified by presenting first many 180° trials and then many 360° trials. It is more complicated if the two types are mixed. Children learn under either training, but it is the second group that retains the learning and can cope with larger numbers of rotations. The more complex training forces the child to discriminate; in Genevan language, "to achieve a structure for the situation." The simpler situation produces only separate stimulus-response connections that lack connections to each other.

How early can we teach a concept? Consider the conservation of number, the idea that number remains the same when position or grouping changes. Piaget says that this rests on the child's attaining the idea of reversibility of the displacement, which, in turn, rests *inter alia* on his motor control and on hundreds of experiences with back-and-forth hand movements; this suggests a grand program of enriched experience in which we try to push back each stage of learning, but we know that acceleration must have some limit. Where? One view is that several radical changes of psychological state occur during development and the timing of these is biologically controlled. The most significant of these hypothesized changes after infancy are (*a*) the point near age 5 where the child allegedly begins to use words to direct his own actions, so that verbal mediation for the first time makes his learning different from animal learning; (*b*) the period around age 8 in which the child masters concrete operational thought, transforming information in imagination in a logically controlled way; and (*c*) the early adolescent period in which formal operational thought with symbolic systems becomes efficient. The first of these hypotheses emerges from the work of Kendler (Kendler & Kendler, 1962) and Luria (Simon, 1957, pp. 115–129), the second and third from Piaget and Inhelder. Of the existence of such transitions there is no doubt, although they may be gradual rather than sharp. The question is, can they be brought about earlier?

Piaget's writings often have given the impression that he regards the timing of these developments as fixed. This occasioned great criticism from

Americans who insisted that Piaget never observed a random sample of the species; the Genevans have recently been hedging their statements with references to the culture of their subjects. More than that, the laboratory has initiated a program of attempts to produce the various conceptual attainments at ages earlier than usual. These studies have had some faint success, but the results seem generally to imply that early training has little value. The best data, because of experimental ingenuity and adequate sample size, are those from Smedslund's (1961) studies of the conservation of weight and substance.

I shall report only one of his highly important observations. He taught children who had not learned that weight is invariant under deformation correctly to predict what would happen in tests such as the following: "two balls of clay are weighed and prove equal; then I roll one out into a snake; now which will be heavier, the ball or the snake?" (This is not a precise description; Smedslund's technique was better.) Success on these tests seemed to show that these children attained the conservation concept a year earlier than usual. But Smedslund made a further test. On some trials he covertly pinched off a bit of clay while making the snake. After the child predicted that the deformed ball weighed the same as the untouched ball, the ball and snake were put on the balance and the snake side went up. These trained children accepted the result. "Oh, it's lighter." "I was wrong." Control children who had attained the conservation principle in the normal way at the normal age did not. They rejected the evidence of the scale, "Did something drop on the floor?" they asked solicitously. These children trusted their internal model of the behavior of weight more than they trusted external appearances. The intensive training, however, failed to produce true conviction about conservation. There is nothing conclusive about these findings. Inhelder is presently conducting trials of various methods for training operational thought, and Smedslund also is searching for methods that will succeed more than superficially.

MASTERY OF A DISCIPLINE

To separate one issue from another in this discussion is like trying to count angleworms in a tin can. Readiness, preverbal understanding, meaningful presentation, transfer—all are part of the same complex. To complete this discussion I must back off and view that complex from one more angle, the purposes of the new mathematical education.

The greatest novelty in the new curricula is not the content, not the instructional methods, not the grade placement of topics. The greatest novelty is the objectives from which all else stems. I disagree violently with Martin Mayer's (1961) assertion that "in the context of the classroom nobody except an incompetent, doctrinaire teacher is ever going to worry much about the 'aims of education.'" I chide David Page for lending Mayer support by providing a know-nothing quote to the effect that "What are your objectives?" is a question on a par with "Explain the universe." Objectives had better be identifiable and explainable if one is to avoid the absurd claim that his methods achieve all ends at once, each in greater measure than any competing proposal. The new curricula, starting from the sound premise that different classroom activities reach different ends, deliberately sacrifice some ends for the sake of others.

Never before was it the aim of common-school instruction to teach mathematics. The school has usually taught arithmetic, seen as a skill of everyday commerce. The only arguments about method in arithmetic were pragmatic ones: does drill, or explanation of the number system, better guarantee ability to keep accounts or to triple a recipe? Secondary mathematics lost all sense of direction when the rug of formal discipline was pulled from under it. Part of it survived by clinging to its pragmatic justification as a prerequisite to engineering courses. The geometry course struggled unconvincingly to pose as a model for everyday "straight thinking."

If I comprehend correctly, the new curricula are trying to teach mathematics as mathematics; to the question "why?" their answer is just a shade more pragmatic than "because it's there." I have no doubt that persons in scientific and social-science pursuits need as much mathematical competence as they can get. I have serious doubts as to how far the average citizen should go in mathematics. I think it very likely that in throwing out practical topics the new programs have gone to an extreme that will produce its own form of quantitative illiteracy and provoke a counterrrevolution. But as psychologist, my role is less to say what should be done than to consider what can be done.

What does it mean to master mathematics "as a discipline?" It has taken close listening at times to be sure that the word is not a return to faculty psychology, i.e., to claims that intellectual effort is good for the mind. But the more sophisticated and constructive reformers emphasize that there are many disciplines, each of them a way of coming to grips with certain types of problems. There is obvious sense in the contention that a mathematician is more competent to solve a new mathematical problem than a bright and educated nonmathematician, and not just because the mathematician knows more theorems. He has an ability to construct models, sense connections within the model and test the internal consistency among premises and conclusions. He has a wealth of apparatus at his command—notational systems, conceptual distinctions, operations. These are used not as the computer uses a formula but as an architect uses all that has been learned from past buildings. To solve a new problem he draws from his store this and that device that might work, juggles them in the air, begins to see a coherence, discards some misfit parts and designs some replacements, and finds more or less suddenly the shape of his mathematical system. This is constructive mathematics; demonstration plays a decidedly secondary role to invention.

The greatest challenge to the psychologist from the new curricula lies here. When it is proposed to teach coordinate geometry in grade 2, the important question is whether this is a better base for some subsequent instruction than an alternative topic. When it is proposed to develop concepts of area by having children count squares within figures, we can assimilate the proposal easily. But when the objective of teaching mathematical method takes precedence over teaching mathematical results, we are led into an area where we have neither experience nor theory.

When faculty psychology was advancing the claim that mathematics equipped one as a lawyer, it was being overly general. When associationist psychology considered transfer as limited to "similar" situations, it withdrew to too conservative a position. Even the theory of transfer through generalizations is timid because it speaks of a very simple mental structure involving just one mediating sentence. The sentence is said to be "meaningful" if the pupil can coordinate it with reality. The formula for the area of a parallelogram, we have said as pragmatists, is meaningful when the pupil can determine areas of parallelograms in various positions and contexts. But the new program identifies "meaning" with the coordinations between this statement and other statements. The formula gains added meaning when the pupil sees how it is consistent with the area formulas for triangles and rectangles, and how it depends on axioms such as that shape is invariant under rotation. These propositional networks form a structure of related beliefs or insights. It is highly plausible that such structures exist in the mind, but we have not learned to appraise them and, therefore, have little insight into the process by which they develop.

One reason we know little about these matters is that we have failed to pursue our measurement of transfer far enough. As I see it, much of the aim of the new mathematics course is to develop aptitude for new mathematical learning. If so, the pertinent test is how well the student can master a new mathematical topic; for any real test we should probably use a topic that requires some weeks of study. This would be evidence of ability to go on learning on his own.

Such a measure of transfer has always been envisioned in the psychologists' definition. All the textbooks tell you that the transfer value of training A is to be tested by a design like this (where the horizontal axis represents practice time needed to reach a proficiency criterion:

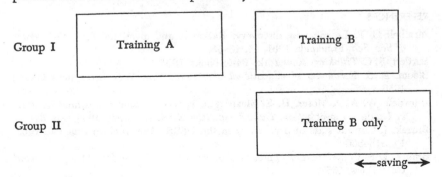

The measure of transfer is the saving in learning time. While this design is used in laboratory research, it has almost never been used in educational studies. As several of the experiments I have cited illustrate, the usual design is

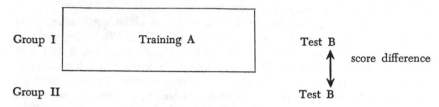

This tells us only whether we have equipped the student to make a quick adaptation to a new situation, not whether we have equipped him to work his way through a mass of material and assimilate it. Studies by the savings design will require much more effort than the usual ones. Perhaps we will find that transfer to a test and transfer to savings in new learning are highly correlated; perhaps training that achieves one achieves the other. Do you suppose, for example, that Gagné's training on how to develop a sum-of-series formula would transfer into improved ability to learn some entirely new process, such as differentiation? I doubt it. And yet that ability to come to grips with the new mathematics is certainly the product of learning, hence a function of manipulable conditions of instruction. We might well devote effort to study how one learns to learn mathematics.

The essential aim of the new curricula is to teach each subject in its true colors, as the specialist knows it: Not as a history of ancient thought, not as a collection of formulas and prescriptions, not as a display of products used by the consumer, but rather as an adventure in organizing ever-new experience. The psychologist cannot but admire the boldness of the conception and the evident art of some of the work. How to collect evidence on the effects of the programs, how to adjust his theories to conform to that evidence, and how to glean from that evidence still better educational methods: these are a challenge to *his* boldness and *his* art.

REFERENCES

Ausubel, D. P. Learning by discovery: Rationale and mystique. *Bull. Nat. Assoc. of Sec. Sch. Principals,* 1961, 45, 18–58.

Bartlett, F. C. *Thinking.* New York: Basic Books, 1958.

Bloom, B. S. *Taxonomy of educational objectives.* New York: Longmans Green, 1956.

Brownell, W. A., & Moser, H. E. Meaningful versus mechanical learning: a study in Grade III subtraction. *Duke Univ. Res. Stud. in Educ.,* 1949, No. 8.

Brozek, J. Current state of psychology in the USSR. *Ann. Rev. of Psychol.,* 1962, 13, 515–566.

Bruner, J. S. *Contemporary approaches to cognition.* Cambridge, Mass.: Harvard Univ. Press, 1957.

Bruner, J. S. *The process of education.* Cambridge, Mass.: Harvard Univ. Press, 1960.

Bruner, J. S. The act of discovery. *Harvard Educ. Rev.*, 1961, 31, 21–32.

Bruner, J. S., Wallach, M. A., & Galanter, E. H. The identification of recurrent regularity. *Amer. J. Psychol.*, 1959, 72, 200–220.

Cronbach, L. J. *Educational psychology.* New York: Harcourt, Brace & Co., 1954; rev. ed.; Harcourt, Brace & World, 1963.

Ervin, S. M. Transfer effects of learning a verbal generalization. *Child Developm.*, 1960, 31, 537–554.

Gagné, R. M., & Brown, L. T. Some factors in the programing of conceptual learning. *J. exp. Psychol.*, 1961, 62, 313–321.

Geldard, F. A. The present status of the laws of learning. *Univ. of Virginia Rec. Extension Ser.*, 1937, 22 (No. 2), 41–45.

Goldbeck, A., & Campbell, V. N. The effects of response mode and response difficulty on programed instruction. *J. educ. Psychol.*, 1962, 53, 110–118.

Greco, P. L'apprentissage dans une situation à structure operatoire concrète. *Études épist. génét.*, 1959, 7, 68–182.

Harlow, H. F. The formation of learning sets. *Psychol. Rev.*, 1949, 56, 51–65.

Hendrix, G. Learning by discovery. *Math. Teacher*, 1901, 54, 200–299.

Homme, L. E., & Glaser, R. Problems in programing verbal sequences. In A. Lumsdaine & R. Glaser (Eds.), *Teaching machines and programmed learning.* Washington, D. C.: Nat. Educ. Assoc., 1961. Pp. 486–496.

Hunt, J. McV. *Intelligence and experience.* New York: Ronald Press, 1961, pp. 266 ff.

Judd, C. H. *Education as cultivation of the higher mental processes.* New York: Macmillan Co., 1936.

Katona, C. *Organizing and memorizing.* New York: Columbia Univ. Press, 1940.

Kendler, H. H., & Kendler, S. Vertical and horizontal processes in problem solving. *Psychol. Rev.*, 1962, 69, 1–16.

Kessen, W., & Kuhlman, C. Thought in the young child. *Monogr. Soc. Res. Child Developm.*, 1962, 27, No. 2.

Kieslar, E. R., & McNeil, J. D. A comparison of two response modes in an auto-instructional program with children in the primary grades. *J. educ. Psychol.*, 1962, 53, 127–131.

Krumboltz, J. D., & Weisman, R. G. The effect of overt versus covert responding to programed instruction on immediate and delayed retention. *J. educ. Psychol.*, 1962, 53, 89–92.

Mayer, M. *The Schools.* New York: Harper & Bros., 1961.

Miller, N. E. *Graphic communication and the crisis in education.* Washington, D. C.: Nat. Educ. Assoc., 1957.

Miller, N. E., & Dollard, J. *Social learning and imitation.* New Haven, Conn.: Yale Univ. Press, 1941.

Osgood, C. E. *Method and theory in experimental psychology.* London: Oxford Univ. Press, 1953.

Silverman, R. E., & Alter, M. Note on the response in teaching machine programs. *Psychol. Rep.*, 1960, 7, 496.

Simon, B. (Ed.) *Psychology in the Soviet Union.* Stanford, Calif.: Stanford Univ. Press, 1957.

Skinner, B. F. The science of learning and the art of teaching. *Harvard Educ. Rev.*, 1954, **25**, 86–97.

Smedslund, J. The acquisition of conservation of substance and weight in children. I-VI. *Scand. J. Psychol.*, 1961, **2**, 11–20, 71–87, 153–160, 203–210.

Spence, K. W. The relation of learning theory to the technology of education. *Harvard Educ. Rec.*, 1959, **29**, 84–95.

7

REVIEW OF CONFERENCE

Andrew M. Gleason

Harvard University

It is appropriate that I begin with a sketch of my own background. I am a pure mathematician who has had some contact with certain areas of applied mathematics but none with either learning theory or psychology. I have been involved with the School Mathematics Study Group, but only at the policy-making level, not at the operational level. The only reason I am here is that several times a week I stand before a group of people who think that I am going to tell them something about mathematics. Of course, these people are all a great deal more sophisticated than the students we have been discussing since they range from college freshmen to advanced graduate students.

While I am supposed to summarize, I intend to load my summary with my own ideas. Indeed, I have been saving some comments which might better have been said earlier.

Yesterday, Paul Mussen called our attention to the differences in cognitive style between one child and the next. One of the sharpest impressions I shall take away from this conference is of the difference of cognitive style between those trained in mathematics and those trained in the social sciences. Words spoken by mathematicians usually clicked immediately with me, while it took a great deal of effort to follow the thought of the social scientists. I presume they found the situation reversed. This fact is certain to impose a major bias on everything I am going to say, but there is no help for it.

It is *de rigueur* that the review of an interdisciplinary conference should note that we have exhibited an appalling ignorance of our subject. We have sketched out areas where more work ought to be done by psychologists and mathematicians, separately and together, and have made it clear that further contact between these groups is necessary. This much is banal, but it remains important. The progress of science requires that one continually strive to maintain contacts between the various disciplines—a task becoming ever more difficult as the sciences themselves fractionate.

I discern three points of contact between mathematicians and those studying the psychology of learning: first, the design and analysis of mathematical models of learning; second, the design and analysis of experiments to test these models; finally, since many mathematicians are actually employed as teachers and have acquired, thereby, a direct insight into the teaching of mathematics, they can offer purely pedagogical advice. The second of these areas, which concerns primarily statistics and experimental design, lies wholly outside of the domain of this conference.

EXPERIMENTS ON MATHEMATICAL LEARNING

The conference heard little concerning learning theory, as such, but we did hear of some experiments on learning that aim in the general direction of a learning theory.

Suppes' experiments concern a form of learning through guessing. No effort was made to instruct the subjects in what was wanted, rather, they were left to deduce this from the simple information that their answers were right or wrong. Without in any sense intending to minimize the ultimate relevance of these experiments, it is clear that they are not likely to give us much direct assistance in teaching mathematics in the near future. Such experiments are the necessary prelude to even the most rudimentary form of a theory of how humans actually learn, but I think this merely underscores the fact that we are very far from a theory that can help us with our teaching problems.

Experiments with learning by guessing have been performed using computers as subjects. Now these subjects are infinitely less sophisticated than any child that can talk, and therefore the experiments will not stand too close a comparison; nevertheless, there is enough similarity so that it is worth summarizing one such experiment with a computer. I refer to the work of Friedberg (Friedberg, 1958, Friedberg, Dunham, & North, 1959).

A small computer was designed in such a way that any way of filling its memory would constitute a runnable program. This small computer was then given a task to perform, such as transferring a single binary digit from one box of its memory to another. Whenever it did the task correctly, the program of the computer was reinforced in the sense that the orders it was using became more likely to be used again. Whenever it failed, the orders became more likely to be discarded. All of this was programmed to be run at high speed within a large computer and many millions of trials were made. (No doubt more trials were made in this one sequence of experiments than in the whole history of learning experiments with animate subjects.)

It was found that for the simplest tasks, such as transferring one digit, possibly with complementation, or the formation of a simple combination of two digits to form a single digit, the machine would find a correct program after a number of trials of the order of 10 or 100 thousand. It never succeeded, however, in finding a correct program to produce an answer involving two binary digits. The density of such correct programs in the set of all possible programs was simply too low for the machine to find one even after several million trials. This was true notwithstanding the fact that the machine was allowed to learn to find the separate parts of the answer first. In searching for a program to do the second part of the problem, the machine invariably lost its correct solution to the first part before achieving success. Even at this microscopic level, the technique of learning by guessing failed because there was not adequate reinforcement to protect what had already been learned.

These experiments indicate to me that if the brain learns by a similar process of random trials, then the individual steps must be very small indeed. In spite of its marvellous complexity, its long electrical response time prevents the brain from making trials on the vast scale of the computer. Consequently, it must have a reinforcement mechanism that is extremely protective of partially correct solutions.

The true function of the teacher is to assist this reinforcement process and the objective of learning theory experiments should be to discover how this process works.

The experiments of Gagné are of a different sort. To me, their most important aspect is that they show that our exterior analytic description of a certain type of problem is closely related to the actual process by which it is solved. In one sense, this is not a very grand conclusion, but consider where we would stand if the experimental evidence were to the contrary. An experiment designed to confirm that a rational analysis is correct is always critical, but spectacular only when the result contradicts reason.

The conference heard three reports of pedagogical experiments, and most of us are aware of other work being done in this field. The main thing that emerges from all this experimentation is that children are much more capable in mathematics than any existing curriculum supposes. I think that this fact has not only been demonstrated, it has been overdemonstrated. Furthermore, it appears to be true in other subjects as well. This brings up new fundamental problems for education. With many subjects heretofore not represented in the primary-school curriculum demanding a place, and with the many old subjects embarking on more ambitious ventures, there is certain to be a conflict over the allocation of instructional time. While we know that children can perform at a higher level in mathematics and other subjects, it by no means follows that they can do so in all of their subjects at once; this, too, will cause a conflict over the design of the curriculum.

Aside from the problems of allocating curricular time and effort between disciplines, there is the problem of what to do within each discipline. Now that we know that children can learn so many diverse parts of mathematics we have a much larger and, therefore, more difficult choice to make and it becomes important that we have a clear-cut idea of what we are trying to accomplish in mathematics education.

After much discussion of this topic at the School Mathematics Study Group there has emerged a philosophy on which the members are essentially unanimous. We should teach everyone to think mathematically to the limit of his taste and ability. This does not mean that we want to make everyone a pure mathematician. We do want everyone to be prepared, both psycho-

logically and theoretically, to use mathematics to the extent that his environment demands. This means, in particular, that he should recognize those
situations in which mathematical thought is demanded. This last point
explains the difference in attitude between the classical mathematical curriculum and the newer curricula. Formerly, we were content to teach mathematical techniques adequate to solve certain definite kinds of problems, some
of which were likely to arise in life and some not. Today we try to teach even
the youngest students the mathematical point of view in the hope that when
he is presented with a problem requiring mathematical analysis he will
recognize this fact, even though it is not marked "Use Mathematics Here."

This change in attitude is accompanied by a switch from technique to
theory. The change is similar to one that is going on today in our engineering
schools. Once, engineering education was primarily involved with a study of
engineering techniques; today, technology moves so fast that a purely technical education becomes obsolete in a few years. This causes a curious situation in the employment market which has obvious repercussions in the
social and economic spheres: this year's graduate may be a more valuable
employee than the engineer with five years' experience. The engineering
schools are meeting this by devoting far less time to technology and far more
to pure theory. Indicative of this trend in mathematics, the conference heard
an eloquent description from Stone of the importance of the function concept in the foundation of mathematical thought and of how it can be introduced into the earliest stages of mathematical training.

This new philosophy of mathematical training leads mathematical peda-
gogy away from one of the most useful psychological contributions to education. The school of behaviorist psychologists says to us, "Define the behavior
you wish to bring about, and we will help you condition your pupils to perform in this way." This is easy if your objective is the classical one of training
students to do set arithmetic problems. It is quite different if one wishes to
train students to "think mathematically," for we admit that the goal is ill
defined and we can offer no objective criteria for recognizing its attainment.
This divergence is no reflection on either the mathematician or the psychologist. It imposes on the mathematician the task of seeking a more operational
definition of his goal, or possibly his subgoals, and it once again reminds the
psychologist that pure operationalism will never solve all his problems.

TEACHING MATHEMATICS

As we approached the question of teaching, four different aspects were
discussed: the students, the teacher, the method, and the subject.

Relatively little was said about the students. Mussen's remark about
differences in cognitive style is important and seems to have been little
explored. There are differences that affect over-all attitude towards mathematics—some like it, others don't. There are also differences within the subject. Some professional mathematicians are highly geometric in their thinking, others are more formalistically inclined. It would not be surprising if

grade-school children were the same. I think a great deal of work could profitably be expended on identifying and measuring cognitive styles. Work is being done, of course, in the related area of testing attitudes toward mathematics.

Somewhat more was said about teachers. One valuable observation was made to the effect that a certain amount of dramatic training might improve many teachers' styles. I would like to stress the importance from the teacher's point of view of a point that was made under method. We talk a great deal about teaching mathematics in a way that is interesting to the students. It is equally important to make it interesting to the teachers. A large proportion, perhaps 90 per cent, of the adult population has an actively hostile attitude toward mathematics; and the proportion is probably not much different among grade-school teachers. If a teacher is insecure and hostile toward a subject, then no matter how sincerely he tries to do his job, some of his attitude will rub off on his students. If mathematics were taught in a way interesting to the teacher, then perhaps some of this insecurity and hostility might be dispersed with a consequent real gain in the efficiency of teaching.

The big thing these days in pedagogical method is called "discovery." It was made perfectly clear that the method is misnamed. In the discovery method the teacher tries to bring about a situation in which one of the real discoveries of mathematics becomes a step within the mental ability of a substantial number of his pupils and then he hopes that one of them will actually makes this discovery. The discovery is really an illusion, but the illusion serves to imprint the whole situation on the pupils by getting them interested and excited. The practitioners of this method have become real artists in the creation of these illusions and the effects have been excellent. It remains to be seen whether less gifted teachers will be successful with the technique. As Page pointed out, the most essential condition that must be brought about is a climate of real interest among the pupils in finding the answers to the problem.

The student of history, biology, or physics is highly dependent on exterior facts, dates, names, or the outcomes of experiments. If he forgets these facts then no amount of cerebration can recover them. Mathematics, on the other hand, has an internal coherence that makes it quite possible to recover a missing fact by analysis. One of the main aims of the discovery method of teaching is to convince the student that he has the power to recover mathematics within himself. There are other schemes, no doubt, that could claim the same, but the rote and drill methods that are so widespread create precisely the opposite impression, for surely the implication of requiring a verbatim memorization of a geometric theorem or a precise form in which to solve a certain type of algebra problem is that the student is powerless if he fails to conform to the letter of the rules given to him. I noted with some pleasure that a minor result of Gagné's experiments was that amount of drill time seemed unrelated to handling his concepts.

Almost nothing was said during the conference concerning teaching machines, yet tucked away in Cronbach's paper is a significant comment that appeals to me very strongly, partly because it tends to reinforce my prejudice against teaching machines and partly because of its inherent plausibility. Cronbach suggests that if the same effort were spent making an ordinary textbook understandable on a sentence-by-sentence basis as is spent in making a teaching-machine program understandable item by item, then the textbook would acquire most of the virtues ascribed to the teaching machine while retaining its admitted advantages.

Finally, there is the question of subject. As I noted above, this is a more important question today than it has ever been before because we now know that there are many parts of mathematics that can be taught to school children whereas in the past only a few parts were even considered. One thing must be borne in mind by the curriculum planner: each course after the grade-school level must be considered from the viewpoint of those for whom it will be terminal. It makes relatively little difference in what order the subjects are taken up for those who will take all of them, but it makes a considerable difference for those who stop part way.

Whenever the choice of subjects for schools is brought up the old controversy of the abstract vs. the concrete appears. The argument that children are unable to handle abstractions is refuted by experimental evidence, but the argument that abstractions are less effective in attracting the interest of students retains a considerable plausibility. Partisans of the more abstract topics point out that an important side effect of the study of mathematics is the liberation of the human mind from the concrete world. When we consider the differences in cognitive style from one student to the next and from one teacher to the next, it seems likely that this controversy will never be resolved.

In conclusion, let me point out that, although the conference was clearly intended to focus on the theoretical aspects of mathematical learning, the participants were far more eager to discuss the more concrete issues. Undoubtedly the liveliest discussion was that concerning how one should teach that $(-1)(-1) = +1$, while not a single voice was raised to address the question of what constitutes learning.

REFERENCES

Friedberg, R. M. A learning machine. I. *IBM J. Res. Developm.*, 1958, 2, 2–13.
Friedberg, R. M., Dunham, B., & North, J. H. A learning machine. II. *IBM J. Res. Developm.*, 1959, 3, 282–287.

DISCUSSION AND DEVELOPMENT OF THE MATHEMATICS OF THE FUNCTION CONCEPT

Marshall H. Stone

University of Chicago

BACKGROUND TO THEORY

The typical proposition with which the whole theory of the function concept is concerned can be expressed in three equivalent forms:

> The [particular] relation R holds between [the objects] α and a;

> [The object] α is in the [particular] relation R to [the object] a;

> [The objects] α and a are in the [particular] relation R.

The sparer symbolism used in mathematics expresses these statements in the corresponding forms:

$$R\alpha a, \qquad \alpha R a, \qquad \alpha a R.$$

The last is rarely used, but the other two are common. For example, it is the second form that is familiar in the case of relations of equality, equivalence, and order, denoted by such standard symbols as $=$, $\equiv$ or $\sim$, and $<$, respectively. Of course, it is necessary to consider not only binary relations—that is, relations between two objects of the same or different kinds—but also n-ary relations among n objects of various kinds. We can always, however, treat such a relation as a binary relation between an ordered set of $n - 1$ elements and another object, where $n > 2$.

The basic definition of a function can now be stated.

DEFINITION: *A (binary) relation* R *is said to be a functional relation or a function if and only if it is true that*
$\alpha R a$, $\beta R b$, *and* $\alpha = \beta$ *imply* $a = b$ *for all* α, β, a, b.

557

When F is a function, there are several new ways of symbolizing the statements $F\alpha a$, αFa, αaF which have been discussed above. The commonest are the following: $a = F(\alpha)$, $a = F\alpha$, and $F:\alpha \rightarrow a$. However, as a certain number of algebraists have observed, it is often quite convenient to write $\alpha F = a$ or $(\alpha)F = a$ in place of the more familiar forms, *and this is what we shall do here.*

In analysis, synonyms for the term "function" are "functional," "operator," and "operation"; in algebra, "operator" and "operation"; and in geometry, "transformation," "mapping," and "application." Some mathematicians would like to maintain distinctions among these terms, for example, by reserving the term "function" to describe numerical relations. It is certain, however, that a single all-embracing term is needed and, if it is not to be the term "function" as some would urge, then the currently leading candidate is the term "application."

The rather long list of descriptive technical terms that must be presented and explained appears in the Dubrovnik Report already cited: identity; argument, independent variable, value, dependent variable; domain, range, support; injection, biunivocal or one-to-one function, bijection, superjection (the shorter form "surjection," correct in French, is very generally used), restriction, extension; graph; evaluation. The graph of a relation R—and in particular of a function—is the class defined as

$$\{(\alpha, a); \text{ it is true that } \alpha Ra\}.$$

Evaluation is the operation of determining the value of a function for a particular instance of its argument and can be described symbolically as $(\alpha, F) \rightarrow \alpha F = a$. The interpretation of this symbolic statement in the vernacular might read, "The object α is converted by the entity (funciton) F into the object $a = \alpha F$.

There are two particularly important definitions needed in developing a theory of functions. One introduces the *composite* of two given functions F and G as the unique function $F \cdot G$ such that $\alpha(F \cdot G) = (\alpha F)G$ for every α or, equivalently, such that $F \cdot G: \alpha \rightarrow (\alpha F)G$. The domain of $F \cdot G$ may, of course, be empty. The other introduces an equivalence relation $\sim$ such that

$$\alpha \sim \beta \text{ if and only if } \alpha F = \beta F.$$

We may note that the formation of the composite is itself an operation or function: $(F, G) \rightarrow F \cdot G$. Two functions F and G are said to be *inverses* of one another if $F \cdot G$ and $G \cdot F$ have respectively the same domain as F and G and act on them as identities, if, in other words, it is true that $\alpha(F \cdot G) = \alpha$ and $a(G \cdot F) = a$ for all α in the domain of F and all a in the domain of G, respectively. When F and G are inverses of one another, it is easily seen that the range of F is the domain of G and vice versa, and that each function is a bijection. As to the equivalence relation $\sim$, the theory of classes shows that it determines a partition of the domain of the given function into mutually disjoint parts consisting of mutually equivalent elements. If the equivalence part containing α is denoted as $[\alpha]$, then the function F induces a new function, $[\alpha] \rightarrow \alpha F = a$, which is easily seen to be a bijection between the class of the equivalence parts and the range of F. The concepts discussed in this paragraph can be generalized to arbitrary binary relations, as is well known; but the generalized concepts are not widely employed in mathematics today—perhaps less widely than they should be.

THE FUNCTION CONCEPT IN ALGEBRA

As stated earlier, in terms of the function concept algebra can be characterized as the study of systems of functions or operations that convert ordered sets of objects, all of the same kind, into an object of that kind. In other words, algebra is the study of operations O such that $O: (\alpha_1, \cdots, \alpha_n) \to \alpha = (\alpha_1, \cdots, \alpha_n)O$. A class of objects and a family of such operations upon them is called an *algebraic system* or an *algebra*. In recent times the comparative study of algebras has assumed great importance. The instrument of comparison is the *homomorphism*— a function H that carries the elements and the operations of one algebra into those of the other, respectively, in such a way that

$$(\alpha_1 H, \cdots, \alpha_n H)\,(OH) = ((\alpha_1, \cdots, \alpha_n)O)H$$

for all elements $\alpha_1, \cdots, \alpha_n$ of the first algebra. Usually, it is assumed that the restriction of H to the operator family is a bijection that remains fixed throughout the particular discussion, and only the restriction of H to the basic class of the first algebra is treated as variable. It may be observed, as a matter of fact, that, if H is extended to the ordered n-tuples by the definition

$$(\alpha_1, \cdots, \alpha_n) \to (\alpha_1 H, \cdots, \alpha_n H) = (\alpha_1, \cdots, \alpha_n)H,$$

the condition that H be a homomorphism is simply that $H \cdot OH = O \cdot H$ (in the domain of O!) for every operation O of the first algebra.

THE FUNCTION CONCEPT IN GEOMETRY

In discussing the occurrence of functions as transformations in geometry, we must start from intuitive understandings of physical observations and progress to abstract symbolic representation so that we can then deal with them mathematically.

At the level of physical or intuitive geometry we therefore propose to single out the Euclidean motions called translations—those motions that preserve directions or, what is the same thing, transform parallel lines into parallel lines. On the basis of simple observations we may infer a number of general principles, such as the following:

1. A translation moves distinct points into distinct points (as does any Euclidean motion)
2. If two translations produce the same effect on a single point then they do so on every point—that is, they coincide
3. There is a translation that moves an assigned point into any other assigned point
4. The composite of two translations is a translation
5. The composition of two translations is commutative—that is, is independent of the order in which they are combined.

The last principle involves somewhat more complex observations than the others and, fortunately, does not play a very big part in most of what we shall have to say. Our aim is to cast these principles into mathematical form with the use of an appropriate symbolism and to use the resulting formal statements as the axioms from which a reasonably interesting mathematical theory can be deduced. It turns out that this is relatively easy to do.

In the formal discussion, the space and its points are respectively a set Σ and its elements π, ρ, σ, $\cdots$. The family of translations is a set $\mathfrak{F}$ of functions S, T, U, V, $\cdots$, with Σ as domain and parts of Σ as their respective ranges. The five informal principles listed above can then be stated formally as axioms:

> *Axiom 1*   (Right cancellation) If $\pi S = \rho S$ then $\pi = \rho$;
> *Axiom 2*   (Left cancellation) If $\pi S = \pi T$ then $S = T$;
> *Axiom 3*   (Transitivity) If π and ρ are given points, then there exists in $\mathfrak{F}$ a function or transformation X such that $\pi X = \rho$;
> *Axiom 4*   (Closure) If S and T are in $\mathfrak{F}$, so is their composite $S \cdot T$.
> *Axiom 5*   (Commutativity) $S \cdot T. = T \cdot S$.

We shall immediately show that under composition $\mathfrak{F}$ is a group—that is to say, that the operation of composition has certain specific properties, enumerated in Propositions 1–3 that follow:

PROPOSITION 1.   *Composition is associative.*

Proof.—This result is perfectly general, without restricting the functions concerned to be in $\mathfrak{F}$. In fact, if F, G, and H are any three functions we have

$$\alpha((F \cdot G) \cdot H) = (\alpha(F \cdot G))\, H = ((\alpha F)G)\, H$$
$$= (\alpha F)\, (G \cdot H)) = \alpha(F \cdot (G \cdot H))$$

for every α in the domain of F; and hence $(F \cdot G)\, H = F \cdot (G \cdot H)$.

PROPOSITION 2.   *If S and T are in $\mathfrak{F}$ there is a unique X in $\mathfrak{F}$ such that $S \cdot X = T$.*

Proof.—Let π be arbitrary and let X be a function in $\mathfrak{F}$ such that $(\pi S)X = \pi T$ in accordance with Axiom 3. By the definition of $S \cdot X$ we see that $\pi(S \cdot X) = \pi T$. Cancellation of π yields $S \cdot X = T$. Now if $S \cdot X = S \cdot Y$ we have $(\pi S)X = \pi(S \cdot X) = \pi(S \cdot Y) = (\pi S)Y$ and cancellation of πS yields $X = Y$.

PROPOSITION 3.   *If S and T are in $\mathfrak{F}$, there is a unique X in $\mathfrak{F}$ such that $X \cdot S = T$.*

Proof.—We determine Y and Z as the unique functions in $\mathfrak{F}$ such that $S \cdot Y = S$ and $S \cdot Z = Y$ in accordance with Proposition 2. Since $(\pi S)(Y \cdot S) = \pi(S \cdot (Y \cdot S)) = \pi((S \cdot Y) \cdot S) = \pi(S \cdot S) = (\pi S) \cdot S$, cancellation of πS yields $Y \cdot S = S$. It then follows from the equations $(\pi Y)S = \pi(Y \cdot S) = \pi S$ and cancellation of S that $\pi Y = \pi$ for every π in Σ. In other words, Y is the identity. Next we observe that $(\pi S)(Z \cdot S) = \pi(S \cdot (Z \cdot S)) = \pi((S \cdot Z) \cdot S) = \pi(Y \cdot S) = \pi S = \pi(S \cdot Y) = (\pi S)Y$, so that cancellation of πS yields $Z \cdot S = Y$. Consequently Z and S are inverses of one another. If $X \cdot S = T$ then $X = X \cdot Y = X \cdot (S \cdot Z) = (X \cdot S) \cdot Z = T \cdot Z$. Hence X is uniquely determined, and we have merely to show that $T \cdot Z$ provides the desired member of $\mathfrak{F}$. But we immediately have $(T \cdot Z) \cdot S = T \cdot (Z \cdot S) = T \cdot Y = T$.

As we have observed above, these three propositions yield the following theorem:

THEOREM 1. *Under composition $\mathfrak{F}$ is a group.*

It is easy to establish a counterpart of Axiom 3 as

PROPOSITION 4. *If ρ and S are given in Σ and in $\mathfrak{F}$, respectively, there is a unique point ξ in Σ such that $\xi S = \rho$.*

Proof.—We introduce Y and Z as in the proof of Proposition 3. If $\xi S = \rho$ we then have $\xi = \xi Y = \xi(S \cdot Z) = (\xi S)Z = \rho Z$. Thus ξ is uniquely determined. That ρZ furnishes such a point ξ is evident: $(\rho Z)S = \rho(Z \cdot S) = \rho Y = \rho$.

There are interesting relations between the space Σ and the group $\mathfrak{F}$ which are worthy of closer attention. For instance, we can use the members of $\mathfrak{F}$ as "coordinates" for the points of Σ by choosing a fixed point σ and determining S_π in $\mathfrak{F}$ as the transformation such that $\sigma S_\pi = \pi$—this transformation exists by Axiom 3 and is unique by Axiom 2. It is a simple exercise to show that the mapping $\pi \rightarrow S_\pi$ is a bijection between Σ and $\mathfrak{F}$. Furthermore the transformation $T: \pi \rightarrow \pi T$ in Σ is mirrored by the transformation $S_\pi \rightarrow S_{\pi T} = S_\pi \cdot T$ on $\mathfrak{F}$, because $\sigma S_{\pi T} = \pi T = (\sigma S_\pi)T = \sigma(S_\pi \cdot T)$. In other words, if we identify Σ with $\mathfrak{F}$ through the bijection $\pi \rightarrow S_\pi$ we are left with the group $\mathfrak{F}$ and the "right group-translations" $S \rightarrow S \cdot T$. This suggests that we can start with an *arbitrary* group $\mathfrak{F}$ with elements $S, T, U, \cdots$ and consider in it the right translations $S \rightarrow S \cdot T$, hoping to obtain a geometrical structure satisfying Axioms 1–4. It is another fairly simple exercise to verify that our hope is realized. For example, the associativity of $\mathfrak{F}$ allows us to verify that the composite of the right-translations $S \rightarrow S \cdot T$ and $S \rightarrow S \cdot U$ is the right-translation $S \rightarrow (S \cdot T) \cdot U = S \cdot (T \cdot U)$, as required in Axiom 4. Since, in general, a group is noncommutative we cannot expect to verify Axiom 5. In other words, Axiom 5 effects a genuine restriction.

Another mapping of considerable interest is the mapping $(\pi, \rho) \rightarrow S_{\pi \rho}$ where $S_{\pi \rho}$ is the unique member of $\mathfrak{F}$ given by Axiom 3: $\pi S_{\pi \rho} = \rho$. It is tempting to denote $S_{\pi \rho}$ as ρ/π, because of the way it is determined; and this notation brings out some interesting parallels with the phenomena which are met in the introduction of rational fractions. Indeed the equivalence relation $(\pi, \rho) \sim (\sigma, \tau)$, defined to hold if and only if $S_{\pi \rho} = S_{\sigma \tau}$ or, in our alternative notation, $\rho/\pi = \tau/\sigma$, is quite analogous to one that is familiar in the theory of the rational numbers.[1] The following properties of this equivalence relation are easy to verify:

(1) if π, ρ, and σ are given there is a unique point η such that $(\pi, \rho) \sim (\sigma, \eta)$;

(2) if π, ρ, and t are given there is a unique point ξ such that $(\pi, \rho) \sim (\xi t)$;

---

[1] The reader will find it interesting to rewrite the entire following discussion in the alternative notation.

(3) if $(\pi, \rho) \sim (\pi', \rho')$ and $(\rho, \sigma) \sim (\rho', \sigma')$, then $(\pi, \sigma) \sim (\pi', \sigma')$.

In fact, the relation $\sigma S_{\sigma\eta} = \eta$ shows that $\sigma S_{\pi\rho} = \eta$ if and only if $S_{\pi\rho} = S_{\sigma\eta}$ or, equivalently, $(\pi, \rho) \sim (\sigma, \eta)$; the relation $\xi S_{\xi\tau} = \tau$ shows that $\xi S_{\pi\rho} = \tau$ (an equation that holds for a unique ξ by Proposition 4) if and only if $S_{\pi\rho} = S_{\xi\tau}$ or, equivalently, $(\pi, \rho) \sim (\xi, \tau)$; and the relations $\pi'S_{\pi\rho} = \rho'$, $\rho'S_{\rho\sigma} = \sigma'$, and $\pi'(S_{\pi\rho}\cdot S_{\rho\sigma}) = (\pi'S_{\pi\rho})S_{\rho\sigma} = \rho'S_{\rho\sigma} = \sigma'$ show that $(\pi, \sigma) \sim (\pi', \sigma')$ or, equivalently, $\pi'S_{\pi\sigma} = \sigma'$ if and only if $S_{\pi\rho}\cdot S_{\rho\sigma} = S_{\pi\sigma}$. Evidently the structure of the group $\mathfrak{F}$ can be regarded as determined by the partition of the set of pairs (π, ρ) into equivalence parts $[(\pi, \rho)]$ and the composition $[(\pi, \rho)]\cdot[(\rho, \sigma)] = [(\pi, \sigma)]$ induced by the relation $S_{\pi\rho}\cdot S_{\rho\sigma} = S_{\pi\sigma}$ in harmony with (3). It should be noted explicitly that because of (3) the relations $[(\pi, \rho)] = [(\pi', \rho')]$ and $[(\rho, \sigma)] = [(\rho', \sigma')]$ together imply $[(\pi, \sigma)] = [(\pi', \sigma')]$. The bijection $[(\pi, \rho)] \rightarrow S_{\pi\rho}$ is an isomorphism—that is, a one-to-one homomorphism. In view of these facts we are led to ask, "If an equivalence relation with properties (1)–(3) is given, can a group $\mathfrak{F}$ be *constructed* from the equivalence parts in the manner just described?" An affirmative answer is implied by

THEOREM 2. *In the set of pairs (π, ρ), where π and ρ are in Σ, let $\sim$ be an equivalence relation with the properties (1)–(3). The relation $S_{\sigma\tau}$ such that $\pi S_{\sigma\tau}\rho$ if and only if $(\pi, \rho) \sim (\sigma, \tau)$ is a function, $S_{\sigma\tau}: \pi \rightarrow \rho = \pi S_{\sigma\tau}$. The set $\mathfrak{F}$ of the functions $S_{\sigma\tau}$ satisfies Axioms 1–4, the function S in Axiom 3 being $S_{\pi\rho}$. Axiom 5 is satisfied if and only if for all π, ρ, σ, and τ the relation $(\pi, \rho) \sim (\sigma, \tau)$ implies the relation $(\pi, \sigma) \sim (\rho, \tau)$.*

Proof.—If π, σ, and τ are given property (1) furnishes a unique ρ such that $(\sigma, \tau) \sim (\pi, \rho)$ and hence $(\pi, \rho) \sim (\sigma, \tau)$. Thus the relation $S_{\sigma\tau}$ is a function. Since $(\pi, \pi S_{\rho\sigma}) \sim (\rho, \sigma)$ and $(\pi, \pi S_{\tau\nu}) \sim (\tau, \nu)$, we see that $\pi S_{\rho\sigma} = \pi S_{\tau\nu}$ if and only if $(\rho, \sigma) \sim (\tau, \nu)$; and it follows from this that $(\rho, \sigma) \sim (\tau, \nu)$ if and only if $S_{\rho\sigma} = S_{\tau\nu}$. Consequently Axiom 1 is satisfied. Since $(\pi, \pi S_{\sigma\tau}) \sim (\sigma, \tau)$ and $(\rho, \rho S_{\sigma\tau}) \sim (\sigma, \tau)$, we see that $\pi S_{\sigma\tau} = \rho S_{\sigma\tau}$ if and only if $(\pi, \pi S_{\sigma\tau}) \sim (\rho, \rho S_{\sigma\tau})$. But property (2) shows that these two equivalent relations hold if and only if $\pi = \rho$. Thus Axiom 2 is satisfied. Since it is true that $(\pi, \rho) \sim (\pi, \rho)$ we have $\pi S_{\pi\rho} = \rho$, and Axiom 3 is verified. If S and T are in $\mathfrak{F}$, there exist ρ, σ, and τ so that $S = S_{\rho\sigma}$ and $T = S_{\sigma\tau}$, because we necessarily have $S = S_{\rho\sigma}$ and $T = S_{\nu\omega}$ and can determine τ by property (1) so that $(\nu, \omega) = (\sigma, \tau)$ or $S_{\nu\omega} = S_{\sigma\tau}$. We then have $(\pi, \pi S) \sim (\rho, \sigma)$ and $(\pi S, (\pi S)T) \sim (\sigma, \tau)$; and by property (3) we conclude that $(\pi, (\pi S)T) \sim (\rho, \tau)$. Thus $\pi(S\cdot T) = (\pi S)T = \pi S_{\rho\tau}$ for every π and $S\cdot T = S_{\rho\tau}$. Hence Axiom 4 is verified. Assuming the same connections among ρ, σ, τ, S, and T, we observe that, when $(\pi, \rho) \sim (\sigma, \tau)$ or equivalently $\pi T = \pi S_{\sigma\tau} = \rho$, we have $\pi(T\cdot S) = (\pi T)S = \rho S_{\rho\sigma} = \sigma = \pi S_{\pi\sigma}$. Since $T\cdot S$ is in $\mathfrak{F}$, Axiom 1 yields $T\cdot S = S_{\pi\sigma}$. On the other hand $S\cdot T = S_{\rho\sigma}\cdot S_{\sigma\tau} = S_{\rho\tau}$. Hence $(\pi, \sigma) \sim (\rho, \tau)$ if and only if $S\cdot T = T\cdot S$. This completes the proof.

The mapping $(\pi, \rho) \rightarrow S_{\pi\rho}$ has the properties previously noted in passing:

(1) if π and S are given in Σ and $\mathfrak{F}$ respectively, there is a point ρ such that $(\pi, \rho) \rightarrow S$;

(2) if $S_{\pi\rho}$ is the identity in $\mathfrak{F}$, then $\pi = \rho$;

(3) $\quad S_{\pi\rho} \cdot S_{\rho\sigma} = S_{\pi\sigma}.$

In fact (1) was established in proving Theorem 2, with σ, T, and τ in place of π, S, and ρ, respectively; and (2) is evident since $\pi S_{\pi\rho} = \rho$. The following question is now raised by what precedes: could we not start with Σ, an arbitrary group $\mathfrak{G}$, and a mapping of the set of pairs of elements of Σ onto $\mathfrak{G}$ with the properties (1)–(3) and construct a family of transformations in Σ satisfying Axioms 1–4 and isomorphic to $\mathfrak{G}$? The answer is again affirmative:

THEOREM 3. *Let F be a mapping from the set of ordered pairs (π, ρ), where π and ρ are in Σ, into the arbitrary group $\mathfrak{G}$; and let F have the properties (1)–(3). Then the equivalence relation induced by F has the properties (1)–(3) indicated in Theorem 2; and the associated group $\mathfrak{F}$ is isomorphic to $\mathfrak{G}$ under the mapping $S_{\pi\rho} \rightarrow (\pi, \rho)F$.*

Proof.—By virtue of property (3), which we may write as

$$((\pi, \rho)F) \cdot ((\rho, \sigma)F) = (\pi, \sigma)F,$$

we see that $(\pi, \pi)F$ is the identity or neutral element in $\mathfrak{G}$ and that $(\pi, \rho)F$ and $(\rho, \pi)F$ are inverses of one another in $\mathfrak{G}$. Thus property (1) allows us to infer that if π, ρ, and σ are given then there is a point η such that $(\sigma, \eta) \rightarrow (\pi, \rho)F$ and hence that $(\pi, \rho) \sim (\sigma, \eta)$. Furthermore this point η is unique because if $(\sigma, \eta) \rightarrow (\pi, \rho)F$ and $(\sigma, \eta') \rightarrow (\pi, \rho)F$ we have $(\eta, \eta')F = ((\eta, \sigma)F) \cdot ((\sigma, \eta')F) = ((\rho, \pi)F) \cdot ((\pi, \rho)F) = (\rho, \rho)F$; and property (2) implies $\eta = \eta'$. Thus the equivalence relation $\sim$ has property (1) of Theorem 2. To obtain property (2) we use the fact that $(\pi, \rho)F$ and $(\rho, \pi)F$ are inverses of one another: to find ξ so that $(\xi, \tau) \rightarrow (\pi, \rho)F$ we choose ξ so that $(\tau, \xi) \rightarrow (\rho, \pi)F$, observing that $(\tau, \xi)F = (\rho, \pi)F$ and that their inverses $(\xi, \tau)F$ and $(\pi, \rho)F$ are likewise equal. Clearly property (3) yields property (3) of Theorem 2 since $(\pi, \rho)F = (\pi', \rho')F$ and $(\rho, \sigma)F = (\rho', \sigma')F$ give

$$(\pi, \sigma)F = ((\pi, \rho)F) \cdot ((\rho, \sigma)F) =$$
$$((\pi', \rho')F) \cdot ((\rho', \sigma')F) = (\pi', \sigma')F.$$

Thus we can introduce the family $\mathfrak{F}$ and infer that the mapping $S_{\pi\rho} \rightarrow (\pi, \rho)F$ is a bijection of $\mathfrak{F}$ onto $\mathfrak{G}$. That it is a homomorphism follows from putting $S = S_{\rho\sigma}$ and $T = S_{\sigma\tau}$ in $\mathfrak{F}$ and observing that $S \cdot T = S_{\rho\tau} \rightarrow (\rho, \tau)F = ((\rho, \sigma)F) \cdot ((\sigma, \tau)F)$. Thus $\mathfrak{F}$ and $\mathfrak{G}$ are isomorphic.

Because of the completely arbitrary nature of the group $\mathfrak{F}$, even when Axiom 5 is introduced and $\mathfrak{F}$ is thereby restricted, but only to be commutative or abelian, it is clear that the properties (1)–(5) that resulted from crude observations on the translations in physical space are far from characterizing the family of translations or exhausting their significant properties. Hence we must look for additional properties and their counterparts for the group $\mathfrak{F}$. Obviously if we use the members of $\mathfrak{F}$ as "coordinates" for the points of the space Σ, every property assumed for the action of $\mathfrak{F}$ on Σ can be translated into a property of $\mathfrak{F}$, and conversely. Hence the geometrical properties of translations in physical space must be reflected in the structure of the group $\mathfrak{F}$. In order to obtain the case where $\mathfrak{F}$ is not only an abelian group but, in addition, a vector system—that is, an abelian group with a distinguished family of internal isomorphisms—we must bring in the similarity transformations in a manner described in detail in Artin's *Geometrical Algebra* (1957). His procedure is to start from an elementary theory of parallel lines in the space Σ and to use this to define the family $\mathfrak{F}$ and explore its algebraic structure. The end result is that the geometrical properties of certain transformations defined in terms of the theory of parallelism are reflected in the vector character of $\mathfrak{F}$ and the introduction of vectors as coördinates in the space Σ. Thus, the present discussion provides a general framework in which so-called affine geometry finds a natural place. It may be observed that in the affine case the equivalence relation $\sim$ can be interpreted as follows: $(\pi, \rho) \sim (\sigma, \tau)$ if and only if π, ρ, σ, τ are the vertices of a parallelogram. It is then apparent why the group $\mathfrak{F}$ has to be commutaitve. The discussion of the completely general case has been carried further by Élie Cartan (1952–55) and specialized to the case where $\mathfrak{F}$ is an abstract Lie group. Thus our treatment has a genuine interest in modern higher geometry as well as in the foundations of elementary geometry.

V

EUROPEAN RESEARCH IN COGNITIVE DEVELOPMENT

Report of the
International Conference on
Cognitive Development

EDITED BY

PAUL H. MUSSEN

1

OPERATIONAL THOUGHT AND SYMBOLIC IMAGERY

Bärbel Inhelder

Institut des Sciences de l'Éducation, University of Geneva

It may seem otiose to try to revive the old problem of imagery in thinking since Binet, Marbe, and Külpe have shown that thought without images is possible, and especially since certain opponents of associationism have gone so far as to deny the very existence of mental imagery. However, contemporary psychology, on the basis of data obtained by neurophysiological and other experimental methods, has broken with the tradition, according to which the image is a residue of perceptions, and has raised imagery to the rank of a signifier. Thus, the genesis of symbolic imagery is seen in a new light.

WHAT ROLE SHOULD BE ATTRIBUTED TO SYMBOLIC IMAGERY AS AN AUXILIARY OF THOUGHT?

It may be asked whether language—without doubt the vehicle of choice for thought—is not sufficient to serve all the needs of symbolic function. Its affective scope apart, language essentially indicates concepts. Yet it seems that there is a large domain that language is not competent to describe except in devious and complex ways, that is, the domain of everything that is perceived (as opposed to conceived). Sometimes it is useful to communicate things perceived, but, above all, it is necessary to retain a large part of them in the memory if future action is to be possible. Recourse to symbolic imagery would thus be necessary every time that past perceptions are to be evoked or future perceptions anticipated.

The importance of symbolic imagery varies according to the type of operation it is called upon to support. It is inadequate for symbolizing logical and arithmetical operations, which, at the higher level, rely on arbitrary sign systems; nevertheless, it provides an important adjunct for the so-called geometrical intuitions, since in these there is partial isomorphism between signifiers and signified, the former consisting of spatial figures, themselves imagined, and the latter consisting of spatial relations on which geometrical operations are performed.

I am grateful to H. and M. Sinclair for their kind assistance in translating this paper.

EXPERIMENTAL TECHNIQUES AND SUMMARY OF RESULTS

The techniques and results to be set forth in this paper are part of a larger study on the genesis of mental imagery that we carried out in Geneva under the leadership of Jean Piaget and in co-operation with an active group of assistants.[1] Experiments involving reproductive, evocative, and anticipatory images were carried out. It is the intention here to concentrate especially on the last group, which bears more particularly on our problem: the relation between the development of operativity and the development of symbolic imagery. In the first set of experiments, children were asked to anticipate the results of the displacement of one figure in respect to another and to imagine successive transformations of one and the same figure. A second set concerned kinetic anticipations in relation to a frame of reference, and a third concerned the part played by anticipation in the development of the concept of conservation.

Methods

The development of symbolic imagery can, of course, never be grasped directly but must be approached through actualizations, such as drawings, gestures, selections from among a series of drawings representing both correct solutions and typical errors of children of different ages, and verbal comments. Along these lines, starting from consonant or contradictory indices, we tried to make inferences about the various kinds of anticipatory imagery. Following our genetic method, we put the same problem to children of different ages, and, from comparisons and the hierarchical arrangements of their ways of symbolization, as well as from the increasing frequency of successful solutions, we tried to extract the laws governing the development and modification of symbolic representation.

I. DISPLACEMENT AND TRANSFORMATION OF FIGURES

Translation of a Square in Relation to Another Square which is Kept Immobile

a) The children (aged 4 to 9 years) were shown two square pieces of cardboard (5-cm. square). The upper edge of the immobile square was parallel to and contiguous with the lower edge of the square that was to be laterally displaced (see Fig. 1).

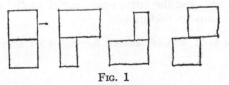

FIG. 1

---

[1] M. Bobel, F. Frank, E. Siolis, and S. Taponier.

First we made sure that the child could actually draw the configurations. Then he was asked to anticipate the result of displacing the upper square from left to right. In terms comprehensible to the child we might say, "If I push the upper square a little bit to the right, can you do a drawing to show me what the two squares will be like?" The experimenter made a gesture to suggest the lateral displacement and requested the child (1) to draw the result of the displacement without seeing the actual displacement, that is, to anticipate the result; (2) to choose from a set of drawings the one that seemed best to represent the actual displacement; and (3) to draw the result of the displacement, but this time after actually seeing the displacement and the two squares in the new position. We asked the child to comment on his trials and errors in order to gain insight into his special difficulties and into the beginning of representative imagery.

From a qualitative analysis of how young children try to arrive at figurative symbols (see Fig. 1) one may educe that the symbol long remains static even in as simple a case as the displacement of one figure in relation to another. The child did indeed indicate clearly by gesture the direction followed by the upper square, but this was only a global, all-encompassing image. When he tried to represent details, however, he sometimes drew the upper square as if it was detached from the lower one, or else—and this was more frequent from 4 to 7 years—he refused to go beyond one of the two frontiers. Thus, instead of conserving the surface sizes, he "con-

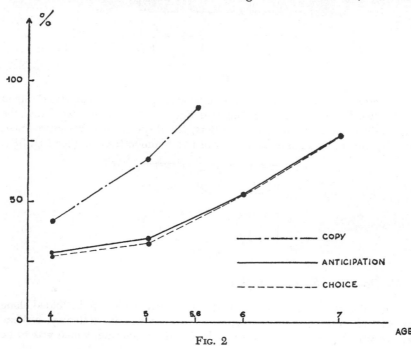

Fig. 2

served" a frontier, that is to say, he rigidly maintained its original position. This kind of "pseudoconservation," which we encountered several times, was not caused simply by difficulties of drawing. This is shown by the fact that in choosing a drawing from among those presented to him the child picked the one that was like his own drawing of the anticipated result. In this experiment, the curves representing the gradual increase in the number of correct solutions in the two procedures practically overlapped (see Fig. 2). The drawings of the final configuration, after the experimenter had actually performed the displacement, presented no difficulties from about 5½ years onward, although among 4-year-old children the drawings showed the same peculiarities as those of the anticipated results among children of 5 to 7 years.

b) A complementary experiment also provided some interesting results. It consisted of superimposing two framed transparent squares of the same dimensions (5-cm. square) and asking the child to imagine the lateral displacement of the superimposed square (see Fig. 3A). This time, young children succeeded in going beyond the outer frontier, but they failed to indicate the inner frontier, thus, in a way, "conserving" the square figure by keeping it intact. Sometimes they drew juxtaposed squares and sacrificed the dimensions; sometimes they deformed one of the squares in order to maintain a common frontier (see Fig. 3A). Everything suggested that the

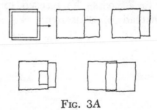

FIG. 3A

child had difficulties in symbolically representing the part that was common to the two figures. If the superimposed figures were circular we found the same reluctance to separate the frontiers; the displacement was represented as a big bulge, thus maintaining part of the common frontier (see Fig. 3B).

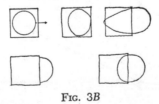

FIG. 3B

Folds: Rotating a Figure through 180°

a) The child was presented with a transparent sheet to be folded along its vertical axis. On the left side, which was to remain stationary, a 5-cm. square was drawn adjacent to the axis. On the right side, which was to be

rotated through 180°, a small round figure (or square) was placed successively at different distances from the axis in such a way that, after folding,
the small figure would appear outside, or inside, or on the frontier of the
larger figure (see Fig. 4). The child was requested to draw what he ex-

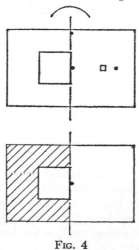

FIG. 4

pected would be the result of the folding. He was asked, for example,
"Where will the little circle be when the book is closed?"

b) The same experiment was done with a square frame placed on a
background surface.

c) The child was asked to imagine the paper being folded in a
straight line at an angle of 45° or 90°, etc., to the vertical folding axis (see
Fig. 5).

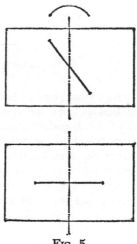

FIG. 5

Two results struck us as particularly interesting.

1. Children from 5 to 7 years showed considerable reluctance to place the small figure inside or on the frontier of the larger one, but the problem became much easier to solve if the large square had an opening (a hole), thus depriving it of the figural quality manifested in the small circles or squares.

2. The representative imagery of topological relations of interiority or exteriority came long before the imagery of the transformation of Euclidian figures, such as changes of direction of straight lines in relation to a frame of reference. The latter form of representation did not become general until fairly late, that is for children between 9 and 11 years. The figurative symbolism seemed to be closely related to the corresponding geometric operations.

Transformations of Arcs into Straight Lines and Vice Versa

A supple piece of wire in the shape of an arc (10, 13, or 24 cm. long) was presented to children aged 5 to 9 or 10 years, and they were asked,

(a) to draw a straight line showing the length of the wire if it were straightened out (by gesture, the experimenter suggested the action of pulling the wire straight by its extremities); to cut lengths of wire equal to the result of straightening the arc; and

(b) to draw successive intermediate stages of the transformation.

The drawings by the young children (see Fig. 6), as well as the cut-

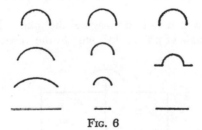

Fig. 6

ting of the lengths of wire, were evidence of an initial difficulty of representing the result of a transformation and of a much more persistent inability to symbolize successive stages of the transformation. Centering his attention on the extremities of the figure, the child first behaved as if the result of the straightening would be equal to the chord of the arc, in other words, as if he had to "conserve" the ordinal relations of the figure's frontiers. Only very gradually, along with the development of operativity, did older children succeed in more or less correctly imagining the straight lines resulting from arcs. When this first obstacle was overcome, there remained the difficulty of representing intermediate stages of the transformation. This symbolization required an operative understanding of the ordinal change of the extremities, the seriation of intermediate stages, and the conservation of length. With progress in operative thinking, it would seem that a new form of imagery developed which captured successive moments of a continuous transformation (like the frames of a film) in order, as it were, to represent the continuity of the transformation in a schematic way.

Comparison of Inscribed Segments (in Open or Closed Figures)

The children were presented with a large variety of closed figures, partially or totally inscribed within one another (see Fig. 7) so that their

Fig. 7

frontiers coincided in one or more points (e.g., a square inscribed in a circle). They were also shown fragments of these same figures as open figures (for example, a semicircle with half the inscribed square, i.e., two chords forming an angle of 90°). The child was to judge whether the total length of the one figure (e.g., the sides of the square) was equal to the total length of the other (e.g., the circumference of the circle). To make it easier for the child to dissociate length and shape, the experimenter suggested, for example, two ants traveling along the two paths.

From a large number of modes of evaluation, which can be linked to development, two extreme cases may be mentioned here. Small children, in accordance with their fixation on the frontiers of the figures, frequently judged the total length of the open figures according to whether their extremities coincided or not, and, thus, considered the straight segments and associated curves to be of equal length. Again, the importance of the frontiers induced the child to judge the length by the inclosure so that any figure on the inside was considered to have a shorter perimeter than the one that enveloped it. The answers thus arrived at were, or were not, correct depending on the shape of the figures. Older children, however, succeeded in anticipating the possible transformations of the figures, which enabled them, for example, to imagine the lines as overlapping when they tried to judge the lengths of the various parts.

II. KINETIC ANTICIPATION OF TRAJECTORY TRANSFORMATION

The Somersault

A tube with its extremities painted different colours was placed on a horizontal support in such a way that part of the tube projected beyond the support. By striking it on the projecting end, the tube could be made to perform a somersault (translation as well as rotation through 180°), so that it arrived in the inverse position on a lower support. After having rapidly performed this movement before the child, the experimenter removed the tube and asked the child to reproduce very slowly the same movement and then to draw the tube in its initial position, in its final position, and in intermediate positions. Finally, the child was asked to draw the trajectories traveled by the two extremities of the tube during the somersault.

From observing the rich variety of symbolic images provided by children aged 4 to 9 years, we would have concluded that, generally, the symbolic representation of the result of a transformation preceded the symbolic representation of the transformation itself. This seemed to command the over-all development of imagery. The drawings (see Fig. 8) show the

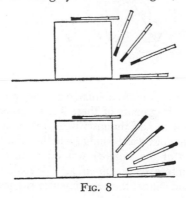

FIG. 8

clumsy way that the children tried to represent the ordinal change of the extremities resulting from this movement. The lag between symbolization of results and symbolization of transformations would seem to be explained by the fact that the child needs to understand what happens during the transformation before he can symbolize it in detail; the transformation image thus seems to be subordinate to operational activities.

Anticipation of the Trajectories of Three Fixed Beads on a Rigid Stem Rotating through 180° (the Axis of Rotation Coinciding with the Middle Bead)

The results obtained in this experiment (Fig. 9), while confirming previous results, provided a remarkable example of the relation between the development of imagery and the development of operativity. Ordinal operations (change of order), which were acquired relatively early (in this particular case at the age of 5), went with representative images, also acquired early, of results of changes of order. Displacement operations, which were arrived at later, went with figurative symbolizations of the trajectories of the beads, which were also acquired later. There were, in fact, 3 to 4 years difference between the image of positions and the image of movements. It would, thus, seem permissible to conclude that the anticipatory images relating to movement transformation do not arise of themselves independent of operative thinking.

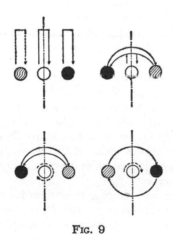

FIG. 9

III. THE ROLE OF ANTICIPATORY IMAGERY IN THE DEVELOPMENT OF THE IDEAS OF CONSERVATION

In order to make a deeper analysis of the relation between the development of anticipatory images and the development of operativity, we repeated a series of earlier experiments on the genesis of conservation of numerical, geometrical, and physical quantity, and compared the child's level of operativity with his capacity to anticipate the transformations and their results. We give here only two examples.

Liquids Poured into Vessels of Different Dimensions

In the experiment on the conservation of liquids, colored water was poured from a cylindrical vessel into another of the same height but a different diameter, and the children were asked whether the quantity of liquid remained the same. The children were also asked to anticipate the level of the liquid which was poured from a transparent vessel into six other opaque vessels of equal height but of different diameters. Finally, the children were asked to pour equal quantities of liquid into vessels of different shapes.

Comparing the various procedures was very interesting. On the one hand, it was noted that for the younger children a rough anticipation was easier than operative conservation, but for the older children the reverse was true: they found operative solutions easier than correct anticipation of levels. On the other hand, it was noted that, of all the children from 4 to 8 years of age, 30 per cent could neither anticipate the levels correctly nor solve the problem of conservation; 22.5 per cent anticipated correctly but without discovering conservation; and 5 per cent, without being able to anticipate correctly, answered correctly the question of conservation; 42.5 per cent showed both correct anticipation and conservation of quantities.

How, first of all, can the failure to anticipate changes of level be explained? While conservation does not force itself upon the child, the younger ones, by their previous experience, as well as by a kind of perseverance, moved toward what might be called "pseudoconservations." As long as they did not see the level of the liquids in the experiment, they considered that the quantities were the same; but when they noted a difference in level, they lapsed into nonconservation. The children, thus, mostly evaluated quantity by its upper limit, that is, by the level of the column of liquid, without considering the width of the vessel. It was as if the children judged more by rigid and partial rules (e.g., same quantity = same level) than by previous experience.

Second, what were the correct anticipations based on and did they constitute a preparation for conservation? Results suggested the hypothesis that a correct anticipation, as a consequence, perhaps, of experience, did not in itself prepare the child for the conservation of quantities; for the same child, called upon to pour two equal quantities into two vessels of different diameters, relied exclusively on the height of the column of liquid. It appeared, thus, that a more or less correct symbolic representation is by itself not sufficient to bring about an operative compensation such as: narrower x higher = same quantity. However, the correct representation of levels will sooner or later become the indispensable auxiliary of reasoning once the child understands the phenomenon of conservation and when, instead of describing what he sees, he starts to explain it.

Displacement of a Stick in Relation to Another of the Same Length

This experiment was done as follows:

a) The child had before him two straight sticks of equal length (say, 10 cm.). One was displaced so that it was almost completely masked by a screen. The child was asked to imagine how far the stick reached behind the screen, and, then, to draw the two sticks as if they were both entirely visible.

b) With the same display, the child was asked to choose from among a mixed group of 18 sticks measuring 0.5–10 cm. (actually 9 pairs), a stick that could exactly fill the space vacated by the displaced stick. Then he was asked to choose another stick equal to the hidden part of the displaced stick; for example, the child was told, "Now find another stick of the same length as the bit hidden by the tunnel."

c) Without a screen, the child was asked whether the length of the stick remained the same after it was displaced parallel to the other stick (a displacement equal to about a third of the total length seemed to give the most interesting results).

The most instructive points for understanding the relation between anticipation and operation may briefly be summarized as follows:

1. The anticipatory image seemed to be quite separate from the preoperative judgment since the imagined representation tended to diminish the length of the mobile stick (which to us seems to be a result of the frontier effect again), whereas the preoperative judgment tended to overestimate the length of the displaced rod under the influence of the movement.

2. The anticipation of lengths seemed to precede judgments of conservation of lengths. Of a group of children aged 5 to 9 (leaving aside fluctuations in estimations and judgments), 25 per cent had neither a correct anticipation nor a sure notion of conservation; 28 per cent succeeded in both anticipations and conservations; 4 per cent had a notion of conservation without correct anticipation; and 29 per cent anticipated correctly, but without reasoning, along lines of conservation.

3. When it came to comparing full and empty spaces, however, judgments of conservation quite clearly preceded correct anticipations. Here, in fact, 38 per cent had neither conservation nor anticipation, 23 per cent had both, 38 per cent showed that they had acquired the notion of conservation but without being able to anticipate correctly, and none anticipated correctly without conservation.

It would thus appear that a correct representative image of the protruding part of the stick was not sufficient to secure the conservation of lengths, the full understanding of which calls for a complete symmetrical system of compensation between empty and full spaces. Nevertheless, it is of interest to note that when the child's attention was drawn to the lengths of the protruding parts, the idea of conservation seemed to be acquired more easily. Children who had done a certain number of exercises in anticipation generally acceded a little sooner to notions of operative conservation than children who had not. It would seem that the image became adequate only when it was directed by operations that were being structured, but image formation, in turn, facilitated the operative elaboration. The experiment thus provided a fine example of the distinction and also of the interaction between the formative processes of images and operations.

THE DEVELOPMENT OF IMAGERY

The Origin of Symbolic Imagery

It is certainly difficult to say exactly when the child's first images appear. Piaget's studies on the origins of sensorimotor intelligence and the genesis of the permanent object would invalidate the hypothesis that imagery appears early, as certain psychoanalysts have contended. Piaget's observations of the development of spontaneous symbolic behaviour in his own children, which have since been confirmed experimentally by our team, lend colour to the hypothesis that imagery is linked to symbolic function, and symbolic imagery arises by genetic filiation from imitative mechanisms.

The earliest observed behaviour implying evocative images is linked to deferred imitation. The child evokes physical as well as human models in their absence. His means of evocation are gestures, attitudes, and movements. Imitative movements seem to become interiorized subsequently in the form of incipient schemes that, in our experiments, are seen as movements and drawing gestures that enable the child to symbolize the models figuratively. This filiation from imitation is, moreover, part of the general process of the development of symbols. From the second year onward, we witness a great development of symbolic function that is marked by the progressive differentiation of signifiers and signified. On the one hand are the multiple signification and the elastic extension, which the child attributes to symbols in his imaginative play, verbal (prelogical) concepts, and evocative imagery; this signification and extension result from assimilative processes of nascent thought. On the other hand, however, the accommodating mechanisms of imitation play a striking role in the constitution of the forms and contents of signifiers.

The fact that the genesis of elementary forms of imagery—far from constituting an isolated process—takes in a series of linked filiations that lead from imitation to symbol formation, strongly supports the modern conception according to which images have the status of symbols.

The Relation between Elementary Forms of Symbolic Imagery and Pre-operative Thought

An essentially static quality was seen to dominate symbolic imagery that corresponds to the level of preoperative thought. This quality generally determines the difficulties of the child in passing from a reproductive image, itself frequently deformed, to an anticipatory image. The static quality of the image is seen particularly in the child's efforts to conserve certain features of the figure while neglecting others and by his incapacity to symbolize the continuous transformations of shapes and movements. Retaining certain typical features of the figure leads the child toward what one might call pseudoconservations and to a certain reluctance to exceed or cross the frontiers.

A whole set of converging indices point to the importance that the child attaches to certain figure frontiers: the translation of a square in relation to another gives rise to a pseudoconservation of the terminal frontier at the expense of surface conservation. As a complement to the conservation of the outer frontier, the child refuses to draw the inner frontiers of a figure when transparent squares are partially superimposed and thus neglects the intersection of the figures. In the experiments on folding, the child similarly refuses to represent the envelopment of a small circle in a square or the intersection with the frontier of the latter as long as the square is a figure and not a background surface.

The most tenacious frontier effect—reinforced as it is by the notional system of preoperative thought—is the refusal to anticipate the projection beyond the extreme frontiers of an arc: the straight line derived from the arc is given as its chord. Another example of the interaction between the figurative and notional aspects of preoperative thought is the systematic way the children have of wrongly judging the total length of open figures by the coincidence of their terminal frontiers. On the one hand, the child centers on the frontiers of the figure and, on the other, estimates the equality or inequality of spatiotemporal displacements by arrival order. The ordinal pseudoconservations, which, in a general way, dominate preoperative thought, are here linked to figural pseudoconservations. Because of its static quality, the imagery fails to symbolize the different stages of a transformation. The almost insurmountable difficulties of imagining the intermediate stages between the arc and the straight line will be recalled, as will the children's clumsy efforts at symbolizing the successive positions of a somersaulting tube.

The insufficiently co-ordinated centralizations and irreversibility of preoperative thought go together with an essentially static imagery. Anticipatory imagery, imitating in fragmentary fashion certain aspects of what is perceived, at first leads to distortion, as does preoperative thought itself. This conjunction seems to involve a form of interaction; figural schematization is in many ways influenced by conceptualization and vice versa, and preoperative notions are, as Piaget would say, "molded in the frame of the image." If symbolic imagery in its figurative aspect always retains a certain static quality, since its role is to imitate and not to construct, operation by its very constructiveness rapidly increases in mobility, and, in turn, acts on symbolic imagery.

The Relation between the Higher Forms of Symbolic Imagery and Operative Thought

With the progress of operative thought, which conceives of changes in a state as the results of reversible transformations, imagery gradually acquires sufficient mobility to become anticipatory; it will succeed, first, in representing the results of figurative or kinetic transformations and, later, the successive steps of such transformations.

In each of the experimental situations, we noted, in fact, a qualitative and progressive modification of figurative symbolization and a remarkable increase in the number of adequate solutions, the two going together with the development and generalization of concrete operations. The hypothesis of a concurrent evolution of the operative and figurative aspects of thought is easily demonstrated, but it still remains to be seen whether their progress is achieved through mutual or unilateral influences. The data available would bear out the second alternative; they show that the formation of operations directs the progress of figurative symbolism, which serves as a support for operative thought.

By examining not only the figurative results but their elaboration as evidenced by the children's trials and errors and their commentaries, we realized that anticipatory images are not simply derived from a spontaneously arising suppleness of reproductive images; the suppleness is, rather, achieved under the influence of operations. The concordance of the results of each experiment sufficiently illustrates the role played in anticipatory images by ordinal operations, in their twin aspect of change of order and serial order. Finally, operative reversibility disengages representative imagery from figural pseudoconservations and orients it toward the symbolization of conceptual conservations.

The study of clinical cases brings an interesting confirmation of the results of genetic investigations. Some children who suffer from deficiencies in figurative symbolization may obtain a quasi-normal operative level; their shortcomings in the field of representative imagery can be assimilated to behaviour belonging to a more elementary level; sometimes they even succeed in compensating for certain lacunae of their imagery, although only by costly deductive procedures. While operativity thus directs the progress of symbolic imagery, imagery that has not yet been made supple by the effects of operativity does not seem to be sufficient to prepare operativity. This is shown by the fact that even the children who, thanks to evoking their daily experiences, can correctly anticipate certain changes of state (e.g., the level of the liquid after pouring into a different vessel, or the distance a stick protrudes after displacement) do not understand any better than the others the conservation of quantities and the compensation of dimensions. If the image is not orientated by operativity, it just does not seem to lead to the understanding of transformations, even if they are figural.

The situation, however, becomes quite different once symbolic imagery is moulded by operations. Images symbolizing the successive steps of figural transformations facilitate the representation of the transformation. The act of symbolically translating successive events into simultaneous spatial images does not only fix the information from which the judgment is elaborated but also serves as a continuous support for the elaboration itself. Although it is true that symbolic imagery, because of its imitative quality, never attains the dynamics of operative construction and does not constitute an element of thought on an equal footing with operativity, it nevertheless fulfils the role of a symbolic tool that is complementary to that of language and, like language, promotes the progress of thought.

In conclusion, we shall consider the relation between operative thought and its symbolic imagery from both the functional and the structural points of view. From the point of view of the functioning of cognitive activity, it would seem that there is, concurrently, a complementary relation and a certain interdependence between the operative and figurative aspects of thought. According to the distinction established by Piaget, operativity consists in transforming, by action or in thought, a piece of reality considered as an object of knowledge. Thanks to a series of reversible operations, the child discovers, for example, the invariability of the quantity, although the matter is transformed. The figurative aspects of thought, on the other hand, are limited to copying, or, more precisely, to imitating in a schematic way the piece of reality. At each moment of development, operativity directs the formation of symbolic imagery by providing it with meanings, and the figurative signifiers, once they have been built up, favor the acquisition and the fixation of information that is food for thought.

By considering the development of operative structures and symbolic imagery, we are entitled to suppose that their modes of construction do not enjoy an equal degree of independence from outside influences. The successive structures of operative thought, as Piaget has shown, are engendered one from the other according to a constant and integrated order. They may be accelerated or inhibited by many external factors; their mode of construction, however, does not seem to be modified by such factors.

The development of symbolic imagery, we believe, depends to a large extent on external contributions. It is as if, in the initial phases, symbolic imagery bore the imprint of motor-imitation schemes from which it stems; as we have shown, the later evolution of figurative symbolism is modified through the progress of operativity.

2

PROBLEMS OF FORMAL REASONING
IN TEST SITUATIONS

Eric A. Lunzer

Manchester University

The reported study is one of several undertaken in the context of a desire to arrive at a clearer understanding of the kinds of advances in reasoning that appear as the child approaches adolescence. How much are these advances sufficiently homogeneous and distinctive to warrant the use of the general term "formal reasoning" in opposition to the term "concrete reasoning," which is characteristic of the achievements belonging to the years between 6 and 9?

THE UNITY OF CONCRETE REASONING

Piaget's studies of concrete reasoning extend over many volumes (Piaget, 1946a, 1946b; Piaget & Inhelder, 1941, 1948; Piaget, Inhelder, & Szeminska, 1948; Piaget & Szeminska, 1941; Inhelder & Piaget, 1959) and over many spheres of thinking. In particular, we may recall the development of the principal invariants of number, length, time, substance, weight, etc., the so-called conservations, the ability to classify objects in terms of precise criteria, the ability to appreciate and respect the transitive property of an ordered series, and the organisation of space in terms of a co-ordinate system based on the primacy and orthogonality of horizontal and vertical axes. Nevertheless, it is not difficult to perceive an underlying unity in the sort of processes that must be presumed to operate in all these manifestations.

I have suggested elsewhere (Lunzer, 1961) that "what develops at about the age of six or seven is the ability to examine two judgments simultaneously and arrive at an appropriate conclusion." Piaget's own interpretation of these phenomena (1957) is very much along the same lines. In particular, in experiments such as those that bear on the conservation of fundamental properties and relations, the child progresses from an intuitive awareness and understanding of the properties to an operational abstraction. The intuitive awareness rests on an unconscious assimilation of a notion such as quantity or length to some one perceptual aspect of the situation in which it figures. For example, an object is judged to be *long* because it projects beyond another; or a collection is judged to be many or more than another

583

because its spatial disposition is more extensive. These intuitive concepts are inadequate and do not relate to the corresponding concepts in adult usage, because the latter depend on an abstraction. It is possible to be quite precise about the nature of this abstraction. It is not, Piaget insists, a mere "reading off" of a particular aspect of the object; it is much more an abstraction, or "fixing," of the real or virtual actions that define the concept. Thus, in the case of number, the action would be the setting up of a one-to-one correspondence, as in enumeration; in the case of length, the action would be the determination of an interval between two limit points, etc. The resulting concepts are first-order invariants that are more stable than the intuitive notions that they replace. At the same time, they comprehend these notions as contributory aspects of themselves.

From the perceptual point of view, such an invariant "operational" concept represents a synthesis of two compensatory judgments. Thus, the quantity of a set of elements is reflected not only in its spatial extension but in the density of its elements. A transformation of such a set that leaves the number or quantity invariant is one in which the two perceptual properties are made to vary in opposite directions: more dense but less extensive, or vice versa. Similarly, in the case of length, an invariant transformation will be a relative displacement, such that the object under consideration will project further at one extremity relative to a reference object, but less at the other. It is in this sense that the operational judgment is essentially a reconciliation of two perceptual judgments.

Yet it is important to note that the "concrete" operational concept is not a mere synthesis of two such judgments, although it could not be entertained as a functionally adequate frame of reference in the absence of such a synthesis. The concept itself is a *precise* relation (or property, the distinction between the two being more of philosophical than of psychological interest) that is determined by the congruent effects of antecedent and postcedent actions of the subject, actions that are usually internal, although some may be overt. Moreover, the recognition of their congruence cannot become implicit, as it must in order to constitute a frame of reference for logical thinking, until the major portion of them is indeed internal or virtual. Thus, in the case of number, establishing the cardinal value of a set of discontinuous elements may entail a real or overt enumeration, involving a one-for-one displacement of the objects in order to establish their correspondence with the ordered and labeled set of positive integers. But such a correspondence is without significance unless the subject recognises implicitly that, as long as the elements remain what they were, equivalence can be *re-established* whatever the disposition of the set. It is these re-establishments that need to be virtual, because it is only in the measure that the subject can *anticipate* them at the moment of his initial enumeration that such enumeration gains its functional significance.

Thus, the first-order concepts, of which conservation is achieved in the course of the years between 6 and 9, are, in fact, relations that are operationally defined.[1] Length is that property of an object that is defined by the measuring of the interval between two chosen extremities; number is that property of a set that is defined by the enumeration of the elements; analogous definitions can be made for such other relative invariants as temporal duration, weight, volume, etc.

The qualifying adjective "relative invariants" is essential. For the present purposes it may be assumed that there are no absolute invariants. The properties or first-order relations with which we are here concerned are invariant through certain kinds of transformations (e.g., length through displacement, number through spatial rearrangement, etc.), and their operational definition depends on the recognition of that invariance (e.g., we cannot measure the length of an object without displacing a standard or a ruler). Moreover, they vary in predictable fashion when certain other changes are made, for example, the cardinal value of a set increases when new elements are added. It is for these reasons that, from a functional point of view, these concepts are more adequate to comprehend the world of objects than are the intuitive notions they replace.

Operational concepts are, therefore, concepts that are defined in terms of the actions of the subject. It is for this reason that the work of Piaget and Inhelder (1948) on classification holds a key position in the research findings that bear on these developments as a whole. In the course of a number of experiments, partly reviewed by Braine (1962), it appears that during these crucial years children learn to think of collections in terms of precise "intensional" criteria that represent the properties that the members of those collections have in common and that distinguish them from other collections. By virtue of such definition, the collections take on the character of logical classes. The child is able to compare overlapping classes and, hence, to reason with consistency. Where, earlier, there was confusion whenever comparisons bore on classes that had some but not all members in common, the confusions are now avoided. Once again, such reasoning involves the reconciliation of opposed judgments (at the simplest level: "x is a member of A because it has the defining property a, but it is also a member of B with the defining property b").

But where, in other experiments, the definitive property of the subject's actions (real and virtual) with respect to the concepts under consideration seems secondary (at least in the experimental setting), here that property (based on the recognition of the precise criteria involved in the

---

[1] This is not the sense in which Piaget uses the term "operational." Piaget's usage refers to the simultaneous awareness of equivalences between transformations that comes as a result of the anticipation of virtual actions and their effects. Such awareness lends to the initial action a precise definition corresponding to the systematic precision of a mathematical or logical operation. Nevertheless, the two usages of the term "operational" are closely linked, since both have the connotation of "well defined within a system."

action of subsuming *all* like elements within a single class) is the primary focus of the enquiry, which is why it emerges with the greatest precision.

All the foregoing may be summarised as follows:

1. Concrete operational reasoning is reasoning in terms of precise concepts.

2. Such concepts always refer to definitive actions, that is, they are operationally definable and operationally definite.

3. Such concepts are rarely elaborated with reference to a content that is entirely novel. They refer to a content that is already familiar, but one that has hitherto been apprehended in terms of "assimilated to" more fluid notions.

4. These fluid "intuitive" notions, or "preconcepts," are determined by perception and perceptual imagery.

5. Judgments in terms of such notions are arrived at with reference to a single prepotent perceptual feature of the situation at any given moment.

6. The new concepts do not entail a loss of awareness of such prepotent features. But they do imply that such awareness is balanced by a simultaneous awareness of other features and, above all, by an awareness of the lawful character of compensation, as a result of which mere transformations effected upon an object or a set of objects do not involve any material alteration (i.e., they involve no alteration in the property that is operationally defined).

At least points (1)–(4) apply equally in all those situations studied by Piaget and the Geneva school to which the terms "concrete operations" have been applied—including the behaviour involved in seriation and the elaboration of precise spatial parameters as well as classificatory behaviour. Points (5) and (6) are particularly applicable to the "conservations." A corrollary of point (3) is that very often the very same term will be used by a younger child with reference to a preconcept and by an older child or an adult to denote a true operational concept. Verbal misunderstandings are, therefore, inevitable to some degree.[2]

In other words, in spite of the wide variety of behaviours that have been analysed in terms of the concept of "concrete operational reasoning," the concept does indeed denote certain essential features that are shared by all and that represent a crucial stage in intellective development.[3]

---

[2] We would remind the reader that each one of these points has been made by Piaget himself (see, especially, "Études, équilibre and perception," the two studies by Piaget in *Études d'épistemologie génétique*, vols. 5 and 7). He is particularly insistent that operations do not depend so much on the appearance of the object as on the co-ordinations of the subject. The key importance we have assigned to the concept of operational definability is not present in Piaget's own writings, but we believe it to be entirely consistent with them.

[3] The use of the term "stage" should not be taken to imply that the development in question is a sudden affair; a child may be able to solve some problems but not others. The term refers primarily to a similarity in the underlying proc-

PROBLEMS OF FORMAL REASONING

How far is there a parallel unity of processes underlying the further elaborations of reasoning that have been termed "formal"? We may recall that Piaget, in his earlier writings, tended to emphasise the verbal character of formal reasoning. Thus, in one important statement of his position, we find a problem of Burt cited as illustrating the type of question that necessitates the application of formal reasoning. The problem is, "Jane is fairer than Lilly; Jane is darker than Susan; which of the three is the fairest?" Piaget correctly pointed out that younger children will tend to interpret the terms "fairer" and "darker" in an absolute sense; hence, they will conjure a picture of Lilly as "fair," Susan as "dark," and Jane as both "fair" and "dark." They will, therefore, conclude that Lilly is the fairest. The problem is contrasted with the simpler form, "Jane is fairer than Lilly; Lilly is fairer than Susan; which is the fairest?" a form of question that can be correctly answered by children of 8. It is obvious that the more difficult presentation of the problem requires that the subject extract the relational signficance of the two statements from what we might term the pictorial evocative connotation of the linguistic forms into which they are cast. To that extent, the correct solution implies an interest in the formal and logical implications of such messages as opposed to their content. It may well depend on the explicit or implicit interpolation of the equivalence, "Jane is fairer than Lilly = Lilly is darker than Jane."

In his more recent exposition of the characteristics of the formal reasoning characteristic of adolescent thinking, however, Piaget (Inhelder & Piaget, 1955) revised his earlier formulation on the ground that to stress the verbal character of formal reasoning as opposed to the concrete character of concrete reasoning might lead us to ignore the fact that it is the character of the problem itself that determines whether its solution will demand formal reasoning or whether it can be answered in terms of the earlier operational level. Not only is it possible to construct concrete situations whose solutions cannot be reached by the "structures" of concrete operations (classifications and seriations, together with the elementary organisation of space and time, and the series of positive integers), but each of the experimental situations devised by Inhelder and reported in this work is an instance of such a concrete presentation of the formal problem. One might add that, by the same token, the second form of Burt's problem cited above constitutes one of many possible illustrations of a purely verbal problem that, nevertheless, does not require anything more than concrete operational reasoning as described by Piaget (with or without the slight change in emphasis argued in the last section).

---

esses of the reasoning ("structure") and, presumably, to an organisation of nervous processes that is common to all and only secondarily to a relative synchronicity of development.

In point of fact, the experiments that figured in the last-mentioned work fall into two distinct groups. The first, including the problems of the pendulum, of motion on an inclined plane, and of the flexibility of a rod, and several others, consists of problems whose solutions are held to require the use of a combinatorial system.

As an example, we may take the problem of the oscillation of a pendulum. The material consists of a length of string suspended from a hook to which the subject can attach one of several weights. The weighted bob is set in motion and the subject is required to note that it moves to and fro with a characteristic period of oscillation. He is asked to find out what determines this period. He can vary the length of the string, the height from which it is released, the impetus (if any) that he himself imparts to it initially, and the weight of the bob. The correct solution of the problem (i.e., the discovery that the period of a pendulum is a function of its length) can only be achieved if the subject can reason that if a particular variable (e.g., weight) affects the dependent variable (period), then the effect (change in period) will appear if he holds all other variables constant and varies only the one he is considering. Conversely, if this procedure is carried out and the result (effect on period) shows no change, he must infer that the variable (i.e., weight, or, more strictly, weight alone), needs to be ruled out as a factor affecting the result. In point of fact, younger children (up to the age of 13 or 14) fail to see the necessity for holding other variables constant. Usually, they are convinced that weight is an important factor and if they discover that the length of the string affects the result they behave as if the role of both variables can be adequately demonstrated by producing an impressive change—that is, simultaneously varying length and weight. Children of 11 to 13 may be led to understand the superiority of the proof by the "method of all other things equal," but they do not adopt it spontaneously.

Among the other situations designed by Inhelder to elicit qualities of "formal reasoning," the following are broadly analogous to the pendulum problem.

One situation is the problem of motion on an inclined plane. The material is a chute that can be pivoted about its lower extremity to alter its inclination to the horizontal; the subject can slide marbles or ball bearings down this chute, releasing them wherever he thinks fit. Beyond the base of the chute is a spring that causes the balls to bounce into one of a series of compartments, depending on the force of impact. Again, the essence of the problem is to disentangle the variables, eliminating weight and size, and so discover that the distance traveled by the ball is a function of the distance up the slide from which it is released together with the inclination of the slide itself. A number of older adolescents are able to reason further that the distance and inclination combine to yield a single independent variable that is sufficient to predict the velocity of motion on an inclined plane and, hence, the distance traveled upon striking the spring, that is, the height of the point of release above the point of impact. Once again, it is clear that the subject who uses the method of "other things equal" has all he needs to solve the problem (at any rate at the lower level). From a formal point of view, the fact that two variables turn out to be relevant, and not one, does not alter the psychological characteristics of the problem.

In the problem of the flexibility of rods the task is to discover and prove that the distance a rod will bend when a weight is placed on an extremity that projects well beyond the point of fulcrum is a function of many variables. In point of fact, those variables that the subject is free to alter are the material of which the rod is composed, its length, its shape in cross-section, its thickness, and the weight of the "diver" placed on the end of the "diving board" (rod). The essential similarity of this problem to the two previously cited is again abundantly clear.

There exists another group of problems, however, that appear to present quite a different psychological problem, but which, also, are not solved before the age of 13 to 15. Thus, a number of experiments devised by Inhelder converge to suggest that notions of ratio and proportion are comparatively late acquisitions. Typical of these is the enquiry into the size of the shadow thrown by a variable object on a screen that is illuminated by a point source of light. The size of the shadow then varies directly with that of the object and is inversely proportional to the distance of the object from the screen. Taking as the object a circular wire loop of diameter D, the interval A between object and screen (with the total distance B from light source to screen, so that the distance from light source to object $= B - A = A'$), and the diameter of the shadow as S, then, with B constant, an increase in D will lead to a proportionate increase in S, while an increase in A will lead to a proportionate *decrease* in S. Hence, with B again constant, an increase in D can be *compensated* for by a proportionate decrease in A. This problem was presented to children of various ages. Successful solution depends on two conceptual systems: the notion of proportion itself as opposed to arithmetical increment (younger children try to subtract from A whatever was added to D, etc.) and the reciprocity that obtains between distance and size of object (younger children are often uncertain whether to add or subtract). (It should be pointed out that the reciprocity is an integral factor of the situation. Measuring the interval A' instead of the interval A does not change the problem from one of reciprocal proportionality to one of direct proportionality since the function involved is B/A and not B/A'. In other words, although A' does indeed vary directly as S, the relation is not one of simple proportionality so long as B is held constant.) Solution of this problem is again taken by Inhelder and Piaget as an achievement characteristic of the stage of formal reasoning (13–15 years).

The above experiment thus involves an understanding both of proportionality and of the reciprocity that obtains between the size of an object and its distance from the light source. A similar experiment concerns the equilibrium of a simple balance. Here there is an inverse proportional relation between the weight suspended from a point on a T balance and its distance from the pivot.

But, it appears that, even when the problem is one of simple direct proportionality, children find it difficult, until at least the age of 11 or 12. Thus, Piaget (1957) reported a series of experiments on the notion of similar triangles of which the following is particularly significant: the subject is shown a pair of similar triangles of which one is substantially larger than the other and he recognises their similarity; he is then shown a triangle (a) of known dimensions beside two lines drawn at an angle to one another such that a set of lines can be drawn between them to complete a series of triangles similar to (a); given the distance along the base of the second triangle from which the third line is to be drawn, the length of the side is a direct proportional function of the length of the corresponding side of the model. Again, younger children try to solve the problem by simply adding the difference between the two bases.

Finally, one might consider at least two of the situations described in Inhelder and Piaget (1955) which appear to represent an opposite alternative to the experiments involving both proportionality and reciprocity. These are the problems of communicating vessels together with that of equilibrium in the hydraulic press. Only the first need be described here. The apparatus consists of two tubes differing in shape and connected by a rubber hose; the system is filled with coloured liquid and the level of the liquid is always equal in both tubes because they are open at the top and therefore subject to the same pressure. The experiment consists of raising or lowering the level in one of the vessels and asking the subject to predict the level of the liquid in the other arm or requiring the subject to adjust the level of the arm that is hidden behind a screen by raising or lowering the other, etc. The principal finding is that, whereas at level IIB, that is, about the age of 9 or 10, children are readily able to discover the identity of levels in the two arms, they are quite incapable of explaining it. It is only at the stage of formal reasoning, that is, after the age of 11 or 12, that they begin to see the level in the hidden arm as a function of a system of pressures partly communicated from the opposite arm and acting in an opposite direction, that is, downward pressure in arm A is communicated as an upward pressure in arm B. But, characteristically, because their understanding is more structured, they are less ready to generalise the equality of levels to all situations. Thus, they find it difficult to predict, or understand, why the levels should still be equal when one of the vessels is much wider than the other, etc. At 14 or thereabouts (no statistical analysis is given by the authors), the subjects begin to give a more adequate account in terms of pressure as force per unit of area, but here the authors recognise that the adequacy of the answers may be partly or largely a result of learning. In other words, the critical development is that that takes place at 11 or 12 and is the ability to understand compensatory forces in terms of reciprocity in their direction.

Summarising this section, it appears that Piaget has pointed to two broad classes of problems the solutions of which are not achieved before the age of 11 or 12 and often considerably later. The first of these consists of situations in which the subject is required to provide proofs of hypotheses by the experimental manipulation of variables, that is, by varying each variable singly while holding the remaining variables constant and noting the effects of so doing. The second consists of experiments in which the subject is required to discover relations, sometimes of direct but more often of inverse proportionality, together with a number of problems that require an understanding of reciprocity in physical systems. It is apparent that problems of proportionality and problems of reciprocity are intimately related, since most physical instances are, in fact, instances of both. At the same time, there are indications that problems that involve only one of these components may be somewhat easier—problems of direct proportionality and problems of simple (nonquantified) reciprocity tend to be solved nearer the age of 11 or 12, that is, toward the beginning of the "stage of formal reasoning," whereas such problems as the equilibrium of the balance are not usually solved until the age of 13 to 15.

PIAGET'S INTERPRETATION OF FORMAL REASONING

The psychological relation between the first group of problems (experimental manipulation of variables) and the second (problems of proportionality and reciprocity), however, is by no means clear. Piaget himself sought to demonstrate a logical interconnexion by (1) interpreting the former as applications of a propositional calculus in which the component propositions were to be considered classes of events and (2) interpreting the truth function as constituting an exhaustive array of the ways in which the separate classifications might be cross-classified. Thus, the statement that to increase the oscillation period of the pendulum necessitates a decrease in the length of the pendulum, and vice versa, may be rendered formally as "p [increases in period of oscillation] implies and is implied by q [decreases in length]"; this statement, in turn, argues the following truth functions: p and $q = T$; not $-p$ and not $-q = T$; p and not $-q = F$; not $- p$ and $q = F$. In other words, a classification of all the possible combinations of events would show that increases in the period of oscillation occur in conjunction with decreases in length and instances can occur in which neither phenomenon is manifest but neither can happen without the other. Piaget argued that the subject who succeeded in manipulating variables experimentally not only showed his awareness of this possible breakdown, but, because he arrived at the (correct) solution and excluded others (e.g., p/q, an increase in period is incompatible with a decrease in length, or p^*q, the two phenomena are independent so that all possible combinations may occur), he must have been aware of every other possible combination in the propositional calculus (16 for combinations of 2 propositions, 256 for 3, etc.). Needless to say, this does not imply that every possible combination is called to mind in solving every problem involving two, three, or more variables but simply that the subject works within the system in the sense that he calls to mind and analyses correctly the combinations that appear relevant or plausible, and is aware of the incompatibility of all the other combinations that he chooses to disregard.

Piaget's interpretation of the essential mechanism underlying the solution of problems of reciprocity and proportionality was also couched in terms of the propositional calculus. The argument was in two stages:

In the first place, it is easy to show that wherever two systems of actions are reciprocally related to one another, any action may be canceled in one of two ways: One is to perform the opposite action, that is, to perform the inverse within the same action system; the other is to perform an action within the related action system to produce a similar effect. Thus, to revert to the example of the equilibrium existing between the levels of liquids in communicating vessels, the action of lowering the level in one by raising the vessel while leaving the other constant may be canceled either by lowering the same vessel, which is simply the inverse action within the same system, or, alternatively, by raising the other vessel, i.e., by performing an action within a related action system, the effect of which is reciprocal to that of the first. Confining ourselves to the same example, it is clear that the system as a whole comprises four possible actions (each of the vessels can be raised or lowered). Moreover, the relations of inversion and reciprocity hold true irrespective of the particular action that is taken as the starting point for these transformations. Hence, from a logical point of view, the four actions constitute a group. One way of seeing this relation is to regard any action within the system as a point on a vector, where the vector represents the particular type of action and the distance on it represents its extent. Disregarding the extent of these actions, we may say that since there are four types of action there are four vectors. Let us call one of these I (identity, the starting-point); then the vector that represents its exact opposite may be called N (negation, raising or lowering in our example); we already know that a third vector, representing a third type of action, will have similar effects to N and this we may continue to call R (reciprocal); the fourth vector is simply the inverse or exact opposite of this: we may call this C (correlative). The terms I, N, R, C, are ways of defining the vectors in terms of one another, that is, they indicate ways of obtaining one from another. The system as a whole is, therefore, a system of transformations within which the following relations hold true: $I^2 = N^2 = R^2 = C^2 = I$; $IN = RC$; $NRC = I$. This is precisely the structure of a four-group.

There is little question that a system of reciprocal actions may usefully be represented in this manner as a four-group. But, so far, no connexion has been established between such a system and the propositional calculus.

In effect, the second stage of Piaget's argument may be rendered as follows: Propositions that constitute the combinatorial system for two or more elementary propositons are themselves such that they can be transformed into one another by means of appropriate transformations, and these transformations, in turn, constitute groups. Thus, any two-term proposition may be symbolised by means of the letters p and q to represent the elementary propositions, together with the symbols "." (and), "−" (not), and "v" (or), to indicate a particular combination. Simple denial of such a proposition has the effect of asserting a proposition that has the same terms except for the addition of the negation symbol (−), where it is absent in the first and its deletion where it is present and the substitution of v for . and . for v. $−(p \text{ v } q) = −p \text{ . } −q$; for example, "I deny that he is mistaken or he is lying" is equivalent to "I assert that he is not mistaken and he is not lying." Since this transformation represents negation, we may justifiably call it **N**. But the proposition $(p \text{ v } q)$ is also related to the proposition $(−p \text{ v } −q)$, that is, substituting negation for assertion without substituting . for v. (The effect of the transformation is a somewhat weak denial of the original proposition; in our example, "He is mistaken or lying" becomes "He is not mistaken or not lying." But it has already been pointed out that Piaget seeks to find a far more relevant application of the propositional calculus to real thinking by interpreting the truth functions of many-term propositions as *classes of events* that exist or do not exist in combination.) That the substitution of assertion for negation, and vice versa, in each term of a compound proposition produces the reciprocal of the original proposition is clearest when we consider propositions expressing a relation of implication. Thus, the proposition "p implies q" is recognised to be equivalent to "$p \text{ v } −q$"; substituting assertion for negation we obtain "$−p \text{ v } q$" that is, "$q \text{ v } −p$," which is the reciprocal of the original proposition. Hence, beginning with the original compound proposition, once again taken as **I** (for identity), we have so far shown how to obtain **N** and **R**. But we may combine **N** and **R** by applying both transformations in turn: the effect is to substitute v for . and vice versa, without changing the signs. (In our example, "He is mistaken and he is lying.") The sense of this proposition is nearer to the original than that of the others and this we may call the correlative. Thus, the four compound propositions "$p \text{ v } q$," "$−p \text{ . } −q$," "$−p \text{ v } −q$," and "$p \text{ . } q$" constitute another instance of a four-group.

In effect, Piaget argues to the psychological kinship of combinatorial reasoning as instanced in the experimental manipulation of variables on the one hand, and reciprocity and proportionality on the other, by pointing to the fact that both processes operate on terms that can be represented by one and the same logical system of relations: the four-group.

There seems little reason to doubt the relevance of the four-group to problems of reciprocity, and, insofar as these are themselves quantified statements of reciprocities, to problems of proportionality. But the application of the same group to compound propositions, although formally irreproachable, seems, from a psychological point of view, to be largely irrelevant. In other words, there is nothing to prevent the postulation of a set of operations by which signs are altered and/or the links between elementary terms are reversed. The effect of so doing is certainly to establish a system of relations that conforms with a four-group. There is, however, little evidence to show that, when faced with real problems, a subject is more likely to shift his attention from a given propositional formulation, for example, "p v q" (implies x), to another within the same group for example, "$-p$ v $-q$", rather than any other combination, for example, p (i.e., "$(p . q)$ v $(p . -q)$"). For instance, in diagnosing the reason for the failure of an engine to start, we may consider first "fuel or ignition" and then "fuel"; we are not particularly likely to think of, "it may be either or neither but it can't be both."

Nevertheless, although Paiget is perfectly aware of the generality of logico-mathematical structures in general and of the four-group in particular (e.g., in transformations of spatial co-ordinates), in his work on formal reasoning he wrote as if what might appear to be its rather artificial application to the propositional calculus were somehow more fundamental than any other. Thus, when analysing the problem of communicating vessels, he wrote, "In such cases, the instruments necessary for thinking go beyond propositional logic to include its fundamental group **INRC**" (Inhelder & Paiget, 1955, p. 134). In terms of the argument advanced in this paper, the group structure of reciprocity derives from the physical relations involved and has little to do with their expression in propositional form, and still less with the need (if any) to impose a group structure on the propositional calculus itself.

Equally questionable, to my mind, is Paiget's attempt to identify the schema of proportionality with the four-group by accepting quantification as self-evident. The crucial argument is given on page 177 of the same work, "The possibility of reasoning in terms of a group structure—**INRC**—indicates an understanding of the equalities **NR** = **IC**, **RC** = **IN**, **NC** = **IR**, etc., the equalities between the products of two transformations. The result is that the **INRC** group is itself equivalent to a system of logical proportions:

$$\frac{\mathbf{Ix}}{\mathbf{Cx}} = \frac{\mathbf{Rx}}{\mathbf{Nx}} \text{ or } \frac{\mathbf{Rx}}{\mathbf{Ix}} = \frac{\mathbf{Cx}}{\mathbf{Nx}}$$

since **IN** = **RC** (where x = the operation transformed by **I**, **N**, **R**, or **C**)." But the equation **RC** = **IN** is the equivalent of a logical statement that the effect of applying the operator **C** to the transformation **I** (or **Ix**), and then applying the operator **R** to the resultant transformation (**C**, or **Cx**) is the same as that of first applying **I**, which leaves it unchanged since it is the identity operator, and then applying **N**, that is, **N** (or **Nx**). There is nothing in this to justify the introduction of numerical multiplication and division. It is true that both apply, but the mathematical statement in terms of proportionality is not a *mere* equivalent to the logical statement of reciprocity.

The summary of Piaget's interpretation of the character of formal reasoning and my limited criticisms of it has been based on his exposition in Inhelder & Piaget (1955). Nevertheless, in order to bring out the essentials of agreement and disagreement, it has been necessary to introduce certain modifications of emphasis. In particular, Piaget's discussion of reciprocity and proportionality is formulated wholly in terms of the four-group as applied to propositions. In other words, the various actions of the system are first translated into propositions and, only then, does Piaget seek to show that they conform to the group structure of compound propositions. We have preferred to separate the notion of a four-group in general from the two applications given in Piaget's work, taking them as parallel instead of regarding one as derivative. And our conclusion was that, whereas the four-group is inescapably bound up with the representation of reciprocal action, it is only by reason of a logician's artifice that it appears in the context of the propositional calculus. Furthermore, some difficulty has been found in accepting the mechanism of the four-group as providing an adequate account of proportional reasoning.

If this criticism is justified, however, the critic must himself accept that there remains a real problem, which is to account for the greater difficulty of the situations described in this work, and, in particular, to discover whether the two types of problem (experimental manipulation of variables, reciprocity, and proportion) share a common psychological complexity or whether each is characterised by its own peculiar complication (as would be the case if a problem were difficult simply because its solution presupposed a certain previous experience).

The matter may be put even more sharply by asking whether Piaget is justified in postulating the existence of two successive levels in the development of logical reasoning or, whether, when the child has achieved the level of "concrete" reasoning and is, therefore, capable of argument in terms of fixed (because operationally definable) terms, his reasoning is *ipso facto* logical, insofar as the problem is not unduly complex (i.e., long) and does not demand experience that he lacks. From this stage on further progress would be a matter of quantitative gains rather than a difference in type of reasoning.

VERBAL ANALOGIES AS AN INSTANCE OF FORMAL REASONING: AN EXPERIMENT

If the term "formal" has a valid scientific connotation, it must refer to a greater elaboration of the structural complexity of the reasoning process, that is, to the interconnexions in the relations that the subject must recognise in the course of his thinking, as opposed to the number of such relations or the content (terms) on which they bear. It seemed reasonable to suppose that, if it were possible to find a third group of problems that was designed to evince such a specifically structural complexity, we might be in a better position to "abstract" any feature or features that might prove common to all three.

The widespread use of verbal test items in the measurement of "intelligence" suggested such a third group of problems. The rationale underlying the construction of such items, insofar as it is not wholly empirical, derives from Spearman's (1923) analysis of reasoning as the eduction of relations and the deduction of correlates. The most typical illustration of such items is the verbal analogy. Accordingly, it was decided to use the analogy in order to construct items involving the structural complexity that seemed the essential component of adolescent reasoning. It was assumed that a simple analogy of the form, "Leather is to shoe as wool is to . . ." requires no more than "concrete" reasoning: the child simply "reads off" the relation between the first two terms and applies it to the third, so discovering (or selecting) the fourth (cf. Peel, 1960, p. 94). It was reasoned that such an item could be made more difficult in one of two ways: (a) by decreasing the familiarity (and increasing the "abstraction") of its terms, for example, "Task is to . . . as problem is to solution," or (b) by introducing greater complexity of form, for example, "Goat/cow/barn is to pig/cheese/milk as wool is to sheep," and especially in such items as "Leather is to soft/shoe/hide as hard/clay/house is to brick." The last of these demands an awareness of the direction of the relation and not merely a recognition of the relation as such.

1. The Test

Following the above considerations, it was decided to construct a test in two parts of which the first would be composed of different types of verbal analogies and the second, of numerical analogies and certain items of series-completion, both designed to elucidate further the nature of the difficulties involved in problems of proportionality.

The section on analogies was made up of 32 items that were divided into four groups as follows:

A. *Eight items of the form* "Black *is to* white *as* hard *is to* steel-stone-solid-soft-blue."—The content of these items was deliberately made relatively simple and the solution involved only one multiple choice. The number of distractors was four for all items. The nature of the relation involved, however, varied from item to item and the position of the multiple-choice term was also systematically permuted. Thus, item 7 was "Wheel-engine-hoot-four-horn is to car as bell is to bicycle."

B. *Eight items exactly parallelling those in A, but with more difficult content.*—Thus, item 13 was, "*Task* is to *attempt-completion-work-end-question* as *problem* is to *solution*," and item 15 was, "*Oval-sphere-round-ring-diameter* is to *circle* as *cube* is to *square*."

C. *Four items of the form,* "a *is to* b *as* x *is to* y," *together with four items of the form, "x is to* y *as* a *is to* b, *where* a *and* b *are given, while* x *and* y *must be selected from a multiple-choice array.*—The number of multiple choices for these terms was three for *x* and three for *y* in half the items and four for each term in the other half. Thus, item 17 was, *"Lion is to lair as set-burrow-dog is to rabbit-kennel-fox";* and item 20 was *"Sheep is to flock as herd-pack-soldier-swarm* is to *cow-bee-regiment-wolf";* and item 23 was, *"Rest-shelter-food-thirst* is to *water-hunger-house-bed* as *clothes* is to *warmth."* While even with three terms to choose from in each part of an item the number of possible combinations is nine and, therefore, greater than the five in groups A and B, it must be borne in mind that even by simple association the subject is unlikely to consider such combinations as *swarm* and *regiment* for item 20, so that the number of effective choices open is considerably less than these theoretically possible.

D. *Four items of the form, "*a *is to* x *as* y *is to* b," *together with four of the form, "*x *is to* a *as* b *is to* y."—The number of multiple-choice terms was varied as in group C. However, the distractors were so chosen that they could be combined in pairs to produce analogies that would be correct if the order of one pair of terms were inverted. Thus, item 25 was, *"Leather is to soft-shoe-hide* as *hard-clay-house* is to *brick,"* where the correct answer is *"Leather* is to *shoe* as *clay* is to *brick,"* but *"Leather* is to *hide* as *house* is to *brick"* would be correct, inverting one of these pairs, as also would *"Leather* is to *soft* as *hard* is to *brick."* Similar considerations apply, for example, to item 31, *"Tank-army-soldiers-land* is to *regiment* as *air force* is to *aeroplane-air-squadron-airman."*

This section of the test was constructed with the following hypotheses in mind:

a) It was presumed that group A analogies would be easier than those of the remaining groups. It was further presumed that the reasoning involved would be of the nature of simple classification. Hence, it was anticipated that, from the age of 9 onward, children would be able to solve such items in principle, even if adventitious factors prevented them from obtaining a perfect score on all the items.

b) It was presumed that group D analogies would be more difficult than those in the other groups. It was further presumed that the increased difficulty would result from the structural complexity of the items and, in particular, from the need to examine and test the established relations instead of merely working to them. To be more precise, it was thought that the activity of testing the several possible combinations to eliminate those that reversed the direction of the relation would imply something corresponding to a separate "monitoring" process. This separate process was envisaged as an essential element in "formal" reasoning. It was, therefore, anticipated that even at the age of 11 few children would be able to solve such items but would begin to discriminate about the age of 12 to 13.

c) It was presumed that group C analogies would require some formal qualities of reasoning insofar as they necessitated a combinatorial analysis. At the same time, considering many such combinations would not occur in practice, it was anticipated that the increase in difficulty as compared with group A was relatively slight.

d) Finally, in regard to group B analogies, it was anticipated that their solution would be more randomly distributed because of the variety of factors involved in the difficulty of the individual items (incidental knowledge, vocabulary, etc.). The average difficulty of the items was expected to fall between groups C and D.

The test also included 33 numerical items, of which 16 were numerical analogies and 17 were series to be completed. These items were included to elucidate the nature of the difficulties children experience in solving problems involving proportionality.

The numerical analogies included several variations, such as the following:

(1) items requiring mere addition or subtraction of a constant, for example, item 33,

$$
\begin{array}{cc}
3 & 1 \\
9 & 7 \\
10 & 8 \\
4 & \quad ;
\end{array}
$$

(2) items requiring multiplication by a constant whole number, for example, item 34,

$$
\begin{array}{cc}
2 & 6 \\
8 & 24 \\
4 & 12 \\
5 & \quad ;
\end{array}
$$

(3) items requiring division by a constant whole number, for example, item 38,

$$
\begin{array}{cc}
8 & 2 \\
48 & 12 \\
6 & 1\tfrac{1}{2} \\
20 & \quad ;
\end{array}
$$

(4) items involving a combination of addition or subtraction with multiplication or division, for example, item 42,

$$
\begin{array}{cc}
8 & 17 \\
4 & 9 \\
3 & 7 \\
(\tfrac{1}{2}\ (X\text{-}1)\ ) & 6 \quad ;
\end{array}
$$

(5) items involving constant exponential powers, for example, item 39,

$$
\begin{array}{cc}
5 & 125 \\
4 & 64 \\
2 & 8 \\
3 & \quad ;
\end{array}
$$

(6) items requiring multiplication by a constant proportion, for example, item 41,

$$
\begin{array}{cc}
18 & 12 \\
10\tfrac{1}{2} & 7 \\
21 & 14 \\
& 6
\end{array}
$$

Items requiring the completion of series were of the following 4 types: (7) additive series, for example, item 49, 3,6,9,12, , ; or item 50, 5, , , , , 15;

(8) serial addition and subtraction, for example, item 56: 15, 14, 12, , , 0;

(9) logarithmic series, for example, halving, item 53, 40,20,10, , , 1¼, or trebling, item 57, 1,3, , 27, 81,; and, finally,

(10) series involving a geometric increase, or proportionality, for example, item 62, 27,18,12, , 5⅓

The selection of these items was governed by the following hypotheses:

e) In spite of the fact that analogies such as items (2), 34 and (3), 38 imply a relation of proportionality between the figures in the two columns, they can be solved at a fairly elementary level, without involving a recognition of proportionality; they can be interpreted as questions of mere multiplication or division in the sense of repeated addition and subtraction rather than as questions involving a functional relation between two sets. Hence, it was anticipated that such items would prove little more difficult than questions involving mere addition or subtraction (e.g., [1], item 33), and would be answered correctly at the level of concrete reasoning, that is, about the age of 9.

f) Conversely, questions such as (6), item 41 can prove very much more difficult to the extent that they involve a functional relation of proportionality.

g) The difficulty cannot be merely a reflection of the fact that the solution of such problems involves the application of two operations (multiplication and division); it reflects the fact that the fundamental significance of the combined operations and the results is not appreciated by children with the mathematical initiation that they are given. Hence, it was anticipated that these items would prove more difficult than, for example, items such as (4), 42 and would be comparable in difficulty to items involving exponential powers.

h) By the same token, in regard to items involving series completion the order of difficulty is, additive series, serial differences, exponential series, and, most difficult, geometric series.

i) Following the widely held identification of problem-solving processes as essentially involving the recognition and closure of "gaps" between the given and the desired (cf. Bartlett, 1958, or Simon & Newell, 1962), the objective size of the gap was deliberately made largest for the easiest items to demonstrate that the number of steps involved in such closure, and, more particularly, the availability of such steps, is of greater significance than the mere size of the gap in relation to the given.

2. Subjects and Method of Presentation

The total number of subjects was 153. They were (*a*) all the boys in a small private school within the secondary-school age range and (*b*) all the boys in the two classes containing the 9+ and 11+ age groups in a one-stream-entry junior school under the Local Authority. In spite of the fact that some subjects were taken from a private and others from a state school, it is safe to assume that the sample was relatively homogeneous in respect to intelligence and background, and somewhat above the general population in both.[4] The distribution of subjects according to age is shown in the following table.

Age.....	9–10	10–11	11–12	12–13	13–14	14–15	15–16	16–17	17 and over
No. Subjects.	17	6	20	17	22	28	13	19	11

It is apparent that the most significant shortage of subjects is in the 10–11 years age group, which proved to be a weakness in the design. It should be stressed that the sole interest of the investigation was to establish a rough index of the level of difficulty of the various types of items, and to make inter-item comparisons. The absolute results can in no sense be taken as norms.

The test was presented as a group written test and was divided into two sessions for administrative convenience and to prevent fatigue. The various types of items were introduced by examples. Every subject was allowed sufficient time to complete the test.

3. Results

(*a*) *Analogies.*—Table 1 shows the gross percentages of success achieved by each age group in solving the four types of analogies.

It is apparent that the order of difficulty of the four groups of items was as predicted, although, overall, group B tended to be little easier than group D and a slightly greater difficulty at the younger ages was counter-balanced by a lesser difficulty for the older subjects. This is precisely what

---

[4] The private school catered largely to boys who, at age 11, failed to reach the examination standard required for admission to grammar school but whose parents wished them to have a fuller education and were prepared to pay for it. Since the proportion of school children admitted to grammar school is of the order of one in five, these boys were still, in the main, superior to the population average. Similarly, the junior school in question was situated in a fairly good residential area and drew its students largely from parents in superior "blue-collar" and middle- or lower-class "white-collar" occupations.

one would expect, assuming the difficulty of these items to be more the result of experience.

TABLE 1

PERCENTAGE SUCCESS IN SOLVING VERBAL AND NUMERICAL ANALOGIES

TYPE OF ANALOGY	AGE GROUP									
	9	10	11	12	13	14	15	16	17+	Over all
A	35	52	69	74	85	85	90	92	93	76
B	11	25	35	46	53	58	65	66	81	49
C	29	38	59	64	75	77	90	84	86	69
D	15	19	43	45	53	50	63	57	73	47

But what is far more significant is that the level of success reached at the age of 9 was far below the prediction, especially since the population was slightly above average in intelligence. In particular, the percentage of success for the easy analogies of group A did not even reach the halfway level until the 10-year age group (which was too small to be very indicative) and did not markedly exceed it until the 11-year age group.

With regard to the principal hypotheses advanced in the preceding section, (a) and (b), the important question is whether, in the light of the results obtained, successful solution of the group A analogies could be taken as indicative of concrete reasoning, while success in group D would indicate a change in the mode of reasoning, that is, reasoning at the formal level.

In order to decide this problem, it is not sufficient to consider the overall percentage of successes at each age level. Since what is at issue is the question of whether the subject is capable of the *type of reasoning* necessary to solve such problems, while the method of testing, involving a selection from multiple-choice arrays, allows a certain amount of freedom for success through guessing or chance, we need some criterion index to indicate that the subject is, in principle, capable of solving the type of problem. Since the eight questions of group A were approximately equal in difficulty (apart from item 1, in which the most obvious association was also the true answer), it was decided to adopt as the criterion the correct solution of at least five out of the eight items by any given subject. Insofar as section D was concerned, the problem of finding a criterion was somewhat complicated by the fact that a number of items were found to include a component of contextual difficulty, while at least two were unsuitable because the solution was not unambiguous. Accordingly, it was decided to select the four easiest items of this group, all of which incorporated the desired structural difficulty and were unambiguous in respect to the correct answer, and to take as criterion that any subject who gave the correct answer to any three of these four items could be regarded as capable of the higher-order reasoning involved. The four items were

"*Nephew* is to *brother-boy-aunt-cousin* as *sister-niece-man-aunt* is to *uncle*,"
"*Milk-calf-large* is to *cow* as *lamb* is to *wool-small-sheep*,"

"*Walk-toe-foot* is to *body* as *wheel* is to *bicycle-roll-machine*," and
"*Tank-army-soldiers-land* is to *regiment* as *air force* is to *aeroplane-air-squadron-airman*."

If we take these as criteria for ability to solve elementary and more complex analogies, the facts appear unambiguous. At the age of 9, that is, when concrete modes of reasoning may be taken to be well established, only 3 of the 17 subjects, or 18 per cent, reached the criterion for group A; at age 10 (with only 6 subjects), the figure reached 33 per cent; but by the age of 11, 16 out of 20, or 80 per cent, reached the same criterion. Thereafter, there is a gradual rise that is of far less importance. When we apply our chosen criterion to group D, we find once again that 8 out of 17, at age 11, 45 per cent, attained the even stricter criterion of 3 out of 4 (with the distractors carefully chosen to fulfil the requirements of analogy apart from direction). Moreover, since the over-all facility level of these questions is, in any case, well below that of group A, the rise in percentage meeting the criterion was only gradual after the age of 11, so that even at 15+ only 75 per cent of the subjects reached this level.

We are forced to conclude that the elementary analogies of group A represent something more than mere concrete reasoning. Indeed, the steep rise that occurs after the age of 10 strongly suggests that these problems involve a type of reasoning, that is, formal reasoning, that is not present at the earlier level and is only elaborated about the age of 11. This is further borne out by the fact that although there are differences in the facility levels between group A and the remaining groups, and the differences are all in the expected direction, even as early as age 11 nearly 50 per cent of the subjects proved able to cope with the structural complexity of group D analogies.

(*b*) *Numerical Analogies and Series.* Table 2 shows the gross percentage of successful answers given at each age level to the two categories of items.

TABLE 2

PERCENTAGE SUCCESS IN SOLVING NUMERICAL ANALOGIES AND
IN COMPLETION OF NUMERICAL SERIES

	AGE GROUP									
	9	10	11	12	13	14	15	16	17+	Over all
Numerical Analogies........	12	23	47	47	69	65	85	78	87	59
Series completion..	25	23	49	42	64	60	67	73	71	55

Both tabulations show a general tendency of percentage scores to increase with age, with the sharpest rise occurring between 9 and 11. There are several exceptions to this, as a result, no doubt, of sampling error, but the over-all tendency is sufficiently clear. Somewhat more significant, because less obvious a priori, is the fact that, whereas the level of success for numerical analogies is less high initially, the final level is consistently higher than it is for series completion. This suggests that, whereas there were several items of series completion that presented little difficulty for the youngest subjects, few of the analogies were in this category; conversely, while there were several items of series completion that continued to present difficulty throughout the age range, there were few such analogies. The discussion of the second argument will be postponed until the relative difficulty of the various types of items have been examined. The first argument is illustrated in Table 3.

TABLE 3

NUMBER OF ITEMS SOLVED BY AT LEAST 40 PER CENT OF
SUBJECTS IN 4 LOWEST AGE GROUPS

	AGE GROUP			
	9–10	10–11	11–12	12–13
Numerical analogies........	0	1	7	8
Series completion..........	4	3	10	8

Nearly a quarter of the 17 series-completion items falls into this category, but none of the numerical analogies.

This finding reinforces the conclusions reached in the preceding subsection: Analogies, whether verbal or numerical, demand a more complex process of reasoning than is available at the concrete level; this is not true, however, of the easiest forms of series completion.

The main interest in this section of the test, however, lies in the light that it throws on the relative difficulty of the various types of items, with particular reference to those involving the notion of numerical proportionality. In Table 4 are given the over-all facility levels (gross percentages of successful solutions by the sample as a whole) for each item in some of several types. In each case, the levels are arranged in descending order. The actual

TABLE 4

OVER-ALL FACILITY LEVELS

TYPE	PERCENTAGE
(a) Numerical analogies:	
Addition or subtraction of a constant.................	87, 73, 59
Multiplication by a constant whole....................	79, 73
Division by a constant whole.........................	86, 77
Combined addition or subtraction with	
multiplication or division.........................	54, 43
Exponential powers.................................	77, 46, 28
Proportional functions..............................	42, 42, 40, 31
(b) Series completion:	
Additive series.....................................	94, 94, 79, 73
Doubling and halving...............................	82, 75, 75
Trebling and quadrupling...........................	52, 46,
Serial differences...................................	58, 58, 45
Geometrical increase................................	28, 23, 21, 19, 16

number of percentages following each category simply indicates how many items were included in this compilation. Thus, there were three analogies involving addition or subtraction of a constant, two for multiplication by a constant whole, and so on.

The specific difficulty of items that involved an explicit recognition of proportionality is borne out by both sets of data. The prediction that analogies involving multiplication or division by a constant whole would be little more difficult than those involving addition of a constant is likewise shown to be correct—in spite of the fact that, from a strictly logical point of view, such items do involve a relation of proportionality, even if it is not recognised by the subject. Moreover, from the fact that series completion involving serial differences proved far easier than the geometric series, it appears that the difficulty of the latter is not the result only of the fact that the solutions necessitated the successive application of two mathematical operations. It is not without interest that even the analogies involving a combination of addition and multiplication were consistently easier for the subjects than those involving a ratio (although the differences were too slight to be significant).

Finally, the suggestion that the objective extent of the "gap" in an item requiring "closure" is a relatively unimportant factor in determining the difficulty of the problem, is sufficiently attested by the facility levels of the following illustrative items:-

Item 50.	5,	,	,	,	,15	$F = 73$
Item 54.	4,	, 12,	,	,24		$F = 79$
Item 60.	16, 24, 36, 54,			,121½		$F = 19$
Item 62.	27, 18, 12,	,5¼				$F = 23$
Item 61.	48, 24,	,	,3, ,¾			$F = 75$

4. *Discussion.* It is apparent that, although the order of difficulty of the four types of verbal analogy was as predicted, the essential thesis of (*a*) and (*b*), that type A analogies would be soluble at the level of concrete reasoning and type D analogies only at the formal level, is not borne out. The outstanding finding is that even the easiest verbal analogies of this form are beyond children at the concrete level of reasoning. The implication that such problems require a different type of reasoning, that is, formal reasoning, is borne out by the comparatively small difference found between the levels of facility of these various kinds of items.

These facts suggest the following interpretation: The error of the original hypotheses lies in the assumption that, when completing such an analogy, the subject can "read off" a relation between the first two terms and apply it. In order to "read" the relation, he must first abstract it from a number of possible relations and then confirm it in the possible solution to the second half of the analogy. Thus, an analogy of the form, *leather* is to *shoe* as *wool* is to *cardigan*, necessarily involves three relations: one between the first two terms, a second between the second pair of terms, and, finally, a third (of identity) between the first two relations. In point of fact, the logical structure of such a system exactly parallels that of a statement of proportionality. This is illustrated in Figures 1 and 2.

LEATHER	SHOE	3	4
WOOL	CARDIGAN	15	20

FIGURE 1   FIGURE 2

In Figure 1, the second-order relation of identity that subsists between the relations that unite the terms in the rows ensures a similar second-order relation of identity between the first-order relations uniting the terms in the columns: Here, leather and wool are united by their common membership in a class (raw materials), while shoe and cardigan are likewise members of a class of the same order (wearing apparel). This structure is exactly parallel to the proportionality in Figure 2,

$$3 \, : \, 4 \, = \, 15 \, : \, 20 \quad \text{and} \quad 3 \, : \, 15 \, = \, 4 \, : \, 20.$$

According to Piaget, the essential operations of concrete reasoning are those of classification and seriation (Inhelder & Piaget, 1959) and their effect is to establish precise relations between terms that are physical objects. From the first section, we may recall that the term "precise" is to be understood in the sense that such relations are definable in terms of a systematic ordering of potential actions which the subject can perform upon these elementary terms. When such relations are established they can be further applied to similar terms, and this explains why a number of items involving series completion present little difficulty at the concrete level since they involve only a continuation of a first-order relation, for example, repeated addition of a constant number. However, when the relations to be established in the first instance are not elementary in character, this mode of presentation no longer facilitates solution and may even make it more difficult, because each term in the series is presented once only while the structure of the series is such that two relations are implied, one with the preceding term and one with the following:

$$a \, : \, b \, : : \, b \, : \, c \, : : \, c \, : \, d, \text{ etc.}$$

Thus, the results of the present enquiry suggest the revised hypothesis that the familiar verbal analogies, as used in intelligence tests, require formal reasoning in the sense that their solution demands the apprehension of second-order relations, or relations between relations, and not merely first-order relations, which are relations between objects. As this conclusion has been reached *post hoc,* it must remain a hypothesis. On the other hand, the fact that numerical analogies present a similar difficulty at ages 9 and 10, while certain numerical series do not, may be taken as some confirmation. Also in line with the hypothesis, is the fact that in the case of verbal analogies children in these age groups are, in general, content to establish a satisfactory first-order relation in selecting the missing term. This explains why item 1 (BLACK is to WHITE as HARD is to STEEL/STONE/SOLID/SOFT/BLUE, solved by 15 out of 17 subjects at age 9) and item 8 (FORK/EYE/LOOK/SHARP/SAW) is to SEE as KNIFE is to CUT, solved by 9 subjects in the same group) were the only analogies in which more than 50 per cent of the 9-year-olds were successful. In the first case, the opposites *hard-soft* formed the most convincing first-order relation even independently of *black-white,* while in the second the concept of an eye as a tool for seeing is such that it would make this analogy one of the most difficult instead of the second easiest; but the first-order association *eye-see* is almost certainly stronger than any of the alternatives offered, so younger subjects accept it and ignore the complication of *knife-cut.*

Except insofar as part of our hypothesis (*e*) reflects the same error as our first hypothesis (*a*), the second group of hypotheses (*e*)–(*i*) is fully confirmed. Since many of the series items and all of the numerical analogies should be taken as problems involving formal reasoning, if the foregoing argument is correct, the question remains why problems involving proportional relations present an added difficulty. The reality of these difficulties is sufficiently clear from a comparison of the over-all facility levels given in the preceding section. It is further emphasized by the breakdown in Table 5, which gives the facility levels of six items involving proportionality at four different age levels.

TABLE 5

Facility of Six Items Involving Proportionality at Ages 9, 11, 13, and 15

	Age Group			
Item[a]	9	11	13	15
41 (NA)	12	20	41	69
44 (NA)	12	30	50	69
47 (NA)	6	25	36	54
46 (NA)	6	40	50	62
59 (S)	0	30	45	58
62 (S)	0	25	32	37

[a](NA) indicates numerical analogy; (S) indicates series.

It was suggested earlier that the fundamental significance of proportional functions and their numerical expression as a combination of multiplication and division tends to elude children for a long time. The reason may be that, when multiplication is first introduced in schools, there is a strong temptation for the teacher to stress that form of the operation that corresponds to repeated addition, since this is easier for children to grasp and also assists in the building of understanding of tables of multiplication. The multiplicand is here seen as an integral whole, and the function of the multiplier is to specify "how many times" this is to be added. In the application of mathematics to science, it is the second form of multiplication that assumes especial significance. Here the multiplicand is seen as a set of units, and the function of the multiplier is to specify a functional relation between each unit and a corresponding (multiple) unit in the quotient. Thus $a \times b$ may be read as, "Repeat a, b times over," but it may also be read as, "For every unit in a, take b units." In this second form, the inverse relation between multiplication and division ("For every b units, take 1") is more immediately apparent. Whether or not this represents a general criticism of arithmetical teaching, it seems reasonable to suppose that the notions of fractions and proportional ratios should be easier to attain to the extent that the relation between multiplication and division is adequately demonstrated in the early stages of learning.

CONCLUSIONS

In view of the extended discussion of concrete and formal reasoning in the first three sections, this one may be brief. In the first section the evidence in favour of the characterisation of concrete reasoning as a unitary process was reviewed and, in accepting its cogency, an interpretation of concrete reasoning was advanced that stressed the development of an ability to construct precise relations that were defined in terms of an ordering of potential actions. In the second and third sections the evidence in favour of positing a parallel underlying unity for processes termed "formal", was considered. While it was easy to identify certain essential features that were involved in the experimental manipulation of variables and the solution of problems involving reciprocal and proportional relations, the question of whether the two groups of problems were further united by a common dimension of complexity was left open. In particular, some doubt was cast on Piaget's own identification of problems involving reciprocity as implying a particular set of relations between *propositions*.

In the fourth section, certain additional evidence obtained from a test designed to bring out the qualities of formal reasoning in the context of verbal and numerical test items was presented. The main conclusion seemed to be that both verbal and numerical analogies required the application of formal reasoning in the sense that the subject needed to establish second-order relations. These findings suggest a general answer to the question left open in the third section.

If the general characteristics of formal reasoning are to be found in the need to elaborate these second-order relations, then it should be possible to trace their relevance to the solution of the two types of problems investigated by Inhelder and Piaget. As to problems of reciprocity and proportionality, the existence of such relations is already clear. Thus, in the first place, it has already been shown that the structure of verbal analogies is identical with that of numerical proportions, while, in the second place, Piaget's demonstration of the relevance of the four-group to problems of reciprocity may be accepted as convincing proof that an understanding of the play of forces in this type of situation requires that the subject reason in terms of

second-order relations such as is implied by the equation IN = RC. Nothing
that was said earlier should be taken as a contradiction of the relevance of
the four-group to these problems; the only point of divergence between the
view put forward here and that advanced by Piaget is concerned with the
question of its application to a calculus of propositions. But problems requiring the experimental manipulation of variables by the method of "all
other things equal" can also be seen as problems that involve second-order
relations. For, as we recalled in the third section, although the mere statement of the proposition "p implies q," or "x is caused by y" does not involve
more than the recognition of primary, first-order relations between terms that
are physical objects or events, the experimental verification of the statement
implies the recognition of what are, in fact, second-order relations between
itself and analogous statements such as "p implies r" (or "x is caused by z"),
etc. More especially, in order to be able to set up an experiment to verify a
hypothesis in this form, the subject must have established second-order relations of consistency or inconsistency between the relation expressed and the
conjunctions of circumstances envisaged in the verification (p and q, not
$-p$ and q, etc.). To put it another way, the experimental verification of a
hypothesis "p and q" entails a recognition of the second-order relation "(p
implies q) implies (not $-q$ implies not $-p$)," that is, however strong the
combination of events in favour of p, it follows from the circumstance that
all the remaining variables are the same as when p was consistently observed, the fact of not $-q$ means that p will not be observed—or the
hypothesis is weakened.

The identification of formal reasoning with the recognition of second-
order relations represents no great departure from a view frequently expressed by Piaget. Thus, he writes (1949, p.15), "[The older child] converts
concrete operations to propositions. They are propositions because they are
not entertained as mere hypotheses. He will thus compose these hypotheses by means of second-order operations such as implication, incompata-
bility, and so on" (our translation), and (Inhelder & Piaget, 1955, p. 254),
"Obviously this notion of second-degree operations also expresses the general
characteristic of formal thought—it goes beyond the framework of transformations bearing directly on empirical reality (first-degree operations)
and subordinates it to a system of hypothetic-deductive operations—i.e.
operations which are *possible*." There is no material difference implied in the
use of the term "relations" in preference to "operations." For, in a system of
transformations linked by precise relations, operations simply represent the
actions or "moves" whereby transitions are effected from one state to another
in accordance with these relations. The term "relations" has been preferred
because it may correspond more closely to the subject's own intuition of the
variables.

It would appear that the simple verbal analogy and numerical proportion provide the clearest model of what is intended, because other psychological factors, such as, number of terms (and, hence, absolute length in the

chain of reasoning), and credibility of alternatives (as distinct from their logical necessity) are minimal.

If this interpretation is correct, however, it would follow that the essential feature of formal reasoning, recognition of second-order relations, appears considerably earlier than is usually allowed, that is, by the age of 11 or 12 (allowing for some bias in our sampling), which is the age given by Piaget as marking the beginning of formal reasoning. Yet careful repetitions of Inhelder's experiments carried out both in Leeds (Lovell, 1961) and Manchester (Jackson, 1965) confirm the much later solution of these problems (mean ages of 13, 14, and 15 for 50 per cent solution being the rule). The comparatively small increase in difficulty between simple verbal analogies in the present investigation and the structurally elaborate analogies suggests that the difficulty of problems at the secondary level should not be measured solely or even mainly in terms of structure.

In the comparison of the difficulty of such problems as "the pendulum" and "movement on an inclined plane," the enquiry already mentioned points to the far greater ease of the latter. From the structural point of view, the two are identical. What is significant is that logical necessity and initial credibility go hand in hand in the second experiment while in the first they are contradictory. A similar argument would account for the resistances encountered in the solution of problems of "false conservation" (Lunzer, 1965). Such an emphasis on *content* as opposed to *structure* finds less support in the works of Piaget,[5] but seems to be required by the facts.

It is clear that the foregoing discussion leaves many problems unsolved. In spite of the recognition of a more or less clear-cut distinction between "concrete" and "formal" reasoning, the transition from one to the other demands elucidation. How far are problems of the analogies variety made easier by preparation for standardised tests?[6] How far may we expect "transfer" of the recognition of second-order relations from one type of situation to another? Such questions can only be answered by further research. But the progressive recognition of distinct factors in the difficulties that may occur in the acquisition of scientific and other concepts should suggest valid techniques for use in the field of education. Among these distinctions, we should include complexity of structure, familiarity with terms, number of terms, and, above all, consonance or dissonance with previously existing notions (credibility).

---

[5] Cf., Inhelder & Piaget (1959), p. 113. "the development of concrete operations, *unlike that of at least the more elementary formal operations* can never be dissociated from the intuitive content to which such operations need to be applied" (translation and italics ours).

[6] The difficulty of these problems for children before the age of 11 is, however, supported by the findings of Burt, cited by Watts (1944), pp. 206–207.

REFERENCES

Bartlett, F. *Thinking, an experimental and social study.* London: Allen & Unwin, 1958.

Braine, M. D. S. Piaget on reasoning: a methodological critique and alternative proposals. In W. Kessen and C. Kuhlman (Eds.), Thought in the young child. *Monogr. Soc. Res. in Child Develpm.*, 1962, **27**, No. 2, 41–61.

Inhelder, B., & Piaget, J. *De la logique de l'enfant à logique de l'adolescent.* Paris: Presses Univer. de France, 1955. (*The growth of logical thinking from childhood to adolescence.* New York: Basic Books, 1958.)

Inhelder, B., & Piaget, J. *La gènese des structures logiques élémentaires: classification et seriations.* Neuchâtel: Delachaux and Niestlé, 1959.

Jackson, S. Master's thesis. Manchester Univer. (in progress), 1965.

Lovell, K. A. follow-up study of Inhelder & Piaget's *The growth of logical thinking. Brit. J. Psychol.*, 1961, **52**, 143–153.

Lunzer, E. A. *Recent studies in Britain based on the work of Jean Piaget.* Natl. Found. Educ. Res., Occ. Publ. No. 4, London, 1961.

Lunzer, E. A. Les coordinations et les conservations dans le domaine de la geometrie. *Études d'épistemologie génétique* (in press), 1965.

Peel, E. A. *The pupil's thinking.* London: Oldbourne Press, 1960.

Piaget, J. *Le development de la notion de temps chez l'enfant.* Paris: Presses Univer. de France, 1946. (a)

Piaget, J. *Les notions de mouvement et de vitesse chez l'enfant.* Paris: Presses Univer. de France, 1946. (b)

Piaget, J. *Traité de logique.* Paris: Colin, 1949.

Piaget, J. Logique et équilibre dans les comportements du sujet. In L. Apostel et al., *Logique et équilibre* ("Études d'épistemologie génétique," Vols **2**). Paris: Presses Univer. de France, 1957, 27–117.

Piaget, J., & Inhelder, B. *Le developement des quantities chez l'enfant.* Neuchâtel; Delachaux et Niestlé, 1941.

Piaget, J., & Inhelder, B. *La representation de l'éspace chez l'enfant.* Paris: Presses Univer. de France, 1948. (*The child's conception of space.* New York: Humanities Press, 1956.)

Piaget, J., Inhelder, B., & Szeminska, A. *La geometrie spontanee chez l'enfant.* Paris: Presses Univer. de France, 1948. (*The child's conception of geometry.* London: Routledge & Kegan Paul, 1952.)

Piaget, J., & Szeminska, A. *La gènese du nombre chez l'enfant.* Neuchâtel: Delachaux et Niestlé, 1941. (*The child's conception of number.* London: Routledge & Kegan Paul, 1952.)

Simon, H. A., & Newell, A., Computer simulation of human thinking and problem solving. In W. Kessen and C. Kuhlman (Eds.), Thought in the young child, *Monogr. Soc. Res. Child Develpm.*, 1962, **27**, No. 2, 137–150.

Spearman, C. The nature of intelligence and the principles of cognition. London: Macmillan Co., 1923.

Watts, A. F. The language and mental development of children. London: George G. Harrap & Co., 1944.

3

THE EVOLUTION OF THOUGHT:
SOME APPLICATIONS OF RESEARCH FINDINGS
TO EDUCATIONAL PRACTICE

Alina Szeminska

University of Warsaw

Before I turn to the substance of my report, I would like to thank you very warmly for the invitation to attend this symposium. It seems to me that it is extremely useful to hold discussions on the evolution of thought with specialists from different countries. Certainly, an exchange of views on research, methods, and theoretical conceptions will be of great value to each of us. Let me, therefore, congratulate you for having taken the initiative in organizing such a meeting.

I am somewhat uneasy about speaking before you. As you know, the tempo of research and publication is not the same for all of us. Internationally, we get to know of each other's research relatively late so that it is entirely possible that the problems central to my research already have been studied elsewhere. To my mind, however, this is one of the purposes of our meeting: to take note of the problems with which each of us is concerned and of the methods we are using to find solutions.

I have based my research on Jean Piaget's theory of the evolution of thought. His conception of the role and development of the operational system is sufficiently known among you so that I can dispense with discussing it in detail here. I would like, however, to emphasize the great value of his methodical research which has . permitted us to go beyond mere static descriptions of the different developmental stages and show their functional significance.

The great variety of research carried on in Geneva, and also repeated in our laboratories, is sufficient confirmation of the existence of the developmental stages and of the characteristic structure of each. The studies in mathematical reasoning and elementary physics, and the experiments in classification, seriation, and induction, have clearly shown the same regularity of structure, sequence, and their transformation throughout the evolution of thought. The elementary schemas become more mobile, acquire a higher level of inner organization, and become, at the end of the evolution, operational systems (groups or lattices).

But this conception of the evolving stages of thought, however fruitful it may be theoretically, has led, it seems to me, to a serious misunderstanding.

By oversimplification, the appearance of the structures that are characteristic of the successive stages have been related directly to precise ages. I hope I do not alter the major ideas of the operational theory when I hold that the ages indicated in the studies of the Geneva school clearly demonstrate the regularity of the successive stages; at the same time, however, the relation between the level of thought and age is much more complicated. The mechanism of *décalages*—shifts within the same or to different levels of functioning—is, I believe, too often neglected by those who interpret the results of the research. Moreover, I believe that the mechanism has still not been studied in depth.

Vertical décalages seem to be linked with age very much more than horizontal décalages. Children of the same age can be found at different levels of functioning within the sensorimotor, practical, or, ultimately, verbal level of development. This led to the formulation of the more general stages of thought: sensorimotor, intuitive, concrete operational, and, finally, formal thought.

But, in addition, Piaget speaks of horizontal décalages: The same child can show different levels depending upon the contents of his thinking. The experiments of Inhelder and Piaget on the development of the notion of conservation of quantities have clearly demonstrated this type of décalage. What is especially important is that, the sequence of development being constant, there is a lag in the formation of the operational stage when the content requires a greater complexity of relations to overcome perceptual or representational obstacles. I believe that décalages are also a result of the influence of other factors such as language and acquired knowledge and the type of activity in which the subject has acquired them.

It seems to us that this problem is important both for the genetic theory of thought and for practical applications. We would like to know how to choose teaching materials in order to activate the development of thought. The basic problem that we are posing is: taking into account the laws of evolution, how can we analyze the conditions or, better, the factors, that stimulate the passage from an elementary to a higher level? The first group of research to be reported consists of the comparison of curves of evolution for the solution of different problems by children of different ages. The problems were first differentiated by the type of mental activity necessary for the solution, such as the definition of the concepts of classification, comparison, explanation, and co-ordination of the relations.

These diverse activities are being studied in relation to different contents, for example, the classification of objects for everyday use, geometric forms, pictures of varied content, and, finally, verbal classification pertaining to ideas in different fields (biology, geometry, grammar, history, and geography). So, too, causal thought was concerned either with current events of life or with facts which the child learned during his classes in biology, history, physics, or geography.

A third distinction of the problems concerns the processes by which the solution can be attained: manipulation, verbal reasoning based on facts directly perceived, or, finally, abstract reasoning.

These researches are actually under way, and in various more or less advanced stages, but all seem to prove that the progress of thought depends on the factors mentioned above.

I would like, first of all, to report briefly on the results of the development of the process of conceptualization.

In an excellent study on the genesis of elementary structures, Inhelder and Piaget have shown how the elementary figural collections are transformed stage by stage and acquire class structure, thanks to the factor of growing mobility of thought.

I have tried to study the functions of the various structures as schemas of assimilation. Since adults assimilate reality to clearly hierarchical conceptual schemas, one can, then, ask the question: when and under what conditions does the child use the concept as a schema of assimilation? I will begin with a situation that is somewhat artificial but that can lead the subject to become aware of a certain aspect of reality. The child is placed before a bag filled with many different objects. He is given no instructions other than the statement, "See what is in the bag!" In observing subjects from 2 to 16 years, one discovers a very clear difference in their attitudes to this situation. Curiously, although the subjects have not received instructions to classify, they begin to sort out the contents; but their behaviour depends upon the structure of the schemas that they are using to assimilate reality. The little 2-year olds begin my manipulating some object that they have drawn from the bag; the next object is included in this motor activity which is transformed by the addition of the new object (accommodation). These sensorimotor schemas give place to the representational-symbolic schemas, which are entirely subjective and are characteristic of the 3- and 3½-year age group. The object drawn from the bag actualizes in the child a representative schema, from which he interprets the next object he removes or, still more frequently, he announces in advance what he would like to take out of the bag in order to "complete" his subjective schema and then, not finding the desired object, utilizes any other object as a symbol. For example, having taken out a little chair, the child announces, "I need a person," but, searching in the bag, he finds a block; he puts it in the chair and says, "There, a man is sitting down." Toward the age of 5, the behaviour changes under the influence of language, which begins to play a fundamental role. The majority of children at this age (79 per cent) only give the name of each object without trying to relate it to the others. Older children, however, are no longer satisfied with such individual identification. The statement, "See what is in the bag!" is sufficient to start them classifying. After having begun, like the younger ones, to name the objects in the order that they appear out of the bag, they try to group them. Some of the children (about 80 per cent of the 9-year olds) observe that "everything is mixed up," and this chaos prevents them from "seeing what is in the bag." So they begin by relating the various objects. In children up to the ages of 6 to 7, the "functional" relations are dominant and the connection between objects is somewhat direct (pencil with paper, doll with nursing bottle, knife with apple). With age, the extension of the schemas is increased. A greater number of the different objects are put together because they are linked in a situation through the same usage or a common position. The subjects try to give a common name to these groupings, referring to them by usage (i.e., "this is for playing," "this is for eating") or by their location in space (i.e., "this belongs in the street," "in the garden," etc.). It is only among 9- or 10-year-olds that one observes a still-increasing frequency of conceptual grouping of the contents of the bag.

In children about the age of 15 we have been able to observe in this experiment a strong tendency to fit all the material into a system of encased classes (*embôitment*), although no assignment was given to do so.

In the experiments in which an assignment to classify objects is given, the stage of conceptual classification is reached sooner. To estimate the level, we analyzed the processes of our subjects by taking account of links among the elements put together, the choice of elements, the relations among the established groups, and, finally, what I call the attitude toward the material. The youngest subjects were not interested in the material as a whole; they put together the objects as they went along and as they saw them, forgetting what they had seen just before; while the older children started out by examining everything, anticipated in advance the possibilities of classification, and went back each time to verify a new class in relation to all the others previously established.

In considering all the different aspects of the subjects' activities, we were able to distinguish six stages, as follows:

Stage I.—Assimilation to subjective schemas, construction of isolated pairs without any concern for relations between the pairs. The choice of the elements depends on the schema constructed with the first element; the following element is interpreted as a function of this schema which leads to a subjective deformation of the selected objects (symbols).

Stage II.—Beginning of generalization without anticipation and without reversibility; construction of long chains of pairs linked by differing bonds.

Stage III.—Beginning of reversibility which still remains partial (incomplete). Unification of the criteria comes afterward. Concrete situations, the common usage, or the accustomed location of the objects, are frequently chosen as criteria.

Stage IV.—Beginning of anticipation. The link is still preconceptual, because even when the subjects express a concept verbally they choose elements that are linked by more elementary bonds between them. For example, they say, "I will take animals," but they choose only zoo animals or farm animals.

Stage V.—Conceptual schemas, anticipation of the whole class, including its extension, with reversibility within the class, but without trying to co-ordinate the different classes.

Stage VI.—Coordinated anticipation with complete reversibility. Search for a hierarchical system of classes.

By following the indices given above, we were able to observe a progression of stages. At the same time, however, the curves of evolution were very different depending upon the material given for classification. For example, with geometric forms in three sizes and four colors, we obtained at the age of 5 to 6, 100 per cent of Stage V conceptualization; the same was true for material composed of common objects (food, toys, miniature vehicles, etc.). However, in the classification of irregular forms or images evoking many functional schemas, among which a choice was necessary, the conceptual stage was reached later, about the age of 13 to 14.

In order to see to what extent the conceptual structures function as assimilation schemas and are, thus, the instruments by which reality is organized, we experimented with free association, according to Busemann's test, and with associations elicited by Zeigarnik's method. When the subject free associated as rapidly as possible, he enumerated the words in a certain order. The sequence of words showed to what degree they were grouped in well defined concepts or linked by some other schemas. It was only toward 13–14 years of age that conceptual groups began to dominate (77.4 per cent), at 8 years of age the conceptual schemas played a minimal role (4.4 per cent). The intermediate ages gave results that indicated a constant progression from the functional to the conceptual schemas.

In the experiments of elicited associations, we observed the same evolution, but it was less regular, because of differences resulting from the specificity of the stimulus words. The older the children, the more frequently was the response word linked to the stimulus word by a conceptual association. At 8 years, 9 per cent; at 10 years, 42 per cent; and at 14 years, 57 per cent of responses could be considered encasement (embôitment).

All the results prove that there are *décalages* as a result of the differences in content to which the conceptual structure must be applied and, also, of the differences according to the type of activity in which the structure must function (identifying what is in the bag, classifying, responding with words as quickly as possible, and free associating). We could also pick other activities such as comparison or definition, which we are now beginning to study from the same point of view. One can say, then, that, even when children possess an instrument of thought (a given structure), they do not always use it. The question arises, therefore: Is it possible to induce the function of advanced structures at an age when the child still does not utilize it voluntarily? Some experiments seem to show that it is possible. In testing the same children with a series of classification tests (varying the material as well as the assignment) we were able to stimulate the conceptual schemas by following a certain order in tests (beginning with the easiest and gradually increasing the difficulty, i.e., the complexity, of the material) but this was successful only from the age of 8 on.

In other research we have also seen that the same child may be found to have reached different levels of development depending on the type of problem. Thus, my assistant, Jurkowski, in his study of reasoning by anal-

ogy, has observed décalage according to the relations necessary for completion. He constructed some matrices similar to Ravens' that were composed of
elements among which the following relations existed: whole to the part of
the whole, causality, opposition, and categorization. The increase of correct
responses and the improvement in the explanations that the subjects gave
were different for each of the relations.

In a study on the understanding and usage of conjunctions, we also
observed décalages according to the different relations expressed by the
conjunctions.

It is still not possible to give a definitive interpretation of why certain
relations are easier than others, although additional research may clarify the
problem. I want to stress, nevertheless, that the increasing reversibility of
development and the schemas of the higher levels do not function identically
in all situations and that the same child may be found at different stages
depending on the problem.

For each problem taken separately, we find always a diminution of
responses characteristic of the lower stages and an increase of responses with
age indicating the higher stages. But the average age for transition to a more
advanced stage varies with the problem.

Moreover, in analyzing the curves showing the progress of the subjects, we were interested to see that for certain problems there were some
very sharp increases and sometimes, also, decreases, of the evolution curve
for the older groups. This observation suggested the hypothesis that the
cause might be found in the influence of school-teaching (the contents of
syllabuses as well as teaching methods). This influence is reciprocal in the
sense that, on the one hand, acquisition of knowledge depends on the intellectual instruments possessed by the pupils but, on the other hand, thought
develops precisely as a function of the process of acquisition of knowledge, which stimulates and necessitates certain intellectual operations. In
order to study the question, we began to analyze the syllabuses and textbooks used in different elementary classes as well as the protocols kept during lessons. It was necessary, in the first place, to see if the different material taught in successive classes made equal demands on the different
cognitive processes.

Three large groups were distinguished in the analysis, as follows:

1. Problems and the exposition of new information related to reality actually
perceived, reasoning according to the perceived facts, and practical manipulation.
We were able to distinguish the following processes in this group:
   a. static description of the data—verbalization of what is perceived;
   b. description of a process while observing the event;
   c. comparison—measurement;
   d. classification;
   e. forming the relation;
   f. generalization through induction;
   g. explanation—the causal relation among the perceived facts;
   h. formulation of the laws after experimentation, prediction of effects.

2. Problems and information that call for memorization concern:

    a. verbal description without demonstration;
    b. names;
    c. definitions—it was necessary to use definitions taken from the textbooks or given by the teacher;
    d. dates, places;
    e. laws, rules;
    f. processes utilized in the solution of certain problems.

3. Problems and information that stimulate and require formal reasoning, conceptual thought:

    a. definition of concepts, classification;
    b. comparison of ideas, of events;
    c. explanation using operations with formal propositions;
    d. argumentation by deduction.

Without going into detail, we can point out that the processes in which memory is essential are still predominant in school. Even in the case where a new idea, rule, or law is introduced by reference to perceived facts, in the course of experiments, the pupil is influenced by the teacher's or textbook's formulation of the problem; he tries to reproduce what he has learned through memory and not by reasoning. Let us give only a few statistics on the types of questions asked by the teacher during lessons in grammar (of the native language), history, geography, and biology, in the fourth and seventh years of school.

Questions involving memory (What do you call . . . ? Give the definition of. . . . Specify the place or time . . . , etc.):

Class 4	90 per cent
Class 7	66 per cent

Questions involving reasoning (What are the differences . . . ? Why can one say that . . . ? What would happen if . . . ? What is the relation between . . . ? etc.).

Class 4	10 per cent
Class 7	34 per cent

In the first four grades (children from 7 to 11 years of age), teaching is based on the intuitive method, in which recourse to perception, or at least to the representation of past experiences, is the rule. But, for the most part (in about 68 per cent of the instances), descriptions and statistical analyses of what is perceived are given. Comparisons are rarely made (19 per cent), while experimentation with induction of causal laws do not account for more than 13 per cent.

From the fifth grade on, teaching relies more and more on abstract reasoning. In physics and chemistry alone the use of experiments is more frequent. The pupil must very often resolve problems dealing with abstract concepts that he has learned verbally and memorized. He is obliged to use formal operations without having had, in the preceding period, the opportunity to learn how to construct concrete operational structures. This explains the great difficulty encountered by some students in the upper grades.

The subjects in these classes are often handicapped in facing problems that younger students will try to attack by using concrete operations. So they give more frequent responses of "I do not know," and "I have not learned that yet," or they try to apply memorized material without comprehension and often inadequately to the problem.

Here is an example of research that illustrates this point:

The experiment involved the principle of conservation of energy. The apparatus consisted of a frame from which were suspended on strings of equal length six steel balls, equal in weight and volume. In the idle state, the balls were in a horizontal line and fitted tightly against each other (see Fig. 1).

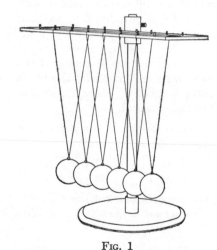

Fig. 1

If the first ball in line was pulled out and released it hit the next one, which transmitted the energy to the next in line, and this one, in turn, to the next, and so on until the last ball in line, which moved out the same distance as the first one had been pulled out. If the first two balls were pulled out and released, the two last balls moved as far as the first two had been moved, etc.

The subject's first task was to predict the effect of the successive experimental situations (pulling out one, two, or more balls). Later, he was asked to explain the reasons for his predictions. He was permitted to see the effects of moving the first ball and then was asked again to explain what he had seen and to predict the outcome of subsequent trials of moving and releasing the balls.

Until 8 or 9 years of age, the subjects were not able to answer the questions after seeing the experiment for the first time, or, even after several trials. Lacking the capacity to perform reversible operations, they could not relate their succession of observations. On the other hand, the pupils in the fourth grade (around 10 years old), who had had no instruction in physics as yet, proceeded by trial and error. They attacked the problem empirically and almost always arrived at the correct prediction but without being able to give a theoretical explanation. They figured out experimentally the relation between the number of balls moved at one end to the number swinging out at the other end, but could only explain the results in terms of force, weight, magnetism, etc.

The pupils in the seventh grade (13–14 years of age) had already acquired some ideas of physics and instead of experimenting to find the solution they speculated on what they had learned and were not able to make adequate answers. They recalled the laws of gravity and accelerated motion, etc., but were unable to apply what they knew to the solution of the problem.

The students from the lycée proceeded very differently, especially those in the upper classes. They organized the experiment in a very systematic manner, interpreting the facts correctly in relation to the laws they had learned of the conservation of energy and the role of factors such as weight, mass, and volume, in the perpendicular movement.

The most gifted students in the highest class of the lycée were able to make correct predictions based on their knowledge of physics.

This research provides evidence that knowledge of physics and ideas learned constitute mobile schemas of assimilation only among older students. On the other hand, poorly assimilated information can become a mnemonic burden which is not only cumbersome but paralyzes cognitive activity in the areas of perception and manipulation.

We have observed the results of the same ineffective teaching—the transmission of knowledge to pupils before they possess the intellectual instruments to assimilate it successfully—in other research involving causal reasoning in the fields of biology and history. We have been able to classify the causal relations that the children learned in three groups, (1) relation of facts learned exclusively through lessons of biology or history, (2) causal relations that were taught in related fields (for biology—chemistry, physics and geography; for history—geography and the native language); (3) causal relations of which one can find analogous examples in everyday life and in the child's personal experience.

In questioning the students we obtained responses that could be classed in three stages, as follows:

Stage I.—Answers referring to accidental facts linked, one to another, more by contemporaneity or coexistence than by causality.

Stage II.—Reference to the causal relation but without comprehension of the passage from cause to effect.

Stage III.—Complete explanations with comprehension of the necessary conditions and of the part played by the various factors which enter into the causal sequence.

For the questions concerned with life and personal experience, the curve of evolution is regular. The percentage of responses in the lowest stage diminish with age while the number of responses in the highest stage increases. The increase is sharpest between the eighth and ninth grades (ages 14, 15, and 16 years), when Stage III becomes dominant.

The curve of responses for causal relations between facts learned exclusively at school is less regular. There are some increases immediately after the lessons during which the teaching of the material has taken place, but in the following year, the curve lowers. This is proof that the acquisition of the knowledge was strictly mnemonic.

Knowledge that was more pertinent to the child and, therefore, facilitated assimilation through understanding, not only remained in the pupils' memories but, in the year following, without supplementary information, was the object of intellectual elaboration. The explanations given by the students raised them from the lower level to the higher level, although the material in question was not taught during that time. The improvement is attributed, therefore, to the evolution of thought processes.

We repeated some experiments on inductive reasoning using the same materials that Inhelder and Piaget described in their work on *The Growth of Logical Thinking from Childhood to Adolescence*. One of my research assistants, Mme Strupczewska, presented the students of the eighth grade (14 to 15 years of age) with tests on the subject of equilibrium of forces on an inclined place, on the flexibility of metals, and some tests on probability. The class was divided into two groups; the first took the tests before, the other some weeks after, learning the physical laws.

The striking fact was that the results did not improve after the instruction. We obtained, depending on the tests, responses indicating that 30–50 per cent of the students had reached the operational stage in both groups. At the same time, we were able to observe that the students who had attained this stage were more successful in a written test on the acquisition of knowledge in physics. There is, then, a direct relation between the possibility of assimilating school information and intellectual maturity.

These examples are sufficient, I believe, to show that it is necessary to make a serious revision of school curricula to adapt them to the intellectual possibilities of the students. This reform is actually under way in our country. A group of educators and psychologists is working on the project.

At the same time, it is necessary to reform the methods of teaching to influence the development of the cognitive processes in order to increase the ability of young people to assimilate knowledge. Several studies are under way to clarify this problem. It seems that one of the most important questions is to uncover a method to facilitate the passage from the stage of concrete operations to that of formal operations. One of my former research assistants, Dr. Putkiewicz, used graphic schemas in the solution of arithmetic problems, permitting him to substitute concrete operations for the formal operations of which the students were not capable. He has obtained substantial results. Students could solve different problems on the semi-concrete graphic) level, but, in addition, after a certain amount of time (3 months) on this teaching method, they could also solve the tasks on the abstract level, using a system of formal operations.

One of our colleagues, Dr. Fleszner, former collaborator of Professor Menchinska in Moscow, demonstrated through interesting research that, although it is important to have the student pass from the concrete to the abstract level, it is just as important for him to be able to do the reverse—to be able to pass from abstract ideas to the practical and concrete. She demonstrated in more than one series of experiments, above all in the field of physical laws, that there are two sorts of abstractions—thoughts that consist of reasoning on abstract ideas and the other that consists of the process of abstraction itself. Students who were capable of reasoning in abstract categories did not know how to solve certain practical problems, because they were incapable of making abstractions from data immediately given.

All these researches prove that, although advances have been made in the study of the evolution of thought, there are still problems that have not yet been resolved. Thus, it is most useful that we meet to discuss the different aspects of this area which is so complex and so important both for theory and for the solution of practical problems in education.

4

PROBLEM SOLVING AND PAST EXPERIENCE

Kjell Raaheim

Institute of Philosophy, University of Bergen

The present report is a presentation of some of my points of view on the study of thinking. The work I have had the opportunity to do in this field has come out of a close co-operation with P. Saugstad; much of my own research work has, as its point of departure, the investigations previously undertaken by him.

If asked to explain what it is that characterizes the study of problem-solving and what are the main questions set forth by different experimenters, one is placed in a situation of some difficulty. Perhaps all one can do is point to the fact that different research workers have been interested in studying how a human being, or an animal, behaves in situations that may be classified as complex or difficult. These would be situations in which there is no opportunity of following already learned modes of behavior, situations in which much of what is encountered is new or unknown, and in which it is rather easy to make mistakes before the goal is reached—if one succeeds in reaching it. It is not easy to present a more precise definition of problem solving that will be accepted by everyone who works in this field. If one turns to the literature one finds that a number of experimenters maintain that a problem situation is a "difficult" situation in which the individual is motivated toward a "goal," but the "road" to the goal is blocked by an "obstacle." Both the Gestalt psychologists and the psychologists influenced by them speak of a "gap" in the "structure" of the situation and maintain that the behavior during the attempt to solve the problem tends toward filling this gap.

I shall argue that the problem situation, although "new" in a sense, is not typically a chaotic situation, but rather one with a fairly strict structure. The situations studied by Köhler, Duncker, and Maier, while considered to be examples of problem situations, seem to be situations in which well-specified rules are set up for the individual's behavior. These rules are laid down in the instructions given to the individual. The goal is pointed out by the experimenter, and the obstacle, or difficulty, may be conceived of as restrictions put upon the individual's choice of implements and modes of attack. The situations are often described as new ones, but often only some of the elements in a given situation deviate from what the individual is familiar with from past experience.

I prefer to describe the problem situation as one "familiar" to the individual: a situation previously experienced or, what, in a number of cases, perhaps, means the same to the individual, a situation that he comes to classify as equivalent to a certain series of previous situations. In the problem situation, however, something essential has taken place, so that the situation here and now is experienced with a *deviation* from what is otherwise a familiar situation or series of situations. The *gap* in the situation, in my opinion, may be best defined with reference to the specific nature of the structure in each case, in such a way that, for each individual, one is forced to define the gap with reference to the specific background and past experience of this specific individual. I shall try, later on, to show how it is possible to determine the way different individuals classify one and the same situation and that this classification is of great importance for their behavior in the problem situation.

The philosopher H. H. Price, in his book *Thinking and Experience* argues that recognition is the fundamental intellectual process. Price remarks that a human being without this ability would find himself in a world that could not be thought of, in which there could be no concepts and, in short, a world containing only new impressions or stimuli to confront the individual. We may agree that, for the existence of higher organisms, it is of the utmost importance for them to have the ability to react to the common features of ever shifting situations, as these situations can be described with reference to some kind of objective criteria. That an organism responds with the same reaction to what are, objectively speaking, rather different stimuli, might result either from a lack of ability to discriminate between the stimuli or from a cognitive ability to render equivalent these different stimuli. In recent years, the cognitive aspect of the experience of equivalence has been stressed (Bruner, Goodnow, & Austin, 1956). Also, in recently performed factor-analytic studies of the structure of intellect (Guilford, 1957; Guilford, Frick, Christensen, & Merrifield, 1957), a number of flexibility factors are reckoned with. Considering both Bruner's work and Guilford's, we come to see that the superior intellect may be thought of as characterized by an ability to relate one and the same situation to a great many different series of previous situations, that is, an ability to make the present experience equivalent to a number of different past experiences. Lack of ability to discriminate may have important consequences in the animal's adjustment to his environment. A cognitive code operation, by which one equates situations otherwise conceived of as different, will, however, leave the individual in a freer position in regard to his adjustment by making him more able to react to minor variations in the situations encountered.

As for my own research in this field, I have hitherto not performed any experiments with children younger than those of the upper grades of elementary school. I have, therefore, personal experience only with the upper levels of development from child to adult. The glimpses to be presented from experiments actually performed with older children may, nevertheless, serve to illustrate my points of view regarding the development and general features of the thought process.

First, I want to give a short description of a rather simple test for measuring the individual's ability to name objects that are *functionally equivalent* to a missing object necessary for the solution of a given problem. I constructed this test as a counterpart to Saugstad's test for measuring a person's ability to name different functions for objects. I have called my own test "The Object Test" (later referred to as the *O* test), and the task confronting the subject is that of listing, within a time limit of 10 minutes, all the objects with which he can replace the object missing in a specified problem situation. Three such problem situations are outlines of which the first is the following: "You are trying to reach a shelf, but it is half a meter too high and you have no ladder. Now write down everything you can think of to stand on in order to reach the shelf."

TABLE 1

MEAN *O* SCORES FOR SUBJECTS AT DIFFERENT SCHOOL LEVELS

High-School Grade	*N*	Mean	SD
5................	16	28.7	10.2
4................	65	26.8	7.6
3................	20	20.8	8.1
2................	22	19.6	5.9

Scores on this test show a tendency to increase with age and level of education. *O* scores for pupils of different grades of high school are listed in Table 1.

The tasks of the *O* test, in my opinion, resemble the task of the individual in a problem situation of the practical-construction type. Consider for a moment Maier's well known double-pendulum problem. The subjects are asked to construct two pendulums that will reach the floor at two indicated spots. All the material needed for the construction of the pendulums is given to the subjects, but something essential is missing: there is nothing for hanging up the pendulums. This is a problem situation that I would characterize as a situation in which the deviation consists of a missing part. The situation is familiar to the individual, or equivalent to situations previously experienced, but, since there is a part missing, the success in solving the problem depends on his ability to find replacements for this part by means of the material at hand. What is, for instance, functionally equivalent to a hook in the ceiling? An individual with a high score on the *O* test probably will be able to perform better in a situation such as this than a person with a low score.

That success in solving problems of the practical type correlates with results on the *O* test, I have previously shown in a study in which the so-called *pea problem* was utilized (Raaheim, 1960). In this problem the subject was confronted with the task of finding a way to transfer a number of peas in a glass on one table to an empty glass placed on another table 2 m. away, the transfer to be done from behind the first table. At his disposal the subject had three newspapers, a string (1 meter long), and a pair of scissors. One finds that the subjects, so far as adults or older children are concerned, in the large majority of the cases try to construct a tube or channel for transferring the peas. One may argue that they conceive of the problem situation as a situation with a missing tube or channel. If an individual has come that far—in other words, if he is able to conceive of the situation as a meaningful whole with a gap consisting of a missing part—his success in solving the problem depends on his ability to find something with which he can replace the missing part. He will be successful if he finds an object that is functionally equivalent to the missing one, or if he is able to construct a replacement by using the material supplied.

We are here touching upon an important point. The solution process may be conceived of as having two distinct phases. The *last* phase is the one accounted for: the filling of the gap in an otherwise meaningful situation. The *first* phase of the process is the discovery of the meaning of the situation. A vague feeling that there is *some* difficulty, that not everything is as it should be, only represents the point of departure for the solution process. The first link in the solution, in my opinion, consists of analysing exactly what the gap in the structure is, what is the deviation from the otherwise familiar situation, or, even, what is the structure itself like or what kind of meaningful situation do we have here? The gap or the deviation can be conceived of only in terms of a specific structure or in terms of a specific type of familiar situation. With a situation of the "missing part" type, the questions to be answered in solving the problem are: exactly what part is missing in which type of situation? and how may this part be replaced?

In the study previously referred to (Raaheim, 1960), I found that some of the subjects with high O scores, in spite of their superior ability to find replacements, did not solve the problem. A closer examination of their proposals for solution gave indications that their lack of success resulted, not from a failure to construct a tube or a channel out of the newspapers, but from a more general lack of awareness of the fact that a tube was missing in the first place. If the situation for these subjects was at all meaningful, it is conceivable that they looked upon the situation as equivalent to a quite different type of familiar situation, for example, one in which something is poured from one container to another by means of a ladle.

In an investigation with children, I found that, to a much lesser extent than adults, pupils in the lower grades of high school conceived of the pea problem as a situation in which the task was to replace a missing tube or channel. In about half the cases the children wanted something that could help them pour the peas from the one glass over into the other. In Table 2, the number of percentage of tube channel proposals on the pea problem is listed for subjects from different grades.

It seems reasonable, now, to ask whether it is possible to talk about a

TABLE 2

NUMBER AND PERCENTAGE TUBE-CHANNEL PROPOSALS IN
PEA PROBLEM BY DIFFERENT GROUPS OF SUBJECTS.

High-School Grade	TOTAL	TUBE-CHANNEL	
	N	No. Proposals	Percentage
5...............	16	14	88
4...............	60	49	82
3...............	20	12	60
2...............	22	11	50

problem "as such" without specifying the implements at the individual's disposal. Is it not the situation as a whole, including the different objects with which the situation can be handled that determines the type of solution? As Duncker (1945) argued, it often seems to be the objects at hand that give rise to the attack decided upon. The objects may be thought to "signal" their use or function to the subjects, and such "suggestions from below," as Duncker preferred to put it, may be considered to play an important part in the analysis of the situation.

One cannot, of course, wholly disregard anything in a complex situation. There are, however, indications that only *some* parts of the total situation are of importance for the individual's conception of the situation as a whole, that is, certain features that the problem situation shares with situations from past experience seem to lead to a classification of the situation in this or that way. In an experiment previously reported (Raaheim, 1961), the subjects were asked to write down what they would prefer to have for the transfer of the peas in the pea problem situation if they were able to choose implements freely. The subjects in one group, while writing down their preferred implement, were given opportunity to see objects actually allowed for the solution, while those in another group had to suggest implements without any knowledge of what was actually to be used later on. There was no difference between the groups as to implements preferred. In this case, the individual's choice of line of attack seemed to be independent of the specific objects at his disposal. While the subjects of both groups were later asked to solve the problem by using newspapers, string, and scissors, their proposals could be looked upon as ways of replacing the part missing in the situation. Although the subjects, pupils from grades 2 and 3 of high school, listed different types of perferred implements, their success in replacing the missing part was found to depend upon the possibilities of the objects actually allowed for solution.

Younger pupils, as already noted, in about half the cases want to have a ladle or similar implement to pour the peas from the one glass over into the other, or, in other words, they conceive of the situation as one with a missing ladle. It is clear that these subjects have a smaller chance of solving the problem than do older pupils and adults who, in the majority of the cases, want a tube, and, then, of course, the only objects at their disposal, or with the greatest possibility of success, can be used to make a tube. This means that, when a situation can be conceived of in different ways, that is, can be coded as equivalent to different series of previous situations, and only one way of classifying it leads to success, the individual who is most flexible will be most successful, if flexibility is taken to be, among other things, the ability to classify a situation in a number of different ways.

Is there any reason to believe that flexibility increases with age? If it does, how are we to get a measure of this ability that will make it possible to equate behavior in one and the same situation to behavior in different series of situations from past experience? Indirectly, one can try to get a measure of this ability by letting the subjects go through flexibility tests of the type used by Guilford and Saugstad. If the subjects are handed an object and asked to write down, or to demonstrate, as many different ways of using this object as possible, one gets a measure of this individual's ability to see mirrored in the object different, functionally nonequivalent objects. In a specific form of this kind of test, which I have utilized myself, the subject is shown a common object together with a list of verbs. He is then asked to look at the verbs to see if it is possible for the object to serve the functions indicated by the verbs. In going through the list he is told to write down on a sheet of paper the appropriate verbs and to illustrate the function with an example of how to use the object. This technique has also been suggested by Osgood (1953).

In some previously reported studies, I found that scores on this function-naming test, called the F test, correlate with scores on tests of general intelligence. Guilford et al. (1957) reported correlation coefficients similar to my own, that is about $+.50$. While I found the mean F score in a group of male high-school students from grade 4 to be 14.6, the mean score among pupils from grade 2 was 11.7. The difference, statistically significant at $p < .001$, indicates that the ability measured by the F test increases with age and educational level.

In Raaheim (1961), a comparison was made between results on the O test and the F test and success on two different problem situations. The first problem was the pea problem already described. The second was the so-called *ring problem*, in which the subject is confronted with the task of raising a gold ring that is lying at the bottom of a shaft (3 m. deep), by using a glass tube (3 m. long and with the same diameter as the ring), a piece of wood, a nail, a knife, and a pair of pliers. The two problem situations may be said to be quite different. As has been argued above, the pea problem may be conceived of as equivalent to different sets of previous situations, either a type of situation in which something must be transferred from one place to another by means of some sort of channel or tube or a situation in which something must be poured from one container into another. The ring problem, on the other hand, seems to lead to just a single general mode of attack, that is, a sort of fishing attack. This becomes clear from a study of the different proposals actually suggested by different subjects. The lines of attack may vary with regard to specific procedure but all subjects, in one way or another, want to try out a fishing attack. On the first problem, the pea problem, one may consider the ability to be flexible important for success. With the ring problem, one has the type of situation that is so arranged that the structure is more rigid and results in only the second phase of the solution process coming into play. The flexibility factor, therefore, should not be of importance here. In the pea-problem study, we found a significant correlation between scores on both the F test and the O test, on the one hand, and the time spent on the problem on the other. For the ring problem, only scores on the O test were found to correlate positively with time needed for solution.

As previously mentioned, F scores have been found also to correlate with "general intelligence," as measured by ordinary tests of mental ability. Not so with scores on the O test. No significant correlation has been found between scores on this test and general intelligence. When the time spent on the two different problems was compared with the subjects' IQ's, we found that the more intelligent subjects were superior to the rest on the pea problem, but not on the ring problem!

In my opinion, we have here examples of two different types of problem situations: It is difficult to find the general line of attack because it is difficult to reach the classification that, in this case, is appropriate; next comes the difficulty of finding the more specific way of handling the situation, for example, finding objects that are functionally equivalent with the one missing. In the other problem situation, the general line of attack seems to be clear for all the subjects: It is not difficult for them to classify the situation as a fishing one and their efforts are concentrated upon the task of finding a suitable replacement for the missing fishing tackle.

In my opinion, it is important to discriminate between two-part processes: (a) the determination of the exact nature of the deviation between the present situation and the situation previously mastered and (b) the handling of the deviation, for example, finding a replacement if the deviation consists of a missing part. It is possible to set up examples of problem situations in which the two factors of difficulty are systematically varied. To make our analysis somewhat simple, we shall describe only the four main types of problem situations. The first is the type in which both difficulties (a) and (b) are small, that is, it is easy to discover the deviation and, also, to handle it afterward. We have examples of this type in the small problems of everyday life and we rather seldom recognize them as problems at all. Your lighter does not work and you get yourself a box of matches. Next comes the type of problem in which it is difficult to find out what is wrong but easy enough to do something about it once you have discovered the deviation. For example, your car stops on the road. You spend an hour or two finding out what is the matter; then suddenly you discover a screw that has to be tightened. The "aha experience" very often belongs to this type of problem situation in which the first factor of difficulty is great and the second, next to nothing. A third category is characterized by the great ease with which the deviation is discovered and by the much greater difficulty of coping with it. Here we have the personal problem of, for instance, a financial nature. It is easy to become aware of missing money but rather difficult to find replacements for it. Such problems might be thought to mean much to the individual's general adjustment and his emotional state. The fourth category, we find in research itself. It is difficult both to decide what is not as it ought to be and to find a way of tackling the problem.

If we are to draw some conclusions from what has been touched upon so far, we might suggest that our main point is that a great deal of the individual's behavior in a problem situation may be explained with reference to his attempts to make up for the difference between the present situation, as he conceives it, and the related situations from the past. For different individuals we have to take into consideration different sets of previous situations. This may mean that, even if adults and children behave rather differently in a given problem situation, the same general rule may nevertheless be the basis of their behavior. With different ways of classifying a situation, what is considered the deviation will vary and, consequently, the behavior in handling the deviation will vary.

With increasing age, there is an increasing accumulation of experience and, we might assume, increasing ability to classify past experience in different ways. Language, as it develops, enables us to take up a freer position toward the environment, and the possibilities of coding our present experiences in different equivalence categories increase.

Even the lower animals, with their instinctive tendencies, may be said to follow the pattern of behavior outlined above. For the animal, recognition of phenomena previously experienced sometimes may be superseded by lack of ability to discriminate between what has taken place before and what is taking place here and now. In some cases this may be fatal to the animal. Consider, for instance, the expression "Wolf in sheep's clothing." In most cases, one should consider it biologically appropriate for the animal to be unable to make finer discriminations. For the cow, grass must be grass even though there are lots of different shades of color.

For a human being, I think, as does Price, that the ability to recognize the past in the present is of fundamental importance for his adjustment to the environment. Price considers that the feeling that something in the new (problem) situation does not fit in with past experience indicates that the individual in question would have recognized the situation if it had been in every respect the same as before. If we agree with him at this point, we should hasten to add that the opposite would not hold true. If we recognize a situation, we cannot infer that we would have discovered the deviation if the situation had been actually somewhat different. We may be wrong when we believe we recognize a situation, and we may classify a situation on untenable premises. For these reasons the individual's behavior in many instances may be said to be pretty "unrealistic."

So it might be with children, for instance. Not only do children make classifications that are "faulty," with the result that they behave in "unrealistic" ways in the situations, but also they sometimes try to use objects for functions that the objects do not possess. We learn from experiments such as that of Luchins with the so-called *Einstellungseffekt* that there is no fundamental difference between the behavior of children and of adults. As a result of an immediately preceding series of similar situations, the subjects classify the problem situations with which they are confronted in the water-jar tasks in a stupid way. Their behavior, consequently, becomes unsuited for the task in question and their mode of attack is as unrealistic as that of smaller children. Such a "blind" organization, without sufficient attention to all details of the situation, I have myself witnessed in an experiment with university students.

The problem situation asked for a way to cross a river when on safari in Africa. Dependent on the distance between the banks, and on the material at disposal (for instance trees of different lengths), the appropriate line of attack is sometimes to build a bridge, sometimes to make a float. The solutions of this written problem, suggested by the students, were seldom based on a careful evaluation of the possibilities in each case. Certain details of the information given seemed to dominate, and the results were pretty unrealistic proposals. Even with a distance of 100 meters the bridge was sometimes suggested. On the other hand, when certain cues in the situation suggested that the current was not strong, the float was proposed even with a distance of only 10 meters and long trees at their disposal. A problem situation presented in writing is not, of course, comparable to a situation in which the subjects are actually at the riverside. But the point is that in using the writing procedure one gets hold of some essential parts of the thought process initiated by the presentation of the material. In a concrete situation, some trial and error may precede the actual solution, and it may be more difficult to get hold of the different ideas that occur to the subjects.

In conclusion, we might state that, in problem situations, adults as well as children behave on the basis of a specific conception of the situation, which is thought to depend on how the situation is seen to deviate from past situations with which it is compared. With both children and adults it is difficult for the observer to get an understanding of how the problem, or difficulty, is conceived of by the specific individual. One cannot hope to reach the whole truth by observing overt behavior. If, thus, a lecturer speaks so fast that his listeners cannot comprehend everything he says, the listeners, who may be trained psychologists, may be wrong in assuming that he is a rather nervous type. The speaker's problem, may, in fact, be better described as that of how to finish his lecture in the alloted time!

REFERENCES

Bruner, J. S., Goodnow, J., & Austin, G. A. *A study of thinking.* New York: Wiley, 1956.

Duncker, K. On Problem-solving. *Psychol. Monogr.,* **58,** No. 5, (No. 270 entire), 1945.

Guilford, J. P. A revised structure of intellect. *Rep. Psychol. Lab., U. Sth. Calif.,* No. 19, 1957.

Guilford, J. P., Frick, J. W., Christensen, P. R., & Merrifield, P. R. A factor-analytic study of flexibility in thinking. *Rep. Psychol. Lab. U. Sth. Calif.,* No. 18, 1957.

Osgood, C. E. *Method and theory in experimental psychology.* New York: Oxford Univ. Press, 1953.

Raaheim, K. Problem solving and the ability to find replacements. *Scand. J. Psychol.,* **1,** 14–18, 1960.

Raaheim, K. Problem solving: a new approach. *Acta Univ. Bergensis, Ser. Hum. Litt.,* No. 5, 1961.

5

SPEECH AND THOUGHT IN SEVERE SUBNORMALITY

NEIL O'CONNOR

Institute of Psychiatry, Maudsley Hospital

The following report describes a series of investigations that were carried out jointly with Dr. Hermelin over the last 4 or 5 years. Cognate studies by other colleagues are referred to where they are relevant.

The major aim and direction of the experiments were to analyze the dynamics of the mental processes in a group of adolescents and children with IQ's of 40 or 50 in order to specify the types of deficits and special abilities that might be cloaked by the over-all description "imbecile." The experiments[1] were organized because the performance of imbeciles is not always of a uniform character and because the nature of damage to their central nervous systems gives us reason to believe that some of their abilities may be more impaired than others. In addition, the nature of the treatment of factor-analysed intelligence-test scores prevents the understanding of the relations among the dynamic forces that operate to create a particular ability or disability. Such factor analyses bypass just those interactions in which we were interested.

At this stage, I should state the relation of this work to the invesitgations of Piaget and Inhelder. In general, our study examined an area not closely related to the main studies of the Geneva School, primarily because it was concerned with the more primitive levels of the child's thinking before he begins to use the logical processes to which Inhelder and Piaget have largely devoted their attention. We might say, for example, that the problem of the egocentric nature of cognition or speech scarcely arises as our subjects are, for the most part, preoperational in their thinking.

We tried to analyse the difficulties that adolescents and children with IQ's of 40–50 display in the following situations: perception and visual discrimination, attention and learning, speech and transfer, unimodal and cross-modal functions, extent and nature of vocabulary, significance of words as signs and as symbols in coding and their relation to immediate and long-term recall, the problem of aids to learning, the question of reading ability, and the total problem of inhibition in relation to input and output. Also

---

[1] The author acknowledges the researches initiated by C. Spearman, C. Burt and P. Vernon.

taken into account were the multiple etiology of defects in imbeciles and its consequent differential damage to the central nervous system that naturally results in differential impairment of functions. It will probably be easier in this report to follow the logic of a recent, more extensive publication.

The first two chapters of the work were concerned with intelligence and thinking, and learning and problem-solving, in the severely subnormal, that is, idiots and imbeciles. The initial chapter dealt with the stochastic relations between functions—relations that are ignored by intelligence theory—and the second summary chapter was concerned with learning and problem-solving and perceptual studies in imbeciles.

In the first chapter, we entertained such possibilities as the failures that defectives might make through not grasping certain visual Gestalts. As an example, our colleague in Cambridge, Alfred Leonard, reported to us that when he presented a display of lights and response buttons to a group of imbeciles they failed to see the connection between the buttons and the lights that would normally have been suggested by the contiguity of the two. This example gave rise to questions about the capacity of imbeciles to discriminate among and compare visual displays. It also raised the question of how visual coding could take place and under what conditions generalisation and differentiation could occur in this group of subjects.

In the second chapter, we considered the important relation between speech and problem solving in imbeciles and discussed the possible difficulties defectives have in recognizing similarities and differences in speech itself. To complete this picture, it is necessary to say at this stage the defectives naturally differ in the patterns of their skills, in the same way as do individuals of higher IQ; the patterns of defectives, to some extent, follow their subdiagnoses, although, at present, such a statement contains more conjecture than verification.

Orientation to the problem of defective thinking is aided by consideration of some of the major observations of previous investigators on the performance and mental functioning of defectives. For example, both Itard and Seguin, two French investigators of the eighteenth and nineteenth centuries, noted the capacity of imbeciles to carry out mental associations within the limits of their attention spans. Such an approach to a consideration of the functioning of imbeciles was not continued after the introduction of Binet's tests in France. A long period—from the beginning of this century to nearly the present day—intervened between the experiments of such people as Seguin and the work that has developed subsequent to 1945. Even at the end of the World War II the study of the scholastic performance of imbeciles had to await the demonstration of their capacity as semiskilled workers. But before this period, in the 1920's and 1930's, studies of IQ and abilities had resulted in the recognition by a number of investigators of the greater capacity of some defectives in nonverbal skills as compared with their verbal abilities. Since then, various attempts have been made to classify defectives into two groups, those with a high and those with a low verbal IQ. It has been supposed that the verbal intelligence score frequently measured a form of intelligence that may have existed before the onset of deterioration; a lower performance score may represent the latter. Alternatively, it was considered that a high verbal score, when accompanied by a low performance score, indicated a possibility of behaviour disorder. Various interpretations of discrepancies between the two scores have been given, but the fact of the discrepancy is the most remarkable and consistent finding of previous workers.

An entirely different approach to the psychological differentiation of defectives is that adopted in America some years ago by Werner and, more recently, by Luria in the Soviet Union. Werner pointed out that defectives showed a greater tendency to inhibition than did normals. Luria's theories and experiments led him to assume that defectives had greater difficulty in learning to inhibit responses, presumably because of their tendency to excitation. Despite the conflict in the opinions of these two investigators, the tendency to divide defectives into excitable and inhibitable groups has been noted by a number of workers. These two attempts at subdividing defectives are not the only ones, but they represent one major theoretical issue in general psychology as it appears in studies of defectives. It should be pointed out also that in the late 1920's Burt drew attention to the fact that the deficiencies noted in mental defectives were of a particular kind and frequently differentially affected mental processes. In this view, reasoning and mechanical memory were more affected, for example, than duration of attention. This statement provided the starting point for the investigations that are presented here. It is, perhaps, worth noting that our opinions differ from those of Burt, but we would like to acknowledge the fact that his statement appeared to be the only one in the field, at that time, that positively suggested the need to study the differential effects of mental handicap.

REPORT OF EXPERIMENTAL WORK

Perception

In presenting our experimental results, I will report first the work carried out on perception among defectives. In every case, when reporting on a particular subject, it is necessary to stress that we have only opened a field of investigation which, it would seem, can be far more extensively developed. In each of our studies we provide examples of what can be done to investigate the perception and thinking and memory, for example, of the severely subnormal or imbecile child, but we do not pretend that the studies are in any way complete or comprehensive.

The first point to make is that surprisingly few studies have been made on perception among imbeciles, although it has sometimes been supposed that defectives were slow in their responses partly because of some kind of perceptual input block. Our colleague Gershon Berkson investigated this possible hypothesis by studying both input and output in simple response situations. By varying with visual and motor apparatus both the complexity of a display and the complexity of the response to that display, he was able to show that variation in the complexity of a presentation could not account for the relative slowness of the performances of imbeciles and the feebleminded but that a variation in the complexity of response *did* influence response speed. Other authors have also suggested that the deficiencies that defectives apparently show in perception are the result, not of fundamental peripheral or central perceptual impairment, but of difficulties in attention. Our own observations of a task involving the recognition of figures presented first visually and then aurally, suggest that the latter, cross-modal method is more effective and results in a higher score. This finding appears to support the view that there is no major perceptual disability in imbecile children. It is possible to argue, on the contrary, that the difficulty defectives have in the use of words may, in part, determine their poverty of perceptual skills. In other words, the fact that they cannot name the features of a display, and, hence, differentiate them verbally, provides them with no firm memory structure to use in conjunction with the visual or auditory or tactile presentation of stimuli.

The accompanying table presents mean scores on tactile- and visual-recognition tasks for four groups of subjects: normal children, normal adults, mongol imbecile adults, and nonmongol imbecile adults. It demonstrates that the capacity to recognize visually presented figures varies considerably between the groups. The pattern for tactile presentations scores, however,

TABLE 1

COMPARATIVE SCORES OF NORMALS AND IMBECILES ON
TACTILE AND VISUAL-RECOGNITION TASKS

Group	N	Mean Tactile Score	Mean Visual Score
Normal children	12	23.37 ± 11.6	24.29 ± 12.6
Nonmongol imbecile adults	12	28.87 ± 7.2	19.25 ± 10.3
Normal adults	12	28.87 ± 7.8	34.37 ± 4.4
Mongol imbecile adults	12	12.83 ± 7.6	22.91 ± 8.4

differs from that for the visual. The difference between normal children and normal adults in visual perceptual skill is a result of education. The imbecile groups, whether mongol or nonmongol, do not profit from such education and show, therefore, the same level of visual skill as do normal children. On the other hand, the column of tactile scores reveals that skills in this field do not develop in the same way as visual skills and that a nonmongol imbecile adult is at least the equal of a normal child in his capacity to discriminate between several different shapes.

These results are taken from an experiment that we designed in order to test an entirely different hypothesis but which, incidentally, produced these results. The figures identified were in each case Greek or Russian letters cut from ⅜-in. plywood. It is noteworthy, however, for the most part, that, although the results indicated backwardness in visual discrimination, they indicated no notable major distortions in the recognition of objects. The same result was indicated by the next perception experiment. It was an attempt to persuade imbeciles and mongoloid imbeciles to match, recognise, copy, and reproduce from memory certain standard proportional or directional figures, such as a circle shaded on one half and clear on the other (a proportional figure); or an arrow pointing right, left, upward, or downward (a directional figure). Defectives did not fail to recognise and match such figures correctly, although mistakes were very frequent in their performance. However, recognition involving memory and reproduction involving memory each introduced an element of error far greater than the errors recorded for perception alone. Mongols showed the same difficulty with reproduction and recall but, in addition, they lacked the compensating tactile skill of other imbeciles.

One experiment, too complicated to report here in detail, led us to believe that the learning of a discrimination by imbeciles results in a somewhat greater specificity than is found in normal children of the same mental age. The experiment involved the differential conditioning of two stimuli on a particular scale. Several scales were used but in each case the differentiation of the two stimuli was more resistant to distortions of the stimuli on the scale by imbeciles than by normal children. For this reason, false generalisation of the stimulus signal appeared to be less possible with the imbecile children than with the control group. When false stimuli intermediate on the scale between the two differentiated stimuli were introduced, the resulting scores for the respective groups showed, as suggested, a greater specificity by the imbeciles. This may be identified by some as the kind of concreteness that often has been thought to characterise defective thinking. If, in fact, defectives display this quality with particular stimuli, the result of which may be their apparent problem in seeing in what way things are similar or the same, it may be possible to aid their differentiating capacities by providing them with more examples of a similar kind so that, through redundancy, further differentiation and, hence, a more complex notion of the concept, may be built up. In any case, it would appear that simple perception is not grossly distorted in imbeciles, and any such supposed distortion cannot be thought to account for their backwardness in the formation of concepts or abstractions.

Words and Communication

It was noted above that the extent and quality of the vocabulary of the severely subnormal is very restricted. Recently, Luria and Zaporozhets questioned the capacity of the retarded to give verbal accounts of their experiences. The logical step, after some investigation of perception, seemed to be to estimate faults in the verbal or secondary signalling system of the retarded in order to determine the extent to which these faults might account for cognitive defect.

Several investigations were used to open the field. Mein, for example, on the basis of ten 10-minute interviews with 80 hospital imbeciles was able to show that their normal individual vocabulary varied between 106 and 677 different words, with a mean of 360 words. Normal children of the same mental age have been shown by Burroughs to have a similar mean and range. Also, the logical structure of imbecile speech followed the same pattern of development as that of normal children as was illustrated by the increasing relative frequency of verbs. Table 2 shows this trend in Mein's

TABLE 2

PROPORTION OF NOUNS AND VERBS IN CONVERSATION OF IMBECILES, ACCORDING TO MENTAL AGE[a]

	3–6	4–8	5–6	6–5
Verbs	18.6	20.0	21.9	20.6
Nouns	31.8	30.8	22.9	21.6

[a]Adapted from R. Mein, A study of the oral vocabularies of severely subnormal patients, II. *J. ment Defic. Res.*, 1961, 5, 52–59 (p. 55).

results. This normality of development is also illustrated by percentages in Table 3. The table shows the number of defectives who describe various objects as "red" when asked the question "What is———like?"

TABLE 3

PERCENTAGE FREQUENCIES OF USE OF DESCRIPTIVE ADJECTIVE "RED" BY IMBECILES AND BY CONTROLS TO DESCRIBE CERTAIN NOUNS

Noun	Normals ($N = 448$)	Imbeciles ($N = 111$)
Blood	85	85
Tomato	80	71
Fire	53	43
Tongue	23	52
Brick	3	28

If, therefore defective speech shows no logical anomalies and, in fact, reflects children's speech, can it be said that imbecile speech lacks semantic connection, as some have suggested? To test the possibility that defective speech follows a sound rather than meaning pattern, we used the nouns listed in Table 3 in a conditioning experiment. Results suggested a semantic pattern of connections. The finding can be given additional illustration by another study. Imbeciles of IQ 30 to 50 were asked to learn two sets of words. If the learning of one set interfered with the learning of the other, a connection between the two was assumed to be shown. There were three groups of words. In the first, words were related semantically; in the second, phonetically; and in the third, not at all. The imbeciles showed the greatest amount of interference with the first group and less with the phonetically related group. Such experiments as these seem to indicate strongly that imbeciles have the capacity to make meaningful associations and to connect words that they know, although the number of such words may be limited. Obviously, there are many practical applications for such information, but at this stage, I will simply mention one, an experiment in the reading ability of such imbecile children.

At the beginning of the experiment, the frequency with which certain parts of speech or certain nouns occurred in the subject imbeciles' spoken vocabularies were recorded and a comparison was made between high-frequency and low-frequency words. A number of the children were then taught to read over a period of 18 months. At one stage, both high- and low-frequency words were given as a reading test. It was found that words occurring in the imbecile's spoken vocabulary as frequently as 74 per cent of the time or more were read by 68 per cent of the subjects; words that occurred less than 74 per cent of the time were read by only 24 per cent of the subjects. Admittedly, this result was complicated by the known fact that short words are more frequently used and, presumably, also are easier to read, but it is clear that some emphasis should be laid on such a simple practical formula in any attempts to raise the level of scholastic performance in this severely subnormal group of patients.

The result of the reading experiment itself may be of interest. In November, 1960, eight children were able to read, on the average, 14 words; by February, 1961, the same group had achieved an average of 30 words; and in July of the same year, 55 words. Toward the end of the year, in November, they had achieved an average of 85 words, and by June, 1962, when the experiment was terminated, an average of 123 words. Their reading was clearly mechanical in some respects but involved comprehension, also, because each word used was chosen from the children's spoken vocabulary and was known to carry a conscious awareness of its meaning.

The Relation between Words and Experience

Up to this point, I have discussed in detail only the relation between words and words; but equally important is the capacity one may or may not have to describe past events in words. This difficulty is particularly characteristic of the cognitive deficit of defectives and might be thought to affect their problem-solving behaviour. For example, in a rote- and concept-learning experiment, the subjects were, in every case, quite unable to describe the process by which they had completed the task correctly. This experiment had been planned to test the capacity of imbeciles to elicit a principle of classification. The test material consisted of sets of a series of two cards, each faced with a picture. One of the two cards concealed a reward. Selection of the appropriate card in each pair delivered the reward. There were three sets of pairs, six pairs in each set. In one set the pairs were not ordered and the correct card was randomly chosen. In the second set the correct card belonged to a series that represented one concept, such as, the concept of a piece of furniture or the concept of more than one. In the third set, the cards were in an unordered series that could only be learned by rote. The first two series could be learned by the recognition of a principle of solution that could be learned after one trial. The test results established the fact that, whereas the imbecile group took approximately 19 trials to learn the rote series, they took about half that number of trials, between 9 and 12, in fact, to learn either one of the two concept sets. It seemed to us, therefore, that it was possible for the imbecile to elicit and make use of a concept as a principle of solution. The point that I wish to illustrate, however, is that only 2 out of the 20 imbecile subjects in this experiment were able to give a verbal description of their procedures, whereas all but two of the control group were able to offer them.

This finding prompted us to carry out another experiment involving the use of three related squares. Squares 1 and 2 and squares 2 and 3 were related to each other in the proportion of eight to five. Discrimination between squares 1 and 2 was taught to a predetermined criterion of discrimination and transfer of learning was taught by testing discrimination between squares 2 and 3. Learning was found to be slower with imbeciles than with controls but transfer was the same for each group and was almost immediate.

When only the first part of this test was carried out and was followed by a reversal procedure, a curious result emerged. If square 1 was first rewarded and square 2 then rewarded in the reversal situation, normals had far more difficulty in the reversal than did the defectives. What conditions enabled the imbeciles to reverse more quickly than the controls? Our impression was that lack of verbal self-direction was involved. That is, when an imbecile solved a problem, he had no accompanying verbal formula in mind; as a result, he could readily switch to a new problem-solving technique as the situation demanded.

To test this hypothesis, we conducted another experiment in which, during the first, or learning, phase, after each successful trial the subject was obliged to state the manner in which he had carried out the task. For example, if he had selected the large square he was then obliged to say, "It is the large one," or "It is the big one." After a series of trials to criterion, each of which was accompanied by this verbal formula, the same routine of reversing the squares was carried out. In this instance, however, the imbeciles were quite unable to repeat their previous fast tranfer and took many trials to learn the reversal. We believe this kind of experiment illustrates the very great difficulty that defectives have in learning verbal self-direction but shows, also, that if such self-direction is made a feature of their education, the symbols, or whatever they may be, that they must manipulate in an imaginative fashion, can be implanted by the appropriate techniques of accompanying action with words.

Coding and Cross-Modal Coding

Recognising the difficulty of defectives in accompanying their mental processes with speech, we considered the problem of cross-modal transfer. This arose in connection with the task in which we were trying the effects of combined speech and motor imitation. The task consisted of obliging the subject to respond to one tap with two taps or to two taps with one tap or, alternatively, to count two after the experimenter had counted one or to count one after the experimenter had counted two. In this experiment, we adopted a procedure suggested by Tikhomirov. Obviously, this kind of response technique could be used cross-modally as well as within the same modality. Thus, if the experimenter counted "one, two" the subject might be expected to tap once, or if the experimenter tapped once the subject might be expected to count to two. The results that we obtained by requiring responses within the same modality or when both modalities were combined, were equal to chance. However, if a transfer was obtained from one modality to the other, then the scores improved significantly. This somewhat accidental finding led us to conclude that the cross-modal reactions were more effective because of the necessity for encoding the response, or, perhaps, because the need to delay gave time to consider the response. It was possible that the success of the subjects in the cross-modal transfer was a result of one or the other of these techniques.

We decided to test whether encoding into speech had made the responses more effective. This was done by using a memory experiment involving the presentation of a series of six pictures. The pictures were presented visually or, alternatively, their names alone were presented. After the lapse of a certain period of time, which varied in different experiments, the same pictures were presented, together with six others, in random order. The task required the subject to recall which of the pictures he had seen before. In the presentation of words naming the 6 or 12 pictures, the task was the same, except that it was verbal and not visual. The cross-modal form of the two tasks was the presentation of the words visually or verbally and their recall verbally or visually. Two separate experiments were carried out using immediate and long-term recall. The results are presented for the visual-visual and the auditory-auditory, as well as the two cross-modal, forms in Table 4. It will be seen that the cross-modal forms were an immense improve-

TABLE 4

MEAN (TRANSFORMED) RECOGNITION SCORES
Immediate Recall   Long-Term Recall

	$(N = 24)$	$(N = 24)$
Sound–Sound....	9.0 ± 9.7	8.5 ± 12.2
Light–Light.....	17.0 ± 21.9	1.3 ± 3.2
Sound–Light....	31.1 ± 24.3	18.4 ± 18.8
Light–Sound....	43.9 ± 23.8	19.8 ± 21.2

ment over the intramodal forms, although there is obviously some decline from short to long term recall in some cases. These results seem to us to provide evidence of the effectiveness of verbal coding in increasing the success of imbeciles' performance on tasks of this kind.

In order to countercheck the possibility, however, we devised an experiment in which verbal encoding could not take place. This was the use of a touch experiment in which the material to be examined and recalled was such that it could not easily be named. Therefore, we used Greek and Russian letters modeled in plywood. They could be presented either visually, without being touched, or by touch, without being seen. In the same way, they could be re-examined after a period of time to determine whether they had been previously presented. The same procedure was followed, using, in this case, 5 shapes, and, in the recall situation, 10 shapes. A standard time of 10 sec., each with 5 sec. between, was allowed for each examination. The letters were naturally not easily named by normal subjects and certainly not by English-speaking imbeciles. In this instance, we reasoned that, because the letters could not be named, they would, therefore, not be encoded, and, whether they were presented tactilely or visually, there would be no possibility of a verbal-encoding nexus operating to increase the facility with which the responses were given. The results that are presented in Table 5 suggest that this is the case.

TABLE 5

MEAN RECOGNITION SCORES

	Normals	Imbeciles
Touch–Touch....	22.0 ± 11.9	31.5 ± 5.7
Light–Light.....	26.4 ± 12.2	19.0 ± 5.9
Touch–Light....	24.6 ± 10.6	19.8 ± 10.9
Light–Touch....	19.8 ± 14.3	19.8 ± 11.8

The table shows that the normal subjects do slightly better than the imbeciles in most instances, with one notable exception that is explicable in terms of the greater skill shown by the adult defectives in touch discrimination over their more junior, but mentally matched, normal controls. I might, therefore, conclude this section by remarking that the bond between the verbal and nonverbal experience of imbeciles is extremely slow in forming but that the bonding process can be speeded up and, if successfully completed, is effective in increasing skill. Translation from one modality to another without change of meaning must, therefore, be encouraged in imbeciles if effective learning is to take place at their level.

Recall

So far, I have attempted to present the operations of transfer coding, as well as perception, in the severely subnormal, or to eliminate some of the problems in these fields by reference to experiments. However, it will be readily conceded that none of the operations so far described would play an effective part in the learning process of imbeciles if material recorded and encoded and even transferred could not be subsequently remembered. The question, therefore, remains whether imbeciles can recall, over reasonably long periods, material that they have learned. As far as clincal impressions are concerned, this should not present a difficulty. The memory of imbeciles and all defectives has been regarded as reasonable, if not occasionally superior, since early clinical investigations. This is a possibility despite certain studies that have shown high correlations between intelligence and recall, providing one takes account of the fact that certain kinds of material cannot, of course, be adequately learned by defectives. So, for example, Miller has indicated that judgment as a function is related to the amount of information contained in the material presented but the memory is independent of this information load. Such indications could conceivably be a relevant consideration in the study of defectives' learning.

In our experiment, following Brogden and Smith, who used verbal mazes with 16 or 24 choice points, we presented defectives with the task of identifying letters from 2, 3, 6, or 10 alternatives and followed this with an immediate memory procedure. As expected, the main result suggested that more alternatives meant slower learning but, even so, recall was the same irrespective of the number of alternatives involved in the learning process. The result repeated the results of another experiment concerning the learning of words with letters of different sizes. We, therefore, had two experiments with a similar result and decided to carry out a third that involved the presentation of material with different frequencies and at different intensities.

In this experiment four subgroups of normal children were matched for mental age with four subgroups of imbeciles. There were 10 normal subjects and 10 imbeciles in each subgroup, involving 80 persons in all. Learning material was presented at two main intensities, 55 db. and 90 db., to each of two groups. In each of the intensity levels, two subgroups received a different number of repetitions of the learning material, 10 and 20 in each case. The material was six pairs of word associates that were learned by serial anticipation. The recall periods were 1 minute, 2 days, and 1 month after the learning phase.

Table 6 shows the results obtained. It can be seen that if the 1-minute period is taken as a learning score, and subsequent scores are seen as recall scores, the differences are insignificant and indicate that, irrespective of the amount learned, recall was adequate in both imbeciles and normals and showed no significant decline over a period of 1 month. The combination of the three experiments, therefore, gave us some reason to conclude that the capacity for recall of imbecile subjects of IQ approximately 38 was at least as good as their other abilities and, in all cases, could be relied on to enable them to retain learned material. I should, of course,

TABLE 6

MEAN RECALL SCORES BY GROUPS AND BY OCCASIONS

	NORMALS			IMBECILES		
db. and Repetitions	1 Min.	2 Days	1 Mo.	1 Min.	2 Days	1 Mo.
55:						
10.........	4.3	4.5	4.4	4.0	4.2	4.2
20.........	5.1	5.1	5.0	4.9	4.9	4.4
90:						
10.........	4.5	5.0	5.3	4.5	4.3	3.9
20.........	5.0	5.2	5.5	5.5	5.4	5.4

add a proviso that their learning in all cases was relatively limited and that we have no information on what would happen if they were required to recall a very great deal of presented material with related intermediate learning.

Subsequent research

It would be possible for me to spend a good deal more time reporting the researches carried out by my colleagues, Peter Bryant and Katherine Mair. Space, however, does not permit me to report much of their extremely interesting work that supplements and develops the findings reported here.

Bryant's work has been mainly concerned with transfer in imbeciles and could be summarized by saying that it is concerned with the effect of instructions on transfer. The original aim of his first experiment was to see whether in imbeciles, specific instructions in an original task would improve transfer in a transfer task that could be solved by the same conceptual strategy. In both the original and the transfer task the reward was always concealed under a card of one particular colour but colour and range of colours were changed in the transfer task. One group was given instruction in the original task only about the particular correct colour. Their transfer scores were then compared with a group who received no instruction at all.

It was found that with imbeciles the transfer scores of those who had received specific instructions tended to be worse than the transfer scores of those who received no instruction at all. With normal children, on the other hand, there was good transfer in both cases; the transfer scores of those who received instruction in the original task tended to be better. These observations were repeated in an experiment involving numbers and again in a more difficult task that involved the combination of one shape and one colour. In the latter case, the difference between the two groups of imbeciles was very marked.

An experiment is now in progress which tests the hypothesis that what is responsible for transfer in imbeciles is the generalisation of those aspects of stimuli that should be avoided, rather than those that should be approached, and that instruction inhibits this former process, thus impeding learning.

Katherine Mair's study is concerned with coding and relates this to the capacity of a group of imbeciles to read. She gave two sets of coding tasks to a group of imbeciles whom we had previously taught to read. Their success in these two coding tasks was related to their capacity to learn to read. As the coding tasks were from sound to sound and from sight to sight, with sets of nonsense syllables, no relation appeared. She then developed a coding task that involved coding from written symbols, or pictured symbols, to a sound, and vice versa. This task immediately revealed a high correlation between the capacity of the imbeciles to learn to read and their capacity to carry out the task. We inferred from this finding that the problem of imbeciles was not, in fact, a problem of recognition or discrimination of shapes nor the discrimination of sounds, but the relation of one to the other.

CONCLUSIONS AND SUMMARY

To make any attempt to summarise the significance of these experiments in imbecile learning, I must try to draw together the various sections of this paper and indicate those that we regard of major and minor importance. The first emphasis I think necessary, is to exculpate the visual and sensory apparatus of imbeciles from any involvement, or any serious involvement, in the extreme backwardness of defectives' learning. There are, of course, obvious differences and deficiencies in the visual patterns and capacity for discrimination of this group and of subgroups within this group. At the same time, despite these obvious differences, the major impressions remain, and the difficulties that exist are connected, for example, with the use of words in the process of naming rather than in relation to perceptual input.

It might also be said that the experiments on recall suggest that it is extremely unlikely that difficulties of memory are involved as a major cause in backwardness. The capacity of defectives, once having learned to recall their impressions, seems to be quite adequate for the limited amount of material with which we have tried to present them. Quite clearly, two major difficulties of defectives are concerned with coding. One is the coding from symbol to sound, cross-modally, and the other is the verbal translation of experience into a verbal account of this same experience. Both forms of coding, which underlie a great deal of our scholastic learning, are extremely deficient in imbeciles, even taking account of their relatively limited vocabulary. I have noted above that transfer of material learned is not handicapped, and the observations made concerning coding—that it can in fact be enforced and increases efficiency when this is done—suggest to us that the processes involved are deficient as compared with the recall processes and second-stage processes, such as memory and transfer. The chief limitations, therefore, in the learning process of defectives would appear to be those involved in the initial stages of learning, that is to say, those concerning learning itself and, probably, attention. Very few of our experiments have been concerned with the question of attention, but other material, from such workers as House and Zeaman and Mary Woodward, suggest that attention is an extremely important element. As we have found this same problem incidently displayed in the experiments reported above, it seems likely that this is the case.

To some extent, the problem involved here might be described as the development of learning "set," and there is some evidence from previous work that, as shown in the experiments we have described, learning set can be developed in this group of subjects but, for the most part, it is not present in the same degree as in normal children.

Summarising this conclusion, therefore, one might say that acquisition seems to be impaired, rather than poor perception, retention, or transfer. Acquisition seems to be retarded largely because of an inability to focus attention on the relevant stimulus features of a display. Such a disability may be largely a question of the lack of expectancy in "sets" appropriate to the task, so that the imbecile cannot begin to learn until he has found out what precisely it is that he should learn. This latter process may take a long time. If, however, verbal coding and the kind of labeling that is used in verbal coding can be enforced, as we have shown, imbeciles can make use of this coding and can increase their learning efficiency as a result.

It may be worthwhile, in conclusion, to draw attention to a report by Ellis of what he considers to be the foundation of certain difficulties in learning in defectives. His view is that diminished activity in reverberating circuits in the damaged central nervous systems of defectives may conceivably account for the lack of activation of such circuits in the presentation of sensory events. Because of this, immediate memory-circuit activation would not continue long enough to enable a long-term acquisition to be consolidated. If the extent and number of these circuits are reduced in the abnormal structure of the defective cortex, insufficient arousal might exist for orientation of a correct kind to take place. Such a model would account for the problem of learning that defectives have and that is partly overcome by increasing the intensity of stimuli. It will be remembered that, in the memory experiment, significantly more subjects from the lower- than from the higher-intensity conditions failed to learn adequately. To achieve adequate set and attention in this group of imbecile subjects, therefore, especially intense displays are required.

I hope that what has been said will be sufficient to make it clear that our experiments, although only a partial attack, begin to provide a possible experimental approach to the subject. I would like to stress, finally, the tentative rather than conclusive character of the studies reported and to point out the need for many more investigations before even the limited conclusions presented here can be regarded as well established. In studying the mental functioning of the severely subnormal, we have used techniques and methods developed in experimental psychology with normal subjects. It is to be hoped that inferences that can be made from our studies may be applicable reciprocally to appropriate areas of normal cognitive processes.

6

THE DEVELOPMENT OF PERCEPTION
IN THE PRESCHOOL CHILD

A. V. Zaporozhets

Institute of Preschool Education
Academy of Pedagogical Sciences of the Russian Federation

During the first years of life perception follows a very complicated pattern of development. The followers of Gestalt theory support the view that a newly born child possesses the basic specific features of perception in ready-made forms. Contrary to their views, however, more and more experimental data are being accumulated testifying to the fact that sensory processes become more complicated gradually, as a result of which perceptive images, appearing at different ontogenetic stages, become more and more orthoscopic, that is, reflect the environments more fully and adequately. We shall try to show here that the increasing effectiveness of solving various sensory problems depends upon the development of children's perceptive activity, that is, upon the degree to which they acquire more perfect means of acquainting themselves with the objects they perceive.

This concept of sensory processes is based on investigation by Soviet researchers (A. N. Leontiev, B. L. Ananiev, P. Y. Galperin, A. V. Zaporozhets, V. P. Zinchenko, and others) who reject (on the basis of Pavlov's reflex theory) the receptory concept of the process of perception, which dominated psychology for a long time. We look upon this process as a certain perceptive action. Important roles in such perceptive actions are played by their effectory components, that is, movements of the hand touching the object or movements of the eye following the outline of the perceived figure. The function of these orienting-exploratory movements is to investigate the object and form a copy—an adequate image of the object—by reproducing its features or forming a "likeness" (A. Leontiev) of it. Motor correction, which is achieved through the movements of the sense organs, probably plays a role in the perception processes analogous to that of sensory correction in the control of complex movements. As we tried to show in another work, making a model of an object with the help of external movements and, in particular, with the movements of receptory apparatus makes it possible for the subject to superimpose, so to say, the created model on the perceived object and, thus, to compare them. The reciprocal afferentation (feedback) from this comparison—the signals of differences—enable the subject to make necessary corrections in the model and to make the copy more precise.

In other words, perceptive actions probably perform not only exploratory and modeling functions but corrective functions as well, providing for an orthoscopic sensory image that is adequate to the object perceived.

I am going to tell you about some experiments that were done by my colleagues and me at the Laboratory of the Psychology of Preschool Children of the Institute of Psychology and the Laboratory of Psychophysiology at the Institute of Preschool Education of the Academy of Pedagogical Sciences in Moscow.

The main aim of the experiments was to investigate the process of the development of perceptive actions and to trace the influence of this development on the formation of sensory images in the child during different periods of his early and preschool childhood.

As is known, the child is born with relatively well developed analyzer systems that are manifested in different general and specific unconditioned reflexes which can be evoked by stimulating the sense organs of the newborn baby. The most important among them, for subsequent sensory development, are orienting-exploratory responses that appear in the form of the child's movements of receptory organs toward the stimuli, fixing these stimuli, tracing their movements, etc. Such orienting responses of a newborn baby are rather imperfect, but the experiments done in our laboratory (M. I. Lisins and L. A. Venger) show that the responses become very sharply differentiated during the first months of life and lead to relatively complicated sensory effects.

L. A. Venger's experiments proved that it is possible to elicit orienting differentiation to complex stimuli, such as geometric figures, in babies 3 or 4 months old. During preliminary experiments, the children were shown two three-dimensional objects (a tetrahedral prism and a ball). It appeared that the duration of eye fixation on each object was approximately the same for all children. Next, one of the objects (the prism) was hung above the cradle in which the child stayed most of the time so that the orienting response to that object would disappear. In conclusion, control experiments were done. Again, the children were shown pairs of objects. In each pair one object was the prism and the other was new (a ball, a cylinder, or a cone). In the control experiments, the children directed their eyes toward the new object and fixed on it for a longer period of time than on the old, familiar object, thus indicating that they had differentiated the objects.

TABLE 1

AVERAGE TIME OF VISUAL FIXATION ON FAMILIAR AND ON NEW FIGURES BY
2- TO 4-MONTH-OLD BABIES[a]

Figure	Time (sec.)
Familiar	17.4
New	37.8

[a]Experiments of L. A. Venger.

But Venger's observations testify to the fact that the movements of receptory organs in a three month old baby are of an executive (the child controls—i.e., executes—the movements), fixing, and not exploratory, modeling character. The function of the movements is to put the receptor into an optimal position for the observation of that or another stimulus, and not to copy or model the features of the stimulus. Our experiments show that the transition from executive movements of receptors to properly exploratory, modeling movements that are necessary for the formation of complex orthoscopic images of perception occurs gradually during the whole preschool period.

In T. O. Ginevskaya's experiments, preschool children were asked to acquaint themselves with some objects on the table by closing their eyes and only touching them. It was found that the character of the tactile movements of the hand changed with age. The younger preschool children (3–4½ years of age) used primitive movements that were not differentiated from working, executive movements. On first touching the object, the children tried to manipulate it (rolling, pulling, and pushing it, knocking with it, etc.) and to acquaint themselves with the objects in the process of such practical and playing actions. Later, the palping actions of the hand are separated from its practical executive actions, but the palping actions are mainly of a fixing character, not exploratory. Trying to find out what kind of an object it is, the child catches it with his hand without using any examining, palping movements (Plate 1A). Children of 6–7½ years of age use, along with the actions described above, more perfect methods of palping the object. You can see delicate palping movements of the hand tracing the outline of the object, determining how solid it is, and examining the material of which it is made. As a result, the tactile images of the child become more diverse in content and correspond to the features of the perceived objects more precisely (see Plate 1B, Table 2).

TABLE 2

METHODS AND RESULTS OF TACTILE EXAMINATION OF OBJECTS
IN DIFFERENT AGE GROUPS BY PERCENTAGES OF CASES[a]

		METHOD OF EXAMINATION			
AGE OF CHILDREN	No. Reaction	Practical Manipulations	Fixation in Hand	Palpitation	Mistakes
3 to 4–6...	9	82	9	—	36
4–6 to 6...	—	48	44	8	41
6 to 7–6...	4	29	26	41	8

[a]Experiments of L. A. Ginevskaya.

Analogous data were found by Z. M. Boguslavskaya, who studied how children of different preschool age groups achieved visual acquaintance with a new object and how they later recognized it among other objects. Under such conditions, younger preschool children cast a very short glance at the object, trying to catch it with the hands as soon as possible and to begin to manipulate it. At the same time, in older children the phase of practical operations was usually preceded by a detailed visual examination of the object, as a result of which they solved sensory problems more effectively.

In the projects of Boguslavskaya and Ginevskaya, the orienting movements of the hand and eye were observed only visually, preventing the investigators from discovering the most general and approximate characteristics of the development of such movements in preschool children.

Later, V. P. Zinchenko, together with A. G. Ruzskaya and others, undertook a more detailed study of this problem using movie films to record manual and eye movements of the children. At the same time, Zinchenko found that there is a great difference in the perceptive actions of children when they recognize a more or less familiar object and when they see quite new, unfamiliar ones. Consequently, we should speak about two different types of perceptive actions: actions of recognition and actions of "acquaintance." In this paper I will speak of the "acquaintance actions" of children.

The palping actions were studied experimentally in the following way: A big, flat figure of an irregular form was fixed behind a screen and the child was asked to examine it tactually for 60 sec. so that afterward he could find it visually among other objects. The experiments were filmed.

A comparison of the actions of children in different age groups permitted us to characterize the stages of development in the tactile movements of the child's hands. The movements of the 3-year-old child were more like catching than like touching. Often small children played with the figure instead of examining it. For example, the child placed his palms on the edge of the figure and pushed it with his fingers. The palm was motionless during the whole period of filming (Plate 2A).

The movements of the 4- to 5-year-old children considerably reminded one of those of the 3-year-olds, but you could see some new elements here. The same catching of the edge of the object with four fingers and the palm was observed, but the hands did not stay in this position for long. Rather quickly, the 4-year-old children started to acquaint themselves with the object more actively by using the palms and the surfaces of the fingers. Fingertips were almost absolutely passive in the tactile process. Usually, the palping was done with one hand only.

In the children 5 to 6 years of age, you could see the simultaneous touching of the figure, the two hands moving toward each other or in opposite directions. But the systematic tracing of the outline of the whole figure was not yet observed. Usually, children confined themselves to careful examination of some specific features of the figure, for example, of some hollow part or some projection, without correlating them or locating their position on the whole figure (Plate 2B). And it was with 6-year-old children that you could observe the systematic tracing of the whole outline of the figure with the fingertips, as if the children were reproducing the form of the figure with their tactile movements by modeling its form (Plate 2C, 2D).

The transition to such more perfect methods of acquainting themselves with an object leads to a considerable increase in the effectiveness of perception. This was revealed in the control experiments with visual recognition of the objects, previously presented for a tactile examination (Table 3). The

TABLE 3

MISTAKES OF RECOGNITION (PERCENTAGES) BY PRESCHOOL CHILDREN
AFTER USING DIFFERENT METHODS OF EXAMINING OBJECTS[a]

METHOD OF EXAMINATION	AGE OF CHILDREN			
	3–4	4–5	5–6	6–7
Looking only..........	50.0	28.5	0.0	2.5
Touching only..........	47.7	42.3	25.0	23.1
Looking and touching....	30.8	21.0	11.5	1.9
Practically operating.....	15.4	10.5	0.0	0.0

[a]Experiments of V. P. Zinchenko and A. C. Ruzskaya.

children under 5 years of age made many mistakes in recognizing figures while 6-year-olds, who had traced the outline of the figure in detail with the palping hand, could distinguish it later unmistakably, in the majority of cases.

The experiments in which the eye movements of children of different age groups in the process of perceiving were filmed, also showed considerable changes in the character of perceiving actions in the course of the child's development. For these experiments, Zinchenko and Ruzskaya used the same figures of an irregular form (30 × 40 cm.). The figures were projected for 20 sec. on a screen that had a hole for a camera in the center. The children were asked to look at the screen attentively so that they could recognize the figures among other figures later (in the control experiments).

In 3- and 4-year-old children, under the conditions of this sensory problem, the movements of the eye were not numerous. The periods of fixation between movements were much longer than in older children. The movements were within the figure and sometimes they followed the central line

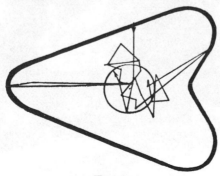

FIG. 1

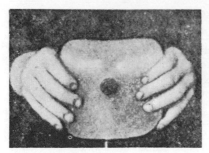

PLATE 2A

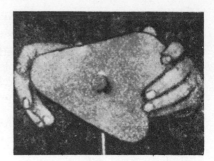

PLATE 2B

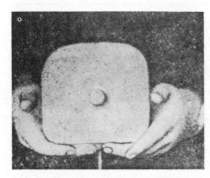

PLATE 2C

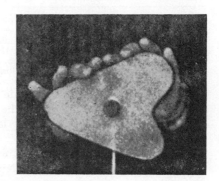

PLATE 2D

PLATE 2E

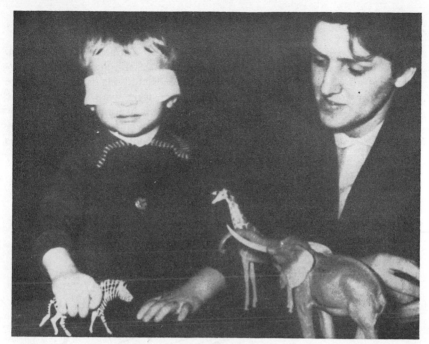

PLATE 1A

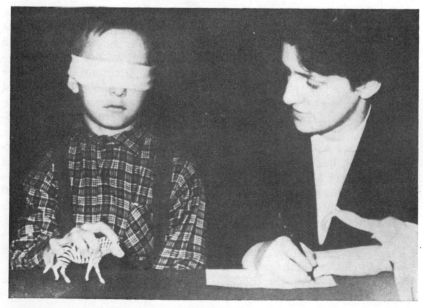

PLATE 1B

of the figure once. Often the subject's attention was distracted by the camera. The movement of the eye following the outline of the figure was not registered at all (Fig. 1). The child's technique of studying is very primitive here, and recognition is very low. Half the answers were wrong, and the children mixed up figures that were quite different in form.

In children of 4 to 5 years of age, the eye movements were also mainly within the figure (Fig. 2). The number of movements was twice as great as

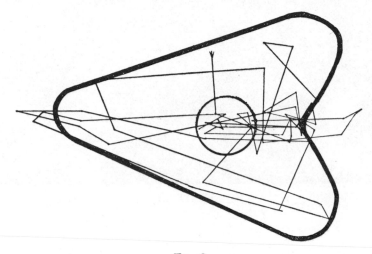

Fig. 2

in the previous group and the time of fixation was correspondingly less. Judging by direction, we think that the movements were oriented to the size and the length of the figure. There were many long movements that were aimed, probably, at measuring the object. Although we did not see movements tracing the outline of the object, in this age group, we did find some groups of fixing points that were close to each other and related to the most specific features of the object. This method gave better results in recognizing the object during control experiments than it did with 3-year-old children.

Five- and six-year-old children began tracing the outline of the perceived figure, but usually they looked at a part of the outline (the most specific one) while the rest was left unexamined. The number of eye movements during the exposure time was approximately the same in the group of 5-year-old children as in the group of 4-year-olds. Many such movements yielded little information to help solve the given problem. These were movements within the figure, for example. Nevertheless, the method was adequate for the child to recognize the perceived object later and the majority of 5-year-old children gave correct answers during control experiments.

With 6- to 7-year-old children, the eye movements followed, in the main, the outline of the fiure, as if reproducing or modeling its form (Fig. 3). At the same time, we could observe the movements across the figure.

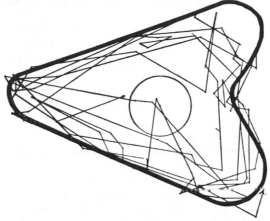

FIG. 3

Probably, these movements also solved an important orienting problem, measuring the area of the figure. The number of movements during the exposure time was greater than that of younger children, and the duration of fixations was shorter.

Using such active and perfect methods of examination, the children gave 100 per cent correct answers during control experiments. But not only this: experiments of Boguslavskaya and others showed that this age group could also solve more difficult sensory problems connected with adequate reproduction of perceived figures in the process of drawing, constructing, modeling, etc.

Although we could have studied the development of perception actions in detail in the spheres of vision and touch only, the results of some of our experiments, as well as some works by other psychologists, gave us the right to think that changes of the same kind could be found in other sensory spheres. Experiments by Y. Z. Neverovich show, for example, that the formation of some probing, orienting movements, clarifying the inner, proprioceptive picture of a motor act, play an important role in the development of kinesthetic perceptions. Investigations by A. N. Leontiev and research workers of our laboratory (Endovitskaya, Repina) testify that the development of methods of active reproduction of sounds will make an important contribution to the genesis of pitch-discrimination in children. The same phenomena were observed by Elkonin and Zhurova in the development of the ability to perceive phonemes, as the modeling of specific features of the stressed sounds, in verbal speech by means of "sounding out" plays an important part in acoustic analysis of a word.

We have given a short description of the formation of perceptive actions in a child, the actions that model the features of the perceived object and provide for the creation of an adequate image of it. What, then, are the conditions and forces that determine the development and improvement of such actions in ontogenesis?

Many Soviet studies show (Leontiev, Ananiev, and Elkin) that the processes of perception are not developed in isolation. Rather, they are developed in the course of the subject's practical activity. In particular, our many years' investigations show that perceptive processes acquire orienting and regulating functions in the activity of a child, and that they develop in connection with the increasing complexity of his activity.

In the early stages of development, more or less correct reflection of reality can only be achieved as the result of practical actions with objects, where sensory processes play dependent, secondary roles. It is in the process of such activity as a whole, including both its sensory and motor components, that an adequate model of an object can be created. This model will be compared with the original object many times, becoming more and more precise and finally leading to an adequate perceptive image. For example, a baby, learning to grasp different things and to take into account their place, size, and form, models (with the movements of his hand) these space characteristics. Later, when he learns to walk, he goes around obstacles and walks in a certain direction, modeling the pattern of his path in his locomotion. The formation of such practical or "sensorimotor" (J. Piaget) models plays, probably, a decisive role in the early ontogenesis of sensory processes which, in the course of modeling, are changed themselves and begin, together with previous signal and starting functions, to perform the functions of reproducing and depicting the reality.

Our experiments show that, where an adequate perceptive image in small children cannot be created by means of visual and tactile acquaintance with an object, such image can be formed in the course of practical manipulations with the object. In the experiments done by Zinchenko and Ruzskaya, children of different preschool age groups were asked to acquaint themselves with flat wooden figures of irregular forms in the following ways: (a) looking at them only; (b) touching them only; (c) both looking at and touching them; (d) practically operating them in the process of inserting them into corresponding holes in a board.

Sensory effects of all these different means of acquaintance were checked in control experiments in which children were asked to recognize (visually) the familiar figure from among unknown figures. The data from the experiments (Table 3) testify to the fact that in smaller children (3 to 4 years old), sensory, "theoretical" acquaintance with a new and complex object gave poorer results than practical manipulation of the objects.

In the process of practical operations children not only distinguished various features of the objects, but also discovered some relations between them.

In Venger's experiments children of 2 to 3 years of age were given the task of trailing a three-dimensional figure through a hole in the experimental grating. It was necessary for them to choose a hole that would correspond to the shape of the figure (Fig. 4).

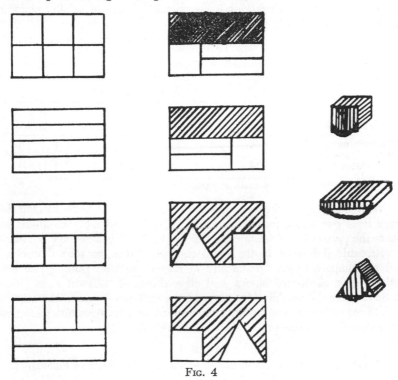

FIG. 4

At first all the children solved the problem only practically by means of trial and error. Two-year-old children stayed at this level even after many exercises. The 3-year-old children often made visual comparisons of the figure and the hole on the basis of practical manipulations. Here the visual perceptive actions "borrowed," so to speak, a method of solution from the practical operations. The child shifted his glance from the figure to the hole several times, as if putting the former on the latter visually, and then gave an unmistakable practical solution, even when the task was quite new and unfamiliar to him.

Results of the same kind were obtained by A. Kasianova in our laboratory. She studied perception and transposition of size relations of perceived objects. The children studied were between 18 months and 7 years of age. There were two boxes before the subject with holes of different shapes and sizes into which he could insert pieces of wood. Under the board was an electric bulb, covered with frosted glass. The bulb was operated by a key fixed outside the box. The situation was such that a corresponding bulb

could be switched on by pushing the button near the big figure (Plate
2E). This was reinforcement for the correct action. Contrary to what supporters of Gestalt theory say, it appeared that the effectiveness and transposition of responses to relations is considerably lower in smaller children
than in older ones (Table 4).

TABLE 4

TRANSPOSITION OF PERCEIVED-SIZE RELATION IN PRESCHOOL CHILDREN[a]

	AGE OF CHILDREN						
EXPERIMENTAL SITUATION	1–5 to 2	2 to 2–5	2–5 to 3	3 to 4	4 to 5	5 to 6	6 to 7
Before training...........	36	18	28	18	9	6	11
After training with practical comparisons of objects...	14	1	5	2	1	1	2

[a]Average of reactions on the absolute size of object.

With the help of the experimenter, the child was made to shift his
glance from one figure to another again, which considerably improved results in the perception of relations in children of 5 to 7 years of age but made
no noticeable difference in the small children. Then we started teaching
them to compare objects practically in respect to size, putting one into
another, cups, cardboard blocks, and other things of different sizes (Plate
3A, 3B). After the teaching experiments, the children repeated the original
series of experiments. The results in perception and transposition were now
higher than those before practical comparison (Table 5).

TABLE 5

DIFFERENTIATION OF GEOMETRICAL FIGURES BY PRESCHOOL CHILDREN
(PERCENTAGE OF MISTAKES)

	AGE OF CHILDREN			
EXPERIMENTAL SITUATION	3–4	4–5	5–6	6–7
Before training.....................................	40.0	32.0	17.0	8
After children were taught to examine the outline of the figure.....................................	11.0	11.0	11.0	3.0

Concluding the review of data on the role of practical activity in the
perception of an object in the early stages of a child's development, I
should like to tell you about some experiments by Sokhina, who studied the
influence of construction on the development of visual analysis in preschool
children. Continuing a well known experiment of A. R. Luria, Sokhina
showed that, without special teaching, children of 3 to 7 years could not discriminate purely visual elements of a complex form; they could not, for
example, say of what parts a given figure consisted. But, after a series of
practical exercises in constructing and creating real structures out of ele-

PLATE 3A

PLATE 3B

ments of different form and size, the children began making a purely visual analysis of the figure, thus anticipating the organization and results of their practical operations. The results of this teaching were widely transferred to new situations and we can see them, for example, in the location of a given element included in complex figures (as in Gottschaldt's figures).

Analyzing various kinds of a child's practical activity, we found that this activity, as a result of specific conditions of human life, bears, from a very early age onward, an "object" orientation; that is, a child uses certain tools and this activity leads to the creation of certain objects. Consequently, practical modeling of the reality as it takes place in games with dramatizations, constructing, drawing, etc., may have an "object" character at very early genetic stages. In these kinds of activities, the child reproduces features of his environment by means of movements and posturings of his own body and by means of surrounding objects and drawing. Such concrete objective modeling, our experiments show, plays a very important part in the development of cognitive processes in general and perceptive processes in particular. Here are some examples.

Boguslavskaya studied in preschool children the development of the visual perception of pictures of concrete objects (a scoop, a vase, an apple, etc.) and abstract geometrical figures. She found that all the younger children (3 to 5 years of age) and a considerable number of the older group (5 to 7 years) confined themselves to very short visual examinations of the exposed object and the subsequent images they created were very incomplete and fragmentary. Using this manner of observation, the children could recognize the object rather successfully according to one or several typical features, but they could not reproduce it in a drawing, for replication requires a higher level of perceptive processes, that is, more complete and detailed sensory images. In later experiments, the children were taught to model the forms of perceived objects out of matches, sheets of paper, etc. The activity was organized in a certain way: it was especially explained to the children that the work should help to acquaint them better with an object and to draw it more correctly later. In these exercises, the models were not the final goal and final products (as is usual in drawing lessons), but were a means of solving certain cognitive and, then, practical problems. After such exercises the effectiveness of perceptive processes rose considerably in all the children, as seen in more precise drawings of the object perceived, although they did not have any drawing lessons (Figs. 5, 6, 7).

An analogous technique of concrete modeling was used by Sokhina in teaching children to analyze visually a complex form while constructing it according to a given model. As is shown in the above-mentioned investigation by A. R. Luria, very often preschool children cannot divide (purely visually) a given object into the elements of which it must be constructed. Usually, they solve the problem in a practical way by trying various combinations until they achieve the necessary result. To raise the level of solving such problems, Sokhina changed the problem a little by paying

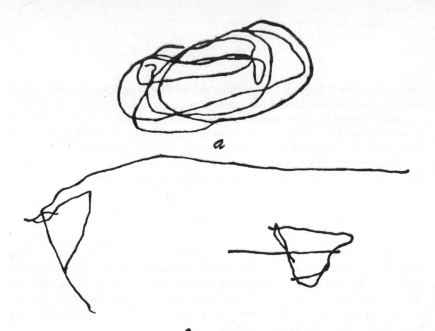

FIG. 5.—Drawings by a 3-6-year-old girl before training; (a) is a cup; (b), a shovel.

FIG. 6.—Drawing by the same 3-6-year-old-girl after training with concrete modeling; (a) is the modeling; (b), the drawing.

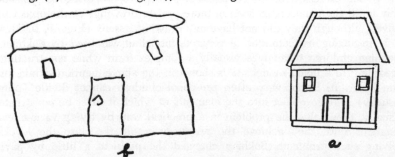

FIG. 7.—Drawing by the same 3-6-year-old girl after training with concrete modeling; (a) is the modeling; (b), the drawing.

the utmost attention to the preliminary orientation to the manner of solving it and not to the practical result.

The model and the elements (flat figures of different forms) were covered with glass and the child was asked to decide in advance what elements he would need to reproduce the model (Fig. 8). Then the experi-

FIG. 8

menter gave the designated figures to the subject and he began solving the problem practically. He learned in the course of the solution whether his previous visual analysis of the complex form had been correct or not. After a number of failures the child usually understood that the problem was difficult and that he had made mistakes in his choice of necessary elements. Then we told him to use the method of concrete modeling to solve the problem and gave him additional elements of white paper corresponding to the figures under the glass; thus, he learned to lay the duplicate elements on the sample and to determine the elements from which the model could be constructed.

Children of different age groups learned to operate with such models in different ways. Three-year-old children could not master the method and the course of instruction did not give any noticeable results. Children of 4 to 5 years of age learned to operate with the paper patterns successfully, but they considered the task and its results to be an independent practical achievement and not a means of solving the next constructive problem. First, they placed paper elements on the sample and, then, quite independently of this problem, began to choose the cardboard figures under the glass that would be needed to construct a new building. In order to induce the subjects to use actual modeling in constructing the building, we had to use some additional methods to increase the value of this problem (constructing a beautiful building by means of parts made of nice, colored cardboard) and to decrease the attractiveness of modeling (using patterns made of simple, soft, white paper). The older children (5–7 years) mastered the method of concrete modeling without any additional exercises and used it adequately to achieve the required practical results.

After this training the level of visual analysis of a complex form was considerably raised in all the children between the ages of 4 and 7. In most cases, they could show correctly the geometrical elements that a given sample could be composed of and where, approximately, those elements should be placed (Table 6).

TABLE 6

INFLUENCE OF "CONCRETE MODELING" ON VISUAL ANALYSIS OF A COMPLEX FORM
(PERCENTAGES)

EXPERIMENTAL SITUATION	AGE OF CHILDREN		
	4–5	5–6	6–7
Before training	23.0	36.0	39.0
After training with concrete modeling	40.0	75.0	80.0

In the described cases, both the object perceived by the child and his reproduction of it were in the same sensory modality. But our studies show that children can start modeling qualities of the specific features of one modality in relation to another modality rather early. Such heterogeneous models are especially important in the formation of an adequate method of analyzing speech and musical sounds. The acoustic sphere is very dynamic and difficult for a child to grasp until he has a model, that is, "materializes" it (as P. Y. Galperin says) in the acoustic characteristics of the space around him and in relation to the objects present.

We had two research projects in our laboratory (T. V. Endovitskaya and I. A. Repina) that showed that discriminating the pitch of pure sounds was extremely difficult for preschool children. The differential thresholds found in these experiments, therefore, are very high. During the teaching experiments, we introduced objects that, by their space relations, created a model correlating tones with objects. Thus, Repina prepared dramatizations in which the heroes were a big Father Bear that emitted low sounds, a smaller Mother Bear with a little higher voice, and a little Son Bear with a still higher voice.

At first, the experimenter and the children presented various stories about the life of this family; then the bears hid themselves in different places and the child was instructed to find them by their voices. It appeared that, after such training, even the younger children (2 to 4 years of age) could easily discriminate the voices according to the tone and, later, to differentiate more successfully other sounds they heard for the first time although they were not connected with any familiar objects (Table 7).

TABLE 7

THRESHOLD OF PITCH DISCRIMINATION IN PRESCHOOL CHILDREN
(DIFFERENCE IN TONE)

	AGE OF CHILDREN			
EXPERIMENTAL SITUATION	3–4	4–5	5–6	6–7
Before training.................................	4.8	3.4	2.4	1.7
After training with concrete modeling....	2.0	1.0	0.85	0.6

I. V. Endovitskaya used a more complicated but more universal model of the correlations between sounds and different heights. She gave to a child a rectangular ruler that was divided into equal squares. The child received a doll, too, which was to jump from one square to another according to the sounds that the child heard (Plate 4A). If the difference between sounds was small, the doll was to jump from the first square to the second. If the difference was bigger, it jumped from the first square to the third, and so on. At first the child did the exercises together with the experimenter and then independently.

The training of children to make such models leads to a considerable increase in the effectiveness of tone discrimination. The use of "heterogeneous" models for such training probably exerts some influence on both sensory and intellectual development.

Logical and psychological studies, carried on by L. P. Shchedrovitsky in our laboratory, show that the transition from object-like models to models that resemble real objects less and less, will prepare the child to replace perceived objects with symbols; this is of great importance for the formation of thinking processes at the preschool age. But the very complicated problem of the formation of thinking that is based on certain sensory impressions, as well as the changes in relations between perceptive and intellectual processes at different stages, will require special analysis, and I shall not deal with it in the present paper.

Coming back to the question of the influence of concrete models on the development of perception in children, it is necessary to stress that, being peculiar analogues of sensory images, the models are not sensory images and it is yet to be discovered how the external modeling is, so to say, "internalized"—how it is converted from external to internal. As is known, a study of internalized intellectual processes was made by J. Piaget in the West; in Soviet psychology, it was started by L. S. Vygotsky and A. N. Leontiev and is being intensively continued by P. Y. Galperin.

The experiments done in our laboratory show that, although there is much in common in the internalization of intellectual and perceptive processes, the process of forming the latter has some specific distinctions. The results of our experiments show that new methods of becoming acquainted with reality are initially started within the practical activities connected with new practical problems the child has to solve. And here, at the first stages, they are methods of accomplishing executive actions, immediately aimed at achieving certain practical results, and it is only later, under certain conditions, that they become methods of orienting-exploratory modeling activity.

For example, N. N. Poddiakov studied the process of forming a habit of operating a relatively complicated mechanism. A child sat at the switchboard and could, by pushing buttons, make, for example, a doll move in different directions (Plate 4B). The subject was given the task of leading the doll around an obstacle and bringing it to a certain point. The experimenter first demonstrated the work of the mechanism, but the children could not understand immediately the principle of its operation. That is why, when they started to solve the problem, they usually began by pushing different buttons chaotically, trying to achieve the desired goal at once. But with such methods, the doll rushed about chaotically, and the necessary result could not be achieved. The difficulties in the practical solution of the problem made the child study the situation and it was here that a characteristic change in behavior took place. When the buttons were pushed, quick energetic movements of the hand became slow, careful, and probing, the movements accompanied by glances toward the moving doll. In other words, just at the moment that the executive actions were becoming orienting-exploratory, an elementary method was being created to test any system of button control.

Analogous changes were observed by Y. Z. Neverovich when she studied kinesthetic perceptions, but in her case the changes were specific to different age groups (they were not only functional this time). The children were asked to reproduce actively in a Zhukovsky kinemometer the movements they had made passively with the help of the experimenter (Fig. 9). A correct reproduction was initially reinforced by approval from the experimenter or a signal from a light. It was revealed that the movements of younger children (3 years of age) were definitely executive and immediately directed to a desired goal. They moved the hand of the kinemometer to a certain point quickly, without any hesitations, and were glad beyond limits if reinforced and deeply sorry if not. We do not see any preliminary orientation in the conditions of the task in this case. At higher genetic stages (children of 4 to 5 years of age) you could observe, along with the described movements, slow, probing movements through which the

PLATE 4A

PLATE 4B

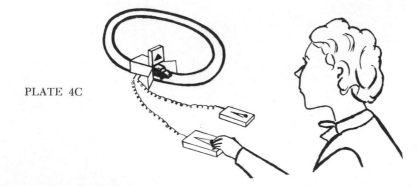

PLATE 4C

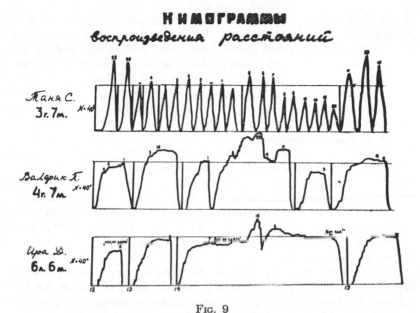

Fig. 9

inner, proprioceptive picture of the task was clarified and a model of the future motor action created.

The data illustrate the convergence of immediate movements of the hand from executive into orienting-modeling. But we also received analogous results when we dealt with indirect actions that led to the creating of new objects and situations. For example, in the experiments of Boguslavskaya, Sokhina, and others mentioned above, it was found that children first mastered constructing, replicating, or drawing as certain kinds of practical operations that led them directly to results they themselves found interesting. And it was only later, when these actions became stable, that you could give them the new functions of examining a situation and of preliminary modeling, for these results can be achieved in the course of experience following executive actions.

Thus, the first and most important stage characterizing the beginning of a new perceptive act is the conversion of a practical executive act into an orienting and modeling one. This is the reason why, at the beginning, a new way of becoming acquainted with an object is usually carried into practice by organs that are capable of performing both practical and cognitive functions, such as by the hands' touching and manipulating an object, or by the muscle apparatus of the larynx, which plays an important role in communications and serves as an important means of analyzing musical and speech sounds at the same time. No longer dependent upon practical activity and having acquired new orienting functions, the subsequent actions of the child undergo considerable changes. For example, each touch and manipulation of the object give the child new information about it. This is why, as we have mentioned, children try at first to use the assimilated practical actions both for practical and cognitive ends. But the cognitive effect of such actions is insignificant, and the actions must be changed and restructured to perform new cognitive functions effectively. This process of differentiating and particularizing perceptive actions, and the subsequent internalization as well, were studied in a number of projects in our laboratory.

A. L. Ruzskaya studied, in children of different preschool age groups, the formation of perceptive actions in discriminating geometrical figures. There were two response keys on the table before the child. At some distance away there was a toy garage with a car in it. A small screen was fixed above the garage on which geometric figures were projected by a special mechanism. When one kind of figure (*triangles*) appeared, the child was to push the left key; he was to push the right one at the appearance of other figures (*rectangles*). The correct choice was reinforced by a toy car's coming out of the garage (Plate 4C).

During preliminary experiments, the children were trained to discriminate the forms by one pair of figures, presented repeatedly. When the differentiation had been worked out, we began control experiments. We projected on the screen different variations of the figures in various positions. All the children made numerous mistakes in discrimination and the number was especially great for children of 3 and 4 years (Table 5).

This testifies to the fact that the forming of perceptive images in such conditions of training is not sufficiently constant and generalized and, consequently, does not enable the child to solve difficult sensory problems.

Proceeding from this hypothesis of the genesis of perceptive actions, Ruzskaya tried in the following experiments to form, especially in children, some ways of examining perceived objects. The children were given cardboard figures which they could touch and manipulate. All the younger children and some of the older group showed rather primitive methods of acquainting themselves with the figures. They moved them from one hand to the other, touched the angles or heaped them up without any careful examination of the figures themselves. It is in this connection that we started especially to teach the children how to acquaint themselves with objects in a more rational way. The child was taught to follow the outline of the figure with his finger, stressing the changes of directions at the angles and counting (one, two, three). The study of triangles was alternated with that of rectangles, and the children learned about differences in their structures, and about the difference in the number of angles and sides. Thus, the child assimilated an algorism of exploratory actions that allowed him to recognize any version of that or another figure independently of its position (Table 5). In the first stages, the function of examining and modeling could only be performed with a palping hand while the eyes played an auxiliary role, that of tracing the movements of the hand. But later the eye became able to solve independently such problems of perception by tracing the outline of the figure as had been done by the palping hand. Very interesting transitional forms could also be observed when the child could differentiate figures visually but his eye movements were accompanied by some movements of the hand modeling the form of the object at a distance, thus organizing and correcting the processes of the visual examination of the object.

Later, the children passed to purely visual orientation. In the first stages the movements of the eye were very extended (Zinchenko) and the child visually traced the whole outline of the figure perceived, modeling its peculiarities in detail. In the last stages of the formation of perceptive processes (after the child was trained for a long time in recognizing and discriminating figures of a certain kind), exploratory movements of the eye became reduced consistently, concentrating on the separate, most informative features of the object. It was at this stage that the highest form of internalization of perceptive process was achieved. On the basis of earlier external models that were created with the help of movements of the hand or eye, for example, and were repeatedly compared with the object and corrected according to its features, there was formed at last an internal model—a constant and orthoscopic perceptive image.

The material substratum of this internal ideal model is, evidently, what Pavlov calls a "dynamic stereotype," a system—a constellation of interconnected cortical excitations—that corresponds to the stereotype of influences stemming from the object.

Now, without any extended exploratory operations, one short glance at the object, the distinguishing of some characteristic feature, can signal into action the whole internal model and thus lead to the immediate grasping of the properties of the perceived object. It is exactly in this form that supporters of Gestalt theory described the process of perception, proving, incorrectly, that it is initial in the ontogenesis and determined by physical laws of the formation of the structure. In reality, as we have tried to show in our paper, a given form of perception is the product of a continuous development that goes on in the child under the influence of practical experiences and learning. It is only a genetic study that can disclose the reflex origin of this perceptive process and its connection with practical and cognitive activity in children.

I should like to stress, in conclusion, that the development of the child's perception is not spontaneous; it takes place under the influence of practice and learning, in the course of which the child assimilates social sensory experiences and joins the sensory culture created by mankind. The adults give the child methods of learning the environment by acquainting him with the systems of musical sounds—speech phonemes, geometrical forms, etc. —that have been developed by man. They also teach him to designate the particulars of his environment, by means of language. As a result, the child assimilates a certain system of generally accepted sensory measures, sensory standards that he uses later in his perceptive activity to analyze the reality and reflect it in synthetic images.

Our studies show that the process of sensory learning can flow chaotically and not be productive. But if you can organize the process in accordance with the psychological regularities of the stage of formation of perceptive actions, the effectiveness of this learning can be considerably raised.

7

THE DEVELOPMENT OF HIGHER NERVOUS ACTIVITY IN CHILDREN IN THE FIRST HALF-YEAR OF LIFE

Hanuš Papoušek

Laboratory for Research in Higher Nervous Activity,
Institute for the Care of Mother and Child, Prague, Czechoslovakia

I count it an honour to be able to represent my Czechoslovak colleagues at this very stimulating conference on the development of cognitive processes and to inform you of some results of our research, carried out in the Institute for Care of Mother and Child in Prague. Since this is the first opportunity for such a wide exchange of experiences, allow me to start with several preliminary comments.

In our country, there is a long tradition of particular interest in child development—it is probably not necessary to mention the famous seventeenth-century pedagogue Jan Amos Comenius—yet we still feel that little has been done to place research on child development on an exact scientific basis, particularly as far as very early development is concerned, in spite of its generally acknowledged importance. It is well known that in early infancy marked developmental changes occur in various physiological or psychical functions and that optimal conditions should be established to prevent deviations unfavourable for the whole further development. This is especially true in regard to brain functions, but there is a question of whether we have sufficient criteria to estimate precisely enough the development of brain functions or the factors that influence this development. Since brain functions gradually become extremely complicated with increasing age, we have another reason to learn more about them at the very beginning of their postnatal development.

In our Institute, there is close collaboration between obstetricians, pediatricians, psychologists, and ontogenetic physiologists, fully engaged in research activity. A child can be followed from birth through the whole of infancy; particularly suitable conditions have been created for studying child development from various aspects, such as, the development of homeostasis, metabolism, respiration, thermoregulation, and immunological reactivity.

The development of brain functions is studied in the laboratories of higher nervous activity led by O. Janoš. From the very beginning we have been interested in both physiologic and psychologic aspects of brain functions without emphasizing any clear demarcation, since the two merge in infants. Thus, you can find in our group psychologists next to physiologically oriented pediatricians using the same methods and interpretation of results. Our main task is the study of age and individual differences in higher nervous activity and of factors influencing the development of higher nervous activity.

We prefer longitudinal studies of infants throughout the whole first half-year, using various methods. Therefore, it is very important that we rear the children in a special research ward, where optimal health and educational care can be given to them and where good control over basic conditions can be achieved. The mothers remain at the Institute for the whole period of breast feeding free of charge and may regularly visit the child afterward. Thus, we have reliable information on health conditions and on somatic and psychic development of every child in our setting.

We are gradually trying to make our methods of investigation thorough and complete in order to enable study of brain functions from all principal aspects, including conditioned reflexes as well as methods for analyzing spontaneous behaviour. For the present, we can summarize some of the studies that are using defensive and food-seeking conditioned reflexes and analysis of waking and sleep in infants.

In the study of defensive reflexes, O. Janos has been using the conditioned palpebral (eyelid) reflex for studying higher nervous activity. This is one of the most constant reflexes in man and enables comparison of data both in premature newborns and in adults. Although recording apparatus for registration of eyelid movements has not yet been successfully designed for the youngest infants, one can obtain objective data about the frequency and latent periods of these reactions with the help of visual observation and a stop watch.

The palpebral blinking reflex is elicited either by stimulation of the trigeminal nerve (opthalmic branch) with a puff of air or of the optic nerve with a light flash. In both cases, we choose the intensity of unconditioned stimulation that elicits the same reaction: complete closing of the eyelids. This empirically determined intensity may vary in individual infants, and, sometimes, even in the course of an examination.

An intersignal interval of 3 sec. between conditioned and unconditioned stimuli (if the child does not respond sooner) is sufficient for identification of the conditioned reaction before applying the unconditioned reinforcement. Difficulties with objective recording prevent using intersignal intervals as short as those used with adults. Longer intervals, on the other hand, would unnecessarily raise the probability of the occurrence of periodic "spontaneous" blinking, although it is rare in infants (frequency of "spontaneous" blinking in infants oscillates between one and four per minute during quiet, active waking periods).

In the category of food-seeking reflexes, I encountered difficulties with the conditioned sucking method and, therefore, I selected a new one, the turning of the infant's head toward the source of food. A special kymograph arrangement was developed for recording movements of the head, total motor activity, and breathing. The actogram of the infant's general movements is recorded pneumatically from the elastic mat on which the infant lies in its crib. Respiratory movements are recorded pneumatically, too, while head-turning is recorded electrically with the help of two potentiometers attached to the axis of rotation of a special frame that turns with the head. By lifting or lowering the axis of rotation of the head frame, the weight of the head can be balanced so that even a small, premature newborn encounters no difficulty in moving the apparatus or maintaining a neutral position; under normal conditions, however, he does not hold his relatively heavy head in a central position during the first months of life.

The experimental procedure is as follows: First, we test whether the conditioned acoustic signal (electric bell or buzzer, located in the midline in front of the child) per se produces head movements. We then establish a conditioned head-turning with milk as unconditioned stimulus, offered from the left by an assistant nurse sitting behind a screen in back of the infant's head. The intersignal interval between conditioning signal and reinforcement is 10 sec. if the child does not respond; if the response is correct, the child gets the milk immediately. We use one session a day, except Saturdays and Sundays, and 10 trials in each session, with random length of intertrial intervals. When establishing the differentiation, we use the bell to signal milk from the left and the buzzer for milk from the right.

In both these experimental methods, we prefer random length of intertrial intervals in order to avoid time conditioning. We cannot be sure that we are identifying the first conditioned responses accurately, since they may be mixed with spontaneous ones, until their frequency increases. We consider it more important to have standard criteria for ending each of the cycles included, that is, the acquisition of the conditioned reflex, its extinction, second acquisition, differentiation, and double reversal of differentiation.

As regards total motor activity or breathing, we are especially interested in the changes occuring with conditioning, for example, increases or decreases so distinct and frequent in young infants being conditioned. We do not insist either upon complete acoustic or visual isolation of the child during experiments or upon completely automatic application of stimuli. On the contrary, direct contact may be important for maintaining the child in an optimal state, or even as a measure of caution during feeding. It is not easy to achieve optimal and comparable behaviour in infants during experiments. Rather complicated organisational and educational arrangements are necessary, particularly, a warm, motherly attitude in a skilled staff, good adaptation of the child to the experimental situation, and continual control over the child's health state and his whole daily schedule to meet the demands of experiments. We examine conditioned blinking during the waking period after feeding, and food-seeking conditioned head-turning immediately after sleep at the normal feeding time.

In the analysis of behaviour, we believe that general description is insufficient and that it is necessary to analyze some individual components of behaviour in detail in order to be able to detect developmental changes or to compare data on behaviour with the results obtained by the methods of conditioned reflexes.

Jaroslava Dittrichová, whose task is to study these problems, has been interested particularly in the development of sleep in infants, but, because of the close relation between sleep and waking at this age period, she has studied sleep and waking simultaneously. Eye reactions, total body activity, respiratory activity, hand movements with toys, and vocalization were recorded. Eye reactions (movements of eyelids and the bulbus oculi—eyeball) were simply observed and recorded by specially coded marks on the kymograph paper. Body activity was recorded by the actograph; respiratory activity, by the pneumograph; hand movements with toys and vocalization (babbling, crying) by specially coded marks. Each minute on the kymograph record was divided into 30 2-sec. intervals; the reactions were evaluated in terms of presence or absence within these samples (of eye movements, body activity) or within 1-min. periods (of frequency and rhythm of breathing, hand movements with toys, and vocalization).

According to these indicators, four main states can be differentiated: (1) a waking state, characterized by open eyes, frequent general body activity, vocalization, and irregular breathing; (2) a transitional state, with decreased frequency of movements and respiration, and with either half-open or alternately open and closed eyes; (3) light sleep, with closed eyes, but still irregular, slow respiration and rare movements; and (4) deep sleep, with closed eyes, slow, regular respiration, without vocalization or general movements. Observations were made continually from 7 A.M. to 10 P.M. Between 10 P.M. and 6:30 A.M., only actographic recording was continued. In some infants, EEG patterns were recorded.

I will first introduce the data from our results on the influence of postnatal age. Since early infancy is characterized by rapid, intensive growth, age is a matter of particular importance. Despite the general agreement among most workers in the field of early ontogenesis on higher nervous activity that the rapidity of conditioning is slower in the very young, experimental evidence is not entirely uniform. Some workers believe that, in newborn or younger animals, conditioned reflexes can be elaborated at the same rate, or even more easily, than in adults. Similar conclusions have been reported in a series of experiments with humans.

We have found that, in the first year of life, the rapidity of elaboration of conditioned reflexes and of differentiation increases with age. Table 1 shows the correlation coefficients we obtained when we compared the age of infants at the beginning of individual conditioning processes with the number of experimental sessions necessary for achievement of the criteria of conditioning, differentiation, and its reversal.

In this connection, another question immediately presented itself:

TABLE 1

RELATION BETWEEN AGE AND No. SESSIONS TO CRITERION[a]

	N	r	p
CR:			
t.......	28	−0.74	<.001
o......	33	−0.62	<.001
a......	55	−0.71	<.001
D:			
t......	22	−0.50	<.02
o......	26	−0.43	<.05
a......	44	−0.58	<.001
Dr:			
t......	20	−0.22	>.1
o......	21	−0.15	>.1
a......	42	−0.35	<.02

[a]CR is establishment of conditioned reflex; D is differentiation; Dr is reversal of differentiation; t is trigeminal reinforcement; o is optic reinforcement; a is alimentary reinforcement.

What age difference by itself is already associated with significant difference in the rapidity of conditioning, that is, how wide is the allowable age span within which we can compare the processes of conditioning? Our analysis, presented in Table 2, shows that an age difference of 1 month or more is almost always associated with a significant difference in the rapidity of conditioning. If distortions resulting from age differences are to be avoided in judging the functional ability of higher nervous activity, then, in the early months of life, the maximum age range for comparison must be less than 1 month. This throws doubt on some previous studies of higher nervous function in groups of infants who differed in age by more than 3 months.

TABLE 2

STATISTICAL EVALUATION OF RATES OF CONDITIONING IN VARIOUS AGE GROUPS[a]

	Age Difference of Groups (Days)	Significance of Speed Difference in Conditioning (p)
CR:		
a.........	15.9 (3.5–19.4)	>.5
a.........	52.3 (3.5–55.8)	<.001
a.........	36.4 (19.4–55.8)	<.001
t.........	43.1 (16.7–59.8)	<.001
o.........	38.0 (18.6–56.6)	<.005
o.........	29.3 (56.6–85.9)	>.1

[a]CR is establishment of conditioned reflex; a is alimentary reinforcement; t is trigeminal reinforcement; o is optic reinforcement.

Besides the quantitative data indicating the influence of age, we can also demonstrate the effects of age upon the qualitative pattern of conditioning. We used Vincent's curves. The average frequency of conditioned responses is shown in individual fifths of the course of elaboration of the conditioned palpebral reflex up to the standard criteria, to show the qualitative differences between two groups of infants who were at different ages at the beginning of the conditioning (Fig. 1). One can see in Figure 1 an

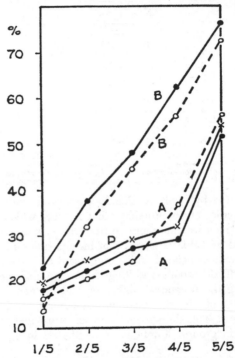

FIG. 1.—Course of conditioning (palpebral reflex). *Horizontal axis,* fifths to criterion; *vertical axis,* frequency of conditioned reactions. *Solid line,* trigeminal reinforcement; *broken line,* optic reinforcement. A, 3 weeks; B, 8 weeks; P, 7 weeks of postnatal age (3 weeks of corrected age in premature infants).

uninterrupted, steeply rising curve in the older infants (B) with no marked effect of different forms of reinforcement (optic or trigeminal); in the younger infants (A), on the other hand, the initial increase is insignificant, but at the end of the second and the beginning of the third month an abrupt increase in reactions appears, as if a marked qualitative change had occured in the infants. This is also confirmed by a comparison of the course of conditioning in premature infants (P), who, in postnatal age, were similar to group B, but, in corrected age, to group A. Their average curve is analogous to that of infants of the same postconceptional age.

During the analysis of the elaboration of conditioned nutritive responses and their dependence on age, we observed a clear qualitative change in associated reactions in the same period. In 13 infants followed from birth, we saw that in the first 2 months of life the conditioning stimulus evoked only quantitative changes in general body activity and vocalization (non-specific associative reactions), whereas from the eleventh week on more specific reactions, which were appropriate to the experimental situation, appeared, for example, various vocal and facial reactions reminiscent of adult-specific reactions—joy, indecision, uncertainty, displeasure.

A similar phenomenon can be seen in the development of behaviour patterns, such as the movements of the hand with toys: they are virtually absent in the first 6 weeks (12 infants observed), occur in 30 per cent of the observation periods from 8 to 10 weeks, and then abruptly and significantly increase to 60 per cent in the twelfth week. After the twelfth week the behaviours increase only very slowly again. The incidence of babbling follows a similar course. According to these various criteria, one can see that around the end of the second and beginning of the third month of life, changes occur that suggest a marked qualitative change in higher nervous function.

Since the first month of postnatal life—the neonatal period—has repeatedly been a matter of great interest to many other workers, it is, perhaps, worthwhile to mention also our data illustrating the age-dependent characteristics of newborn infants. If we compare the Vincent's average curve of attainment of the stable food-seeking conditioned reflex in newborns (Fig. 2)

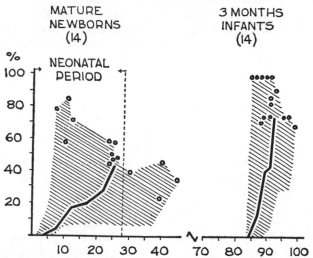

Fig. 2.—Course of conditioning (food-seeking reflex) to criterion. *Horizontal axis,* age in days; *vertical axis,* frequency of conditioned reactions.

with that of 3-month-old infants, we see that it is flatter and, even in the last phase, does not approach the percentage of positive reactions of the older infants. About two-thirds of the newborns achieved the standard criteria of five consecutive positive reactions within the newborn period.

The first conditioned reactions, usually weak and with a long latency, appeared by the first week of life. Newborn infants first achieved the criteria of stable conditioning at 7, 10, 11, and 12 days. Also, after extinction and renewal of conditioned reflexes, differentiation was completed by 6 weeks of age when a bell signaled that the milk came from the left and a buzzer signaled that it came from the right. In the diagram, the polygon into which individual curves of conditioning fall is striped. Pavlov considered the rapidity of conditioning an indicator of the strength of the process of excitation. From this point of view, our data would indicate relative weakness of this process in newborn infants.

A similar conclusion can be drawn from the analysis of waking and sleep. The waking state takes up about 10 per cent of the newborn infant's day (47 per cent in the twenty-fourth week, $p < .005$) and is strikingly intermittent. The newborns persist in continuous waking on the average of only 6 min. at a time, as apposed to 64 min. in the older infants. A considerable portion of the newborn's day (35 per cent) is spent in a transitional state between waking and sleep. This portion falls to 17 per cent in the twenty-fourth week ($p < .01$). Similarly, in newborn infants, the total time spent in light sleep is longer.

On the other hand, the duration of deep sleep is the same in newborns as in 24-week-old infants (about 20 per cent of the day), although its course is not so continuous. The frequency of intervals when the eyes remained closed less than 10 min. is 62 per cent in newborns, and falls to 44 per cent in the twenty-fourth week ($p < .005$). Thus, even sleep is sporadic during the first weeks of life and becomes consolidated only later.

Marked individual differences are apparent already in the neonatal period, as shown, for example, in the rapidity and course of establishing the conditioned food-seeking reflex (Fig. 3). It requires further study to discover whether these differences represent differences in functional maturity or are qualitative differences in fundamental brain functions. Similar individual differences have been observed in conditioned defensive reflexes and in the criteria of sleeping and waking. Thus, it seems clear that the development of individual differences in higher nervous activity can be followed from birth, although this has been previously denied.

The conditioned food-seeking reflex gave us a new key to further interesting problems. Its basic component—the turning of the head—presents a suitable example of a simple and easily analyzed movement, which, according to the cephalocaudal principle, starts functioning early in ontogenesis and can be used as a good experimental model for studying the earliest development of later, voluntary activity. Even the bilaterality of this response is advantageous, since it enables us to test the influence of different variables under ideally comparable conditions. We can, for example, study the influence of two kinds of reinforcement in the same child and during the same session, reinforcing the conditioned reflex with different stimuli from each side.

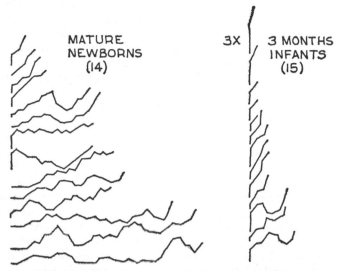

Fig. 3.—Individual differences in conditioning (food-seeking reflex).

Depending on the form of reinforcement, this movement can also become a part of defensive behaviour or orienting activity. (In this form, it has been used by J. Koch in our laboratories since 1960.) When associated with alimentary reinforcement, the head-turning is often accompanied with marked associative reactions, such as vocal or emotional reactions, changes of respiration, and general movements.

We have also tried to study the conditioned character of these emotional reactions. In 11 infants, 4–6 months old, we established a differentiation in which the infant received sweet milk from the left with a bell signal and a bitter solution from the right with a buzzer signal. His responses to these fluids were appropriate and quite opposite, in terms of facial or vocal reactions. Soon, the infant began to react with the same emotional manifestations to the acoustic signals alone. The bell produced signs of satisfaction, the buzzer signs of distaste, frowning, etc. Then we switched the signals, and the infant was offered bitter solution with the bell and milk with the buzzer. He rejected the milk and spit it out, but accepted the bitter solution eagerly as long as the bell was ringing. Only gradually did the infant learn to readjust his responses. It was obvious that, already at this age, the conditioning stimulus can overcome the immediate effect of reality.

Finally, in a further series of experiments in 4- to 6-month-old infants, we attempted to work out an experimental model of the first developmental stage of a voluntary act. We reinforced the same stimulus with two kinds of milk according to which side the infant turned his head, that is, sweetened milk from the left and unsweetened milk from the right. The infant soon differentiated between the two milks and turned his head only to the left. We then reversed the milks, with unsweetened at the left, and the infant gradually switched over and turned only to the right.

It would be difficult to analyze these observations in detail in this paper. We can only summarize by saying that the infant's behaviour, resembling purposeful activity, develops as a complex conditioned response at the level of the first signaling system and depends on externally applied experimental conditions.

We have not yet gone far enough to elaborate some general principles of the early development of higher nervous activity. On the contrary, we are more or less at the beginning of our main work, having found the first paths into this uncertain but fascinating area and having collected the first data about the subject of our interest. We have been working out some further methods to elucidate the development of brain functions even from other aspects, such as the development of vegetative and electrophysiologic correlates of conditioned reflexes, the development of orienting reflexes and emotional manifestations. This task has not yet been carried out. If the first step was to concentrate on the effects on individual differences of the development of brain functions under normal conditions, the next will be to study factors that can influence this development. These steps are, of course, not simple, and that is why we appreciate so much the opportunity to discuss the problems here.

8

THE FORMATION OF THE CONCEPTION
OF IDENTITY OF VISUAL CHARACTERISTICS
OF OBJECTS SEEN SUCCESSIVELY

Zofia Babska

University of Warsaw and
National Academy of Science, Warsaw

Two questions were of interest to us: first, at what stage of development is the child able to reflect, or take cognition of, the identity of visual characteristics of objects; and second, how does the child arrive at the stage.

The literature on the subject provided too little information to obtain the answers. On the one hand, there was little material on the subject, and, on the other, many contradictory statements were found within what material there was. Contradictions were noted in the results of different experiments and in the conclusions drawn by different authors; they appeared, even, in statements of a normative character that referred to the age at which the child was able to perceive or discriminate between various types of visual stimuli.

I have been looking for the sources of these contradictions, most of which appear to be in the terminology used and in the manner in which the statements are formulated. Terms, such as, "perceive," "discriminate," "recognize," and "imagine," that are used in general formulations lack precision. They are not sufficiently well defined in meaning, are too general to be useful as descriptive terms and are of little value as theoretical ones.[1]

The question of terminology is related to the manner in which statements are made. Examples of such statements are, "The newborn infant is not able to discriminate colours;" and "He develops the ability to discriminate four basic colours when he is one year old." When we read such statements, questions immediately arise: Does the newborn baby not discriminate any attributes of colours? Is there no form of the child's activity that, under direction, would give evidence of colour discrimination at an age earlier than 12 months? Can the child over 1 year of age discriminate colours under all conditions? Are there no conditions in which the child under two years is able to differentiate shades of colours?

Statements such as those given in the preceding paragraph mainly tell us only about the changes in the *object* of cognition with the progress of

---

[1] The point of view expressed here is discussed further in Babska (1958).

age. This, in our opinion, is one of the essential sources of contradictions in the general normative formulations.

Apart from the question of the *object* of cognition, there is the question of the *form of activity* in which the object occurs, and this also changes with the age of the child. The infant behaves as if cognition of already known differences between stimuli must occur afresh over and over again. For example, visual stimuli already discriminated within the framework of orienting activity must be discriminated anew when emotional reactions are involved; the child must learn once more to discriminate the same stimuli in feeding activity, such as sucking, and still again in verbal responses.

One observes that at an early age each child must learn for himself, as it were, to discriminate visual stimuli; there is not a single, integrated "baby mind." This observation is closely related to Gershuni's findings that the same person's thresholds of sensitivity vary according to the different kinds of reactions that are used to measure them.

It is clear that contradictory generalizations of a normative nature may be formulated if one does not take into consideration the type of activity that is influenced by cognition. If, for instance, one's statements are based upon the verbal reactions of the child, it would be correct to claim that, as a rule, children around the third year of life start to discriminate four basic colours and that children in the first year of life do not discriminate them. Another author, basing his statements on orienting reflexes, would claim to have found colour discrimination in the first months of life.

Still another source of confusion in statements referring to developmental phenomena is the failure to consider the conditions under which the cognition of a given factor finds expression in a given form of activity. An example may be cited in which the Gesell form-board test is used. A 16-month-old child can put a circle into an opening of the same shape only if the circle is placed in front of the round opening. If the form board is turned around so that the circle is in front of the square opening, the child of 16 months will make an error. A few months later, however, he will be able to solve the problem correctly under the same conditions.

Empirical data show that the types of conditions that are helpful for the finding of correct solutions to various types of problems or tasks, or that are effective in improving the level of performance, change from one age to another.[2]

In addition to the points discussed above, it is essential to call attention to the changing *function* of cognition in relation to the activities of the child, that is, the function of cognition as it changes in the process of regulat-

---

[2] Cf. the results of Piaget's investigation in which he permanently changed the experimental situation (the essential feature of his "clinical method") and tried to determine how it influenced the child's level of performance. Cf. as another example, the investigations of Goldstein and Scheerer (1941) with aphasic adults. They introduced various levels of assistance in solving difficult problems.

ing the child's relations with his environment. Thus, for example, visual stimuli function in the newborn to evoke activity (innate orienting reflexes); later, the stimuli may function to inhibit activity; and, still later, to direct it. The mediating functions of visual stimuli become more and more complicated with age.

A review of the literature on this subject (Babska, 1958) has led to the conclusion that research results should be organized around certain essential topics when empirical data is presented, as well as when general conclusions are drawn from them. These topics are, (1) the object of cognition; (2) the form in which cognition is expressed; (3) the conditions under which cognition takes place; and (4) the function of cognition. This proposed scheme is merely descriptive, of course, and has no direct reference to any psychological theory; it can, however, serve as an adequate basis for an explanatory hypothesis.

Although the schema is not new or original, it is not universally recognised. This can be seen by looking through textbooks in which statements (e.g., general normative formulations) are infrequently given in the suggested form. The failure of authors of empirical studies to take the topics into account often leads to results that cannot be compared with those of other studies or of other investigators.

✿   ✿   ✿

One of our investigations that is described later was concerned with one area of the development of cognition in the child. (The area will be defined more closely within the schema proposed above.) The subject of the investigation was the signaling function of the external appearance of objects. Visual clues on screens were used as signals of the hiding places of objects. The experimental activity was the child's search for the hidden objects. In addition to testing all subjects under constant experimental conditions, we introduced a number of modifications. The specific features indicating the hiding places were shapes and colours appearing on the surface of a screen. The child's discovery of the objects depended upon whether his activity was guided by his ability to relate the identity of successive visual clues.

As has been stated, the literature does not give us a clear-cut description of the stage at which a child is able to identify the external appearance of objects, either in the form we have investigated or in any other; nor has it clarified how the ability is achieved. Later in this paper we will return to the information that this study provided. At present, we will proceed to describe our experiments.

INVESTIGATION OF CHILDREN'S ABILITY TO RELATE VISUAL IDENTITIES

Ninety children were tested in six age groups: 1 year and 6 months (1–6); 2 years and 3 months (2–3); 3 years (3–0); 3 years and 6 months

(3–6); 4 years (4–0); and 5 years (5–0). Each group consisted of 15 children. Each child was given 3 tests and 8 trials in each test, so that a total of 270 experiments and 2,160 trials were available for analysis.

The materials consisted of four identical grey-coloured boxes and three sets of square-shaped white cardboard covers. On the first set of covers, a hen, a horse, a woman's face, and a cat, one object per cover, were drawn in dark outline. On the second, geometric forms—a circle, a square, a triangle, and a star—were cut out from black paper and pasted on. On the third set were circles of identical size but of different colours, red, green, yellow, and blue (colour, brightness, and saturation were roughly the same). In each of the three experiments conducted with each child, a different set of covers was used.

The experimental procedure was as follows: First, each child individually was shown one box with the cover on and turned toward him, for 2 sec. Then the cover was removed and the child looked at the toy lying in the open box for 2 sec. Then the box disappeared from the child's view and, after approximately 15 sec., the child was faced with four closed boxes arranged in a straight line, each with a different cover from the same set. In one of these boxes the child had just seen a toy hidden. The experimenter asked, "Where is the toy?" and asked the child to give it to her.

In the next trial (trials took place at intervals of about 1½–2 min.), the boxes were rearranged and the situation was repeated with a new box. No box was placed in the same relation to the other boxes on any two successive trials. Each box was given to the child to "recognise" twice during the experiment. Each box was placed in each of the four positions twice during the experiment.

On two successive days, the child was presented with very similar tasks. The only difference was in the covers on the boxes. On the first day, the covers with hen, cat, horse, and woman's face were used; on the second day, the four geometric figures; and, on the third day, the four colours. On three successive days each child was given a total of 24 trials. In each trial, ranging from 1½ to 2 minutes, 10 important steps were distinguished, and the child's behaviour was recorded in terms of the steps.

The experiments I have just described were preceded by about 300 similar ones conducted with 56 children in the second and third years of life. Those experiments were exploratory in nature.[3] They were conducted with different groups of children. In some, various changes in the experimental design were introduced, and, sometimes, many different versions of the experimental procedure were tried out with the same child. The modifications of the design were as follows: (1) The boxes, from among which the child was asked to recognise the one previously shown him with the toy inside, were not rearranged in successive trials; in each trial of the same experi-

---

[3] The results were briefly presented in an article (Babska, 1959), and were described and extensively analyzed in a monograph (Babska).

ment, the position of the boxes was unchanged. (2) In some experiments, the child saw first the toy and then the cover on the box into which the experimenter put the toy. (3) In some experiments, the child was given play names for the figures on the covers of the boxes, for example, the red circle was named "the ball." (4) The number of trials varied in some experiments from 4 to 12. (5) In some experiments, other kinds of covers were used. (6) Sometimes the experimenter inhibited the child's choice for a while by holding his hand. (It was intended, in such a situation, for the child to consider his choice a moment.) (7) For one group of children, in all 8 trials of 1 experiment, the toy was always kept in the box with the same cover; only its position in relation to the other three boxes was changed. As 12 covers were used, 12 experiments were conducted with each child.

With the exception of the modifications just described, in all other versions of the experiments the children were presented with the task of finding a hidden toy, without special training, after seeing the screen and the toy behind it only once. It is important to take into consideration that the children were expected to recognise different-looking screens in several successive trials (visual characteristics of the screen varied from trial to trial).

The experiments were arranged in such a way that the visual "cue" for finding the toy was the *relation of identity*. One may say that the child could have used the shape or colour of the object on the cover of the box as a "cue," but I will try to show that this was not so.

The experimental situation called for the child to find the toy. The toy was always in one of several boxes that differed in visual characteristics and that was shown to the child in the second part of the experiment. The box was identical with the one in which the child had previously seen the hidden toy. This was the only constant and, at the same time, the specific characteristic of the box containing the toy (differentiating it from other boxes). Recognition of this characteristic in searching for the toy always led to success, that is, to discovery of the toy.

The box containing the toy possessed other characteristics at each trial in addition to the essential and specific one, such as characteristics that were always present but that were common to all the boxes and not specific to the one box containing the toy (i.e., the shape of the box). Other characteristics differentiated the box containing the toy from others, but only in a given trial, for example, the position of the box in relation to the other boxes—in different trials, the box containing the toy occupied different places. Even the specific "absolute" visual characteristics of the box with the toy—differentiating it from other boxes—became accidental. In various trials the toy was hidden in the box with varying covers. The directive, "Look in the box with the red [or other] cover, and you will always find it," would be in error. The cue for discovering the toy was always the relation between the outward appearance of one of the boxes among which the child looked for the toy and the appearance of the box in which the child had previously seen the toy, that is, the relation of identity. "Look always for the toy in the box that looks the same as the one in which you saw it hidden directly before"—this was the only directive that guaranteed success in every trial of the experiment. If the child used another cue he might have been able to find the toy in some of the trials, but not in all.

From our arguments up to this point, it appears that the correct solution of the task might, in fact, be taken as the expression of the child's ability to take cognition of the relation of identity of visual characteristics of objects (screens) as well as of the ability to regulate goal-directed activity.

The investigation provided descriptive and normative data showing the stages through which the child passed in improving his approach to the solution of the task. An analysis of the data, particularly of the type of errors made (Babska, 1963), became one of the sources for developing an hypothesis that explained the changes occurring with age.

The changes occurring with age in respect to the number of correct choices is illustrated in Figure 1. The percentage of correct choices increased from 27.5 per cent at the age of 1–6 to 93.3 per cent at the age of 5–0.

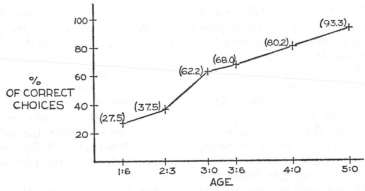

FIG. 1.—Increase in percentage of correct choices with age.

The increase in the number of correct responses was not regular over the years. This is illustrated in Figure 2.

The greatest increase in correct choices came between the ages of 2–3 and 3–0. In the preliminary, exploratory investigation, it was found that the greatest interrelation between the number of correct responses and conditions (various modifications in the experimental situation) came around 2–6. Such modifications had little influence on the level of performance below 2–3 or above 2–9.

Judging from the rate of increase of correct responses and the kind of relation found between the number of correct responses and the experimental situation, we distinguished three stages in the development of the child's

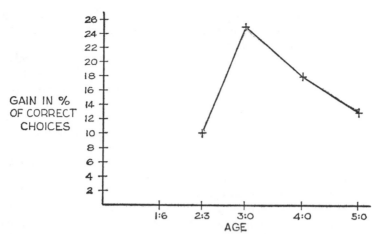

Fig. 2.—Average gains in percentage of correct choices in intervals of 9 months to 1 year.

ability to conceptualize identity. The outstanding features of the child's behaviour in the three stages are as follows:

Stage I. The correct choices occurred only with chance frequency. The most common error was that of preference. In more than 80 per cent of the experiments, the children opened the box in the preferred position in 50 per cent or more of the trials.

Stage II. Certain modifications of the experimental situation produced a great number of correct responses; others did the opposite. The sort of covers used (geometric figures, colours, pictures of animals) and the introduction of names for figures on the screens, are examples of the variables that influenced the type of responses in this stage.

Stage III. This stage was typified by the occurrence of correct choices in the most trials. The examiner had the impression that children already knew, at this stage, how to solve the task and that errors were caused by factors such as lack of attention. A change was noticeable in the kind of errors made from the fourth year of life onward.

❋   ❋   ❋

The question arises: Is it useful to distinguish stages, such as those mentioned above, in the continuum of development and growth? Can they be used to describe the developmental changes of various other kinds of abilities? Some of the characteristics of stages described above, we think, can be generalized. They are as follows:

In stage I performances giving evidence of the existence of the relevant ability did not occur. There are, relatively speaking, no circumstances or conditions to evoke the given ability. Nothing can help the child. What we observe may be termed here *lack of ability.*

In stage III there are no conditions, relatively speaking, which can prevent the child from giving a correct performance. There are no circumstances that would prevent the child from solving the given problem. What we observe is *presence of ability*.

Stage II is the middle one in which one may observe close relations between performance and conditions. In some conditions a high level of performance can be achieved, while in others the opposite is observed. An examination of the relations mentioned above can give us criteria for diagnosing the level that the child has achieved so far in developing the given ability.[4]

If, in analyzing the development of abilities, we were to accept these stages, certain consequences would follow in psychological diagnosis. Instead of stopping with the statement that John's ability indicator is 102, we would say that he will perform Task A only if condition type 1 existed. We would also say that no conditions exist in which John is able to solve Problem B and that no conditions can prevent John from performing Task C.[5]

As we have said, approximately 3 years of age is the important period in the development of the child's ability to direct his searching activity by relating the identity of the visual characteristics of objects presented successively. At this age, the child passes from the second to the third stage in the development of this ability. Let us now refer to certain information from the literature dealing with the characteristics of the child at this age. Stern and Stern (1931) claim that not until the end of the third year can the object of the child's cognition be characteristics and relations. This corresponds to the results of Heidbreder (1926), Hicks and Stewart (1930), Hunter and Bartlett (1948), and Luria and Polakowa which show that only after age 3 can children direct their activity by some general principle of action. We consider the direction of activity by the relation of identity to be such a general principle. The results of our investigation also seem to agree with the findings of Szuman (1948) that the level of goal-directed and effective activity achieved by the 3-year-old child is based upon recognition of the results of his own action and upon his discrimination of effective and non-effective means and ways of action.

❋   ❋   ❋

How can one explain the child's passage to the stage where he can direct his activity on the basis of identity of the visual appearance of screens presented successively? The hypothesis that we accepted maintains that this stage is genetically linked with the previous stages of searching reactions. In the first 9 months of life the child is interested in an object if it is before his eyes. If, for example, it is hidden behind a screen, he immediately stops looking and does not try to find it. Only in the ninth or tenth month does he

---

[4] Compare "preliminary" and "full" organization of stages in Piaget's work.

[5] We expect that such descriptions of the level of development of abilities would provide a good point of departure for educational work. It should help answer the questions: Will the child profit from any influence at all? Is it necessary for him? To what kind of changes in the child's performance should it lead?

search actively in this situation, that is, remove the screen (cf. Stern, 1930; Buhler, 1931; Piaget). Piaget says that the searching reaction in relation to a hidden object is the consistent outcome of a long period of the child's visual, motor, and tactual accommodation to situations that he meets. The searching reaction, as described above, undergoes further transformations.

At about the age of 1 year the searching reaction may, in my opinion, be defined in the following way: The disappearance of an appropriately new and small object from the child's view behind a screen constitutes a stimulus evoking a search at that place. The length of time during which the child searches for the hidden toy is, at first, in the order of seconds at most, but at the age of 3 years may be in the order of days.[6]

The child's behaviour in response to the disappearance of an object, as described above, is common among children at around the twelfth month of life and is stable (i.e., not extinguishable in natural conditions) for a number of months. It is an expression of a common, stable structure. In the light of Piaget's research, this structure seems to me to be clearly acquired and is based upon a number of motor-conditioned reflexes that have been formed in appropriate conditions in the natural and common-life situations of the child.

Since the searching reaction at the place where the object disappears functions repeatedly, new associations that mark a new stage of development are formed. This is expressed in the emergence of searching reactions that are directed by definite visual characteristics of the screen. If, thus, in the course of its functioning, the searching reaction is reinforced (i.e., the child finds the toy) only when the child looks behind a screen of a given appearance, apart from its place, this may lead to the formation of a conditioned, motor reflex, that is, the emergence of a screen of given visual characteristics may begin to evoke the appropriate action leading to the discovery of the toy (cf., Frank, referred to by Piaget; Lejkina; Szipinowa and Surina, referred to by Lublinskaja; Welch, 1939; Zaporozets). The fact that the searching reaction directed by the visual aspects of the screen appears later in ontogenesis (second and third year of life) does not appear to be accidental, in the light of facts and analysis.

The functioning of the searching reaction directed by the visual aspects of the screen also produces occasions for the creations of "unnecessary associations." Thus, if the child, directed by the visual aspects of the screen, finds the toy, he might "unnecessarily remember" where the toy was and continue to look for it in the same place in the next trial. This type of association arises with ease at the beginning. Having been achievements of former stages (i.e., of the first 9 months of life), they now inhibit progress

---

[6] The maximum length of delay of which a child is capable depends on a number of factors, e.g., the number of screens used in the investigation, and the time interval between the individual trials. For a detailed discussion in the literature dealing with delayed reaction, see Z. Wtodarski (1958).

and hamper the child's passage into the stage where search is directed by the visual aspects of the screen. With age (in the second and third year), there is a steady decrease in the length of the training period that is necessary for the searching reaction to be directed by visual aspects of the screen.

How can we explain this considerable decrease of training time in relation to age? In our opinion, at least two factors have a direct influence.

The first factor is the passage of the child's nervous system to a higher functional level. Here I have in mind the achievement of relative functional excellence in the processes of nervous excitation—the improvement of internal inhibition—as well as the emergence and intensive formation of the second signal system, the verbal system.

The second factor is the shift, in the second and third year of life, from considering as of major importance such attributes of objects as place to attributes such as visual characteristics. Many observations give evidence that, starting from the end of the first year of life, visual characteristics of objects become more and more important to the child. For example, as soon as a child sees an object he prepares to grasp it in various ways, depending upon the shape. Depending, also, upon the visually recognised structure of the object, the child sets itself to manipulate it in various ways. Even stronger evidence is the naming of objects while looking at them. These facts begin to be typical of a child only at the end of the first year of life. There are incomparably fewer types of behaviours in the first year of life than in the later years to give evidence of the significance of the outward visual aspects of objects to the child.

From the examples given above, it may be seen that visual aspects of objects acquire significance when they occur in new forms of child activity (e.g., manipulation) as well as when they occur in new forms of adult influence upon the child (linking words or names to the child's contact with objects); these recur with increasing frequency after one year.

In particular, the visual aspects of the *surface* of the object (e.g., colour) take on meaning in verbal interchanges between adult and child. The external shape of objects takes on significance for the child from the end of the first year of life, since he feels them to be different when picking them up in his hand. The surface colour and composition of coloured shapes do not ordinarily take on meaning in natural conditions during the first year of life, but, from the second year onward, they do. Objects of similar shape but different colour composition are repeatedly named differently by the adult and are used in various ways by the child in imitation of the adult.[7]

The probable result of this process is that the visual characteristics of objects, having acquired meaning as a certain category of phenomena,

---

[7] It is not known whether, given completely different conditions of life, or given a strong, artificially applied reinforcement of colours and shapes of objects in the first year of life (adapted to the given level of development), the visual aspects of objects would not take on significance for the very young child.

apart from their concrete quality in each individual contact, come out ahead in the competition with other characteristics of objects, such as place occupied. Hence, they begin to attract the attention of the child. If the object itself becomes important for certain reasons, it is apparent to the child that this is so because of its visual appearance; formerly, this was apparent to the child in the same situation because of the place occupied by the object.

If it is accepted that the object seen by the child is a complex stimulus, the components of which are visual characteristics and place occupied by it, it would seem, on the basis of what has been said, that, as a result of various associations (including verbal), visual aspects become the strongest components in the combination for the child around 3 years of age and cease to be masked by other components, such as the place of the object. As a result —when the child is stimulated by the entire complex stimulus—his orienting response is evoked by the strongest component, that is, by visual characteristics. If the whole complex is reinforced the child associates its visual characteristics with the reinforcement (cf. Pawlow, 1949, lecture 8).

Under some conditions, children in the second year of life can find the object hidden behind one of a few different-looking screens after previously seeing the screen and the toy behind it only once. However, if in successive trials the toy is placed in each trial behind a different-looking screen, only children over the age of 3 years solve the problem correctly.[8]

Let us suggest, now, an explanation of how the child achieves this stage. If one accepts that the association between the concrete visual characteristics of the screen and the toy explains the correct responses in the successive trials, then one must accept as well a consequence of this assumption—that each such association is inhibited in a very short time. If it did not disappear, but continued to exist, in the next trial, the child would look for the toy behind the screen of the same visual appearance as the one that hid the toy in the preceding trial. We have observed, however, that children over 3 years in several successive trials correctly looked for the toy behind the screens that looked different in every other trial. Should we assume that in each trial a new association was formed that inhibited the association of the preceding trial?

The functional efficiency of this form of searching, which we have observed in our investigations, its stability (relatively independent of the inhibiting influences and its common occurrence at age 3), suggests to us that this form of searching is the expression of a pattern of brain function that is characteristic and stable at this age. It is as if visual characteristics of objects, as a given category of phenomena, become "permanently" the "stronger component of the complex" as a result of various connections entering into the life experience of the child, and, consequently, other components become relatively permanently inhibited. The new structure is

[8] Cf. Stern's (1927) statement that only the child in the third year of life is capable of recognising what it has seen only once.

characterized by the following reaction: If an object is hidden behind a screen of a definite visual appearance the child searches for the object behind the screen that is identical in appearance. From the objective point of view, the reaction thus described is directed by the relation of identity of the appearance of screens given successively. No actual association is necessary for its emergence. It is the expression of an existing "permanent association" of a "categorical character" that develops ontogenetically as a result of many different experiences.

The passage to this stage is, in the light of our discussion, linked causally with prior stages. In the earlier stage, the child was able to use as a cue the position of the screen and, in the succeeding one, the concrete characteristics of the screen (e.g., colour). The achievement represented by the earlier stage seems to create the possibility of gathering experience necessary to pass to the next stage.

The interpretation of the development is based upon the view that development occurs by means of the formation of nervous system "functional structures," which become enduring at a given stage of growth and typical in all similar life conditions. The formation of these structures results from the transformation of preceding structures in the process of acquiring a given category of experiences. In relation to psychological changes in early childhood, it seems profitable to make use of knowledge of the function and development of the higher nervous system of the child and, in particular, of the formation of instrumental conditioned reflexes. Such were the sources for our explanatory hypothesis.

In the child's activity, which was the subject of our investigation, the main role was played by the visual analyzer. The work of this analyzer is recognized as a very complicated function that is very closely related to the essential changes in the development of cognition.

The child's passage to the stage where it is possible to recognize the relation between visual characteristics (in our case, the relation of identity) is, in our opinion, not so much an expression of the improvement of the visual function itself. Rather, it is the expression of a given level of the development and integration of the analyzing and synthesizing functions achieved by the brain at this level of the child's life.

REFERENCES

Babska, Z. Kształtowanie sie odzwierciedlenia cech wygladu przedmiotów we wczesnej ontogenezie w zbiorze: Z problematyki psychologii i teorii pozania [The formation of reflexion of visual characteristics of objects in early ontogenesis]. In, C. Nowinsky (Ed.), *On Problems of Psychology and Epistemology*. Warsaw. PWN, 1958.

Babska, Z. Development of object identification in one- and two- year-old children. *Vop. Psikhol.*, 1959, 6, 131–138.

Babska, Z. Skłonności perseweracyjne w stosunku do pozycji przedmiotów jako funkcja wieku [Persistency in choice of the object on the basis of its location as the function of age]. And Uprzywilejowywanie pozycji środkowych i prawych przez dzieci przedszkolne [Preference of some positions as the factor modifying the distribution of choices in recognition tests for pre-school age]. *Stud. Psychol.*, 1963, No. 5.

Buhler, C. Zum Problem der sexuellen Entwicklung. (On the problem of sexual development.) Z. *Kinderhk.*, 1931, 51, 612–643.

Goldstein, K., & Scheerer, M. Abstract and concrete behavior: an experimental study with special tests. *Psychol. Monogr.*, 1941, 53, No. 2.

Heidbreder, E. F. Thinking as an instinct. *Psychol. Rev.*, 1926, 33, 279–297.

Hicks, J. A., & Stewart, F. D. The learning of abstract concepts of size. *Child Develpm.*, 1930, 1, 195–203.

Hunter, W. S., & Bartlett, S. C. Double alternative behavior in young children. *J. exp. Psychol.*, 1948, 38, 558–567.

Pawlow, I. P. Lektsii po fiziologii [Lectures on physiology]. Moscow: USSR acad. Med. Sci., 1949.

Stern, W. Psychologisches und Jugendkundliches vom Ersten Internationalen Kongres für Sexualwissenscheft [Psychological and child study material from the First International Congress for Sexual Science]. Z. *päd. Psychol.*, 1927, 28, 96–104.

Stern, W. Psychology of early childhood up to sixth year of age. Trans. A. Barwell. (6th ed.) New York: Holt, 1930.

Stern, W., & Stern, C. Erinnerung, Aussage und Lüge in der frühen Kindheit. Monographien über die seelische Entwicklung des Kindes. II [Memory, testimony and lies in early childhood. A monograph on the mental development of the child]. (4th ed.) Leipzig: Barth, 1931.

Szuman, S. Rozwój psychiczny dzieci i mł odziezy [The mental development of children and adolescents]. (2d ed.) Warsaw: Nasza Ksiegarnia, 1948.

Welch, L. The development of discrimination of form and area. *J. Psychol.*, 1939, 7, 37–54.

Włodarski, Z. Reakcje odroczone u człowieka [Delayed reaction in man]. *Przeglad Psychologiczny [Psychol. Rev.]*, 1958, 1.

INDEX

INDEX

Abstract general terms or concepts, 41-51
Ajdukiewicz, 495
Allen, 418
Anderson, Alan R., 463-64
Animism (concept), 9, 13
Apostel, L., 109-10
Archives de Psychologie (Swiss journal), 5, 10, 78
Artificialism, 7
Artin, E., 461
Associationism, 97
Atkinson, R. C., 498, 500
Austin, G. A., 85

Bang, M., 19
Barker, R. G., 342
Bartlett, 67, 111, 536, 684
Baughman, E. E., 224
Beberman, 538
Bekhterev, V. M., 276
Bergson, Henri, 4
Berkeley, Bishop, 243, 257
Berko, J., 333, 337-40, 370, 434-35
Berkson, Gershon, 636
Bernoulli, James, 456
Bernoulli, John, 456-57
Bertalanffy, von, 26
Binet, Alfred, 5
Birge, J. S., 409, 416
Blankenship, A. B., 369
Bleuler, Eugen, 5
Bloom, B. S., 536
Boguslavskaya, Z. M., 649-50, 657, 663
Boole, George, 52

Bourbaki, 20
Bousfield, W. A., 409-10
Bower, G. H., 500
Braine, Martin D. S., 13, 585
Briggs, G. E., 416
Brogden, 643
Brown, L. T., 540-41
Brown, R. W., 204, 244, 313, 324, 340, 370, 411, 412, 429, 434-35
Brownell, W. A., 534, 537, 542-43
Bruner, J. S., 75-76, 83, 85-86, 536-37, 541, 624
Brunswik, E., 76-77, 79, 83, 88
Bryant, Peter, 644
Bureau International d'Education, 8
Burroughs, 638
Burt, 5, 587, 635
Busemann, 615
Buss, A. H., 171-72

Cantor, C. N., 409
Cantor, Gordon, 188-90
Carmichael, L., 13
Carnap, Rudolf, 52
Carroll, J. B., 412
Centre International d'Epistémologie Génétique (Geneva), 11, 12
Chatenay, Valentine (wife of Jean Piaget), 8
Chomsky, Noam, 335, 341, 342, 363, 400, 402, 409-13, 429, 432, 446
Church, A., 445-46
Claparède, 5
Class (concept), 40-51
Cofer, C. N., 440

693